THE COMPELLING STORY OF AN INVENTOR,
HIS DREAM, HIS DESTINY AND…

THE GREED OF A DIME

BY STEPHEN E. MOOR

Copyright © 2001 & 2018 & 2019 by Stephen E. Moor
Copyright Registration Number TXu 2-149-908

Printed and bound in the United States of America
ISBN 978-0-692-09504-1 (soft cover)

Published by World Class Inventors LLC
All rights reserved, including the right to reproduce this book
or any portion thereof in any form whatsoever.

Book design and layout by Stephen Moor
Cover design and artwork by Robert Cipolla Graphics
Back photo Stephen Moor

Other books by Stephen E. Moor
The World Class Inventors Handbook

For more information about the author and videos:
Please go to worldclassinventors.com
or look me up on YouTube.

The original version (First Edition) of this book was embarked upon in September of 1997 and was completed in December of 1999.
It was originally written for an audience of one… AlliedSignal/Honeywell International.

This current edition has been updated and revised to reflect the fact that I would sue Honeywell over the theft of my Intellectual Property.

On July 1st, 2002, as a Pro-se Plaintiff; I filed a nine-count Complaint against Honeywell in Federal District Court, Newark, NJ.

After four-plus years of pre-trial, Honeywell would settle with me on the very eve of my jury trial; September 1st, 2006.

STEPHEN E. MOOR v. HONEYWELL INTERNATIONAL INC., et al.,
case # 02-CV-03142 JAG.

Court filings & pleadings can be found on www.pacer.gov

This book is dedicated to Jesus, the lover of my soul.

To my wife Patti, for being the wonderful wife that she is.
To Jaclyn and Matt, the children that fill my life with joy unsurpassed.

Me and my best girl. Feb. of '83.

She had almost a million miles on her when we had first met.
A 1972 Kenworth K100 single sleeper; 350 Cat engine with a 15 speed trans.

Upon graduation from college, I went out and bought this beauty.
Possessed by a dream... and for the life of me I couldn't shake it.
After a short stint of driving for other people, I threw all caution to the wind and went out and mortgaged my soul, in order to go over-the-road unfettered.

Little did I know where this journey would lead me...

CONTENTS

INTRODUCTION — vii

PREFACE — ix

THE PROMISE — xv

1	THE PHONE CALL	1
2	PRELUDE TO THE DANCE	18
3	THE DANCE	33
4	THE CALL…, LONG OVERDUE	51
5	MEETING THE ENGINEERS, A CHRISTMAS CHEER	67
6	WHO CHANGED THE FORMULA?	86
7	SO YOU WANT TO MEET ME AT THE AIRPORT?	99
8	A GUEST OF HONOR	126
9	OUT HERE WITH THE BIG BOYS	150
10	CUTTING THE COVENANT	165
11	THE LONG HOT SUMMER	204
12	THE INDEFENSIBLE LIE	229

PROLOGUE — 271

CONTENTS

PART II

13	THE AFTERMATH	275
14	THE ROLL-OUT	276
15	I'M GONNA BLOW THE BRIDGE!	282
16	A FEIGNED CALL FROM THE CHIEF	284
17	WHO THREW GASOLINE ON THE FIRE?	287
18	THE GRAND THEFT	289
19	IT'S… WAIT AND SEE TIME	292
20	SURPRISE, SURPRISE…, SURPRISE!	294
21	WILL YOU MEET ME IN SEPTEMBER?	296
22	I'LL MEET YOU AFTER THE SHOW	298
23	A CHRISTMAS PROMISE	304
24	NOTHING HAPPENS BY CHANCE	307
25	DO THESE GUY'S EVER RETURN PHONE CALLS?	310
26	BETRAYAL AT THE BEACH	312
27	IT'S A MATTER OF TRUST	317
28	ETHICS FROM A SPEEDING CAR	323
29	FRAM BRAND MANAGEMENT	325
30	AN INDEPENDENCE DAY LETTER	331
31	FOCUS ON THE CUSTOMER	334
32	A FOLLOW UP TO A PLEA	336
33	A MESSAGE FROM THE ARMOR-BEARER	338
34	WHY DON'T YOU JUST DROP IT?	340
35	THE LAST ATTEMPT & SEVEN GOOD REASONS	344
36	A MORNING WITH THE STAKEHOLDERS	349
37	PREACHING AGAINST THE CHOIR	360
EPILOGUE		374

INTRODUCTION

This is a high stakes adventure that promises to take you deep inside of one of the largest and most powerful corporations on earth, Honeywell International. It all begins with a starry-eyed inventor who was in possession of two very valuable patents and a truckload of trade secrets. Though an industry outsider, he would be the one who would uncover the disruptive billion-dollar market opportunity. He would also be the one who would bring to life a technology that had been lying in plain sight…, the one that the industry experts had been blind to. As it would be revealed, both the engineers and the marketing gurus within this tight-knit industry were caught flatfooted by this young innovator as he beat them to the punch, by squarely staking his claim to it. The ensuing chain of events would put in motion an inventor's journey that would end up morphing into a Nantucket sleighride of hellacious proportions.

As this success story begins to come unglued, it will unquestionably strike at the very heart of the American dream, capable of making even the most casual observer step back and wonder.

From the onset, there was nothing harebrained about his plan. All he ever wanted, was to license his patents and watch his product grace the retailer's shelves. His sole ambition was to provide a solid future for both he and his family. It was never about fame or notoriety, because those sort of thoughts never crossed his mind.

As he traveled deeper and deeper inside the behemoth, it would become apparent that time was quickly running out for him. Like the rushing of the oceans tide, this monstrous Company was turning rouge and he was not in a position to stop them. One thing was for certain…, he had to strike a deal before the giant corporation could no longer restrain itself, and if he failed…, they wouldn't hesitate to eat him alive.

Author's note:
What you're about to explore is a book within a book.
There's a front-story and there's a backstory.
The personal photographs will truly make this come alive.
Enjoy!

YOU SHALL KNOW THE TRUTH
AND THE TRUTH SHALL SET YOU FREE
JOHN 8:32

PREFACE
ABOUT STEVE AND THE STORY

Before I launch into the story, I'd like to give you some background information about myself and what possessed me to write this book. I first began this journey as a backyard inventor. I conducted market feasibility studies by climbing over every square inch of my tractor trailer rig, often times fixing the lumbering hulk in the pitch dark and bitter cold..., hundreds of miles away from home. I conducted prototype development in a cluttered one-car garage. My office was the kitchen table and my word processor was a yellow legal pad. I communicated by letter, fax and telephone. Everything was done old school and manually, because there were no computers around when I first set out in the mid 1980's.

After my research had been completed, and the patents granted, I picked up the telephone and called upon a Fortune-38 Company, a shiny city set upon a hill. Thus, began the process of selling a billion-dollar idea over the telephone to the Fram oil filter unit of AlliedSignal; soon to be known as Honeywell International. At the time, Fram was the largest manufacturer and distributer of automotive oil filters in the world.

Over the course of time, my two humble patents would end up becoming benchmark patent citations recognized by the entire oil filtration community. As of this writing, my patents have been cited some 159 times by the USPTO, making me the most cited sole inventor in the history of oil filtration.

My inventions came to me by pure inspiration, but as Edison once said, "That's only the smallest part." After lots of hard work pushing tractor-trailer rigs over the road for hundreds of thousands of miles and turning lots of wrenches on them, I began to distill this idea of mine. In the final analysis, it was total dedication fueled with an insane amount of persistence that drove me to make my efforts pay-off.

The main thrust of this story is about the journey of a backyard inventor. Of how I got my foot in the door of a world leader on a cold call, of how I sold them a disruptive concept that was about as foreign to them as landing on Mars. Of how I made it into Walmart and the other majors throughout North America..., where my two oil filter products would grace their shelves for over a decade.

My journey as it first began, was filled with such anticipation punctuated by episodes of sheer out-of-body joy. Yet despite such promise and positive energy, it would end up morphing into an unforeseen nightmare of incalculable proportions. Through no fault of my own, I would come within a razors edge of losing everything that I had worked so hard for!

Little did I know that my business partner Honeywell, had other plans for my future. Before this journey would end, I would be sucked up into a raging storm that was spawned out of their immense greed. Unbelievably..., my parting gift for the privilege of spoon feeding all of my coveted technology to both their engineering and marketing departments was their calculated theft of my intellectual property.

If life was fair..., and we all know it's not... I should have chalked up the most patents in the world for this category.

As this drama begins to unfold, it will become all too apparent that Honeywell by their own actions genisised this incredible story. I just happened to be the one who penned it.

To this day, I am still forever grateful that I was able to come out the backside of this tornado in one piece. So now, I'm going to set the backdrop of how this book actually came to be, and the pivotal role it would play as I worked my way up the forbidden mountain.

The Greed of a Dime took me a year and a half to write. I began putting all of its myriad of details down in September of 1997 and completed the work sometime in December of 1999. Writing this book was not a part-time effort. My writing schedule was as grueling as anything I've ever done…, six hours a day… six days a week.

In early autumn of 2001, I commissioned a short print run of this book. My mission was to get the book that your about to read into the hands of Honeywell's powerful CEO. It was my deepest hope that it would paint a picture that the upper brass could not possibly disregard. It was that fall when I finally got up the nerve to deliver the book to Honeywell. I can say with absolute certainty, that this book reached its intended target, because I hand delivered a copy to Larry Bossidy's personal assistant in the foyer of the corporate headquarters in Morristown.

By some reckoning, I guess I could have been viewed as a somewhat worldly individual, however, when it came to the battle that I was about to wage, I was no more than just a babe in the woods. I guess that's why I stubbornly clung to the hope that Honeywell would one day open their eyes as to what I had been so desperately trying to telegraph them. Regrettably, they chose to keep their eyes tightly shut, despite being in possession of my play book well in advance of the big game.

Their non-response was what any thinking person would have expected, yet I clung to the hope that they would see the error of their ways. In the final analysis, they couldn't give a tinker's damn whether I would ever go public. Nor were they the least bit concerned about the liability they might one day have to face should we meet in a Federal courtroom. Truth is, large corporations are not self-governing entities like the social justice experts want us to believe they are. These huge multi-nationals never seem to be held accountable for their actions like you and I have to, and it's proven just about every time you look at the news. They don't fear repercussion. They don't fear public disclosure, they don't fear the government and they certainly don't fear a lawsuit that could tarnish their reputation.

During this same period, I had been shopping for legal counsel, because I knew something was terribly wrong. Just how wrong I wasn't exactly certain. The only thing that I could be sure of, was that Honeywell knew full-well what they had schemed behind my back. It was those missing pieces that fueled my resolve all the more to get to the bottom of it…

The only way I can put it, is that Honeywell didn't want any part of acknowledging what they had done to me as an honorable business partner. My book was summarily ignored and so was I. Well so much for that.

I knew in my heart of hearts that I been left no other option, but to sue the bastard's. As fate would have it, I would sue Honeywell as a Pro se plaintiff in Federal District Court in July 2002. I was 42 years old then. A husband and the father of two young children, married to a first-grade teacher. At the time, I was making a living as a straight commissioned real estate agent, selling houses on the

Jersey Shore. And my wife Patti, well..., let's just say that she wasn't killing it as a first-grade teacher.

The fact was, I woefully lacked the upfront two-million-dollar cash retainer fee needed to secure a law firm capable of taking on a Company the likes of Honeywell. So, I chose the last possible option. I quit my job and mortgaged our home which we had just paid off, and I would sue Honeywell all by myself. Bolstered by my wife Patti's insane loyalty and grit, she didn't hesitate to risk it all. She kept the home front together, as she pulled the sled with the reins securely in her teeth. Meanwhile, I taught myself to become the Holiday Inn Express's version of a lawyer. It was all in preparation so that I could do battle in Federal Court against the onslaught of the 9th of largest law firm on the planet, that boasted 1,100 lawyers on staff; two separate 30-man law firms and Honeywell's 250 in-house attorneys.

The Greed of a Dime would become a crucial piece of Discovery in the lawsuit that I filed against Honeywell in July 2002. I can assure you, Honeywell and their minions of lawyers read my story. As I mentioned in the *World Class Inventors Handbook*, I did the unthinkable from a legal standpoint, I granted their attorneys an additional six-hour session to depose me on this book! Legal suicide I know..., but I didn't give a tinker's damn. I had to make certain that they had no ill-conceived delusions that I would blow apart like some cheap watch under their up-coming cross examination. They videotaped my every deposition for later study and to show the jury in the event I couldn't keep my story straight.

It goes without saying, that I meticulously documented and vetted this entire account so that it would mirror image the huge document trail that my inventors journey had generated. I had but one goal in all of this... This book was my last hope to stop the madness... Stop their scofflaw behavior and put an end to their insane denials and ridiculous defense tactics and put an end this maddening lawsuit. But that wasn't to be...

They were so pissed-off that I had dared to throw a rock at the charging bull elephant they'd become. Besides, by now it had become purely business-sport to them. And the shareholders..., well, they would never find out that the Company was spending several million dollars in an attempt to crush a puny business partner that had the unmitigated balls to stand up to them. The one who invented the product that the Company touted, was **"the most significant innovation in oil filtration history."** The one they made the national television commercial for. The product that made it into two separate annual reports. The one that they rolled-out at SEMA twice. The one they had to put in theft-proof packaging, because 750,000 units were stolen out of Walmart during the products initial roll-out..., that one.

They simply couldn't help themselves now. Knowing that the gauntlet that I would be forced to endure had the power to drag me on down into the depths of hell. And it did..., little by little each passing day. Our pre-trial lasted four grueling years before I was finally awarded a date for my jury trial. They did all this in order to crush me morally, financially and spiritually. And they didn't spare any of the horses. It was a full court press, and it was all-out effort to make me tap out before the big game. To their utter amazement, it didn't happen, so they ended up settling with me on the very eve of trial for millions.

What you can't fathom, until you've lived it, is this... A court battle of this magnitude with a major corporation, is tantamount to the siege of Leningrad in the middle of a Siberian winter.

Just so you know, during my lawsuit, I personally took the deposition of nearly every one of the main characters in this book. I took seven depositions in all. In addition to that, I allowed them to depose me twice. The sweet irony… All of our collective sworn testimony dovetailed perfectly with what had been memorialized in this book years earlier and beyond!

Nearly two decades have passed since I penned this book, and I still have quite an emotional charge regarding the whole ordeal. In case you're curious, here's what I found most compelling about the whole thing…, it was the journey. For me, it had always been about the journey. And with the journey came the magic rocket fuel that propelled me ever forward…, the dream. In the end, it had always been about being in love with the dream.

You see, there's nothing quite like being propelled by your dream, especially if it's real! Here's a pro tip: your dream is capable of taking you places and emboldening you to do things that you might not otherwise consider.

'So why release the book now, after all these many years have passed?'

Simply put, "To everything there is a season, and a time to every purpose under the heaven."

Inventing, widget building, and product marketing have become very popular topics on both the internet and television. As popular inventing continues to go mainstream, so will the many myths that are invariably going to spring up around it. There's an entire industry that's focused on helping inventors out with their ideas; all of course for a fee. With the prospect of financial independence tied to a dream, comes many overinflated promises and lots of inaccurate information. The scary thing, is that many of these services are charging some very hefty fees and are dispensing inaccurate information for the privilege. That's where a starry-eyed innovator with a dream can be taken advantage of. There's so much blue sky being spayed about, and from where I sit, that's really bad.

As for the television scene, I could have only of wished to have teamed up with a well-connected and highly capitalized 'Shark', that for a percentage, would have taken me by the hand and led me up the mountain. And I have to totally level with you…, that's what I wanted! I gladly would have accepted an easier way out, had one been offered! But at the time, there were no easy-way-outs to be found, so I had to go it alone…, or not go at all.

Don't be fooled…, what your viewing on TV is rare! Though it's uplifting, and it makes for great entertainment, it's not reality either. What I'm trying to impress upon you, is that nearly every one of you dream-driven innovators will be making this treacherous climb up the mountainside alone…, just like I did.

My climb was arduous, and it was gritty… and in all probability, so will yours. My friend, that's the other side of the entrepreneurial game, and I thought that it would only be fair to share this reality with you…, since I can.

Don't misconstrue what I'm saying here. The inventor's journey is without doubt, the absolute thrill of a lifetime! It is an experience that needs to be savored just like a fine wine. However, the mountain range that you'll be scaling is daunting, and it's fraught with innumerable hidden pitfalls. In plain language, you'll need a seasoned Sherpa capable of getting you safely to the summit and it's something that you should be mindful of.

I've already climbed these mountains, and I've done so at the highest level of difficulty imaginable.

On the one hand, I've made several million dollars, yet on the other, I've lost tens upon, tens of millions that were rightfully mine. So, if I could give you some sound advice, I'd start off by inviting you to come take the journey alongside me.

Come… Come take a practice run at living out your dream as you put yourself in my shoes. Let's climb these mountains together. It's imperative that you get the lay of the land well in advance before setting out on this sort of a journey. Take my word for it…, it's impossible for you to begin to fathom the twists and turns that an innovator's dream-driven journey can present.

To answer, 'why release the book now?'

I've been sitting on this book for far too long. It needs to be brought out into the light of day and enjoy a life of its own, especially if it's to provide anything of value to the person who has a wanderlust for adventure or a good idea to hatch. That said, I'm compelled to leave you with a truth that Jesus passed along while he traveled about, "But no one having lit a lamp sets it in secret."

I guess it's high time I that I heed His advice. It's my time to take this book out from under the basket from which it has been kept all these long years. My hope is that you get an opportunity to read it. May you enjoy the thrill of the ride. May you share in my every emotion that abounds around every twist and turn of the journey. May you be helped and inspired by it. May you learn all of the lessons that you need to learn before you set out on your own journey, wherever that may take you.

We were inseparable.   spring of '83.

Owning a high-mileage tractor can make for some marathon wrench turning sessions. After driving 2,000 miles a week or more, this is what I could look forward to. Old school, paper log books, pay phones, CB chatter, trucker's strikes and lots and lots of miles.

I was young, determined, and rather invincible.

THE PROMISE

I was walking in the pocket of a sandy cove that the waves had carved out between the granite boulders of the jetty and the beach. The signature left by the most recent storm. The wind was driving hard out of the west pushing the billowy white clouds further and further to the east, out over the Atlantic, across the backdrop of a steel gray sky. I was chilled to the core as those winds came driving across the beach trying their best to strip me of my warmth. It was late in November of 1985, after a Thanksgiving that never was, and a Christmas that wasn't going to arrive that year.

My father lay at home wasting away from the throes of terminal lung cancer. He was going to make the trip before too long and I wasn't certain how much longer he could hold on. As for myself, I was feeling rather lost, dogged by a spirit of depression and the uncertainty about the promises of life.

To complicate matters, I was temporarily unemployed and feeling a bit like a failure having come off the road for all this madness. Not long ago, I traded my seat behind that big eighteen-wheeler I used to push, in exchange for the lure of big city money. The fool's errand of trying to deceive myself hadn't quite worked out, so I quit my brand-new job as a commodities broker. It wasn't a natural fit anyway…, yet I was still reeling. Quittin' didn't come naturally, and I could of counted on two fingers the number of times that I had actually quit anything.

Despite all the turbulence, I was in the process of breaking out, but as to where and how, I wasn't exactly certain. For some time now, there had been this gentle prodding that had been flashing across my thoughts like some uninvited guest. The best I could tell, it was a sliver of an idea…, just the tiniest wisp. However, its calling was relentless, as it beckoned me to open it up and explore. True to form, I had done my best to ignore it…, I was pretty good at that you know.

From the earliest days, I was accustomed to having goals, a plan of attack and especially now that I was being thrust into a new era, I wouldn't hear of getting side tracked with some bothersome idea I didn't have time for. Somehow, the imminent passing of my father from this world into the next, was rearranging my priorities and becoming the impetus for a change that was about to take place in my life. The change was inevitable, I could sense it in my being…, yet at the time, it was neither anticipated nor was it welcomed. Unbeknownst to me, that gentle Voice I was hearing was about to gain a position of higher prominence in my life.

As I walked along the cut in the shoreline with the coffee colored waves breaking onto the sandy beach, my eyes focused on the flotsam and jetsam which had collected in rafts, a reminder of the previous night's storm. Every now and then I sifted through the rubble with a sweeping foot, hoping to uncover a treasure. It was akin to what I was attempting to do with the jumbled thoughts in my unsettled mind.

Walking a little further on down the beach, just as I reached the jetty rocks… It was there that it finally broke loose inside of me. In a moments time I surrendered my opposition, and in so doing, the dream had been imparted. It would be the dream that I'd ride… It'd be the one responsible for shaping the chapters that lay way off in the distance.

I was about to undergo a sea change in my life and chart a new course, but to exactly where I wasn't sure, except I'd do it with a 'damn the torpedoes' type of conviction. All I knew, was that I had just agreed to take on this vision and I was in the midst of running through a set of gears like none other I've ever known.

Climbing up the rocks to get a better vantage point of the sea and sky, I looked for a spot affording me some shelter from the driving winds and perhaps invite some feeble rays of sun to warm me. I sat down and leaned out of the wind trying my best to quell the jumbled messages and emotions that were still wreaking havoc. After sitting still, a while, I couldn't help but notice how calm the sea was inshore, in direct contrast to the whitecaps and turbulence further outside. I sought out this realm of calm for myself, I needed to have a talk with the Lord.

Oh, I knew God all right. I imagined I knew Him pretty well from the time of my childhood. As a matter of fact, I supposed I knew Him better than most. And I also knew that the little Voice that I was hearing and doing my best to ignore, was His. His voice was gentle and calm, like that of the inshore sea. It was my mind that was raging out of control, like the whitecaps out there, surely a result of operating outside of His will for my life.

During the course of our conversation, I had become acutely aware that the large chunk of granite I was perched upon He had made along with that huge body of water that halts at the shore with all the creatures in it, …and the sky above. Knowing that gave me immense comfort. Suddenly, my mind began to drift out on the magnificence of this God of mine and a calming peace came over me as the troubles in my mind that I held onto so tightly, began to leave.

I decided at that moment, that I was going to accept the dream, and all that the quest might have in store. The Lord and I needed to go over the ground rules, for which we did. I made a covenant with Jesus that day on the inlet jetty, and I was determined not to break it. The deal was sealed, the idea was freely given, and it was now mine to freely pursue.

And as for my part of the bargain, it had just begun with my acceptance. The faith part, and the real work lie ahead. My job now was to trust, and of equal importance, work, work with all perseverance as if my very life depended upon the outcome. I wasn't the least bit concerned, He was the guarantee and would insure our mutual success.

A couple of weeks later my dad died. I had made my peace with him to the fullest extent of my ability. Sadly enough, my dad never let anyone get too close to him and I was certainly no exception. And, I'll have you know, just because he was dying, he wasn't about to change the rules for anyone, not even me, and I counted myself his buddy.

CHAPTER 1
THE PHONE CALL

Nearly a decade had come and gone since the idea was imparted and the promises had been exchanged on the rockpile that juts out into the Atlantic.

It was early January 1994. I had a great Christmas and I had a lot to be thankful for, but I couldn't wait for the new year to get under way. I wanted to make the phone call, it was all I could do, not to think about it. My destiny was centered around this phone call and I had rehearsed it a thousand times in my head over the past few months. I would live with these phone calls well in advance of my making them, sometimes for several months before ever making one. It had everything to do with timing and how my strategy would play out. Subsequently, these belabored calls would become part of my being.

In the game that I was about to play you might get one chance to paddle out into the lineup, hoping to navigate the killer surf with the big boys. If my phone call was not fielded by a receptive individual on the other end of the line my future attempts of communicating with that particular company would be over, before it could ever begin. My experience up to this point had already taught me that much.

So, on January the 5th, 1994 I walked into my kitchen asked the Lord for His help and guidance and picked up the phone and placed a call to the main switchboard at Fram, a division of AlliedSignal in Rumford, Rhode Island.

To put things in context, AlliedSignal was a Fortune 38 Company and was powerful enough to merge with Honeywell International and absorb them into their existing business framework. The deal was consummated in December of 1999 and Allied took on the Honeywell name for branding purposes. Allied's top management, including the CEO would still be running the show after the merger took place.

It was well into the morning, but not that close to lunch I reasoned, as my mind wanted to go tilt from the adrenaline rush. My body tingled from the anticipation mixed with real fear.

'The person I needed to speak with should be in, shouldn't he?' I reasoned that it should be a guy, but in actuality, I didn't even know who I was going to ask for. There was one thing at this point I knew for sure, I was capable of articulating to the switchboard operator who I needed to speak with once she identified that person's title.

All this over a stinking phone call! 'You can't be serious?' Oh, but I am! The stakes were huge, the mountain was great, my inexperience was apparent at least to me, and the fear…, the fear of failure was crushing! I tried to overcome it the best way I knew how, but I had to admit, I was simply terrified! I had already blown the previous six months courting Purolator Oil Filters and they had already dropped the ball sometime back, in large part due to a lack of vision and their own demons of fear that lived within their corporate structure.

I called on Champion Labs another huge oil filter manufacturer, and they didn't see the value in my innovation either. I had gone so far as enlisting a friend of mine deep inside the filter business to make a connection for me at another big player, Dana Corp.'s, Wix and so far, he was coming up empty handed. They didn't exactly say no at this point, but if Wix was going to make a decision, they were sure moving like molasses on this one and I wasn't waiting around for them to figure it out.

At that point, it was anybody's guess, if Wix would ever come around and my crystal ball was on the fritz.

At this juncture, I wasn't feeling too positive as to how this journey was going to wind up. I was trying to hear from God, but He wasn't talking. Well, I guess in fairness to Him, if He was talking, I sure wasn't listening very well. I was too preoccupied with anxiety and my own ability to get me over the top to hear much of anything. My sites were fixed on the mountainous waves on the horizon and I was too busy wondering if I was ever going to make the paddle out.

So, if I may, here's what I was up against. There are only four major automotive oil filter manufactures of any consequence in the U.S. and I had already called on two and thus far, my efforts had won me a couple of 'thanks, but no thanks' letters.

In the patent world of the small-time inventor you actually request these 'Dear John' letters, not because you're a masochist or something, but because you need documentation in case your product by mere coincidence happens to find its way onto the retailer's shelf in the next couple of years without your permission. These letters would be the benchmark proof needed to support a nasty and very expensive patent infringement law suit. The letters I received back from these companies would invariably detail the various excuses and pitfalls surrounding such a novel filter product and justify the company's rejection.

I didn't even bother with the 4th player, General Motors even though they owned AC Delco, who made oil filters. They were just too big to bother with. At the time they were the biggest company on the planet. It would have been like dealing with a mid-sized country, and even I was smart enough not to attempt that.

As I mentioned previously, the third company out there was Wix. Though they had been contacted, they weren't exactly biting at the moment, so that left me with exactly one company remaining. At the time, Fram was the largest automotive oil filter manufacturer on the planet and I was one phone call away from my destiny.

I didn't have any personal contacts at the Company, and I didn't even know who to ask for! I was flying on instruments only, and mind you, in some very heavy weather.

The phone rang a few times before a pleasant operator manning the switchboard answered automatically, "AlliedSignal; Fram Division." After a brief explanation to the receptionist, my call hurtled towards its target, a Mr. Kevin Gill, Manager of Product Marketing; Automotive Filters. The whole while before he picked up, I thanked my lucky stars that I had been able to sidestep the engineers. With that knowledge in hand, my confidence level automatically began to rise, bolstered by the fact my best chance to explain myself lie in talking with someone in marketing first!

"Hello, Kevin Gill," his voice shot out at me. I was his target now and I could feel it. This guy seemed so strong and I was on the verge of going into hypoglycemic shock from the tension.

"Hi Kevin, my name is Stephen Moor and I have recently been granted a patent on an oil filter. I would like to know who I could speak to about it?"

I knew darn well that I wanted to speak to him. I needed to speak to a salesman that could entertain a dream, or at least a semblance of one. I needed someone with an open mind that wasn't apt to sport an opinion concerning something he didn't know anything about.

The game that I was caught up in was akin to playing a board game, where the roll of the dice determines the space you land on, and quite possibly the final outcome. Of course, at least to me, the stakes were much higher than any board game I could ever imagine.

We're talking the effort and pain of attaining two patents outside my sphere of formal training, in the arcane field of oil filtration, and in an industry, that had not seen any appreciable change in over a generation. And that doesn't even begin to take into account the enormous amount of time, and the investment of my life's force over the last decade or so. Notwithstanding the thousands of dollars spent and not realized.

No…, to me, the game was more like walking through a mine field trying not to find out the difference between a claymore and a toe popper. Prematurely landing on the space marked engineer, could hurt a lot…, or even be deadly.

Most of the engineers that I had dealt with over the years were plodders, deadpan types, requiring a loaded gun to their head to evoke a response. Besides, I wasn't looking for some guy to debate the obvious with me now. I couldn't be bothered with the inane details such as 'could this thing be built?'

I already knew the answer to that one! All I needed now was for someone to agree with me about something on a much higher order. That there was a hungry market of consumers out there, just waiting for this type of oil filter!

I was determined to take Kevin's temperature right up front. I'm not all that aggressive, but my patience had almost run out for this round and the suspense was driving me mad. I was setting myself up for the shot. I was in 'all or nothing mode' as I prepared myself to gauge his interest, enthusiasm and nerve. His initial response would be telling, and it wouldn't take much for me to know whether an intelligent dialog was going to be on the menu or not. I wasn't taking anything out on him, it wasn't even possible for it to be personal, it was just that I was so darn torqued up from the demanding journey thus far. The journey up the side of this mountain so far had been nothing short of exasperating.

"Is that, so?" he said. "Why don't you tell me a little bit about it and we'll go on from there," he shot back at me. Right from the get go, he exhibited a vibrant self-confident attitude. I couldn't help but wonder if he was thinking… 'Ok, hot rod, sell me.'

"I received a patent for my idea back in May of 93', it's for a Teflon treated oil filter. The additive market in the U.S. is huge! It's probably bigger than your Company's gross oil filter sales. You do about half a billion dollars a year in filters, don't you?" I said, kind of probing.

"Yeah, that's about right, you're in the ballpark," he said, validating the accuracy of my half statement.

I could tell I was peaking his interest although his response was guarded. 'He had to be interested, didn't he?' The idea was so simple it begged the obvious. The market was burgeoning with potential. As I awaited his response, I couldn't help but think, 'this idea was great, and it was mine!' There was no mistaking it, I was pregnant with this dream and could feel myself coming unglued. I just had to share with him the vision that had been consuming me for the last several years. As my anxiety melted away, confidence and certainty took its place, bolstered by Hope.

"Hey Steve, filters are supposed to remove things from their environment the last time I checked. They're not supposed to add stuff. How are you going to sneak that past that public's perception? I think that's a pretty major sticking point my friend. Don't you? Well, maybe not for you. Obviously, you got a patent on this thing," he said genuinely trying not to bust my bubble, while at the same time sensing I knew the lay of the land, whereas he didn't.

His strong questions were laced with doubt, a product of his experience in the business. I could almost sense immediately that he was challenging me to engineer a way out of this line of reasoning. He wasn't being arrogant about it, nor was he trying to put me on the defensive. Probing, that's how I read him. Probing… And that was ok by me.

"Kevin, I have two patents on oil filtration, not just the one I am calling you about," I added, if for nothing else, but to hopefully lend some credibility to my case. I was quite certain that there weren't too many people out there walking around with not only one, but two significant utility patents in the field of oil filtration. Hey, at least I was impressed! But, as the saying goes, 'that and a buck will get you a cup of coffee.'

"For lack of a better term, I refer to them as additive treated oil filters. They both have stuff added to them. They both perform their primary functions like every other filter is designed to do, which is to filter the oil. However, they have a secondary function which is to add a beneficial additive to the lubricating system. Do you know where I got my idea from?"

"No, I don't. But why don't you tell me, this should be good," he said, spurring me on, somewhat amused with me by now.

"About ten years ago I was changing a coolant filter on my Kenworth K100 tractor. I used to be an over the road truck driver and then in a moment of insanity, I went out and bought my own tractor. My job description instantly catapulted me into the world of being an owner operator. I didn't have any special training as a mechanic, but if you don't want to go broke, you better learn how to turn a wrench. And you better learn how to do it fast. I had become quite proficient during that learning curve, so much so, I overhauled two tractor rigs before I got out of the business.

"Anyway, I was replacing a coolant filter one day. You know, the kind that a big diesel engines use. I'm sure you're familiar with this kind of filter. It prevents the formation cavitation bubbles in the cooling system, which if left unchecked, can bore microscopic holes into the walls of the cylinder liners?"

"Yea go on," he said. "I never heard about a little air bubble that was able to bore through steal but go ahead." By this time, I was getting the vibe that my explanation might have been over his head already or perhaps too convoluted for him to totally grasp the magnitude of what I was about to tell him. After all, he didn't know where I was going with this one, but I certainly did. And the punch line was gonna be great.

"It just so happened that I bought this Fram coolant filter from a truck parts counter out on the road somewhere. When I opened the box, there was some sort of white powder on the bottom of the box that looked very suspicious to me. I shook the filter and heard something rattling around in there and more of this powdery stuff came flying out. I thought that I bought a defective filter and took it back inside and told the guy at the parts counter about it. I was pretty green as a mechanic then. Apparently, the counter man who sold it to me didn't have the slightest clue what was going on with it either. So as the filter lay on the counter with all this white powder coming out, we both stood there staring back at each other, like two dogs at a new pan.

"So, I asked him if he wouldn't mind grabbing the service manager of the shop. To make a long story short, the lead mechanic came out in his greasy coveralls and picked up the filter in his hands and gave it a quick shake. Without skipping a beat, he told us both that the powder that was coming out of the filter was meant to be in there, and that it was a beneficial additive of sorts and that it did what I told you about concerning the little bubbles. Anyway, that incident had stuck in my head for many years. Eventually I filed for a patent based on that concept, except my idea was aimed at oil filters.

"I filed for my first patent, because of what I had discovered that day at the parts counter. I used the same concept embodied in that coolant filter. Isn't that kinda neat?"

"Yeah, I'd have to say so. So, what on earth possessed you to get involved in oil filters, anyway? You gotta admit, it's kinda unusual. I mean it's not the kind of thing you get out of bed one day and say to yourself, 'hey, I think that I am going to invent a better oil filter today.' Right?" he asked, now trying to get into my head.

It was obvious that I had captured his interest, and that was just fine by me. All he needed to do was to ask, and I'd be glad to talk on the subject for hours without coming up for air. His genuine interest at this point began to give me hope. I lived on hope, like a junkie that lives for a dope fix. That's all I had propping up my dreams at the moment, Hope. He certainly wasn't aware of my plight, but the little bit of hope that he was tossing my way was big enough for me to float upon. For today it would be enough to keep me above turbulence that this maddening quest had spawned. At this point I had a least nine years of my life invested in this enterprise, venturing almost everything, without much of a reward. All I had to show was a couple of worthless patent plaques that hung on my living room wall as a testimonial. I had basically put my own life, as well as that of my wife's, in a perpetual holding pattern on account of this pursuit.

"Well," I said. "Being an over the road trucker you learn a lot about efficiency if you're paying attention. It's not a game, the work is dangerous, and the profit margins are real thin."

I was always so proud to recite the fact that I once belonged to that motley fraternity. It never seemed to have the effect on others as it did on me. For me, it was one of my greatest achievements and life experiences to drive those big trucks across the country. It was still in my blood.

He seemed to have the time, so I took advantage of it by launching into a brief but thorough treatise on oil filtration and the science of oil tribology. I respected the fact that he was a marketing guy and not an engineer, so I was careful how I related those principals to my invention. After enlightening him about my basis in reality from an engineering standpoint, we got down to the real business at hand…, marketing.

"You know Kevin, the Teflon treated oil market in this country is huge!

I refer to it as the 'designer oil market'. It is very similar to the craze Perrier has created in the spring water market in recent years," trying to plant the seed that I was on the brink of sharing with him the same type of stand-alone market.

"I'm starting to see your point," he said.

I could almost see the beginning of a smile coming over the phone line as he volunteered, "You know Steve, if what you're telling me is true, and I don't have any reason to believe otherwise, you just might have something here." He was still thinking out loud half muttering and grumbling to himself.

My ears couldn't help but perk up when I heard him give me a me glimpse of his cards, as he got caught up in my enthusiasm. "It's amazing! Why the heck didn't our guys think of that, it's been right under their noses the whole darn time!"

I lived for moments like this. There weren't any promises made, no contracts signed, just a little affirmation. To me, this acknowledgment of the obvious was like a big hug and long overdue.

"So, you're starting to see the merit in this idea," I said, biting my lip, hoping he wasn't going to take away my high.

"Yes, I do! It sounds very interesting and if you don't mind, I'd like to explore this a little further."

Then almost reflexively, he caught himself and gave me the obligatory corporate line, "Of course you know that I can't make you any promises to you Steve.

"From what I understand, our guys in R&D may have played around with additives, but I don't know how far along they've taken it. I do know that Fram is seriously considering a step-up value-added filter line at this time, but we haven't been able to identify a definite product type as of yet," as he took me into his confidence.

Although he was being tactical, his statement struck a chord in me, to be more precise, a raw nerve. Because, if Fram's engineers were playing around with additives, it wasn't because they were a bunch of random geniuses. No…, that wouldn't of been the reason. It would go a lot deeper than that. So, I let him in on a little secret…

"You know, I called on your Company just about six years ago to the month Kevin, regarding my first patent. I worked with a guy by the name of Bruce Kennedy. Do you know the guy?

"I believe that he held a marketing position lateral to yours; something like Manager of New Product Development."

Kevin replied, "No, I can't place him, Steve. No…, I don't recall the guy at all. I was in the field at that time out in Long Island. I guess for some reason our paths never crossed."

"What were you doing out in the field," I asked, hoping that this guy wasn't just some marketing guy hatched out of a corporate vacuum.

"I've been with the Company about thirteen years and I've just come inside in the last few years or so. I guess you could say I got a promotion of sorts and was transferred up here. I've logged over nine years out in the field." His response was firm and not bloated with false pride. "I was a field rep servicing our automotive accounts."

"Yes!" I exclaimed to myself giving him the go head sign in my kitchen. This guy was self-assured. He'd been there and didn't need to put up a front about it. He had real world experience and I could sense that he was still fresh…, still in the game.

I was so psyched! I was compelled now more than ever to let him know about my last sales call that I paid on the Company. I wanted to share with him about the ship of fools that I had run into my last time out. But before I could do any of that, I wanted to close the loop concerning his background. I needed to feel secure in whom I was going to confide. After all it was my phone call, and I have a funny thing about petting on the first date, even though I might have been so inclined.

"Hey by the way, what's your educational background anyway?" jumping at the chance for him to give me a better idea of who I just might be dealing with. He told me that he went to St. John's University in Queens, and got an MBA by going nights at N.Y.U. Good I thought. He's done it the hard way just like myself, the guy's not a weakling. I knew I wasn't, and I had the scars and the mileage on my young soul to prove it.

"Kevin! One quick question, how old are you? You sound kinda young."

"Is that good or bad Steve, I don't know?" he fired back, trying to gauge my rather personal line of questioning."

"Please don't misunderstand me, I think it's good. No, I know it's good!" I said, full of anticipation. "And I'll tell you why. It's just that I've been dealing with these older guys that are towards the end of their careers and they don't seem to have any guts or vision anymore. Unfortunately, at least most of the people I've dealt with seem about as excitable as a dial tone. Do you know what I mean?

"I'm not very well acquainted with the American corporate landscape, but there's some sort of a disease that these guy's pickup around mid-life. They appear to hang around in their careers long enough, only to languish until death, while at the same time hoping to retire on some stupid golf course in Florida? Am I missing something, or perhaps, I just don't get it?"

He broke in and jumped up on my soap box, "I'm thirty-seven and I am not just here taking up space either. I have a job to do, and I am paid well to do it. I am not averse to risk if it can be justified, and I'm not afraid of losing my job, just because of a bad decision I could make."

"You sound kinda young yourself, how old are you anyway?" he asked, in return.

"I'm thirty-five, and I gotta tell ya, I'm way behind schedule, I planned to be much further along by now. This thing has really eaten up the clock." Boy I was so glad to be talking with some young buck for a change. That just served to reinforce the vibes I was already getting from him.

Kevin wanted to hear about my last contact with Fram. Apparently, he had the time and I was thrilled to oblige. He encouraged me to recount the story, so I did. Besides, I'm sure that he needed to do some more sifting himself, before he could become more comfortable with me as well. I'm positive that he wanted to make sure that my expulsive conversation wasn't the manifestation of some nut case. Hey, I was out to prove that I was in fact real…

I started in… "As I said before, I called on Fram about six years ago and spoke with Bruce a couple of times and forwarded him a copy of my first patent. He looked it over and expressed an interest in my concept. He sent me out legal disclosure letter for me to sign, before he would even set up a meeting."

Somehow, I didn't feel that it was necessary to go into further detail pertaining to the patent with all of its minutia. But for the moment, that's what Kevin wanted me to talk about, so I had to follow his lead, despite the fact that it wasn't what I wanted to get into for the sake of time.

I was compelled to tell him something more personal. It was concerning the shabby treatment I had received at the hands of the chief engineer and his sidekick, the Head of Manufacturing. That day stuck in my craw, even after these long six years. The episode was the epitome of "Not Invented Here." To this day what had occurred during that meeting over lunch still seems like an alien abduction to me and I couldn't wait to spell it out for him. But that had to wait, because before we could go any further, he wanted to hear about the claims behind my first patent.

"I told you how the basic idea came to me, so now I'll give you some detail of what it's about and its applications. The filter was designed to be employed primarily in a secondary by-pass operation, like the systems found on class eight trucks. More or less, this filter was designed for heavy-duty diesel applications, you know…, tractor trailers, buses, construction equipment and the like.

"The premise behind my filter's improvements were pretty basic, but not always clearly understood by the people in this field. 'Oil doesn't wear out; it just gets dirty.' It gets dirty when it comes into contact with the operating environment from soot, dust and wear metals etc. The main offenders are the particulate contaminant's and acids. Chemical contamination especially, wreaks havoc on the oil system.

"The filter wasn't designed to be set up directly in series like a primary or full flow filter, but to be hooked up in a parallel arrangement, hence a bypass operation. Today, the standard bypass filter is only capable of filtering down to around five to ten microns in size at best. And back when this patent was issued, the best filtration rate for a by-pass filter was certainly above ten microns. Fifty percent of an engines wear occurs from particles around the five-micron range and below. The point is, I know how to manufacture a one-micron absolute bypass filter in a cost-effective manner."

Kevin chimed in, "I see your point, about oil not wearing out. Though I gotta admit I never thought about it before. So, what about it? That's been done, before hasn't it?"

"No, it hasn't! And it certainly hasn't been done using my way of going about it. Yeah, there have been a few efficient particulate filters that had gained some limited success on the market, but there's more to the story of how oil breaks down.

"During the lubricating process, the oil becomes acidic. This acidification occurs over time due to a couple of things. First, there's internal condensation that can occur inside of the engine that mixes with the sulfur by-products present in the fuels. Second, there's the blow-by that gets past the piston rings due to the pressures created during the combustion process. These and other by-products of the combustion process breaks down the oil from a chemical standpoint and it inhibits its performance to lubricate efficiently. This is one of the main reasons why oil has to be changed periodically. It's because of chemical contamination as much as anything else."

"Okay…. Okay! I get it! I'm starting to see what you're talking about. That does kinda sound novel to me after all. I can't ever remember hearing about anything like that before," he said, with a sincere ring.

"Hey, go ahead, you got my interest on this thing, I'm following you. I'm starting to see the evolution in your thought process with this newest patent of yours."

"Did you know that when oil is formulated it's not just pure crude stock," as I baited him with one of my loaded questions.

"I don't know? What do I know about oil, other than we make filters that filter it when goes through a motor? I'm in sales remember? I'm not a scientist or an engineer. My job is to evaluate ideas, then figure out if the consuming public is willing to spend their money on it once it's on the shelf," he said, flexing his muscles.

"I know, I know. Now look! The standard motor oil that you buy off the shelf with the SAE and API designations is comprised of at least thirty percent additives in the formulation and by now, I'm sure that the percentages are higher. In case you're not aware, motor oil isn't a hundred percent refined crude stock. It's formulated with at least thirty percent other additives, like detergents, viscosity stabilizers, anti-foaming agents, there's a long list of stuff. And not to complicate matters, we're going to completely dismiss the fact that Mobil 1, is a fully synthetic motor oil. You get the point?

"Well anyhow, acid formation in motor oil breaks down the alkaline based additive package through use, and over time makes the oil acidic or 'sour'. That's because the oil is only capable of holding so much acid before the PH balance gets out of whack. This can be borne out through oil analysis in a test to determine what's called the TBN, total base number. It is a good way to let the operator keep track of the health of the oils additive package. Only fleet managers that are attempting to stretch the PM, (parts and maintenance) intervals between oil changes would pay careful attention to TBN.

"I hope this stuff isn't too dry for you, some of the details…, I mean? But you wanted to know, and it's the crux of the improvement. I got my patent on an additive treated oil filter that would combat or neutralize acids that form over time in the oil. This filter would be pre-charged with a specific amount of this additive package that would restore the oils alkalinity. So, if the oil could be kept clean from a particulate standpoint, and it's entirely possible with the proper filtration, you could most certainly extend the PM safely. And that's already being done right now in many fleets by the use of conventional filtration that incorporates a more efficient secondary by-pass filter design. But here's the kicker Kev, if you could restore the TBN of the oil, you could extend the PM ten-fold. Then you'd really have something a lot more efficient."

"Wow, I didn't find that boring at all," he said enthusiastically. "Where the heck did you pick all that stuff up?"

Feeling a little self-conscious, I replied back, "I don't know, just along the way I guess. Anyway, you see it was always my contention that it wouldn't bore a fleet manager who was trying to stay on the cutting edge of fleet maintenance. These guys are looking for every legitimate way to reduce downtime and operating costs for every unit in service."

Eager to know, he asked, "So what did our guys say about it when they brought you in to look at? What did you say…? A few years ago, or something?" he said, trying to recall my visit.

Not wanting to sound rude, I replied, "Six years ago," driving my point home.

"All right…, all right," he said. Swiftly sensing that situation still carried an emotional charge. "So, what did they say, I've got to hear it?"

"I'll never forget it Kevin. We all piled into Bruce's compact car and they took me out for lunch to some Sizzler joint. We chatted the whole time in the car about oil filters. I'm certain that we must have sounded like a bunch of nutty kids talking about girls, there was so much enthusiasm. And this was after we sat upstairs in some sort of a small conference room on the second floor for the first hour talking about the same stuff. The mood was that of exuberance.

"So, when we got to the restaurant we were still talking like we were having a mini convention or something. This went on all through lunch, till about the time the last cup of coffee was being served. Then out of left field the chief engineer leans across the table and looks at me square in the eye," and says, "I don't think you have a patent on this filter!"

Kevin didn't even wait for another drop of air to come out of my lungs as he exclaimed, "You've got to be kidding me, right?! So, what did you do? What did ya say? I don't want to come across like a complete ass, but you had a patent on the thing, didn't ya? I mean that's what you said. After all, isn't that why those guys were supposedly meeting with you! Wasn't it?" He couldn't contain himself, he was so floored. "Hey, who were those clowns anyway," he asked, wanting to know.

"I don' t remember their names. I have a letter floating around here in one of my files with a bunch of guys names referenced at the bottom.

I'll have to look it up and let you know the next time I talk with you, ok?"

Still not able to let it go, he half mumbled under his breath, "I can't believe that this happened! So, what did you do?" he said, rushing me along to the outcome.

"I pulled out my briefcase from under the table placing it on my lap and started flipping the locks open when he stopped me. "That won't be necessary Mr. Moor, I have every reason to believe that you don't have a patent on this idea. Oh, shoot I thought, we've just gone from Stevie old pal to Mr. Moor. I was dumfounded. You know!"

"I guess you were man! What a circus aye?" Kevin said, feeling my pain and confusion brought about by the simple desire of bringing something new to his industry.

"Anyway, I had heard about this N.I.H. thing that big established companies sort of adhere to and it was starring me straight in the face on a that sunny day in April. I thought it sounded too farfetched to be real, kinda like the cops having a blue wall of silence sort of thing. But this wall Kevin, it's very real, let me tell you!"

"Steve, what the heck is N.I.H.?"

"Your serious, right Kevin? You mean to tell me that you don't know what N.I.H. stands for?"

"No! I swear to you! I never heard of it before," he said sincerely dumbfounded.

I explained to him that N.I.H. meant 'not invented here' and that I had heard the term used for the first time by a friend of mine, the ex-VP of Engineering for Purolator.

"Sounds kinda dumb, doesn't it?" Kevin replied, as he tried to make it go away.

"Sure, it does, at least on the surface," I said. "But then again, maybe it's not so dumb. Look at it this way. Let's say that you are the ones who are controlling the overall market and you come across a technology that might prove out to be beneficial, but you don't own it. It's owned by someone else. And if that person is small enough, you'd have no problem blocking his entry into your world. In the end Kevin, it's the big players of the world who control what consumers' end up purchasing, now isn't it? So, I guess maybe it's starting to sound kinda real."

"Holy crap, I guess so. But Steve…, what did you do when he told you to put your briefcase down? So, did you put it down like a good little trooper?"

"Yes, of course I did. What do you think that I was going to do? Start a fight with this guy and blow any chance of ever being able to approach the company again! Not a chance! I wasn't about to let my emotions blow this one for me, not after all my hard work!

"There's only four players in this business, remember? What if I came up with a better improvement next week, and I wanted to come back?" I asked, being facetious.

"Besides, my head was already past tilt when he pulled that stunt anyway. I didn't begin to know how to defend myself against such an asinine statement like that. I tried, believe me, but it was of no use. I even brought up the fact that I had mailed a copy of my patent to Bruce. I even interjected something about a conversation I had with the patent examiner in Washington, DC after this patent was issued. Nothing worked! And I was damn sure that he had a copy of my patent lying on his desk back at the office. And if he hadn't of already read it, then why would the chief engineer of Fram be giving up three hours of his precious schedule anyway? For what?

"You answer me that one?" I fired back, swallowed up by the account of my own tale. "He didn't care, the meeting was over, Pal!" I said, rather angrily.

"Wow." He said, his mind completely blown. There was no doubt in my heart that he knew for sure, that with a story like that, I was indeed for real.

"Steve, I believe you Buddy, but I just have to ask, what was Bruce and the other character doing while this was going on?"

"All I can say was that Bruce was simply hog-tied. I only got a glimpse of his face, because he was seated next to me and I couldn't take it all in. All I can tell you is that he looked about as lost as I was. It was rather obvious to me that he didn't have the slightest idea that this was going to happen. And I most definitely got the impression that if he knew that it would of turned out this way, he would have done his best to have spared me of it.

"And as for his side kick, the Director of Manufacturing, he remained motionless. Stone cold, if you know what I mean?"

Kevin's reply was, "Hey that sounds spooky. Doesn't it you?"

At that point, I wished that he could have shielded me from the pain that I had to endure back then, but Kevin was nowhere to be found around Fram's headquarters at that time. For the moment, all I wanted was his understanding to ease the vestige of this old wound..., a wound I had tricked myself into believing was long since healed over.

I was quickly coming to believe in my heart that Kevin was going to become my liaison to this Company..., there was something different about him. I could sense it. And as important as that seemed, I was still under a self-imposed mandate to lay down some ground rules that we both would have to abide by.

I was fully aware of the fact that this guy was holding the power to unlock my dreams, if it was meant to go that way. That was all the more reason why I wanted to be right up front with him.

I didn't want to be played with..., not by him, not anybody. I had tested him to my satisfaction and was sure that I could end up trusting him. 'Anyway..., what real choice did I have?' 'Cause that's just how the game was going to have to be played... On the fly.

Besides, my gut instincts were telling me, that he knew that I was real, and that he might consider taking a gamble on me as well. I just needed to further prove to him that I wasn't some nut job that would wind up getting him into trouble someday for all of his efforts.

There was silence for a long moment. The story seemed to have a numbing effect on the both of us.

Finally, Kevin broke the silence. "Hey man, I'm really sorry that this happened to you," he said contritely. "I apologize on behalf of AlliedSignal Corporation and the entire Fram Division. This isn't what this Company is about. This shouldn't of happened to you at all."

I was touched, and I could just feel it in my spirit that he meant every word. "Thanks for your understanding Kevin, but it's eaten up six years of the clock. Time that both the Company and I won't ever get back. "But I have what I feel is an even a better idea now," I chimed in optimistically. "I just gotta have your word on it, that you'll never hang me out to dry like the last bunch of guys did. I know it wasn't his doing, ...I mean Bruce. He was out gunned for sure. He seemed about as helpless as I was. He didn't see this thing coming either. It was all over his face when the engineer dropped the bomb. You know Kevin, this was just the engineer's way of telling me that I didn't belong out in the heavy surf with the big boys. I'm not that naïve. But let me tell you something, that's still not enough to extinguish my dream."

"Kevin, I just gotta ask one thing of you… Please don't ever try and hype me or lie to me. Okay? It's just not worth it to either of us," I said half threatening war and half pleading for him not to break my heart this time around.

"I won't. You have my word on it. I'll never lie to you, it's not my style Buddy. That's for losers. Listen, I got to go now. I have a meeting in a few minutes," he said abruptly, as if he looked at his watch and wondered where the last forty minutes had gone.

The courtship ritual between the two young bucks was rapidly drawing to a close. I was feeling that great joy, the kind that surpasses any drug. It was welling up from deep with inside of me. The fact that Kevin was in the process of telling me he'd had enough, didn't seem to matter. Lord knows I certainly left him something to ponder about. The idea… The stranger on the other end of the line… His company…, and perhaps most of all, himself.

As for me, I had experienced so many good things during the course of this phone call, I could literally stay high for a week.

"I am very interested in your idea. I see the merit of it." Just then he shared it with me…

"We're looking for a new step-up filter concept and we don't have one nailed down as of yet, because to be truthful with you Steve, we don't have a solid concept. This just might fit the bill. Send me a copy of your patents and anything else that might be helpful. I am going to need all the ammunition I can get when I go to the engineers."

"Gee, thanks a lot Kevin. I'll get this out to you in a few days and I'll call you in a couple of weeks," was about all I could get out, as I felt the tears of joy beginning to well up.

Hanging up the phone I gave a huge shout for joy. It was so strong it shook my kitchen. The guy I just got off the phone with, didn't have the foggiest idea of how happy he had just made me. I couldn't wait for my wife Patti to get home from work, so I could share the news with her. We were about to enter a new phase of the quest and go to places we had never been to before!

I spent the next two days crafting the most important sales letter of my entire life, losing count somewhere after my twelfth revision. Finally, I was able to take the volumes which had been running around in my head and condense them into two short pages. I could only hope that my message was compelling enough for my new found contact to rise above the statuesque and risk his neck for an outsider's idea.

Dear Mr. Gill, *January 7, 1994*

I would like to thank you for giving me the opportunity to speak with you in reference to my patent #5,209,842 on January 5, 1994.

Your open minded and inquisitive demeanor was very much appreciated. I would like to share with you a brief synopsis of how I see this patent's concept in the scheme of the marketplace.

It had nearly been a generation since the advent of the spin on automotive oil filter. This innovation has spawned many of the technological advances in the fields of motor, lubricant and filter design.

Full flow oil filtration is almost impossible to improve upon in its present operational capabilities due to its design constraints.

The media is the determining factor. The only way to get around it is through by-pass filtration, of which we will never see in an automobile environment.

Fram, however, has taken the full flow automotive oil filter to the outer edge of the operational envelope with its premium high efficiency glass media. This product certainly has its appeal for the sophisticate, and the consumer looking for the best in advanced media performance. I don't know how big this market segment is, nor do I know how profitable it has been for you. By the same token, I do give your organization credit for attempting to innovate in such a rigid environment. The prior art in the field of oil filtration is by no means replete with newly issued benchmark patents, a fact we both are cognizant of.

The Teflon treated oil market in the U.S.A. is huge! My source calculates it to be in the hundreds of millions of dollars with healthy growth for the foreseeable future, and a possible doubling in size!

The PTFE material incorporated in 90% or more of these formulated products is DuPont's Teflon. PTFE has been blended with oil and sold as an enhanced super lubricant for almost twenty years.

Teflon has one of the lowest friction-coefficients of virtually any material known to man. A highly technical fact that the general public has assimilated as common knowledge. Teflon has a natural affinity to settle out of suspension when mixed with oil. (As a footnote, the prior art contains several patents on detailing the complexity of keeping PTFE in a colloidal suspension.) Therefore, the products on the market that claim one treatment with PTFE will last 50,000 miles is a fallacy. These products make this claim to justify their twenty-dollar plus per quart price tag. This filter patent counteracts this claim in reality by releasing the Teflon particles over time: hopefully over an oil change interval or some part thereof. This filter does not make any 50,000-mile claim, in fact it is good for one 3,000-mile lube interval and avails itself for repeat business.

On the retail side, NAPA carries Slick 50, and so do many other auto parts chains and independents alike. The retail giants such as Walmart and K Mart, carry this product as well. The Slick 50 marketing campaign ranges the full gamut from TV, radio and print, boasting they have sold over fifteen million copies to date, (at an average cost of $30 per quart).

Product recognition is right out there in the open and the cement that holds this industry together is the rock-solid trademarks of DuPont and Teflon. I recently saw a NASCAR race sponsored Slick 50 with Texaco as a second seed sponsor! Teflon treated oils are being sold by infomercials and are being hawked by the Home Shopping Network and QVC as well!

This product is simple for several key reasons. This filter will be featured as a premium line product with the specific purpose of being able to add a useful and valuable dry lubricant to an automotive lubricating system. It is foolproof because the filter does the work, not the consumer. There is no need to heat the engine, put in a quart less of lube oil, then put in the quart of PTFE treated oil, and the drive the car for the next fifteen minutes. This situation is inconvenient and overwhelming to most car owners and is a significant impediment for new business. Despite these factors, the product still sells fantastically!

This filter would be rather simple to manufacture and therefore, opportunity costs to tool up would be minimal. If this product was priced right, the (competition and market maker) would be decimated, because you could undersell them and still have a high margin filter product line!

I have sent you all the pertinent documentation for you to examine. The possibilities are awesome; I hope you draw the same conclusion.

I let the obligatory waiting period pass, clicking off ten days or so before I would allow myself to call him. Only God knew when I was going to reach him again, which of course left me no other choice than to hope that it would be sooner than later. The passage of time was not a simple thing to deal with. No, not at all. Especially after setting my sights on knocking off the king of the Teflon treated hill…, Slick 50.

It was late in the day on February 12th, 1995 when I had finally reached him. Over a month had passed since our fateful initial conversation. This type of turn-around time between communications, was part and parcel of the big wait. It was great to be talking with Kevin once again.

"Hi Steve, how are you! Sorry it's been a while since we last talked, but I've been traveling a lot and it looks like I'm going to be on the road a lot this quarter. Maybe the next one as well. I hope not, but who knows? I certainly don't," he said.

I replied back, "So they got you runnin', huh Kevin." My mind was reeling, trying to glean through every bit of information that might be coming my way.

"Yes, they do, my good man," was his reply. "Hey, I got your letter right away with your patents, and I read it all. And don't think I didn't, because I didn't call you right away. I've just been really jammed," he said, sounding frazzled.

"I knew you did Kevin," I said, trying to offer him my understanding of his situation.

"I'm sure you must be a busy guy. So, what did you think?" I asked fishing. I was always fishing.

"Hey it was great! What can I tell ya! It was just what we had talked about wasn't it? Except just down on paper and a tad bit briefer," he said, ribbing me.

"I didn't mean to be all over the place when I first talked to you, but ya gotta admit, there was a lot of information," I offered, somewhat defensively.

"You did a great job, really! I just have a little trouble here in paradise now, but hopefully it should work out. Anyway, it had better darn well workout," he said, with quite a bit of emotional charge.

'Oh boy', I thought, bracing myself for disaster. 'What's he gonna say next?' Whatever it was, it didn't sound too promising. At times like this I had no choice but to sure up my foundation, vigilant for any sign of impending disaster. The many hard lessons learned early on had regrettably knocked most of the stars out of my eyes.

I called on my faith. Let's face it, that's all I had to go on at this point in the game. This entire dream, this situation, was so far beyond my control it wasn't funny. I tried to live by a simple axiom through this entire saga. Do my job and do it to the very best of my ability in a timely fashion and at all costs and don't fall prey to fear and worry.

God was in control, because I certainly was not. I incessantly fed myself on that truth. He was the one responsible for planting and nurturing this filter, which had become the vision of my soul. I lived with this vision for over a decade and we couldn't be separated now. I was consumed with it.

So, the question would invariably arise, what was to come of this present situation? 'Was it another stinking lesson of how to cope with failure?' I wasn't sure. However, what I was sure of was that I didn't come this far to fail, even though my mind kept screaming it! But I wasn't biting. No matter what storm clouds started to emanate from Kevin's mouth, I knew that they weren't the product of his manufacture. I was sure of it.

Besides, he wasn't aware of the source backing me. "Kevin," I said, "You might as well be blunt with me, I assure you, that whatever it is, I can deal with it."

He burst out, "It's those damn nudniks in the engineering department," as he let loose. "They're giving me some flack about this idea," he said, rather dejected. "But I am not done with those guys yet, believe me Stevie."

My heart dropped to my feet, as his words penetrated my being. Don't get me wrong, faith or no faith, you still feel the arrow pierce you on the way in, and you definitely feel it as it passes on out. It's how you handle yourself during the attack that counts, I kept telling myself.

"So, what did they say?" I asked, feigning that I wasn't affected by the news.

"They don't like it…." His voice trailing off. "They said the stuff was snake oil. That it really doesn't work," he added. The disappointment in this voice was evident and he didn't bother masking it.

I was keenly aware of the fact that although he and I didn't even remotely know each other, nonetheless we were beginning to share a kindred bond that had been initiated from the onset of our first talk. There was no denying it, he had taken a shine to me, and to my idea.

"Hey Kevin…, is it dead?" I asked, regaining my courage while at the same time trying to cheer him up. The compassion he showed towards me was uplifting.

"Because… if it ain't dead, I'll close the bastards," I shot back, wanting a good fight with the engineers.

"No… Heck no! It ain't dead by a long shot! I ran it by my boss and he saw the merit in it. I ran it by some of the other guys that I know and can trust, and I'm telling ya…, the things got some genuine interest!" his demeanor beginning to rise.

"Who is your boss anyway?" I asked.

"A fellow named Peter Ross."

"How is he? You know what I mean? Is he open-minded? What's he like?"

"Oh, he' fine. He lets me do my own thing. He lets me do the job I'm paid to do."

"Well then, that's great. At least you don't have to worry about locking horns with your boss."

"Who, Peter?" he replied. "No way. We get along just fine."

I was definitely seeing a ray of hope after he shared that important insight. I said to him, "Listen now, take it from me, one salesman to another, don't worry about the engineers. All we have to do is isolate their objections and proceed from that point. Okay? I mean… I'm willing to do that much, are you?"

"Yeah, of course I am. It's just that you make it sound so simple. And I wish it was. You know, talking to those guys, I mean..."

I knew he thought that I was operating in some sort of vacuum, but I wasn't. I was just confident that I'd be able to handle those people, was all.

I asked, nudging him along, "So what do the engineers need so that they'll get on board?"

His reply to my stupid question was rather obvious. "Facts man! Facts! You must have that kind of information around that you could send off to me. Don't you?"

"Actually, I don't have the kinda information that you're going to need." I regretted being so candid with him, but I wasn't left any other choice. The truth was premiere.

"Well my friend, I gotta be straight with you. Unless you can produce what we need in order to convince these guys that what you have is real, we're dead in the water. I just want to know that. I'm not playing any games with you Steve. Okay?"

For which I replied, "Well then, can I ask you a stupid question?"

"Yea sure, I don't care. Go right ahead!"

"Those guys have a whole department at their disposal, right?

"Yea…"

"So, you mean to tell me that they can't take some junior engineer from some place, you know, a go-for, and assign him to do the research for this project instead of me? I mean after all Kevin, the possibilities we discussed, the sheer potential of the thing is enormous. In light of everything that we've discussed, they're not motivated to at least invest that much of an effort to find out what I've told you is true!" I asked, sincerely incredulous.

"Yea I was right! He shouted back through the phone at me. "You are crazy!" he said with a sarcastic chuckle.

"They don't like it man! Get it!" Taking the liberty of asking me a stupid question himself, he asked, "Now why the heck are they going to expend the time and effort to support something they don't like? You're a smart guy, so figure it out for yourself!" Boy that sure had the ring of finality to it, leaving me no choice.

"Well you've made the situation pretty obvious to me. I'm just going to have to get my butt in gear and get this material. You know Kevin, I never dreamt that it would be necessary for me to have to convince a major company about something they should already be up on. I was sure all along that this idea would be a no-brainer. But I guess it's not.

"I don't want to get longwinded Kev, but when I was dealing with Purolator, they wanted me to provide them with a full-blown test study. It was going to clock in at about two hundred and fifty grand. The basic analysis was going to tell us that Teflon when mixed with motor oil is slippery and that people are willing to put into their engines to the tune of a half a billion dollars a year. 'Why?' Because it works.

"I wasn't about ready to do that for them, and I'm darn sure not willing to do it for you guys now," as I muttered under my breath. "Yea sure, spend a quarter of a million dollars to prove a point only to have a company tell me that they still weren't interested…, no way am I that stupid.

"Besides, any fool should be able to look at the established up and running Teflon treated oil market and determine that much. But, I guess we're not dealing with just any fool here, huh Kevin? 'Cause we're dealing with Fram's Chief Oil Filter Engineer, I dealt with him before, remember?" One thing for sure, I was still not in receipt of my healing yet, unable to resist taking a shot at him.

Kevin said, "Hey my friend, let's hope that it doesn't come to that, because if it does, I guess you'll be about finished. But anyway, this is what I have to do now… I have to send you back the materials that you sent me," he said, sounding rather sad to be putting me through such a stupid exercise.

"I don't want to, but I have to. It is some sort of legal thing, a company policy."

"I know." I replied, trying to make him feel better. "It's a form of sending me a 'thanks but no thanks letter.' It's okay, I've been there before."

"Yeah whatever. Don't worry about it," he said, trying to get me off the subject. "It ain't over till it's over. You know how the game is played," he offered.

I replied, "I sure do…, but can I ask you one more question? Did you at least make a copy for yourself?"

"Now what do you think, Stevie?" was his immediate reply.

"Okay my friend," I said to him, "The ball is in my court and I had better hustle and find you some published test studies that will prove my point. That's going to be about the best I can do, 'cause I ain't paying for some huge company's test study."

"That's what we are going to need at the very least," he said, trying to be as positive as possible. "Remember, you don't have anything to prove to me, I have faith in you. When you get my letter don't let it bum you out, ok?"

"Hey! I won't. Thanks for all of your support. I'm just gonna go out and do this thing. I won't be calling you much except to say hello and to give you an occasional update."

"You go right ahead and be my guest, your call is always welcome. I'll always have time for you unless I'm in the middle of something, you know that."

I did 'know that,' and I was strengthened by his belief in me and the fervor he was showing towards my filter. I set my face like flint against the buffeting winds of rejection. I was going to accomplish what needed to be done.

"Stevie, I gotta run now. I'll be in touch Buddy. Don't you worry!

I'll be building consensus as I go along. Good luck!"

I was left no choice but to do my job. That meant that I had to commit to scouring the entire planet manually to find the valuable test studies that would be able to put me over the top. To say that it was a herculean task without the aid of the internet, would surely be an understatement. But after several months of hard digging I finally got what I needed. I was ready to get back in the game...

Salmon River in the fall of '94.   Pulaski, N.Y.

Solo fishing excursion in search of the land-locked giants.

CHAPTER 2
PRELUDE TO THE DANCE

Through the years, the love of the outdoors grew in me as I matured into manhood. That was certainly one of the purest gifts that my dad had imparted to me. I was drawn with equal fervor whether it be to the mountains, streams, lakes and woods or the majestic ocean with all of its changing moods.

It was getting on to be late September, and here at home on the Jersey shore we were enjoying the blessings of an Indian summer. It's a brief time of year when natures beauty is surreal. A time when sun and sky play off the warm clear waters of Atlantic and the crisp surf breaks into aqua-marine jade. And it was time for me to get ready and head on up to the Salmon River north of Syracuse, NY, to intercept the fall run of the land locked king salmon. The fall of 1994 was fast approaching, and I had been building a relationship with Kevin for the past nine months. We had been moving forward toward our objective of providing the engineers the type information that would hopefully prove our point conclusively, that Teflon treated oils had scientific merit.

Over a month ago I had sent Kevin a collection of six independently published technical papers. These various papers summarized the studies performed by different engineering groups employing the scientific method using S.A.E. (Society of Automotive Engineers) and API (American Petroleum Institute) guidelines to arrive at their results. Their findings were conclusive and significant. The results demonstrated that PTFE (polytetrafluoroethylene) or Teflon, had a beneficial effect when mixed with motor oil for lubricating purposes.

I had searched high and low to obtain this material. The fact that I had turned up anything at all in my search was miraculous indeed. As it turns out, this field of enhanced lubricating additives is an arcane field to start with and experimentation with PTFE is even rarer yet.

Keep in mind that I did all this research manually, by phone, letters and library. I didn't have the luxury of the Internet at the time. I'm not even sure if this stuff can be retrieved off of it now, but as of yet I couldn't be bothered to find out.

I hadn't talked with Kevin since I had sent him the package other than when I called him to make sure it had arrived. He told me that it had arrived, and that he had passed the information along to the engineers. There wasn't much else that he, nor I could do at this point, except wait patiently for their response. But that was over a month ago. I couldn't help but wonder what was going on after all my hard work.

'Did my missile hit the intended target? It had to, didn't it? Those guys couldn't be so stubborn and that blind as to disregard the indisputable facts, could they?'

I reasoned that they sure were capable of dismissing the truth, but that they weren't going to do it in this case. Not with Kevin looking over their shoulders.

'It was just that they needed time to go over the data. Right?'

This odyssey was turning out to be a testimony of my ability to dole out time like it was an inexhaustible commodity and I was seriously contemplating canceling my fishing trip this year due to everything that I had in the works with Fram.

Well darn it, I had decided that I wasn't going to go along with it any longer! I was going fishing come hell or high water. Just like I had done for the last eight fall salmon runs. I decided that I wasn't going to hang around and become a prisoner of some darn phone call that may never come.

My wife Patti knew that I had been working hard trying to keep all the balls in the air. She felt that it was best that I take a few days off to clear my head and go enjoy myself fishing. Not that she couldn't use a break from her exhaustive schedule either, raising two young children and holding down a full-time job as a first-grade teacher.

Patti is a very selfless person and routinely donated her life force to me in an effort to keep me as energized as possible. My quest had become hers. Most of the time she was at a loss to help me, however, she gave me her most precious commodity, her undying support. Patti was intuitive enough to know that after a short fishing trip, I'd return with new life pumped into me, ready to jump back into the raging battle.

I had reserved a room for a couple of days above Tony's Bait and Tackle shop for the middle of the last week in September. I thought that I had better call Kevin and let him know what I was up to, so I put a call into him a day or so before I was scheduled to leave for New York…, just in case.

"Hi Kevin! It's Steve Moor, how are you?"

"Hey, great Steve! How are you doing buddy?" he shot back full of enthusiasm. This job of his was like an opiate or something to him. I could tell he got high off of it. At times, I had to wonder. Here I was, this free agent, an entrepreneur, an inventor with no strings to hold me back and this guy's enthusiasm was so infectious that I was tempted on several occasions to trade positions with him.

I asked him, "What's going on concerning the test studies that I sent ya? The engineers have had that stuff for over a month. Haven't they?" I said, matter of fact. It wasn't going to do me much good to get excited and hot under the collar with Kevin, the delay wasn't his fault.

"Yeah, I know…, I know. What can I tell you? I agree that they've had plenty of time to take a good look at the materials. I'm just gonna have to put in a call and see what's up with those guys."

"That's fine by me. I'd like to know what's going on as well, if you know what I mean. But that's not why I called you."

"It isn't?" he asked, sounding puzzled.

"No, it's not." I felt kinda self-conscious at this point telling him that I was going fishing. In some weird way, I felt like I was cheating on him, leaving him in the fray at his post.

"I'm going to take the next few days off and go salmon fishing in upstate New York."

"You are! That sounds cool, I wish that I could go with you! Hey! I thought that salmon was a west coast thing? You said, you're going to New York State?"

"That's right. There's plenty of salmon right here in Lake Ontario and they happen to migrate up the Salmon River that runs through the small town of Pulaski every fall."

"So… Did you call, to let me know about the salmon run?" he said, ribbing me.

I said, "Nice try, I just called to let you know that I'll be out of town for the next few days. I'll be home Friday night. It's been a month now, and I just kinda have a premonition… I know that you don't subscribe to that sort of stuff so to speak but indulge me on this one. Okay Kev?"

"Okay, yea sure. I'm going to talk with those guys. I guess anything could turn up in the next few days. Hey…, you know that I am squarely on your side Buddy and that I'd be the last one to doubt you."

"….and Kevin, if you need me for any reason call my house and talk with my wife. She gets home from work every day at about four o'clock. Or you can leave a message on my machine and I'll get it. I talk with her every night when I'm away from home."

"Sounds good my man. I hope you have a good trip. I'm going to give the engineers a call and I'll talk with you after you get back. Take care."

The fishing was excellent, and the weather was almost as nice as what I had left behind at home. I fished in a tee shirt even though the beautiful foliage suggested otherwise. I was fortunate to find the river with perfect conditions. Beautiful, with clear water, bright sunlight with plenty of huge salmon holding behind boulders and laying up in pools making it a dream, to sight cast to them.

Every night while I was gone I called my wife. And every night that I called she would say the same thing. "No, he didn't call today, and he wasn't on the recorder either."

I had only spoken with him a few days ago and everything seemed all right then, if you could say that. Yet somehow, I had this feeling gnawing at me that he was going to call. There was something brewing, I just knew it, that's why I fought so hard with myself to justify leaving for the trip in the first place. I wasn't sure why, but I could just feel it deep down inside where I lived.

That premonition gently dogged me the whole time that I was gone. I really wasn't sure if my mind had been playing some sort of trick on me or not. Or was it the guilt of leaving my little family behind while Daddy decompressed for a few days. I wasn't exactly sure, but I called Kevin first thing Monday morning. It was totally out of character for me to have done so without a legitimate reason, I'd never done anything like that before.

As fate would have it, he was in his office and picked up the phone. I thanked the Lord that he wasn't in some inane meeting or out running the road.

"Hey Steve! Where the heck have you been!" he screamed into the phone. He was so loud, I thought that he was going to bite the bottom out of it.

"I've been trying to get a hold of you!"

'Gee,' I wondered to myself, how could that be possible? I checked in at home every day and I'm sure that my answering machine was working, and my wife knows how to take a message. Besides, if he needed to speak to me bad enough, I was sure he'd keep calling until he reached Patti. He wasn't bashful, that much I was sure of.

What I am going to propose might sound a little crazy and out of character for Kevin, but maybe he was just trying to reach me in his mind. He sure hadn't left behind any tangible signs of his trying. It was really kind of weird for this guy who was so methodical to be acting this way.

Normally, I would try to explain myself and communicate my way to the bottom of something, but he seemed so worked up. So, I decided to pass on that option, knowing that it was better for me to just keep my mouth shut and listen.

Hopefully he was going to tell me what was going down quicker than I could ever piece together what was happening. Out of breath, and more or less shouting, he blurted out, "The engineers are coming in from all over the damn country and Canada to meet here this Friday! In Rhode Island!

The senior VP of Marketing for Fram is going to be present along with a lot of other people. There are going to be people from engineering and manufacturing, and a team from marketing is being assembled as well! There's even going to be someone present from legal! They are all going to be in the same room at the same time! It's unbelievable Stevie! I can't believe it!" as he continued to shout.

Continuing, not able to control himself, "You don't know man, but this never happens! Steve...! Can you come?" It was as passionate of an invitation that I can ever remember receiving in my life. He was pleading with me and it was mind-boggling. In its wake, I can remember going blank...

I replied matter of factly, "Yea sure, but I have to check my schedule."

He screamed back through the phone at me, "What are you crazy! What the heck do you mean, check your schedule! You can't be joking, are you?" He was ranting now, his voice getting raspy. "This is it Bud! This show ain't never happening again! Not here, not now and not ever! I seriously doubt this will ever happen again in either of our lifetimes..."

The moment about to unfold was not only mine, but in some respects, it was his as well. And he wasn't trying to twist my arm nor bully me, but he wasn't going to take no for an answer. Kevin was too much of a gentleman for that, besides that, he was too smart. What I really think he was doing was trying to see if I had lost my mind. Because, perhaps, I temporarily must have. My lackadaisical response had thrown him a curve he couldn't handle. My reply was never meant to hurt him, but I could tell that I had inadvertently wounded him.

"What's the heck is the matter with you Steven? This is your big moment. You have to come! This is what we've been waiting for. I've scheduled you in for two hours!" My lackluster response left him perplexed as his hurt rose to the surface.

Even at this nebulous juncture in the project he was already assuming his protective role as my co-partner. A role that I would freely share with him, co-birther of this revolutionary new oil filter.

Even to this day I don't know why I gave him such a ridiculously nonchalant reply, like, "I would have to check my schedule."

'After all that's why I had sacrificed my career path to become a real estate agent, wasn't it?' So that I could answer the bell at moments like this without being beholden to forty-hour a week time clock. Who was I kidding anyway? I didn't have a rigid schedule to keep and Kevin knew that as well as I did. It would have been impossible to have babied this process along without the luxury of flex time and I knew it.

Besides, I wanted this thing so bad that I would have missed the birth of my first-born child for this moment. 'Yet how could I have been so glib when he first told me of the news? I don't know?'

Looking back at it now, the only plausible explanation I could give was that I was just worn down from the battle at that particular time. In a way, it didn't matter that I had just come back from fishing. Or that I had just spent three days in God's country standing in a river up to my belly landing fish my father had only dreamt about.

All I can tell you is that apparently; the balm wasn't strong enough to free me from the thoughts about the filter... the filter! Oh, how it played through my consciousness relentlessly. I tried turning these thoughts over to God, I knew that's what I should do about this thing, but I was helpless.

No doubt I was indeed possessed of this thing and behaved rather foolishly, by playing hard to get..., and with Kevin of all people.

Fortunately, in the mist of my self-introspection, I came abruptly to my senses and realized that I wasn't only hurting myself, but Kevin as well. By this time Kevin was not only an ally, but I considered him a friend.

Grabbing hold of myself, I shouted back as if from the dead, "Of course I'll be there! I can't believe this is happening! My focus returning, "So when did all of this come about? The meeting and all!" I asked, once again backed by all the enthusiasm that had propelled me thus far.

"I'm glad you finally realized what I've been trying to tell you," he said, truly relieved. Adding, "You really had me going there for a moment Buddy. You know that?"

"I'm sorry Kev, I didn't realize…" I said, apologetically.

"Don't worry about it now, it's forgotten Steve. Let's talk about what is going down on Friday," he said, all business now, putting the tryst behind us and taking charge of the situation. Confident as ever, he began to describe what was about to transpire while I listened on in awestruck silence.

"A couple of days ago while you were gone, I believe it was last Thursday, I got wind of this memo floating around. It's really weird, but this meeting materialized out of thin air. The top engineering and manufacturing staff is flying in from Ohio, Indiana, Canada and other places to have some sort of a big meeting here. Us guys in marketing weren't exactly included in this get together of theirs when this thing first began you know."

I interrupted him at that point, "Kevin, don't mind me jumping in, but the last time I worked with the Company, the engineers were all based out of Rhode Island?"

He replied, "Yeah I know that, but a couple of years ago they were relocated to a new research and development facility out in Perrysburg, Ohio. There's hardly an engineering staff left here at all. They've all been shipped out."

What he said didn't exactly make sense to me, so unable to resist I asked, "But what are they doing out in Ohio when the main corporate office is back here in Rhode Island?" Trying to get as accurate picture of the company as possible.

"Most of our manufacturing plants are located out there, in Ohio and Indiana, out there in the rust belt. It just makes sense that they are closer to the points of production and as close to Detroit as possible. You know what I'm talking about?" he said, sounding anxious to get back to where he was before I had interrupted him.

"Okay, so what exactly are they doing coming here?" still trying to get every detail that I could.

"You know; I really can't answer that."

"Why?" I asked.

"Because Steve, frankly I really don't know, or I'd tell ya. Come on now, would ya?" his patience wearing a bit thin. "All I know is that they are coming to corporate to have this big meeting, but that's really not important now. Oh, I guess it might be, I'll find out for you latter. Okay?" he said, indulging me a bit. "It's not like it's a top secret or something, all I have to do is ask. I'm sure it's not that much of a mystery.

"But listen to me, all that really matters now is that you are going to have two full hours to be able to explain yourself to these guys and everyone else in the room!" Adding, "I think that's great! Don't you?!"

"Yeah sure, but I've never done any public speaking before. I've never given a presentation like this either," I offered quite sheepishly.

"You'll be fine! Are you kidding? This is going to be a piece of cake for you," he said with all sincerity, building me up for the event like a good trainer.

I asked him, "Should I change anything in my approach?"

"No! Absolutely not!" Not allowing me another chance to finish my self-recrimination.

"What if I get excited during my spiel and kinda let loose on the bunch during this whole thing? You kinda know how I can get." By this time Kevin had endured about enough of my self-effacing bull as he could stand and proceeded to set me straight.

"Steve, cut the crap, this thing is in your blood, you know it inside and out. Do you think for one moment that there is anyone in the room that knows more about this thing than you do? Well..., do ya? I sincerely doubt it, so come on now, okay! Besides, excitement sells man. You closed me. Didn't ya?"

"Okay, okay..." knowing he was right. I certainly had the ability to present my case. I was up to the job and we both knew it.

"Kevin, changing the subject for a minute, who is going to be present at this meeting from marketing? Is your boss Peter Ross going to be there?" I asked inquisitively.

"No. He's not going to make it. He's traveling out on business to the west coast."

"Is that going to matter?" I asked, trying to get a solid grip on the dynamics that existed between Kevin and his boss.

"No not at all. I wish he could be there, so you guys could meet each other, but it's really not that big of a deal, he's on board, I already told you that. But his boss will be there, the Executive Vice President of Fram. Now my man, that's pretty damn important." As he fell silent, he then added, "That's for sure...!"

Unable to resist, I asked, "What's this guy's name?"

"Jack McGrath. He's a pretty good guy and he's got an open mind. He's interested in what you have to say. As a matter of fact, since Peter's been away, he's the guy I went to when I had heard that the engineers were coming to town and he is the one who orchestrated this thing for your benefit. Are you starting to get the picture?"

"Yes, I am," I replied, beginning to see how this production was coming together. "Gee that sounds pretty positive. Doesn't it, Kev?" I asked, wishing the presentation was a thing of the past, and that I could forego the whole ordeal of giving a major performance.

"It sure does my man. Stevie, if you get Jack's blessing, you'll be on your way!"

It was special times like this, that drew us both closer together. Kevin seemed so altruistic about the whole thing, he didn't appear the least bit threatened or jealous about the prospects of my succeeding, then again... Nor was I so naïve as to what might be on his agenda. He was entitled to reap whatever reward he could from the success of this project and as far as I was concerned, if he was going to bless me with his efforts, then I certainly wanted to see him rewarded in spades.

You know, I had been working on this patent thing seemingly alone for what had felt like an eternity. Only Patti, my soul mate; Kevin my new-found ally; and a few select kindred spirits were able to fathom the enormity of my success if it were to come to pass. And I am not talking from a financial standpoint. That was still quite an unknown and would yet to be revealed until much later on. My monetary rewards would squarely be set in the hands AlliedSignal along with their Fram

Division as to how they were willing to deal with me and my invention, because at this point I didn't have a clue.

"Hey Kev, I got a question for you. Is this engineer the same guy I met six years ago when I called on Fram? Is he still with the Company? And what about his sidekick, that Indian looking fella in manufacturing? Will he be there?"

Kevin let out a raspy laugh as he bellowed out, "You really crack me up man... The head of manufacturing's name is Henry Dorsett. And by the way Steve, he's the Head of Manufacturing for the Autolite Spark Plug Group Division. And one last thing, I don't recall him being of Indian abstraction," he said sarcastically.

"And if the engineer you met with six years ago was Tony Coronia, then he'll be there, because he's still the Chief Engineer for the Fram Filter Division. But it really doesn't matter this time Steve, don't you see that? There's going to be a ton of people in the room. Don't worry, it's not going to be like last time. I assure you, it's impossible!"

"Okay, I guess you're right. Ah..., I know you are," I said, trusting him.

As usual another call came in, invading our interlude. It was Kevin's secretary reminding him that he had a meeting in ten minutes.

"Hey Steve, I gotta run in a few. I really hate cutting you off like this man," he said apologetically. "We'll get to spend some quality time together when you come up. Okay?"

I replied, "I'm fine Kev, but I just have two quick questions for ya." He said, "Okay, shoot."

"The only thing we didn't cover at all was the part about legal. You said something about legal. Something to the effect that someone from the legal department was going to be there."

"Boy! Am I glad that you reminded me! It's really important and I forgot all about it with all the other stuff that we've been talking about. Look, I am going to give you this person's name and extension, do you have a piece of paper and pencil handy?"

"Yea sure. Fire away."

"I'll spell it for you... Dianne Newman, extension 3648. Got that? It's really important you talk with her. It wouldn't hurt for me to transfer you over to her office when we're done. She's probably got some legal documents for you both to discuss and go over. I'm sure it's nothing out of the ordinary, no big deal." He said, making light of formality.

"No problem, I be glad to talk with her. Just one last quick point. I am going to drive up the night before the meeting. I think that would be best. It's a healthy five-and-a-half-hour drive for me to get here without any unforeseen traffic problems. Where's a good place to stay?"

"Oh, I already have a good place lined up for you to stay. Talk with Jodi my secretary, she's going to get directions for you and confirm all the arrangements."

"Steve, I gotta run Buddy. Okay? I'll be in all this week, so give me a call before you come up. Hopefully, Thursday night I can catch you and we can go out for a beer or something. I'm really looking forward to meeting you."

"Same here Kev. I'll catch you later."

When Kevin dropped off the line he transferred my call over to Dianne Newman's office. The phone rang a few times and the pleasant voice of a woman picked up, "Hello, Dianne Newman."

"Hi Dianne, my name is Stephen Moor. I'm working with Kevin Gill. I have a patent on an oil filter that the company might be interested in, perhaps for a new product," blurting out all starry eyed. "I am scheduled to attend a meeting this Friday, October 7th. Kevin told me that we needed to speak to each other as soon as possible."

"Okay," she said. "That's fine Steve, I trust that everything is going along smoothly for you."

"Yes, sure. Kevin's been great to work with," I said enthusiastically.

The extent of her response was a ho-hum, "Oh." I remarked to myself that 'she obviously didn't share the same feelings towards him that I did.' If I had only known at the time what lie in store for me, I would have armed myself with a machine gun. But you have to understand something, on a journey such as this, there aren't any crystal balls.

She then asked me a question that threw me off guard. "So, what can I do for you?" At that point, I stopped short to catch my breath as I ran the response through my mind, 'she's supposed to be telling me what the next step is, not the other way around.'

I was baffled and thought that perhaps I didn't make myself clear enough the first time, so I repeated myself again for her benefit. After all, I heard her flailing away on the key board of her computer the moment she picked up the phone and she was still going at it like a fish slapping on a bank.

When I began to restate my business she stopped typing and appeared to know what was required. "Oh, I need to get a 'proprietary information agreement' sent out to you right away. Do you have a fax machine?"

I replied, "No I don't own a fax machine, but I have access to one at the real estate office where I work. I'll give you that fax number and you can send it there."

"Very well then, I will be faxing you out a copy of this agreement as soon as I can. Please feel free to look it over and if you have any questions or changes you might feel are necessary we can go over them after you have received it. Okay?"

I told her that was fine with me and I would call her as soon as I read over the document and asked her to transfer me back to Kevin's secretary.

The fax came through the next morning at eight o'clock. It was my habit to be in the office early and I was able to receive this document as it was coming through, before any of my well-intentioned co-workers had picked it up.

Sitting down at my desk I read it over carefully. The contract was simple enough, though I'll be the first to admit that I am not a legal mind. I mulled it over in my head as to whether I needed to consult a patent attorney before signing it. Oh, it wasn't like I couldn't of rustled one up somewhere, but I just decided against starting the meter running at this juncture for a couple of reasons.

To start with, I would characterize my relationship with Fram at this point as pre-courtship. The prospect of a commitment especially on their part was way in the offing. Secondly, I earnestly wanted to go into business with them and was I prepared to trust them at face value. And by the way, the vast majority of my trust had been placed in Kevin. Even though he was a company man, I felt that he would keep the playing field as level as possible for me. If there was one point of contention I found in the agreement, it was under paragraph one… "If the Proprietary Information is orally disclosed, it must be reduced to written form and delivered to Allied within thirty (30) days of such oral disclosure."

I wanted this time period to be extended from thirty days to sixty days especially on my behalf. My line of reasoning was that the flow of proprietary information was going to be from me to them. After all, I was bringing them the idea in its entirety and not vice-versa and I wanted the extra time to cover myself, if I needed it. I was hardy chained to a typewriter in my basement.

I called Dianne later on that day and told her that I had agreed to the contract except for one minor request, pertaining to the time frame for the oral disclosure. She in turn had no problem with that request and faxed me out an amended contract with the revised change.

It was late Wednesday afternoon by now and I had just received the final version of the agreement by fax. Dianne told me that it wouldn't be expedient for her to send me out the originals to sign at this late date and that it would be just fine for me to sign them the morning of the meeting.

With all of that behind me, the thought of making a presentation in front of all those people started to loom up bigger than life.

I headed down to the furnace room in my basement which doubled as the projects archive, to get some important papers. The prospect of the impending presentation began to press in upon me with an anxiety that could kill, if I let it.

I began to sort through mounds of files trying to recall where I had last remembered seeing the files I had come down to retrieve. There were dozens upon dozens of files strewn about several shelves and a work bench that contained anything pertaining to my patents, including all of my hand-written patent manuscripts.

As I rooted through my most recent files, a sense of relief came over me as the test studies I had just compiled appeared. I sorted through about a dozen or so of them and put the ones that I needed aside. I pulled out all of the material that I had gathered from DuPont and anything concerning Teflon, putting those materials aside as well. Although my grasp of the subject matter was solid, I was determined to spend the next couple of days cramming for nothing short of an inquisition.

Wednesday evening had rolled around, and Patti and I found ourselves lying in bed talking. It was the night before I was about to leave for Rhode Island and the house was quiet as the kids lay sound asleep in their rooms. Finally, we were able to carry on a sane conversation without them interrupting. However, I could see that the moment was going to be short lived, Pat was starting to fade fast, and our time alone looked like it would be coming to an abrupt halt. I hurried to get my thoughts out before sleep took her off, but before I had the chance, she fell asleep. My heart went out to my gentle worker, who was totally played out by the demands of her day. Patti could work boy. It was scary at times. She could outwork most men I knew. Often times making me feel rather guilty at how hard she could pull the sled. I gave her a gentle hug, so not to wake her, wishing her good night.

Although mentally drained, I was still too wound up to sleep. I didn't want to study anymore for the meeting, and no amount of guilt could motivate me to do so. So, I slipped out of bed, thinking Patti was sound asleep. As I began to quietly dress in the dark, she broke the silence with a sleepy whisper, "Where're you going honey?"

Softly, I replied, "To the canal. I'm too wired. There's so much going through my head, I can't sleep now."

Half asleep, in a gentle motherly huff she said, "You better go to sleep now. You have such a long ride ahead of you tomorrow." With that, I gave her a kiss on the cheek and told her that I loved her.

Cooing, she warned, "Be careful, and good luck."

As I walked out the door I was greeted by the still night, absent of any sign of the moon. The warm, clear the night air, radiated the magnificence of the heavens above. The garage door broke the silence as I reached in to grab my fishing rod, long handled net and tackle bag.

Our house was close to the canal, a man-made ribbon of water about a mile in length, perhaps a couple of hundred feet wide, hemmed in on both sides with steel bulk heading. It was great stretch of water that held a large population of striped bass that were especially cooperative during the spring and fall, before migrating out to the ocean.

Stripers for the most part are nocturnal creatures and that made it possible for me to pursue them while most fishermen stayed at home sleeping.

In the midst of loading the gear, my thoughts suddenly turned to Patti, and her concern for me being too tired to drive to Rhode Island the next day. As I closed the back hatch of our Dodge Caravan, I began to drift back… Eying the family transporter in the dark, I was reminded that it was hardly a substitute for my beloved Kenworth K100 tractor, the one with that big CAT engine and 15 speed transmission. As I opened the driver's door to get in, I thought back to the thousands of hours I spent float-shifting through all those gears, mesmerized by the other worldly whine of her turbo. It was a memory that had been fading fast, as my life sped on. Yet somehow, there was a vestige that remained. I couldn't help but remind my humble little van, that the big KW and I used to take off from this very spot, heading out for many a midnight run. Heading for destinations far out into the night.

That time was well in the rear-view mirror now, but every once in a while, the truck driver in me would come out, untethered by some environmental cue. Uncontrollably…, certain things would trigger my longing to get behind the wheel again. Like a bad habit, it was still in my blood, these long ten years. Being an over the road trucker was an important part of my past. Like a tough old friend, it played an integral part in the forging of my character. To be sure, the business had taught me endurance along with how to be self-reliant and fiercely independent.

Sadly, the only traces of that life which remained, were some old memories accompanied by a few stubborn oil stains that still marred driveway.

I drove over the bridge looking down at the water as I headed towards my favorite spot. From atop the bridge looking down some forty feet below I could see that the tide was beginning to run out of the bay heading towards the ocean. I hadn't fished for a few days and I was eager to get into it again, having heard that the outgoing tide had recently produced some nice fish in the twenty-pound class.

My heart raced with anticipation as I approached the canal. It was a season of anticipation for me. In a couple of weeks, I'd be donning my neoprene waders and waterproof kayakers jacket prowling the surf line in the middle of the night. Like a skilled predator, I knew every changing cut along the beach. Whether alone or with a proven buddy, I'd stalk the stripers feeding amongst the waves during their migratory run south along the coast.

The night air was scented with the sweet smell of the salty brine as it drifted off the water and for a brief moment I was loosed, free of the pursuit of the great filter chase. My mind, like the bay running down the canal, was emptying out into the peaceful black night.

Thursday morning, I got a hold of Kevin and told him that I planned to arrive in Rumford late that evening, around nine or ten o'clock. I told him that I wanted to hit the George Washington Bridge and the north bound Cross Bronx Expressway as much after rush hour as I could. He understood exactly and wished me a good trip, although he regretted the fact that my plans wouldn't allow for us to meet before my big day.

You see, at this point, after nine months of talking on the phone and doing our best to make this opportunity unfold, Kevin and I had yet to meet each other face to face. He informed me that he would be too busy lining things up in the morning, so that even a quick breakfast would have been out of the question.

"Hey Steve upon your arrival at headquarters tomorrow, the receptionist will know to ring for me at the meeting. Okay? Then I'll come and get you and bring you up to my office where you're going to have to wait for a little while. Is that all right? Are you with me Buddy? Because trust me, there is a method to my madness."

By now he intuitively knew me well enough to feed me all of the information beforehand, so I wouldn't slow him down with a barrage of questions. "Here it is. Say these guys finish their business early, and there's always the remote chance that they might, well…, I want you around and ready for 'em. I want to get you as much time as you need."

I must have driven my parent's crazy when I was growing up by asking them 'why' all of the time, and I guess things weren't much different now that I was an adult. "Kevin if you don't mind, can I ask you why?"

"Yes, sure." Then he added for my edification, "It's just that I want to keep their stream of productivity flowing. Or maybe I can get you another fifteen minutes or half hour. It just might make the difference between success and failure. I don't know what's going to happen, I just want you to be there and primed. You know, vintage Steve!"

As our conversation was winding down I told him, "I'm fine with whatever you say Kev, you're my guide on this safari and I'll do whatever you think is best. I'm set, if you are. I'm looking forward to all that tomorrow has in store for us both," I said, excitedly.

He replied, "Whatever that means. Yeah me-too Buddy."

Sometimes my approach to this situation was just a bit too ephemeral for him. I don't blame him at all, he didn't know by what technique I was climbing this mountain. I had withheld that side of myself for a more appropriate time.

I spent the rest of the day reading and going over the test studies along with the other related materials. I was bent on knowing this stuff inside and out. The last thing that I needed was to be put on the spot by some engineer or chemist that might have been brought in for the occasion just to test me.

The task was daunting, and this situation could have put me past overload if I would have allowed it. Although I was well versed in this field, I still found it no small consolation that I had to address a room full of experts. At least I anticipated they'd be experts. It was my manner to always, whenever possible, to over-prepare.

Looking on the bright side I had my presentation down fairly well. I certainly had enough time to prepare for it during the course of the last several years, and more specifically in the last few months.

At this point in time I had found myself eight full years into the odyssey and I'd been living vicariously for this moment to arrive all along.

I arrived at Fram's headquarters in Rumford, Rhode Island at about a quarter to nine on the morning of Friday, October 7, 1994. The morning was clear and crisp, and it was setting itself up to be a beautiful day. I had the benefit of an enjoyable ride up that culminated with pleasant room and a good night's sleep.

During the previous evenings drive, somewhere in northern Connecticut, my presentation took on what I felt was its final form. I was primed to go. My heart raced, fed by the anticipation of the moment, not to mention aided by the adrenaline that was already copiously flowing. As I got out of the car that morning at Fram's headquarters, my eye caught the corner of the building and this incredible feeling of Deja vu came all over me.

'Yeah, I know that I was here in the late spring of '89,' I told myself, as the debate raged on in my head. I can't explain it, but I was compelled to walk towards the south-east corner of the building and away from the front door. It was so weird, this place looked more than familiar to me, almost like I had been here in a previous life…, a dream seemed more plausible, I reasoned.

'Your acting like an idiot,' I told myself. 'You don't believe one lick in reincarnation and you certainly don't prescribe to that previous life fable either.'

Rounding the corner by the employees parking lot, I looked at my watch. 'Oh good, I still have ten minutes before I go in.' By now curiosity had gotten the better of me. The little drainage ditch and service road, the warehouse type building in the back, they all looked so familiar. As I turned around to begin heading for the main entrance and it suddenly dawned on me!

'You had a delivery here when you were trucking! So that's why it was stuck in your head and you couldn't shake it loose.'

Really, it was no big deal and I didn't put much stock in the fact that I had been here before on non-filter related business, but I had to marvel in a sense how coincidental one's destiny could be. I must have made a delivery here sometime in the early eighties, as best as I could figure. Then I mused, 'was this whole episode part of my destiny? Like the guy in the mail room that eventually becomes the company's president?' I didn't know the answer to that one and I didn't see how it could possibly affect the outcome of today's meeting either.

In flash, it had all come rushing back. I was driving for an owner operator at the time. She owned a couple of International Trans Star single screw tractors, which she had leased to North American Van Lines special products division, hauling primarily new furniture. One day while I was revisiting North American Training Academy, the tractor trailer driving school that I had graduated from in Newark, Delaware, she happened to show up with one of her rigs looking for an able-bodied graduate.

It just so happened that I was visiting the school taking a refresher course since I couldn't find a driving job the year before.

Back in 1979, when I got my articulated license or CDL, driving jobs were scarce and companies frowned upon hiring young inexperienced drivers like myself which was due primarily to their illustrious insurance carriers. So anyway, as it turned out, she hired me on the spot and I ended up driving one of her rigs. Meantime she, her boyfriend and her dog went with the other truck.

I was almost to the front door of Fram's headquarters and was finishing up that run in my head. '…That's it, I had a partial load of office furniture that I dropped off here. Yup it was Fram all right. My final destination was in Maine that following morning, Bar Harbor to be exact, some sort of laboratory facility out there. 'I'll never forget driving through that fog, as I struggled through it all night,' recalling as the door behind me slammed shut.

Walking over to the receptionist I thought, 'I'm in Fram's world now… I wonder what Kevin looks like?'

About ten after, this guy comes bouncing through the glass security doors staring hard at me.

"Steve, is that you man!?" he said, kind of squinting, as he looked me straight in the face for the very first time.

"I guess so," wanting to bust him a little. "You see… if you would have let me come up here before, and we had lunch together, like I had offered, you'd of at least of known what I looked like."

Smiling, he replied, "It doesn't matter one bit at all, what you look like my man," ribbing me back. "I'm just really glad that you're here and that you could make it!" shaking my hand, as if he had just run into Dr. Livingston somewhere on the Dark Continent.

Kevin had been in the meeting for a good hour before my arrival and I could tell he was glad to be out for a little while to stretch his legs. My arrival made him visibly happy, you could see it in his gate as we walked down the hallway. I can remember walking just a tad behind him, like a little boy would do his dad. I might be the inventor, but this was his world and his domain. I was pleased just to tag along.

As we proceeded up the stairs, heading towards his office he greeted some of his co-workers as they floated by. I watched their every move, the looks on their faces as they greeted each other…, analyzing their exchanges, sniffing the air so to speak. I had a deferential respect for Kevin, he truly was going shape up to be my only guide as I penetrated the machine for the first time.

"Hey Steve, I want you to meet this guy," as we entered his department area. "I work alongside of him, except that he's in the spark plug end of it, you know Autolite."

We worked our way past a few empty work stations till we came upon a cubicle with this guys back turned towards us. He was working away at his desk and didn't notice us behind him. Kevin tapped him on the shoulder and as he turned Kevin greeted him, "Hey Paul…, I didn't mean to startle you. I just want you to meet somebody. This is Steve Moor, the inventor of that Teflon treated oil filter I've been telling you about."

He stuck out his hand and I shook it, "Hi Paul. It's nice to meet you," I said.

Then Kevin and Paul talked for a minute or so before we headed towards his office. "He's really a good guy and he knows his stuff, too bad he's involved with Autolite, I could use a guy like him on this project." Just before his office was a little alcove occupied by his secretary Jodi. And after a brief introduction, I was whisked into his office. He jumped onto his computer, checking his company's inter-office email as he simultaneously opened an inter-office envelope. I could see first-hand how frenetic he was. Rummaging through some papers on his desk, he grabbed a photocopy of some sort of article. It was as if he had just found the treasure map that he was looking for.

Grabbing the phone, in the middle of dialing he said, "Read this," as he shoved the papers towards my chest. "I think this is going to be really good, a friend of mine that works in the company faxed this article to me earlier this morning."

I sat back in the chair and proceeded to read a two-page article from the October issue of Motor Trend Magazine entitled, *Navigating the Maze of Friction-Reducing Formulas*. He was still on the phone as I began to devour the article. As the words began to jump off the page, I was barely able to contain my joy. It was if this unsolicited testimonial was ready made to bolster my cause!

I hadn't even made it halfway through when he covered the phone with his hand and leaned over his desk, "Looks like you're enjoying it, huh…. What do you think? I didn't get a chance to read it yet myself," as he hopped back into his call.

"This is awesome Kev! sporting a big smile. "My God, if I had known any better I'd swear that this guy wrote this article just for me." Reading on a little further I thought to myself, 'maybe he did…'

Covering the phone again, with his hand, "Okay, that's good!" He began to take charge like a marine drill sergeant. "As soon as I get off the phone, we'll go down to the photo copier and run off enough copies for the entire room. So, you think you can use this, huh?" Smiling.

I replied, still marveling at the windfall of information, "Yeah, you bet I can!"

By the time he got off the phone I had finished the article and was sufficiently charged up to take on the most skeptical opponents of Teflon treated oil.

As a matter of fact, the Fram Filter Division was cited in the article as performing tests to find out whether this material would clog their filters media. Fram's own internal testing conducted in 1992, proved that this material in no way impeded the natural flow of oil through their filters.

I was certain that restricted oil flow due to the addition of the Teflon could indeed be a major objection posed by the engineers. Now I could remind them of their own test study, should they happened to press the issue. The fact that Fram had completed their own test study on this very subject was news to both of us, especially to Kevin, since he wasn't aware of it and he worked for the company!

We headed down the hall to a central photocopier, because the one in his department wasn't cooperating at the moment. While making copies, I asked him if he was going to read the article.

His reply was a hurried, "I'm not going to have time. As soon as we're done making copies for the group, I have to get back to the meeting to see when they'll be ready for you."

I said to him, wanting his support, "Are you sure that you're not going to be able to read this thing? Kevin it's truly incredible."

"I'd love to Stevie, but I don't think that I can manage it. I should have been back at the group at least ten minutes ago," as the copier was in the process of churning out the twenty or so copies we needed.

Glancing over at me with a big smile, he offered, "Take it easy, you read the thing. You know what it's about, and that's what counts. I'm sure that you'll be able to fill the group in, if the occasion arises," sporting a sarcastic grin. Sometimes I just wanted to give his neck a good wring, knowing at times that he got a sadistic pleasure outa watching me do the high-wire.

With that, he asked me to go hang out in his office. Bundle in arms, he headed down the stairs to the meeting in progress. Before I entered his office to prepare for my wait, I stopped to chat with

Jodi for a moment. "Hi Jodi, Kevin went back to the meeting for a while, and he said that he will come get me when they're ready." Then I added, "It's pretty neat for us to have been involved in such a relationship without ever meeting each other until today."

She spoke up giving me a polite smile, "Yes, it is. Kevin's told me all about you. He speaks very highly of you. You know."

"Well that's great, because I feel the same way about him. I sure hope that this thing works out today, I've got a lot riding on it," I added, classically understating my position.

Jodi replied, trying not to divulge her boss's true position, "I think he does too."

She then asked me if I cared for a cup of coffee before I went into his room to wait. With that I thanked her and said that I had plenty at breakfast.

Kevin's office was a neat and tidy affair. An eight by ten area comprised of heavily painted masonry block out of vintage 50's architecture. Spartan by design it had only a couple of small shelves displaying some of the products that he was affiliated with. The view from the offices second story window was its only redeeming feature. Down below was a small treed meadow covered in well cropped dark green grass.

Looking down at the peaceful landscape, I instinctively spent my remaining moment conversing with the Lord, thanking him in advance for my success.

Canal striped bass. fall '94.

Chasing this majestic prey would steal many hours of my sleep during the fall run. I'd pursue them from the beach starting from around November into January.

CHAPTER 3
THE DANCE

"Hey Steve! they're ready for you Buddy!" Kevin boomed, as he entered his lair. The silence was broken with finality, as his presence took over the room.

"Okay," I said, grabbing for my briefcase. "Let's go do it! I'm ready to do battle."

We didn't talk at all as I trailed behind him to the conference room that had been set up for us on the first floor. As we entered the room I caught a glimpse of all the different faces gathered around this huge elliptical table. Once inside the room, there left little doubt, all eyes were on me, as my skin seemed to register their penetrating queries. All the members present were men, and I thought it rather unusual that I didn't sense any hostility coming from them. I sensed that they were more in amazement than anything else.

Remember, it wasn't every day that they were assembled to have an outsider lecture them about the future of oil filtration, let alone a real estate agent with a couple of oil filter patents.

"Good morning everybody. It gives me great pleasure to introduce to you, Stephen Moor the inventor of what I feel is a very unique and I hope viable new oil filter for us. Steve and I have been collaborating on this project for the last several months and I would like for him to tell you in his own words what it's all about."

'Oh boy,' I thought. What an introduction, I felt as if I had been setup for celebrity status with that intro. I could only hope that I would do this moment justice.

Kevin then walked me over to my seat, a little to the right of the head of the table. Though he sat across from me, he was seated far enough back that he was out of my direct line of sight. So, if I wanted to see him bad enough, I would have to crane my neck back and then I could only pick him up with my peripheral vision.

'That Bugger,' I thought. 'He's really letting me take the wheel of this thing alone.' I reached down for my briefcase, put it on my lap and unsnapped the locks.

'Gee that's farther than I got the last time I met with this outfit,' I thought trying to make light of the situation running through my mind.

Just then Kevin broke in for what I knew was to be for the last time, "Steve, I'd like to introduce you to the people present here today, going around the table and starting with the gentleman seated directly to your right."

The guys directly on my right were mainly from the engineering and manufacturing side of the business. I remember sitting next to someone from the heavy-duty side, who had been flown in from one of their production facilities in Canada.

As Kevin moved towards the middle of the table on my side, he introduced me to the head of manufacturing. 'Oh shoot! That's one of the guy's that I had met with on my last patent. That was the lead engineers side kick!' I couldn't afford the luxury of letting any petty or vindictive feelings towards him erupt inside of me. And I certainly wouldn't have allowed that to happen anyway. 'And besides, if I was looking for exoneration, I would just have to sell them right here and now..., wouldn't I?'

There was so much electric in the room, you could feel the anticipation. It was apparent, they actually wanted to hear about my revelation! I was shocked! 'So where was N.I.H.?' He had to be here somewhere? Well if he was, I'd spot him before too long.

When he got to the head of the table on the far end, Kevin stopped at Jack McGrath, and introduced him as the Senior Vice President of Fram and the Head of Marketing. I studied him well, while at the same time doing my best to conceal my efforts.

Apparently, Friday was Fram's dress down day and he was wearing a navy-blue V-neck wool sweater with a white cotton shirt. His countenance projected that he was the man in charge, but a kind fellow.

Suddenly Kevin stopped, as if instinctively, "Jack…, Dianne Newman's supposed to be here, isn't she? I could have sworn I saw her name on the roster." Immediately I heard a couple of chuckles and a brief flurry of comments were bantered about the room concerning her. I didn't pay any heed to them, since the room was filled with all men, I dismissed it as being a guy thing. Nonetheless, I was thankful for the fact that it loosened up my audience and took the pressure off me before I was about to go on.

As I enjoyed the brief moment of levity, I do recall that the bulk of the jabs were being aimed at her habitual tardiness. One jab in particular that I remember, was to the effect, 'that she never arrives for a meeting unless she is at least fifteen minutes late.' Mr. McGrath adeptly acted as if he hadn't heard the remarks and smoothly provided her an alibi.

Kevin picked up where he had left off and started down the other side of the table. This side of the crew was mainly comprised of people in marketing until he got to the gentleman seated directly across the table from me, the chief engineer! 'Oh my God, there he was!' As my eyes caught his, I could feel the blood rushing to core of my guts. He didn't seem the least bit phased by my presence, as he politely smiled a, 'good morning, it's nice to meet you.' I couldn't help but remark to myself that his smile was akin to that of a Marine drill sergeant smiling at a new boot with long hair and an earring.

I was floored! It was the head engineer who sat across the table from me that day at lunch six years ago! The very guy who told me that I didn't have a patent on my last idea. 'Did my facial expression and sudden loss of blood pressure give me away?' Surely it must have!

'The guy couldn't be that dense?' But somehow, I wasn't sure if he made me. I fought to regain my composure using every psychological axiom I could use to justify his non-reaction to me. Finally, I settled on the most obvious, 'hey if it didn't bother him, I was going to do my best not to feel self-conscious about it either.'

Looking back on that day, in all honesty, I couldn't believe that the man didn't know who I was. It just didn't seem plausible to my way of thinking. It was simply impossible that he had no recollection of our previous encounter. I'll bet you that in all probability during his tenure as chief engineer, he had never met with an industry outsider like myself to explore a new idea for an oil filter! Ever!

Kevin's master of ceremony job was winding down and it was show time. "Huh Steve, why don't you first tell the group a little bit about yourself leading into the patent and your view of the marketplace. Then, you can close it out by telling us how you envision its manufacture. When you're finished, I guess we'll open it up to some Q and A. Is that Okay?"

"That'll be fine Kevin, thank you very much. I would like to start off by saying that I am very privileged in being invited here today to speak with you all about my oil filter.

"I received a U. S. patent for it in May of 1993 and it is the second patent that I have received in the field of oil filtration. I received my first patent on oil filtration in June of 1988. The first patent that I was granted pertains somewhat more to the heavy-duty aspect and does not particularly lend itself readily to automotive applications."

In an attempt to bolster my credibility with a touch of levity, I added, "You know I've been working with Kevin for the last nine months on this concept. I've had to provide him with all the pertinent information before he'd ever consider permit me to address a group of his peers." The room was silent as they listened intently as they waited for me to reveal some grand kernel of wisdom. Then rather unintentionally, I roasted Kevin in a single line, "What I am saying, is that Kevin ain't no lay-down. He's more like a good junk yard dog than anything else. What I'm really trying' to say…, is that it wasn't easy getting here."

Well, the room broke out with laughter and the comments and barbs flew around the room, this time unrestrained. O'l Kevin sat back in his seat turning beet red, defenseless against the heckles of his co-workers.

There was no doubt about it, I had arrived at the dance. I was up and rolling, the nerves had shaken out, the anxiety that this moment had created vaporized and the mountain didn't appear so insurmountable anymore. Sitting on the edge of my chair as if I was ready to get up, my mouth and brain worked in unison, like a well-oiled machine. My eyes met with theirs, cutting deep into their souls and I can only describe it as giving the presentation of my life.

In keeping with Kevin's outline, I digressed momentarily sharing my background in sales with them. "I know that real estate sales people are looked upon as maybe one notch above the urchins that sell used cars. Unfortunately, as true as that may seem, there are a lot of very good and honorable people in real estate sales industry, and I happen to be one of them. For the last seven years I have been self employed as a real estate agent, and before that I was a commodities broker, so I know enough about sales to be dangerous," I said trying to come across as self-effacing as possible.

Then I added, "And I have done this full time straight commission, supporting a wife and two small kids." Hoping that would lend some degree of credibility and dispel the myth that all real estate agents hide out at the office drinking coffee and eating doughnuts.

Moving quickly ahead, I informed them that I had been an over the road truck driver and owner operator with a few hundred thousand miles under my belt. "Due to the margins being so thin in trucking, I was always looking for a means to get as much efficiency out of my equipment as possible. One of the major areas as you might expect is fuel efficiency and engine performance. P.M. intervals and the prevention of subsequent premature engine wear play a big part of any operations bottom line. Almost by default I had learned to become a skilled mechanic in order to survive in that business. I guess that I just kept my eyes open for possible solutions along with an open mind, and kind of stumbled onto these ideas.

"Obviously, I felt strong enough about it to pursue them to the point of filing for two separate patents on the subject." As the words slipped out, I couldn't help but remark to myself, that was an understatement if I had ever heard one.

At this juncture, I discussed both of my patents in quite some detail which sufficiently intrigued my audience. I guess they weren't prepared for the real estate agent wearing a suit and polished wing tip shoes to unload on them like I had. My sorted background replete with the various journeys I had logged, went a long way towards earning their respect. They were nearly disarmed, and the room was still, as I finally invited them to peek under the tent.

Kevin, that stinker, had known all along that I was capable of making this happen. That's why he insisted that I address the group and not he.

"With all of that in mind, I'd like to let you know why I'm here. Fram wasn't my first choice of companies to bring this filter to…"

It was a heck of a way to start a sales presentation, buts that's how I felt led to do it. Once I had seen the chief engineers contorted scowl hidden behind his seemingly benevolent smile, I chucked any semblance of my previous presentation out the window. I was going to take this one in on instruments only!

'Why not?' My whole mission had been operated as an all-or-nothing premise from the beginning, and I didn't think now was any time to change my tack.

"I went to Purolator first. And I gotta be honest with you, they're the company that shoulda jumped on this thing like a bass on a bug. But unfortunately, they couldn't see the forest through the trees.

"When Pennzoil spun them off in 92' I made it my business to get a hold of their stock prospectus and it proved to be very enlightening as I read it through. You see, they had divulged some very salient points concerning the oil filter market and their role in it.

"They concluded that seventy percent of all the oil changes done in the U.S. are performed at installed sales sites. They went on further to state that they enjoyed seventy percent of that market. And you know…, somehow, I kind of believed them.

"And just in case you are not so inclined to believe that, I can assure you that the type of information that gets put into public offerings is scrutinized by the Securities and Exchange Commission during a company's due diligence period. The Commission would frown upon any information that would be found to be inaccurate. So, I have to deem this information as being accurate. Besides that, over the last few years, I had become very close to the ex-chief engineer of Purolator, so I am somewhat intimate with the landscape of the automotive oil filter market in general."

Suddenly, one of the younger engineers raised his hand like he was flagging down a cab in the city. "What was this guy's name? I used to work for them in Tulsa back in the late eighties."

Kevin leaned forward like he was somehow trying to protect me from any pre-mature line of questioning. I caught sight of him for the first time out of the corner of my eye and as I did so, he said, "Go ahead Steve, tell him who it is."

"But gentlemen he's still got a lot of ground to cover, so if you don't mind if at all possible, could you please hold your questions until he's finished. I don't want to get us side tracked."

As I started to speak I craned my neck over towards Kevin as he sat back in his chair. He looked all right, so I proceeded. "His name is Richard Dye. I believe he left Purolator around 1991, just as Pennzoil was putting the company on the block. I worked with him on my first patent and I really think that Purolator may have gone for it, had the company not been put up for sale. Mr. Dye found himself in a position to reevaluate his future with the company and I guess he felt it best to leave and go out on his own.

"The engineer that took his place was a guy by the name of Alex MacLean. Unfortunately, when Dick left, the new chief engineer threw the baby out with the bath water…, that being me and my filter. Does that check out?" I asked, willing to expose myself to whatever level of scrutiny it would take to get the job done.

"It sure does." he said, with a ring of satisfaction. "It sure does!"

I knew that I had a limited amount of time and a lot of stuff to go over, but I was on a saturation bombing mission. When this talk was over, they were going to know that I was an expert in this field and it wouldn't be relevant where I got my information from, or that I might of paid for it with my own blood.

"Getting back to the installed sales. Whenever I've had the opportunity to look in the garbage cans at garages, and believe me I've looked in hundreds, I see mostly white housings and precious few orange ones. I am certain that you guys don't do much volume to speak of in the installed sales arena. So, if I am wrong, please correct me!" I said, begging for a response.

Jack McGrath chose to affirm me on this point.

Jack was graced with a pleasant demeanor and I could only hope that I was right. This dog and pony show was mainly directed at him for the moment, he was the one who had the juice in this room, not the chief engineer.

"Everything that you've said so far Steve is correct," he said with a smile, nodding his head.

I knew that I would be walking a tight rope from the moment I had ever mentioned the fact that my concept was indeed better suited for their main competitor other than Fram. At this point I would have been burnt toast if Mr. McGrath had any sort of an ego problem, but thankfully I had read him correctly. He was going to allow me the privilege of sewing up the patient before it jumped off the table.

I stopped talking as I heard the door behind me open. Dianne Newman had arrived onto the scene. I didn't want to turn around and make the poor woman feel self-conscious, after all, she was a good forty minutes late.

As she passed where I was sitting, she paused momentarily and made a gesture somewhere between a curtsy and bow. That suit of mine must have really stuck out in this crowd, as she zoomed in on me.

She worked her way up to the opposite end of the table, clutching her writing tablet that identified her as belonging to that ignoble fraternity of scribes. Sitting down, I could hear her inform Mr. McGrath that she was in the middle of something important and that's why she was late. Her explanation was quite audible, seemingly intentional, like she wanted to inform the whole room that she had been in the middle of something terribly important that had required her undivided attention, unlike this once in a career gathering.

Settling into her seat, the room got quiet once again and it was my cue to continue what had become a mini treatise on 'oil filtration with regard to a manufacturers approach to market share.'

In my endeavor to enlighten the group as to my real-world experience I was about to draw upon my previous experience with Purolator once again. It was the only company I had any demonstrable contact with, concerning this patent. Not withholding the fact, that it was the only company in my estimation that could the undertake a project of this magnitude, besides Fram of course. But before I worked my way back to Purolator, I wanted to at least show the boys that I had done my homework and that I had demonstrable proof that I had made the rounds within the industry. So, I started off…

"Champion Laboratories is a large manufacturer of high volume lower end filter products such as Lee, Champ and STP to mention just a few filter brands they manufacture. I called on them nonetheless and had spoken to their chief of engineering, John Gather. He sent me back a nice 'thanks but no thanks', letter informing me that the public would not be interested in a step up, premium priced oil filter. In effect letting me know that the public is happy to consume what they were presently being offered." That brief account made it fairly clear that I knew how another one of the major contenders viewed the industry. But as far as I was concerned, that wasn't enough. I wasn't going to stop selling until everyone in the room was convinced that if Fram and I teamed up, we could catch the entire industry flat footed!

Moving forward, I briefly alluded to the Hastings Filter Company. "They are a small company out of Michigan engaged in the metal stamping business as well as the oil filters. I spoke to someone at the company, but I can't recall who, since I was just fishing at the time and not too serious about pursuing them concerning this venture. I only mentioned Hastings to you guys, so that I could at least point out, that the company didn't even make my first cut."

Naturally, I wasn't about to mention the little visit I had paid on Fram six years' prior either! A move like that would have been suicidal, so I preferred for the moment to keep that dirty little secret amongst the parties involved, knowing full well that Kevin had nothing to gain by mentioning it either.

So that left me Wix and I wasn't about ready to mention them at this juncture either. And I had my reasons…

Anyway, Wix was a reputable filter manufacturer that was a wholly owned subsidiary of the Dana Corporation, located in Toledo, Ohio. They made a very good aftermarket filter product, and I had used their filters extensively when I was trucking. They sold their filters under their own name, yet at the time, they weren't very good self-promoters. However, on the flip side, they did well over one hundred million dollars' worth of volume, manufacturing filters that were sold under the NAPA name, short for National Automotive Parts Association. At the time, NAPA was the largest automotive retail chain in the USA.

Now that bit of information definitely interested me, and it should have piqued Fram's interest as well, but it seemed like Fram was too damn dense to even begin to evaluate their own competition. As for me, I was already quite convinced that with all of the new marketing possibilities that my filter was sure to create, it would be a great stepping stone for Wix to make a run at a public debut.

Yet for the time being, I didn't mention how I felt about Wix. Simply because, they weren't my ace in the hole, and I didn't have anything concrete going with them at the moment. Nonetheless, they were the only trump card I was toting. I just prayed that I didn't need to play it. As you can see, I was talking to Fram now. They were the only game in town, and I knew it!

So, I launched in, "I have to be honest with you, Purolator wanted me to fund a test study to prove the contention that Teflon when added to oil makes it lubricate better. But I was already one up on them. I had already been in touch with South West Labs, a premier certified testing lab out of Texas. And if you don't mind, I'd like to tell you a little story…

"After explaining to South West Labs what I wanted to find out, they came back and told me that a cursory test study would certainly run in the quarter of a million-dollar range, with the sky being the limit. I was familiar with E.G. & G. another lab of the same caliber, also located in Texas and got a similar response.

"It didn't take Purolator long to turn sour on my invention. In one of the final conversations that I had with Mr. MacLean, he was kind enough to inform me that the concept was too risky for his company to get involved with.

"Quite naturally their people didn't know anything about the material to start with. And secondly, they weren't convinced that it worked like the makers of the product said it did. At this point in our relationship, I knew deep down inside that even a full blown certified test study wouldn't be enough proof to convince them.

"And since I don't like taking no for an answer, especially when I'm right, I took one last shot at 'em, because he didn't appear like he was going to blow me off the phone quite yet. So, this is what happened, '"I said to him, you know Mr. MacLean, I have been in contact with both E.G. & G. and South West Labs, and for about a quarter of a million dollars…, you can find out what I already know, that this stuff works!"'

My eyes caught Mr. McGrath's as I finished the exposé. His eyes betrayed his excitement, and the impish smile he gave me confirmed it. He had caught hold of my vision!

The rest of the engineers sat back quietly as I looked around the room. They were in a quasi-state of arrest after hearing me take on one of their own, even if he was one of the enemy.

'After all, who did I think I was?' I wasn't skilled, nor practiced in the art of oil filter manufacture. But what I had said had merit, bordering on being one hundred percent accurate.

Even old fish face who sat across the table from me was silent except for an anguished cough that erupted every now and then. The engineers kept silent, as they obediently followed the chain of command.

And I wasn't finished yet.

"So any way," I continued, "Mr. MacLean finally sent me a letter. I have it in my briefcase and I'll be glad to show it any one who is interested. It merely sums up that without a test study, Purolator and I were going nowhere.

"You know, it's kinda funny, Mr. MacLean had used my own information against me in the letter, letting me know how much the test study would cost," I said, with a sarcastic jab.

Just like I had previously done with Kevin, I was compelled to let these people know to their faces that I didn't want to be used, nor did I care to be set up. And that I intended to deal with them honorably and ethically and that I would expect no less from them… ever.

I had laid the groundwork for the close and I'd like to believe the group from Fram's marketing team knew what I was about to do.

Even though I hadn't been able to see Kevin face the whole time, I was confident that he hadn't missed a beat and I would have gladly of done this thing all over again, just to have seen his body language. I was preaching oil filter marketing like a house afire.

With Jack in tow, I started the finale. "You guys could have this thing! I just got done telling you that I've had a dialog with every major company in the business during the course of the last year, and none of them want it!

"And just in case you might of missed it, I went the distance and have already presented their mind sets toward change. So just as a reminder, I'm telling ya that they just won't hear of it! If you just listen to me, I promise you, this thing could be a monster and you're going to catch your competition asleep!

"The Teflon treated market is huge! I bet it's almost as big as your gross sales in oil filters! However, there are a couple of things that I have a hard time understanding. For starters, how come nobody in the filter business has paid the slightest attention to the additive treated oil business? That thought absolutely boggles my mind!

"Petrolon has been selling Slick-50 for years and probably racked up a couple of billion dollars in sales without any serious challengers! Heck they've been in business since 1978, and I think we'd all know by now if their product harmed engines? Don't you think?" I asked, just begging for a response.

"If that be the case, wouldn't the big three auto makers come crashing down on them for warranty problems?!

"You already know the answer to that one, being original equipment manufacturers yourselves.

"What about the Federal Trade Commission? Wouldn't Slick-50 be a dead ringer for a truth in advertising case, if the stuff were purely snake oil?

"Here's what we have. This filter is like a Reese's peanut butter cup. The filter housing is the container and the media is the delivery system that distributes the Teflon elixir!

"And I have the patent on this system!" I was now crowing like a proud rooster in a barn yard.

"I know how to make this thing," as I started to get a little ahead of myself. "It would be simple and wouldn't require any retooling for your existing filter design! The startup costs from a manufacturing standpoint would be insignificant!"

There…! At long last, after being pent up for so long, I had finally been able to say it!

I laid it all out. You would have to of been brain dead to have missed the simplicity of it all. By all accounts I should a been home free, walking in tall cotton as I acknowledged the cheers of the crowd. But this wasn't like some dumb movie… 'Cause, the room fell silent!

And I had just blown myself out, like a forest fire in a back draft, I had nothing left to offer.

The silence in the room was deafening until it was finally broken by the head engineer's cough. 'Oh shoot, he's disturbed,' I thought. And now he's coming after me.

In a half-mumbled growl, he offered, "I don't like it…!" No one in the room dared say anything at this point. This was between him and I, as we readied to square off. And as far as I was concerned, that was fine by me.

"Mr. Coronia," I said very calmly and deliberately. "What exactly don't you like about it sir?"

There was a long pause, as I waited for him to articulate his disagreement. "I just don't like it," he said, repeating himself again.

I was at a loss for words. I needed something more substantial to respond to other than just his raw emotion.

Oh, what the heck, I had to do something. This guy was acting like an emotional boob and I wasn't about to let him pull me down, so I blurted out… "I sent Kevin six bona-fide test studies, in hopes of satisfying any technical qualms your group may of had concerning this material sir."

Mr. Coronia didn't speak again for the moment, however his displeasure in this situation was still very apparent as it spilled all over his face.

It was now Dianne's turn to chime in. It wouldn't be very long before her first statement would belie her as a grandstander of sorts. "Mr. Moor, Teflon or PTFE as it's also known is a Fluoropolymer, isn't it?"

I responded, "Why yes, of course it is." Waiting to see where she was going to let that one take us.

"Well," she said, "Isn't that material carcinogenic? And wouldn't it have an adverse effect on exhaust emissions?"

"Good point Dianne," I said, keeping my cool. Inside I was being eaten away by her rather stupid overreaching. But moreover, I was upset because I could see that she was the type who wouldn't have thought twice about wasting what precious time I had left to sell the group what should have been the obvious. And that was no snap judgment, because if she had bothered to read the materials that I had sent Kevin, which obviously she hadn't…, she would have already known the answers to all of those questions!

"I'll make you a copy of it after the meeting," I said. "The designation of this material as being carcinogenic is nowhere to be found on the 'material handling data sheet'. And in reference to your second question, one of the test studies specifically concluded that the addition of PTFE didn't have any deleterious effect on tail pipe emissions. Emissions were unchanged," I added somewhat defensively.

Just when I thought I had successfully dispatched with her, she asked me another question as if she had been left unfulfilled by her first line of questioning. "Isn't the used motor oil going to contain some of the Fluoropolymer residue in it? I don't think that would be safe unless we can determine otherwise," she said, rather authoritatively.

It was my distinct impression that Dianne was not against the project personally, at least not at that specific moment. It was more like she was an annoyance more than anything else. I would find out quite sometime later, after some detective work, that might not of been the case exactly. It would be much, much worse!

"Dianne, I'd like to address that point, if I may. I am sure that all of us in the room are aware of the fact that Federal EPA back in the 80's declared used motor as a hazardous waste. Laboratory tests have shown that when drain oil was put on the skin of rats it caused cancer. So, I guess we can all agree, that presently, every drop of used motor oil that comes out of a spent Fram oil filter is presently a potential source of cancer. So, let's first agree, that your used filters are toxic to begin with. Okay?" I said lobbing that bomb straight back at her.

"That's why there's now governmental guidelines in place for the proper handling and disposal of both used motor oil and spent oil filters. I don't think that the addition of Teflon, and by the way, Teflon is a plastic, is going to add significantly to the toxicity of used motor oil. Especially in the minute amounts we are talking about here. And one more thing if I might. Don't they coat the bottom of frying pans we eat off, with this stuff?"

At this point my intention was to totally disarm her. "This material had been in use and found to be harmless in this application for at least sixteen years that I know anything about. If indeed, its formulation with motor oil posed any significant health problems to humans, the DuPont Company, the main supplier of this material would have ceased making it available for that purpose a long time ago."

Before I knew it, I came up out of my seat. "Is there anyone present here from Allied's Fluoropolymer division this morning?" as I began calling out like some town crier. Heads began turning as they searched the room for an expert, for which neither Dianne nor myself were qualified as such. There was no referee to be found. "I guess since there's no expert to be found in the house, why don't we table this discussion for the time being," I offered, wanting to move on. I had to get back to the head engineer, while I had the chance, while there were still witnesses around!

"I am more than willing to let your world class experts in your chemical division determine the fate of this additive. Why don't we let them tell us whether it's safe or a deadly toxin? And if they come back and tell me that it's too toxic to play with, I'll scrap my patent, pick up my ball and go home. Does that sound ok by you Ms. Newman?" What I must have said worked, because it shut her up as she began to write furiously upon her tablet.

Once Dianne had been quelled, the engineers started coming forth asking me various technical questions pertaining to what exactly was going to be in the filter. And other serious questions like, how did I propose to build such a product. And for a few moments, I totally lost myself talking shop, embracing the men who actually build filters for a living, readily sharing with them my many ideas.

And the naïveté!!! Because I did all this before I had even signed any type of Proprietary Information Agreement. Perhaps maybe I shouldn't have, but I did. And I guess I did because I went to this meeting with the full intention of not only signing such a document but going into business with the largest oil filter manufacturer in the world before the day was over!

Besides, I knew going into this, I had sixty days to reduce my disclosures in writing, according to the Proprietary Information Agreement. I put those ominous thoughts aside and kept on selling, knowing… hoping and trusting that the Company couldn't… No! They wouldn't allow themselves to stoop so low as to steal my trade secrets.

Despite the dubious circumstances created by Dianne and the head engineer, I still felt that no matter what, Jack McGrath along with Kevin, would be honorable enough to cover my back door.

I told the group that my patent specified DuPont's MP 1100 Teflon micro-powder, with an average particle size of three microns. "To get the Teflon to release itself gradually I made mixture of Teflon and a carrier oil forming small balls, kind of like when you make pancakes and you have little batter balls that keep floating around. The material would be applied on the dirty side of the media. When the oil hits the agglomerated masses, the pressure generated inside the filter along with the shearing action of the hot oil would physically separate the smaller masses and single particles allowing them to pass through the media. Therefore, allowing the material to gradually pass through the media and enter into the motors lubrication system. It's really quite simple," I said.

"And if you don't like that material, I have another material that DuPont specifically told me about when I was doing my research. There is a product called SLA 1612, made by Acheson Colloids out of Port Huron, Michigan. They are proprietary blenders of this material. They take DuPont Teflon that is .34 microns in size and held in a colloidal suspension with a 50-weight solvent neutral carrier oil. As a matter of fact, Slick 50 gets their material from them and so do the majority of the other Teflon treated oil manufactures."

Just then, one of the engineers from their manufacturing plants asked me how I proposed to manufacture this filter.

I told him, "This is how I envisioned its manufacture, when the finished filter is coming down the line just before the packaging station there is a plunger that comes down on the top of the oil filter." Using the palm of my hand I pressed it down on my clenched fist placed sideways simulating an erect oil filter.

"The plunger comes down and as it does seals the top of the filter while it injects a metered amount of the material into the input side of the filter. This has to be done with sufficient pressure, because it has deliver this material past the anti-drain valve which is already in place."

He interrupted me, "Excuse me Steve, that all sounds fine, but our filters come off the line tapping plate down. They all get placed in the box that way. So now, you want us to package them with the tapping plate facing up?"

"Yes, and that's not a big deal," I said enthusiastically. "We can fix all that by putting a curlicue in the line just before the filling station. They're simple and they work, I've seen them in action at many a plant I've delivered to as a truck driver. I've seen cans coming off the line, or past the labeler, they then go through the curlicue cage, and the orientation of the can changes by 180°. It's magic!" All he could say was, "Hum, I see your point, that's not such a big deal!"

Then I went on to say, "Besides, you're going to be making a wet filter here, so it would only stand to reason that you would want the tapping plate to face the sky to avoid any potential leakage. Also, this filter should be sealed, with a top. Perhaps a peel away foil top like a yogurt cup or something. That would definitely keep the material inside the filter. Or I guess you could shrink wrap it. The Japanese have been doing that for years on their original equipment filters sold through the car dealers."

One of the other engineers smiled and said, "Gee Steve, that sounds like you've got damn near everything covered."

The marketing people were nodding their heads in approval as well. But somehow, I could tell this wasn't their show. For the most part, they barely spoke up and I found that rather odd. Especially since this project was already earmarked as Kevin's baby and my appearance this morning had been backed by Jack McGrath. 'Or was it because they assembled with such short notice that they weren't up to speed on what was actually taking place?' I never got a chance to question Kevin on that point.

By now I could see that it was about all the head engineer could take, as he chimed in on cue. He started in with, "I don't like this thing," again.

Running down my options, I felt pretty secure in the fact that I had said just about enough to have made my point. As far as I could figure, up until now I had been more than forthright illustrating whether this patent of mine had any merit or not, so I let it rip…"Don't take this personally sir, but I don't really care what you like!"

The room seemed to reel back, and another hush fell over it as I threw down the filter gauntlet. Not wanting to give him time to react, I thrust ahead with my frontal assault. "You see that article there in front of you…, it's a feature article, and it's not outa some rag, but it's out of this month's Car and Driver Magazine. It states that the consumer loves this material and that many people loyally swear by it. So sir, not to be disrespectful to you, I really don't care what you like. However, I do care what the American consuming public likes! And as I told you before, they like this stuff to the tune of a half a billion dollars a year!"

Shuffling my papers around, I began closing my briefcase. I don't know, I guess I started moving, as if I was going to get up and leave. To this day I don't know if I was actually going to leave, but that's what my body was doing, as if it had been left on auto pilot.

Without further concern, I continued my assault on the lead engineer..., like an angry hornet. Precarious as it might of seemed, this was how I had to play the game. The balance of my entire future was now invested in my next move whether I liked it or not! It was maddening, like Russian Roulette, one bullet in the chamber type of deal.

"I haven't even begun to call upon Wix yet. I've left that up to an intermediary up until this point, but he ain't me! I think I'll just take my leave now, and I'll give them a call tomorrow."

Then it rang out…. "No, you won't! You are going with us," Jack McGrath shot across the room, taking the helm as he rose to his feet. "We're going to do this."

He didn't elaborate, he didn't explain, he didn't need to. It was done!

Dianne jumped in instinctively, at least she had come prepared to do that aspect of her job. Looking back on it now, it would be the first time…, as well as the last time that I would ever experience her doing the job she was being paid to do. "Steve, we are going to need some time to check out the viability of this project and of your patent. That means that we are going ask you for your cooperation in granting us a reasonable amount of time to do what needs to be done. Is that okay with you?" she asked.

"Yes of course Dianne! I'll cooperate to the best of my ability. I'd like to say something if I may. This isn't about me here, this is now about us… It is about us taking on your competition in battle and using this product to decimate them! As far as I'm concerned, they've all had ample opportunity to get on board and they've all seemed to of missed bus," I added, dropping my weapon.

"So, will you give us 60 days? That will get us past the Thanksgiving Holiday," she asked.

My reply was instantaneous, "Why yes, of course."

The chief engineer grumbled like a smoldering volcano and was doing so in a language I couldn't quite understand. Yet somehow, he managed to communicate to Dianne that 60 days wouldn't be adequate for the engineering department to act.

She came back to me, almost apologetically at this point and asked me for more time, for which I agreed. "Will you give us 90 days?" Her demeanor seemed to get humbler as the request for time got larger.

I was pretty metered, knowing full well in the grand scheme of things that my time was a commodity, something to be used for the benefit of all. My response was again, "Yeah sure, why not?"

Again, the volcano across the way grumbled as he telepathically told her to ask for another thirty days. At this point I had granted the engineers a staggering 120 days to figure out if what I had just told them was a figment of my scheming and perverse imagination or not. During the course of this shakedown, I could feel my mind getting out from under me as I logically tried to run this situation through my head. 'Did a Fortune 38 Company doing eleven billion dollars a year, specializing in aviation, chemicals and automotive aftermarket products need to be coddled, so they might determine the obvious?' Aghast, I couldn't believe what I was witnessing for myself, deep in the belly of this mighty ship.

My fuse was lit, but well concealed as I began, "Mr. Coronia, I know that you are the Chief Engineer of the largest filter company in the world, and I realize that you are a very busy man and that you must have a lot on your plate at any given moment. But I wanna ask you a personal question? What in God's name could you possibly be working on right now that could be any bigger or hold more promise than what I just brought to you today?!"

"I'll tell you what," I said looking right down the table at Jack McGrath, "If you don't want to aggressively take this thing on and give it the priority and the respect that it deserves, I'm gonna pick up my ball and go home."

Without a moment's hesitation, Mr. McGrath jumped in trying to pry the engineer and myself apart. I guess we might have looked like two kids wrestling in the dirt.

"That's it! We are doing this I tell ya! We're on board and we are going to give this situation all the respect and priority it deserves," he said, as he began to stir in his seat.

"Mr. Moor, I have to apologize. But regretfully, I have another meeting that I have to run off to." He began to rise from his seat, and as he did, he looked directly down the table and smiled at me before he began to address room, "We're doing this! So, I want you to give this man whatever he wants."

As he made his way down to the end of the table where I was seated, he stopped momentarily and looked at me square in the face, before once more confirming his words with an out stretched hand. I rose to shake his hand, which he held out in partnership and as his flesh pressed against mine, our eyes met up close, and we made covenant… "Don't worry young man, I promise you, we won't drop the ball."

Before he had time to exit the room, Dianne had gotten me up to 180 days!

When Jack left the room, the meeting was essentially over. I was heartsick that he had to leave so early, I really wanted to meet him up close. For now, I just had to be satisfied in knowing him from afar, as the man who was willing to take a chance on an unknown like me, willing to stick his neck out by going into business with me. Little did I know, I would never have the chance to meet with him. A few months' latter I was saddened to find out that Jack had left the company. From what I had gathered, he had been pushed out in a power play. What a crying shame. Surely, the project, as well as I personally, lost a great ally in him.

The Company put on a cold cut buffet that ended up to be the informal culmination of the great gathering. Dianne excused herself and went up to her office to attend to weightier matters, begging off on a sandwich, saying she'd already brought her lunch.

"Steve, I'll be upstairs in my office for the rest of the afternoon. When you are finished come on up and stop by and we'll sign the documents," she said cheerfully.

Kevin told her that we'd wrap this up in about an hour or so, and that he'd send me on by. The chief engineer and his side kick stayed off to the side and pretty much kept to themselves, as I held court informally with a couple of engineers intrigued by prospects of bringing to life a new filter. They told me that they couldn't ever recall taking part in such a project and that nothing exciting like this had ever happened to them during their careers as filter engineers. I can tell you, they were visibly excited about the roles they hoped to be playing. I can remember distinctly conversing with a production engineer on the heavy-duty side. My heart bubbled with joy as I envisioned myself being able to get close to those big trucks again! I even had visions of Fram producing filters under my previous patent once this project proved itself successful in the marketplace. I was intoxicated with the dream.

As we all broke into small groups and munched away on cold cuts, hard rolls and potato salad, the room was a buzz with shop talk. Kevin was in a huddle formation in the corner of the room with a couple of guys from marketing, politicking amongst the various players, building consensus…, he was always building consensus. I had come to know that was his strength. As for me unchaperoned, I was left to happily discuss the finer aspects of proper oil filtration with some of the engineers.

These were the guys I would have naturally sought out anyway, perceiving they needed to spend some time with me on how to build it. They were the ones that needed the proper guidance, they unwittingly held the success or failure of this project in their hands, not Kevin. So, in the precious amount of time allotted us, I gave them what I felt was crucial for them to know, praying all along we'd have a follow up session real soon! My demeanor radiated self-assurance clothed in humility, as I went over the crucial aspects of the filters design. If they failed to grasp what this filter was all about and took too long to perfect it or brought it in over budget I'd be dead! And in that case, there wouldn't be any resurrection from amongst the dead.

At this particular juncture, I didn't have a concern about marketing. True, they had a long road ahead of them, but with Kevin as the lead sled dog they'd make it to their destination. I was sure of it! Besides, Kevin and I were growing closer by the moment and I could almost communicate with him telepathically. He knew what my vision was, and he was intelligent enough to know that he should embrace it to the best of his abilities…, that's if he wanted to succeed.

After about an hour or so we broke up, it was Friday afternoon. I was glad that I didn't have to trade places with those engineers, as I watched them gather up their gear, preparing to catch their flights back home. I had a myriad of thoughts flood my mind as I watched these loyal company men prepare themselves for the ride out in the van to the airport.

By comparison, I had the far better portion, only some papers to sign and a long victory drive ahead of me. I was unfazed by the imminent fact that by the time I headed for home, my five-hour drive would blossom into eight, due to the Friday evening rush through Connecticut and New York. But it didn't matter at this point, nothing did. All I knew was that I had won! Driving home with my trophy in hand would be a pleasure even if it took all night.

Kevin and I headed up the stairs, heading for his office. When we were out of sight of the others, he gave me a pat across the middle of my back. I could feel it reverberate throughout my entire body, as I looked into his smiling face. He looked so darn pleased with the whole thing I didn't even have to even ask. But self-conscious me, I couldn't let the opportunity get by without begging the obvious…

"So, hey Kev, what do you think? How'd it go?"

After all my years of being placed in situations where my best never seemed good enough for the old man, I couldn't help, but to find myself fishing for Kevin's approval. Though I felt kinda stupid asking his opinion of something that I was sure had already hit the mark, I guess out of my own weakness, I gave in.

Kevin, unaware of my pathos, gladly obliged…, oblivious to my wounds of put down, fear of failure and the sarcasm that crisscrossed my soul.

"You were awesome Dude! You were stellar!"

I replied almost autonomicly, "You think so, huh?"

He was still very much high on the moment himself, besides, it was natural for him to give it to me anyway. "You killed 'em man! What can I say Stevie! We're going into business together!" as he grabbed me across my shoulders and giving me a good squeeze.

"Look, I got a couple of things to catch up on. I'm going to bring you over to Dianne's office, so you guys can take care of what needs to be taken care of, okay? So, when you're done, come back to my office so we can chat for a few. Then if you don't mind Steve, I haven't seen my wife and kid much lately, so I'm going to see if I can't split out of here early today. If that's all right with you?"

I said, "Yeah, sure. Of course."

As we arrived at Dianne's office area he left me off outside her door, because she wasn't to be found. So, I just hung around and chatted with one of her secretaries, while waiting for her to materialize.

After we had been talking a good while, Dianne came from around the corner and ushered me into her office. At first glance, it was a cramped little space, cluttered with papers lying in piles all over the place, like that of scatter-brained professor. But that smell! Instinctively, my eyes surveyed the room until I met up with the half-eaten remains of a runny tuna fish sandwich that happened to be sharing the window ledge with a beat-up toaster oven. Apparently, she must have just warmed the thing up, making the whole darn room stink like a chum slick.

Dianne proceeded to walk directly to her computer and sat down, opting to fidget on her keyboard instead of addressing the business I had come to her office for, and in so doing, sat down with her back towards me. I drew a momentary blank as she began dividing her attention between that infernal computer of hers while picking away at that pile of tuna, oozing out from between the two slices of bread.

It seemed like an eternity as I watched on in disbelief, overcome by a building flood of offending thoughts that began accosting my mind. I can still remember standing there, staring down at her desk, feeling the joy of the moment being sucked out of me as I allowed her natural ability to be rude dominate my being. I'll tell you, something about our first meeting that day was awful fishy, and it wasn't the tuna!

I found myself in some sort of freakish time warp as she chose to separate us with her back while flailing away at her keyboard. As my humiliation boiled over into righteous indignation, I asked myself a perfectly legitimate question. 'Was that anyway to treat the new business partner that she had just been entrusted to handle?' I thought not!

Suddenly, without warning, the clouds began to part, and the bright light of reality started to come steaming in. In a moment s time, 'that give away the farm' euphoria had been stripped off, and with it, went the hollow victory I had won downstairs only moments earlier!

'Hey wait a minute!' Seemingly, I had caught myself just in time! 'This wasn't how this was supposed to be going down!' To state the obvious, AlliedSignal and I were on the verge of signing a proprietary information and joint technology sharing agreement for both my patent and trade secrets. And that of course was true! But what was also true was that they were about to tie up both me and my intellectual property up for the next six months. They were about to own me!

Something was happening to me, for which I had never planned. For the first time in memory, I could feel myself being confronted with the terrible feeling of entrusting my baby to someone else! The handing over of my idea to the big boys was being done with so much callousness on their part. And jumping into the frigid waters with Dianne had more than sobered me up! I was beginning to feel like such a fool! For the most part, I had invested all of my ten long years figuring out how to get here and had spent precious little time preparing for it! And now here it was…, the moment had come upon me!

I couldn't shake it out of my head, something was missing. 'Where in God's name was their 'good faith' deposit! Where was the money? Was I supposed to let them try this thing out for size, just because I was so eager to get here?' I didn't think so! As far as I was concerned, that didn't have a thing in the world to do with why they were not conveniently offering to compensate me for that privilege!

At least in the state of New Jersey, you can't even make an offer on a piece of residential real estate without a show of good faith embodied in a deposit. It's called 'earnest money'! This Company was about to suck my brains dry for the next six months with the intentions of creating a revolutionary product without so much as offering me a dime at this point. I was shocked, as the reality came crashing in! 'What should I do now?'

I truly didn't know. As a matter of fact, I can tell you I hadn't really paid that much attention to it until now! And I guess Allied figured that if I was stupid enough not to ask, then they weren't about to offer.

But wait a minute! I don't want to come across the complete fool, because I did ask! I had already discussed this point with Kevin before I had come up for the meeting and I remember asking Kevin if I was entitled to a pre-licensing agreement fee if the Company and I were to sign some sort of an agreement.

Now there they were, lying on her desk in plain sight… The contracts that we were supposed to sign. I couldn't help playing back Kevin's response in my head, as they stared back up at me. "Well Stevie, they pay ball players walk on fees, don't they? I'm sure they're not going to give you even a fraction of what those guys get, but still, they should give you something. But Steve, I don't want to sound like a jerk here, I have to tell ya that's not my department.

"Seriously though Buddy, you're going to have to discuss that with Dianne when you get up here and she's going to have to get that one from her boss. You know what I mean?"

Her back was still turned, and I was feeling really uncomfortable. I was compelled to do something, so I flicked open the latches of my briefcase hoping to grab her attention. Taking out a copy of my patent, I was placed it on her desk in plain sight. Apparently, my shuffling around was enough to break her concentration, as she pulled away from her keyboard.

She finally turned 'round to face me. And with a smile meant for nothing more than disarming me, she said, "Now, where are we?"

"Shoot, she's asking me?" I just wanted to strangle her. What the heck could she possibly be thinking, 'where are we?' I fought with everything I had, to keep it together. I wondered to myself, 'this lady has got to be kidding! Was she a lawyer or something, I just knew it! Because she was behaving just like some of the winners that I had jousted with over petty real estate deals.'

My curiosity had gotten the best of me, I just had to find out. "By the way, Dianne are you a lawyer per chance?" I said, playing to her vanity.

Her reply was slow and deliberate, as if she had to think about her response, "No I'm not..., but I perform much of the same work for the Company as a lawyer would." Then she added in a moment of levity, "But they don't pay me like a lawyer," as she chuckled.

Looking back with 20/20 hindsight, what a stupid ass I was. I had gone on a fishing expedition for clues on how she ticked, and she volunteered the essence of her being. But I missed it. What she had revealed to me in that little sentence was telling, and my missing it, would cost me dearly down the road. As it would prove out, this woman's passion was practicing law without a license.

I replied, "Oh so you're not. So, what exactly is your title and what do you do."

I must have landed squarely on her hot button, because she beamed, "I am the Head of Strategic Planning and Worldwide Development for Fram. It is my job to negotiate contracts for the various product groups under the Fram/Autolite names."

"I see. Do you travel much?" I asked, truly interested to find out where exactly she fit into our equation.

"Yes, I do. My job keeps me very busy. I travel the world for Allied negotiating for the Company's various interests. Another function of my job is to chart out future programs the Company will be following, like this filter of yours that we will be working on for example."

"Getting back to my filter. Shouldn't I be receiving some sort of earnest money for my six-month involvement with the Company?" I asked, trying not to be too forward. Yet, it was my full intention to make it known to her that I believed that my compensation at this point was not only protocol, but fair.

Her face dropped in response to my question, almost as if I made an improper advance towards her.

"What do you mean by that request?" she asked, indignantly.

Dianne's response sent me reeling inside. Her reaction to my benign question was downright personal. For a moment, she led on like she was the chief financial officer of the company or something, and that I had just tried to defraud her.

"I don't know if we've made any provision for your compensation at this point Steve," she said, concerned. "I know as of this time, that I haven't considered it myself."

Coming back without hesitation, I replied, "Well I have, if you don't mind. So why wouldn't a company as big and powerful as AlliedSignal not have considered something so basic as offering me an up-front fee for the privilege of exploring the possible viability of my patent over the next six months or so. You know Dianne, the profit potential of this filter is massive. Besides, it shows not only good faith on your guys part, but intent."

I had come this far so I couldn't let it rest. "Now let's assume for a moment that I'm Boeing, and that I'm dealing with Allied. Would they receive the same treatment as myself under these circumstances?"

"I don't know. I don't do business with them personally, Steve." With that, there was no further response from her, she just tacked 180 degrees, as if the subject had never been brought to the floor.

From here on out, she just let her body language do the rest of the talking for her and I could tell that the subject wasn't open for discussion any longer.

Almost immediately we were in the mist of ratifying the pre-licensing agreement. During that process, I attempted to make some polite small talk, but as it turned out, it wasn't worth expending the effort.

Despite the tension I felt inside, I was yet compelled to ask her once more about the earnest money, realizing that it was going to be more or less an exercise in futility. Even if she tacitly agreed, she'd still fall back on that old, 'it's up to my boss routine.'

The last thing that I desired was to get Kevin embroiled in this situation. I felt that he had done enough to get me this far along, so asking for his help in this situation was out of the question at this stage in the game. The last thing that I wanted, was for Kevin to think that I was an ungrateful whiner. After all, I had gotten my foot in the door and perhaps I should a been grateful enough just for that. 'Cause let me tell ya something…, there was no two ways about it, that's exactly how AlliedSignal felt!

"So, Dianne? Will you find out for me about an up-front fee for the agreement? You know, like a signing bonus," I asked, taking every pain to be as polite as possible, so as to avoid provoking a visceral response from her once again. I even offered her an out in advance, "Why don't you run my request by your boss after were finished signing."

Her reply was sedate. At this point she was only going to pay me lip service. "Yes sure, Steve. I'll ask him and then get back to you in a couple of days or so. Would that be all right with you?" she asked, knowing full well I had nowhere else to go.

There was no doubt about it. I was about to get trumped on this one.

The signing of the paper work was routine and was over with the flick of the wrist. Our business had concluded. There wasn't the remotest indication that a check would be forthcoming, and I was perceptive enough to realize at least that much.

In a way, I was about to enter into an irreconcilable marriage with an austere giant of a bedfellow. The last thing that I needed, was for them to roll over in the middle of the night and crush me…, forgetting that I was lying there next to them in the same bed.

From the very onset, the victory started out as bitter sweet. Despite my joy, I was tempered. I was beginning to sense that I was up against a new set of ominous forces out there lying in wait for me.

I beat it out of her office to say my good-byes to Kevin. I wouldn't see his smiling face again for the next seven months.

CHAPTER 4
THE CALL…, LONG OVERDUE

The October strategy meeting with the Fram team was quickly becoming a memory, and for the moment, the only piece of unfinished business facing me was whether I was going to be compensated for entering into the pre-licensing agreement or not. I had been patiently waiting a few days for Dianne to inform me as to how the Company intended to handle this matter.

Shortly thereafter the answer came back. Allied's official position was that I was not entitled to any pre-licensing fee for having entered into a proprietary technology sharing agreement with them. Although intuitively, I already knew that was going to be Allied's official response, it still didn't add up to my way of thinking.

The way I figured it, I was entrusting my confidential blueprint to the largest oil filter manufacturer on the face of the earth, and at least according to me, that had to count for something. Furthermore, not only was my intellectual property patented, but I was more than willing to demonstrate over the next six months its validity, even to the point of them telling me "no".

And if that wasn't enough, I had already made my intentions quite clear from the very beginning…, I was on a mission to show them how to gain entree into the Teflon Treated Oil market, unopposed! Allow me to put things in perspective. The market I was positioning them for was fast approaching nearly half a billion dollars a year in sales, a market that could easily eclipse Fram's domestic automotive oil filter volume!

I had it all mapped out. It was up to the decision makers at Allied to determine whether they wanted to pursue this untapped bonanza or not, it was really that cut and dry.

With all due respect, I was acutely aware that I might be viewed as just some clam digger from the Jersey shore who had been selling real estate for the last seven years, but that shouldn't of had any bearing on their stinginess. While on the other hand, I wasn't pretending to be some industrial genius either, promising to turn the field of oil filtration on its ear. No, I wasn't that starry-eyed, just realistic. After all, the compensation I sought would only be fair in light of my future contributions, now that I was about to tell them everything.

So, like it or not, that was the position I found myself in. You just had to be there.

Getting back to what Dianne had told me. "It simply was not the Company's policy to compensate individuals like myself at this stage in the game." Well that was their position and I gotta admit, it was a kind of a hard swallow. But it would be up to me now, to take it or leave it. I wasn't in shock, just disappointed.

As I surveyed the situation, I knew that I couldn't very well pick up my marbles and leave like some pouting baby, for God's sake. It had taken me ten long years of incredible persistence to get to this point, and my very soul was invested in this endeavor! Notwithstanding, it was way too premature to be thinking such idiotic thoughts.

Besides, I had to look on the bright side, they had already bit, and now it was up to me to make the best of it! So, I let the issue drop right then and there, resolving never to bring it up again.

My determination had become stronger than ever to cooperate with the Company to whatever degree that they would work with me. We had a lot of work in front of us and I just had to see this thing through. I certainly couldn't afford to dwell on the negatives and I wasn't about to acquire that bad habit now. Instead, I chose to forge on and make my way up this side of the mountain.

So, for the moment I consoled myself, placing my trust in the fact that I was doing business with the largest filter manufacturer on the face of the earth. And I must confess, for the time being, it seemed to have been working. However, as the journey progressed, the need for reality checks would become more and more frequent, and I would find that my consolation would eventually turn to disappointment.

"You know Pat, Thanksgiving is next week, and I haven't heard a thing from the engineers yet. It's really getting to me. It just doesn't add up. They've been allotted six months to figure this thing out and they've already eaten up a month and a half! What could be going on?"

"Maybe you should call Dianne honey, don't you think? she said, pulling the covers up to her chin. Just the thought of speaking so soon with her was starting to become a sore point with me. I didn't care much for Dianne. Perhaps we had gotten off on the wrong foot, but after our initial introduction, I wasn't finding her especially gracious.

"No honey," I shot back, "She's more involved in the legal side of the business," I said defensively. "She doesn't have anything to do whatsoever with whether the engineers are going to call me or not. My business with Dianne centers around this pre-licensing agreement and I'm sure that I'll have to deal with her down the road when it comes time to negotiate the final contract." That much I was sure of, since Kevin had already taken the guess work out of that one.

I said all that, trying to appease my sense of responsibility, in order to justify not having to deal with her. After all, I was the one looking for reassurance, not Patti. She was just doing her best to comfort me and give me some guidance.

I didn't have it out for Dianne, quite the contrary. I just had a keen sense that I'd be much better off, just to steer clear of her. She was just plain old confrontational, and it wasn't in my make up to lock horns at the drop of a hat with another person, especially not this stranger who had just popped into my life!

It's hard to put into words, but I couldn't help but feel that she was boxing me into a corner and a fight or flight mechanism was beginning to brew a storm inside me. As best as I could tell, she was offering me no other choice than a show down and I didn't want that.

'And over what,' I thought, 'ego?' I guess… Since she obviously perceived herself as some despotic gatekeeper or something. But one thing was for sure, from where I stood, I wasn't about to fall prey to my emotions and blow the opportunity of a lifetime! And it was my opportunity, not hers!

The kids were sound asleep by now and the pressures of the daily grind were fading and by this time, so was Patti. I didn't fault her, she was up at dawn every day with the two little ones and would let me sleep in the extra hour or so, usually with the bedroom door left wide open, the shades up and kids running about. I'm not quite sure how that extra sack time was charged against my account, all I knew was that I paid dearly for it.

I rued the fact that I preferred the nights.

"So why don't you call Kevin in the morning and ask him to call the engineers?" she said, trying to free my soul from this quandary.

"I spoke with him last week, remember? He told me that the engineers would be calling me any time now. So, I guess I'll have wait for them to call. There's nothing more I can do for the moment, I've waited this long."

With finality she said, "Okay honey, I guess you know what you're doing." Sleep was more of a pressing need for the moment as she began to drift off.

As I lay awake in bed I could hear the geese flying over as they followed the fly-way south, guided by the stars. The bedroom window was open a crack and the cool air was settling on my face. The warmth and security that I got from lying next to my best friend wasn't any match for the turmoil that was playing out in my head. The rhythm of her breathing was long and deep, she was fast asleep now.

I grabbed the remote and flicked on the Weather Channel and the local weather came up, wind out of the west at 8, clear and thirty-six degrees. It was a quarter after ten and the following morning was a work day for the both of us. I debated as to whether I would stay in my warm bed and toss and turn for the next hour, because sleep seemed like a long ways off. I had enough nervous energy to burn, so I slipped out from under the covers without waking her and began to dress in the dark.

I didn't get as far as my long underwear before she tossed a bit, turning towards me half asleep, mumbling like she'd done on a thousand other nights, "Where you going?"

"Fishin."

"What time is it?" she asked, with a twinge of 'are you crazy?'

Like it really mattered. I never had a set time or pattern as to when I was going to fish, other than I made it a point to go after the wife and kids were asleep. But during the fall striper season, the hour was irrelevant as long as it was past dark and so long as the fish were running. Somehow, I'd always managed to find the energy.

The beautiful thing about my freedom was that Patti graciously allowed me to have it. I always had my space from the very beginning of our marriage.

She knew where I was going, but she was still compelled to ask, more out of duty than anything else. She was also aware that if she needed to find me for any reason, she'd have to send for a posse, having no idea how much running and ducking was involved to hook up with my elusive quarry.

"It's early baby, a little after ten. Now go back to sleep, I'll be back in a couple of hours if there isn't anything happening."

She rolled over again, barely getting off, "Okay sweetheart, I'll see you when you get back. Don't be too late, careful please."

I slipped out and went into my daughter Jaclyn's room to check in on her. Somehow that little treasure appeared more precious when she was lying there fast asleep, all cozy and secure in her little bed. I pulled the golden hair out of her face, running my hand across her forehead as I did. Suddenly, her eyes popped open, she stretched and gave me a smile that would keep me warm for the rest of the night.

After whispering in her ear and kissing her on the cheek I told her that I loved her, then continued my rounds towards my son's room.

This situation was entirely different, akin to nitroglycerin. Gently, I opened his door and tiptoed up to his crib just to make sure the kid was covered and breathing. Matthew was just 13 months old. Only a few short months ago all four of us were prisoners of a colic nightmare that lasted for five straight months! But that was long in the past, as I looked down at him, eternally thankful for having a healthy beautiful son, who would one day be able to buddy with me. But for now, I dare not touch him! If he woke up before I got out of the house, all hell could break loose and the party would be over.

Making a hasty retreat from his room, I gently closed the door behind me.

After grabbing my hat and coat from the closet I made my way to the fridge and grabbed a slug of orange juice out of the container. The tide chart hung on the refrigerator door pinned up by one of my wife's corny magnets. Most likely some kid in her class gave it to her for a present. The chart was a fixture there and would be of service to me for at least nine months out of the year. I was always mindful of the ebb and flow of the tides; it was integral part of my life. The ocean was a constant source of delight to me. I fished her during one season and rode her waves on my surfboard during another.

Grabbing the well-worn chart in my hand, I scrutinized the small type searching to locate the date. My eyes locked on to the line I was searching for, dead low was at 1:45 am. I smiled as I tucked the chart back under the magnet. 'Great, outgoing water.' It was my favorite tide to fish. Glancing down at my watch I saw that it was after 10:30 already, it was urgent, I had to get moving!

The house was dark and peaceful as I rushed through the kitchen and moved down the hall way and out through the garage. Hastily, I grabbed my gear that was lying in its corner making my way out into the night. Peering upward into the black sky I noticed only a small sliver of the waning moon remained, rimmed by the shimmering stars.

The night was gorgeous, and the conditions held the promise of a fantastic evening ahead. I remarked to myself, 'at times like this, who needed sleep!'

I stopped at Seven Eleven and grabbed a 12 ouncer, needing a jolt of caffeine, besides it helped take the chill off, as I nursed it by the side of the van. The temperature continued to drop as the gentle breeze whipped around, blowing straight out of the west. The parking lot was well lit, bright enough to play a night game, so I decided to tie up there, instead of struggling on the inky black beach with a flashlight hanging out of my mouth.

After some sorting out of my surf bag and making sure I had the essentials at my disposal such as the flashlight and pliers, I donned my waders and jumped back into the van. My secret spot was only a few miles down the road as it beckoned me. Ok..., maybe it really wasn't so secret, but it just made me feel good to believe so. It was more inaccessible than anything else, because all of the property along that stretch was privately owned, and the Mantoloking cops monitored the situation closely. So, if you didn't have a place to legally park your car, you didn't fish it.

Without a care, I tossed my keys under the seat and started off toward the beach. The path leading toward the ocean cut through what was once a stand of black pines and hundred-year-old bayberry trees. The air was infused with an aromatic balm that reminded me of Christmas, as the trees rustled in the gentle breeze. The ocean was remarkably silent as I neared the crest of the dune. As was typical for late November, the westerlies reduced the inshore waters to that of a lake.

Once over the crest, I caught a glimmer of the giant pond. About a hundred yards or so to the south appeared an interesting a cut in the shoreline, but in the blackness, I could barely make it out even from the top of the dune.

The stars were out in full force, but their faint shimmering was hardly a match for the darkness. The row of million-dollar oceanfront's perched atop the dunes gave no light as they stared down at the beach. Cold and dark, their owners had long since packed up and left the warmth of summer behind.

I walked along absorbed in heaviness, as I scanned the water looking for any signs of life. The ocean seemed flat and desert like, almost a mirror image of how this situation with Fram was making me feel. For the moment I didn't see any signs of life as I walked along the shore the line.

My self-imposed isolation couldn't quell the incessant din that was playing on in my head. The battle raged on like that of two opposing teams trying to take the field at once.

I won't deny it; I had obsessed about this filter in one way or another since '85. Now I was focusing on just another emerging facet in what seemed like a never-ending saga. Perhaps that was true, but this time it was different I kept telling myself. Much different, as I tried to elevate my hopes.

Because now, for the first time in nine years, this was a different kind of wait. We were in business! I was waiting on what I had to assume was a cadre of professional filter engineers that were about to call on me. And that was all well and good, but what I truly found mind boggling was that a company with such prowess was taking so darn long to call. And the scary part of it was…, I knew they needed to! The wait at times, was almost more than I could bear…, yet I knew they had to call.

As so far as it was demonstrated to me, once the information would begin to flow, it was going to be a rather one-sided affair. It would be flowing in one direction, from me to them.

The dominant team that played in my head was known for their incessant pursuit of the filter. Its soul was propelled by the hard driving forces of accomplishment, destiny and the invention. They wanted to take the field, and they wanted to take it now! They were an unbelievably persistent lot, they didn't know the meaning of words like 'quit' or 'can't' and 'what if', they wanted to battle it out right here and right now. It mattered little or nothing to them that I was out here for the purpose of refreshing my soul and to fish… Not to obsess!

I glanced out over the bar and sized up the structure, trying desperately to let the other team take the field. This was the team that sought out peace and tranquility. This was the team that truly enjoyed nature and loved exploring all of her hidden secrets. And it was this team that was desperately seeking its time on the field, after all it was their turn to play. The first team with all of their heavy demands was truly draining.

A sandbar some fifty feet from the shore was beginning to show itself with the ebbing tide. With enthusiasm, I waded through the trough in order to get it, with the water nearly up to the top of my waders. This moat if you will, was only a few yards wide, but had to be forged if I had any intention of reaching the fish. After negotiating the steep face of the backside of the bar, I proceeded out another twenty yards or so before stopping after the water was comfortably up to my groin.

Still, no signs of life yet, as I looked around in the dark.

Reaching into the breast pocket of my waterproof kayakers jacket I pulled out the mini-flashlight and shined it on the water out in front of me.

"Bingo!" Beneath the surface swam a myriad of sand eels. They darted all over the place as the light penetrated the gin clear water, giving their silent presence away. The anticipation inside of me now rose to a fevered pitch. I pulled back my sleeve and took a quick peek at my watch, it was 11:15. 'Great,' I thought. 'It's still early and I had plenty of time to wait them out!' The bass had to sense that their dinner was here, after all, they were majestic eating machines. They had to be schooling just out over the bar, foraging dinner. I was certain of it. Before I took my first cast my mind was made up, I was gonna fish here tonight. The situation held too much promise to even consider another moving to another spot.

Cocking my rod back, I made a cast out past the edge of the bar. I was using a small yellow wooden lure called a needle fish, deadly when the stripers are feeding on sand eels. The plug's streamlined profile aided by the following wind made it a good ways out there. I barely cranked the handle when… Bang! I saw the silhouette of a splash against the inky blackness, as the bass smashed my plug with the fury of a small freight train. The initial 'bump' or 'strike' made this pursuit worth it all, as the drag screamed on the light spinning outfit I favored. The fish made a respectable run, then held the bottom before doing so another time or two. I pulled against the fish stretching the line taught so that I could better estimate his size. It was pretty apparent that this fish wasn't the thirty pounder that I was stalking, but still not a shabby fish, in the ten-pound class I imagined, more than capable of putting up a decent fight on light tackle.

As the fish tired, I reeled it in close to me, as I deftly prepared to grab it from the waist deep water. This part of the game was kinda hairy. When the fish was within a few feet I'd keep it at bay with my rod tip and reach for my light. I needed both hands free for the next part of this maneuver, so I'd stick the light in my mouth while trying not to gag.

Grabbing the line with my hand I'd coax the fish towards me waiting for an opportunity to grab the fish's lower lip with my thumb and forefinger. With a striped bass that poses no problem at all, since they don't have any teeth to speak of, but what really could really pose a problem was the three pairs of needle sharp treble hooks that hung off of the plug. The art was to lip lock the fish before it could shake its head and plant one of those hooks through your hand, in which case, would no doubt require a trip to the hospital's emergency room.

The other alternative was to pull the fish all the way back to the beach and unhook it on the shore, though it was much safer, I rarely opted for that unless the fish was badly hooked. It was too much of a hassle to walk all the way back in.

I had a great reverence for these fish and through all of this pulling and tugging, hooking and unhooking I always made it a point to release them with minimal amount of wear and tear.

And so, it went. This event repeated itself over a dozen times or so until the tide switched, and the fish shut off completely. The feed was over now. The fish were gorged and that was fine by me. By this time, I was looking for a valid excuse to quit anyway so I could justify walking away from this session. I needed to go home and get some sleep.

It was now half past two in the morning when I walked off that bar, content. Having kept the other team off the field for a few hours was a real blessing. My peace had returned, as I climbed the dune, calling it a night.

The phone rang late one Friday afternoon, Patti had been home from work for a little while and we were hanging around in the kitchen chatting about the events of the work day. Like most hard-working Americans, I loved the feel of a Friday. Just knowing that it was the beginning of a two-day respite for Patti, put me at ease. It was my wife who had weekends off. Not I…, though I would be the last person to begrudge her of that.

The calling she followed confined her to the classroom teaching thirty first graders the rudiments of reading, writing and arithmetic. One thing for sure, it was essential for her to recharge her batteries for a couple of days at the end of her work week. Personally, I couldn't quite fathom how she handled it. Very few people I've come across outside the teaching profession have any concept of the stress that a diligent elementary school teacher endures.

On the other hand, my situation was quite different. I was a salesman on straight commission, working nights, weekends and ah…, 'flextime'. Therein lies the panacea for all the would-be entrepreneurs, flextime! Work your own hours! 'Right?'

Well, that's sort of an oxymoron. I always wondered how you could work your own hours around other people's schedules? The answer to that one is, you can't!

Yet, I still didn't want a nine to five'er either. I knew that if I had a rigid work schedule that didn't permit flexibility, I wouldn't be afforded the luxury of babying my patent and pursuing my dream. So for me, the choice was simple, I had to go with flextime. I needed the flexibility of adjusting my schedule at the drop of a hat, to play the whimsical invention game.

Ring… ring… I was standing by the phone and looked over at Patti and said, "You wanna get it Honey?"

She looked at me, as if I was half crazy and shot back, "No!" Her eyes bulging wide as she gave me this incredulous look, saying, "You get it! You're standing right next to it for heaven's sake!" She just shook her head at me, unable to hold back her smile.

I was only teasing her. Our marriage wasn't built upon either one of us carrying on like indentured servants around here, we were two separate individuals that functioned as one.

I smiled back at her, still teasing as I picked up the receiver grumbling, "You know I hate this darn phone," I mouthed, just out of earshot of the person on the other end of the line.

"Hello, is Steve Moor there?" came a sort of poky Midwestern voice. Patti was still in the middle of her lifting her arms and sporting an impish smile, as I turned to face her with the phone tucked under my chin.

"This is he," I replied with a casual seriousness, readying myself to shake the would-be solicitor off the line. It was after five, around supper time and as was often the case, our peace would be invaded by these disrupting marauders.

"Well hi Steve, this is Gary Bilski from Allied Automotive."

Patti listened intently, straining to know who was responsible for spoiling our quiet moment as she fixed her gaze on my now very sober demeanor. Standing there almost frozen, she tried to figure out who was holding me captive on the other end of the line.

"Good afternoon Gary, so you're from AlliedSignal," I replied, just for Patti's benefit, letting her to know who was on the other end.

"What can I do for you Gary?"

"Well," he replied, "I have a copy of your patent here, and I'd like to go over it with you a bit. If you don't mind?"

I shot back, "No problem, I'd be glad to answer any questions for you."

If you can believe it, I still wasn't able to put two and two together. I had no idea who Gary was, or why AlliedSignal would be calling me now. The timing of the call threw me for a loop, besides, I was expecting a call from Fram, not AlliedSignal.

My mind began to race, as I thought to myself, 'what could this guy be calling me now for?'

Immediately the flood gates opened, and the demons came rushing in, trying to find a place to settle. They were quick to attack and never bothered to ask permission if they could! They were there at every turn, dogging me every step of way, just looking for an opportunity to suck the life blood of hope out of my soul.

The situation was problematic, due in part to my realism. For starters, I was acutely attuned to the fact that I was a participant in a game that was bigger than any other I had ever played. Keep in mind now, this guy on the other end of the phone was calling me in my kitchen. My briefcase that was still lying on counter and was brimming with real-estate matters, not engineering materials relating to the latest developments in oil filtration technology!

And the stakes! They were incredibly huge! I had a decade of sacrifice poured into this thing and I was looking to score and to score big. That's right! My sites were fixed on earning a well-deserved royalty check that would arrive at my house every quarter. Hopefully those checks would allow both Patti and I to walk away from our jobs and permit us to raise our children together the way we saw fit, not by the hefty dictates of our employment responsibilities. In a real sense, you could say I wanted to win the lottery, except I was endeavoring to earn it, since I didn't play the lottery much to speak of. The reality of it was, I was structuring my own lottery, except it was something that I was going to win on purpose.

The vehicle I intended on using was my patent and my ability to market a disruptive consumer product. And the concept…, well it was nothing short of magnificent! Now all I needed was a partner that would back me up. And if that could be arranged…, we'd both win big!

So you see, I didn't know yet who that guy on the other end of the line was, but I did know one thing for sure, either he was carrying a 'Yes' that would keep us alive for yet another round, or he was carrying a 'No', in which case, the death rattle wouldn't be far behind!

At this very moment the demons were creating a tumult, setting me up for the 'No,' employing all their wiles to crush me with Fear…, Doubt… and… Unbelief!

On the other hand, all that the Lord had promised me was present as well… Quiet and calm…, a type of peace barely recognizable set against the backdrop of the din going on inside my head. The Lord was always such a gracious gentleman. And in these moments of extreme chaos and pressure, He would always speak the same few words to me, which would rise up from deep within in my heart, "I didn't let you get this far to fail my son."

That was it! That was all I needed to hear, as I latched on to those words. At once I chose those words to agree with, and not the others that repeated over and over, the ones that kept repeating… "This is it…, it's all over for you…, they don't want it…, you're gonna fail!"

Instantly I regained my composure as my self-assuredness came rushing back in a torrent.

"Hey Gary, if you don't mind, what's this all about?" I asked, wanting to find out what the caller had in mind.

He replied, "Oh I'm sorry, didn't I tell ya? I'm with the engineering team out here in Perrysburg, Ohio," masking his bobbled introduction.

I was immensely relieved to find out who it was. His Midwestern accent put me to ease and I was doubly pleased that it wasn't some quick talkin' metropolitan hotshot.

"So Gary, let me get this straight, 'cause I'm a little bit slow sometimes. Are you the engineer that has been assigned to the Teflon Treated Oil Filter project that I have the patent on?

"Yup. That's me," he replied matter of factly.

"You see Gary, you gotta bear with me for just a second here, if you don't mind," not wanting to sound too much like Colombo. "But I'm having a hard time placing you at the meeting back in October? I was kinda expecting Tony Coronia to call me, you know, the Senior VP of Engineering."

The point is, Gary had not attended that meeting. Because if he had, I would have remembered that…, since I had made it a point to visit with every one of the engineers in the room. During this phone call, I thought it best not to get into the particulars why he wasn't present. So, I let it ride…

"Oh, oh! I got ya. He's my boss," figuring out what I was driving at. "Believe me, he doesn't get involved with this sort of stuff."

By now I guess, my query as to why he was calling me started to spill over and make him a little paranoid.

"Okay! Okay!" raising my voice an octave with approval. "I get it now. It's just that it's been such a long wait and I didn't know specifically who was gonna call…, I mean you personally, you know?"

Switching gears, "Darn! It's already been a month and a half since that meeting we all had, is there a problem? Kevin said, you guys were gonna call me, but I never expected that it would take this long."

"Kevin?" he replied. This guy was still so laid back he was virtually unaffected by my barrage. "Oh, you must mean Kevin Gill?" he said, repeating Kevin's full name, and for who's edification I wasn't sure.

"Yes!" I replied, "Kevin Gill! I've been working with him for quite some time now. He's a great guy!" I added. Now I said that because I truly meant it, but it wouldn't hurt to go on a brief fishing expedition anyway. I was always interested to see if the people that Kevin worked with felt the same way about him as I did.

Gary gave me a rather stock reply, showing little if any emotion, "Oh he's a good guy."

Taking into consideration Gary's tone level, his answer was good enough for me.

"So Gary, what exactly is your position at the Company, if you don't mind me asking?"

"No, not at all. I am the Senior Engineer for Passenger Car Filter Development for AlliedSignal's Fram's filter division out of Perrysburg, Ohio. That is our main research and development facility for oil filters."

"Wow," I said trying not to blow smoke at him. "That's quite a title. Have you been with the Company a long time?"

"Yeah. I've been with them quite a while." That answer seemed to of tired him out.

Patti gave me a thumbs up and a wink. Clutching my briefcase, she waved at me and tiptoed out of the kitchen, so I could be alone.

I still felt quite strange concerning the timing of all this. Somehow, I just couldn't quite make sense of this untimely call, as I struggled to put the whole thing into perspective. The notion that Fram's lead project engineer was reaching out for me at supper time on a Friday evening I thought strange enough, but to be contacting me a month and a half into our pre-licensing agreement was well beyond my comprehension!

Looking back at our initial meeting in October, Fram seemed to be so insistent that they were going to need every bit of the six months I had given them, and then some. I can remember, like it was yesterday, going back and forth several times in front of the group, as the lead engineer kept prodding Dianne to wrangle more time out of me. All I can say, was thank the Lord for Jack McGrath, the Senior VP of Fram, when he came to my rescue that day by putting an end to that auction. I can still remember how he stopped the bidding by assuring me in front of the group that "they weren't going to drop the ball." The signals I had been given at that time by Mr. McGrath were clear, Fram was in a hurry to get this thing started, and they were committed!

On the other hand, I was now somewhat relieved that Gary was on the other end of the line. Knowing that at the very minimum, the engineers would require my guiding touch to help them jump-start this project.

Flashbacks of that presentation now came rushing in. What really stuck in my craw, was the fact that during that presentation, I couldn't help but recognize that the engineers assembled hadn't proffered a single original idea which might have brought this filter one step closer to fruition. And to be frank about it, I caught them all flatfooted, just like I had previously caught every one of their competitors. The only difference being, before the meeting took place that morning they had more than likely been admonished by their chain of command to at least give me a fair hearing before condemning me.

And believe me, it wasn't as if they were playing it close to the vest either…, I am not that naïve. I know what I witnessed that day, and I'm here to tell you, that their enthusiasm during that session couldn't be concealed! But, like I just said…, so was their obvious lack of input.

So, after the dust had settled and the fanfare long over, I came away from that place more convinced of something I had known for quite some time. That the abundance of information which was about to flow, was going to be one way…, from me to them. It was that obvious. It was now going to be my job to guide them. I was the one who was going to responsible for getting them up this mountain…, and I was determined now more than ever to drag them up if need be.

That's why at this particular phone call was so disconcerting! First, there was this major time lapse which I hadn't been able to come to terms with. And now to complicate matters, the prospect of starting a project of this magnitude so close to Christmas, when employees routinely go missing in action, and their heads are stuck under the preverbal Christmas tree, just added to my paranoia. Simply put, this undertaking could lose momentum before it ever got started.

The impromptu invitation to begin the communication process somehow wasn't how I envisioned myself interfacing with the engineers either, so I just had to ask Gary one more time why he was calling me. 'Cause it was driving me crazy!

"So where do you want to start Gary?" I asked, turning the subject back to business.

"Well," he said taking a long pause, "You really have quite a novel idea here. I'm used to working with filters that remove material, if you know what I mean? You know…, this one is kind of a new for me."

"I'm sure, believe me Gary, I know. I've spoken with enough engineers in the business to have realized that much. You guys are purists. A filter is supposed to filter stuff out, not add it, right?" I was certainly obliging him with an answer that he could relate to. If he proved to be like all the rest of the engineers I had bumped into along the way, I was certain that this was how he would approach this filter as well. It was tantamount to a filter engineer's credo.

Chiming in immediately, he said, "That's right!"

With that, he fell directly into the same old mindset trap as the other engineering experts. And yet to me, the concept was so simple, begging the obvious.

You see, every engineer I had ever jousted with, without exception had been hard pressed to even consider the possibility, that maybe…, just maybe…, oil filters could provide a multifunctional purpose. And at first blush, Gary was turning out to be no exception to the rule…, sporting the same kinda thinking I'd already been exposed to.

"Ok, but let me ask you a question," I said. "If filters are just supposed to take stuff out and never add anything, then what about coolant filters? You know the spin on types that large diesels and class 8 trucks use. I'm talking about the ones that for all intended purposes use the same filter paper found in your standard spin on oil filter."

I wanted to compare apples to apples on this one, so I her rip. "The basic difference here Gary, is that coolant filters are designed to filter the cooling water, much the same way an oil filter are designed to filter oil, with one minor difference. The coolant filter in this case contains an additive that performs a specific task. It's basically the same concept, except we're talking oil filters here," I spouted out uncontrollably, not able to resist hyping him on my concept!

"Which, by the way, let me ask you Gary, are you familiar with what I am talking about? You know, the coolant filters with the white pelletized material inside of them?"

"Yes sure, but I'm not aware of them specifically. My expertise is in automotive side of things and not the heavy-duty," he said, coming across a little pressed.

"Well Gary, I can't recall exactly what the chemical composition of that stuff is, but I'm familiar with what the material's supposed to do. It's designed to dissolve over time and disseminate throughout the entire cooling system and after it becomes integrated within the cooling system, it's supposed to inhibit the formation of cavitation bubbles that can occur due to vibration. The vibration in large diesel motors can cause the formation of small bubbles within the cooling system that if left unchecked, are capable of boring pinholes through the cylinder jackets. As a matter of fact, I've installed Fram coolant filters on my own rigs before."

"What do you mean your own rigs?" he shot back inquisitively.

"You don't think that some real estate agent dreamt up these patents of mine by selling houses for a living do ya?" I replied, teasing him.

"I don't know?" he said, missing my humor. I didn't get to talk with Kevin much the other day when he called. He was in the middle of something and didn't have much time. All he said is that you had been calling him and that you wanted to know when we'd be calling you."

"I remember him telling me that if we needed to set up a meeting with you that it wouldn't be much of a problem, that you had a flexible schedule, because you were a real estate salesman or something like that. Like I said, he didn't go into much detail other than he thought that you were sharp and knew what you were talking about, not a bull singer type.

"So Steve, tell me, do you sell real estate, or do you own trucks?"

"For the last several years I've been selling real east estate full time for a living. But during the early 80's I was a professional over the road truck driver and on more than one occasion I owned my own rig. In that job you get a crash course in mechanics real fast. Either you learn or go broke that much quicker. So, if you're wondering where I learned about oil and filters, that's where I got my start, learning how to turn a wrench to keep my rig going."

"Wow, that's interesting. How long did you do it for?"

"A little over three years."

"Why did you get out? Did you like it?"

"That's a long story Gary. But I'll tell you I had a love-hate relationship with it. The hours were incredible and so was maintenance and overhead. There was no real money in it to speak of after expenses and what I really miss about it now, was the driving part. Oh, how I loved the feel of driving a rig."

We spent the next few moments discussing some of the details relating to how I envisioned the manufacture of the filter as well as some of its performance aspects and by the time we had finished this discussion, I had a pretty good sense that he realized I hadn't dreamt this stuff up in a vacuum.

Suddenly, he popped the question, "So what's your schedule like next week?"

Though long awaited, I didn't anticipate his sudden invitation. My immediate inclination was, 'you name the time and date, and I'll be there,' but I knew that I couldn't make that sort of a commitment, at the drop of a hat, flextime or no flextime. I still had enough of a schedule to contend with.

I asked, "Well, when did you want to meet with me?"

I could hear Patti open the door to my son Matthew's room, he was crying up a storm in the back ground as he awoke from his late afternoon nap wanting a bottle. Patti stuck her head into the kitchen, as she rocked him in her arms trying to assuage his discontent. Whispering over his cries, she said, "How's it going honey?"

Covering the phone with my hand I said abruptly, "Excuse me for a second Gary."

"Fine hon'… He wants to meet me next week! What'll I tell him?"

She looked over at me with a determined smile as she leaned over to grab a bottle from the fridge, "Just tell him you'll be there, as soon as you can grab a flight!"

Walking over to the microwave to heat his bottle she looked back over her shoulder and gave me a look of encouragement that only a soul mate could. The baby's little head was tucked under her chin and he started to coo as he recognized the bottle in momma's hand. "I'll be out of here in a moment honey. I'm so excited for you!"

Getting back on the phone, "Sorry about that Gary, my little boy just got up from a nap and my wife had to grab a bottle for the little monster." I said, jokingly.

He broke out with a chuckle, "I know what you mean, I have a couple of small kids myself."

For a moment the dad's in both of us took center stage as we got side tracked talking about parenthood for the moment. "How many kids do you have?" I asked.

"Two."

"Oh great! How old?"

As it turned out Gary had two young children, a boy and a girl near the same age as my kids. We traded a few war stories that we both had in common being young fathers along with the ongoing sleep deprivation experiments the kids had been putting us through.

He told me that his wife was expecting their third child before the winter was out, so I congratulated him on the upcoming birth of his healthy new baby. Nearly in the same breath, I told him that I had my hands full with two, for which he was quick to agree.

"My little boy is a shade over a year, and for the first five months, the kid was terribly colic. I don't know how my wife and I came out of it with our sanity. And you know, today the boy is perfectly fine, but a little volatile, if you know what I mean."

"Yeah, I do," he said. "We never had a colic kid, but we've heard stories."

"All I can say, is that I hope you never have to go through it."

"Me too!" he said, with uncertainty.

I wasn't being callous, but in the middle of our conversation this cruel thought came flashing across my screen. Well, maybe it wasn't so cruel... I was persuaded that it was more realistic than anything else, after all I could relate. There I was myself, smack in the middle of this vortex of child rearing, at a point where the energy drain was so tremendous that I couldn't help but wonder how his own family life at the moment could affect his performance on my project.

And it didn't require an expert to figure it out either, he was juggling the same hats that I was; father, husband, job and bills. And by the sounds of things, I could tell it wasn't any easier for him than it was for me. Obviously, this was life, and neither of us was complaining, but it did impose its pressures and limitations of which we both had to face. I realized immediately, that we were both going to need each other's help and cooperation if we were ever going to give this embryonic filter of mine a chance at life.

"So what day is good for you next week Gary?" I asked, caught up in the moment.

"My schedule is booked during the earlier part of the week, but I'm looking ok from Wednesday on. Do you think you can make it?" he asked, with a hint of excitement.

I was getting good vibes from this guy and I liked him already. He didn't appear hung up on the fact that I wasn't a professional engineer type, or from his industry. Gary came across as hospitable and anxious to see if this thing was going to work. And as far as I could tell, if it did, that was gonna be all right with him too. I was relieved that he seemed the type that wasn't about to make me miserable, on account of fact he had a job to do.

So far, this was all that I could of hoped for and once again it all seemed to be happening!

"I'll tell you what, I'm gonna try and shoot for Wednesday" I said, full of wishful thinking. "It's too late to reach my travel agent now, or I'd would! I'll have to try and get her tomorrow, and if I do, I'll give you a call. But now that I think about it, just keep in mind that this is Christmas time and my chances of getting a flight to anywhere at the last minute is going to be slim. So really, the best I can do is to call you as soon as I can with a few flight times. Is that okay?"

"Sure, that sounds fine Steve. Let me know when you can make it and I'll fill you in on the rest of the particulars."

"Hey Gary, before you go, I need to know what airport I'll be flying into. Where's Perrysburg near anyway?" I asked.

"Oh? We're located about twenty-five minutes or so from the Toledo airport. So, you'll be flying into Toledo. Okay?"

"Yes, sure. I gotta grab your work number I don't have it, and by the way, in case I have to reach you after hours or over the weekend, would you mind if I grabbed your home number as well? I mean if it that's ok with you?"

"Yeah, sure. But I'm not gonna be home Sunday until late, I have a family function that we have to go to."

"I hear you loud and clear on that one. I'll try to get you tomorrow if I can.

By the way, give me your wife's name so I can address her if she picks up the phone when I call."

"No problem with that. She picks up the phone more than I do!" he said chuckling.

"Well Gary, it's been great talking with you and I'm looking forward to meeting you personally as soon as I can catch a plane and come out, so that we can get this thing rolling.

"I just have one little question that's been bothering me, if you don't mind? It won't take but a moment.

"Why did it take so long for you guys to call me anyway?"

"That's a good question. All I can tell you, is that were working shorthanded with the downsizing that's been going on around here and all. And I guess that we're just busy."

"Okay, that's good enough for me, I'll let ya go now. I'll be in touch. Bye."

Actually, that wasn't a good enough excuse for eating up a month and a half.

Busy…! 'On what'?!

I didn't know?

I couldn't fathom how this project especially with its time constraints didn't rate over Fram's routine engineering duties. I just couldn't figure it!

'How many truly novel concepts were they working on besides mine?' I already knew the answer to that one and that's why I couldn't let it alone. None!!!

But I'll tell you what… The deeper I went inside, and the more I got to peek under the tent, the less I could make sense out a what I saw. Nonetheless, when I hung up the phone my soul was brimming with joy. I was stoked! We were finally moving ahead now, and I was thankful for that, despite the lingering doubts I had concerning the Company's way of doing things.

Again, I refused to dwell on the little fires I witnessed breaking out, preferring to just extinguish them. All I really wanted was to be grateful for the big picture.

"Hey Pat!" I yelled. "Come in here! I'm going to Toledo Baby!"

My travel agent happened to be closed on Saturday, but I reached her first thing Monday morning and asked her to book me the next available flight for Toledo. But unfortunately, just as I suspected, it would take some doing to get me a round trip flight on such short notice. Subsequently it wasn't until Tuesday when she finally managed to find me an airline that would fly me out. The only catch was, it wasn't leaving until the evening of December the 12th, a good two weeks away!

The plan was that I was going to meet with Gary on Tuesday morning and then head back to Jersey in the afternoon. That was my only plan other than driving out to meet with him. I hadn't run it by him yet, but later that afternoon I gave Gary a call at work to firm up what I had come up with.

"Hi Gary! It's Steve Moor. How are you doing?"

"Great Steve! Boy, that was quick! How'd ya make out?" sounding kinda revved up at the sound of my voice.

"Under the circumstances, okay I guess," saying with a long pause.

"What do you mean?" he asked, sensing my uncertainty.

"The best I could do was Monday December 12th. It's an evening flight so we'll have to meet Tuesday morning. I hope that's all right? Because if it's not, I'll be just as glad to drive the five or six hundred miles out, so we can meet earlier. Believe me, it's really no big deal for me to drive out and see you. Besides, aren't we cutting this awfully close to the Christmas holiday?"

"Na, don't worry about that Steve," he said. "The thirteenth looks just fine, that'll work for me and besides, that will give me plenty of time to set everything up.

"Hey! We're gonna put you up in the Marriot Courtyard, it's a pretty nice place. We use it quite a bit when we have guests from out of town come in," he said, sounding quite pleased with the way things had turned out.

"Oh, I'm sure that hotel will suit me just fine," I replied. "It's gotta be more accommodating than the sleeper I used to live out of when I ran the road," joking with him. Without exaggeration, I would of gladly slept in a rest-stop for the privilege of meeting with him in the morning, if I could have.

I wasn't a seasoned business traveler by any stretch…, you know…, with the plane, the rental car, the hotel, the important meetings. I'd much prefer a dispatcher telling me that I had to get my load to such and such a place, by a certain time and date. And as long as there was a road, I'd get there without so much as a second thought. I'd done that hundreds of times, and to put it bluntly, I didn't relish the prospect of this sort of business travel.

"So, Gary, I'm going to arrive at 7:30 PM on Tuesday night and get to this hotel. Right?" I asked, wanting to know the details.

"Yes, that's right," he said.

Asking, "Is it close to the airport, 'cause I want to know if I need to be renting a car?"

"Oh, it's about fifteen minutes from the airport and you won't have to bother with a cab or a rental car, the hotel runs a shuttle bus and you can catch a ride on that," he added, eliminating my next question.

I wanted to ask him about the meeting. He hadn't really elaborated much about it, except he thought it was a good idea for us to meet in the event I had any important information that might be useful to the Fram engineers. The evening we first spoke, he had hinted that the meeting was going to consist of just him and I, perhaps one other guy. The prospect of sitting down with Gary and sharing with him all of the intimacies of my filter didn't in the least bring on stage fright, but if at all possible, I wanted to keep it that way, preferring not to go through a full-blown presentation like I had done back in October. I sincerely wanted to pin him down on this, because if it wasn't so, I at least wanted the opportunity to prepare for it mentally, and of course study.

"That pretty much answers most of my questions except one Gary. I assume that you can pick me up in the morning and take me to work with you, right?" I said hoping.

"I was about to suggest that," he said. "And if you want, we can meet for breakfast, so we can get a jump on things."

I replied, "That would be perfect, I would like that very much. What time do you want to meet?"

"I'll meet you in the lobby at 7:15, is that all right?"

"Yes, that's fine by me," I answered, segueing into the final details of our meet. "Hey Gary, by the way who's coming to this meeting," I asked.

He paused momentarily. Nothing obvious, like he was groping for an answer or anything, so of course, I didn't pay it much heed. Besides, what would it matter if he told me that I was going to address one hundred engineers in an amphitheater. 'What could I possibly do to change that anyway?'

Casually he responded, "Oh…, just you and me. Maybe just one of the other fella's that I work with might stop on by, but I promise you, it's going to be real low key," he said, reassuringly.

"Okay, Gary. I'll give the hotel a call sometime Monday afternoon and confirm my reservations. Look forward to seeing you Tuesday morning on the 13th."

Caretta Trucking   Caretta 'coast to coast'   mid '80's.

Truly a world-class fleet and operation for its day.

During my research and development phase, I conducted an extensive multi-year test study on a one-micron secondary-by-pass oil filter that would provide the foundation for my benchmark '901 patent and the many filter breakthroughs to follow.

Famous for running high-mileage teams from the Eastern seaboard to California & back. A two-man team could routinely complete a 6,000 mile turn in less than a week.
Top flight equipment powered by Cat's iconic 3406's & big cam Cummins w/13 speeds.
Glorious 'left lane' cabovers; Kenworth's, Peterbilt's & Freightliners.

Sadly, they would end up going bankrupt…, yet another victim of unbridled deregulation. Now they're just a fading memory like so many of the great ones of that era.

CHAPTER 5
MEETING THE ENGINEERS, A CHRISTMAS CHEER

Rush hour… The heavy traffic was moving at a brisk pace and as could be expected, there was no shortage of commuters turned race car driver, doing their fair share of drafting. Included in the mix, was a steady stream of big rigs that accentuated the landscape. This night the interstate was awash in diesel wagons hurtling down the boulevard, cutting through the darkness bedecked in full regalia, with their chicken lights a blazing.

It was the night before the scheduled meeting in Ohio and I was in the truck lane motoring northbound on the Jersey Pike heading for the airport. Pressing on, I began wishing real hard that I wasn't stuck behind the wheel of some dumb Dodge Caravan. Then out of the side-view mirror it appeared…, this massive silhouette creepin' on up behind me. As he swung her out into the left-lane, I began rolling down the window in order to get a better listen. He was justa' gettin' it…, it was obvious that this driver was intent on makin' time. As the hulking Studio Sleeper nosed up beside me, I could feel the huge pressure wave she was pushing come right through my window and brush the side of my face. The beautiful sound was unmistakable, as the 3406 under the long hood of the W900 purred with all of 500 serious horses. As he put his foot into it once again, I could hear the distinctive whine of the big Cat's turbo spooling-up as he floated through yet another gear. Stayin' up with him, was now out of the question. Before long, there was nothing left but his sailing mud flaps and the red reflection of his maker lights bouncing off his shiny barn doors.

To my way thinking, it was simply amazing, how something so graceful could pull such a massive loaded trailer so effortlessly. 'It was crazy,' I thought. 'How could something as pedestrian as a big truck passing me, have the ability to transport me back into another dimension?' Actually…, I already knew the answer to that one…, 'I still had the fever pretty bad.'

Oh, the memories! Though I never drove a beauty such as that, I still had memories none the less, and savored them as I headed towards the airport. My mind was occupied with the past…, a past that I had left out there somewhere, back in another life.

The appointment was upon me, the long week of refresher-cramming was quickly drawing to a close, and the opportunity to momentarily drift back was a welcomed respite. With the facts down cold, I was confident I was capable of answering just about anything that Gary might have in mind, or anyone else for that matter, concerning the manufacture of my filter.

For the moment though, I was somewhere else…, traveling in a different dimension. The ongoing issue wasn't settled yet and had surfaced once again. The question being, 'did I want a long nosed conventional or a flat faced cab over? Invariably, being out on the highway would as always, reopen the debate that had been a constant over the years. On the surface that might have sounded a little absurd, but my childhood obsession hadn't been put to bed as of yet. Let me assure you, I had left a part of me out there a while back. I had run the road before.

Back then I was single, barely a man in my early twenties. It was my senior year of college and I wasn't taking your typical sabbatical, hitch hiking across Europe for a year. With me it was different, my disenfranchisement with higher learning released me to temporarily pursue an obsession. Back then, I traded my seat in the classroom for that of an air ride seat behind the windshield of an eighteen-wheeler. As it would prove out, that was only a taste. I headed back to school to finish out my senior year and receive my diploma, only to do it again for a couple of more years after I graduated.

The drill was simple. I'd say goodbye to my folks, then shove off, plying the highways and back roads of the lower forty-eight. I'd be gone for a good two months at a stretch sometimes. Destination…, anywhere in the continental United States. I viewed myself as a sailor of sorts, putting out for a voyage. My ocean was terrestrial, and the steering currents were the ribbons of asphalt and concrete. I sailed alone, but rarely was lonely, seldom afraid and always expectant.

Now, after many years of being away from it, I still couldn't shake the vestiges of that white line fever.

Every time I got out here the question would always arise, 'was I ever going to get another chance to get behind the wheel of a big rig again?' I desperately wanted to know the answer to that question. Personally, I couldn't see how that could ever be arranged, my life was so different now. I had become a husband and had grown up to be a father, not the type to so readily leave my brood for even a few days. I was far from being a young cowboy any longer, responsible just for myself. Consequently, some dreams die hard, I guessed the little boy in me was still alive and well.

These days my time spent out on the road always seemed to be so short lived, and this night was no exception. Newark International lay just down the road a piece. Glancing down at my watch, I had an hour and a half before the flight departed, and I was running out of road fast. Caught up in the moment, I felt as if I had it in me to make it all the way to Ohio that night. I would have much preferred it over the plane ride.

The industrial belly of the Garden State was lit up like up like a Christmas tree as I pulled off the interstate and into the airport's parking lot. Although the business day was almost in the can, I couldn't resist grabbing the day's edition of the Wall Street Journal as I worked my way towards the boarding area. I didn't care for the papers much, but occasionally I was interested in seeing how the movers and shakers of the business world were getting along without me. In some weird sort of way, I had always wondered what it would be like join in on their game, knowing full well that it wasn't for me. The notion of being immersed in that sort of a battle on a daily basis would have left me drained and wanting for what I already possessed.

As time progressed, I was becoming more and more attune to my destiny, and it wasn't to be found in that forum and I didn't require a soothsayer to inform me that my future dreams were inexorably locked up in this filter. The responsibility of allowing it to have a life of its own rested squarely upon me and my ability to communicate clearly with the engineers.

The flight out to Ohio was an hour or so, giving me enough time to thoroughly take my mind off what the morning would bring. For the time being, the flight served to stave off the guilt that I should still be studying instead of reading the newspaper. Besides, as it turned out, the newspaper was an antidote for the anxiety that was steadily building within me. As fate would have it, yesterday's news posted the quarterly output and sales forecasts for the automotive industry and seeing that information in print only served to bolster what my soul already knew. The market potential for this filter was massive! It was an unexpected confidence boost that I sorely needed. After all, I told myself, 'I was truly on to something that played to an enormous market place and Fram needed it more than they realized!'

As I looked for the hotel's shuttle bus out in front of the terminal there was a blanket of snow on the ground, it was a lot colder out here than it was back east! Jersey's weather seemed more like the Carolina's than this stuff. Just then, I got a shivering thought, 'if this cold front hits home anytime soon, the striper fishin' would all be but over.'

There it was, over there, waiting for me. I found it rather comforting, as I climbed into the van. All I wanted to do was get to the hotel, so I could check in and grab a quick bite before settling in for the evening. By a little after ten I was studying once again for what I had hoped would be for the last time. I couldn't foresee any reason why I would ever have to pour over this material like this ever again.

With all of my papers spread out, I propped myself up in the middle of the bed reviewing the entire file until I fell asleep, sometime past midnight.

The time was seven fifteen in the morning and I was seated in a large smushy leather chair down in the front lobby of the hotel. I had been waiting only a couple of minutes before Gary came through the set of double glass doors, signaling an end to my waiting. Almost immediately we had locked onto each other's gaze, caught in a moment of instantaneous size me up, disarming the other with a smile.

'Was this the guy I was supposed to meet,' I wondered? 'It had to be! He was right on time, and besides he looked like he might be an engineer,' I thought.

I was in the midst of freeing myself from the grip of the chair as he made his way over to where I was seated. "Gary?" I asked, not totally sure it was him.

"Hi Steve. It's nice to meet you," sticking out his hand. "How was your trip out?"

"Oh no problem, everything went smooth," was my reply. "I don't get to travel like I used to," I said, trying to ease us into a light conversation. "Do you travel much? I mean on business for Fram?" I asked.

"Yes, I do, but not as much as I used to."

I piped up, "Yeah, I guess traveling on business must get a little bit old after a while. My experience is very limited, and I guess maybe I'm better off."

"I'd say so," was his reply. "Hey, how was your room? I hope it was okay?" he added with genuine concern.

"Just fine Gary. Thanks for asking. Do you know where I can grab a cup of coffee around here, I could use a jump start at this hour."

"Yeah sure. They have a decent menu here and we have plenty of time. Do you want to catch some breakfast?"

My reply was, "That's fine by me, lead the way."

We both sat down and had a leisurely cup of coffee as we waited for our eggs to come out. So far there wasn't the slightest hint as to why we were together. It was pleasant just to sit there as we eased into the morning, chit chatting about each other's kids covering familiar ground.

Out of nowhere with a mouth half full of eggs he blurted out, "So how did you come up with this idea, anyway? You don't have a background in engineering do ya?" asking with a puzzled look, as he scrunched his brow.

"No, I don't, but it's kind of a long story," I said.

"That's all right, we have time," came his reply.

"I'm sort of a jack of all trades," I began... "Unfortunately, a master of none so far. I've done quite a few things, and I've already been down my share of blind allies so to speak."

He began to pump me. More out of sheer inquisitiveness I expect, than motive. And what I was about to tell him was good for him to know.

Keep in mind now, this fella sitting across the table from me was the Team Leader for Fram's Passenger Car Filter Development. Out of nothing more than respect, I figured he was entitled to know a little bit about my background. Like how I had formulated this patent and arrived at my business plan. Besides, I didn't want him to think that I was some gunslinger that just came in from out of town and that I was going to rewrite the book for him.

"Well Gary, I haven't had what you could call a predictable career path. Before I go on, I assume that you went straight through college and got a job right away in your chosen field of engineering. Right?"

He replied, "That pretty much covers it, this is my second engineering position."

Somehow, I always was a little envious of my contemporaries who had these career paths etched in stone. Their lives always seemed so ordered, so secure, as opposed to my life so far, which more or less reminded me of an odyssey. Don't get me wrong. Odyssey living is truly the spice of life, however this constant exposure to the unknown can get more than a little nerve racking.

"Okay, well that's where we kinda differ you might say. I started out as a pre-med major and by the time my junior year came around the more advanced courses in math and physics cut my legs out from under me. I was determined to be a doctor, but I was hamstrung by my aptitude in math. So regrettably, it left me no choice, I had to drop out of that program. I became a psychology major instead."

That little scenario invoked sort of a blank stare of puzzlement from him. "Why'd you do that? That was kinda far removed from your biology major wasn't it?"

My reply didn't require any pondering; I had gone over it a thousand times since. "It was the easiest way out for me at the time. All that mattered at that point was to get my diploma and get as far from academia as possible. You could say that I had become disillusioned with my failure, school..., the whole darn deal. I might add, I was a bit broken hearted over the whole thing.

"This might sound a little weird to you, but I really wanted to be a doctor from the time that I was a little kid. The math thing at this stage was an insurmountable obstacle that came at a time which left me no other choice, but to bag it."

He seemed to be enjoying my little saga and asked me to go on. So, I continued, "I had always been sort of independent and made my own decisions if you know what I mean. For instance, I put myself through a top flight all male Catholic high school. Then I paid my own freight through college. I called my own shots, right or wrong. I had always paid my own way, from the time that I was a young kid. 'Cause of that, my parents gave me a lot of latitude to chart my own course in life. You know what I mean? My only regret was that I always wanted a mentor. Maybe if I had one, I wouldn't of made so many wrong turns. I don't know? Who knows?

"So anyway, I was attending the University of Connecticut and at the end of my junior year I had just about enough of school, so I withdrew for a year and went trucking. I hooked up with this girl from Pennsylvania that needed a driver for a tractor trailer she owned."

His eyes bulged like saucers, grinning "Are you serious?" he said, amused.

"Of course, I'm serious," to which I replied, "That's only part of it. That chick owned two tractors! She was an owner operator and owned two tractors that she leased to North American Van Lines. She, her hound dog and boyfriend took the one tractor and I took the other. That's how I got my first road job."

Well that was it. Gary couldn't contain himself now. He started to laugh, unable to hold it back. I guess he felt a little self-conscious for laughing, so he apologized for it. "The part about the hound dog really got to me," he said, trying not to laugh.

"Oh, don't worry about that," I told him. "You can laugh all you want, I know it sounds a little funny, but that's how I got my big break into trucking. Then eventually over the course of the next few years I owned a couple of rigs myself, and man let me tell ya, that's when the real education began. The breakdowns. I wasn't much of a mechanic before I started, but I sure was a fast learner!"

"I see," was his reply. "That makes a lot of sense to me. More like hands on field training, I guess," he chuckled.

We still had a good half hour before heading out for the meeting and by this time I was feeling quite comfortable with him, he was a real likable fellow. Gary was still intrigued as to how I, as an outsider, managed to dream up this idea for a new filter, let alone get a patent on it. In his polite manner he continued to pump me.

Before long, he was up to speed on my first patent and I managed to cover most of the ground that had gotten me to this point.

During much of the time we had been talking, that gentle Voice in the back of my mind kept prodding me to pin him down on who was going to be in attendance at the meeting. I ignored it until it would stop no more.

'Why was that of such importance anyway?' It really wasn't going to change the outcome of the facts one way or another and it certainly was the one variable that I couldn't control.

With no time being opportune, I popped the question as we got up from the table. "Hey Gary, not that it really matters to me, but who's gonna be at this meeting besides you and me?"

He was in the middle of fumbling for his credit card to pay the bill when I asked him, so he didn't respond right away, so I just let it go at that.

As we made our way out to his car we walked through the parking lot without so much as a word. Unlocking the door with his key he got inside and reached over the passenger seat to unlock my door, then motioned for me to climb in. I opened the door, stowed my duffel bag on the back seat and sat down. Then as he stuck the key in the ignition, he glanced over to me and answered the question that I had asked him back there a few minutes ago.

"Well, there's going to be you and me and maybe another colleague that I work with that might be stopping in. It's not going to be anything much. We'll probably finish up in a couple of hours and you can be going on your way."

"Sounds all right with me," as I picked up my briefcase, swung it around and placed it alongside my duffel bag in the back. I replayed his answer over in my head one more time to be certain. Sure enough, that's what he had told me when we spoke on the phone last week, at least it was consistent.

The ride to the research facility was about twenty minutes of nondescript highway miles. I felt relaxed and enjoyed the ride as I stared out the window at the gray wintry landscape. Gary was asking me about my real estate career, but I wasn't as obliging as before. To me, my involvement in that business had been nothing more than a means toward this end. Real Estate sales as far as I was concerned was a bloody little game that required much sacrifice and my heart was never truly in it for a variety of reasons. More often than I'd care to admit, my time was wasted by strangers and there was never any compensation for all that wasted effort. It was a treadmill of sorts, where the virtues of honor and loyalty commonly ended up on the trash heap. In order to get me through it, I much preferred to view myself in my heart of hearts as more of technical sales rep. in the making, rather than a real estate salesman. Besides, I didn't want anyone along this journey to pigeonhole me as a real estate salesman, whose sole expertise was selling houses for a living.

It didn't take much for Gary to realize that wasn't my favorite topic, as he backed off on that line of questioning.

The facility was located off by itself, and stood out from the distance, on the barren treeless lot. It seemed like it was situated in the middle of some farmer's field. As we approached it off the interchange, Gary pointed it out to me with a degree of pride.

"This is where I work," he said, as his excitement level continued to rise by the moment. The way we had been carrying on it appeared as if we had been partners working on this project for the last six months. You couldn't of guessed it, but our relationship was at best a couple of hours old, and that would have included our phone time. Gary didn't appear the least bit jealous or threatened by my entrée into his domain, and he wasn't compelled to hide it either. As for me, well, I was more than pleased that the chemistry between us was there.

Suddenly in the form of a manifesto, and unsolicited by me, Gary offered these words of encouragement just before the car came to a rest in the lot, "Hey Steve, I gotta tell you that this is a first for us here at Fram! You know, we've never done anything like this before. I mean, we've never looked this hard at anything from the outside before. And I've gotta tell ya, we're all pretty excited around here about it!"

I had already gleaned as much, long before he had experienced that epiphany. Anyway, I already knew what he was saying had to be true, nonetheless…, it was decent for him to say so.

Yet those words out of the mouth of the senior project leader of the largest filter company in the world had the effect of melting my heart. Despite that, it was so hard for me to accept the fact that something as dear to me as this was actually coming true! I just had to ask him, "Do you really mean that Gary?" as I watched my grandest desire unfold on the big screen.

"Heck yeah, Buddy! It sure enough is, or you wouldn't be here. You can believe that!"

I was once again lost in the midst of pinching myself, making sure that I wasn't in the middle of some sort of pleasant dream when all of a sudden… I was overcome with stark terror!

My duffel bag…! Where was it? My samples were in there and I needed them! I spun around only to find the bag where I had left it, lying on the back seat next to my briefcase. Ok. No biggie. It was just one of those crazy thoughts, you know, the kind that seizes you in a moment of irrational fear. I'll tell you, it was one heck of a way to convince me that this moment was real and that indeed, I wasn't dreaming at all.

Out of sheer relief and exuberance I shouted out, "Gary! I almost forgot to tell you, I brought you a couple of different samples of the Teflon!"

"You did?!"

"Yeah. And I also brought along the material handling data safety sheets!" Well, you would have thought that I had brought along the Holy Grail or something.

I really made his day when I told him that I was going to leave him some samples of the 'special sauce' for him to try out.

Before I knew it, we were walking down the hallway of a relatively new Butler type building. I'd have to say, that it had a lot more contemporary styling than the 1950's era facility that housed Fram's headquarters back in Rhode Island.

Gary walked briskly down the hallway, heading towards his office a few paces in front of me. Upon entering his small office, he let me know that he was just going to drop off his jacket and grab a pad.

"Come on follow me, we're going to sit in this room over there," as he pointed to an open door down the middle of the corridor.

"Do you need to use the men's room?" he asked.

"No, I'm fine. I went back at the hotel before we left. Thanks."

He seemed a little nervous now, but I didn't pay any attention to it. I just thought that the whole situation was making him a little nervous, as it did me.

"Can I get you another cup of coffee, then?"

I replied, "No thanks, my back teeth are floating."

Unaffected by my quip he said, "Okay then, follow me." All of a sudden, he appeared more serious now than he had been all morning. I kinda had this shooting thought, 'if just the two of us were meeting, then how come we were not sitting down in his office? Well too late…

I followed him down the hallway and into a small conference room where five men stood milling around talking quietly, then as we entered all eyes turned on us. As natural as you please Gary's first move was to introduce me to all five men present, as we all began reaching for each other's hand.

Whew… I took a deep breath. 'What do we have here? I thought just the two of us we going to meet!'

Right off the bat, I remembered two of the guys distinctly, the other three I had never laid eyes on before.

There was no getting around it, one of the men present was my nemesis of sorts, Mr. Anthony Coronia, VP. of Product Engineering. He presided over the entire shooting match for Fram.

We had already made each other's acquaintance on two prior occasions. For the most part we barely tolerated each other, and I was more than a little uncomfortable as we greeted each other through our thinly veiled smiles. Mr. Coronia made no bones about it, he believed that I didn't have any right to conduct business in his world, and he wore it out on his sleeve.

Then there was Bijan Kheradi a nice enough guy, Fram's Manager of Filter Materials, Perrysburg, Ohio. He seemed familiar, I must have met him back in October, at the big hoe-down that kicked this thing off.

So, what if I had walked into a booby trap?! Now, certainly wasn't the appropriate time to be analyzing what was taking place. To be honest, it all happened so quickly and so smoothly, I wasn't afforded the luxury of getting in touch with my emotions at that moment, there simply wasn't any time left for that. Whether I was feeling scared or aggrieved wasn't important now. I went on full alert.

The fact of the matter was that the meeting was planned by them and not by me. My part in the whole thing was to show up, and to disseminate the information. It mattered little what the circumstances might be, or if I was under pressure. That wasn't the criteria for which I was about to be judged. Believe me, at this point my hands were full, just trying to remember the guy's names and their areas of expertise.

The next gentleman that I was introduced to I'd never met before, either. His name was Gordon Jones, Director of Filter Engineering, Perrysburg, Ohio. The next gentleman was Greg Vackle, Professional Engineer, Manufacturing Services; Stratford, Ontario, Canada. From what I could gather he was like the plant manager for Fram's Canadian manufacturing facility. He seemed to be an affable fella and I had not met him before either. The last gentleman in the lineup to be introduced was Ronald Rohrback; Ph.D., AlliedSignal Corporate Headquarters; Morristown, N.J. After his introduction, I really started to ask myself some serious questions. 'Like for starters, what were the odds that a Ph.D. from the corporate headquarters just happening by?'

Not too shabby a turnout for some itinerant inventor who peddled real estate for a living, huh! It wasn't the time to dwell on that, nor to get cocky. I was too busy praying under my breath for Jesus to help me. And believe me, I needed His help now!

The room began to settle down after we all found our places at one of two long cafeteria style tables. The tables ran lengthwise and divided the room into halves, in effect, it was a low budget facsimile of a horseshoe conference table. At the front of the room was a white writing easel that separated the tables punctuated by an institutional looking wall clock, the kind I used to stare at when I was in school.

For a moment, the guys talked shop amongst themselves and it seemed as if I had stumbled into old home week or something. Before long, it had become pretty apparent that they were all assembled here for a specific purpose. This gathering was no coincidence and it was a far cry from the casual exchange that Gary had been eluding to. This guest of honor could only watch and take it all in before the festivities would begin.

Harmless enough. Ron, the Ph.D., was seated at the other table directly across from me and in my mind, he wasn't the type to stand out in the middle of crowd. They all kinda blended in together, forming sort of an engineering malaise.

Gary was seated at the same table as I, but up at the head with Greg seated between us. He was out of eye shot from me…, surely the umbilical was being severed. Before I knew it, the shop talk came to a halt and they began talking this corporate stuff, launching into a 'who's on first routine.' It was quite foreign to me as they jockeyed amongst themselves who was going to be the scribe, who was going to be the time keeper and who was going to be the leader. An air of seriousness prevailed as they seemed to auction off these roles, while at the same time it appeared as if we were all about to join in on some kind of game. Little did I know...!

"I know you all met Steve. Steve came in last night from New Jersey to share with us about his Teflon Treated Oil filter that he has a patent on. We are going to take a look at it now and see how feasible it would be for us to develop and manufacture it. Now Steve has a quite a bit of experience with Teflon and additives and I'm sure what he has to say is going to be helpful to us."

That sure sounded like a rather ominous introduction, if I ever heard one. Especially the part that 'they were going to take a look at it and determine the feasibility of the whole thing.'

And I can attest to the fact that the setting wasn't provided with the intention of warming one's heart either. In the meantime, my mind began to multitask, as surveyed my surroundings. For the briefest of moment's, I got caught up studying the neat rows of cinder blocks that made up the walls that had been slathered in a thick skin of shiny white oil paint. The room's ambiance appeared about as austere as the occasion was shaping up to be. This space sure wasn't giving off any warmth, as its coldness made an attempt to penetrate my soul.

Looking up, I couldn't help but notice the rectangular stainless-steel clock framed in the middle of the front wall looking down at me, its purpose no doubt, was to warn all comers that their time would be limited, as I knew mine was.

'So, is this what it's all about?' I wondered? 'I hoped not!' It was way too late now anyway. No one had to tell me, but I'd be willing to take odds that up until this moment these nice gentlemen hadn't put themselves out to even consider the possibilities that this filter held. The somewhat lackadaisical attitude that obscured much of this filter's birthing process was here this morning and I could sense its glib presence lurking just beneath the surface. That was something that I had to deal with. And I'm certain, that I wasn't over reacting to the moment. I was truly an outsider looking in, and I was taken aback as to what I was observing.

Acutely aware of this, I had no choice in the matter. I could see that I had an obligation to jump start this project. For me, it was way more than just showing up. There wasn't any time afforded to even begin and analyze the circumstances besetting me, it was all happening so quickly. There was just too much happening round about me for my limited faculties to digest, leaving me no choice other than to play this hand like I had played every other…, flat out! The moment was at hand, all I could do was take it in and file it away. Besides, there was still a case of nerves waiting on me and before long it would be show time!

Craning his neck over in my direction Gary said, "Hey Steve, didn't you mention out in the lot that you had brought us a couple of sample materials?" nervously asking, just to make sure.

I could tell that he was feeling more than a bit uneasy here. 'Could it possibly of been that his butt was on the line? Or was it, because he walked me into this setup without so much as a hint and now he was feeling a little bit guilty about it?'

I couldn't be sure why he felt that way. And I didn't have the luxury of time to psychoanalyze him.

I just hoped that the boy finally got some religion and woke up to the fact that nearly two precious months of our pre-license agreement had gone by the wayside! So, if I caught him in the throes of some soul searching, that was all right by me. Right about now, I just hoped the monumental foot-dragging of which he had been so much a part of, was giving him just a taste of the pain I had been enduring all along.

Anyway… He had no choice in the matter now, he was going to have to hang on to his seat like the rest of everybody else in the room…, including myself. We were all about to take the ride together, because I was prepared to either fly like an eagle or go down in flames in front of the whole gang.

"Good morning gentlemen," I said, forcing myself to open my mouth and shake out the nerves. "It's good to be here meeting with all of you this morning. As you know, I have come to discuss my patent on a Teflon Treated oil filter. I'll be glad to explain it to you as well as share any other ideas that I might have concerning its development and manufacture."

Pausing for a moment, I leaned over in Gary's direction, "And yes Gary, I brought along a couple of different samples and some of the other materials I thought would be helpful."

With that, a smile broke across his face and he sunk back in his chair saying, "Oh good Steve, so that means you brought along an extra copy of your patent as well, I hope? Mine's floating around my office somewhere."

That was all the cue I needed, giving me an excuse to bury my head for a moment as I searched for my composure. Hunching over my briefcase already straddled on my lap, I flipped through my files searching for copies of both of my patents, just in case. And I can tell ya, I wasn't coming up for air until I had secured the both of them.

After a moment I exclaimed, "Here they are! Sorry I don't have enough copies for everyone in the room, I only brought a few." I was forever giving out copies of my patent along the way to different personnel at Allied/Fram. Sometimes I reminded myself of a neurotic Japanese business man at a convention, who frenetically goes about handing out business cards to anyone he might bump into.

But let me assure you, there was a method to my madness. I was just making sure that there was no room for argument or debate, whether now or in the future, that this idea had originated with me. I had put into circulation throughout the Company as many copies of my patent as I could, trusting that it would be sufficient evidence one day if the need ever arose to establish my authorship.

Unable to resist the shot, I added, "You know, Gary, I didn't expect to be meeting with all these different faces, if you know what I mean?"

With that, I got a self-conscious chuckle out of the group, as they all seemed to catch my drift.

Maybe they thought they had the deck stacked, I don't know. But in reality, other than being told from the onset who was going to be in attendance, I preferred to look at it from the bright side. It meant that now there was going to be more than just one person responsible for what I was about to impart to the Company, and that in my opinion, could only be a good thing.

I passed what I had brought along over to Gary and he thanked me, saying that he was going to have them run off during our coffee brake sometime around ten. At that point I glanced up at the clock, and it was just a little past eight thirty. 'Oh Lord, we had a long way to go before coffee.'

I opted not to bring along too many glitzy visual aids for this presentation not wanting to turn my presentation into a dog and pony show. So, I didn't pattern my approach after one of those Kinko's television commercials, figuring these guys already had enough cellulose in their diets. Besides, my audience wasn't going to be easily wooed with a bunch of well put together paper anyway, that's why they had a note keeper.

Better or for worse, the material was locked up in my head and I chose to impart it to them orally, so I thought it best to hit them with my big gun right off. At my feet, lay my duffel bag. Reaching down, I grabbed the two samples and placed them on the table in front of me. Jokingly I blurted out,

"Sure glad I made it through customs with this stuff! This one sample looks more like cocaine than anything else."

The boys caught the humor in that one and laughed a bit, easing me into the presentation.

Gary chirped in, "Darn good thing you didn't get stopped. I don't think that stuff is regulated by the airlines. They might not of appreciated you flying around with that fluorinated hydrocarbon on their airplane."

I couldn't help it, as I reached over and looked at him rather dumfounded more than anything else. "What do you mean by that Gary?"

"Oh nothing. Nothing at all. It could be flammable is all. That one containers got oil in it."

Letting that one go by, I shut my mouth, thinking, 'Well if that was true, then the nylon duffel bag I was carrying around was about just as flammable and shouldn't of been allowed on the plane either.'

Placing my hand on the large plastic can, "This material is called MP 1100, it is a dry micro power made by DuPont. It's got an average particle size of four microns, small enough to be able to flow through your most efficient full flow filter without causing any noticeable restriction."

Next, I held up the shiny metal container holding a material produced by Acheson Colloids, comprised of sub micronic Teflon particles held in colloidal suspension by a fifty-weight solvent neutral carrier oil and I explained what that was. In turn, I was quick to remind this new group that I had already made mention of this material back in October's meeting. Adding that Acheson was the only formulator that DuPont approved of when it came to the blending of their Teflon for use in automotive applications. And that it was through both my extensive research and my business relationship with Dupont that had led me to the existence of this material, since it wasn't at all available in the public domain.

Now I want to set the scene from a legal standpoint… This is very important regarding the proper handling of trade secrets.

This occasion was the second time I had formally told AlliedSignal that Acheson Colloids SLA 1612 was my trade secret as it would specifically apply to treating an oil filter with this material. Though it wasn't specifically cited in the body of my patent, that was of no legal consequence, since I had already disclosed it as my trade secret under the protection of our signed Proprietary Information Agreement and our Test Marketing Agreement; better known as our Trade Secret Agreement.

Just so you know, I had already memorialized this fact in writing and had sent a certified copy to Dianne Newman under the previously established, 60-day time period. I also made it crystal clear that the disclosure of this material as well as anything else that I would be sharing with them would all considered to be my closely held trade secrets. And of course, I would later memorialize my disclosures that I would make to this group and would send Gary a certified copy as per the agreements that governed my disclosure of proprietary information.

Any fool could have figured out that I had traveled out to Perrysburg, for the express purposes of teaching AlliedSignal/Fram how to make a Teflon treated oil filter. And the only way I could do it, was by systematically divulging my various trade secrets. Not to be cocky…, but as a group, they were unstudied, uninitiated and unprepared for what I was about to disclose. They were clueless, and once again, I caught the experts in this field flatfooted. Period!

Since most of these guys were not at the October meeting in RI, I found myself having to once again go through an entire presentation from scratch. I wasn't at all thrilled about it, but that didn't matter. As a skilled salesman capable of closing a deal, I knew that I'd be dead in the water if I couldn't isolate their objections. So, I systematically began to position them in my mind, as I began the process of dispatching them one by one.

So, I started where one might expect… at the beginning.

Like it or not, I knew from my past experience, that filter engineers, at least the automotive filter engineers that I had encountered in the past, didn't take kindly to the notion of putting anything foreign inside of a filter. Simply because, 'filters were designed to remove particulate contaminants from oil and not add anything,' end of discussion.

Knowing that…, my first order of business was to overcome that objection completely, or there'd be no going forward until that fire was put out. Anything that might have altered their conception of what was supposed to take place inside of a filter could invariably cause a fight, regardless of whether they had even read my patent or not.

And by now, I was absolutely certain that none of them hadn't bothered to do that cursory chore prior to my arrival. The fact that Gary was going to make copies of my patent for the group, said it all.

But in all seriousness, the mere thought of a filter having a dual role was more than most engineers could mentally handle, before their brains would go tilt. Even if the transformation was as benign as my improvement suggested. The very concept cut crosswise against a very long held and ingrained tradition that was as old as oil filtration itself!

"What size does your Extra Guard filter down to?" I quipped, asking a facetious lead off question.

Before anyone had time to offer a response, I volunteered the answer, "20 microns at best. Right?!" The engineer's heads casually looked about the room at one another, their eyes doing most of the talking, consensus reached. It was a no brainer of a question for sure, but I had to, I was building…

Taking the nod from Greg seated beside me I was off again. "In the trucking business, where I got my training, we referred to full flow primaries as 'nuts and bolts filters."

Ron chimed in, "How so?" he said, protectively.

'Oh darn!' I thought. Looks like the party was about to get started. 'Was my confidence a bit too unbridled for him?' I wasn't sure. That certainly wasn't my intention. All I knew, was that I had this stuff down cold and I had been living it for so long! Well, by now, any vestiges of stage fright had long since vanished and by all indications, it appeared like I had exposed the dominant one in the bunch! And I would of never of guessed it either! If there was a protagonist in the crowd, I would have placed my money on the VP. of Engineering. If anyone made me feel uneasy, it was this guy and I certainly had my reasons. But at this point he just stood in the corner of the room by the door with his arms folded across his chest, taking it all in, as the Ph.D. strolled onto the mat, preparing to engage me.

For the time being I wasn't so concerned. I knew where I wanted to go with this one, and he'd have to follow, but before I could go any further, I just had to know…

"If you don't mind my asking, what do you have your Ph.D. in Ron?" Curiosity had gotten the best of me, and I couldn't let it rest until I could get an idea where he fit into the mix.

"Not at all," he replied. "My concentration is in the material sciences, on the research level," he added, shedding some light.

"Oh," I replied, "So you're a research scientist." Thinking to myself, 'what kind of research?' I wasn't even sure what material science was, and I was sure feeling too uneasy to ask. All I knew was that it was awful coincidental that he and his cadre just happened to land in this cornfield in the middle of Ohio, for such a casual meeting. And that still really bugged me.

He matter of factly replied, "Why yes I am."

Attempting to loosen him up, I offered, "That's kinda unfair sticking you in a room with all of these filter engineers, isn't it?" I smiled, but he wasn't going for that one.

Little did I realize the magnitude of the statement that I had thrown out there so flippantly. As of yet, I was a long ways from being able to ascertain what his intended mission was that morning.

"Well Ron, in the heavy-duty field, and class eight trucks in particular, it's pretty much the norm to have by-pass oil filtration. Generally, the better by-pass filters get down to about 10 to 12 microns compared to the full flows with a 20-micron rating. That's all I meant."

"I still don't follow you. What did you mean by nuts and bolts?" he said.

"I'm sorry, you'll have to excuse me, that's more or less fleet manager's lingo. Most of the premier fleets that I knew anything about during the time I conducted my field trials wouldn't consider running a unit without a 750-secondary by-pass filter on board. All I meant by that was, full flow filters usually filter out the larger particles and let the smaller more damaging ones pass right on through. What I'm saying, and maybe your colleagues will back me up, is that the particles in the 1 to 5-micron range are generally the ones that do the most damage. They behave, sort of like micro fine lapping agents that get in between the close tolerances of the moving parts causing the most engine wear. And I don't need to tell you that a micron is a 39th millionths of an inch.

"Aside from which, none of the major filter manufactures produce a by-pass filter rated at one micron at this time. That's another totally untapped market as well," I added. And that concept dovetails nicely with my '901 patent.

"But please, don't let me get side tracked on that subject now. Because I hold a completely separate patent on a one-micron additive treated oil filter that lends itself beautifully to the heavy-duty side."

Justified, I continued on a little further, intentionally directing my treatise in Ron's direction, assuming that he was the filtration neophyte in the assembly. By now, I was hoping that under this veiled approach, some of my knowledge base might rub off on the engineers and soften up their thinking. I wasn't at all sure if it was going to work, but that's the direction that I was led to go in.

"Ron, if you don't mind, I'd like to sum this up," as I began to address his question. "A full flow primary filter is the first mechanical line of defense on an automobile's engine when it comes to keeping the oil clean. Now due to certain design constraints, inherent in all full flow filters, they aren't capable of trapping the Teflon particles in this size range once they've mixed in with the lubricating oil.

"Notwithstanding, even today's most efficient by-pass filters like the ones found on big diesels wouldn't be able to filter out this material either, so this concept would no doubt fit in with the heavy-duty diesel side as well."

After I finished speaking, there was a momentary buzz in the room, accompanied by a series of nods and grunts as the engineers conferred amongst themselves, verifying whether I knew what the heck I was talking about. There seemed to be little cause for debate, so we continued on.

"Okay, I see what your telling me. I'm just not so familiar with the mechanics of oil filtration, that's not my area of expertise," he volunteered.

"I wasn't totally aware of that; I hope you didn't mind."

"No. Not at all. On the contrary. I found what you had to say quite interesting."

"Okay, great! I was just trying to establish from the onset that this material wouldn't be clogging your media, that's all. And for the rest of you guys…, sorry I took the long way around the mountain."

Almost instinctively, I stuck my head down and began to feverishly root through my briefcase without so much as 'an excuse me.' I pulled out the Motor Trend article that Kevin had given me back in October and looked through it, until bingo! The clincher!

"Oh, not to belabor the point, but this article which appeared in the October 1994 issue of Motor Trend states that in 1992, the Fram Filter Division conducted a test to see for themselves if Slick 50 or their competitor, Tufoil would clog their filters. The article went on to say that the particles in these formulas would be able to freely flow through their filters. Well you get the point."

Just then, Gary called out, "Steve! Could I see that article! I remember Kevin mentioning something to that effect during a discussion we were having a while back, but I never got a copy of that for myself."

"Yes sure, Gary," I said, handing him the article, trying my best to conceal my absolute pleasure. "By the way," I asked, "Do you have a copy of Fram's original study? 'Cause I'd love to take a peek at it."

Just then, Gary's face went blank as he leaned past Gordon, looking me square in the face he replied totally lost, "I don't remember it? Do any of you guys?" As he looked around the room.

It was amazing, but true! Nobody in the room could recall any such study! And if anyone had, they surely did a masterful job of playing dumb.

'So, I guess it was just as well that I ended up delivering my little treatise, I mused.' It reinforced the article that Gary was about to copy for the group and it was going to bear out exactly what their own study had already proved…, that's if they could ever locate it.

Sitting back in my chair, I drank it all in, savoring the moment. There was no room left for debate on that issue, hopefully we could move along toward designing the prototype. Just then, I had a rather alarming thought come racing across my screen, 'could it be possible that Motor Trend had the unmitigated nerve to reference something as credible as this study without ever verifying it beforehand?' I thought not!

On the other hand, and equally as ludicrous, 'was it possible for these top Fram engineers to all draw simultaneous blanks concerning a test they had performed only a couple of years back on the very same material that I wanted them to deliberately put inside of their filters?' I wasn't sure, but it was really unsettling that the collective recollection of this test ever being conducted had evaporated into thin air.

Changing gears, Gary took the lead by asking Gordon a pointed question. "Hey Gordon, how do you suppose we get this material into the filter?"

"I'm not sure," he replied, looking in my direction.

Gordon was the production engineer from Perrysburg and seemed especially inquisitive as to how I envisioned the mass production of this filter. Quite natural for a guy in his position.

"Hey Steve," as Gordon spoke up from across the room, "I can only imagine just how much work you must have put into this concept. But it would really help us along if you could share with us some of your best ideas as to how we should go about production on a large scale. Have you given any thought to that?"

"Thanks for the compliment, Gordon. I'd be happy to share with you how I made my prototype and I'll go from there if you don't mind. Hopefully, I might be able to offer you some helpful ideas concerning how you might want to consider setting up your line."

The last thing I wanted to do, was to give a presentation with my guns blazing, so I had to approach this whole thing cloaked in humility. I surely hadn't anticipated telling those guys how to go about their business. To the contrary, what I had expected right out of the box, was that they were going to tell me how they envisioned manufacturing it, since that's what they were doing every day for a living.

But that's not what happened. They wouldn't settle for anything less than me sharing my personal vision and findings for this product…, so I let rip.

"Here's what I did. I rigged up a hydraulic pump off an old tractor and set up a variable pressure loop on the work bench in my garage in order to test the media for restriction. For example, I'd weigh out a gram of the material then combined it with an ounce of straight forty weight motor oil, forming a mixture. I liken this mixture to pancake batter with those little batter balls that float around in the bowl. Except in this particular trial, I wasn't looking to get rid of the agglomerated masses and form a homogeneous mixture. The intended effect was to wind up with these agglomerated masses present, because they are key with regard to the time release mechanism that I put forth in the delivery system. What I expect to happen is for a proportion of this material to be held back by the media, let's say about two thirds. This portion will pass through the media over time, in effect promoting the time release aspect of the delivery system. Meantime, approximately the other third comprising some of the smaller masses and free particles are going to flow through on the first pass or so. The pressure, temperature and the swirling action inside of the filter will break apart the agglomerated masses over time and eventually all the material will end up dispersed in the oil.

"After these initial bench-tests checked out, I ended up strapping several of these pre-charge filters to my own car's engines and I'd cut them apart at various intervals in order to get a visual. It all seemed to check out and verify my claims.

"What I want you to notice is this, the filter now acts as a container for the material, so you don't need to pour it out of a bottle, like you would a bottle of Slick 50. Since the material is concentrated, it doesn't matter whether the oil has been changed or not. No adjustments have to be made to the oil level either, which is a hassle. So, there won't be any need to subtract the quart of engine oil to compensate for the addition of the extra quart of Teflon treatment. And finally, the filter acts as a delivery system, allowing the material to assimilate into the lube system gradually over time.

"I realize that might smack a little of marketing, but it's not entirely. I just figured out how to replace a twenty-dollar bottle of Slick 50 and substitute it with a step-up Fram oil filter that can be purchased for a fraction of the cost, while providing the same benefits. It's simply how I envisioned the utility of the improvement."

Not in a million years did I believe that my brief overview would have evoked so much discussion amongst the engineers as it did. A spurt of enthusiasm came over the four of them as they bantered about how they might go about making this filter. I was encouraged as their discussion took on a life of its own, while they relegated both Ron and myself to watch from the sidelines.

Meantime, Ron occupied himself as he thumbed through the Motor Trend article which left me free to focus in on the engineer's chatter. I was forever trying to come up with the missing pieces to the puzzle they were searching for. I knew that I possessed blueprint, I could only pray that it would line up with what they needed to hear. As I listened, I distinctly heard each one of them say in their own vernacular, "We have to make this filter as simply and cost effectively as possible."

So once again it was posed to me, "Steve, how do you envision that we make this filter? You must have an idea…, no?!" Gary asked, hoping I would at least be able to provide a track for them to run on.

"Sure, I do!" replying confidently. I had something worthwhile to contribute. "I don't know if I ever had mentioned this to you or not Gary, but I became pretty good friends several years ago with a guy named Richard Dye, the ex-Chief Engineer of Purolator. Anyway, he owns his own filter manufacturing facility now, in Fayetteville, North Carolina and I went down there once a few years back to visit with him. So, I have seen what a filter line looks like, and therefore I have a pretty good idea of how one operates. Based on that, this is what I envisioned… You would first need to install a hopper where the oil and Teflon can be blended. As the completed filter moves down the line, a plunger passes over it and pumps a metered amount of the mixture into the filter. Right after this station is another one, where a foil top or cap will be placed on it, just like at packaging plant that fills containers, like yogurt or a small fruit cup. The final step is boxing, then out the door!"

Greg, the plant manager from Canada, wanted to know whether it would be feasible to get the material past the anti-drain back valve while it was in place by using this method. He wasn't so sure if the pressure required to pump the material past the anti-drain back valve would damage the valve in the process or not.

To which I said, that I doubted it very much, since it is made out of flexible nitrile rubber. But out of common sense and respect, I offered to Greg, that they would be in a much better position to determine such a thing.

And so, the debate went on along those lines for a while until Bijan brought up yet another stumbling block, this time based upon Fram's current means of production. Up until now, Bijan hadn't asked me a single question. But that didn't mean a thing, 'cause so far, I hadn't caught any of these guys napping. I more or less likened his quiet demeanor to that of a large coiled snake waiting in the grass. It was just a matter of time before he'd let me know he was out there. Believe me, each one of those guys was more than capable of asking questions they felt important.

"Stephen," he said, "In case you are not aware of this, our filter's come off the line with their tapping plates facing down. So how do you propose we get the material into the filter body, let alone past the anti-drain valve and onto the media with the filters upside down?" asking, with a genuine concern.

'Hum,' I thought. 'Where have I heard that before? No matter...' There was no time for reflection now…, realizing that question had come up somewhere before. I just couldn't recall for the moment.

All I can say…, was that I spent many a night staring up at the constellations trying to iron out all of these potential manufacturing dilemmas, and hopefully it was about to pay off. On a countless number of long casts into the darkness, I worked on the production line's layout, as I would slowly retrieve the lure back from the inky depths. Forever obsessed on how I would keep the 'ramp up time,' and 'opportunity costs' down to a bare minimum.

We hadn't even begun to address those cornerstones of production yet, but I wasn't about to shy away from that topic either. It would be an issue of paramount importance to any company that would take on the manufacture of a new product. If the alterations to their production line proved too involved, meaning much more than the simplest alteration, I'd be out the door before a prototype would ever be considered. And let me tell you something, nobody in the room had to offer me that bit of advice!

"A curlicue," was my reply, as I looked across the way at him, smiling.

His brow wrinkled up as he looked back at me as if I had made a wise crack. Nobody in the room got it either, as they all went dead like they had been mysteriously unplugged. Perhaps I didn't call it by its proper name, but none the less to me, it was a 'curlicue.'

"You know, one of those stationary cages built into the line that turns the cans over a hundred and eighty degrees. They have to be cheap and readily available. You get it, don't ya? You still look kinda lost Bijan."

"I don't quite follow you, a 'curly cue," he replied still puzzled. I could tell that he was hung up on what I called it, more than anything else.

"If you don't mind, let me try and illustrate. Keep in mind that I have been to lots of factories, back in my truck driving days. I've been in all kinds of plants and by the way, I love plants and I'd really love to see yours sometime.

"Anyway, I used to haul Carnation evaporated milk out of dairy country in New York State. And on their line as the cans would come past the labeler, they went through this cage that was twisted like a 'curlicue' that positioned them right side up for boxing."

With that, a smile broke out across his face, and just before he was about to tell me he understood, it suddenly came rushing back…

I remembered sharing this very same insight concerning the line with the group back in October. Ignoring the recollection, I quickly forged ahead, putting aside the fact that he had been part of this very same discussion at that meeting as well. Perhaps he was still wrangling with the concept of changing the filters orientation.

Launching in headlong, "I'm fully aware that every filter that comes off your line does so with the tapping plate down. That's primarily why you end up boxing them that way. Right?

"But, think about it for just a moment, the filter that I'm envisioning here is an entirely different animal and it's not something that's going to readily fit into your mindsets regarding its production, at least not at first blush, but allow me to try.

"For starters, this filter is going to be pre-charged with a mixture of Teflon and oil, so it's gonna come off your assembly lines wet! Certainly, this is a first for any filter manufacturer and that includes you guys. So, the best way to avoid any foreseeable problems, as well as for the ease of manufacture, this filter has got to be produced and boxed with the tapping plate facing the sky. I realize that it's the exact opposite of what you've been used to doing, but it's going to be simple to implement.

"First off, this filter is going to require a protective cover in order to seal all those holes in the tapping plate, just in case the material wants to seep out. And it doesn't take a genius, but somewhere along the way, these filters are going end up getting tossed upside down, and they could be laying there for a long time. It can't be avoided, so it's an inevitability that I've already accounted for. Just so you know, my patent cites several potential methods for sealing the tapping plates in order to deal with this issue."

Interrupting myself, "Just a little trivia for you. I got this idea from the Japanese automakers, when I once bought a genuine Toyota filter made in Japan. Not only did it come in a box, but it was shrink wrapped to boot. How's that for packaging?' I laughed.

"But that's not exactly what I'm thinking here. In my estimation that's over-kill and way too expensive. What I've envisioned is much simpler and cheaper. The tapping plate gets sealed with a peel-off foil top, much like the ones that go on a fruit cup or yogurt. Another possibility is a very thin plastic cap or lid, like the ones you put on a coffee can once it has been opened. At any rate, either one could have graphics on it, and it certainly would perform the job. As an aside, it would provide additional platform to re-emphasize your brand…, and of course be yet another first for you guys.

"Now, I realize that cost is everything. That's why in my opinion I'd opt for the foil, it'd be cheaper in the long run. That is unless you can find a source that might already produce generic plastic caps that would already fit onto your various size cans. In that case, it would eliminate the cost of tooling up, then I'd consider going for the caps."

Sometime a little after nine-thirty, Mr. Coronia attempted to slip out of the room without anyone's notice. I caught his untimely exit out of the corner of my eye, which caused me to stop talking before I could finish.

I don't know, maybe I was wrong…, but I got the distinct impression that he had heard just about all he could stand. More than likely, he had spent the better part of his life in the business and he wasn't considering a 'new and improved anything,' especially not from an outsider who sold real estate for a living. That must have been a bitter pill for that poor guy to swallow, but when those corporate fellas back east told him that he better make this thing happen, well…, let's just say he must of been red lining!

It was never my intention to ruffle this man's feathers, let alone try and get even with him this time around. And believe me, I could have cared less that he had pulled that "not invented here" crap on me six years ago over my first patent. Back then only a very limited number of people at Fram were aware of my patent, so it was convenient for the chief engineer at that time to summarily dismiss my patent as something of a fluke. But now it was entirely different. This idea of mine had already made it up to the brass level, and this time there wasn't going to be somebody to look me square in the face and tell me that I didn't have it covered.

Now by some quirk of fate, but more like sheer tenacity…, I was back again! And not because of some foolish scheme, or anything so stupid as trying to get even.

For now, I could only think upon what improvements that he might have personally come up with over the long course of his tenure in the business. 'Were any of them significant enough to wind up in a finished filter?' I didn't think so, but one things for sure…, my improvements fell way short of moving him.

Before he had a chance to turn around and mount the doorway our gazes had locked on to each other, like two pairs of heat seeking missiles.

Gary, picked up immediately as to what was happening and readily excused his boss's premature departure, saying that he had other pressing matters to attend. For his part, the chief engineer flipped me an impish smile and wished me well.

"I hope to see you later Steve, before you head back," Mr. Coronia offered, turning for the door. He hadn't quite made it all the way out when he paused for a moment, then looked back at me once more before bidding me, 'good luck.'

It struck a chord deep down inside of me as his body language broadcast from the portal of the doorway back to where I was seated…, 'remember young man, Houdini's final stunt.'

I muttered to myself in response to his parting gaze, before pressing on, 'and you sir, better remember, it ain't over…, till it's over.'

Picking up where I had left off, I hurried though the rest of my summary. It was just a matter of going through the motions now. I guess deep down I was hurt by the chief engineer's disapproval of my innovations, and not having his blessing made me feel all the more uncertain of my filters future, because no doubt, he still wielded a lot of power around here.

After regaining my composure, I continued where I had left off, "Next, taking an old syringe, I pumped the liquid past the anti-drain back valve, into the dirty side of the filter. That's where I want the treatment to originate, on the input side of the filter.

"So that's about it guys. I never claimed that it was complicated, just novel. Kinda like a Reese's Peanut Butter Cup," I offered slumping back in my seat, still licking my wounds inflicted by the chief's obvious disapproval.

CHAPTER 6
WHO CHANGED THE FORMULA?

The burly PhD's hand came crashing down with a loud thud, as it made contact with the top of the table. With a stout voice he exclaimed, "God darn it…, it's great to see an entrepreneur!" He paused a moment as he gathered his thoughts, leaving me to wonder what he was about to say next. "You know…, it's really great to see some outside blood in here finally! It's about time we started getting some innovative ideas flowing back into this place once again!"

It seemingly happened out of nowhere, that's what made it so bizarre. The last I could recall; I was staring down the barrel of his line of questioning. Then without so much as hint, the Company's point man does a complete one eighty. Suddenly, he's standing tall with me, affirming to the rest of the group just exactly what I had brought to the table! It was nothing short of miraculous!

There was no mistaking it, he was addressing me! His eyes locked onto mine, struggling, he tried to act dignified, but to no avail. He couldn't. A broad smile had already broken out, and by this time was commandeering his face. At that very moment this unsolicited gesture began to communicate volumes to my heart and it meant more to me than anything he could of put into words. I understood the meaning of his smile and quite naturally so did he. For the briefest of moments, we communicated telepathically, you could say more like 'heart to heart'! Somehow the presence of other engineers sitting alongside us in the room didn't seem to matter anymore.

Evidently, not only had I survived, but I managed to make it through what had played out to be a full-blown interrogation session, complete with opposing council. After it concluded, I felt more like I had been deposed, than asked to share. More like an adverse witness than that of a cooperating business partner. And now for my reward, I was bestowed his stamp of approval. And in no uncertain terms, in front of his peers no less! Of course, from my perspective, the outcome of the contest was more than justified.

After all I had brought the business plan, the manufacturing plan and the marketing plans for this project, where none had existed before my arrival. I had presented all of my material with a total commitment to integrity and honesty. Above all, I operated on faith. Faith in myself and faith in the words of which the Lord had already spoken to my heart, long before I ever set out on this trek. Those words loomed up large and repeated themselves many times that morning during the fray… "I didn't take you this far to allow you to fail."

Try this flashback on for size…

As the morning progressed, I couldn't help but notice that both the frequency as well as intensity of Ron's line of questioning was being kicked up several notches from where he had initially started. He began to press me all the harder concerning the technical aspects of the materials in question.

Having little choice in the matter, I dismissed his offbeat scientific questions as more of an annoyance than anything else, thinking it was just his way of participating along with the engineers. Then during a particularly grueling foray he posed a rather obscure question, having to do with the molecular weight of the material…, something crazy. I didn't have the answer to such a question and no amount of rooting through my files was going to save me at this point either. And let me tell you something, this wasn't the first time that I didn't have the answers for him!

My mind was sent reeling in a sheer moment of helplessness, 'this wasn't supposed to be happening to me… I was losing control! Then it finally began to dawn on me!

'…Oh my God,' I gasped! 'What was going on here with this guy? And what the heck did I get myself into!' I felt like some stupid little toad that found himself in a pot of hot water, with the heat being turned up slowly, on my way to being boiled to death.

When I finally collected myself, it dawned on me that I was in the middle of an audition for AlliedSignal, the giant specialty chemical company and not Fram, the filter maker!

Apparently, it was the first order of business on the Company's agenda all along. And at this juncture, it went a long way toward explaining why I was in the process of facing off against some chemistry expert who had forgotten more about chemistry than I ever knew.

It was all starting to make sense… As best as I could figure, Allied had flown in one of their top experts and sent him on a fact-finding mission to ascertain if Teflon, which had been around for fifty years, was able to perform the job that the published research, some of which I had already furnished AlliedSignal six months ago had demonstrated. And what I really found mind boggling, was that AlliedSignal itself had an up and running four billion dollar a year chemical division with a sizable Fluoropolymer business which already produced their own PTFE (Teflon)!

So again, this left me with an unanswered question…

'Why didn't I get a call from Allied's research department in Morristown, immediately following our October meeting if they wanted to ask me questions of this nature?'

'Why didn't their top-shelf fleet of chemists investigate such a basic question, after they sold tons of the stuff?'

I had to assume, that questions such as those must have already had answers to them. Perhaps that might of made too much sense. I was only an hour and fifteen away by car and I could of easily of met with Ron or anyone of his colleagues from Allied's chemical department. If this was how a behemoth of a corporation chose to do business, then so be it. But I couldn't help but wonder now, what kind of games were being played?

No matter. Like I had previously pointed out, it wasn't mine to pick or choose the exercise. It was theirs.

The exchange between Ron and I, was far from over yet, and I had surmised that there was gonna be no dancing around this gate keeper. The situation had been reduced to its most elemental issues and I clearly recognized that it was a priority thing now, as we continued on. The design phase would most certainly have to wait, until I could satisfy his probing inquiries.

At one point, there had been up to five other engineers present in the room and their participation had for the most part, been overshadowed by the line of questioning that this man had required me to field. After the smoke cleared, I realized that I had been sucked headlong into a match that had been carefully orchestrated long before my arrival here this morning.

Thankfully, I never really believed that we were going to meet alone, even though that's what Gary had tried to feed me. Though I had ridden atop the turnip truck many times in my life, I was at least smart enough to know that product development from the ground floor up and assembly line alterations, weren't going to fall within the purview of one individual. To have believed that little fairy tale, would of resulted in an unmitigated disaster of my causing. You know…, the one where the inventor gets caught flatfooted, by the company that he's trying to sell his disruptive idea to.

Believe me, there was never a chance of that happening. I came prepared for this meeting as if I were trying my own defense, and in a very real sense, that's what I had been doing that morning. Luckily, I had been pouring over this material from the moment I got off the phone with Gary, nearly two weeks prior…, and I hadn't come up for air, until sometime after midnight in my hotel room the night before.

I knew full well my limitations, so I prepared accordingly…, like any overachiever should.

AlliedSignal pitted me against their version of Goliath, a burly interrogator that went by the name of Ron. For my part…, I came bearing a briefcase full of papers, a couple of benchmark patents and some highly prized Teflon samples. My would-be opponent haled from the Signal's corporate research facilities located in Morristown. …He would be armed with a Ph.D. in material science.

After a while it had become more evident that this gentleman's assignment was to ferret out the veracity of the information that I was delivering to the Company. There was no mistaking it, if the facts contained within my patent were found to be bogus, or if my trade secrets backing this enterprise were found to be worthless… or I if had gotten this far by deceit…, then it would be his job to stop me, and to kill it…, right then and there.

I had been thrown into the middle of an unannounced final exam, not some meaningless grammar school pop quiz. My only defense was to stay cool and provide him with the facts and answer the questions directly, which I did. There was no bull slinging this boy…, only science would do today. To which all I could say was, 'thank God I didn't take this meeting with Gary too lightly.'

So, I guess after nearly two hours of intermittent grilling, Ron had come to the same conclusion as me. That what I was offering AlliedSignal, was indeed very valuable!

Peeling back the onion even further, I realized that I was incapable of neither dreaming up the proceedings nor the outcome. As the circumstances unfolded, I could only wonder how David must have felt when he saw Goliath's body collapse and fall to the ground in a heap. The moment was nothing less than awesome!

It was a little past ten, when Gary by consensus, stopped for coffee. The room cleared out as we all got up and strolled out into the hallway to this little cubby by the water fountain. We stopped and congregated in front of the coffee pot and all of the fixins'.

I wasn't much in the mood to talk with any of the guys, as I propped myself up against the wall, still punch drunk from my cage match with Ron, doing my best to sort out how I had done back there. For the moment, I was just content to stare at the hand-written sign that was posted above the Colombian votive, made of stainless steel and glass. The signage let everybody know, that on this faraway outpost, all were expected to be on the honor system here, 'coffee $0.25.'

Drifting deeper into introspection, I remarked to myself, 'how cheap this outfit was to make their employees pay for a lousy cup of coffee.' With that came another very sobering thought, 'what was it going to be like when it would come time to talk money with these chaps…, that's if I ever got that far?'

The boys were milling around, nursing their coffees, when Gary came up to me and offered me a cup.

"Hey Steve, can I buy you a cup?" he asked, not the slightest bit in touch with my quandary.

Reaching into my pocket, I felt for a quarter and reached towards the can as he placed his hand in front of mine, waiving me off.

"Steve don't worry about that, really, it's been taken care of already. "Thanks Gary, I appreciate it."

Although it was none of my darn business, I was sufficiently agitated by just about everything that had taken place this morning..., so I had to open my big mouth. "Hey Gary, so what's the deal about paying for the coffee? What's with the quarter?"

"Oh?" he replied, "It's a long story but, the coffee situation around here kinda got out of control if you know what I mean."

"Wow," was about all I could muster, because I wasn't in the mood for anymore jousting. So, I let it drop. Just then, Greg strolled over and began to engage me in a conversation about heavy-duty, also quite unaware of the pain the booby trap had inflicted upon my trust of them all.

About fifteen minutes had gone by and it was time to hit the bricks once again, so one by one, we filed past the pump and topped off our Styrofoam cups. I could only hope that I was in the home stretch, but there was no real way of telling what lie up ahead.

Finding my chair, I was confident that I had done my best up to this point, but I was tiring of the game, wanting to turn the tables. So far, in pouring out my heart, I had purposed to give this man as well as the others what they came seeking, whether solicited or not. But even after all this, I was left stymied as I watched those guys play their hand with a patent lack of emotion. It seemed like so far everyone had checked their passion for this new voyage at the front door, which left me no choice, other than to guesstimate where Ron and the others stood.

Over the last couple of hours, I had endeavored to clarify twenty years' worth of claims, erroneous and otherwise. Claims that had not only been made by Slick 50, but by every other Teflon treated oil purveyor that had followed them down the pike. And frankly, I gotta admit, many of the claims proffered by some of the elixirs were outlandish enough to make a seasoned filter engineer's skin crawl, which only left me to wonder what was going through the minds of my engineer friends as well as my expert questioner.

All I knew, was that it was my job to spell out the truth and dispel the rumors by sticking to the scientific facts as much as possible. In a very real sense, I was on a crusade..., a crusade to debunk this material as 'snake oil' and work my way through a maze of hype which had sprung up alongside it. My hope was, that by this time next year, Fram would be offering for sale throughout all of North America a brand-new line of Teflon treated oil filters that I could proudly associate myself with as the inventor.

Flipping through some papers, Ron turned the floor over to me, and I don't rightly know how I got started, but I dredged up an incident that had long since been dormant. The parallels were uncanny, and I couldn't resist. So, spurred on more out of desperation than inspiration, I unloaded...

"You know," addressing the group, "I've had more than a few conversations with DuPont on this matter over the years. As a matter of fact, the container of MP 1100 sitting over there on the table they sent me."

Ron lifted his eyes off of his papers and focused his attention keenly on me. I'm sure he was wondering where I was about to take them, which all the more seemed to reinforce my premonition that this little get together still focused on us.

"I can remember back, it was a while ago, right around the time that my patent went co-pending, that I put a call into DuPont, one afternoon. I was searching for technical stuff as well as any other information that would demonstrate that this material when mixed with oil made it slipperier. I must have talked to a half dozen people in the Fluoropolymer department before hooking up with the right guy, an engineer by the name of Johnson.

"Anyway, not only was he kind enough to share some of his knowledge concerning the material, but that afternoon he shared with me something of a higher order, his perception of how the automotive industry viewed DuPont and this material of theirs. It was quite insightful.

"He went on to share this anecdote with me that nearly mirror images some of the skepticism that I've picked up on this morning as well. So, if you'll indulge me for a moment, I'd like to share it with you all."

I wasn't about to throw a temper tantrum, but by this time I sure wanted to. And if it would of helped, I would have. These boys left me no real option at this fork in the road, so I began driving, drivin' hard at their ivory tower.

'What was this all about anyway?' For starters, I held the patent. No one else in the room did, or anything even close to it for that matter! Obviously, nobody else from one of the big five filter companies had seen fit to file for one like it either!

And for all the obsession… At the very least, you would of thought that they'd of given me a little credit here. Surely, I wasn't so naïve as to be unprepared to engage them at this level without being able to back up what I had brought to the table. A move like that would of been absolutely insane! To even think you could get away with a stunt like that would have been the height of stupidity!

'And where the heck was Kevin?' I wanted to wring his neck for setting me up like this! 'Wasn't he a part of this as well?' I wondered.

'Oh, I couldn't be sure. I was just too aggravated to even think straight. It must of been the water out here,' I mused.

The indignation inside of me was about to explode! This was turning out to be, too big of a joke. Nobody in the room had done their damn homework concerning this project. Nobody, except for me! And by this time, I was so passed indignant, I was about to cram it down their throats.

Well, for the time being, the four engineers remained sidelined for a time, like a bunch of wallflowers at some high school dance, mesmerized by the press of Ron's frontal assault. But before it was all over, I'd see to it that they'd get their chance at me as well. I hadn't come this far to let a refresher course in chemistry stop me. I had come here with prototypes on my mind!

Starting in again, "There's one thing that I know for sure. Teflon and oil has been marketed to the public by Slick Fifty since the late seventies, and it's going to be 1995 in less than three weeks. All ya need do, is look as far as the racing circuit for your proof. The up and coming sponsor of NASCAR's premier racing events is none other than, Slick Fifty! This stuff is legit! The hundreds of millions that it generates each year, etches that one in stone…, at least for me it does."

One of the engineers chimed in, "Steve I hear you, but does it work? We know that there is a market that calls for it, but does it work?"

Hearing what he said, I shut my mouth for a long moment and ruminated. My future was held somewhere in the balance of my reply. 'He sure sounded like he was one of Ron's silent backers,' I thought. At last I knew where they wanted to go, and I was more than happy to take them there.

I let 'em all have it, "What about the six studies I sent to Kevin back in August?! That was over six months ago! As a matter of fact, from what I was told, it was those very studies that put me over the top and resulted in the October meeting that I was invited to back in Rumford. That's why we have a test marketing agreement, isn't?"

Let me tell you something, as I endured this inquisition, I wasn't sure why I had a pre-license agreement with them at all! This Company wasn't on the move, it was flat-footed!

"If you guys don't mind my asking, didn't any of you read them? The test studies I mean."

At that moment Ron broke in and sufficiently put an end to that line of questioning. By his tone, I knew better than pursue it. Apparently, I had caught all of them with their pants down.

"Anyway," quick to change the subject, "Bear with me a moment so that I can finish my story about the engineer from DuPont, it will only take a moment." The room got quiet in a hurry as the spotlight was once again removed from them and shown back on me. Notwithstanding, this group had lots of manners and they were rather amused by my flat-out candor. That in of itself was telling.

"He began by telling me, that DuPont believed that Teflon enhances oils lubricity, at least his sector did. For which I said, 'I knew it!' As you can understand, initially, the Company wasn't so quick to offer that kind of information to an outsider such as myself when I first came asking for proof.

"Then I told Mr. Johnson about a previous phone conversation that I had one day with this lady who was in charge of marketing department for Teflon. Naturally I was up front with her about my patent, and I even mailed her a copy of my patent upon her request. I told her that I was in the process of marketing my patent to a major oil filter company and that it would be a feather in both of our caps if she could send me any published test studies. I could perhaps license my patent and she could with my help, sell a lot of Teflon to this large client that I would introduce DuPont's product to. I told her that short of me paying for a test study, I was searching for published scientific papers that would bolster the claims made by my patent.

"Now get this! This is what she told me, and I quote... '"It will definitely take me longer to get permission to send you these test studies, then it will for you to find them on your own."' I was floored!" I told them.

"So, I asked her if she could at least point me in the direction of where I might inquire about such materials. Apparently, there was no problem with that, until she began riffling off addresses over in Israel, the Netherlands and places in eastern Europe. (For the reader's sake the time frame was 1989-90, there was no Internet to help with any research, my research was all done manually).

"So needless to say, I didn't pursue that avenue at all. I wouldn't of even known how to address the darn envelope to places like that for God's sake."

They all got a big laugh out of that one. And I was confident that they wanted to hear my punch line, as badly as I wanted to deliver it. So, I continued on, but before doing so, Gordon who had been rather sedate the whole morning chimed in, "What about the engineer? What did he have to say?"

"Okay," I said. "Now I'm gonna come to the part that's gonna blow your mind. Gettin' back to the engineer, I said to him, '"What's the problem with you guys? I mean DuPont owns Conoco, for goodness sake. It would seem that if a chemical company owned a major oil company, and the chemical division found a way to enhance the properties of a product the oil company produced, you would think that it would be a no brainer to modify the product to make it better. Wouldn't you think? That's got to go on all the time, doesn't it?'"

"His response was, '"Well yeah, but not in this particular case. If we were talking about additive packages or something else, perhaps. But not Teflon.'"

"Why?" I asked him. "Believe me I didn't have the foggiest idea of what he was about to tell me next."

"'Oh, I don't know, he replied. They kind of told us to keep out of their business, and that their oil is plenty slippery enough just the way it is.'"

"I could hardly believe it, as I gasped at what he had told me, saying to him, you gotta be kidding! You mean to tell me that a wholly owned subsidiary like Conoco, can tell the parent company DuPont, to stay out of our business just because we might not subscribe to your science!"

"His reply was, '"That's about the size of it.'"

"We went on for a while and talked about oil additives for a while and then I popped a question that I just had to have the answer to, 'Don't you guys want to sell as much Teflon as you can?'" I asked.

"His reply was forth coming, '"Why sure we do.'"

"Okay," I said. "You are DuPont. So haven't you presented your case to trade associations like MEMA for instance, (Motor and Equipment Manufacturers of America)?"

"'As a matter of a fact we have,'" was his reply.

"Well, how'd ya do?" I asked.

"'Not so damn good,'" came his reply. "'We attended this one meeting awhile back and tried to present our case, but they didn't even want to hear what we had to say.'"

"What did you do? I asked in unbelief.

"Then he replied rather matter of factly, '"We had no choice in the matter, they weren't interested in hearing what we had to say, so we packed up gear and left.'"

As I continued to address the room, I did my best to sum it all up for them, "Here's what I am trying to say to you guys. There is such a thing out there called 'Not Invented Here.' I happen to know what it is, because I've stared it in the face first hand, and I've done so on more than one occasion. The fact of the matter is, as ridiculous as it might sound, it can not only occur within a specific industry, but it can also occur within the same company!"

In a veiled attempt, I wanted them to know that I had already obtained the marketing departments blessing already, but I was going to be needing theirs, before we could ever hope to proceed. Moving in for the close, I employed every bit of conviction I could muster, as I went for broke...

"Perhaps a better example is synthetic motor oil. Mobil One was out in front of that one for almost a decade, before any of their competitors in the petroleum world ever bothered to follow suit. You mean to tell me that the other leading oil companies didn't understand the advantage of synthetics at that time? Come on now, hardly!

"But here's the key, if you look at it for a minute. If the consumer perceives that there is an inherent benefit that is derived from an improvement, sufficient enough to cause them to make a purchase, they will do so every time! Now what's your problem!" I asked, unable to restrain my passion.

"The research already bears it out! Teflon when mixed properly with oil makes it more slippery. It's a fact! DuPont knows it! They're just not promoting it 'cause they lack the passion!

"I kinda get this feeling that somehow, if you guys accept these facts as being true, it by virtue makes you less of an engineer or something. And that would be the furthest thing from the truth! Besides..., who am I to ask AlliedSignal to compromise any of its engineering principals anyway?

"Oh, and one last thing... I got this one question that's been burning inside a me. Why must there be so much opposition to a new and improved that might very well be your next home run!"

I was right, and I knew it. It had to be said, and I was glad of it. The room fell silent as they digested my oratory. Sitting back in my seat, I positioned myself for a barrage of incoming.

Time seemed to have stood still, as I went over the rationale in my mind. After all, if it was proof they'd of been looking for, at least there was no doubt in my mind I had provided it.

But believe it or not, that wasn't even the real issue we were facing at this particular moment. It never really was. Truth be told, there were several more issues I could have handily identified, but they were up against something different here..., the killer of all dreams. At this point, nothing much could be accomplished until we faced the cornerstone of their opposition... Fear! Like so many others before them, it was the Fear of Failure that was holding this crew back! And it was so palpable, I could smell it!

Without so much as a warning it vaporized. The pensive fog that had surrounded them had broken, shattered by Ron's congratulatory outburst, as he broadcast it about the room. "Steve, I gotta admit, I'm not just a little bit jealous. I wish I had come up with this idea. It's a very good one, and it's gonna fly! I give you a heck of a lot of credit for being so persistent, young man."

Leaning back in my chair, I got a glimpse of Gary's face, as he beamed at Bijan across the way. Greg, seated beside me with his hands folded gave me a thumbs up, as I attempted to get Gary's attention.

Momentarily, the room was filled with an indescribable joy and I had all I could do, not to get drunk on it! There was little doubt that everyone present, was more than a little relieved that this foray had come to a happy conclusion. As for our reward..., for the five of us which had remained..., we had broken through..., broken through a few of those barriers of fear, doubt and unbelief and laid them to waste. We were home free, at least for the moment.

The filter of the 21st century was beckoning our efforts to sit down and map out the manufacturing phase. It was time to design her in earnest. I couldn't help but be reminded of all the creativity that was wasted back there fighting off the demons attached to our fuselage, as they tried their best to make us and crash and burn. With a resurrected hope, maybe..., just maybe..., we were free to pursue the promise set before us.

There wasn't much else to say for the moment. The information that I presented them was so simple you needed help to misunderstand it, of that much I knew. I wanted them to chew on it a while nonetheless, because I was too busy trying to sort out my brain from the force-feeding session I had just been put through. Folding my hands behind my head, I slumped back in my chair commenting to myself that I was blessed to still be in the game.

Gary bent forward and leaned past Greg, getting me into full view. "Steve?" It was the first time we had communicated since my break through, and he was all smiles.

There was never any doubt in my mind concerning Gary's motives, he was all for this project having a life, but it would have to fly on its own merits. Though I wasn't in any of those guy's shoes, I certainly was all for that, not wanting to be accused of forcing my good intentions on anyone.

Gary was no different than anybody else in the room that morning. They all worked for Allied, and there were careers and families to look out for. In this game, that I was now very much a part of, I got the definite feeling that there wasn't going to be any corporate hero types emerging any time soon, and that included Kevin as well. Nobody was willing to stick their neck out for anybody on this project, and I wasn't expecting any preferential treatment. The protocol was rife with the stark reality that if some poor hire made the unfortunate mistake of backing the wrong horse, there'd barely be time for a wake, as they'd be sent packing. Caution was never thrown to the wind by any of these company men. Because lurking about every decision was that dreaded monster, Fear of Failure. It was my distinct observation that such a monster dominated most of their thinking processes while they were on company time.

Apparently, with all the posturing over, Bijan became more assertive as he invited Gary to think for a moment, "Hey Gary, taking into consideration our present line configuration, and in light of what Steve has already proposed, how are we going to get this stuff into the can? I'm still wondering."

Gary let go a belabored, "Yea I know," as he emptied his lungs, heavily in thought.

"I conceptualize what he means about the hopper and filling station with the plunger and all, but I'm afraid that upgrade alone will shoot our budget," Bijan added, with genuine concern.

"Hum, I hear ya on that one," came Gary's reply. Gary was in the game all right, but let's just say he wasn't aglow with optimism.

"What do you think Greg? You're running a lot of PH8A's up there, aren't you?" referring to Fram's major filter plant up in Canada.

"Hey Gary, what does that mean?" I interrupted, before Greg could even get a word out.

"Nothing really Steve. It's just a popular filter model we make. I just referred to it because we have a lot of experience with it in larger runs. So, when we make this one, we'd like to base it off of that line speed is all. Do you follow?"

"Loud and clear sir," I replied, happily. "Greg, I apologize for jumping in on you like that… I'm sorry."

"That's all right Steve, believe me I understand."

"Yeah Gar, we run a lot of them. I have to think how we can go about this for a moment," was his reply.

Again, I was pleased, while filled with trepidation at the same time. Sensing all too quick for my own good, what the next obstacle was all about. The tenor of the groups focus was changing right before my eyes. And yes, it was wonderful at last to be watching these guys begin to operate in their element, but what was happening really wasn't about the placement of a conveyor belt or a pumping station. I wished it could of only of been that simple.

Without so much as a hint, they mounted a Herculean attempt to engineer past AlliedSignal's penny-pinching ways. My presence in the room didn't seem to matter either. By adoption I was brought into the inner circle of their society as I sat in on their brainstorming. It was certainly understood that my input was every bit as valid as the next guys. At last we had gelled into what I had wished for all along…, a team.

"Hey guys," as I worked my way in, "It's about the coffee pot, out there isn't it?"

Greg leaned forward and put his face in mine, asking me if I had lost my mind or something. I told him of course that I hadn't.

I explained, "What I mean is this, it's all about money, ain't it?" I couldn't help but notice that the largest filter company on earth doesn't deem it productive to supply its finest engineers with coffee is all!" A self-conscious laugh from the guys filled the gallery.

Continuing, "Hey really guys! I figure all the improvements to the line and essential upgrades could be done for less than a couple of hundred thousand dollars, and that would be for the whole show. So, what's that to a filter division that grosses about a billion dollars a year?" Moaning out loud for the first time, "I don't get it?"

It became obvious that Gary didn't want me to take what was going on any further to heart as he said, "Don't worry about it Steve, we'll figure it out. We have time."

"Okay," was my reply, "I'll trust you guys for it," as I began to feel my ownership again, for the first time in a long while.

"Like I really have a choice in the matter," I said humoring them all. "But I'll have to remind you that this thing is supposed to roll out by next November. The Show is less than eleven months from now, and I've already been promised the Show!"

For the uninitiated, the Show was a code word for the SEMA show, held every year in Vegas. The largest automotive aftermarket trade show of its kind in the world. And it happens at the end of every October, just like clockwork. The marketing department at least had enough insight to realize that they had a major hit on their hands, so my product was to be rolled-out with as much fanfare as they could muster.

Just so you know, the SEMA rollout for any new automotive product can't be topped.

Right then Gary jumped in. I guess that perhaps I was heaping too much on his plate…, and too fast under the circumstances. It was obvious in his reply that he was more interested in covering his butt at the moment, more than anything else, "Well…, it's a little too early to say anything about that Steve, but with a little luck, we should make it."

That feeble charge for the hill quickly began to fade, as the turmoil created by AlliedSignal's half-hearted attempt to fund this project took hold. Somehow, I drew strength from the fact that the firestorm beginning to brew inside of me, was due more to the parent Company's austere money mentality than anything outlandish I had authored. I was relieved that the goings on weren't birthed due to a flaw in my patent, or some insurmountable quirk embedded in the manufacturing process that I had put forth.

Once again, the engineers locked in and began throwing out amongst themselves the various ways in which this material could be assimilated into the finished filter. I sat on the sidelines taking it all in, resting on fact that at least for the moment, I knew where they happened to be going with my baby.

Sitting back in my chair, I watched and listened as the engineers continued their discussions, remarking to myself how good it felt, now that the barrels of Ron's big guns had been silenced. Every so often he'd stop taking notes and would jump in, questioning the foursome. In so doing, our eyes would meet every now and then, smiles exchanged. We had become allies.

'It was squarely up to those guys now,' I thought, as they bantered about every conceivable idea that had to do with getting this material into a finished can. As the master mechanic and visionary of this thing, I stayed out of it and let them run their own course, ever mindful, that if they strayed into the impracticable, I'd be there and swoop in with a final solution.

However, the big question was, 'Were they gonna treat the media inside the can or out? Was it going to be dipped or sprayed? Were they going to make it, or have one of their suppliers make it?' The possibilities went on infinitum, as Gordon flailed upon the big white writing tablet, directing the 'action items' around like a well-seasoned traffic cop.

For the life of me, and I don't know whose big idea it was, but before anyone had the decency to consult me, they began talking about making a mixture of Teflon and grease!!! 'Making a mixture the consistency of toothpaste I heard one of them say.'

Naturally I cringed! 'What should I have done?' Something rash like jump up to my feet and start screaming 'hey, you guys gotta stop! Don't go another step further, you're way outside the scope of my patent, my trade secrets and anything else that I've taught ya!!!

Whether intentional or not, they had indeed let themselves stray outside the realm of anything I knew woulda even worked. And yet, it appeared all so innocent..., nonetheless, it was happening right in front of my eyes!!!

'Should I of opened my mouth? Should I have pointed it out or what?' They were all big boys, I reasoned, and knew what they were doing. I decided that it was for the good and welfare of the team, that I should hold my tongue. I reasoned that they needed enough rope, so that they could attempt to do it their way. They were going to fail, and I needed to let them fall flat on their faces, 'cause if they didn't, they'd be left chasing their tails past the engineering deadline and the project would be cast aside on the trash heap. It was killing me, but I had to let them get it out of their system. So decided to let them fail.

I saw how they were floundering, witnessing this thing sputter, before it could ever get off the ground. So, I dealt with this questionable incident like I had dealt with every other..., alone and very much dependent upon my long-range vision.

I know that I've said this before, but it's worth mentioning once again. I was responsible for getting the Queen Mary safely to her birth..., and I was pushing her with a dingy.

Leaning forward past Greg to get a better line of sight, I could see Gary nodding his head. "I get it, yeah sure! As it comes down the line we could have some sort of wand place a dollop of this grease on the inside rim of the can. Then as usual, the filter assembly gets placed inside. You know," he said, sounding as if the puzzle had been solved, "That might just work!"

From that moment on, the chosen method of delivery was this Teflon and grease sort a mixture, that was going to be either placed into the can or applied to the media at some given point in the process. All of my practical ideas had been summarily thrown out the window without as much as a thought! It was all done for expedience sake..., in the name of ramp up time, opportunity costs and money.

I didn't object to their lunacy, because I didn't have much sway at this juncture... I was up against the money factor. So, whichever was the 'easiest, cheapest and quickest way,' was going to win out.

Anyway, I kept telling myself that it didn't matter. I had to force myself to believe, that I was in their good hands now. It was an even trade I mused..., after all, these guys had already spent the better part of the last three and a half hours listening to what I had to say as the inventor. For what it was worth, they had allowed me to run my leg of the race, now it was my turn to let them run theirs. They held the baton and at least they were finally running with it. The question remained, 'did they start the race off limping?' We'd soon find out.

———————————

It was getting to be past noon and our business was wrapping up, except for the niceties. The boys pressed me to stay for lunch, as I pulled out my plane ticket to confirm exactly when I had to leave. I had a choice between a 1:40 departure or 7:30 that night. I opted for the earlier flight.

Some moans went up from the group, "Come on Steve, after lunch you can tour our facility and take a look at what a real test bench looks like," somebody offered.

If I could have visited one of their manufacturing plants, I certainly would have stayed! 'Cause that would of given me a window into their manufacturing soul, and I couldn't of put a price on that! But no such gift was offered, so I opted to skedaddle.

"Look guys, I really appreciate the offer, but aren't you sick of me by now?" I asked, half serious. "After all, I've been talking here for the last several hours, and besides, if I wanted to see a test bench all I'd have to do is stick my head out the garage door and look at mine," being smart.

"Are you serious?" as Greg and the rest of em roared. By now, Greg must of thought that I was a wild man, "So tell me about this test bench of yours, I don't believe it," he said, with a big grin.

They all huddled around as I told them how Wolfgang my machinist friend, who was a bona fide wall-jumper from East Germany, had given me this hydraulic auxiliary pump off of an old tractor of his. "I used it to create the oil pressure within the system, so I could perform my restriction tests." After I finished explaining it, I offered to send them a video of it in full swing.

As we walked down the hall saying our farewells, we passed Mr. Coronia. The caravan stopped momentarily, as he plied Gary how it went. "It went well Tony..., very well! We learned a lot from Steve, and I believe we are on our way!"

He replied, "Oh I'm pleased." As I stretched out my hand to reach his, all I could think about was that at long last he and I might become allies. Gazing into my face, he offered, "Well done there young man," as he struggled within himself to congratulate me amidst his total befuddlement. Surely, he thought I would have been dispatched with.

I couldn't help but think of the king when he came to check upon Daniel, after having him sent off to spend a cozy evening in the lion's den. Only to find him alive and very much intact in the next morning. And who could of blamed him, knowing what I had just been up against.

'Dear God, it felt so good to be alive and thriving!' I was so blessed to be afforded the privilege to chase my dream with the unbridled hope that I had placed in my own future. Believe me, at a time like this, after the mountain had been climbed, I was at my most vulnerable.

From a worldly standpoint, I should of been taking notes, taped the meeting, brought lawyers, accountants and advisors of every ilk. And maybe, that's what I should have done. But I didn't.

'And you wanna know how far I would have gotten wearing a well-worn defense like that?' I assure you, as far as the Signal was concerned..., not very. More than likely, I wouldn't of gotten past the front door! The game they were playing wasn't rigged in my favor, so you can forget about it! I wouldn't of even made it past the secretary out front!

Despite my many disadvantages, I also happened to be at my strongest. For I wasn't holding onto any vendettas from the past and not harboring any malice for all their many foul ups which seemed to be automatically charged to my account! I was just as happy to enjoy the moment and to forgive all the fallible players that I had been involved with along the way. But that doesn't mean that I was a complete trusting fool either, not by any stretch. I was blessed with a good memory.

Motoring down the road towards the airport, Gary for some odd reason brought up his boss, the senior VP of Engineering. Not being able to withstand that particular button being pressed, I shared with him at length what had happened at his hand six years back. Now it wasn't that I didn't forgive the man, that wasn't the case at all. I did so as much to let Gary know what I had already been through, and what it had taken for me to be in an automobile with the senior project engineer of the largest filter company in the entire world. I guessed that it was just my way of letting him know that I would go ballistic this time around if there was the hint of any such a repeat. Notwithstanding, it wouldn't hurt for him to have a little deeper insight as to whom this obscure little inventor might be all about.

As the story progressed, he took on more and various whiter shades of pale. I swore to him that I was telling the truth. I owed it to myself to let him know one last time that I was as serious as a rattlesnake bite and that I wasn't going to tolerate any underhanded or unfair treatment by the Company this time around.

As it turned out, Gary would be the first employee in a long succession at Allied that I openly made this promise to. Promising that my cries would reach all the way to the CEO, Larry Bossidy if need be.

I know he heard me loud and clear that afternoon, I just don't know if he quite understood just how serious I was.

The filter test bench in my garage.	late '80's.

After treating the filter prototypes, I'd run them for extended periods to see if any negative effects on oil flow and media restriction would show on the pressure gauge.

The license plate on the wall was given to me by another trucker out on the road.
It used to hang on the front bumper of my KW.
When I came off the road, I stuck it behind the wires and it hasn't moved since.

CHAPTER 7
SO, YOU WANT TO MEET ME AT THE AIRPORT!

While sitting at my desk one morning, going through the endless reams of ridiculous paperwork in duplicate and triplicate, Norma, my secretary hollered out from the photocopier room, "Hey Stevie, there's a woman on the phone for you…, a Dianne Newman from AlliedSignal." My preoccupation with the nearly meaningless shuffle came to an abrupt halt. I could feel my galvinistic levels rise a notch with each succeeding breath as my heart began to pump. Just sitting there with my heart a pumping, I sat there and stared at the blinking light on my phone.

She called out again from the back, "She's on line two. Did you pick up?"

Hollering back to her, "I got it," reaching for the phone.

'What the heck could this woman possibly want with me?' Wondering, as I struggled within myself to take her call. It was roughly 10 am on a Thursday morning somewhere around the second week of March 1995. It was cold outside and there was a remnant of snow hanging around, hardly able to melt due to the cold damp weather that was lingering on.

The office was always so cold and damp on days like this. There was a heavy layer of cold air that hung just about ankle level, emanating from the frozen water under that shanty of a building we called an office.

As I picked up the phone, almost by reflex action, "Hi, how are you Dianne?"

"I'm fine," she replied.

I'm thinking, 'darn, we're making good headway', she's fine. I mean that's what she told me. 'Right?'

I knew that I was fine, more often than not I would be. It wasn't my curse in life to fall prey to viscous mood swings. And talking about mood swings, now that's one thing seven years in the real estate business will get you, a ringside seat watching many an adult being negatively controlled by their emotions.

"How far are you from Morristown?" she asked, out of the blue.

"I don't know, about an hour and a half," all the while wondering to myself where she was going with this one.

"I'll be in New Jersey tomorrow for business. I have to meet with a gentleman, before he leaves to go back to India."

'Yeah, so what the heck does that have to do with me,' I thought.

"I have some unfinished business that I have to wrap up with him," repeating the statement for the second time, seemingly trying it out on me for effect.

I had a terrible habit of drinking coffee on an empty stomach first thing in the morning after I got up and I'd chase it later with another cup and routinely wouldn't eat anything at all until one or two in the afternoon. This particular morning my stomach was turning to begin with and my newfound set of nerves wasn't helping the situation very much, as I waited for her to get to the point.

"I'm going to meet him at Newark International in the morning, he's staying with his parents near there. How far are you from Newark anyway?" she asked.

"About an hour and a half," I replied.

"So, you're about the same distance from our headquarters in Morristown as you are from the airport, aye," definitely trying to feel me out this time. "Well I'd like to meet with you tomorrow before I go back to Rumford. What's your schedule like?"

I knew I could be free, and if it wasn't, I could clear the decks if necessary. Anyway, it didn't matter, this was AlliedSignal calling and I wasn't about to allow my growing negative feelings towards Dianne get in the way.

"Well, I'd like to meet with you in the morning. I'm meeting with this fellow and I want to fit you in either before or after him. It's your choice. What would you prefer? Would you like to meet me at nine o'clock or eleven?

"So, can we meet at the airport...? Is nine too early?"

Stammering a bit, "No, it's ok," still trying to figure out her motives.

"Anyway," she continued, "I just reviewed our pre-licensing agreement and we have approximately two weeks remaining before it runs out.

You don't have a problem giving us an extension at this time, do you?" My reply was to the point, "No, I don't."

The six months that I had originally agreed to was never etched in stone on my part and besides, at this point I really had no other option, but to give the Company an extension. For me to have done anything less, would of been asinine.

"So you see, I thought it would be good if the two of us got together so we could extend the agreement," while in the same breath asking, "Would you be all right about giving us another two-month extension?" The phone on my end went silent for a moment as I thought about it. "Gee..., that would push us out near the end of June wouldn't it?" I said, half out loud, still thinking to myself.

"Yes, I imagine you're right Steve."

After quick reflection, I realized I had little choice in the matter, knowing full well that the engineers hadn't come up with a suitable prototype as of yet. "Yea, sure, I'll give you another two months Dianne."

Now it was my turn to play dumb and ask her a few questions. "Hey Dianne, why can't you mail me the extension, it's not like I'm going to change my mind or anything. Better yet, fax it to me right now, I'm in my office. I'll sign it and fax it back to you right away. You can always put the hard copy in the mail latter."

Continuing, "Why do you want to meet with me anyway?" I asked, still not a hundred percent certain. 'She couldn't of just been calling about the extension. Na, that was just too straight forward, there had to of been an ulterior motive. Besides, I hadn't ever let on that I was going to ask for a release from our agreement anyway.

She was cat and mousing me at this point and I thought it rather childish. I just wanted her to get to the point of why she was calling me after five long months! Up until this point, my contact with Dianne was almost exclusively limited to our meeting back in October when I had signed the pre-licensing agreement. Subsequently, we had only a couple of brief conversations which pertained to my receiving a pre-licensing fee for the signing of that agreement. And as I mentioned previously, that had gone nowhere. Other than that, my contact with her office was limited to housekeeping issues such as the reimbursement for the two business trips that I taken so far to meet with Company personnel.

Then out of the blue, she began, "I thought it was time that we..., I mean both you and I, might start the negotiating process." You know the Company has shown some interest in your ideas and your patent and I just thought that we might move along," she said, almost in a passing fashion. It really bugged me that she would be so petty by downplaying the Company's interest and I did my darndest not to let her see it.

"Well that's great! I felt that the Company would come to that conclusion," I replied, trying not to burst wide open with pride! I certainly couldn't allow myself to get caught up in the moment either, just because she had finally decided that it was time to fill me in on the obvious. Surely, it must of been killing her to give it to me.

More importantly, I thought it was really bizarre for a company such as Allied to have waited all this time, before even gauging what my future demands for my intellectual property package might be. Believe me, that in of itself was more of an immediate concern than having to deal with Dianne's crazy up and down personality.

Just so you know, this deal went far afield of just the licensing of my Teflon treated oil filter patent to them. There was my '901 Additive treated oil filter patent, that was thrown into mix as well. There were trade secrets behind both of these patents that had to do with the manufacturing nuances, additives, methodology and the list went on and on..., a mile long. Not to mention, of how I spoon fed Fram/Allied my marketing insights and how I would reveal the present mindset of their competition and their product's trend metrics.

In pouring out my guts under the protection of the Proprietary Information Agreement and the Test Marketing Agreement; which just happened to be a Trade Secret Agreement on steroids, I had given them enough information to keep their patent department busy for the next two decades.

Just so you know, I brought AlliedSignal/Fram the entire package, the entire plan. I had everything and they had nothing as far as the IP and the business plans were concerned. For my part I needed them for their ability to manufacture, distribute and to promote. The stark reality, that's what any inventor/licensor is seeking when shopping for a fair and equitable license.

Here's the point, I wasn't Paul Newman and I knew it. I was at least smart enough to know that I was incapable of getting this bottle of salad dressing on the shelves all by myself. So, obviously, I needed a partner like Fram/Allied to partner with. However, keep this little something in mind..., even though I had to spill my guts in order to entice them to go into business with me, that still didn't entitle them to one scintilla of my IP! The only way that they were entitled to use any of my IP was under a an agreed upon, signed and binding license agreement! Period!

Now I'm a flexible guy, and I would have met her at a gin mill, a truck stop, or anywhere else for that matter. That should give you an inkling of how bad I wanted this to happen, but nonetheless, the way in which I was now being approached really bothered me. It just didn't sit right with me to do business with a Fortune 38 Company at an airport, when we could have just as easily of met on Company property with a degree of formality and some suitable notice of course. Believe me, I don't want to sound like a sentimental kook, but I only planned on doing this once in my lifetime, kinda like getting married. So, I didn't feel that it was out of line to do things proper. That aside, I was still dubious as to why she seemed to want and put so much distance between us and the Company facility. The late December meeting with Ron and the engineers was still kinda fresh, that scab certainly hadn't had time to heal-over yet.

Keep in mind that Ms. Dianne was the Head of Strategic Planning and World-Wide Development who represented a four-billion-dollar business unit of a Fortune 38 Company. Simply put, I didn't feel that twenty-three hours' notice was proper protocol, and neither would it be proper to draw up this deal on the back of a paper napkin either. I really couldn't justify how the chain of events were unfolding and she wasn't helping put my mind to ease about it either. And to add insult to injury, I wasn't all that thrilled to be playing second fiddle to some guy from India that was in a hurry to catch a flight back home. I'm sorry, but I felt that this deal of mine required her respect as well as her undivided attention.

I'm a terrible liar! Maybe because I don't have much cause for practice, but I gave it my best shot. "Well Dianne, I have to double check my schedule before I can absolutely commit myself to meet with you tomorrow."

I didn't give her a reason yet, as to why I couldn't attend. I just told her there's a good possibility I'd be there, but I needed to confirm it was all.

As she began pressing me harder, I got another glimpse of that little control problem of hers, the one that I had run up on, last October.

Before she got too huffy, I broke in, "I call you back around lunch time to let you know for certain if I can make it or not? That should give you plenty of time to firm up your appointment with the other guy you're meeting with."

Tersely she said, "Call my office and leave word if you are available to make it. If I'm not in, leave word with my secretary."

As I was just about to hang up the phone, she shot out, "You know Steve, Larry Bossidy, our CEO is very interested in this project and wants to know where we stand on this matter between us. As a matter of fact, I am going to be meeting with him in the next week or so, and he wants a report!" She threw in 'between' us like it was something personal, between her and I. Not between AlliedSignal the Corporation and myself. That subtle but rather obvious intonation began to send shock waves through my being as she began to put an odious spin on things.

Right about that moment, I really wanted to launch into her and tell her how I really felt about the situation, but I dared not. Thinking to myself, 'nothing like waiting for the last minute for you to call, with your bowels in an uproar! And no less over your sloppy management of my life's work lady!'

Yet another great lesson came to mind, one I had learned well, while earning a living as a straight commissioned real estate salesman… 'Guard your emotions and watch your tongue, people aren't big on accepting retractions after you've taken their temperature for them.'

"Gee Diane, that's really great that Larry's interested in this project, being the CEO of such a large company and all. I'll just have to do my best to meet with you at the airport. I'll give your office a call around noontime and let you know." We both finally said our good byes and hung up the phone.

Norma was on a cigarette break in the coffee area in the rear of office, as I walked back to grab a cup of water from the cooler. "So, who was that woman?" she inquired, rather protectively.

"Dianne Newman from AlliedSignal," I said.

"Yeah, so. What did she want?"

"You know Norma, AlliedSignal! You look lost Normie. Fram the oil filter company remember!" I repeated, like I had expected that little tidbit of information to have been tattooed on her brain. Norma was a great secretary and conducted herself as if she was the personal secretary to all fifteen of us that worked out of the office. Not only that, this very feisty young grandmother was a special friend to me and was a good sounding board and confidante. I valued her opinions and her insights that she readily shared with me as we charted the milestones of my saga.

"Oh!" she exclaimed. "That woman! So, what did she call you about?" intuitively aware of the fact that I had just been accosted.

"They want to start negotiations with me!" I said, brimming with feelings that only landing the big one could give. But in truth, my emotions were tempered in the of knowledge that I was going to have to do business with someone that I was quite sure, wasn't wrapped too tight.

"Oh, Honey that's great! So, come now, talk with me for a moment," as her eyes gave away her genuine excitement. Norma was truly happy for me, even if it meant that I could soon be liberated from this job, and perhaps in the process, sever our bonds.

"Do you believe the nerve of that woman? What the heck are women doing in business anyway if they can't cut it," I said, letting my opinion get the best of me.

"Now, now, Mr.! Don't start with me on that subject," she said. "So, she's a nut! You can handle her! I've seen you handle plenty of nuts around here," as she began getting a little impatient with me, because she knew my character.

"She wants to meet with me tomorrow at Newark Airport! And if that's not bad enough, with less than twenty-three hours' notice. Can you believe it? Meeting her at an airport and not at the Company's headquarters in Morristown. I just can't figure it.

"On top of that, she's making me dance around some guy that's supposedly catching a plane home, back to India. What the heck does that have to do with me anyway? I can't believe that she's starting off with me this way," I lamented wanting to blow. "I'm so angry I could chew nails!"

Lamenting out loud, "I have to work with her…, I just know it. I've already tried to see if I can work with someone else, but so far it's been a no."

I wasn't whining…, and I certainly wasn't any wallflower when it came to difficult negotiations. To be sure, I had logged more than enough experience dealing with some extremely difficult individuals during my tenure as a real estate agent. However, this situation could not be compared to some fleeting real estate deal, that would pass in a matter of months…, only to be forgotten. This without question, was the business deal of my life, and it would have lasting effects for the rest of my life.

Normie, as I was fond of calling her, understood completely the situation I was in. "So, tell her you just can't make it. Reschedule the whole thing and meet with her at the Company, if that's what you want. I'll tell you Stevie, I wouldn't be too thrilled about meeting with her off company grounds myself, especially if that's the way she's going to conduct business."

So, after that quick chat with the coach, I decided to call Dianne's office and bow out of the meeting due to scheduling problems. Calling back around noon, I got her secretary Jackie and told her of our earlier phone conversation, and about the possible meeting in New Jersey, that Dianne wanted to schedule for the next day. I asked her to please tell Dianne that I was going to a wedding on Saturday that was being held out of town and that my wife was in the wedding party. I conjured the whole thing up, the rehearsal, everything! Oh, how I cringed! It was the damnedest lie, if I ever told one!

"Tell her I'd be happy to meet with her next week, and I would even be glad to make the trip up to Fram's headquarters to save her any inconvenience. Just tell her that it would be impossible to meet with her tomorrow!" Jackie, like a good sport took the whole message down.

After my floor time ended, around one o'clock or so, I left the real estate office for the short trip home. When I got in, I was greeted by my baby sitter who watched our two-year-old son a few days a week while my wife and I were off at work. Barely in the front door, she started hollering for me, "Steve! Steve!" calling out in near panic. It was a flustered call for help, not unlike Edith Bunker would emit after Archie had just got done dumping on her.

"Oh Steve! I am so glad that you're home. I just got off the phone with this woman who was yelling at me. She wanted to talk with you, but when I said that you weren't home..."

Mary Beth was really upset, acting as if she had done something terribly wrong, like dropped the kid on his head.

"She just kept on yelling and giving me orders. She was so mad and upset with you. I don't know..., she said that you were supposed to meet with her tomorrow, and then you called and canceled, after she had already made plans to meet with you! Oh Steve...! She was really going berserk on me. I didn't know when you'd be home, so I couldn't tell her. Besides, I didn't have any idea what she was talking about anyway?

"Are you in some sort of trouble? I hope not," she added, deeply concerned.

"No, I'm not. Not at all! Thanks a lot Mary Beth. Don't worry about it a moment longer, everything's fine."

'I can't believe that she called my home and starts reaming out my baby-sitter,' I muttered to myself in utter disbelief.

"Do you believe that kind of behavior," as I began to revisit the call I had received back at work.

Mary Beth had been a friend of mine long before I was married, and now she had become like a grandmother to our two children, a sweeter more loving person you'll never find. However, there was one little personality flaw that would occasionally drive me absolutely mad. You see, she could be a tad bit on the naïve side, when it came to sizing people up. Occasionally we would have friendly arguments over that subject, especially when I would drag myself in from work, all bloodied from a horrific real estate episode. And as was usually the case, even after I got finished with a blow by blow, she'd be left in a state of disbelief that grown adults could carry on in such fashion.

I wasn't quite sure what it was about her, but Mary Beth had a very hard time relating to the darker side of human behavior. Needless to say, that alone was enough to get me going, but when she began to proffer all sorts of inane excuses for it, well, let's just say things between us could get pretty heated.

Today however, was very different, because she wasn't making any excuses for Ms. Dianne.

The phone call that she had intercepted out of the pit, the one intended for me, seemed to have done a wondrous job of clearing up her condition of rose colored glasses.

"What are you going to do?" she asked, still all shook up. "You have to meet with her, don't you?" she said, still not able to fathom that I wasn't in big trouble.

"Yeah, I have to meet with her. But I just don't know if it will be tomorrow is all," still weighing the situation.

Mary Beth replied, "I don't blame you one bit. She's is a very fresh woman. How can she be in the business world, Steve?" It was so obvious that even the baby-sitter had enough sense to know something was terribly wrong with the whole picture.

My reply was simple. "She can, and she is. Don't take this personally Mary Beth, but I think that you're sometimes better off sticking to children, then with adults, if you know what I mean."

"Your right," she said. "I really wouldn't want to do what you do for a living. Between this patent stuff and your real estate job, I don't know how you keep from going crazy."

I thought it best to call the guy I was working on this project with. It's was always a crap shoot to reach him anymore, with all that voice mail doing the screening these days. Whenever I reached him right away, it always seemed to be like such a bonus.

Saying a little prayer, I dialed Kevin's number in hopes of by-passing his secretary telling me that he was in another meeting. Or getting his voice mail, only to be informed that he was out of the office traveling again. Much to my relief, he picked up the phone. I poised myself, readying to tell him of the bizarre goings on.

There always was a certain feeling of security when I would talk to Kevin about our joint venture, despite the fact he always seemed so preoccupied and so darn hurried all the time. And it wasn't like I called him every day, or even once a week! I respected the fact that he was doing his job, and I was doing mine. However, I would call him from time to time, to discuss new findings I may have come up with or strategize with him concerning the impending birth of our revolutionary oil filter.

It was my patent, and my idea for sure, and Kevin never begrudged me of that fact, he was certainly able to let me have that. In my estimation, Kevin was a skilled handler, a talented individual and well-liked by his peers. In my eyes what really set him apart from the crowd, aside from having a stout backbone, was that he could make a decision unlike most corporate types I had run into thus far. He was my entrusted guide, leading me on this safari, deep into the dark regions of the mega corporation he worked for.

"Hey Kev, it's Steve, how ya doing?"

"Ok man how are you!" he shot back right at me.

He was up every time called, like he was running on adrenaline or something. "What's up? What's on your mind?" knowing that I never called just to have a mindless chit chat session.

"Dianne called me this morning around ten o'clock," I said, not letting on yet about anything.

"Oh, that's great! So, what did you two love birds have to talk about this time?" Taking the occasion to bust me.

"Yeah sure," I said, giving it back. Like you ought to know. I'd love to see how you'd handle her."

"No thanks, my friend. I got enough to handle already!"

He seemed to listen intently, as I laid bare the gory details of the mornings call, though he allowed himself the privilege of making a few snide comments along the way. No matter how dire, I couldn't help but be amused by the sarcastic spin he'd put on the situation. He had a way of making me feel like he was mediating between two kids on the playground that didn't know how to get along but should of known better.

Kevin really liked me, and I knew that. And I also knew that I was in a situation that I could win, and perhaps win big if only I played my cards right. Likewise, he knew darn well that I wasn't about to let some short-circuited individual screw up this situation for me either. 'And you know something?' All I could do was hope that he was right. However, later on…, she would have things in store for me, that would lie unforeseen by the both of us…

"I know. I know. So, she's a ditz! And she certainly doesn't appear to be handling things right, but what do you expect from me?" hoping to assuage my distaste for her school girl tactics.

"Doesn't appear to be handling things right!" I said, angrily repeating his words. Yet I couldn't help but to feel rather self-conscious, because the last thing I wanted to sound like, was a whiner in front of him, respecting the fact that he was also in a tough spot. Not only did he work for the company, but he's was what you would call a consummate company man! In his case though, I viewed it more of something to be proud of.

With that he began to offer me some advice, "Don't meet with her if you don't want to. I understand completely man, but believe me Steve, I know you're much better than that! Look Buddy, I'm gonna give it to you straight, it's certainly to your benefit to meet with her no matter how pissed you are! Now you said that she left her home number with your baby sitter for you to call her at home tonight. Right?

"Wow that's a little bit much! You still don't even have my home number yet!" unable to control another contorted laugh. Then in an act of diplomacy, he offered, "Ah… what the heck. Let her stew a little while, then give her a call tonight."

"Okay," I agreed. I was reluctant, but I agreed. I had asked Kevin to intervene between us on a previous occasion already, but with no success. And before our tenure was over, I'd ask him at least another time or two.

So far, he'd always been there for me, as a sounding board and as source of guidance, but he just didn't want to push the matter any further by removing her from the loop! Simply put, it was her job to meet with me, and no one else's!

It was the last thing that I wanted, but all I could do was try and relate to how Saint Paul had asked the Lord three times to remove the thorn from his flesh. The Lords reply was simple, "My grace is sufficient enough for you."

My wife Patti got home at about 4:30 from her whirlwind tour of teaching thirty first graders the essentials of how to make it to second grade. I loved my wife dearly, and I never had any difficulty communicating my innermost thoughts with her. But when she blows through the front door after a day's work, well…, it's nearly impossible to get her whole attention, let alone even a little part of it. Her arrival was always like an obstacle course of sorts.

There's a five-year-old daughter who needs to be greeted. Then there's the three-year-old son that has to be reassured that mommy's home for the day and isn't going to leave again. Sometimes there was Mary Beth, or Patti's parents who moved across the street to check in on. Often times, it was a tall order to see how everybody's day worked out. Then finally there would be me. Without fail, I was the one who was supposed to be patient and grown up enough to wait for the dust to clear before I could talk to mommy. But sometimes, and not very often, I would need to be first. And of course, I was having one of those days that I really needed to talk to her. A major event was developing in our lives that would affect our little family's destiny. An event that I had pursued with such a high degree of determinism, it was a wonder it hadn't already overtaken us.

"Patti!" I exclaimed. "Pat, Pat…! AlliedSignal called me today at work!"

From the moment she'd hit the front door she'd be into doing a million things at once. And today was no different.

"Follow me," she said, waving her hand in a big sweeping motion as she worked her way into the bedroom. The kids and the commotion had subsided for a while and for a brief moment, I would have an opportunity to tell her what had happened, that's if I didn't get to long winded.

"So, tell me, what's going on?" she said, picking up on my excitement.

"Who called, Kevin?"

"No... Dianne!"

"Dianne?! What does she want? You guys haven't talked to each other in ages," she said, stopping what she had been doing. "Is something wrong Honey?"

"No, not really. She wants to meet with me tomorrow at Newark Airport to begin negotiations for my patent."

A look of relief filled her face, "That's so fabulous honey, you're really gonna do it! This is what you've worked so hard for. This is what we've been waiting for! But can I ask you a stupid question?" Her eyes squinting, as if trying to figure out the answer before I could give it to her.

"Sure," what is it?" I said.

"Why are you meeting her at an airport? Shouldn't you be meeting her in Rhode Island or Morristown," she asked, as if she was able to read it right off my face. "Are you sure there's not something wrong?" Without another word from me, the look of joy on her face began melting into contemplation. She wasn't about to play poker with me.

"That's just where she wants us to meet Honey. I didn't like the sounds of it at first either," as I launched into a through debriefing of the full day's events.

Patti always understood, and rarely questioned my judgment when it came to this quest that I'd been inexorably tied to. So, in the end, she agreed with Kevin that I should meet with Dianne, even if it was at the last minute, and even if it was at an airport. The two people I trusted most on this matter, including the one who knew me best, both said the same thing, 'that I was a bigger person than to give into some petty mind game she was playing.'

So, it was agreed, I was going to the airport.

I called Dianne at home that night like she asked. I placed the call to her at about 7:30 p.m. and she picked up the phone. Although I had rehearsed how I was going to handle her, I still wasn't sure how to go about it. In my mind, she was still totally out of order showing a complete lack of professionalism and tact. Beating up on my baby-sitter like that, was just beyond my comprehension.

'Would she be ticked?' I didn't have any way of knowing. And what did I care anyway, after all, it wasn't like I had foisted my rude behavior on her.

Actually…, I did care. Immensely! I was about to cut the covenant with a Fortune 38 Company, that happened to own the largest oil filter division on the planet, Fram Oil Filters. Of course, I cared! What was brewing here was madness, compared to the relationship I was enjoying with Kevin. And by this time, I was well on my way to cultivating the respect and cooperation from the engineers and production department as well.

'So why did my relationship with this woman have to be so dysfunctional?' My only answer to that one was, because she apparently wanted it that way!

I could vaguely make out the dim light way down the line, as my freight train of dreams groaned in the distance. I wasn't about to let my emotions let me fall prey into Dianne's hands, just because I wanted to hate her. I couldn't allow it! The force of hate opposed everything that I stood for as a God-fearing person, and besides, I wasn't going to allow something that low-level ruin my dream.

I blurted out, "Hi Dianne, I was asked to give you a call at home tonight," as it came pouring out of me before I had a chance to think. My salutation was more an autonomic response of sorts caused by my uptightness, I guess.

"Oh, hi Steve," came her terse response, absent of any malice. There wasn't any sign of the battle raging on in her, at least not like the one that she had successfully created in me.

"Well… Do you think you are going to make it tomorrow? At the airport I mean?" she asked, like a well-mannered schoolgirl.

"Yes. I'm going to meet you there at nine o'clock in the morning. That's why I called you early enough this evening, so you could tell the other gentleman he'd have to meet you at eleven. Because, I definitely won't be able to make that one."

"That's great Steve! Don't worry about him, he'll be just fine," as if to reassure me that I hadn't inconvenienced the kind man from the far away continent. She really seemed to have a thing for this guy and that bothered me. Maybe she just thought he was so nice because he was going to become easy meat for her table once the real matter of business started. I had no way of telling.

'Could she really be that stupid,' I thought? 'No, she couldn't be! Or then again, was she?'

During my tenure in sales, I've had enough dealings with people of this kind man's extraction to know that behind their generally pleasant demeanor lies a very astute business style that hails from the third world, where survival is no joke, but a daily consequence. I couldn't believe how she seemed to pander to him, while at the same time run over me. I couldn't quite figure out why she was so bombastic towards me. It drove me crazy. To this day I don't have any substantial answers, only assumptions as to why she would have wanted to become my worst nightmare.

I felt like I owed her an explanation why I was going to end up meeting with her, so I finished my false alibi. "I called my wife at work to see if our Friday would be open, because of the wedding that she was to be in on Saturday," I said, neatly sowing up my white lie of earlier in the day. "I'm sure you know how it is, being married. I always check in with my wife before making plans, so I won't mess things up. I'm sure you understand what I mean, you being married and all," I said, giving her the benefit of the doubt, that she had to of found a mate by now.

That was certainly a stab in the dark, because I didn't know for sure if she was married or not. My odds were fifty-fifty, I was comfortable with that, so I just waited for her reply.

"Yes, I am married. Except, I never check in with my husband when it comes to my business dealings."

"You don't?" 'What a chance for me to get inside her head, 'I thought, feeling my tension dissipate. I was on the verge of hopefully obtaining some useful insight as to how this Vulcan might operate. Being euphemistic, I commented to myself, 'this woman might be able to be reached after all.'

Before I was able to pat myself on the back she started to elaborate further. "Business always comes first, the other things aren't as important, so they can wait."

Even I was stunned by her answer. "Okay! I guess we both have different priorities going on here. I just want you to know something for the future. As far as our business dealings are concerned, I will always put my family over business. And I will always check in with my wife before any business trip…, no matter how close, no matter how important. You got me on that one, don't ya?"

'So much for my psychology degree,' I thought.

"I don't know what happened to me today, it was just that I've been under so much pressure lately and had so many things going," she volunteered, bending a little under the weight of my ground rules.

It came out of nowhere, her pseudo apology I mean. Yet I was still so disgusted, I barely acknowledged her lame attempt at an explanation. I've never been very big on excuses, and for heaven's sake, take another look at this gal's title! 'How come I didn't have a job like hers,' I wondered.

Anyway, the conversation petered out after she told me to meet her at the executive suites across from Continental Airlines in terminal C. I asked her if the place was suitable for doing business and she assured me that it was, something designed for business travelers on go. You know the business traveler who happens to be married to the road. Something romantic to that effect.

I can remember thinking to myself, 'gee lady, like I'm really a world class businessman and traveler. Like a clam digger such as myself, would really know about this sort of thing!' In going over her belated explanation, it might have set better with me if perhaps she had initially communicated that small detail to me from the very beginning. But she didn't. Apparently, communication wasn't her strong suit.

I'm telling ya, when she first told me that we were to meet at the airport, I literally envisioned that we were going to meet at some bar or burger joint off the concourse. Besides, I still was overly suspicious that Allied would conduct a business meeting of this magnitude off of Company grounds.

That night as Patti and I lay in bed discussing the bits and pieces of our day, I was somewhere else thinking about tomorrow.

Hitting my stride, I located my strategy. Flinging off the covers I jumped up and straddled the middle of Patti's stomach. "I'm not going to give her any numbers tomorrow," shaking Patti's shoulders for effect. "I want Dianne to convince me why I should go with her Company and not Purolator or Wix.

"Dianne needs to sell me on the fact why I should go into business with them. We wouldn't be meeting tomorrow if they weren't interested…, now would we?" I crowed. "I'm going to make her sweat a little and let's see how she likes it. I'd love to see if this deadline thing with Larry Bossidy is true anyway," as I slid off of her, pulling the covers over us.

Patti humored me as she chortled, "That's right Honey, you tell her…

"What time do you want me to get you up in the morning?" she asked, as sleep began over taking her. Patti was that quintessential morning person and she derived a degree of masochistic pleasure getting me out of bed early.

As we both started to drift off to sleep in each other's arms I thanked the Lord for giving me such a loyal and supportive partner to go through life with.

The prospect of the morning drive to the airport filled me with excitement. My trip was going to allow me some long overdue quality time on the turnpike and permit me to once again savor all that big iron as they sailed on by.

I arrived at the airport making sure to give myself ample time to park and find my way to the place where we were going to meet. I got to the meeting spot a good ten minutes early. I could feel my palms starting to sweat and my stomach already had that hollow feeling in it from nerves.

Dianne was my adversary, and I held her fully accountable for the perverse relationship we were having. The amazing thing about it was, I had only met her briefly on a prior occasion!

I was on my best behavior that morning. I told myself to weigh every word and to assay every move. I wanted to see if I could win her with kindness and today was gonna be my big chance to win her over. I even prayed about this whole situation in the car on my way to the meeting and was sure that I'd be ready!

Dianne seemingly appeared from out of nowhere, as I paced the floor engrossed in heavy thought. Sometimes when I get in these situations that require great resolve and purpose I can get pretty introspective. She probably caught me in the middle of counting how many carpet fibers there were in the mosaic I was staring at.

Startled, I lifted my head and made eye contact with her. She was late, and I was early. That one-upmanship stuff was of little concern to her, I assure you. I greeted her first with a jovial, but sincere, "Hi Dianne, how was your trip?"

She replied with, "Okay I guess," coldly as she clutched a bunch of loose folders tightly to her chest. That was barely all we spoke. She kind of waddled down the corridor with her bag swinging off of her arm, as she made her way to the check in clerk for the executive suite she had rented.

Thinking to myself, 'what a defensive posture, incredible body language!' Dianne clutched her papers tightly to her breasts like some young co-ed strolling along a college campus in a wholesome 1950's film. Her posture to the untrained eye didn't reflect all of the subliminal turbulence below the surface. I can tell you for certain, that she was clutching her gear for protection, more like a shield than anything else. 'A shield from what!' I anguished. 'I got a heck of a lot more riding on this deal than she would ever have in ten lifetimes!' I followed her down the hall to the clerk's desk.

We weren't going to speak until she was ready, that was evident by her body language. She was punishing me for yesterday, and I knew it. However, undeterred, I delved into some harmless chit chat in an attempt to loosen her up.

The room we went into was a ten by ten windowless cubicle, exuding an ambiance a notch or two above a minimum-security jail cell. 'Gee, this should be fun,' I thought to myself, putting my yellow pad and beat up gold Cross pen down on the table.

"Where should we start now?" she inquired of me, plopping down her bundle on the round little table in front of us. Settling into her seat she asked me once again, "Where should we begin?"

I sincerely wanted to clear the air with her concerning how she made me feel during our previous conversations. That's where I wanted to begin. I wanted to change the tone of our relationship from this point on, so we wouldn't be so doggedly adversarial and counterproductive.

Normal would have suited me just fine!

"Dianne, I want to ask you a question. I kinda get the feeling that when I say it's black, you somehow feel compelled to say it's white. Am I missing something here?" Am I bothering you? Because, it seems to me that I am ticking you off, or something?" So much for my deliberate attempt at business etiquette.

Unfazed by my lead in, she replied, "No…, no. It's just that I've been under a lot of pressure lately. I've been extremely busy. I have to leave for Russia next Wednesday for an important meeting. I've got all these deadlines, of which this is one of them," she said, looking for sympathy.

I could tell that she was a company man through and through, but of a different ilk than Kevin. It all was so transparent and in a strange sort of way. I pitied her. I had already pegged her as the kind of person that would blindly slit her wrists and bleed for 'them' in hopes of attaining that almighty accolade. In reality, companies like Allied don't give out accolades to people like her anyway. The ones who blindly do their dirty work. Their thanx lies in the fact that they're fixers.

I couldn't relate to her blind worship of the corporation that she served. Her conduct towards me as a future business partner was anything but genial or cooperative. I was left without any plausible explanations for the situation I was thrown into. I couldn't read the landscape. I was left with no choice except to believe that she was incompetent and sloppy and kept people at bay with her confrontational style. I had witnessed this kind of behavior many times before in my real estate career, exhibited by real estate agents, brokers and lawyers. But to be treated like this by an emissary of AlliedSignal? Come on! It couldn't be! I just had to be wrong!

My feeble attempt to clear the air didn't work any magic, of that I can assure you. And apparently, my prayer time in the car went hurtling down the drain the moment I opened my mouth.

Dianne took out her pad and began writing on it. When she had finished, she passed it clandestinely across the table to me without saying a word. I looked at it closely, there were three lines drawn across the page: up-front money, price per piece and volume.

After a moment, I passed it back to her. "Put one more thing on that page," I told her plainly. "Total buyout."

She replied, "Okay sure, what did you have in mind?"

"I'm not sure what I have in mind at this moment, but I sure don't want to limit my options at this point either. Is it possible to be compensated with stock options instead of cash?" I asked.

"I'm not sure about that Steve? I'll have to check in with my boss concerning that on Monday, when I get back into the office. Is that okay with you?" she said, trying to oblige me at this point.

"Shouldn't we get into some numbers concerning what you might want at this point?" trying her best to reel me in.

"I would really like for you to tell me about the Company before we go any further," I said.

"What would you like to know?" she quipped, as her tone level started to drop. She was perceptive enough to realize that we were a long ways off before I was about to discuss the money.

A simple query like asking her to share some pertinent information about the Company was enough to set her off. And I didn't much care that she wasn't up for sharing time either. She was going to share with me whether she liked it or not, because this is what I had come for, nothing else. I didn't come to talk money. I only came to reinforce the value of my contribution. I was going to make it obvious to her that she was dealing with an expert in the field of oil filtration, and that I was quite capable of setting a realistic value on my intellectual property package. I was armed with all sorts of information gathered diligently over the span of a decade, of which I can assure you, she didn't have the slightest clue. Some of the areas I knew about with confidence were: filtration, oil filters, manufactures, markets, margins, royalty rates, materials, tribology, automotive, trucking and heavy-duty. …And the list went on a mile long from there.

I started out, "You know Dianne, one of the axioms that I lived with intimately and on a daily basis was a little something called N.I.H. Industry has a habit of being set in its ways and isn't actively seeking out any ideas that originate from the outside. I really don't know how much you may be attune to it, but it's referred to as 'Not Invented Here.' I've cut my teeth on these three little words, and I now realize that it requires a lot more than just the ownership of a patent, trade secrets and a novel idea to entice a manufacturer to go into business with you.

"I contacted Purolator in June of 93, and I did that for a reason and I'd like to tell you why. I did so, because I knew for a fact that they are the largest player in the installed sales market. When Pennzoil was spinning them off in '89, their stock prospectus was quick to point out that the installed sales market made up seventy percent of all the oil filter sales which occurred in the United States.

"And following suit, Purolator was quick to claim that they enjoyed over seventy percent ownership of that market! I think installed sales is the future of the oil filter business, and the trend bears this out.

"So, what is Fram's presence in this market?" as I began to launch out on my fact-finding mission.

"Our strength isn't in that market place. We have the greatest presence in retail, such as Walmart, K Mart, Pep Boys, Trac Auto, Auto Zone, Western Auto, Target and the like. We dominate the retail market," she said confidently, trying to circumvent my initial assertion.

"That's good to know, I wasn't exactly aware of that. So, tell me Dianne, what is your market share?"

"At this time, we have approximately twenty-eight percent of the total market."

"All right, so you marginally have the largest share of the total market right now. Is that correct," asking again as I prepared to jot that information down on my yellow pad.

"Dianne, I'd like to get back to my original question about the installed sales market if I may? I'm assuming that Fram's share can't be very large in light of the fact that Purolator's Group Seven filter takes up such a large chunk of that business. Am I correct?"

I was asking totally legitimate questions of a future business partner, but I could see that my basic line of questioning was already starting to annoy her.

"So why are you so interested in the installed sales market and Purolator anyway?" She asked, sneering at me while twirling her pen.

"Let me give you an example if I may," trying to enlighten her as to what exactly I was driving at. "I'll use vacuum cleaners for an example. Let's say that there are approximately a dozen notable manufactures that participate in this market. Okay? And the price range of their products vary from eighty dollars for an inexpensive compact model with few options, to over a thousand dollars for a Kirby or an Electrolux that can do just about anything except your dishes.

"What I'm trying to do, is to try and quantify how that consumer driven market works? I want to ascertain why a Kirby can cost a grand, and a Eureka doesn't. Don't you?" I couldn't help but get excited, as I prepared to win her over with this a little utilitarian analogy.

"No. No, I don't! I don't care about vacuum cleaners! And furthermore, I don't care to know anything about them either. I don't vacuum, and I haven't done so for all the years that I've been married," she scowled. What does that have to do with oil filters anyway?"

I never intended my analogy to be sexist, that wasn't my point at all. It was just that at one point in my life I came within an inch of my life of becoming a Kirby vacuum cleaner salesman, was all! I thought I knew a little something about why someone would pay a grand for a vacuum cleaner and happily live out the rest of their days with that beautiful all-aluminum machine. I wanted to establish the concept of value with her, then demonstrate to her where the present-day consumer would be most likely to show up to buy this value-added oil filter of mine. In short, I felt the best place to sell an oil filter like mine would be in the installed sales market. In places all over the country, like Jiffy Lube, Grease Monkey, Pep Boys, K Mart, Firestone and Good Year!

Though we had gotten sidetracked, I couldn't let her go now. I just had to know the rest of her story. "Well then who does the vacuuming for you?" I shot back innocently, figuring I might as well get that much out of her. Maybe it would provide some useful information toward shaping the psychological profile that I was trying to piece together.

'So, what,' I thought. I just had to know who vacuumed her house for her, if she didn't. I certainly hadn't intended for my analogy to upset her in any way. My intentions had been pure, and I wasn't trying to be a chauvinist either. And I don't even think she took it that way.

"This might sound a little crazy Dianne, but at one point in my life I entertained selling Kirby vacuums door to door," trying to explain why I had used the analogy. "He's done it ever since we've been married. As if it would be a pox on her, "I've never picked one up," she added indignantly.

"Okay…, okay! Forget the vacuums for a minute. I was just trying to get out of you why I should go into business with Fram and not Purolator. Or Wix… or Champion Labs for that matter. I think I know why I should go into business with you guys, but for now…, I want you to tell me! What I'm doing here, is giving you an opportunity to sell me. And if you can't, and we can't get along civilly here, then I might as well get up now and leave!" I slammed her, and she needed it. I would of left, and that wasn't a threat.

Apparently, she got the message. "Okay, what is it that you needed to know?" her demeanor changing on a dime, as if we had just been seated for afternoon tea.

"I wanted to know what percentage you do in the installed sales market, and if you plan to grow that business, 'cause whether you see the method to my madness or not, I'm convinced that it's crucial for our future success."

"Well as I said before, we do very little in the installed sales market. Maybe about three percent," she offered rather offhandedly. "Again Steve, our emphasis is in retail. Our margins are much higher there and we make a lot more profit per unit. We don't have many private label customers."

"How many private label filter customers do you have?" I wasn't bashful about asking a question such as that. I believed the Company should have shared this sort of information with me a long time ago!

"Just a few that I know of, off the top of my head. Quaker State certainly comes to mind; we do about fifty million dollars a year with that account in filters. We make filters for Ford Motorcraft as well as some for Pennzoil. As for the rest of the details, I'm not really sure. That's not my department…"

I had to ask myself, 'if she didn't have all the facts necessary for me to negotiate with them intelligently, then how was I supposed to make them a rational proposal?' I knew quite a bit about Purolator already, and had gleaned some additional interesting information from their stock prospectus. I was definitely now comparing the market strategy as well as the strengths of the two companies.

'You know, a company's best tool to keep you flatfooted during royalty negotiations is to keep you in the dark', I told myself.

Dianne broke in again, "Steve, are you aware that our profit margins are the highest in the industry. Purolator might sell a lot more filters than us, however their overall profit ratio is much lower than Fram's."

"That's interesting to know. It makes sense to me. Purolator manufactures about twenty-five or so private label brands for other customers. Just like Maxwell House Coffee which Kraft Foods owns would certainly have a private label business." There I went again with another analogy. I could only hope that this illustration would have a softer landing than the one about the vacuum cleaners!

"Exactly!" she exclaimed, as we began to see eye to eye. For the moment I was exuberant inside. Her unsolicited cooperation made me feel like flying.

"You know, Purolator just got bought out by a company called Mark IV out of Buffalo, NY. I am sure that they are in the middle of restructuring and wouldn't be receptive to any new innovations at this time. I think they have financial troubles besides," she chirped, trying to draw me away from any further mention of Purolator.

What she didn't know, was at this time, any thoughts of doing business with Purolator had long since been a dead issue with me. However, from a business model standpoint, that certainly didn't preclude us from discussing their market strategy…, nor their market share. Because like I said, like it or not, Purolator was following the trend set by the consumer. Installed sales was what he customer wanted!

The 'do it yourselfer' market was eroding…, even as Dianne and I spoke! And the D. I. Y. market was the one Allied Automotive seemed to be married to…, for a whole host of reasons I couldn't quite identify, other than the retail margins. More than anything else, I was on a mission that morning to find out why that was the case.

Of course, I knew that retail enjoyed higher profit margins. That was about as elementary as breathing! The point was… If retail was dying on the vine, and I knew that it was… Its higher margins in effect would be meaningless, five-years out!

Besides, if my filter was positioned in the installed sales market, the profit margins would be the same as retail! So why weren't they capable of charting a dual course and attack the installed market with a value-added product, that would be their key to entrée? …The one that would give them a completely new and untapped retail venue? How blind could this outfit be. I was seriously beginning to wonder…, and I was more than a little bit scared of their stupidity.

I answered, "Okay, sure I can understand that. I've called on a couple of companies in the past during periods of restructuring or a leveraged buyout. It's a mess. They wouldn't be receptive to buying the first wheel ever invented, if you offered it to them. Anyway, I've already talked to Purolator almost a year ago and our talks died on the vine after only a few of months. It became a dead issue."

Dianne broke out in a smile before I had a chance to finish that statement, acting as if I had given her some huge negotiating chip by mistake. That wasn't what happened at all. My intention was to share with her the facts, even if they weren't obvious to her. Besides, I had told Kevin along with the entire group about this a long time ago.

Perhaps if she hadn't arrived nearly an hour late to that meeting back in October, she would have been able to of heard first hand my experiences concerning Purolator. 'Do ya think she had the good sense enough to find out what she might have missed that first hour? Or perhaps do you think somebody might of bothered to fill her in?' I thought it rather bizarre how something as important as this, never got relayed to the one single person responsible for handling me. So much for detail I guess.

I went on further to say that I had I called on Champion Labs and spoke to John Gather, the man in charge of the engineering department. He told me flat out, "That the consuming public wouldn't pay the extra money for a step-up oil filter such as mine!"

I dearly wanted to get across to this lady that for an outsider, I was indeed somewhat of an industry insider. That I was an intelligent and honest player. I wanted her to respect me during our tenure. In return, I would show her my cards, if she'd show me some of hers. It never was my intention to go into business with Fram and beat them out of a single thin dime. It was about sharing and doing so with honor and integrity. It was about taking the filter world by storm, together as a team! That's what it was about, at least it was to me.

And believe me, that's how Kevin and I approached this project. Despite my earnest desire to do so, I never earned her respect. But I'll share with you a little bit of what I did earn… One day in the not so distant future, I'd find myself on the receiving end of the stuff that only nightmares are made out of!

"So, do you see the Company moving in the direction of installed sales?" still focusing on that point with great emphasis, because that's the way I saw the oil filter market going, and going fast. The last thing I wanted, was to get stuck with a behemoth bucking the markets trend, if you know what I mean.

"I guess so, Steve. But I can't say for sure. Hopefully your new filter will influence a positive change in the direction of our marketing strategy. That's if what you are saying is correct," she said trying to offer me some hope for the future.

"Oh, I can assure you what I am telling you is correct! Anybody can see that the United States is rapidly becoming a service economy. Okay, I guess you've given me about all you can on that subject. Besides, it's not my position to sell you on that fact. I guess I'll have to leave that job up to my filter, once you've alerted your customers that it's gonna be available."

'So, what was I supposed to do, grab her by the throat and tell her that she was in the presence of a visionary?' I didn't think that would have been appropriate.

If you don't mind, let's leap ahead two decades. Apparently, I may have been right about the DIY landscape after all. Back in mid 90's when I called on Fram, absolutely no one I had met at Fram changed their own oil! And that was back in 1994-1995. Today, virtually no one changes their own oil…, except perhaps, those with a screw loose… and that would of course include me. I've never had my oil and filter changed by anyone. I may just have an oil filter fetish.

Fram has since been sold twice, and Purolator many times more than that. Virtually every oil filter brand out there is now made by the private label giants Champion Laboratories or Mann+Hummel. Independent oil filter manufacturing is now a thing of a by-gone era. I guessed I was right…, but nobody cared to listen. Together, both Fram and I missed the lucrative installed sales market. ...Oh well, so much for hitching your star to someone else's wagon.

I had decided to change the subject now, because she was just treading water. I was satisfied that she didn't have anything more to offer me on the subject. The truth of the matter was that I was going to go into business with them, whether I really liked it or not. As it turned out, they were the only game in town at the moment, and besides, they were at least moving forward. Albeit, sometimes I had to wonder.

"Let's talk about what you do overseas and Canada, you know the rest of the world. Fram's an international player, aren't you? What's your market share like worldwide?"

She had to think about it for a while, before coming back to me with, "Yes we are. Yes, we do business internationally, and we have business relationships set up all over the world."

"That nice to know. Why don't you tell me about the percentage you control outside the Continental U.S."?

"Why do you want to know that anyway, Steve. It really doesn't concern you. Does it?" as her demeanor began heading south once again. That question, though not by design, surely put her on the defensive.

"Well it does affect me. 'Cause, I want to be compensated for every filter that rolls off your assembly lines worldwide. Now I'd call that a concern, wouldn't you," trying not to sound smug. Dianne could be astute when she wanted to, and now she was trying. "Are you covered by any foreign patents outside the U.S.?"

"No. I am not. As a matter of fact, I am only holding a U.S. patent for this invention. I haven't filed any foreign patents and I'm certain that the filling period for that has lapsed long ago. I never intended to file for Common Market nor Asian coverage. It would have cost more money than I could ever get my hands on. And in good conscience, I didn't want to bring any investors on board, because I couldn't guarantee anybody a return on their investment, knowing in advance how risky it would be to sell this concept to a major company."

"Hey Dianne, not to be rude or anything, but I already gave you a copy of my patent back there in October. I'm positive that I disclosed to you at that time where I was covered."

"No, you didn't."

"Didn't what? Give you a copy of my patent, or inform you as to my coverage?"

"The coverage part." Somewhat flustered, "Oh I have a copy of your patent somewhere in my office," as she threw me this look at me, like I was some sort of boob.

"Okay let's just drop that, let me get back to something here. Look..., Purolator tried to paint me into a corner by requiring me to pay a quarter of a million dollars to finance a test study for my technology and I didn't go for that either."

She just didn't get it. As a matter of fact, she could of cared less that she happened to of been dealing with someone who happened to be a little bit savvy.

Then I decided to pose what I felt was a serious question for her to ponder. "Do you realize the odds that I have had to overcome for me to be sitting across the table from you. It's awesome," as I folded my hands behind my head and leaned back in my chair and giving her a big smile. "Let's say it was about a thirty or forty million to one shot, okay?"

It was getting late and we had maybe a half an hour left before the nice gentleman from India would show up for her eleven o'clock. I was looking for one more carrot if I could get it, and at the moment, I was certainly falling short of making any real headway by trying to impress her with my own self acknowledgment. She wasn't interested in any human-interest story here. And I'm sure that as far as she was concerned, it probably amounted to little more than self-aggrandizement on my part.

"We could pay you a royalty for anything sold in Canada," she blurted out.

"Oh yeah? Why is that?" I asked, totally baffled by her sudden offer.

She then went on to explain that AlliedSignal Automotive does not differentiate between the sales which occur in Canada from those sales which occur in The United States. "The sales figures of the two countries are not separated. They're lumped together and at this point we couldn't break them down if we wanted to. Not with the present accounting system we have in place. So, you'd be paid for any filters we sell in Canada and that's that," sporting a gratuitous smile.

Incredulous, I just had to ask her if she wouldn't mind repeating the whole thing over again for me. "So, you're serious huh? You mean to tell me that a company like yours doesn't separate sales figures between Canada and the United States. Is that correct?"

"Yup," she said, shaking her head in acknowledgment. "We don't differentiate between the sales that take place on the North American Continent."

The opportunity was ripe, so I took the shot, "So who carries Fram in Canada?" I surely didn't have a clue at the time. And since she had just thrown in Canada, it would of been nice to get an idea what kind of volume I could expect.

"Canadian Tire, they're like a large hardware chain that sells a little bit of everything. We're in solid with them, we own them so to speak!

"Both they and Walmart do the lion's share of the retail business in Canada. That's about all I can tell you. I'd have to check with accounting to get the kinds of figures you are asking me for."

"Okay. So, tell me about Europe. What do you do over there?" I asked hoping to get an answer.

"In Italy we do business with a large aftermarket manufacture called Sogi Fia. They pretty much make up the majority of that market. Selling to the common market nations and such. There is a large German company, but we don't do much with them and their name escapes me now."

I would later come to find out that company was none other than Mann+Hummel.

I asked, "Do you own any manufacturing facilities over there? Do you own any filter manufacturing plants?"

"No. No, we don't. We have a licensing agreement with Sogi Fia. I believe we own a thirty-five percent interest in them."

"So, you don't manufacture oil filters overseas per se and yet you guys claim to be the largest oil filter manufacturer in the world, huh? I guess the market isn't so lucrative over there, where gas is a couple a few bucks a gallon. I know that there are plenty of cars, but I would guess that the consumer doesn't have the same discretionary spending power as an American. Am I right?"

"Yes, you are. Things are a lot more expensive over there, oil filters included."

"What's your margins on filters over there, Dianne? With Sogi Fia?"

"We have licensing deal where we license our Fram name to them. We get about five cents per filter sold.

I was absolutely dumfounded! "You mean to tell me that you guys only get five cents per filter! That's incredible to my way of thinking. There isn't any room in there for me, even if I was to get a royalty. How many of these things do you sell a year? I mean what could it possibly amount to!" She responded rather candidly, "Not very much. Not very much at all, volunteering maybe around fifty thousand dollars a year."

Well that about settled that debate! I was used to making almost fifty grand a year selling real estate, albeit that was during a good year. At this point I certainly wasn't poised to make a pig of myself. Besides, from the sounds of things, they hadn't done a very good job cultivating Europe anyway.

I told Dianne I didn't want to screw up their deal any worse than they had already done so. To think…, a mega company likes of the mighty Signal earning a lousy nickel a filter, just so some company could plaster their name on the side of a filter can. I still couldn't believe it?! So, I let the European arena fall by the wayside for the moment, until I could verify whether she was telling me the truth or not.

Just so you know, this scenario for what it's worth just reinforced why I had only pursued patent protection for the U.S.! The rest of the world, even the civilized western world and the Pacific rim nations didn't generate the magnitude of sales found in the U.S. markets and I knew it!

It's sort of amusing now to look back upon our meeting that day, because when I gave her back Europe and the rest of the world, it left her rather stupefied. No doubt regretful, she put her head down as if it was some big loss for me to not of taken the bait. In the final analysis, I was glad to have jettisoned this disguised opportunity over the side, since it would be one less thing that we could fight about going forward.

Our two-hour meeting was coming to a close. It was almost zero hour for the poor man from India to show, and he musta been on her mind. "What about India?" she blurted out passionately like it really was important to her.

I had thought long and hard about this filter way before I had ever met Dianne Newman or even dreamt about negotiating this filter a new home…, so I was on autopilot on this one. "You can keep India. As a matter of fact, Dianne, you can keep China, Mexico and the rest of the world. You're not doing any filter business there anyway by the sounds of things. And besides, most of the third world is riding around on bicycles and mopeds right now, barely able to feed itself! What are they going to do with a Teflon treated oil filter in a developing third world nation anyway? These developing nations won't be ready to buy something like this until long after my patent has expired."

As for me, I had been right by not focusing my efforts on the rest of the world after all. Really, she didn't have any right whatsoever to boast that Fram was a world leader, that was for sure. And as for my initial gut reaction to forgo the costly filing for patent protection on a worldwide basis…. Well, let's just say that I was spot-on about that one.

I didn't invent the lightbulb here, and I certainly wasn't under any delusional visions of grandeur that I had. I knew one thing and I knew it to the very core of my being… 'America was the Walt Disney of the world.' A market place not only destined for my product but poised for it! A market place about ready to explode which would make me richer than my wildest dreams, that's if this Company had the smarts to support it properly.

The Indian showed up promptly at eleven o'clock, just like I knew he would. His arrival curtailed any further dialog that might have developed between Dianne and me. It was just as well; I had gotten about all I had come for. Besides, I was confident knowing that I had been able to glean just about as much information from her as humanly possible.

As Dianne turned her wiles towards the tall attractive young man, I couldn't help but wonder what she had in store for him. Unless he was good, and I mean really good, he would be out manned and out gunned.

Dianne was quickly onto her next assignment, and true to form, she was ignoring me as if our two hours of playing chess meant little or nothing. I headed for the corridor as she poured herself all over this poor chap like a hot libation.

My departure in progress must have momentarily broken in on her concentration. As I walked down the hall I could hear her yelling after me. I stopped and turned around only to catch her as she gave me a big wave from down the other end. Not skipping a beat, she shouted, "Call me Monday with your numbers, I need them for Larry! I leave for Russia Wednesday morning."

I couldn't wait to get in my car and head on down the turnpike, knowing that the big rigs would be out in full force. I was looking forward to the short trip on the big road, 'cause if I was lucky, it would mercifully transport me back to another place and time. However, before I could liberate myself from this morning's madness, I had an airport flashback to deal with. It went a little something like this…

After we settled into the office cubicle, Dianne began furiously scribbling on her legal pad. When she was done, she turned the pad around and slowly pushed it under my face. It was a poor rendition of a hustler in some cheesy movie shaving a few points off a bad debt. Under the royalty column was Allied's initial offer…

After a momentary glance, I pushed the pad back from whence it had come. I politely told her, that 'she could stuff it.' I made it clear that any further talk of money was now tabled. Aghast, I dearly needed to know what the motivation behind their offer was.

They offered me ¢1 a copy.

Stupid me…, I foolishly assumed that Ms. Dianne was going to show up with some of the necessary information that would allow for a fair negotiation. Apparently, she must of forgot to bring her data points. As for me, I showed up with my detailed valuation, and I was more than prepared to negotiate my royalty in earnest. Regrettably, I spent the next couple of hours suffering through a dog and pony show that I could have easily of done without.

Here's what really got me. Supposedly…, I was going into business with the largest filter company on the planet. As such, we were both obliged to negotiate for the privilege of creating a saprophytic union, where each of us promised to not to suck the life's blood out of the other. What I sorely lacked in order to negotiate a fair *royalty rate agreement* was the following: Allied/Fram's marketing, business and manufacturing plans; including their packaging, promotional, and planogram strategies. Of vital importance was their sales venues and attack plans…; complete with numbers, costs, margins, customer base, profit splits and milestone projections.

Knowing what they were going to do and how they intended on doing it would have allowed me to at least feel like I was negotiating with my eyes open.

The jousting between us would only heat up after the airport episode.

I called her back, Monday morning like I said I would, but of course, she was unreachable. I had spent that entire weekend ruminating about what I should start the negotiations off at, knowing what the numbers should be based upon. The size and the scope of the market potential for this filter was awesome, I was confident that it was capable of generating at least half billion dollars in the near term and it would be certainly within the realm of possibilities to eclipse the billion-dollar mark if they would only allow themselves to follow my vision!

I knew good and well, that it was Dianne's job to downplay any notion of those kinds of numbers. Being aware of her mission, only severed to ratchet up the anxiety of having to make this call. And unfortunately, I already knew her battle plan. I was going to be forced to start the bidding against myself, and the prospect was maddening. The anxiety that this was creating inside my head was overwhelming. No doubt I was being punished for refusing to talk about money at the airport, but that wasn't going to happen, not after being offered a penny a pop.

She on the other hand was more than likely refreshed from her weekend away from the office. I'll bet that Dianne hadn't given this matter more than a fleeting thought…, if at all. And why would she, it was only another assignment. Besides, this matter to be dealt with would have little foreseeable impact on her career, at least as far as I could tell.

Precisely my point. This situation was by far the weightiest matter I had ever faced in my entire life and I was going up against a machine-like individual, capable of short circuiting without so much as a warning. 'How was that for fate?' I thought.

I had done my best to get what I needed out of Kevin, but that turned out to be a dead end as well. Though our relationship was solid, and I wouldn't hesitate to ask him nearly anything, he was at a total loss when it came to feeding me the sort of info I just laid out. Now you have to understand something, Kevin was great, but his utility as far as these matters were concerned was extremely limited. Much of what I needed in order to make this a fair fight, was apparently way above his pay grade…, information he wasn't privy to. What I required, would have to come from Allied's brass, and I got that sinking feeling it wasn't ever going to happen.

I placed another call to Dianne well after lunch, still hoping to catch her, sometime around two o'clock that afternoon. If she didn't pick up the phone or catch me this time, it would be her loss, not mine. After all, she was supposed to report to the C E O concerning our negotiations before her Russian trip. I did all that I could do for the moment, leaving a detailed message with her secretary, Jackie Stevenson.

A return call never came on that Monday like it should have. Dianne was still running true to form. Her style of doing business with me was textbook boiler room. Always creating this great sense of urgency with grave consequences if a decision wasn't arrived at immediately. Yet there was always one part of the equation that would invariably be missing…, her follow through, and that was a dead giveaway. Somehow, I remained puzzled, but I gladly accepted the precious few extra hours she allotted me to fine tune the missile I was about to shoot across her bow.

Kevin and a good friend of mine in the filter business had already offered their sage advice, telling me that I shouldn't expect more than a nickel per copy sold. To me those numbers were absolutely insulting based upon the sheer potential of the thing. Though the both of them may of had good intentions, neither one of them had put in a fraction of the legwork to have come up with their paltry valuations. So, like everything else, it was up to me to fully evaluate this thing.

Drawing upon lessons learned, I came into this exercise somewhat a seasoned player, having witnessed firsthand what the demon of greed was all about. It was during my tenure in the real estate business, I learned what a full-blown money grab looked like. My policy was never to be a pig, and I certainly wasn't going to become one now, just because I was on the threshold of a mega harvest.

———————————

I finally got a hold of her Tuesday morning.

"Hi Dianne…, I put in a couple of calls into you yesterday, but never got you," I said laying out my defense.

"Oh, I know. I had meetings all day." Without so much as a flinch, she blurted out, "So where do you want to start? I mean, what would you like to be paid?" she said, immediately correcting herself.

I have to admit, there was brief a moment of hesitation as I jammed the shell in to the barrel of my gun. Swallowing hard, I lobbed the shell across the Signal's mighty bow…. "I was looking for 2.5 million up front and thirty-five cents per filter," trying to sound self-assured. I had to try…, as the words of both Richard Dye and Kevin Gill kept playing, on what must have been an endless loop. I owed it to myself. After all, I was the one who had researched the opportunity, they hadn't, not by a long shot.

As far as I knew, there wasn't another soul on the planet who had. 'So, what was an extra uncontested billion-dollar a year market worth to a Fortune 38 Company doing 14 billion a year?' I wasn't any accountant, but two and a half million dollars seemed to me peanuts!

There was a long silence. Real long. All that kept running through my head was that proverbial adage…, the cornerstone of all negotiations, 'The one who talks first loses!' Boy that one took over and now began playing.

It seemed like several minutes, though it wasn't anything close to that, until I could hear my stupid mouth breaking the silence, saying, "What's your position?"

That was one of the only times in memory, that Dianne was glad to ever hear me talk. She appeared relieved, that I broke the silence. Without hesitation, she switched modes and went directly on the defensive, "We can't pay that. That's not realistic Steve!"

Oh, how glad I was to hear her throw on that part about being realistic. That was my middle name, and now more than ever, I was compelled to explain realism from my view point. "Dianne, I hope you don't mind, but I would like to justify my starting figures, and try and get a feel for where the Company is. I can substantiate my numbers if you let me."

"As we had discussed on the previous occasion, I know you guys sell about a hundred million oil filters per year. And we have already acknowledged the fact that the gross volume for the entire North American market was somewhere north of four hundred million units per year. Right?"

She had been listening intently and was agreeable thus far. At this juncture, I also knew the approximate number of the total gross sales, broken down on a company by company basis as well.

Keep in mind now, that I never saw this information in print. I compiled it over a lengthy period of time and this information was exclusively given to me by word of mouth. Nor at any time did Dianne or Kevin, or any of my other contacts ever pass along in writing these facts and figures authenticating this data. For the most part I was relegated to take these figures at face value, and hope that they were accurate. Assumptions and educated guesswork was about all that I could rely upon for guidance.

The information that I sought in order to make an intelligent decision, was closely held..., exclusive to the industry, and never shared with the outside world. Nothing short of industrial espionage was going to pry that information loose, there was no way I could ever expect getting my hands on it. And Allied had already demonstrated that they would never divulge that to me..., despite what I was bringing into the deal.

"I know that this filter would be a valuable weapon for increasing Fram's market share, especially in the arena of the installed sales market where you have little, to no presence, Dianne."

"So how do you justify those figures you gave me, they are way more than we can ever pay you," she added, again for emphasis.

Well I began, "Jiffy Lube claims that they do fifty-million changes per year, and that's just one quick lube franchise! The trend for installed sales is on the rise and it's going to eventually bury the 'do it yourselfer' market and you guys along with it, if you don't tool up real soon. You have no hope of cracking this market. You know why, because you don't have a product capable of doing it. That is, unless you team up with me and my patent and everything else that I've brought to the table!" I spoke those words, rife with conviction. They were by no means meant to be taken as a bluff or to be misconstrued as false bravado. The entire plan was mine. That was my contribution. Their part was to make the thing..., market it and get it into the distribution chains that they already controlled. As for future growth..., any fool understands that success begets success.

Her reply was a sobering, "I don't think so."

"What do you mean?" I said, trying my damnedest to get her to see my point. Purolator with its Group Seven filter, along with a whole host of other private label brands that it manufactures is doing seventy percent of the existing installed sales business. Champion Laboratories for the most part is picking up the rest of the pie. Installed sales is out pacing the DIY market sixty..., forty as we speak. What do you mean, I don't think so!"

"We just don't view the market the way you do Steve and are not prepared to pay you that kind of money for your patent," she said. Not a single word of mine had registered and I knew it.

Thinking to myself, 'shoot she is stubborn, and so foolish to boot.' I quickly reevaluated the situation and took my focus off of her for a moment, realizing that she wasn't acting as an independent thinker in this matter. It was becoming more and more obvious that she was getting her marching orders from the top. I knew that her orders were coming from Allied/Automotive, a multi-billion-dollar automotive division. Purveyors of Fram oil filters, Autolite spark plugs, Garret turbochargers, Horton clutch fans, Bendix brakes and air dryers... There was a whole laundry list of brand name products that made this one of the most powerful divisions of its kind on the planet.

The reality was, I had my calculations based upon my diligent research, but unless Allied/Automotive was willing to share exactly what they were going to bring to the table, I'd just be left with educated guessing. By this stage in the game, there was little doubt that they were doing their best to keep me in the dark. You would think that I'd be privy to at least something..., since I signed the same non-disclosure agreements they had. But I have to be honest with you, during the course of our relationship this Company never shared anything with me that I would ever consider proprietary or secret.

Just so you know, if either one of us were accused of violating those agreements, either party was capable of dragging the other into Federal Court.

Obviously, the Company wasn't being very fair, by expecting me to put an actuarial value on my life's work without getting more of a definitive look at what they were prepared to do for me! So needless to say, that left me in the precarious position of starting high, and then do something I wasn't so happy about at all…, stalling. I had to stall, at least for the moment, until I could gather more information. My best hunch was, that the longer our relationship went on, perhaps the more I could learn.

Just so you know, based upon my very limited information, it was way too early for me to even consider putting a value on my patent and intellectual property. At this juncture, I found myself being inexorably drawn into a game that I was now, obliged to play. Their game plan was to paint me into some corner.

For starters, the engineers were still floundering and had to yet to develop a realistic prototype…, and who knew where that was going? And the Company's list of foibles, just went on from there. But the catch…, and there was one… They had now decided that they wanted what I owned rather badly, despite all their playing 'hard to get.' So now, to add insult to injury, my test marketing, or pre-licensing agreement was about to run out on them. This situation clearly made them uneasy, since they had already done a pretty good job of sizing me up and had come up with the most important element of the deal…, me. They knew I wasn't the kind to go quietly into their night.

The scary thing about negotiating with an automaton like Dianne, is that no matter how convincing, or well-grounded in logic your argument might be, they're likely to never see the light, it's simply not their function. Even Kevin, who had his whole heart and soul into this project, and at least by my standards, was a formidable marketer, was totally incapable of reigning her in.

It wasn't like I was Michael Jordan here, about to sit down to talk with Nike. I could feel myself beginning to fold a bit…, and I did everything in my power to resist the temptation.

"Ok, I see that you're not even going to give me a counter offer, so despite my better judgment and as a sign of good faith, I'll bid against myself. One point five million and twenty-five cents a filter."

Again, there was a long silence. And again, like a stupid ass, I broke it.

I was a better salesman than she could ever have hoped to of been, but still I violated a major tenant of sales. I spoke first. But before I berate myself, let's realize that this wasn't like the negotiations that you read about in the Wall Street Journal or something. That's so much bull, where you have big against big, 'so where's the disadvantage in something like that,' I wondered.

Heck, this enterprise didn't even resemble the pabulum I was used to practicing in residential real estate sales. At this point the only basis for negotiation went something like this, 'hey I'm real big, and we both know that you're puny, besides you have a snowballs chance in hell of ever producing this filter and getting it onto the shelves without us, so whata' ya going to do? Fish or cut bait?'

"Oh," she said. "Steve…, your still way too high. We aren't prepared to compensate you like that at all."

The 'at all' part had a somewhat chilling effect. Maybe what my friend, the ex-chief engineer of Purolator had told me was correct. Maybe his analysis wasn't tainted against me, just because I was a rank amateur playing now in the big leagues. I just couldn't know for sure.

'And what if Kevin was right?' I had tried to pump him about the money on a couple of occasions, trying to gauge the Company's position on the matter, but he wasn't all that much help, other than eluding to what the Company 'might' be willing to pay me. I had all but dismissed his responses, because he didn't appear like he was capable of giving me their bottom line. The fact was, I still was convinced that their figures were ridiculously low. So as this exercise dragged on, it was becoming more apparent that I hadn't any palpable choice left in the matter, and I knew it. …More importantly, she knew it.

However, do to all the chaos which surrounded the project, time was still on my side. It was only the middle of March and she would be gone starting tomorrow for at least ten days. Perhaps I could buy some time. Put her off until such point that I could justify my giving in to their meager offer, whatever that might prove to be. The only option I could exercise for the moment, was not to come crawling.

I could put up some carefully thought out resistance and they've already come to expect much out of me. However, the bottom line was this…. I knew better than to push them too hard, or they unquestionably would try and eat me alive. That's what really scared me about this tight rope act.

"Well Dianne, I still think that a million and a half dollars up front is reasonable. And like I said, I want twenty-five cents a copy," restating my position.

"I don't think it's doable at these numbers," she replied.

I interjected quickly to end the thing, "I'm sure that we'll be doing business, but I need to get some more information from you guys in order to make a better decision. Why don't we let it keep until you get back from Russia?"

She then replied, "I'd like to, but there is that little matter I mentioned to you about last week."

"What was that?" I said, playing dumb.

"You know, Larry Bossidy. Larry wants to know where we stand on this situation."

"Oh… That's easy," I replied. "Tell him that I am sure that we are going to go into business together, but I need to be better informed before arriving at any final numbers. Tell him that we are gonna do business and tell him that I'm trying to figure out what would be fair compensation for positioning his Company in a billion-dollar a year business."

"Okay if that's what you say. I'll just have to pass that information along to him. I'll be calling you as soon as I get back from my trip," as she hung up the phone.

At this juncture I had to seriously wonder, 'Was she really telling me the truth about Larry Bossy's interest?' All I knew about Larry, was that he was busy attempting to turn this industrial manufacturing behemoth into a productive streamlined modern company poised for the twenty first century. At least that's what the papers said. All I knew, was that he was in the midst of gutting tens of thousands of jobs at a clip, and he was bailing blood by the bucketful.

'So, how in God's name could he have the slightest interest in an oil filter I wondered? And if he was, how was he going to pull out his wallet and pay me what was reasonable under the present circumstances?'

I knew that my idea was great and could be very lucrative for the Company, but does a guy running a fourteen-billion-dollar entity with eighty thousand employees care about my deal? I didn't tend to think so. But, I couldn't rule it out entirely. Certainly, he knew how to make money, coming over from General Electric Capital, a protégé of the vaunted CEO, Jack Welsh. Maybe by some chance he saw the opportunity. I could only hope so…, yet judging by my handlers, I'd lay odds he was clueless as to what this filter could actually add to his bottom line.

So, when it came to Larry, I rather believed that Dianne was playing to my ego, trying to blow smoke up my pant leg.

At last our interlude was over. I could again focus my attention on what Kevin was orchestrating with the marketing team, and once again I could begin filling in any gaps for Gary Bilski, the lead engineer in charge of the product's development. One thing remained a constant, this Company was like a kid playing with a pack of matches, it was a full-time job putting out the fires of their making.

CHAPTER 8
A GUEST OF HONOR

This year's gray winter seemed to move along with an almost deliberate expedience as the trees laden with bud signaled the impending change. However, in stark contrast, the project appeared to be stuck in a deep freeze, like some ice clogged river, struggling within its banks trying to reach the open sea. At least that was my perception of it all.

It was now April and Fram had all but consumed the one hundred and eighty days I had granted them under the pre-licensing agreement, resulting in more questions than answers.

Over the last few months I had logged several conversations with Kevin in which I had expressed my deep concerns regarding the engineering department. For some inexplicable reason, they seemed incapable of developing a suitable delivery system for the filter as of yet. I remained baffled over the situation only to turn to Kevin, who was well aware of the situation, but still unable to give me much solace on that score, himself having no authority over the engineers.

I don't know how the one was related to the other, but for some reason, it made it all the more unbearable for me to muster the courage and ask him how his department was faring on the marketing front. It was as if I was shell-shocked, afraid to open my eyes for fear of discovering what further mess might be brewing.

For the most part, rarely did I press him beyond his reassurance of, "We're on track Buddy, it's coming together." Invariably, that would be the response I would receive whenever I would ask him, 'how things were moving along?'

Really, he wasn't doing anything different than I hadn't done on a thousand different occasions at my job. Like, when I would reassure my real estate clients during their transactions that everything with their deal was going to turn out all right, even though at the time, things sure didn't appear that way.

To me, a deal was a deal, so what if mine was wearing a different face? 'Should that of mattered?' To trust was to trust. The way I saw it, Kevin was still the Sherpa, leading the trek up Mount Allied.

Until, one day during a particular phone discussion without so much as a hint, came, "Hey Stevie! We're making pretty good headway man. Things are starting to shape up around here. I know it may not look like it to you, but believe me, we are," he said beginning to plead his case.

"Anyway, we're going to have a major marketing session scheduled in the not too distant future, looks like the second week of April," he said offering me a peek under the tent.

"Oh really?" I said, not wanting my enthusiasm level to rise too quickly despite the fact I was in dire need of some encouragement from somebody, and preferably someone from Allied. I was becoming desperately weary of the game. As if it wasn't enough just to watch the engineers grope along, I had to be ever mindful of Dianne lurking in the background. She had the uncanny ability to reemerge at any time and without warning, as the bungling 'Attila the Hun.'

"Yup. That's right," he continued. "And I think the right thing to do is to invite you up, so you can see for yourself what's going on around here." Again, he paused for a moment as if he needed to collect his thoughts. "You can consider yourself, the guest of honor. How does that sound to ya Buddy?" he said more than happy to move over and share the stage with me.

"Well, what do you think?" as he gushed with enthusiasm.

The moment had decidedly won me over and I could suddenly feel my confidence in the Company returning. The very prospect of witnessing first-hand how a world leader such as Fram went about the structuring of a marketing campaign thrilled me to no end. I couldn't wait to see how things were done.

The truth of the matter, I considered myself more of a marketing guy than an inventor. In my way of thinking there were lots of people out there with patents but were their ideas good enough to have a life of their own, was the real question! I always viewed the inventors journey this way, 'to invent something is one thing, to be able to successfully market it, is yet quite another.'

Once again, I allowed myself to be transported through the haze and past the swirling mixed signals that ran constantly through my mind. Again, I let the trust I had placed in Kevin propel me yet deeper into another facet of the dream. 'Was it was coming true?' I wasn't sure, I could only hope.

The last time we had talked, Kevin had told me to give him a call in about a week, and he'd be able to let me know when the meeting was gonna be scheduled. At that time, he would be able to formally invite me up as a team member. He was just that way about this stuff, like sending me out formal letters of invitation every time I was invited up. I got a kick out of him and it made me feel so welcomed.

'Oh, I know,' I'm not that much of a clam digger... In all probability it was more a formality to cover his butt than anything else, but I chose not to view it that cynically. Besides, he was a heck of a lot more efficient than the other two departments I had been dealing with, and I still thought it rather a nice touch.

Finally, after several tries, I got through to him sometime around the end of the first week in April. "Man, you are a hard guy to reach," I boomed into the phone. "I sure hope your wife has an easier time tracking you down than I do!"

"Hey, my friend, how are you?" he chimed back, glad for the call. "And you need not bring my wife into this, she does all right for herself! She's got my private number and you don't!" he said, busting me. As far as I could tell, there wasn't any such line.

"Oh, by the way I'm glad you called," his playful tone becoming more serious as the master delegator in him began to emerge once again.

"I have this marketing meeting firmed up for the eleventh of this month at nine o'clock. Can you make it!?" Now he was sounding more like my handler, asking me if I could make the drop.

Not giving it a second thought, I shot back, "Of course! I wouldn't miss this for the world. It's going to be awesome," I said, unable to hold back my excitement.

"I don't know about awesome. I guess it depends on what you mean by that, but it's happening, and you need to be here for it," he said.

"Kev?"

"Yeah?"

"I'm not trying to bust you, but how come you seem so torqued up about this meeting? You're almost acting like you did back in September, you know? Before I put on that presentation in front of all those people. Remember?"

"Of course, I remember! How could of I forgotten something like that already, you nudnick!" I was beginning to get the feeling that this meeting was going to have serious implications, as Kevin made his intentions known in between the fun and games.

"Stevie, in all seriousness Buddy, this meeting is the first formal meeting of its kind for this project…."

"What!?" I could feel myself wanting to jump into the phone. "What do you mean by that? You mean to tell me that you guys in marketing haven't met over this thing yet!" Fearing the worst, I began to feel myself coming a little unglued.

He didn't allow me to run much further with that thought and uncorked me before I built up anymore steam. "Hey Steve, calm down would ya! It's not like we haven't met yet or anything. What I was trying to say was that we haven't assembled like this before, you know as a team. It's not like there hasn't been any smaller focus groups set up to look at the different areas of the process. Like I told you, this thing is under way. Okay?"

Feeling a little embarrassed I said, "I'm sorry Kevin, I didn't mean to dump on you. It's just what your Company's been putting me through…"

Fully capable of understanding where I was coming from, he didn't let me get another word out before saying, "I know. Unfortunately, you have been through a little more than either of us had expected. Who knew? But trust me, before you know it, we'll put this all behind us. This thing is going to be a blockbuster!" Well that's all I had to hear. I didn't like getting all worked up anyway, and least of all, with him.

"So anyway, what I wanted to tell you is this, when you come up your gonna be able to join in with pretty much the entire marketing team. I thought you'd like that since you're such a stickler for details," he said beginning to laugh. "Besides, it's still your play book that we're running with and I feel that you are entitled to see what we're doing with it!"

I felt like a jerk distrusting him back there a moment ago, even though I hadn't actually verbalized it. For now, that left us nothing much else to go over, except a quick rundown of the meeting's itinerary along with some brief housekeeping issues.

Sensing that his other irons in the fire needed tending, I started to say good-bye. As usual I couldn't resist, "Can we meet for breakfast, Tuesday morning? I think it would be great if you could bring along your boss, I'd love to meet him." As of yet, I had never met Kevin's boss, Peter Ross.

"That sounds like a great idea, Steve. I'll tell you what, if it's doable, we certainly will. But right now, I can't commit to it. All right? I know that the both of us will be pretty busy setting this thing up, so call me Monday and I'll let you know."

The morning of the big meet found me sitting by my lonesome staring out onto a busy intersection in Rumford. From my perch high upon a stool, I nursed a cup of coffee in the relative peace behind the plate-glass window of the restaurant. I wasn't thinking about much, just watching the commuter traffic build to a crescendo. The early morning sun brightened up my little part of the world as it came streaming in from the southeast, radiating the promise of a new adventure that would begin in about an hour or so.

I bent my head down to take a lazy sip when I heard that distinctive rumble out front. It was a cross between the sound of jet turbo and a coffee grinder. Slowly, I lifted my head, just in time to catch the profile of all seventy-feet of magnificence, as it strolled on up to the intersection. The vibes emanating from the large Cat engine stirred my soul, as she purred from her moorings, secure under the hood of the long nosed Peterbilt 379 conventional. I caught myself remarking out loud, 'My God what a glorious piece of engineering! Double sleeper with the dual stacks, all chromed out against the backdrop of the jet black Imron paint job.

'Someday' I thought. 'Someday when my filter would be nearly as common as standard equipment on big diesels like this, all across North America I'll be able to get me one just like this.' It would be my crowning achievement for my patent to be accepted by the heavy-duty diesel community and at least by my reckoning, that day didn't seem too far around the corner. Hopefully upon its' arrival, it would be my ticket to roam the boulevard once again. This time in style.

All to quickly the light changed and the rig gently lurched forward, the driver swinging her wide, so he could make the tight right-hand turn leading down the ramp onto the service road. With deft precision he guided her onward, as her huge trailer followed obediently behind. Just before the trailer dipped out of sight, the angle of the sun caught the shiny stainless-steel barn doors, throwing a beam directly my way, sending me back…, back into deep contemplative thought. Once again, I began to ponder all that I had been through these last few months and all that it entailed for me to be having this solitary cup of coffee here in Rumford.

The receptionist at the front desk extended me a cheerful greeting as she asked me to sign the visitors book. For an instant I fumbled for the pen that I swore was tucked away on the inside of my coat pocket.

"Would you like a pen sir?" came an obliging voice.

"Ah, no Mam. I have one on me here someplace. Thank you." Looking down at the sign in sheet made me chuckle inside. Deliberately, as I signed my name, I stared at the blank where it asked, 'what company I represented.' Thinking about it for a moment, I wrote it down with a contented smile, 'Myself.'

"Young man. Is there someone in particular you are here to see?"

"Yes Mam. A Mr. Kevin Gill," I replied, looking down at my watch. I was a good fifteen minutes early.

"Okay. "I'll buzz him for you. You may have a seat over there, if you'd like.

The answer came back that he would be down in a few minutes, so I excused myself, preferring to wait outside and take in the brilliant spring day. It was a good while before Kevin came walking out the double security doors after me. His white cotton shirt sleeves already rolled up, a sign he had already been workin'.

With outstretched hand and big smile, he greeted me, saying, "I know what you mean, I rather be out here, than cooped up in there for the rest of the day. So, how's everything going Buddy?" putting his arm around my shoulder giving me a good squeeze. "Was your room and everything all right?"

"Yeah sure," came my reply. "I hope all is well with you and your family."

"Ah, thanks for asking. They're all doing fine," he said.

In short order he moved right to the heart of the matter… business. "Hey, we have some time before the meeting gets underway, let's run upstairs. I gotta check up on a couple of things. Then I want to stop in and introduce you to my boss, Peter. He's a pretty good guy, I think you'll like him."

I followed behind Kevin as once again he led me through his domain. We mounted the stairs, blowing past cohorts and finally past Jodi, his secretary, ending up in his little ten by ten control center. I enjoyed a candid moment as I spied this frenetic being pounding out an interoffice e-mail and returning calls. Commenting to myself, 'this poor guy's office didn't go very far in dignifying the zeal that drove him to produce like he did for this Company.' For the very first time I understood in no uncertain terms why he was always so hurried on the phone with me. He was truly a mad man.

Giving a courtesy knock on the already opened door, Kevin walked us into his boss's office. Bent over a pile of paper work was a relatively young man sporting nappy head of pre-maturing gray hair.

"Hey Peter!" he announced in a respectful tone, "I'd like you to meet someone!"

His friendly eyes smiled at me as he stuck out his hand, "You must be Steve Moor. The inventor."

"Yes sir," came my somewhat stiff reply.

At that moment Kevin chimed in, "That's not really necessary Steve, the sir stuff. Pete's a real regular guy. Aren't you Pete?" as we all began to smile.

"I'm glad you could make it today, he said. "We have a lot of ground to cover, it should be real interesting."

His room was at least twice the size as Kevin's and he must of rated, because it was also carpeted. Strewn about the room were neat little piles of papers and folders. For lack of a better guess, they must have represented the different projects he was overseeing. His system kinda reminded me of my own, where I'd have my stuff lying all over the floor. No shot intended, it must have worked! After all, he was the Vice President of Marketing for Fram. Not too shabby a post for a guy in his mid-forties.

I watched askance, as they momentarily huddled together, trading in hushed tones something about Quaker State and Slick-50. I was so preoccupied with my own concerns that I simply wasn't paying their conversation much heed at the time. And before you knew it, we all began shooting the breeze regarding some marketing questions which I had brought up.

Then I hit him with my pet peeve, the 'installed sales market'.

"Peter," I began, "What's your feelings concerning the installed sales market?"

Not having a clue what I was driving at, he answered, "What do you mean by that? That's an awful broad question."

My objective was to get out of him first hand, how Fram viewed this marketplace and their role in it. I felt that it was crucial for both the viability of this filter as well as for the future of Fram to be heading aggressively in this direction.

"Well Peter, what I meant by that is this. Jiffy Lube as of right now, in 1995, is doing fifty million oil changes per year. And from what I've been told, Fram sells approximately one hundred million oil filters per year in total. Give or take.

"I am not a true insider like you guys, and I don't pretend to be one either, but I have sufficient knowledge to realize that the market is going that way. The installed sales market is only going to pick up momentum in the next few years. And if I'm wrong, please tell me. 'Cause I don't care if you hurt my feelings, I'm a big boy."

"It's not about hurting your feelings Steve. You are right, but..." I braced myself for the 'but' part. In my experience the 'but' part was rarely intended to go my way, nor was it seldom reassuring.

I was desperately trying to get out of him if they planned on using this new filter of mine to gain market share in this arena. Up till now, Kevin was straight forward with me about nearly everything, but somehow, I detected him waffling whenever I brought up the subject of installed sales. I was taking a calculated shot by going over his head, by going right to the horse's mouth…, but I had to. Besides, I'm sure Kevin realized that I had to be true to my own vision, even though we somewhat disagreed on that issue. 'At least I did it right in front of him,' I mused.

On the other hand, if Kevin had ever felt threatened by me or thought that I was some sort of a loose cannon type, he never would have allowed me to wander amongst the Fram machine as freely as I did.

Peter continued, "We aren't too keen about the installed sales market Steve. That just hasn't been our strength in the past." He said it so matter of factly, so as not to invite my further input which began to make me wonder. So, if I heard him right, he told me that I should find this day interesting, well, I sure hoped that he meant it. Because as far as I was concerned, now was as good as any time to start!

"How come you guys aren't so keen on installed sales? Are you that willing to let Purolator and Champion Labs have it all to themselves?" I asked, as my passion for that subject took hold of me.

"Well it's not as profitable, not by a long shot, at least compared to selling to the 'Do it Yourselfer's' in places such as Walmart and Pep Boys. The profit margins on those filters sold in the Installed Sales Filter Market are so thin, it's hardly worth our effort Steve," he said, indulging what he must of reasoned was my naïve line of questioning. After all, I was an outsider. Right?

Somehow, I still didn't quite get it. 'Why would the top filter outfit in the world be so insistent upon chasing an ever-shrinking market?' I just had to know, so I decided to have one more run at him before letting the situation drop. I had to be careful here, obviously, the last thing I needed, was to get off on the wrong foot with Kevin's boss! "So, Peter, I know you're a busy guy and the meeting is going to start in a few minutes, but wouldn't you…., I mean Fram, like a surefire avenue that would allow greater entrée into this market?"

I just stood there and studied the look on his face a moment, before concluding it was safe to go a little further. "You know Peter, if Fram institutes this marketing program right, this filter will enable you guys to not only meet your margin requirements, but it will enable you to increase your unit sales volume substantially as well! And as a bonus Pete, the marketing campaign will breathe new life into the Fram brand name all at the same time!" There it was, I had said it. I had laid it out for him in nearly one breath!

Indulging me for what I felt might be for the last time, he said, "That would be great Steve. I guess we'll have to take a closer look, at some other point in the future." My heart dropped, as his voice trailed off, as I did my best not to show my utter disappointment. I knew where I was, for God's sake!

My idea had been circulating around this place in one-way shape or form since January of 94'. And don't kid yourself, I was keeping track of the time! Sixteen months had elapsed since I had put that first call into Kevin and I was certain that Peter was one of the very first to know.

I had enough sense to realize that our little chit chat was over, and I was beginning to get scared. Somehow, I got a nasty little feeling that going into business with this outfit was gonna be like pushing the Queen Mary with a row boat.

At about ten minutes of nine, Kevin and I walked shoulder to shoulder into a large conference room located on the east side of the second floor. There were already several people seated around a large conference table talking in low tones, sipping on diet soda and coffee. As we entered the room all eyes turned automatically toward the new arrivals…, us. Before Kevin had a chance to introduce me, I had already greeted everyone with a bashful smile and a twinkle in my eye. I can't emphasize it enough, I was once again in their world, only a visitor. It was imperative that I earn their individual respect first hand. My actions and the way I conducted myself carried much greater weight than my fleeting notoriety as the inventor ever would have.

Kevin, the gracious, yet commanding master of ceremonies bellowed out, "Good morning guys, I'd like to introduce you to Steve Moor, the inventor. He's been working all along with both myself and with Gary in engineering, so please consider him as another valued member of the team."

'What could I of added to that introduction?' It was part and parcel why Kevin and I got along so well. He was remarkably secure in whom he was and the job in which he had set out to accomplish. In a starry eyed kinda way, I likened him to a young Lee Iacocca during his formative years at Ford Motorcars. Maybe that analogy was way over reaching as to the comparison, but what did I know.

I didn't recognize anybody, as I scanned the room except for Gary. Before I realized, he grabbed my hand with gusto, as much to say all was well with the world. "So how are ya doing Steve!"

"I'm doing fine Gary. How about you?"

What I really wanted to do, was to squeeze his hand until it turned blue. Then ask him a question, 'like what the heck was going on with the engineering department!' Before I knew it, I had become a prisoner of this insane engineering flashback…

When I had left Gary in mid-December, I was told that the research on the delivery system would be in full swing after the start of the new year. I was convinced that unless there was some sort of a miracle, the engineering department would be tripping over itself in a vain attempt to do it their way. They were under a mandate to develop this system using the cheapest and easiest way possible. To my way of thinking, they were only destined to fail.

Around late January, early February, my premonitions were confirmed. Unfortunately, I had been proven correct…, and I didn't want to be.

According to Gary, "Steve, we've been working with this paste that we made by mixing grease along with the dry micro power which you gave us, you know, the sample of MP 1100 from DuPont? When we put this paste into an oven and bring it up to temperature, say somewhere around 180° F, the same temperature as hot motor oil, it seems that the grease doesn't want to cooperate. It's not readily melting at that temperature. After we boost the temperature up significantly it begins to melt and forms a gooey mass, sittin' there on the bottom of the can."

Due to the engineering mayhem out in Perrysburg, Ron Rohrback, the Ph.D. from Allied's research facility in Morristown began reaching out to me, hoping that I could figure this thing out for them.

I can remember distinctly that this PhD chemical genius didn't have anything much to offer, in way of a solution for their failing delivery system. The engineering phase was approaching meltdown status, and Gary had a real hot mess on his hands.

Just so you know, when I first met Ron, his name was nowhere to be found on a single oil filter patent. As of today, he is the proud recipient of several additive treated oil filter patents, much of which genisised from my IP and trade secrets. You know, I've always regretted not deposing him.

'So, was I hearing these self-appointed innovators correctly?' Because, I thought I was! They were both telling me, that my filter's delivery system was a sloppy mess…, and it didn't look like it was ever going make it off the launching pad.

But wait a minute! This delivery system was Fram's brainchild now, it wasn't mine! Remember, cost, ease of manufacture, Allied's self-imposed production constraints?! For God's sake, the engineers had strayed far afield of my design platform, and that's exactly why they were failing!

"What about the various delivery systems that I disclosed to you guys, Gary?" I asked, searching for an answer.

"Oh, we've looked at it a bit, but it also ended running down the media and settling down the side of the can."

Jumping in, I couldn't help it, "So did you try spraying the filter media under pressure like I had specified?" Right about then I was feeling like I had called a plumber to put in a sink and he put in a toilet instead! That's exactly why I felt so helpless. Rarely if ever, did I have to call upon people to fix things, or do things for me. I was so used to being able to fend for myself. But this was totally different. These guys were supposedly the biggest and the best in the world at what they did. Besides, it wasn't like I could go out and make my own oil filter and get it on the shelf like a bottle of designer salad dressing.

"Well my God man, why didn't you spray this stuff on under pressure? You got to impregnate this stuff into the media's matrix on the dirty side of the filter, just like I told you. Remember?"

He could sense my anguish and gave me some sort of excuse that they didn't have the equipment, or the time and money to devote to this enterprise. He carried on interminably, telling me, "Don't worry Steve, we'll figure it out, we've got time."

As our conversation progressed, I became decidedly more uncertain whether these guys would ever get this right, despite already having been spoon fed by me back in both in October and December!

It was nearly all I could bear, thinking about what might be taking place in the engineering lab. During this debacle, I carefully weighed all of my options. Yet, the timing still wasn't quite right for me to jump in and take control as their big-rig of failures headed straight for the ditch. So, I chose to bite my lip and watch the unfolding madness from the sidelines for just a while longer.

But no matter what…, no matter how impudent the engineering team would prove to be…, I still possessed the key that would insure that even they'd be able to make this thing work. I had still had a doozy of a *trade secret* that I'd end up force feeding them at the eleventh hour. It would come in the form of a little silver can…, and it would end up saving the entire project.

In the final analysis, this situation would require my direct intervention in order to save the engineers from themselves. And that's exactly what I'd end up doing.

…My head a spinning, I pulled my hand out of his and found a seat across the table from the lead engineer. Ironically, before the marketing extravaganza would end, Gary would end up telling the marketing team all what Steve had brought that day…, in that little silver can.

Kevin was milling around the room still visiting with the various individuals now assembled. I sat off by myself, trying in vain to review the meeting's agenda, I was scarcely able to resist the interplay of the team members as they discussed the project. Looking down at my watch, I noticed that it was five minutes before the meeting was officially about to begin. Almost instinctively, I began to run down the list of attendees. To the best of my accounting, there were six people missing. Somehow Kevin must have caught my vibe, because mid-way through his conversation with one of the field reps he called out, "Has anybody seen Peter? He is coming, isn't he? And what about Dianne and Karen, and the others? It's almost nine." The group returned a blank stare, tendering a bunch of "I don't knows', they're all supposed to be here."

Just then Peter came through the door, chatting away with this attractive middle aged blonde woman. She was wearing a violet leather mini skirt and vest ensemble with yellow trim. Wow! That was certainly a bit racy, compared to the ivy league cotton attire I had seen so far around here. I had to stop for a minute and wonder if she was in violation of the dress code.

As they took their seats amongst us at the large conference table, Peter took the helm, asking the group if we had all been introduced. For my edification, he introduced the lady he had arrived with as Karen Borger, Fram's in house media expert. So far, she was the only woman in the crowd.

"Is everyone here yet?" he asked the group, trying to get the meeting underway. I heard somebody vouch for three of the absentees, but by my count, there was still one more person missing.

Just then, Kevin spoke up, "Anybody heard from Dianne yet? She's supposed to be here."

Again, reminiscent of the first meeting, there came an unsolicited barrage of commentary from the gallery, heading right her way.

In the middle of the flurry, I glanced over at Kevin for his reaction, only to be met with a stern look. Apparently, he hadn't asked for her whereabouts for my benefit, just so I could witness her co-workers skewer her from behind for the second time. Again, this crew like the last one, didn't hesitate to give it to her; in front of a me, a total stranger, no less!

I derived little consolation from the foray, knowing that I felt the same way towards her as did her peers. Nonetheless, I was glad to know that the storm brewing between us wasn't just something I had dreamt up.

Symptomatically, Dianne's superior, this time in the form of Peter Ross, came to her aid, excusing her tardiness due to some overriding business issue. What an enigma! And one I'd better learn to deal with, I reasoned! The very thought that it was my fate to negotiate with this individual was enough to steal the moment.

With all that behind us, Peter began to formally introduce the nine of us who had made it to the meeting thus far. To my thinking, it was quite a team, comprising first off of Peter and Kevin. Two of Fram's top ranking sales and marketing executives. Then there was Steve LaVellee another Fram marketing guy just under Kevin and a trusted cohort of his.

Geoffrey Skog, their senior in house graphic artist who was going to responsible for the graphic design of the new filter along with its newly designed box and support materials.

Karen Borger, an ad campaign specialist, responsible for the story boards and instrumental for the commercials that Fram was going to launch on behalf of the new filter. From what I could gather,

her job was crucial as to how the upper brass in Southfield, Michigan and Morristown, N.J. would later view this project.

There was Tom Taverna, senior field rep with whom Kevin was first chatting with earlier. A senior field rep who understood the retail market, having logged over twenty years handling major east coast accounts like R& S Strauss for Fram. Sitting next to him was another field rep of similar experience in that of Tim Lukasiewicz. Those two guys had been buzzing since I laid eyes on them. I wanted to make it a priority to get inside their heads before the day was out. I had done my own preliminary field studies gauging consumer demand, but I wanted to get a feel for how these guys saw things. No doubt these guys were pro's and could get a lot closer to the sources than I could ever hope to. I couldn't wait to see what they had to say about the whole thing!

The engineering department was represented by Gary Bilski, the senior engineer on the project. To round out the group, I was invited. The only non-AlliedSignal attendee, contributing to the group as only the inventor and visionary could.

Last but least…, there were the other three guys who were no shows, along with Dianne who was in the building somewhere, but unaccounted for.

In true AlliedSignal fashion, the group broke into its corporate rendition of the 'who's on first routine' again. You know, with the time keeper, scribe, etc. It was my second time watching it, and I have got to tell you, it looked as foolish as it did the first time when the engineers performed it for me.

Looking down at meetings agenda, I soon realized why Kevin had asked for Dianne's whereabouts. No wonder! She was slated to speak first.

I was encouraged to actually see it in print, the first matter of discussion was in fact, "The Bossidy Meeting!" I guess what she was telling me back in March must of had an element of truth to it, after all. Larry was truly aware of this project and about my filter!

Maybe she wasn't just hyping me after all!

I couldn't help it, but I was really proud of the fact that the CEO of a mega corporation like AlliedSignal was aware of the birth of my new product. For the briefest of moments, I allowed myself to indulge in a fantasy, wishing that I could one day meet personally with him, perhaps someday over lunch; especially after the filter proved itself a success, on a balance sheet of course. I would have considered it an honor to have met with him.

Suddenly, that fantasy came to a screeching halt as my foolish emotions gave way to the hard facts. 'Hey wait a minute!' He didn't know about this project merely because he was some benevolent benefactor. Or because it made him feel good to pay attention to the budding development of a new oil filter. No, that wasn't it at all! This thing had the potential to reinvigorate the sleepy Fram brand name as well as position him in a market that could approach a billion dollars a year worth of new revenue. That's why he was so interested.

With that, a smile came to my face. 'Yes, thank God, Larry was after all watching the show.' Albeit he was watching it from afar, atop his perch back at headquarters, but make no mistake, he was still watching it.

So, if I was aware of this revelation, it only stood to reason that all of the little workers involved along the way must of been aware of this fact as well. 'Gee,' that was a sobering thought. It kinda put me somewhat at ease, as I began to recall the time in Gary's car, when I let him know that "I'd go to Bossidy if I had to!"

'Well that's good!' I mused. That promise I made to him back there must of had some teeth in it after all. Perish the thought. But in the event that I needed Larry's help, he'd at least know what I'd be talking about. I could only pray that it would never have to come to that, but if I had to, it was a promise I intended on keeping.

I sorely wanted to analyze the next two issues slated on the agenda, but before I had gotten a chance, Kevin had deftly nudged Peter out of the way, changing the flow of the meeting. And he wasn't doing it to save Dianne's bacon either. His intent was to focus the groups energy towards the task before us. Believe me when I tell you, this project had thoroughly gotten into Kevin's blood! And I'd like to remind you of a little something here, if it wasn't for his passion this meeting would have never of taken place! I was just hoping against hope that he'd be able to infect Fram with his enthusiasm.

At that juncture he started to mention something about Southfield. I didn't rightly know at the time what Southfield meant exactly, except it was a town in Michigan. And I wouldn't have known even that much, if I hadn't dropped a load of office furniture out there years back. So quickly, as not to miss what he was about to say, I scanned the other two topics that Dianne was responsible for. I dearly wanted to see what role she'd play and how she would function in front of this group in light of our tenuous relationship.

While straining to listen, I persisted in reading the next two headings when I stumbled upon the part, "Test Market Agreement Status."

'Hey, wait a minute!' For a moment I forgot about everyone else in the room. I couldn't believe what she was skipping out on. It was her duty right up front to discuss the status of the inventor with the Company! In layman's terms, that meant that she was supposed to report on how we were progressing towards a final agreement in front of this very group. Well..., we weren't even close. As a matter of fact, she had summarily stopped talking with me!

'Oh,' I thought, 'maybe, just maybe, it would come out in front of the group that our talks had broken down and that Fram was proceeding with an entire marketing plan for which they had no idea what my compensation would be.

In my opinion, that shouldn't of been a variable left up in the air at this late date, because my compensation needed to be figured into their cost of production by now! And besides, they really didn't have the right to be planning the future of something they didn't own as of yet!

I realized it was a long shot, but perhaps our inability to agree at this late date would indict her, and just maybe..., she would have to be replaced. 'Ah', it was just wishful thinking on my part. As it would turn out, this Company wasn't aware of the collision course it was on.

Predictably, Dianne was nowhere to be found and it looked like she was off the hook once again.

Immediately Kevin started talking to Karen, asking her how she was coming along with the story board, for the brand-new television commercial that she was working on. I listened intently to the information, as it started to swirl about the room, trying my best to glean every last detail of what was being said. From what I could gather, there was going to be a crucial presentation that was scheduled to be put on in Southfield before too long. Caught somewhere between suspense and ignorance, I garnered Kevin's attention and proceeded to blurt out a question. "Excuse me Kevin, I know we must have touched upon it before, but are you guys really going to make a television commercial for this filter?"

From across the table I spied Karen smiling at me, knowing she had caught my childlike delight.

"Yes, that's right Steve. I told you that we were," defending his attention to detail. Well, I guess he had mentioned it before, but it wasn't like it was so much a reality then.

"Okay Kev," came my reply. I have one more quick question on something I'm not quite up to speed on." "Go ahead." He replied.

"What is this Southfield, that keeps popping up?"

At that point Peter jumped in, wanting to move along. "Steve..., Southfield is where AlliedSignal's Automotive Aftermarket Corporate Headquarters are located. It's a suburb close to Detroit." He went on to say that it located out there so it could be in close proximity to the big three auto makers. Something to the effect that it made it easier for the Company to stay in close contact with their major customers.

Again, the exchange between the three of them heated up, as they feverishly discussed the project's budget. What I heard them talking about didn't make good sense.

'Why?' Because it didn't!

As I listened, I got more nervous by the moment. Oh, their intentions were well meaning..., but from the sounds of it, they didn't have any concrete source of funding for the project as of yet! I couldn't help but to recall how the engineers had been going through the same motions back in December, as they tried to figure out how to manufacture this thing on a shoestring. Never did I want to believe that this same demon would be found here as well. I wanted to listen in more, but I almost couldn't, because my heart was so heavy with doubts now, I thought it might explode.

I remarked to myself, 'guess that's why I never really had the nerve to press Kevin how his department was doing over these last few months when I would call.'

Burying my head in the meeting's agenda I read on, looking for refuge while staring right at the... "Engineering Update"!

'Oh God,' I prayed. Not wanting to face what the engineer intended on sharing this morning. He still had to be behind schedule, and I knew it. Before I had an opportunity to reflect upon another thought, I felt myself being swept away into the throws of another one of those engineering flashbacks.

Pondering the situation, I stared right through him as he sat across the table from me. He appeared very much at ease, taking everything in stride. I gathered that to him, his plane ride out here from Ohio was just another pleasant junket the Company had sent him on.

Don't get me wrong, I really liked him. But the delivery system that had been entrusted to his care was a far cry from being completed. Believe me, the last thing on my mind was to make this personal.

As I fumbled through the meeting's agenda, desperately trying to figure things out, I happened upon page seven. There it was, the time line for the entire project, laid out in plain sight. The plant tooling was scheduled to get under way in less than three weeks, putting us into the first week of May. There was no way!!!

It just so happened that three weeks prior to this morning's gathering, I had sent off a certified letter to Kevin. The letter memorialized delivery system that I had gone over in quite some detail with Gary. The improvement was mine, therefore I felt it necessary to put all of my major contributions and upgrades in writing. I can remember sending this letter to cover my back door more than anything else.

Under the edict of the Proprietary Information Agreement, it was essential that I notify the Company in writing within sixty days of disclosing any proprietary information outside the scope of my patent. Technically, if there was a change to the delivery system for example, which might end up in the finished filter, it would be imperative that I document my authorship if the idea originated with me.

On the flip side, should the unthinkable occur… In the event that the Company had engaged in changing a major aspect of the filter in order to go around my patent in an orchestrated plan to defraud me…, well at least I'd have grounds for legal action such as patent infringement, misappropriation of trade secrets or falsifying the oath of inventorship.

Just so you know, later on down the road, Allied/Honeywell would wind up doing exactly what I had feared the most. And that's why I would eventually sue them.

That same letter dated March 16th, 1995 had another intended purpose as well. I purposely took the occasion to register my protest against the Teflon and grease delivery system which the engineers at this late date seemed so hopelessly enamored with. Additionally, for my future protection, I warned Kevin that the engineers had already wandered way outside the scope of my patent and trade secrets by exploring their own versions of a delivery system without ever telling me point blank that my system was not practicable.

As an aside, I took great pains to craft this letter as tactfully as possible and I had my reasons. Chiefly, because right before my eyes, I was watching the most prominent oil filter engineering team on the planet drop the ball!

'What should have been my response?'

'To fire a harsh warning shot across their bow?' Hardly! That would have only exacerbated the situation, and quite possibly, it would have killed the project with a simple; 'sorry, we tried, but it doesn't work!' I definitely got the impression that innovation didn't happen to come flying off the drawing board around here, and I didn't want my innovation winding up on the trash heap.

Things around there were just that tenuous. Lest you need reminding, the Senior VP of Engineering, was no big fan of mine and he was a simmering caldera, just waiting to blow. If Gary ever went cryin' to him over his foibles, I'd be thrown out on my ear quicker than you please.

So quite naturally, my sixth sense during this period was working overtime, trying to massage this situation on multiple fronts. Although the engineering team may of been excited about the possibilities, it still couldn't make up for their lack vision and their ineptitudes. Most importantly, the fire in their bellies needed to come up several notches, in order to overcome the simple challenge of how to get the stupid Teflon into the can!

From my observation, there was only one person truly dedicated enough to stoke the boilers on board this mighty ship…, and that of course was Kevin.

As the looming waves of chaos battered the mighty ship, it appeared that they left port without the necessary fuel to reach the other side. The fuel that they were lacking was start-up money… Somehow, captain Larry, thought he was going to make this voyage based upon 'good intentions'.

Yet my father, who was just a humble mailman, had enough sense to teach me early on, "that the road to hell was paved with good intentions."

The truth was, it would require a full-blown miracle to get the adequate funding in order to assure this project's success. And the forecast ahead… Well, it was calling for heavy seas.

Nearly an hour late, Dianne came bouncing through the doorway in her classic schoolgirl persona, clutching a load of disjointed papers to her breast, once again shielded by her notepad. Approaching Peter, she smiled briefly for the group then bent down and proceeded to whisper in his ear loud enough for the benefit of all, as to why she was late, and why she couldn't possibly be expected to stay.

Our scheduled break would have to wait as Peter handed the reins directly over to her charge. Her arrival presented me a toss-up between the lesser of two hurts. Having to endure watching her bobble through her duties or subject myself to the engineer, who would assure the group that everything was moving along smoothly, when I knew otherwise.

I keenly eyed her, as she selected a spot near the head of the table, though far enough off to side where I didn't have her in complete view. Unlike the others who had been speaking that morning, she chose to stand up while addressing the group. Laying down her files, she looked my way and as politely as you please, presented me this big smile with all the trimmings. "It's such a pleasure to see you this morning, Steve! Welcome to the group. I hope you had a pleasant trip up?"

All that would come to mind was, 'you chameleon.' I didn't hate her. Like I said before, that was against my principals to hate anyone. Besides, I truly didn't.

"Did I dislike her?" Yes of course, but not enough to wish her any harm. More than anything, I viewed her as some hell-bent automaton, who one minute was as nice as ice cream, and the next, a bombastic liar. To my chagrin, I had been unable to find a happy medium with Dianne, as it was impossible to predict which one of her personalities would be in control at any given time. It was like dealing with the seven faces of Dr. Loa.

"Dianne, why don't you start off by bringing us up to date with your last meeting with Larry Bossidy?" Peter asked.

"Well," she replied, as an air of self-importance started to rise within her, "I spoke with him not too long ago, before my trip to Russia." She traveled the world for this Company and wanted to make sure nobody in the room forgot that little detail.

"Larry expressed a lot of interest in the project and felt that it was just what the filter category needed. "More of a consumer driven product that would set itself apart from our premium Extra Guard line!" For a moment, I couldn't help but to think to myself, 'if you wanted Larry's attention boy, well now you got it.'

Hunching over, she placed her hands on the table, glancing from side to side before disclosing her next revelation to the group. It was written all over her face, she must have gotten pretty close to the flame the last time she had communicated with the boss, "You know, Mr. Bossidy has expressed his concerns to me that this filter must be brought in on schedule. It's very important that we meet the target date of 'Industry Week' this upcoming November, not like you all need reminding, but that's a little more than six months away. I'm sure you're all aware of that fact; nonetheless, I assured Mr. Bossidy that we'd be ready."

That was the of it! She exhausted the contents of the big meeting with the boss in nearly a single breath. I was amazed at how little real information was actually conveyed, as it certainly left me wanting. And looking around the room, it was apparent that the group shared those same sentiments as well, their faces communicating; 'yeah, so big deal, we already knew that much!'

Sensing her delivery had fallen flat, she added, "Oh and one more thing, he's really into this filter you know! He mentioned to me that he would like to have a part in how it's going to look," making an attempt to cheer the group onward.

Instantly, a symphony of unrestrained groans went up from amongst the crowd against any such thought.

Still trying to hold onto her enthusiasm for the boss's input she blurted out, "And yeah, he thinks the box should be gold!" Only to be met this time head on with some very real objections from the graphic artist and media expert.

Apparently, it had been enough to push most of the group over the edge, then outa nowhere it started. "Hey Dianne, does AlliedSignal's logo have to be plastered all over the filter and the box this time?"

I can't recall exactly who raised the issue, but it sure sounded like it had the makings of a mini Boston Tea Party. "Yeah Dianne," someone else chimed in, "We do our part around here and what do we get for it? A cut in our budget for all our efforts!"

'Wow…!' I had no idea what was brewing beneath the surface, waiting for her reply.

"You know good and well that everything we make gets the AlliedSignal logo placed on it," as she summarily skipped over the budget gutting. "Especially something like an oil filter!"

"Then does it have to be so conspicuous this time around? Because it's really going to detract from the art work on the filter," someone else bravely offered.

By now Peter had about enough of this, as he instructed the group that the Allied logo would not only appear, but it would be in accordance with the proper scale already set forth by the parent Company.

Come to think of it, they were absolutely right! I didn't want Larry's involvement in this process either, that certainly wasn't where he was needed. I would of much preferred that he just put his money where his mouth was, knowing full well that it would require a lot more than a gold box and an AlliedSignal logo to insure this filter's success.

Apparently, Geoffrey Skog had been diligently at work on the graphics with the blessings of Peter, Kevin, Karen and the group and it had already appeared as if the color scheme had all been but settled; the filter was going to be black. And if the group, other than Dianne and Larry had any say about it, so would the box.

After the group settled down, Peter asked Dianne to run down the next item. Up to this point I had just kept my mouth shut, taking it all in, as I wrestled to keep my emotions in check while the various bombs of disappointment went off around me.

"Dianne?" Peter asked inquisitively, "How are you making out with DuPont?"

"Oh fine. I have a call into them," she said, rather importantly.

I wanted to jump the gun, and I badly wanted to say something, but I couldn't. No, not yet. So, I had to settle for repeating to myself, "I've got a call into them," under my breath. For the sake of the project, I could only hope that she was further along than she was letting on. After all, Dianne had received this assignment six long months ago, during my October presentation!

"Well if you don't mind, could you please bring the group up to date." Peter said, trying to cajole more of a detailed response from her.

"As you know, Allied is considering the options of whether we should co-brand our new filter product with that of DuPont's product, Teflon. If we proceed that way, DuPont will grant us a license, allowing us to use their brand name on our product as well as our packaging." Adding, "But we aren't quite sure if it is worth the effort..., number one. And number two, do we really want to go into business with a competing chemical company at this time?"

Without hesitation, Kevin jumped in like a Pit bull. "I think if the price point for the material is there, who really cares if we go into business with a competitor. It's not like they're going to hurt us in any way." He said it with so much conviction, that the vein on the side of his neck was popping out.

I looked around the room and noticed that most of the group were shaking their heads in agreement with what Kevin had just said. Nonetheless, before too long, a full-blown debate had ensued as to whether Fram would be better served by having DuPont Teflon on the can or not. The issue at hand was simple, 'should Fram opt for the use of the real thing or could they afford to compromise and use the generic substitute PTFE to launch a brand-new product?'

From where I stood, if Fram chose to go with PTFE simply because they thought it might of been cheaper, it would have wound up getting them exactly what they paid for..., nothing! At this juncture, my concerns weren't the issue here, I wasn't in charge of this matter, Dianne was!

Over the next several minutes I agonized whether I should open my mouth or not. Desperately, I tried to detach from the room, now a buzz. I watched on in a state of horror, as the marketing experts and filter industry insiders discussed a concept which only belayed the fact that when it came to this market, they were still on the outside looking in! I was still very much the source, and I was now compelled to act.

It was more than obvious to me that by this late date, that Dianne had barely put together the rudiments of a trademark licensing agreement between AlliedSignal and DuPont, which left me absolutely speechless! I just couldn't take it any longer, as I sensed an oncoming lull in her presentation. So, I waited for an opportunity, before wading in.

"You know, I have been in touch with DuPont over the course of the last few years..., relating to several key issues pertaining to my patent. One of which, was the licensing of their trademark for the use of their Teflon product." Suddenly, all eyes turned my way and the chatter in the room trailed off, before I even had time to finish the sentence.

"I had discussed with them at length, the rather critical issue of licensing their Teflon trademark, to me. As a result, I am licensed to use it myself, right here and now! I brought along a copy of the trade mark agreement in my briefcase. Let me explain something to you. First off, you can use their trademark if the product you are manufacturing has at least fifty-one percent of their material in it. Secondly, the user must display the mark according to the nomenclature the DuPont Company specifies, just like you guys would, when you license out your technology. That's no big deal, right?

"Thirdly, the use of their trademark is free if the aforementioned criteria has been followed. Oh, and one more thing, and I'd like to let you in on a little secret..."

Kevin stared across the table at me trying to conceal that nasty little grin of his, doing his best to act ultra-professorial in front of the group. He knew that I was up to something, it was written all over his face.

"What is it Stevie? Tell us what it is. Maybe it can be helpful to the group, after all you're the guy who's been studying this stuff for a longer than any of us."

"Thanks Kevin. I appreciate that. This will just take a minute…

"You know… When I first began studying this material, naturally I didn't know a thing about it. And you would of thought that the first place I'd go looking for information on PTFE would be DuPont. And you'd be dead wrong, because by design…, they were my last stop.

"And you wanna know why? It's because they are the leader when it comes to this material and its applications, and I didn't want to become unduly influenced by their world-class leadership in this industry! Besides, I knew if anybody had the answers to my questions they would.

So what I did, was shop all the other major manufactures in America first. Of major consideration was: virgin material of the highest quality, extremely small particle size and of course, price. Coincidentally, I can even recall contacting AlliedSignal as a potential source for the material as well. And do you wanna know what Allied sells?

"Well I'll tell you! You guys sell PTFE. You don't sell Teflon and you can't. You know why? Because, you didn't invent it and you don't own the rights to the name.

"Now let me address brand recognition. Does the consumer even know what PTFE is? I really doubt it! But I know for a fact, they certainly know what Teflon is!

"So, do you know where my search ended up leading me?

You got it…, straight to DuPont! You can't beat em on price, quality, particle size. And you certainly can't beat them when it comes to name recognition!

As I continued to unload all over Dianne's six months of inexcusable foot-dragging, "Come to think about it, I'm not even sure if AlliedSignal actually manufactures the particular material required for this application. And I'll tell you what, they don't support any colloidal formulations such as Acheson Colloids SLA 1612. And I'll prove it to you!

"Ron Rohrback, and Gary knows him from our December meeting… Anyway, he's one of Allied's top Ph.D.'s out of Morristown and we talked extensively out in Perrysburg, and we've since talked over the phone several times. And you wanna know what, if Allied produced a suitable material for this project, he would of been all over it. But he wasn't. So, allow me to simplify things for you. Dupont Teflon is the only game in town!

"So, what am I saying here? DuPont either directly, or through one of it formulators provides ninety-five percent of all the PTFE material that ends up in the Teflon treated oils sold in North America. The way I see it, you can't justify reinventing this wheel unless, you could either come up with a better co-branding strategy or come up with a similar formulation yourselves. But at this point, I happen to be convinced you can't do either."

The room fell dead silent. It would be a moment of truth of sorts. I slid back into my seat, determined to wait them out in the heavy silence. My little treatise was never intended to show up Dianne, but like a misbehaving kid, she hadn't even begun to do her homework assignment.

'So, what was I supposed to do?' I was the visionary here…, not her and not no one in the room! It was simple, I wasn't going to allow her nor anyone from Allied to screw up my co-branding strategy!

Just so you know, co-branding today is very common, but back in '95 it was rare. Actually, it was cutting edge marketing. Prior to me calling on the Company, neither Fram or AlliedSignal ever co-branded another consumer product. Notwithstanding, they had never done so with such a powerhouse as Dupont and Teflon.

In the final analysis, it wouldn't have bothered me if I had to do the entire assignment for her, or the whole damn team for that matter. I gladly would have, if they just would of let me. My goal had never changed, I just wanted to see the job get done and get done right.

Given a few moments, the chatter picked up, and once again the volume returned. Same subject, different heading. As if to signify the change in direction the conversation became laced with corporate jargon such as, strategic buying units, commodity research teams, pooling of Company requirements and the like. The course had now been plotted in DuPont's direction, as the group determined how best to identify how much preexisting business was already being transacted between the two giants, in effect trying to sharpen the price quotes I had already furnished Allied. As this piece of business wrapped up, the issue had been settled, the new filter would be wearing DuPont Teflon on the side of the can. Amazingly enough, this truly a simplistic decision could have been worked out between Diane and I many months ago…, that's if she had only have asked.

Dianne was starting to fidget a bit as she reached for her bundle of papers. I guessed that she was readying to leave like she had previously announced. "Dianne I'm aware that you have to leave in a moment, so we'll be brief. How are we moving along with your negotiations with Steve?" Peter asked.

Rising to her feet, she bent forward and looked down the table at me. "I don't know? How are we doing? Steve?" she queried, sporting a devilish smile.

She was masterful as she lobbed that innocuous question my way. What was I going to say in front of the group? 'That she was an impossible jerk that didn't do her job!' I was trumped but good, as I began to fumble for the right choice of words.

"I don't know? I guess okay." Came my stiff reply, knowing instinctively that my response wasn't going to cut it with this crowd. I could feel their eyes zeroing in on me. The moment was surely going to require more solidarity than that wimpy response. "Oh, we're trying to come to a meeting of the minds. We've have our moments…, but we'll agree, of that I'm sure. You can count me in. I'm definitely on board." It killed me, as I felt it roll off my lips.

The position I found myself in left me with very little wiggle room. The situation required that I demonstrate my undying commitment towards the project, while at the same time forced me to turn a blind eye on the many evident shortcomings. In that instant I made huge trade, opting for honor and showing goodwill towards all the employees of Fram, which just so happened to of included Dianne.

'Oh, I had the chance! I could have bloodied her with truth in front of her peers, but at what expense?' My honor and me looking like a cry baby? No thanks! So, I let the opportunity for a contest pass unnoticed.

Just so you know, it was a judgment call that would eventually cause me to suffer Hell itself, a little further on down the line.

Invariably, the group must of had an inkling of what Dianne was putting me through, but nobody really knew what was actually happening to me at her hands, with the exceptions of Kevin and Peter. I'm sure that the rest of the group felt that what I was going through was just the cost of doing business with Fram.

It was done. She picked up all of her papers and bid us farewell. As she passed behind Peter she looked over his shoulder and called over to me, "We'll be talking Steve, real soon."

Yes, without question it was unfair! I looked up only to be met by her pleasant smile, noting that it was still intact. Somehow, it just served all the more to reinforce her victory. Approaching the doorway, she glanced up at me one last time. "Have a nice trip back."

The two salesmen returned in tandem, back from their trip to the soda machine, chatting away as before. There was a good ten minutes before the meeting would crank up again and I wanted to find out what those guys could be talking about like two little kids. In the temporary absence of any major distractions preying on my mind, I made an earnest attempt to eavesdrop on them. They were talking about the "Nationals… the Nationals?"

'For goodness sake what was that?'

As I listened a while longer, I finally figured it out in my lightning fast mind that they must of been talking about a race of some sort. Then one of the guys threw a hat on the table and they both clamored over it, like they were about to dissect it, or something. Sitting motionless, I did my best to become invisible, trying to figure out why a hat could be so captivating, as they whispered back and forth to each other.

For one thing, they were sure enough laboring over every minute detail about this nondescript cap, like it was some work of art to them. The fabric, the visor, the strap, should it be ventilated, should it be this, should it be that. I gotta tell ya, it was bizarre, the attention they paid to this dumb hat!

By now I was getting plain old nosy.

I overheard Tom mention Atlanta a couple of times, and I heard the other guy mention John Force in the same breath. I'm no gear head, but even I was aware that he was a giant on the NHRA drag racing scene.

Just then Kevin wandered over and gave me a couple gentle pats on my shoulder. Leaning forward as if to protect me, he asked in a confidential tone, how I was doing.

"All right, I guess." Grabbing his arm, I tugged on him, so I could whisper in his ear. "Those two guys across the way over there, they're talking up a storm over that hat and something about Atlanta and the Nationals? What's that all about, if you don't mind?"

Pulling up a seat, "Oh that's a hat that they have been working on for a promotional."

"Promotion of what?" I asked inquisitively.

He then looked at me with this stupid grin, like I shoulda known better, "The Grand Nationals in Atlanta. We've been the main sponsor of that event for the last several years. They're running in a couple of weeks and that hat is one of the freebies we'll be giving away down there. They've been working on it for some time now."

I couldn't help it, as I stared at him like a dog at a new pan! "You mean to tell me, that's their job?!"

Picking up on my tone he scowled at me as much to say, you dummy, just one of em'. I got the message.

"Hey guys, don't let me interrupt what you have going on, but Steve here is interested in what you're doing, being that his filter will be featured at next year's Grand Nationals. I guess by this time next year; he'll be getting a hat of his own. Isn't that right Steve?" He got up and slid the chair in under the table with authority, making a crash, as if to drive home that point home to those two guys. Then in another graceful move, he let them know that I had a few questions for them, as he disappeared.

"Hey Tom, Kevin tells me that you live in Jersey. It's quite a commute to Rumford isn't it?" I asked, trying to break the ice.

He replied, "It's really not that bad, I only have to get up here a few times a month for meetings."

"I figured as much, I was just kidding. Let me ask you something! In all honesty, what do you think about the concept?!

"What concept?" came his sober reply.

"You know, the concept we've been discussing here all morning, Teflon inside of an oil filter." I said, earnestly fishing for this seasoned field rep's sentiments.

"I think it's pretty good. Slick 50 has been around for a long time and it sells, doesn't it?"

Stunned, but getting his drift, I replied, "Well…, yeah." His response had said it all.

"Okay," I said, trying to mask my disappointment of his assessment.

"So, what about your accounts?" hoping for yet another angle. "Did they express an interest in carrying the new line? I know Kevin has already told me that there are already several major retailers who are willing to buy it already…, sight unseen!"

Pausing for a moment, he then offered, "They are going to take a look at it, they're a pretty tough bunch, you know." I then realized all he was doing was humoring me, like I was some sort of neophyte.

"Are they?" I replied, just about ready to give up on the two. 'No doubt jealousy must have already gotten to their hearts.' I sorely had to restrain myself from getting on a soapbox at this point. All I wanted to do was let them know what it was like to sell, and I mean to sell from ground zero! I was hurting of course, but I was more disappointed by their blatant lack of fire in their guts for the project. For me to have inquired any further would of been begging, and I wasn't about to do that. Any fool could of seen that they were too wrapped up in that silly hat of theirs and the upcoming fling in Atlanta to be thinking about much else.

However, I couldn't resist a parting shot. "Do you guys think that your customers are a harder sell than what I've had to face in order to close Fram on an entirely new filter line?"

In unison they both spit and sputtered before one of them blurted out, "Of course not!"

"I didn't think so," came my reply. Getting up, I left them alone, so they could beat the hat some more before the meeting resumed.

Just so you know, the Double Guard never made it into either Strauss Auto or Kmart. The irony, both Strauss and Kmart already featured both Fram oil filters and Autolite spark plugs, so entrée into these vendors should have been a given, since they both serviced these accounts. That left me only to wonder, '… just how good were these two guys at their jobs anyway?'

Unnoticed, I slipped out of the room to pay a visit to the soda machine and collect my thoughts. As I blindly stared at the selection, I nearly forgot what I was out there for, it certainly wasn't for a soda. The more I thought about it, the madder I got as I began to think about it. 'The last great thing this outfit did, was to come up with some corny marketing slogan of the early seventies, "You can pay me now, or pay me latter."

Oh, how foolish I was. Letting those two plodders cut my heart back there. I kicked myself for being so weak. The stage set before me, left little doubt that there was certainly more to come, once the meeting would resume. I could only wonder as to what.

The three demons of "Fear, Doubt and Unbelief" were hot on my trail once again, and I knew it. I was out in this lonely hallway for a reason, to square off with them. In so far as I was concerned, this morning's meeting was one big manifestation of their work. Confusion! A textbook example of how the right hand didn't having the foggiest idea of what the other hand was doing. Not needing any further proof, I called up for reinforcements… Jesus. He was the only one I knew in the miracle business.

Upon my return I grabbed my seat just as Peter was calling the group to order. "Okay people. Settle down please. At this time, I think it would be appropriate to give this filter a name before we go any further. Don't you? I don't know how you feel, but I'm getting kind of tired referring to this filter as some 'thing' or 'filter'. You get the point, I'm sure. So how about breathing some life into this thing, Oops, see what I mean!" he said, with a confident smile.

"Let's all turn to page six of the agenda and get on with the christening."

There were twenty-four names from which to pick, and the room automatically broke out into a free for all. From my far and away vantage point, I watched the Lilliputian struggle, as they tried to lay hold of some brand immortality…, hotly contesting the moniker of the new black filter. After all, this name was intended to be around for a long time, 'hopefully longer than some of their careers,' I mused.

For my sake and the future well-being of my baby, I hoped it would be nurtured and become a productive member of the Fram family, at least for the next seventeen years. Incidentally, that happened to be the remaining number of years left on my patent, granted me under the United States Patent Office. And let me tell you, never for a moment did I entertain settling for a contract that would specify anything less.

As it turned out, there were a lot of really silly names that appeared on list, clearly half of them were outright stupid. With the likes of; Infuser, Injection Filter, Servpro...

Thankfully after the dust had settled, reason prevailed! I was proud to meet the beginnings of my new child, a jet-black filter, poised to ring in the new millennium in oil filtration… THE DOUBLE GUARD!

'Finally,' I sighed, after all we'd been through, the filter had a proper name given it, ironically just in time for me to run headlong into the next topic on the agenda, "Status of Slick-50 / Quaker State"?! The ink hadn't even dried on Double Guard's name before I realized that a scenario of heart stopping proportions was afoot, capable of snuffing out its life. Suddenly, the fate of the filter was akin to Moses set adrift in a papyrus basket hidden in the reeds!

During my visit to Peter Ross's office earlier, I recalled overhearing them mentioning that Slick-50 had been put in play, but I had my installed sales blinders on at the time, so I didn't pay much attention to it.

Then suddenly it dawned on me! I mean, who was about to acquire Slick-50! My Lord Almighty it was Quaker State! There it was, staring me right in the face, in black and white! The very same guys who were doing fifty million dollars' worth of business this year with Fram were now going to buy the largest Teflon treated oil company on the face of planet!

'Do ya get it?' I asked myself.

'Yes of course I do,' came my hollow reply. 'Well it doesn't require an advanced degree to figure it out, Quaker State might just be throwing their hat into the Teflon treated oil ring! Maybe they've decided that it was high time for them to make a Teflon treated oil filter themselves and guess who they'd ask to manufacture it for them?!' Fram!

My fate, along with the new born filter, precariously hung in the balance. If Allied acquiesced to such a request, I would certainly be thrown to the dogs, patent or no patent. And as for you litigious arm chair quarterbacks out there… Well, the notion of instituting a patent infringement suit against the likes of one of these two giants, wasn't something to be viewed as some Hollywood movie.

Although Fram was sloppy at times, there was no way to tune up for such a court battle. Besides, it wasn't as if the Company wore its confidential information out on its sleeve for guys like me to read anyway. So, believe me when I tell you, though I had my ear to the railroad track, there was no way to see this train coming.

My mind was being pelted with disbelief, as I surveyed the landscape. 'What were the odds of making it through this ordeal intact?' If there was ever a time I was out manned and out gunned, this would have surely qualified! All I could do was pray. Under my breath I called out, 'No Lord! They can't take my life's work, not right in front of me, remember what you planted in my heart!' Remember, I'm calling to mind your word to me. "That you would not allow me to come this far to fail." 'So now God, if you don't mind, I'm including that to mean being stolen from!'

I leaned back in my chair and addressed the monster… 'Bring it on!'

The black thunder heads moved in and I reckoned the storm couldn't be far behind as Peter leaned over in Gary's direction, "Gary, you've been following the Quaker State developments, haven't you?

Lifting his head to meet Peter's glaring question, "Well yeah, kinda," came his startled reply.

Peter continued, "I just thought you might have been following that situation closely since you're our point man, in charge of bringing the delivery system on line…."

"Steve and I have been talking… About several various delivery systems… Here, I brought some handouts describing in some detail what we've been talking about so far," reaching for his folder.

There it was, for all to see! "Step-Up Filter Design Status," detailing the concept along with the design parameters. Amongst other things, it harmlessly diffused the paste debacle while highlighting the silver bullet I had already transferred over to them via my trade secrets. Front and center was Acheson Colloids SLA1612 Teflon formulation! It was a move, by the way, that in the end would save the project as well as keep his career afloat. Although the handout was the handiwork of engineer, that didn't discount the fact that it was the product of all my research.

"So, Gary? What's this stuff going to cost us to treat each filter?" Kevin bellowed out getting into the fray. The last thing he wanted to see come of this was this product wearing a name other than Fram's, which also by the way, would have included the green logo of Quaker State. Nor did Kevin relish the possibility of seeing me getting throttled in the pursuit of the bottom line either.

"Oh, about eighty-five cents a shot," the engineer replied.

"Are you serious, man!" Not the least bit bashful about his concern. "Is that the best we can do on the price?!"

Gary just peered over just as sweet as you pleased, to meet Kevin's skepticism head on, "Why yeah? We may be able to shave something off that price, but we won't be able to do so until Dianne gets back to me with some figures. Like how much business Allied does with DuPont and stuff like that. And you guys, you have to let me know what kind of a production run you anticipate for this filter as well. But I can tell you, it's not going to drop by more than... Well, let's say a dime."

"What about burnishing the tapping plate to remove those ugly pickle stains? I want that tapping plate to really shine!!! If we go with that red outer gasket, that thing will really look high performance," Kevin added, with childlike excitement!

But this day Kevin wasn't about to hide anything from me, I could see his tone had become laced with doubt. It was the money issue and I knew it; the monster had reared its it hoary head once again. It was amazing! By all appearances, Gary seemed unfazed by the fact that in one felled swoop, the cost of the Teflon treatment was about to swallow up nearly all of the money allocated for the filter's entire upgrade!

I had to really hand it to Kevin. Amidst the panic and confusion brewing over the utter the lack of funds, this brash young man didn't hold back from reaching for yet another important feature for our sorely underfunded filter! "And since this is going to be a wet filter so to speak, we better equip each one with an anti-drain back valve. Don't you think Gar? What could it cost, a few cents, maybe a nickel apiece?"

"Woe, wait a minute Kevin! You know that we've only been allotted around eighty-five cents for the entire improvement here!" Peter said, putting an abrupt halt to his subordinates shopping spree. "...And that would include something for the inventor here," he said grinning. Then looking over at me as much to throw me a bone... Like I should get paid for my contribution he added, "Whatever that might be?"

So, as it would seem, the storm of great magnitude spawned by the bottom line, dictated by the clinking of nickels and dimes had passed me by, sparing me of its heartless fury. So, for the moment, I'd been granted a reprieve, and Allied would pass on forming an alliance with Quaker State and Slick-50. It was clear, AlliedSignal didn't want to share this market with anyone!

In a reversal of roles, Allied was now on board with me, as they jettisoned their fifty-million-dollar client over the side in favor of what I had brought to the table!

So, I guess AlliedSignal's insatiable quest for the bottom line precluded such an arrangement from ever taking place. Ironically, the process which could have so easily eaten me alive a few moments ago, happened to of spared me, by dispatching the uninvited interloper. I was still numb from it all, sort of like a frog, caught in the middle of a hail storm. It would be the only time I'd be thankful for Allied's unbridled greed.

For a moment I found safe harbor, as the hurricane spawned out of raw business advantage, finally blew itself out.

To sit there, knowing that with a dollar and a dream I had triumphed over the fifty-million-dollar account was truly something to behold. My God had indeed shown up that day to see me though.

However, when it was all over I was left with one nagging question for Him, 'Lord how is this tightfisted outfit ever going to pay me?'

CHAPTER 9
OUT HERE WITH THE BIG BOYS

It seems like only yesterday, that I was a boy standing on the beach, watching the double over head surf breaking in rhythmic lines of perfection. The silhouettes of the guys out in the lineup looked like a bunch of seals, as they bobbed up and down on the pulsating swells. Every so often, in a moment of perfect timing, a member of this floating wolf pack would break away and partake of the ocean's ecstasy. I can remember holding my breath and watching in sheer amazement as the rider and his board carved across the huge wall of water. As to that day, my recollection is clear, only the big boys were out.

It wouldn't be so long after that, I'd find myself standing on the crest of the beach with the early morning sun in my face, eyes squinting as I spied the relentless surf, pounding in the bright sunlight. Surprisingly, there were already a handful of guys out at this particular beach break, noted for grudgingly allowing few opportunities to paddle out against an endless onslaught of surf.

I wasn't quite sure how they had made it through that thick whitewash, to the calm water out beyond the roaring breakers. Occasionally there would be a lull, but ever so brief. It was the only means that could provide the edge necessary to make the hundred-yard paddle. The answer to that riddle and the only possible way out was, patience.

The tail of my board stuck firmly planted in the sand as my arm pulled it close to me, like she was my best girl. We stood there watching together, waiting silently for fifteen minutes or so, alone.

It was my job to spy out an opportunity to get us out there beyond the breakers as my heart pounded the whole time. The adrenaline rush was crushing, even for a high testosterone adolescent, not yet sixteen.

The white water of last big wave was heading towards the beach and I could sense that this was the time. Running full speed off the bluff, the board and I flew headlong over the shore break in a graceful belly flop. I began to paddle with every fiber, pulling myself up and over, then through the lips of the building succession of waves. Just as the board pierced through the lip of the next oncoming wave, I'd open my eyes once inside the watery envelope, only to be met by the sun's fractured rays which looked like chards of glass fluttering all about.

Every muscle in my body worked in unison, pulling me out through the backs of the thick waves, avoiding the certain disaster of being dragged back over the curl, and sucked over the falls.

My shoulders screamed from the punishing workout and my lungs felt as if they were catching on fire. Just when I imagined I could go no longer, I popped through the clean-up wave in the last set, landing me into another world. All of a sudden, the ocean mysteriously appeared so peaceful, as if the paddle had only been a bad dream.

I sat up on my board and filled my lungs with a long soothing breath, craning my neck to see over the heaving swells, surveying the territory. Apparently, my arrival in the lineup had gone unnoticed. It didn't matter to me anyway; I wasn't out there for attention. The fact that I was green didn't bother me either. I knew just knew that I belonged..., out there with the big boys.

It was the mid May of 95'. I had put some twenty years behind me now, yet that memorable occasion in the big surf remained a vivid memory. I was a full-grown man with plenty of responsibilities, yet many parallels remained the same. Again, I found myself standing on a bluff of sorts, staring out into the distance, straining to find the rhythm of yet another turbulent system. This game too, was dominated by the big boys, but of a different kind. Nonetheless, it required the same kind of skill learned as a kid, paddling in the heavy surf…, most notably, timing and patience.

My mind was becoming more and more preoccupied with thoughts about Fram. Things were moving along satisfactorily, I guess. Anyway, that's what I was being led to believe. However, my gut instinct was telling me otherwise, as I would find myself mired in some serious moments of doubt from time to time, watching the various processes at work.

A few months back, Kevin had informed me that the Company and Jack McGrath, the Senior Vice President of Marketing had parted ways. I didn't dwell on it at the time, but I was saddened to of seen him let go, for I was convinced that the Double Guard had lost a loyal ally when he left Fram.

His departure left me feeling hollow. Jack's pledge of support given me, during that fateful day back in October of 94' was gone now.

Along the way, the project would suffer other devastating casualties as well. I sensed in my being that the backing for the project was mysteriously being eroded. Subsequently, I would be powerless to defend myself against their inevitable onslaught that might be awaiting.

By now it had also become obvious, at least to me, that Fram hadn't ever collaborated with an outside inventor before, such as myself. It also became apparent they lacked much of the necessary organizational skills required for a successful new product launch as well. The situation became progressively more troubling, as I began contemplating whether Fram even possessed the ability to bring this product to life at all. 'But what could I do?'

At this point I was in so deep…, my investment so great.

Keep in mind that I know what I'm talking about. I know what I had witnessed, having been an integral participant in the birthing process of this would be revolutionary oil filter, now dubbed, "The Double Guard."

As it turned out, I had gained most of the member's confidence from the outset, so in return, the team unabashedly brought me deep inside the project as a full-fledged member.

'And why wouldn't they?' After all, they were running with my playbook.

So just for the record, I wasn't like some kid trying to get a peek under the circus tent while the elephant was in the throes of giving birth. I was present long before the baby's head started to crown, in fact I was counted as one of the original midwives entrusted to deliver the baby!

Beset in front of me was an engineering team that had not completed its manufacturing profile as of yet, and a marketing team that was woefully underfunded. So, as you might expect, the blatant mistakes and inattention to detail that I had witnessed from both teams were at times more than I could stand. Yet I bit my lip, I had to, propping myself up all too often with, 'this is only an oil filter made out of metal and paper. Don't get too excited here!'

'Come on now, be realistic,' I'd keep telling myself. 'You've witnessed many a flawed performance during your real estate transactions, Dear God Steve, get a grip! And you know full well that the people entrusted with the launch of this thing are all imperfect creatures too. Just like yourself.'

'But this wasn't some residential real estate deal gone awry on the Jersey shore, darn it!'

What was going on here was of a much higher order. This was supposed to be a high-level marketing and manufacturing thing. I was on the threshold of going into business with one of the most powerful companies on the face of the planet. Oil filters were their forte. Besides, this project was borderline science, for heaven's sake!

So, in the spirit of cooperation I repressed my critical observations, tucking them safely away and out of sight. We were at a point in our relationship where we couldn't be reconciled from each other now, we had merged as one. Our relationship was like that of a chemical reaction, the catalyst had long since been introduced, the ensuing result was inevitable. And I didn't profess to have the power to stop it.

Yet, I forced myself to ride upon the great wave of all their promises. I had been assured along the way by all, that my oil filter was destined to grace the shelves of every major automotive filter retailer across the United States and Canada and so I chose to believe in them.

Double Guard would be born. It didn't matter how much maneuvering it would take on my part…, I would see to it!

In the worldly realm of business, Kevin supplied my only solace, yet even I knew that his ability and zeal for the project wasn't enough to shoulder the load single-handedly. Yet, I still believed that if anybody was able to convey my vision to the Company, it was him. In my estimation, if this project was left to fend for itself without Kevin's personal oversight, it would have surely atrophied and died on the vine.

As if to make the situation even more ambiguous, I have to tell you there was a genuine feeling of electricity in the air. It was an undeniable fact; the Double Guard project was somehow beginning to show signs of reinvigorating the sleeping giant as it began to stir from its thirty-year slumber. The Fram brand name mounted an attempt to move beyond its last great achievement of the past…, a dated television commercial!

What I saw taking place was more than a catchy sales pitch to rally behind. It was a birthing… Of something tangible, of something real. A product that the division could proudly stand behind. Even I heard rumors that people close to the project were coming into work with a renewed sense of vision, a new sense of purpose.

There was genuine revival going on, something great was being born, and we all knew it!

On the heels of all this madness I found myself deep in the belly of a vortex. The timing couldn't have been worse as I paddled out. I wasn't left any choice; the negotiations were about to begin…

Dianne and I had barely kept our flimsy lines of communication open since our airport rendezvous back in March. Yet thankfully by some act of fate, I had been temporarily spared from a one on one with her when I was up for the marketing meeting in April.

There was no doubt in my mind that she wasn't the least bit phased by the patent lack of communication either. In her heart of hearts, she knew that I was going to come along, that was a given. That shouldn't of been any great revelation, since I had never made that a mystery anyhow. Besides, any fool could see that I was the pursuer and not the pursued.

The tension inside of me was mounting. It was not as if I was a greenhorn when it came to this business of articulating a position for which I then had to negotiate. For the life of me, I just couldn't get a handle on how I was supposed to deal with Dianne. It just wasn't fair.

She stood squarely between me and the rational business contract I sorely needed, which would no doubt secure the future prosperity for both me and my family. I was more baffled than angry. Yet I didn't despise her, though maybe I should have. She had truly morphed into a schizophrenic gatekeeper, keeping me out despite the fact I'd already been granted a security clearance.

Finally, around the end of April as it started getting down to the wire and Dianne and I began to speak with each other with more frequency. We needed to consummate an agreement we could both live with, but as usual, the pathetic excuse for negotiations would break down before we'd even get started. In the aftermath of the imploding talks, we wouldn't communicate with each other for days and weeks at a time, depending upon how much time was left on the clock to resolve a particular issue.

I found myself calling Kevin with greater frequency now, and I can assure you that it wasn't to discuss something of importance any longer, like the marketing plan. I was now pursuing him in the hopes of gaining some insight as to how I might go forward with Dianne. I just wanted to get this ugly relationship between Dianne and me over with, and arrive upon an amenable, but fair agreement for both Allied and myself.

For the life of me, and you can call me naïve, but I never even considered that the negotiations for money would have ever created such heartache. If I had known in advance, that would have been the case, and had foolishly placed my initial energies there, I would have been doomed from the start.

My treasure had always centered around finding a suitable partner, then being able to convey to them what I had was something worth pursuing. If the truth be known, the situation I was now facing was such a negative and costly detraction.

Unfortunately for us all, it effectively precluded my involvement in the marketing strategies that were so crucial if this new filter was to spearhead Fram's triumph over their competitors.

One morning around the middle of May I found myself sitting at my desk in the real estate office, my mind obviously off somewhere else. Motivated to shed my terminal career as a real estate agent, I pulled out my phone card and dialed up Kevin. I did so in hopes of shedding a career which had increasingly become my master, not the other way around.

"Hey Kev, it's Steve. How are ya doing?" I asked.

"Okay, my friend," he shot back enthusiastically, "So what's on your mind?" Intuitively, he already knew that we hadn't much new ground to cover at this point.

"Kevin, I hate like the dickens doing this…" I said, "But I got nowhere else to turn," feeling more than a bit self-conscious.

"And what do ya mean by that," he said immediately offering me his support.

I replied, "It's the stupid negotiations. It's impossible! Oh, not the damn negotiations, but her. I can clearly say it's white and without the slightest provocation, she'll say it's black."

Feeling exasperated, I added, "You guys want to go into business with me, don't you? It's not like your outfit is perfect either. Far from it you know."

My frustration pushed me further and further, I had to let all the poison out. "We're all in this together, we only got each other at this point and you know it!" I shut my mouth for a moment and allowed him to probe the depths of my anguish. He had gotten pretty good at this by now.

Although he had to know where the hurt was, he was slow to reply. Knowing him as I did, I'm sure that he was sorting through the birthing malaise of this filter from my point of view. Whatever the marketing team wasn't accomplishing at the moment could be straightened out. And he knew that I believed that he was good for it.

And the engineers... So, what if they were plodders, I could push them along. Besides, there wasn't a soul around the camp that didn't believe that I'd reach in and pull the baby out with my bare hands if I had to.

There was no doubt that I was driven, and that this baby was mine. I freely chose to give it up for adoption, to a better home. Based upon the facts, I chose the Fram Family, the lineage of the AlliedSignal Clan, backed by billions upon billions of powerful dollars. They not only had the wherewithal to produce this filter, but they had the juice to have it wind up on the retailers' shelves all across North America. There was no way an individual like myself could ever of accomplished such a feat, even with the aid of some serious backing. It was impossible to go this one alone.

The answer should have been clear to him by this time. The problem had to focus around the adoption agent and the ensuing proceedings. And if I was out of line, he'd be in my face about it. You can rest assured, Kevin wasn't bashful, there was a lot of Pit bull in him.

"Steve, I'm sorry that you have to deal with this woman. I know that she can be difficult at times..."

Interrupting him, I screamed. "Difficult! You gotta be kidding me!" I started to unload, but it was his turn to walk on me.

"Okay, Okay! You're right she can be downright impossible to deal with at times. And everybody around here knows it. But she's still here, and I can't do much about it without creating a heck of scene. Do you understand me?" he said, in exasperation. "If you really insist, I can try and have her removed from this case for you. But I'm telling you, it won't be pretty!"

Kevin wasn't aware of it, but he was playing directly to my sense of self-sufficiency and I couldn't resist the bait. I didn't need my hand being held by anybody, and that included him. The last thing that I wanted was to be labeled as a complainer and a cry baby that needed to have a lot of tender loving care in order to make a business deal fly.

"You can't take her place..., can you?" I moaned, pleading one last time.

"No, I can't Steve," he said emphatically. "Hey..., I'd love to, but I can't. How would that look anyway? Now wouldn't that be viewed upon by the higher ups as the fox in the barn?"

"You mean hen house?" I said, laughing at him.

"Oh, don't be a wise guy. You know damn well what I'm saying."

Well, I knew what he meant, but nonetheless I was perplexed. "What do mean? You still represent AlliedSignal and you work in a high-level capacity for Fram don't you?

"Then for God's sake, how can you be accused of any sort of indiscretion by negotiating with me? You're still a company man."

He got a little hot about that one, as he fired back, "Yeah, so what about it? I am, and I'm proud of it."

"Well…, I'm the inventor darn it," I exclaimed, "Not the enemy, remember?!"

We weren't angry with each other, it just seemed that every time Dianne's role in the negotiations were brought up he seemed to be at a loss when it came time to explain why I had to put up with this insanity. The vibes that I was picking up were ominous. There was something brewing just beneath the surface, but it wasn't as if it was in plain sight.

I couldn't figure out what it was or where it was coming from just yet. Just take my word for it, all the cards weren't on the table at this point and I knew it. My choices were simple, just play on, or get up and walk out with absolutely nothing.

I'm going to go out on a limb here, but you have to understand the situation I was in. I had long ago given AlliedSignal the innermost workings of my patents, the keys to my trade secrets, my marketing and business plans…, and I do mean everything. Just like some fancy meal kit that would arrive in the mail. I even acted as technical support, like when you get stuck and call the eight-hundred number for support. If I walked away, they would make the filter anyway… and without me. That was a total given.

Laws of any kind in this game don't mean squat, when it's a mammoth corporation against a sole inventor. So please don't get hung up on the starry-eyed notion that we are supposed to be protected by our legal system, because ofttimes, we are not. And in the game, I was playing, everything was done out of the public eye, which complicates matters exponentially. Please don't be foolishly idealistic here, this is how it works…, even in our beloved America!

My only option at the time would be to wait for the product to appear in the open market, and then mount a campaign to sue a Fortune Fifty Company. Trying to find either the two-million-dollar cash retainer for such a campaign or a law firm brave enough to take such a case on contingency would be tantamount to climbing an even bigger mountain than the one I was in the process of scaling.

To be clear, this is how this particular 'game of dare' works. 'We're gonna run over you, but if you'd like, go ahead and sue us…, because we'll amass a king's army against you.'

"All right, okay!" he shouted through the phone, trying to stave off my onslaught. "You're right, what can I tell you. But if we let this thing get too crazy here, it could blow up in both our faces!" He wasn't elaborating, and I knew better then to ask him to do so at this point.

Hearing the frustration grow in his voice, I backed down knowing that he really wanted to help, all at the same time knowing that he was really powerless to do so. Attempting to sure up both of our spirits, I drew an analogy of how this mess related to a similar situation, when a man as tough as nails asked his friend for a similar favor.

"Hey Kev… All this madness aside, did you ever hear the story about Saint Paul's thorn?" I asked, in a half serious tone.

"Paul's what!!!" Immediately he seemed to lighten up, musing at my impending analogy.

I repeated myself once again, as I tried to make light of our world of human frailty and discord. "You know, St. Paul of the Bible. He had a thorn in his side.

"Don't tell me, you don't know who he is? He's the guy who wrote better than half of the New Testament."

"Yeah, so what about it! You know something Steve, you really crack me up. Like that's really got something to do with what's going on here right now. But you might as well go on and explain it to me, 'cause I know you will. I just hope it's going to make you feel better. Besides, I don't have the foggiest idea what you're driving at anyway," he said.

I couldn't resist busting him back, "You mean to tell me that a good Irishman like yourself doesn't know this story?"

"Hey… I believe in God man," he said defensively. "But this stuff isn't my forte, like it might be for you, ok? So, go on. I want to hear about this guy's thorn."

"Okay. To make a long story short, Paul had personal contact with Jesus sometime after He had ascended back to the Father. Paul, you know, had a personal encounter with the Lord after being knocked down and blinded on the road to Damascus."

"Why? That's a heck of an intro, wouldn't you say?" He said, musing.

"Yeah well, Paul was on his way to persecute the church and I guess you might say that he had it coming to him. Anyway, that's a long story… Anyhow, much later, after he got really tight in his relationship with the Lord, Paul began to suffer this constant harassment by a fallen angel. And this demon tormented Paul to the point where he asked Jesus, who by this point was not only his Lord, but a most dear friend…, to get him off.

"Do you wanna know what Jesus said back to him?"

Listening intently, he replied, "No I don't, but I'm sure you're gonna tell me anyway?"

I paused for a moment, hoping that the answer might sink in. "Jesus said to him, '"Paul my grace is sufficient enough for you."'

"Put another way, Jesus told Paul that he possessed the tools and the ability to take care of the situation himself just fine. Jesus let him know that He was there for him, but it was up to Paul to overcome the situation himself.

"Well anyway, that situation kinda reminds me of us. I keep coming to you, asking you to please handle Dianne who happens to be a big thorn!"

"Don't you see the parallel?" I asked, hoping he'd grasp what I already knew. Dianne was a demon of sorts, a demon that I'd have to battle on my own. And it didn't seem to matter one bit that the rest of the project members and I got along like family, because no one from AlliedSignal was prepared to get her off my back. And that included my dear friend Kevin.

"You keep telling me that I can handle her," I added.

He replied, "It's kinda weird, but you know something, that's what I've been telling you all along!"

"I don't know, I just thought you'd appreciate the insight, since I am convinced that this woman isn't going to be judiciously removed from this situation. Not by you, not by Peter…, not by anybody." Little did he realize, but the analogy that I had just laid out for him was more or less a fatalistic summary at this point.

"Yea I guess, perhaps O'l St. Paul was right," he quipped. "You got the tools baby and you got the power. And unfortunately, you're gonna have to handle her. I'm here for ya Buddy, but this is between you and her now. After all Steve, like I said, you do possess the tools to handle her my friend."

As time passed, he and I talked more frequently, and we took it upon ourselves to begin roughing out the framework for my compensation. And I might add, we did this despite his better judgment.

I wasn't being greedy, nor was I drunk on the opiate of illusion. Clearly, there was no advantage for me to pretend as if I had invented the lightbulb and that I wanted to be paid the world for it. That was never the case, and if I acted as such, a company like AlliedSignal would come crashing down on me, like a bass on a bug. The whole time my only objective was to be paid what was fair. That was relative of course, because I knew beforehand that Fram was going to be the bigger winner. Trying to be sensible, I didn't let that bother me, because that was just the way of the world and I wasn't about to change that formula.

There wasn't any pre-license compensation in my case as I stated before, and I still felt that the Company from the very beginning was in violation of the rules of engagement. From my personal experience, earnest money; when tendered up front, becomes the cement that binds the two parties together and sadly we lacked that now more than ever. They were freewheeling with my deal!

So, I had passed on the earnest money eight months back when Dianne told me that it was out of the question. By my way of thinking, the earnest money would have been valued at a few hundred thousand dollars based on the potential value of the proprietary information I had given Allied. But that was all a dream now. Like a shaky marriage heading for the rocks, I was beginning to feel like I was doing the lion's share of the giving. Although it was a healthy eight months into the operation, I was still bottle feeding the engineers.

I had exerted considerable effort seeking higher counsel but no matter what, it still boiled down to my own judgment. And by the way, no lawyer was going to save me at this point, the only solution they might offer was for me to walk from the situation. I was in pain, but I didn't want to walk, quitting wasn't what this journey was all about.

You might ask, 'why not? You certainly could have done something.'

My response is quite simple, 'I was already pulling this boxcar with my teeth and I was convinced that it wasn't the appropriate time for a lawyer to enter the picture on my behalf. 'Cause if I did something predictable like that, Allied would of folded up their tent long before they ever would let my lawyer past the front door.'

All I could do at this point was to fend for myself, because in the end, no one shared that foxhole with me during the incoming barrage of ground fire. Not my wife. Not Kevin. Not nobody…, but God. And I have to tell you, even He seemed very far removed at times.

During my pursuit of the holy grail, I made contact with a very special person by the name of Richard Dye. Initially, I made contact with him sometime back in the summer of 1988. At that time, he was shepherding the engineering department for Purolator Products, you know; the guys that make Purolator oil filters. You know, one of the largest oil filter companies in North America…, that one.

We had become fast friends during the process and had kept in touch throughout the years spanning the course of both my patents. If there was anyone I could refer to as my coach in the field of oil filtration, it would be Dick. And for me, when it came to the oil filter business, he was as close as I would come to having a mentor. What I was going through at the moment was critical and I needed to reflect upon some of the valuable insights he had shared with me over the course of our association.

Anecdotally, when it came time to make my first sales call and hawk my newly acquired patent, his company wasn't the first stop. At that time, I had employed a peculiar methodology for selecting the pecking order of who I was going to contact first. I had four prospects lined up, and with the exception of Purolator, they were more or less scattered about the eastern half of the U.S.

Logistics figured heavily into the mix at that time, because I wasn't so inclined to put on a road show that included air fare. Things were pretty lean back then, which pretty much eliminated the prospect of long distance travel for the time being. So, when Purolator had moved from my back yard in Jersey, to Tulsa, Oklahoma a couple of years earlier, they dropped to the bottom of the order.

Back then, in my utter naïveté, I believed all that was necessary to entice any filter company was to just simply tell them about my improvement patent and they would go for it! I believed that for a couple of basic reasons; pure lunacy and that viable utility improvement patents for oil filters simply weren't being granted.

To which I can now say, 'how idealistically blind and stupid could I have been?' However, in my own defense, I hadn't met the great equalizer as of yet... N.I.H.

Anyway, I called on Fram first because they were within driving distance and the closest company to my home.

I know, I know, 'how sophisticated!' But that figured heavily in my decision to call upon them first. And what followed next, well..., we've already covered much of that ground.

That behind, I needed to call on my second prospect, Purolator Oil Filters. That phone call began my association with their Senior Vice President of Engineering, a man by the name of Richard Dye. And what a nice guy, talk about not being threatened by an outside with an idea! I can remember our very first conversation. I addressed him as Mr. Dye out of courtesy as I normally would of course. But before long, he admonished me from calling him by his last name.

"I have a first name Steve, please call me Dick. I don't go by that Mr. stuff," I recall him saying.

Dick wasn't the typical stuffed shirt engineer type either, devoid of personality. I found him extremely knowledgeable and empowered to do the job he was hired on for.

The company had picked up and moved out to Tulsa, but he still kept his home in Jersey and perhaps, that's what created the opportunity for us to eventually meet. Although a good nine months had passed, my ability to wait things out, finally paid off. During one of his hurried trips back East to meet with a major vendor, he so kindly invited me to meet with him for lunch at Bennigan's on route 22 in Union, N.J. sometime in August of '89.

I got to the restaurant before him and parked my car and waited for his black Cadillac with Oklahoma plates to show up. I wasn't waiting too long before he arrived. He got out of the car with that, 'I'm looking for the person I've never met before kind of gaze, as he spied the parking lot for my black Honda. I rushed out of the car armed with a yellow pad and hurried over to this man the size of a fullback. Catching sight of me before I reached him, he called out, "Steve, is that you?"

I rang out, as our eyes met, "Yes, it is Dick, how are you!"

"Just fine," as he extended me his hand in friendship. "Say let's get inside where its cooler. Darn, it's hotter out here now, than is back home in Tulsa. And let me tell ya, it gets mighty hot back there."

The hot August afternoon was oppressive, with the humidity running at eighty percent. We had already begun to sweat like a couple of pigs as we headed for the air conditioning.

"So, what your telling me is that you don't miss that good old Jersey humidity," trying to get a rise out of him.

As we walked in, his eyes went to and fro looking for a hostess to seat us. I could tell that he was on a tight schedule and he seemed wound up like a top. Finally, the hostess came into sight and waved us forward. Relieved to be out of the heat, he said once again, "I don't miss this humidity one bit at all. I'll tell ya."

We sat down and ordered a couple of large iced teas and began a lively exchange. I had to pinch myself, as a flood of emotions came coursing through my soul, scarcely able to believe who was seated across the table from me, sipping iced tea. Dick held eight patents in the field of oil filtration and his talents were an amalgam of engineering, marketing and strategic planning. His role was more like that of a sweeper back in soccer than that of chief engineer, where he covered the backfield for Purolator. The face that I saw was one of a strategic thinker and marketer rather than that of an engineer with myopic vision. In my eyes, I knew without being told, he was one of the great ones in his field.

For the last year we had only known each other over the phone, knitted together by only a series of hurried conversations, as I pressed to entice him about my first patent…, the '901. I couldn't help but be reminded of the endless massaging which I had often times dispensed to sell an indifferent buyer, a home. I worked with more home buyers than I cared to mention, spending sometimes a year or more with them before they actually bought a home off of me. And believe me, many of those sales, I considered myself lucky to have been able to put in the closed draw.

"So Steve, tell me about what went on between you and the boys at Fram." Asking me to recount a story that was now over a year old. I could tell, he was beyond curious to get the inside track why they didn't bite on my first patent…, the '901. "You know, the time Tony Coronia told you that you didn't have a patent over lunch."

Well that's all I needed. I launched into that story without skipping a beat. I told him the story from the beginning to end, because I had only told him bits and pieces about what had gone on. I'm sure he wanted to hear the whole episode in context, since all I ever shared with him before was fragmentary. And I was free to do it, because it wasn't as if I was squandering my valuable phone time on something that didn't directly affect our business relationship. I'm sure he was also conducting a bit of a fishing expedition of his own, anxious to find out why Fram, their chief competitor, had walked away from an apparent opportunity to gain market share.

So, for the moment, I was more than happy to indulge him, because if there was a lesson to be learned in my retelling this story that afternoon, Dick would most assuredly point out the value of this experience.

As the tale progressed, he stopped me dead in my tracks. I was at a point in the story when I had communicated to Fram that I had a patent.

"Now Steve, explain to me exactly what you meant, by that you had a patent," he said, laying a trap like a Confucius master would for his pupil. "Was it pending, was it co-pending or had it already issued?"

My response was immediate, and I knew the lingo. This part of the game as far as I was concerned was elementary. "I know what you're driving at." I responded wanting to get to the finale. "At the time I called on them, my patent had already issued. I had paid the Patent Office my fee and I had already received an official copy of the patent. Besides Dick, I know the difference between co-pending and patent pending. So, between you and me, I wouldn't of bothered calling anybody with a patent of mine that was just pending, or even co-pending for obvious reasons." Not needing to waste time reciting the obvious.

"Okay. Good answer, I'm just making sure. You don't mind now, do you?" he said, acting fatherly.

"Of course not," as I began to proceed with the rest of my story.

When I finished with the whole saga, I was expecting Dick to bestow on me some great treatise on why the engineers at Fram told me that I didn't have a patent despite the obvious fact that I had one.

He sat back in his chair and took a long drink of his iced tea and smiled at me. "You don't know what's going on, here do you?" He was smiling at me, as I foundered, lost in the moment. I was bewildered by his response thus far, and I guessed that it was all over my face.

'I was so darn trusting; a flaw in my upbringing,' I supposed.

Leaning over the table, as if I was trying to physically pull it out of him, I said pleading, "Come on Dick! Tell me now, would ya!"

He still sat back in his chair and ruminated for a moment, kinda like a country boy sitting on the front porch chewing on a stalk of grass. After a long pause, he slowly and deliberately spoke three letters… "N.I.H."

I shot back at him, "N.I.H.! What the heck is N.I.H.!" trying to hold back a nervous laugh. What's that supposed to be, a secret code or something."

"Well, you're not too far off, Steve. It's an abbreviation for 'Not Invented Here'. Don't you get it Steve? You have a new idea and it may be valid. Personally, I think it's got a lot of promise, or I wouldn't be here having lunch with you today. But you're out here with the big boys, and if they don't want you around, well you're just gonna have to forget it unless you can bring this filter to market yourself! And we both know that the filter market isn't like selling a pet rock or a chia pet."

"I agree with you. I learned about this sort of stuff back in college, it's called an oligopoly. It's a situation where there are only a few players and there is very limited freedom of entry due to cost impediments, or access to marketing outlets." I had to laugh to myself, as I spewed out this text book macroeconomics definition that somehow managed to be filed away deep in my memory.

Dick responded, "Hey! You're about right, that's about the size of it. "Let's see…" I watched him intently as he conjured up the players for me. You have Fram, Purolator, Wix and Champion Labs. That's about it for the automotive filter manufacturers. Right?"

"Yea, I guess so. What about Hastings, do they have any market share?" I asked, inquisitively.

He replied, "No, not really. Not worth mentioning anyway. Besides, they're too small for your project anyway. You're going to need to team up with one of the big boys to get this one off the ground Stevie. Your best bet is Fram or us, and it sounds like they've already shut you down pretty good!"

"Can I go back to them and try talking with someone else? You know bypass the engineers?"

Looking about as cold as he did serious, he offered me some sound advice, "It would be the kiss of death."

Dropping that one like a hot rock, I asked, "What about A.C. Delco?"

"So…, you want to deal with one of the largest corporations on earth, do you? I don't think so, he added with a sour twist. "If you think we're bad, well you'd be in for a real shocker dealing with those guys. Don't forget Steve, we sell to those guys!"

"Not that I would, but couldn't I try to approach Fram again?" I asked, still unable to resist the temptation of acting the stupid school boy. Oops, it had already slipped out, so I braced myself for his answer.

Besides, I was trying to sell him now… And although Fram was a distant memory, I wanted a better explanation than for him to just tell me that it was the kiss of death.

He replied, "Now what do you think Steve? Let me tell ya a little something, just so you might understand. The well has already been poisoned, it's not worth the aggravation for you. I'm talking to you from experience now. You'll never get back in."

Dick was right, and I knew it. 'Cause I had already tried contacting some woman over at Fram who I was told was Bruce's superior in marketing department after he had sent me 'the thanks but no thanks letter.' And you know something, it was rather peculiar, but for some reason I had developed this acute mental block as to who this woman might of been. For the life of me, I couldn't recall her name. All I can really remember is that I had called her office a couple of times and got her secretary, as I tried to maneuver around Bruce.

However, I do remember one thing. Bruce warning me in our very last conversation, that this person told him to advise me that she never wanted to be bothered by me again!

Just so you know, it took me an eon to figure out this piece of the puzzle…, but that woman was none other than Ms. Diane. Apparently, we had a subliminal history that had latched onto my fuselage from the very beginning. Down the road, I'll let you in on another worldly detail.

The tension was mounting inside of me as it was time to pop the question.

I don't know, but I guess I must have asked him a question concerning the restriction of oil flow and he was in the middle of a through explanation discussing burst pressure of the average spin on filter housing, or something to that effect… My mind was running away with me and for the moment and I could barely pay attention.

I was being barraged by anxious thoughts. 'What about us? What was to become our relationship between Richard Dye, Purolator and myself? Were we going to go into business together? We've been talking to each other for the last year or so… But were we going to get down to the business of making this filter come alive or what?!'

I thought we would. Anyway, I sure hoped so, but I couldn't say for certain where we stood. Only he could. I reached deep down inside myself. I had to dislodge the demon of rejection that had been trying to make a cozy home for himself there.

He finally finished his treatise on the finer points of flow restriction and burst dynamics when I interjected, "Thanks Dick. That was a really neat explanation you gave me about flow restriction." Boy, I was glad that this wasn't some dissertation that I was going to be tested on in the morning, because I barely followed a word of it, too preoccupied by my own agenda.

"But I got another question for you on an entirely different subject, if you don't mind?"

"You do?" He said, with a big grin, taking another forkful of his Caesar salad.

"Yes, I do." I prefaced it this way. "Don't take this the wrong way, but what's going on with us?" As I began to put the words into his mouth, I asked him in the affirmative, "You see the merit in my patent, you said so yourself..."

He still looked happy, chewing away on his salad and didn't appear the least bit phased by my line of questioning. I kept telling myself, if it's meant to be, then it's meant to be, so I was just going to have to be blunt about it.

"Are we going to go into business with my filter or not?" The question landed there with a thud, begging for an answer…, his answer. So, I just shut my mouth and determined not to speak until he answered me.

After a long swallow he looked me square in the face and readied an answer. "I told you that I think your idea has merit. And I believe that it is really novel and that there could be a market for it. And if I didn't think so, we wouldn't of been talking for as long as you and I have been. However, I have to be honest with you, I've had just so much on my plate this entire year that I haven't been able to give your idea the full consideration that it truly deserves.

"I'm sure you're aware, but there is a whole host of things that have to be done in order to bring something as big as this off the ground Steve. I gotta level with you, your concept is more than ground breaking. For instance, before a launch could even be considered, I would have to do a lot of networking with the people within my organization. Frankly I just haven't been able to do that so far, because of all the other duties the company has piled on in the last year."

As he spoke my mind was racing a mile a minute trying to ferret out everything that he was telling me. If he was telling me the truth, and I had every reason to believe that he was, his assessment wasn't too terrible. And it wasn't as if he had told me that after careful consideration of my idea, he just didn't see the market potential nor the feasibility of the whole thing. So far, I could live with that.

Let me point out that I wasn't being self-deceived either, because he wasn't telling me anything like my idea was a long shot. Not at all. In fact, what he was really telling me, was that he was just too darn busy at the moment to do anything about it! And that included building consensus amongst his peers. Timing as to this, or any endeavor when it comes to a sale as complex as this one is paramount!

Being the way that I am, I still needed him to elaborate. "Okay Dick," I said rather relieved. "I'm kinda happy that you've said that my idea has merit. I mean you could have told me to forget about it and go on to the next idea. But you're not telling me that, right?" asking him flat out for his assurance.

"That's right Steve. You've got a good idea there," he said, not mincing any words as he picked through his salad.

Pushing further, "So what you're telling me, is if you had more time to concentrate your efforts on my idea and could build consensus amongst your cohorts at work we might have something here? Correct?"

He replied, "Yup, that sounds about right." Well that made me feel a lot better, at least I felt that I had a better than average chance of pulling this off.

Suddenly I could start to feel this upwelling from deep within my belly, it was the force of joy. I was being overtaken right there in my seat and the puny demon that went by the name of 'The Fear of Failure,' had left me without so much as a good-bye. How rude!

Dick and I spent the next hour talking about some of the major accounts he was calling on and all that it entailed from the stand point of the VP of Engineering, turned marketer. We also covered the landscape of the oil filter market and the strengths and weaknesses of the various players as we casually formulated a marketing strategy for a filter such as mine.

I can remember pumping Dick towards the end of our meeting as to how many filters he felt could be sold per year. My heart soared when he told me that I could expect upwards to twenty million units being sold per year at somewhere between a nickel to dime per unit to me. Those kinds of numbers really made the odyssey worthwhile in my view. But so far, they were just numbers, and this was all going to be one gigantic pipe dream if Dick couldn't free himself up, to start the ball rolling at Purolator.

As we headed out to the parking lot I probed him further before we parted. I asked him point blank, "Dick my future is riding on this one, what's going on with your schedule? Are you going to be able to clear some of your calendar so that you can explore the feasibility of my patent?"

Albeit, what he and I had discussed over lunch was soothing enough for my insecure soul, but it really wasn't nearly certain enough for me to know that a deal could be had. What I needed from him at this moment, out here in the sweltering parking lot, was a commitment. I waited for his response, as he pulled open the door to the Caddie throwing his jacket onto the front seat. Leaning on the front door, he bent over and smiled at me. I could tell that he enjoyed my company and had a warm spot in his heart for my tenacity and my ability to pursue a dream.

"Steve," he said. "There's a lot of stuff going on at the office and I am busier than a one arm paper hanger right at the moment, but I am hoping that things will change shortly. As I told you inside, I do see a lot of merit in your idea, and I want to pursue it further. All I need is the time. I hope things work out, believe me, for both our sakes. Nothing would please me more than to see Purolator introduce a revolutionary new oil filter and to know that it came from you.

"Look, I definitely understand where you're coming from and I don't blame you for being a little impatient with things and the way they've turned out so far. But I want you to understand something, you have to know that there are forces at work here that are way beyond my personal control…

"That's all I can elaborate on for the moment. You'll just have to trust me on this… Okay?"

How could I of possibly responded to all of that? I realized that he was a very busy man and last thing I thought was that he might of been putting on some kinda front. He couldn't of been! Almost every time I called his office and got his secretary he was either in a meeting all day or traveling around the globe!

My choices at this point were slim to nil that I would be able to interest another company in my '901. Besides, I didn't want to disenfranchise Dick in any way shape or form. I was positive now that he was personally supportive of my idea.

Yet for some reason, I still had my suspicions. The fact that he couldn't act, really bothered me. I was at a loss. I didn't understand corporate culture, and I was the farthest thing from being a fortune teller that you'd ever want to meet.

Somehow, I just knew that there was something lurking out there beyond my understanding for the moment, and Dick wasn't volunteering neither. As usual I knew my place and I didn't have the unmitigated nerve to ask. I wasn't going to push him, I knew better. So I let it drop, as he got into his car and drove away.

Just so you know, Purolator was in the throes of a major corporate upheaval. Dick would soon leave the Company for greener pastures and Purolator itself, would be sold off and acquired by another suitor. The opportunity of ever selling my '901 would be lost in the mayhem as another VP of engineering would soon take Dick's spot.

So much for luck and timing. The odyssey of mine would continue and the Lord would give me yet another more disruptive patentable idea, I just didn't know it as of yet. As I've said before, I'm not much good when it comes to reading tea leaves.

Me at 50 and still charging.	fall of '08.

Carving out a bottom turn on a rare, yet perfect south swell with my custom 9'0''.
The Jersey Shore in the fall, simply wonderful.

CHAPTER 10
CUTTING THE COVENANT

That morning was truly a first for me. Not only did I have breakfast with Kevin for the first time, but Peter joined us as well. Upon the conclusion of our little get together, we formed a little convoy, and followed each other back to Fram's headquarters. Soon thereafter, Peter wished us both good luck with Dianne, then went his own separate way, leaving me no choice but to follow Kevin. We beelined straight for his office, undoubtedly to go over my compensation for what would be the last time before hooking up with Dianne at nine o'clock.

As usual, Kevin assumed the form of a whirlwind once he made it inside his office, tending to a host of perfunctory items he normally would have accomplished if breakfast with me hadn't gotten in the way. Apparently, laying there on his desk happened to be a message waiting on him that he couldn't possibly ignore, so he asked me to stay put in his office for a few, while he dispatched with "this small fire," as he put it.

Before long, I got bored pacing in this modified jail cell he called an office, so I wondered out front to grab some coffee and chat with Jodi his secretary.

"How's it going Steve? You're getting to be a real regular around here," she said with a smile.

"Yea, I know. I'm thinking about filing an employment application," I said jokingly.

She kinda mumbled under her breath, "I don't know if that's such a good idea."

"Hey Steve! Can I grab you a cup of coffee or something?"

"Sure, why not. Just a half a cup please, I'm gonna have bladder control problems if I drink too much more of that stuff this morning." Changing the subject, I offered, "Ya know, I'll be meeting with Dianne and Kevin in a little while. We're supposed to hammer out a licensing agreement this morning," I let slip out nervously.

Empathetic, she offered, "Yes I know, good luck with Dianne! I just looked at her and gave her an understanding smile, not wanting to start anything. "Kevin's really proud of you and all that you've brought to the Company." Adding, "he's really gonna miss you, you know."

Lifting my head up from my cup, I met her with what must have appeared to of been a look of stark terror. Before I could even speak, she had covered her mouth, "Oh my God! He didn't tell you yet, did he? I was sure he had, please forgive me!"

Without ever having a chance to respond to her anguished plea, I was then transported headlong back to curious situation that occurred during breakfast that morning.

There was a nice little restaurant attached to the Marriot where Kevin and I had planned on meeting for breakfast. I arrived first. That wasn't so unusual, as I picked a quiet spot in the corner of the place, overlooking the bustling traffic. When seven thirty rolled around, no Kevin, 'it was really unlike him to be late,' I thought. Then out of nowhere, peering around the corner of the empty dining room I catch Peter Ross, Kevin's boss looking right towards me!

As if to flag him down, I raised my hand and yelled over to him, "Hey Pete!" That move surely caught his attention, because before I realized, he was leaning over the table wishing me good morning. At about this time I must of had a million thoughts running around my head as to what might be going on.

In the middle of him pulling up a chair to join me, I let loose with what had to of sounded like a stupid question, "Do you have any idea where Kevin might be?" As tactfully as possible, I volunteered that I was supposed to be meeting with him for breakfast this morning.

Just then a smile broke out on his face. Sensing the uneasiness of it all, "As a matter of fact I do, Steve. He gave me a call late last night and said that he had something which had to be taken care of first thing this morning. It just couldn't wait, so he asked if I didn't mind sitting in for him, till he could break free. Hoping you wouldn't mind."

What could of been my response other than, "Of course not Peter…"

Call me paranoid, but intuitively I just sensed that something was going on, but I hadn't even the slightest hint as to what it might be. So…, trusting soul that I am, I dismissed it, not wanting the hassle of reading into something that may not exist. Besides, I assured myself, 'it would be a great opportunity for just the two of us to get to know one another better anyway. And just the same, I really wanted the chance to feel Peter out privately as to how he wanted to approach the marketing campaign for the Double Guard.'

Looking back…, boy what a set up! I had been neatly introduced to my new handler like a baton pass in some relay race, and admittedly, I was totally blind to it! Now I'm not saying it was right, not by a long shot, because it sure wasn't. But I got to give it to them both, 'cause that fifteen minutes alone with Peter went pretty smooth.

'And so, what do you think occupied our time as we waited for Kevin to arrive? Why, installed sales of course! I was an installed sales lobbyist of sorts. That was my undying position as to where the true success of this project lie, as well as the future of the Double Guard itself.

Returning from my psycho-journey, I grabbed Jodi's hand, "Jodi, it's all right! I'm sure he was going to tell me all along. I guess he was just waiting for the right opportunity. It's not like he's a liar, right? I'm sure he's got his reasons for not telling me yet." My words didn't help her much, the discrete secretary was still reeling from her indiscretion.

Putting aside my own pain, I spent the next few moments trying to make her feel better as I began, "So Jodi, you may as well tell me…, when's his last day?"

"Friday." She said sadly. "I'm gonna miss him," sounding like she was about to cry. "All of us around here are going to miss him terribly."

"Oh," I said. "So, he's leaving Friday? You mean this Friday, right?"

"Yes Steve, this Friday."

'Dear Lord', I thought trying not to choke. 'That was only two days from now! Talk about cutting it close Kevin!'

There was absolutely no way to describe what I was feeling inside! Perhaps shock? I had no way of knowing. 'It just didn't make sense to me, he loved this Company.' And to think, this all came down on me within thirty minutes of a meeting where I was about to sign away my rights to a life's work.

I couldn't stop thinking about it. 'He gave them the best thirteen years of his life.' Furthermore, he loved this filter, nearly as much as I did, often referring to it as his greatest professional achievement. 'Why then was he leaving, and what did he know?'

The whole situation made me reflect upon my own commitment to a career. I hadn't given any one company thirteen years of my life as of yet, and the way I was cranked, I couldn't see how I ever could. The only career I felt passionate enough about, was that of breathing life into this filter.

"Hmm... So, he didn't get fired, did he?" trying to lighten her up with a smile.

Kevin had been her boss for some time now, and her eyes betrayed the hurt.

"No!!! Of course not," she said defensively. "He's going to another job."

Just then Kevin walked out and smiled at us both. Our little conversation was over now, as he summoned me into his office, closing the door behind.

Once inside his office he apologized for attending to other business, and as for me, I did my best to hold everything together. "Say, how'd you do with your little fire?" I asked. "Did you put it out, I hope?"

His labored reply came back, "Oh, it was nothing much after all," as he leaned way back in his chair and folded his hands behind his head. For a moment he just went blank and stared into that darn computer screen of his.

He was hurting, and I could sense it. I figured, my plight was just one more detail for him to anguish over now, along with the other burdens he was carrying. All I could do was hope that he would level with me before the day was over, because if he didn't, his betrayal would have cut me to the bone.

Succumbing to the pain, I disassociated myself from our friendship for a minute, as I began to size him up. Concluding, he was sharp enough all right. But by no means did I ever feel outclassed. 'Oh, he could have gotten over on me of course, just like a lot of people I had already encountered. But he would really have to be a dishonest liar to outmaneuver me on this one, especially when it was time to figure out what was best for the welfare of this filter's success.'

Breaking free from the malaise, I felt the need to move on with my life, which meant, talking about 'the money.'

"So Kevin, honestly, the best your outfit can do is a lousy fifty grand in up-front money, huh?" not in the least, wanting to minimize Allied's greed!

"Steve. Like I told you over the phone the last couple of times, fifty-grand is all they are going to give you. I don't have any control over that. Believe me when I tell you, I tried to get you as much as I could, but those bean counters have some pretty damn sharp pencils around here. I think you'd at least be aware of that by now."

"I can see that for sure," I replied. Still lamenting, "Allied probably spends more sponsoring a ridiculous golf outing than what they are about to pay me in up-front money for this thing," feeling myself wanting to go off.

"You know Kev; the bastards didn't even give me a lousy dime for the pre-licensing agreement... And then on top of it, they had the unmitigated gall to tie me up for another couple of months just, so they could assure themselves that this venture was a hundred percent guarantee. And like a dummy, I've gone along with the whole charade, without hardly a whimper!"

Interrupting me, he said, "And I think that was wrong! They should a at least given you something, and I think you already know how I feel on that issue." He just sat there patiently, hands folded behind his head, listening to what I had to say, knowing good and well that I wasn't the milquetoast type, who reveled in the art of wailing.

There was some real poison in my system which had to be bled out at this time, and I'm sure he figured that he better endure it, if there was ever going to be an agreement signed that morning.

"Oh… and one last thing. I got a few more items to cover. Just listen to me for a moment and put yourself in my position before you speak would ya? …Okay?

"I'm going into this meeting knowing for a fact that the engineers haven't perfected a delivery system yet, right? A system that they can't seem to get straight! A system I put together in my garage for God's sake, and they haven't figured it out yet! And that's just for starters…

"Then at breakfast, we have Peter fighting against me concerning installed sales, which I know for a fact is the way to go, especially if you guys think you're in a consumer driven filter market which you all claim to be.

"Remember Kev, I studied this thing out, long before I ever called on you guys! For heaven's sake, you filter companies hadn't even considered a Teflon additive treated oil filter before I received my patent and came calling on you all!

"Oh, and another thing… I'm up here to supposedly enter into a licensing agreement with you guys and who does Fram pick as their representative? One of the biggest scofflaw's I ever run into in my life…, Dianne! And if that ain't true, how come you jumped in here at the last minute to cut this deal with me? You're doing her job for her right now! Come on now Kev, everyone knows it! It's so obvious she's crazy, that's why the woman gets such a wide berth around here."

He leaned forward and placed his hands on his desk. All he could do, was to look at me with that stupid grin of his.

'What could possibly be his reaction to all I said?' He was way too smart to argue the facts with me. Aside from that, I had him dead to rights and he knew it.

"I understand where you are coming from my friend," he offered apologetically. "True, there's been some mistakes along the way, but you didn't have to come along for the ride either, you know," as he began to get up from his chair and make his way around.

"I love ya Buddy, but that's an awful cheap shot," I said. "You know I really didn't have any other place to go." I was wearing thin from the incessant cover ups and repeated exposure to the Company's endless parade of blunders. I had to do a reality check and ask myself a rhetorical question. 'This was Fram I was dealing with, right?'

"That's precisely my point, Steve! Don't you realize they're smart enough to have figured that one out already? And yes, all by themselves! Mistakes aside, nobody, and I mean nobody, in this entire industry has the juice to pull this one off, except Fram! And don't let anyone kid you on that one either, my boy," as he looked me square in the eye showing his ire like that of a wolf over a piece of carrion. With that, he made me a most solemn pledge. "I want you to remember something Steve. Nobody's gonna be able to do this job like Fram! Not Purolator, not Wix, not nobody!"

Just so you know, during my lawsuit Honeywell didn't use this book against me much, even though I afforded them every opportunity to dissect both the book and me. In the end, the best they could come up with was the previous two paragraphs, where I stated that I didn't "have any other place to go." It was totally laughable, but that was their justification for the malfeasance that I would endure at their hands. Their lawyers loved reminding me, 'that my own words stated that they were the only game in town.' So, because of that, I shoulda just of sucked it up and been happy. Think about that one…

"Look man! The real money isn't in the up-front dough anyway..." he said, trying to reason with me. "You know that, as well as I do! Come on now, isn't that why you fought so hard for your dime?

"Well you got your dime! You're getting a dime a copy for every filter that rolls off our lines, just like we've agreed to. And remember, that's a flat dime, not to be discounted as the volume goes up. In the scheme of things, you did pretty darn good my man."

Under the circumstances I let him bring me back to where I belonged, earth…, where all of us fallible creatures roamed. "It's not that I'm being a pig here Kevin. I just wanted to be treated fairly…, was all. We both know I'm not Michael Jordan here, talking to some cereal company who's gonna just lay down for him. Allied's going to make the lion's share of the money, as they should, it's only fair, but I just thought…"

Moving from behind his desk he came over to me and put his arm around me, giving me a good squeeze, talking in my ear as he did. I just hung my head like a good trooper and stared at floor while his voice penetrated my soul. "Look Steve, I'm gonna make you a millionaire outa this one. I already told you that. Maybe not this year, as he gave me a good squeeze, "Or the next, but certainly not before too long!

"I see us doing about three, maybe four million copies this first year. Then it's only gonna build from there if we support it right," he said, speaking from his heart.

Pulling away from the warmth of his hug, I tendered a rebuttal, "Hey Kevin, I think your figures are a little low. Don't you?" still wanting to carry the fight on a little further.

"How so?"

"I figured sales were going to be more in the five million range the first year and we should be at ten million copies by year three, that's all. And let me make myself clear about something, I'm strictly talking retail here, I'm not including installed sales nor heavy-duty."

Putting me off, "Well I'm not about to argue that one with you now, we don't have time. Anyway, you could very well be right about that, Steve. Who's to say? Anyway…, I really must hand it to you man, so far, you've been right on the money on just about everything.

"So Steve, let me ask you something? Are all systems go here or what? Because if they aren't, please say so, because now would be the time."

I still had a lot more rolling around inside of me, like if you can fathom this one… Peter at breakfast was still talking about the Quaker State Slick-50 deal, in terms as if it still had some real bearing on whether Fram was going forward with my licensing deal or not! Unbelievably, that was thrown into the equation just before I was ready to sit down and cut the covenant!

And there was the issue of my heart. Still raging on, as I debated whether I should come right out and tell Kevin that I was already aware of his clandestine departure. I sorely wanted to find out what that was all about. But now wasn't a good time for that. I could see that he had gotten himself pretty worked up about the money and all the rest. Besides, we were too close to Jodi's office for comfort, not wanting to see her suffer any fallout because of her innocent slip.

"Everything's fine Kevin," I volunteered, knowing we had to strap ourselves in tight for the ride ahead of us.

Just so you know, the sudden and drastic lowering of my earning projections wasn't the result of miraculously getting religion or something. Nor, was it as far-fetched as suddenly being educated on the facts by Allied/Fram's management, because that wouldn't hardly be the case either. My figures had to be adjusted so that I would be more in sync with my licensee's defeatist attitude, and so I could better accommodate their insanely low performance standards that they set for themselves as world leaders. Up until this point, I had done my absolute damnedest, to guide this lumbering ship into its birth, but to no avail. ...Any fool could of seen that I lacked the herculean muscle to perform this task.

"Okay then!" he said, as a welcomed smile broke out across his face. "Let's go try and find that artist before we get tied up with Dianne.

"I really want to show you the box. I think you'll really get off on it!"

Once again, I found myself trailing behind Kevin, as we motored through the corridors of Fram's Corporate Headquarters. 'Darn, this guy was always so hurried,' doing my best to keep up with him. He was leading the way again, like he always had, especially when we were on his turf. But this time it was different. The picture I was piecing together as a result from this morning's episodes was suggesting that things between us might forever be changing. I was left no choice, other than to acknowledge the fact that my days of following his lead and trusting him implicitly were rapidly drawing to a close.

"Hey Kev, what's the big hurry man?" I shouted out, trying to mask my rising emotions. "Don't you know how to operate at any other speed around here besides hyper?" I called sarcastically, to his back, wanting him to slow down.

Not skipping a beat, he looked back over his shoulder grinning, "No! You do want to see the artist before our little get together this morning, now don't you?"

"Yeah sure! I can't wait to see what the box looks like," I said like a kid on his way to the carnival. "But does that mean we gotta run through building like two idiots to get there?" I added.

The heavy aluminum doors burst open, as his shoulder slammed into them with a jolt. We entered a quiet courtyard that separated the two buildings where a couple of picnic tables for the employees had been placed. The day was setting up to be warm, as the late May sun came streaming through the trees on that Rumford morning.

I caught up to him and tugged on his shoulder. "Hey, grab a seat for a second I want to talk with you for a moment," trying to sound unassuming.

He looked at me with those big green eyes of his smiling, "Yeah sure, what's on your mind. It's not Dianne is it? Because, like I told you over the phone yesterday, today's meeting is more or less about going through the motions. It's all been agreed to, remember?" he clucked sporting a self-satisfied grin, like it was already a done deal.

I couldn't take it. I felt like I was going to cry, and I really didn't want to..., not in front of him. The anger brought about by the antics of the morning had receded and was now replaced by a wave of gut wrenching sorrow. Shielding my eyes from his, I stared down at the ground, pushing the dirt around with the tip of my shoe. I didn't really know where to begin as I fought to keep my voice from belaying what was rolling around deep inside of me. "Hey Kev," I began, "I know…"

I caught him out of the corner my eye, staring out into vacant space, eyeing the trees gently swaying in the warm breeze. "I know," came his hushed reply. His mind was obviously somewhere else.

I remarked to myself that it was the first time I ever saw this dynamic guy in such a deflated state.

Still not able to bear looking at him, I lifted my head and stared straight at the side of building while repeating quietly once again, "Kev I know…."

This time he gave me a pat on my knee a couple of times and said the same thing, "I know Buddy, I know."

Feeling the frustration, as I fought back the tears, I mustered the strength to look him in the face. "You don't get it, do you Kev?" By this time, I was overcome by emotion, barely able to finish. I thought for sure he would have caught the heaviness of my heart, as it was oozing out of my very pores. But he didn't, and it was just as well, because it made it easier.

He shot back, vintage Kevin, "Hey man, so you know, but I don't know what the heck you are talking about? Okay. So, if that makes any sense to ya, you might as well let me in on your little secret, I'm not a mind reader here."

His callous words came to my aid, and helped chase those foolish emotions from my heart, as I regained my composure. "Well," I said, "For starters, let's just say that I know that Friday's going to be your last day at work!" Dropping the bomb.

"Oh my God! How did you find that out?! I mean… Of course, I was going to tell you, but it wasn't going to be before your big meeting this morning. It's not like you don't have enough stuff on your mind.

"Please Steve, you have to trust me on this one, I was just trying to look out for you is all!"

I could see now, that he was the one hurting, as he fumbled for the right words and finding few. I'm sure he must have felt that I caught him red handed in a lie. And I couldn't convince myself a hundred percent otherwise, yet I wanted to believe him. For the life of me, I never had this guy pegged as a liar.

It was my turn now to give him some comfort as I grabbed his knee, giving it a good shake. "It's all right Kev, I trust you. Don't even consider it. Hey, it's not like we're two little children. If a better opportunity came up for you and your family, you'd have to go for it, or you'd be a fool. You're worth it," I said reassuringly.

"That's why you're leaving? Isn't it?"

Knowing I hadn't turned on him, I spied a sheepish smile starting to emerge. "Yeah, but look, I can't explain it now, for obvious reasons, one of which we don't have time. But I promise, when we are finished with our business today, I owe you a beer and an explanation. Are you all right with that one?" he asked, just to make sure. "'Cause if you are, let's go see Skoogie, and have a look at that box!"

The walk across the courtyard seemed like an eternity, as we made our way shoulder to shoulder. The little stroll seemed to reinforce the bond which had been forged between us on the battlefield of this project all the more. Somehow, I couldn't help but to be reminded of Jack McGrath's premature departure and how that bruised me, but Kevin, he was my soulmate on this one. I felt like he just took a direct hit and was leaving me forever, without time for a proper farewell.

Reaching out, he grabbed the handle of the door and just stood there on the concrete landing before taking aim. Staring me square in the face, he said, "Please don't think I'm dropping the ball on this one, 'cause I'm not. I've done the very best I could on this one Steve," in an attempt to give me one last dose of reassurance before he pulled open the door. "This baby's in the pipeline now and it's gonna fly!"

My head was in a tail spin as we walked down the hall and up a flight of stairs to the artist's office, only to find that he wasn't around. I was in a lot of pain, but I knew I had to go on, for my own sake now, and for that of my little family waiting for me back home.

The hour was fast approaching, and it would be only a matter of a few moments before the three of us would be sequestered in a small conference room up on the second floor of the main building. There we would pledge our word and cut the covenant, ratifying the licensing agreement.

For now, all I could do was watch, as Kevin rummaged through the artist's folio, swearing under his breath, like he owned the joint. Desperately, he searched to put me in touch with the goods, making a valiant attempt to bolster my spirit before the mornings meeting got under way. Within a few minutes, the pack rat found what he had come looking for, grabbing the 11x17 color copy, handing it over to me. "Well! What do ya think?" he said, taking a step back, giving me plenty of breathing room, so I could pore over the giant-sized layout of the box.

"It's gorgeous," I exclaimed, my face lighting up.

"Sorry Steve, I know it's only a color photo copy for now, but he's working on the proofs."

"It's all right by me Kev, it's still so beautiful! Skoogie really outdid himself on this one," as I held it up to the sunlight.

"You're sure that they won't screw it up now that you're leaving?" I muttered, paying half attention to what I let slip out, still very much captivated by the artist's handiwork. I couldn't believe it, at long last I was actually holding something in my hand that was tangible, even if it was just a sheet of paper!

"No, they can't," came his reply, tinged with melancholy. "I've brought this thing so far along that even they can't screw it up! Steve, just about everything's been done, there's only some loose ends left to be tied up."

"Okay." I said, as a determined smile broke out. "Let's go meet Dianne."

Upon leaving the artists office in building B, we traveled across the courtyard in silence, heading towards the mornings final destination, the meeting. Once again, my ravaged soul yawned open, as an uninvited memory, laden with disappointment from the past, flashed across my screen.

'Think about it Steve, this wasn't the first time that something like this has ever happened to you,' as I started to chide myself, like somehow I was actually responsible for the sudden turn of events.'

I began to reflect upon a situation that paralleled this event rather closely, although it took place some years ago, recalling distinctly, that things hadn't fared nearly as well for me back then. You see, Dick Dye had pulled this exact same stunt on me when he resigned from Purolator Oil Filters.

In a bizarre twist of fate, I guessed it was now Kevin's turn to act it out, as he repeated the same maneuver almost to the letter, as he too prepared to leave his post, without giving me so much as a whisper of forewarning.

Back when Dick left Purolator, his subordinate Alex MacLean moved up the ranks to fill the void left by the lead engineer, then only to drop any further investigation of my '901 additive treated oil filter patent. That move left me to wait it out on the sidelines, only to watch, as my baby got tossed out with the dirty bath water. 'As for my reward?' Well I got to watch over a years' worth of collaboration go right down the drain.

Over time I would come to realize that the new guy was just distancing himself from the projects that might have borne any semblance of his predecessor's, regardless of merit. I viewed it as a cannibalistic move that didn't make good sense, kinda like when a bull alligator eats it's young.

However, with regard to Kevin, I didn't know what to think. All I knew was that this time, my ship of dreams was losing yet another good captain.

'Was there someone waiting in the wings to take his place?'

I didn't think so. I hadn't run across any other Kevin types since I had begun dealing with this outfit, so I guessed that wasn't even a remote possibility.

'So, as before, was I wrong to depend on one man to see me through?'

I wasn't sure. But from what I had experienced from my second time around, it seemed like these big corporations seem to breed good men very grudgingly. 'So, if they only had one man to give me on the project, namely Kevin…, then they only had one man to give,' I reasoned. That's at least the way I saw it.

'So… Should I of folded? You know, pack up my grip and leave before I got in any deeper, because right about then, I wasn't so confident about the rest of the hired help?'

That option didn't look so promising either, considering I still wanted to get to market yesterday!

But like the man said, "This baby was in the pipeline now! Even they can't screw it up." The Double Guard was going to be a reality after all. 'Wasn't it…?'

The brutal storm which had come between us had for the most part blown itself out, as Kevin and I climbed the rear stairwell of the main building together in silence. The gale force attacks, which had only moments before torn at my dreams and assaulted my emotions were now gone, without so much as a trace. With every step, I could feel the remnants of my future plans slipping a bit further beneath the surface as they plunged for the bottom, like the twisted wreckage of a once mighty vessel.

I was relieved to find that she wasn't here yet, the conference room was still empty. Walking over to the window, I stared out for a long moment before grabbing a seat. I was locked in a race against time, as I struggled to sort out of the whole ordeal before the real show would begin.

'So, was this the way it was supposed to go down?' I wasn't sure, as I pondered the details, which to me had become stranger than fiction, if that were at all possible. Furthermore, I was compelled to ask myself, 'why did a journey with such great promise, have to wind up being so painful anyway? So bloody.' For the moment, I was short on answers, but I swore to myself that before it was over, I'd know!

Out from the corner of my eye, for what I knew was going to be the last time, I spied my partner, turned pseudo-betrayer. He sat quietly across the table from me, immersed in his own universe. The prospect that he wasn't gonna be around to share in the glory of what we had both worked so hard to accomplish tore at my very soul. On the opposite end of the spectrum, I wanted to smash him for jumping ship at such a crucial time. Still, I wasn't blind to his plight either. I knew all too well that 'glory don't feed the bulldog!' I could only wish him Godspeed, and hope that this new better paying job of his would reward him for his talents better than Fram had.

So there he sat…, that resilient bugger, the quintessential company man. Still very much forging ahead with his future plans, handling all this around him, like it was so much water off a ducks back. For a moment, I wished that I might suddenly be able to grow skin as thick as his, it sure would of come in handy right about now. The inventor was about to face off with him and Dianne, bruises and all. And there was certainly no way around that one!

Annoyed, Kevin got up and slammed his chair into the table, "I'm going to look for her, damn it! It's almost a quarter after," he barked, then glared over at me, like it was my fault or something. No sooner did he get up, then in she came. Right on time, 'late!'

"Good morning gentlemen. I hope I didn't keep you waiting long, but the contracts were just coming through the fax machine a few minutes ago and I hadn't reviewed them as yet. I know you'll understand that I needed a chance to review them," she said trying to make light of her ill preparedness. I was impressed. This was shaping up to be her closest on time performance since the airport.

"Right now, my secretary Jackie is running off some copies and we can begin reviewing the document as soon as she brings them over. It shouldn't be more than a few more minutes. Is that all right with you?"

I sat there silently, studying their body language, prepared to wait, for as long as it might take. Then out of nowhere, came this ugly spirit of doubt, quick to remind me that I had entrusted over a decade of my precious destiny to this Company and now it rested squarely in the hands of these two people seated in front of me.

My mind went reeling in several directions all at once, as I weighed out how badly I wanted this contract. Things were starting to move along quickly now. I attempted to fire off a prayer under my breath, but before I could take a stand, the uncertainty of it all came crashing on in.

I reflected on the fact that I was still receiving distress calls from the engineers…, not too comforting a thought at this juncture either.

And to complicate matters, while over breakfast that morning, the talk turned towards the Quaker State and the Slick-50 deal. I was still getting mixed signals, as Peter eluded to the fact that it still wasn't a total given that their fifty-million-dollar account had headed south. I got the distinct impression that they weren't completely out of the running either and could end up being the spoiler. The way the conversation was unfolding, Quaker State could just as easily reemerge as a contender for the project, thereby knocking the Double Guard off its shaky perch. It was imperative I beat Quaker State to the punch, even though I held the only patent and its trade secrets for a Teflon treated oil filter. Let me tell you, the pressure created by that situation alone was nearly enough for me to sign almost anything.

Then there was the illustrious timeline. From the very onset, my gut had been telling me that the project had gotten off to a sloppy start, especially when it took the engineering department two months to initially contact me. But now as it appeared, both the engineering and marketing areas weren't capable of making up for lost ground. I found myself left virtually powerless in the process, hemmed in by a 'don't ask don't tell' mentality that seemed to be an integral part of Allied's corporate culture. And believe me, it wasn't like I didn't ask, because I always was.

'I don't know?' The Fram team was known to be kind of evasive when it came time to sharing some of the more intimate details concerning the areas in which they were fumbling the ball. My inquiries regarding these incidents would oftentimes be met with the Company line such as, "Things were all right and going according to plan, and not to worry." Assurances such as, "Remember Steve, you're dealing with Fram here, we invented the business, remember?"

'So where could I of gone anyway?' I was in a position where I had no choice, but to put my trust in the Company. The more I thought about it, the more I realized that my position was no different than that of a patient lying on an operating table waiting to be cut open.

Then of course., there was Dianne! 'Did I really stand a fair chance, dealing with her on her own turf, especially now that Kevin was halfway out the door?'

By this time the answer was, 'not a chance!'

'So why pretend?' I had to get an agreement today, while Kevin was still around or perhaps I'd never get one at all!

Oh, and while I'm on the subject of not having Kevin around. I was prepped all right, if that's what you want to call it! Never being spoken to in advance that Peter was about to step in for him.

'Yeah, yeah, I was confident that Peter was going to do his best.' And from what I could see, he was a nice enough guy. But that's precisely my point! I didn't know him, and he didn't know me. We were two strangers thrown together and nothing was about to change that. Besides, Peter didn't birth this project with me, Kevin did! Not only was this a peculiar way for Kevin to sever our relationship, but it was a damnable way to impart my business strategy to someone who was supposedly going to carry the ball.

So, for what it's worth, I felt that Peter was hardly a suitable replacement for Kevin on the project, although at the time I couldn't put my finger on why. I felt bad about that. Like I wasn't giving the guy a chance, wanting to believe that my relationship with Kevin was getting in the way, so I placated myself into believing things would turn out right, after all he was Kevin's boss.

Again, my gut instincts were right, little did I realize that waiting on me just a tad down the road, would be the full-blown manifestation of this seemingly inconsequential changing of the guard.

So, with all that figured into the mix, I knew better than to leave Rhode Island without an agreement that day. And by the way, I hadn't lost my mind as of yet, not by a long shot. I was determined more than ever to get an agreement, however there was just one caveat I would insist upon… 'It had to be fair!'

———————————

"Do they check out?" Kevin asked, his serious tone yanking me back into the room once again.

Dianne looked at him askance, "Excuse me Kevin? Of course, they check out. What do you mean by that anyway?" she asked, puzzled.

"I just want to make sure that what the man has agreed to, is in the contract is all. After all, we gave him our word before he took the drive up here to meet with us this morning. That's all," he said, coming out of his seat a little, meeting her head on.

I couldn't help but smile at him, 'go get em Kev,' I thought.

"Of course, they check out," her voice trailing off, glaring at him like he had become some sort of a turncoat.

"So Steve, Kevin tells me that we're agreed that you are to be paid ten cents for every filter we manufacture, is that correct?"

"Yes, we've agreed to that."

"And you have accepted the fact that you will be paid fifty thousand dollars in upfront money, is that correct?"

"I agreed to that as well. But I got to tell ya Dianne, you guys have a heck of a nerve offering me fifty grand for all this. I want you to know that's how I feel about it, right up front. I'm gonna take it, but I'm not too thrilled, if you know what I mean."

I didn't plan on venting, but I couldn't resist a parting shot. "You know, this outfit spends more sponsoring a lousy golf outing, than what you're about to pay me. And I'm turning AlliedSignal onto a billion-dollar market, that's if you're smart enough to go out there and get it."

She just sat there and grinned. Her thick hide made Kevin's, seem like boiled chicken skin. "Do you remember back at the airport, when you weren't so inclined to negotiate with me?" she asked.

I replied, "Yeah…, I had my reasons for that."

"Well, if you think fifty thousand is a low figure, you might be interested to know what I was authorized to offer you per piece that day.

"What?" I asked, not so amused.

Waiting a moment for the full effect, she spitefully blurted out… "The penny per filter I offered you, was in fact our top offer."

"I remember that, like it was yesterday," I sneered. "That's why we never talked money that day, remember? Anyway Diane, let's get on with it," I said, glancing Kevin's way, as much to say, 'thanks for the setup Buddy.' About all he could do, was just sit back in his chair and take cover, hoping that the two of us weren't about to go at it.

"It's true Stevie. It's true," he broke in. "That's what they wanted to start the bidding off at, but they ended up giving you a dime man!" His excitement drove him nearly across the table, trying to remind me of that fact. "Don't ask me how you ever got it out of them, I still don't know! Maybe, it was God? Anyway, you hit a home run on that score, believe me!"

He had such a beautiful way of backing me off, 'I believe they call it being told what you want to hear.' It didn't matter anyway, I had already promised him that I was going to behave like a good trooper during our little get together, and I intended on sticking to that.

So not wanting to get too cantankerous, I rather flippantly threw one last jab, "That wouldn't of surprised me at all. Maybe that's why I wasn't so hopped up about discussing my compensation with you that day," wiping the smile off her face.

Just then Jackie walked in with the contracts. I had never met her before, nonetheless I knew her as that kind voice on the other end of the line. You know, the one just before I'd be put through to the lion's den.

After she handed the contracts to her boss, I stood up and reached for her hand. "Hi Jackie, Steve Moor. It's a pleasure to finally meet you!

My courteous jester seemed to catch her off guard as she blushed, sticking out her hand. Grabbing hold, I wished that this kind soul could somehow make it all better as she greeted me with a reassuring squeeze.

Dianne lifted my copy of the contract up in the air, signaling for me to unloosen her secretaries hand. I could tell she was annoyed that I had the nerve to fawn over the help before such a momentous occasion. Apparently, my full attention needed to be directed towards her, as I grabbed my copy and sat down.

'Whoa, what gives around here?' I wondered, scanning the time stamp on the top of the front page. 'Was it just me, or was it just the way things were done around here?' It seemed like every time I turned around, people were waiting for the last possible minute to do their jobs.

There it was, *May 31, 1995   8:56 AM Allied Auto Law #1702 P. 11*. The fax number printed on the bottom of the page tipped me off that this document wasn't prepared by her.

"Hey Dianne," I said with a puzzling look, "Where did this contract come from? I thought by the sounds of things, that you were going to draw it up."

"Oh, no," she replied rather defensively, "Whatever gave you that idea?"

I didn't want to get involved in a spitting match now, for God's sake. I don't know, except she had always led me to believe that she was in total control of the contractual process and that she was going to draw it.

"Well, pardon me," not wanting to start. "Then would you be so kind and tell me where the 313-area code originates from, and perhaps who drew this contract?"

"Sure. It was drawn at AlliedSignal's Automotive Corporate Headquarters in Southfield, Michigan and the attorneys name is Gus Hampilos. Is there anything else?"

"No thanks. You answered my questions for now."

"Good then. Shall we move on?" she said, eager to begin her presentation of the contract.

I nodded my head and gave her the go ahead. The front page was boilerplate, as one might of expected, the addresses of both parties including some basic definitions and my patent number of course, 5,209,842. 'So far so good,' I thought, as Dianne went through motions.

Just so you know, the basic parameters of this contract between myself an Allied had already been thoroughly hashed out prior to my arrival. I was expecting a straight forward and somewhat clean contract. What would end up being presented to me that day was anything but. Had I of known what they were about to present me, I would have skipped the contact presentation and would have had it sent directly to my lawyer.

As an aside, if I had gone that route, I would of never of found out about Kevin's impending departure until long after the ink was dry!

You haven't the foggiest clue of the shit storm I was about to wander into…

I don't know why, but she reminded me of a real estate agent, as she nervously presented a bogus contract to an anxious set of sellers. I was in the seller's position now. Studying her every move as she did her level best to soften me up for the impending hook, that I intuitively knew just lie ahead. As a presenter of contracts myself, I knew exactly what she was doing, as I watched her work her way through the fluff. Like any seller…, all I really cared about was the bottom line.

The contract specified that I would receive my royalty checks every quarter, 'fair enough,' I thought, until we moved a little further on down the page. Before long, my suspicions had been confirmed! 'Remember the fifty thousand dollars in up-front money?' Well, they were still willing to pay me that sum, except the Company as it turned out, seemed to have a hard time letting go of it. They wanted to pay me the money after 120 days from the effective date of my contract!!!

My first instinct was to get insulted, but that would have only made matters worse. So, I skipped over the festering details of how my 180-day pre-licensing agreement had by now blossomed into 220 days of non-compensation and confusion.

Emblazoned into my thinking was a kernel of wisdom imparted to me by a first-generation, born of Italian immigrants. For the briefest of moments, I reflected upon some insight imparted me by a dignified old man. A soul who got his first taste of life in Newark's, First Ward. A guy who suffered great prejudice throughout his early years at the cruel hands of the other nationalities who had colonized the land long before his parents had arrived in America to start a new life. A man who joined the C. C. C. Camps under Roosevelt, when at age sixteen, left his blind mother and crippled father behind so he could earn enough money to provide for them. A guy yet barely seventeen, who ran off to join the navy the day he buried his father, leaving all of his worldly possessions to his sister. A guy who never gave it a second thought that he might not make it back from the raging battles in the Pacific Islands to reunite with his sweetheart, the one he married the week before he left for the big one. A man as tough as nails, yet as gentle as a newborn, who still carried many scars that didn't want to heal, even now that he was old.

That man I'm referring to, was none other than my wife's father, now seventy-nine years young, a guy I would still advise against getting into a fist fight with. And as God would have it, He sent a good loving man my way shortly after my father died to help me pick up the pieces.

As we went over things before I left, he grabbed my hands and buried them in his huge mitts in an earnest effort to remind me of the facts of life. "Remember Steve, I got a lot over you. Now watch these bums. And whatever you do, don't let em take your kindness for weakness!"

"I won't Tony. I got a good idea what I'm doing."

"You're no dummy anyway Steve…, I know that. But remember just the same what I'm telling ya, these guys make it a practice of chewing people up and spittin' them out. I didn't put in forty years at Westinghouse for nothin'. We'll talk after you get back."

"Now Dianne, let me ask you a question and correct me if I'm wrong. AlliedSignal proposes to compensate me a hundred and twenty days after we have a fully signed and executed contract?"

I looked over at Kevin as he sat there motionless, then I turned once again to Dianne. "You guys are serious, right?"

She looked at me, and played dumb, like a real pro. For a moment there, I had to wonder if this outfit promised to pay the Indian back at the airport with a year's supply of curry and rice.

"No, Steve. That's rather standard," as she rambled on about something stupid, like it fit into their billing cycle.

"Well, we might as well start right here, if it's all the same to you," I said, guarding my emotions.

Batting her eye lids, she inquired, "Do you have a problem with the hundred and twenty days Steve?"

"As a matter of fact, I do! Let's make it what it should be," I said calmly. "Let's make it payable in ten business days. Okay?"

Immediately she sputtered as if she was about to make a withdrawal out of her own personal bank account. Flustered, she looked over at Kevin, with those pleading eyes of hers, desperately wanting him to advise me against such a perishable request.

Calmly, he replied, "Dianne, how would you like to be kept waiting for your next paycheck?"

"But…"

"Hey, you asked me, and I'm telling you. This Company, I'm sure has the ability to write him a check certainly within ten business days, he added sarcastically. "Come on now, let's just agree so we can move along here, we have a long way to go."

Without any further commentary, she duly noted that change on her yellow pad. It had been agreed to.

Under the next section: **3. ROYALTIES**, *there it was, under **3.(b)**, my dime! I was to be paid $0.10 for every filter **made in*** the U.S. during each such reporting period. So far so good, but as I turned to the top of page three, Canada was conspicuously missing! Searching on, it became apparent that there was also no reference made to distinguish the automotive royalty from that of the heavy-duty either!

Not sure what to do, I kept my mouth shut and waited for the right opportunity to log my objection, since I considered the heavy-duty market to be a completely separate entity from the automotive. And coincidentally, so does every filter manufacturer on the planet! I knew all too well that any truck filter was going to sell for three times as much as an automobile filter. 'After all, the Company's profit margin on those filters would be at least more than double, so why wouldn't they want to compensate me accordingly?'

So in turn, I was fully expecting to receive at least twenty cents apiece for every heavy-duty filter that rolled off the line, reasoning it would only be fair.

Things were starting to proceed a little too fast for me now and what I was about to lay my eyes on next, hadn't even remotely occurred to me.

Little did I realize it, but I was well on my way to getting my mind blown!

I left the Canadian issue and the heavy-duty market where they lie bleeding, opting to come back for those wounded later.

This chicken-hearted outfit was now proposing to tie both me and my patent up for the next three years for a grand total of two hundred and twenty-five thousand dollars! All of a sudden, I started to get this sick feeling, that this clause was specifically put into the contract to compensate me in the event that Fram fell flat on their faces. Just in case they failed to successfully seize the billion-dollar opportunity I had so carefully laid at their feet for the last seventeen months!

I can tell you this much, I certainly wasn't in this game for a lousy couple of hundred grand! Let's try and put this into perspective, I had a seventy-thousand-dollar mortgage on my forty-year-old ranch house waitin' on me back in Jersey!

Let me tell you something, I wasn't in this thing for thousands or even hundreds of thousands. Not for a moment! That never would of been sufficient motivation to put my entire life…, and that of my precious family's on hold, while daddy lead them through a decades long journey through this mine field. I knew realistically this run on Broadway was worth somewhere around thirty million dollars to me and several billion dollars to them!

So, here's how the contract read:

Fifty Thousand for the first year.
Seventy-Five Thousand for year two.
One Hundred Thousand for year three."

Not wanting any part of Dianne, I turned towards Kevin as much to say, "Et tu, Brute?"

It was now going to be his turn to sputter, as he tried his best to convince me that this clause was inserted in there for my protection. '…More like to try and buy me off in the event of a disaster,' I thought.

"Hey Kevin! So, did you have prior knowledge of what was supposed to be contained in this contract?"

"Ugh, no… Not really, Steve," he said rather sheepishly. I knew darn well he was privy to much of what was being presented before me that morning, he just wasn't about to show his hand.

"I sure hope not, I shot back angrily. "Because it looks here like you guys are scared to death, poised like you're ready to fail or something! You got a heck of a nerve offering me this insulting insurance policy, Kev! It's worth peanuts to me. I'm not in this thing for a couple hundred thousand dollars either, and you above all people should know that Kevin! If you guys feel so inclined like you're gonna fall at the starting gate, then why don't you offer me something fair like three million dollars. Not two hundred and twenty-five thousand over three years, for God's sake!"

Dianne interrupted, apparently miffed I was grilling Kevin, while she was being left out.

"Steve, now you know we aren't prepared to make you any such offer like that."

"I know all about it Dianne," I said in abject disgust. Looking like a crazy man, I leaned over to her and offered, "So let's play on your pathetic terms. I want a hundred thousand for each of the three years, making it an even three hundred thousand dollars. And if you do screw it up, I want the patents and all of my trade secrets back! Okay?!

"That's right Steve, let it drop. Let it drop Buddy," he said relieved.

"Oh, I don't know about letting anything drop quite yet Kevin. So how 'bout it Dianne, three hundred grand, okay?"

"I don't know?" she said, stalling.

"Well good," I politely offered. "Why don't you go over there and call whoever, and I'll just wait here for you to return with their response." She just batted her eyes and looked at me kinda dumfounded. I'd have to admit, I enjoyed watching her squirm a bit, now that she was unable to perform her magic tricks in front of Kevin, like she had done in private with me. I was just banking that Kevin hadn't completely sold his soul as of yet.

"Now Steve," Kevin chimed in trying to settle the air. "She'll check it out, okay Buddy? But you know that she can't just get up and call somebody and get an answer like that for you. Now you know that! So, come on, let's say we move on. I promise, she'll check on it. Won't you, Dianne?"

Relieved, she offered, "Oh yes of course."

"If you don't mind Dianne, I'd appreciate it if you would jot that down on your yellow pad there, just so you don't forget. Because I'm not going to forget to advise my attorney, so he can take this up with Allied's attorney.

"Oh, and one more thing about the insurance, like I said, it's really not important, because you're not going to fail, however it is a matter of principal with me now. So, I'd like to tell you a little something Dianne, this is not just business to me, its personal. So, if you guys drop the ball, and Allied screws up and ruins my dream, I promise you that my story will get out to the entire civilized world. Now that's what I call insurance, not what you're offering me!

"Just so you know, we're both carrying policies now. But like I said, it really doesn't matter, because you guys aren't going to fail. Right Kev? Because you're not going to fail. Right?"

She didn't know what to make of that statement, of course she didn't know me well enough either, nor did she care to. But let me tell you something…, he certainly did!

Kevin chuckled a little under his breath as he smiled, perhaps glad in knowing I was just as passionate about my baby's new life as the day I first called on him.

By the same token there had to be more. I could only wonder how much he actually knew, and as to why he was bailing out of Fram in such a hurry. One thing for sure, he wasn't about to tell me what was going on, not yet at least. He was just as intent on me signing as ever, 'it was his job, remember?'

A little further on down the page was that billing cycle thing again. Apparently, the big boys were going to require a full sixty days to pay me after each quarter would end. Dianne told me it was just normal accounting protocol, so I went along with that request despite my better judgment. The fact remains, that in this day and age of computerized everything, they would know down to the minute, how many filters rolled off their lines. Never in my wildest dreams, could I be convinced that they would need sixty days to perform that task.

'Who were they kidding,' as I swallowed hard, fending off the insult of having me…, the living breathing inventor, lumped in with the accounts receivable like that. And I told Dianne so!

Un-flapped by my commentary, she proceeded to move further on down to the bottom of the page, to the next section:

4 NO REPRESENTATION OR WARRANTIES

"***4.(a)*** *Licensor (that's me), makes no representation or warranties, express or implied, that the exploitation by AlliedSignal of Licensed Patent does not infringe any other patent right or other proprietary right or alleged right of any Third Party."*

"***4.(b)*** *LICENSOR MAKES NO REPRESENTATION OR WARRANTY, EXPRESS OR IMPLIED, REGARDING THE MERCHANTABILITY OF LICENSED PRODUCTS NOR THE FITNESS THEREOF FOR ANY PARTICULAR PURPOSE."*

As she finished reading the aforementioned warranties, even I, in my lightning fast mind was satisfied with the Company's intent, as spelled out in those two paragraphs.

"That sounds good to me Dianne, I mean sections ***4(a)*** *and* ***4(b)***. I'm certainly not a lawyer but that sounds fair. But don't worry, I've already retained a good attorney to go over this contract with Allied's, so this contract won't end up too one sided, if you know what I mean."

The reality of it was, it was never my intent to infringe on anybody's patent in the first place. 'So, if it was ever my intention to defraud anybody, wouldn't you think that the United States Patent Office who issued the patent would have denied me during their search and examination process?' The answer of course, would be 'yes.' And that's coming from someone who's been through the patent granting process twice.

"Oh that's fine Steve, I wouldn't have expected anything less of a fellow like yourself." Hidden in her tone, she as much called me a distrusting pain in the neck. Kinda like telling me, 'go on now little boy, run to your lawyer, but watch yourself, don't trip and fall now!'

I didn't care how she felt! At this point, just the prospect that I wasn't going to ever have to speak directly to her ever again, was enough grace for me to endure whatever she might want to throw at me this day. I mused, 'after today, if she wants to talk with me, she'd have to do it through my lawyer, who by the way was charging me over $225 dollars per hour just for the privilege. At any rate, I was glad to pay it, just to be freed of her tactics!' That lawyer today, would bill out at $500.

'Of course, I needed a lawyer! To have thought otherwise would have been absolutely crazy! Besides, if I had gotten wind that Kevin was leaving ahead of time, I would not have been sitting there that morning without one, whether they liked it or not! I wasn't that stupid.

'So why didn't you go home, as soon as you found out that Kevin was leaving the Company?' Simply put, I couldn't. The missile was in the silo, it was fully armed, and the target was locked in. Believe me, the countdown was in progress when I had arrived that morning.

I can't emphasize it enough, but the little stunt that Kevin pulled by leaving the Company without giving me the benefit of the doubt, put me in a very compromising position that day. And clearly, it hurt my position terribly.

Apparently, I had trusted him more than he deserved. But it was too late now. In his zeal to chock one up on his resume and tidy up his career, he somehow forgot about me. He forgot about our bond. 'I guess the concept of trust went out the window in light of reeling me in now for the Company.' The manner in which he chose to part ways with Fram was about to cost me my very soul!!!

It was time now to go back and retrieve the wounded and address the Canadian issue that was so blatantly missing in action, under section ***3.(b)*** on the bottom of ***page 2***.

"If you guys don't mind, can we flip back to the bottom of page two, last sentence under ***3.(b)***, where it says *made in the U.S., during each such Reporting Period.*

"Dianne, you specifically told me at the airport back in March, that due to the Company's accounting methods, Canada was not differentiated from the U.S. At that time, we had agreed that I was to be paid for every filter made in the U.S. and sold in the U.S. and for every filter made in Canada or sold in Canada. You called it a throw in.

"Now do you remember that?" I paused, yet no response.

"Because I do!" As I began driving at her once again. "I expect to be paid for every filter that gets sold in both the United States and Canada! And no loop holes now!" I said with a determined look. I was inflexible on that point, as well I should of been.

"Well," she stated slowly, playing oh so innocent, "I can't exactly recall now, it was so long ago."

I looked over at Kevin, feeling like I was being beaten in front of a crowd of onlookers. "Hey Kevin, help me out here man! You know darn well about this conversation! Are you gonna back me up or what?" looking at him, while wanting to strangle the both of them.

He turned towards Dianne, playing the diplomat. 'Leaving, or no leaving, he was still gonna be on company time till Friday afternoon,' I thought.

"So Dianne, how come that's absent from the contract?" he asked trying to referee.

"Uh…, uh, I don't know?"

"Well, don't you think you should?" inquiring with a sarcastic bite. "Come on now, you must of given the particulars to that guy in Southfield who drew this thing up. Now wouldn't you?" he said, angrily.

"After all Dianne…, we did promise this man a few things ahead of time and I think we are at least obligated to follow through on them. Now don't you think?"

'Well at least he hadn't left me out to dry on that one. I was glad he hadn't fallen that far from grace.'

Exasperated, she began to panic. "I don't know? What do you think?" It was as if I was watching her revert back to childhood or something right in front of my eyes. I wasn't able to make her out…, either she was totally lost, or she was projecting her personal greed onto my deal. Anyway, one thing for sure, I knew that it was absolutely killing her to open the sacred till at the company store.

Impatient now, "Hey Dianne, this guy ain't no dummy here. Write down on that yellow pad of yours what he just said and give it to him, so we can be done with it. Okay?"

"What about paying him for what we sell elsewhere?" she persisted, as if she was in a deep fog?"

"I don't know!" he said, barking at her. "You ought to know the answer to that one! This was your assignment, not mine! Damn it!" The scene was tense enough to cause the vein to pop out of the side of his neck once again. Despite the Tomfoolery, I couldn't help but get a chuckle out of witnessing that one.

Now it was my turn to jump in, but before I had the chance, my mind was sent reeling back to a prior phone conversation I had with Dianne only a short while ago…

I was in the real estate office, doing my floor time one morning, when Norma let me know that Dianne was on the phone.

"Good morning Dianne," I said, wondering why she was calling me? It wasn't like we were discussing my contract any longer, because Kevin had basically assumed her role, by doing her job, at this point.

"And good morning to you Steve." Came forth a salutation as pleasant as pie. My God I thought, either she's a schizoid or I was one. She was so sweet? 'What did she want…, I mean need?'

"What can I do for you, Dianne," I asked.

There was a long pause, so whatever it was, she needed to find the right way to serve it up. I just sat there patiently, expecting anything from her at this point.

"Steve, do you have coverage for any other countries besides the United States?" she inquired, not the least bit self-conscious that she was asking me such an elementary school kid question.

"No. I am not covered by any other patents Dianne." I was shocked by her gall. The question was so telling. Somebody else might of rubbed her face in the mud for that one, but I tried not to play the game of life like that. However, I wasn't beyond playing dumb, and wondered how much further she'd go to incriminate herself.

"What do you mean by that?" I asked.

Clueless… "Well, what I want to know is, have you filed for any patent protection other than that of the U.S.?"

"No." Recalling the fact that we had already gone over this ground back at the airport.

"And why not, may I ask?" she said, prying.

"Because I didn't have the money at the time. Messing around with foreign filings could easily mount upwards of a hundred grand or so. I'm just a small-time inventor, selling houses for a living. Remember?"

"Well I'm sure you are doing all right," she said cutting me off, summarily dismissing what I had just mentioned about the overseas filings.

I shot back, "Dianne I didn't use that illustration, just so I could cry poor mouth to you. So why don't you let me finish?"

Now she seemed aggravated, because I wasn't telling her what she wanted to hear. "All right, go on."

"Dianne, I have to level with you. During the open file period, I wasn't sure if I was going secure an American filter company that was capable of seeing the forest through the trees. Let alone a foreign one. So why would of I filed for outside protection? In my position, you gotta be a realist you know."

"So, what does that have to do with filing for overseas protection," she huffed, not catching on.

"Hey, I'll be the first to admit it, I didn't invent the light bulb here. So, let me ask ya, are you a betting man?"

"Well, I don't know?" she said, rather lost

"Would you of gone out on a limb and filed for any overseas protection if you had been in my shoes?" I asked.

Apparently, she had digested my rhetoric, then after a long pause… "Ah, no."

"I thought you might say that," I said, with a chuckle. "Besides, the statute for filing for international protection has long since lapsed. So even if I licensed the patent to Allied today, we'd still be barred from filing for international protection, even if we wanted to.

You know Dianne, I really don't want to tell you your business, but these are exactly the types of questions that Allied should have aggressively explored the day I sent Kevin my patent in back in January of 94'. Not something you should be asking me in May of 95'. We might of had a chance to file back then, but certainly not now!" I paused for a moment.

She was silent. Apparently, she had been stung by the salience of that truth, knowing that 'it was all water over the dam by now.'

Still, there was no further response from her, so I offered, "Like I told you at the airport back in March, the market is the United States, anyway. It's the Walt Disney of the world."

"Oh, I see," she murmured foggily, not in the least bit moved by my assessment of the situation.

"So, you don't have any other protection, is that correct?" as if repeating the question for the third time would change things. It was rather apparent she was on a prospecting mission, hoping to turn up some sort of a find. But to me, it was a pathetic last-ditch attempt at doing her job. Yet in some weird way I felt sorry for her, as I thought, 'man, if anybody was a day late and a dollar short, it sure was this gal.'

"That's correct." I offered rather fatalistically. "We were both locked in now, unable to change the course of things now, even if we wanted to."

"Okay, fine. Oh, by the way, would you mind sending me up a copy of your patent? I've seemed to of lost mine. Thanks. Click." In true fashion, she had dropped off the line in a huff.

Of course, I was beyond stupefied. 'So why don't you try and explain how the Strategic Planning Officer of one of the largest companies on the face of the globe had the unmitigated gall to call me and ask me questions that I had supplied to her over eight months ago in her office?

'Questions that an aggressive company would have asked from day one? And please, if you can, explain to me how this individual had the brass to ask me for a copy of my patent? Not in the least bit humbled by the fact we were at point in our supposed professional business relationship in which we were no longer able to effectively communicate due to personality conflicts?!!!'

So, like a good little trooper, I sent her off a copy of my patent along with a note via certified mail. The date, May 12th, 1995. Yes, I could of faxed it, but I wanted to send it certified just for emphasis…. And to possibly use this against her if I needed to one day in the future.

My mind landed hard, as it came careening back into present time. I hurried to return to the situation set before me. "Dianne, I thought I had made myself quite clear back at the airport, when I decided not to be compensated for the rest of the world. I thought that I had made myself quite clear that I was just looking to be compensated for the United States and Canada."

She began, "Okay, I just thought…"

Then just to shut her up and to get moving, I said, "All right, if that's how you feel about it I'll just have to remind my attorney to include compensation for the rest of the world! You heard her Kev, she wants me to get paid for everything sold worldwide. I ain't made out of money, so I guess I'll take her up on the offer!"

By this point, our going back and forth had gotten Kevin a little chapped, so he bellowed out over our exchange, "Okay Dianne! I have no problem if you want to compensate the man for the entire world. I happen to think he's entitled to it anyway, so I hope you're happy now? Can we please move on?"

To keep things consistent, she was reticent to give me what I wanted and thought fair. Instead she did her best to satiate her desire to do things her way, even if it meant giving me something I didn't even want for the asking. But this time I took her up on it!

It was getting close to lunch, so we decided to forge on ahead to page four:

5. PATENT INFRINGEMENT

*"**5.(a)** In the event a claim of infringement of a patent has been asserted against AlliedSignal by a third party as a result of AlliedSignal's manufacture, use or sale of Licensed Products, Licensor shall make "Reasonable Efforts" to assist Allied Signal in modifying the Licensed Products to the extent to avoid such claim of infringement. Further, Licensor shall make "Reasonable Efforts" to assist AlliedSignal, at AlliedSignal's expense, in defending any such claim."*

"That seems fair. Let me see if I'm right here," as I looked directly at her. "So, let's say Purolator decides to make a similar filter. No, no…, stop! Let's use Quaker State instead, now that they have just bought Slick-50! I think that would make a much better analogy, don't you Kev?"

"Hey Buddy," he sneered, "Do whatever makes you feel better. I was fine with the Purolator one," he offered clearly unamused.

"Okay, so let's say Quaker State goes out and puts Slick-50 in an oil filter and slaps their name on it, you know co-brands it, like we're doing with DuPont. Almost like you were considering doing with Slick-50 before Quaker State moved in and put them in play. Anyway, AlliedSignal would want me, as the inventor to come to their aid." Thinking out loud I continued, "And I guess by doing so, I'd essentially be coming to my own aid as well, now that you think about it."

Edging her way in, "That's right Steve. I think that sounds very fair, don't you? You see Steve, we are not the bad guys here after all," she said feeling quite proud. Unable to let the moment go, she continued embellishing the obvious, "You see, even if this product inadvertently infringes upon somebody else's product, Allied is prepared to modify your product to avoid any infringement. We are just requesting your assistance in doing so at our expense, of course!"

"Like I said Dianne, that seems fair. It's nothing more than what I would of expected Allied's position to be anyway."

Kevin just sat back in his chair, basking in the rare moment of consensus. "Well if you guys liked that part so much, why don't you read on. What do ya say Dianne?"

6. PATENT ENFORCEMENT

"*6.(a.)* *In the event either Party discovers tangible evidence of the manufacture, use or sale by another of a product which infringes any claim of Licensed Patent, the party that discovered the evidence shall notify the other Party promptly in writing upon such discovery. Such notification shall include all such tangible evidence discovered by the notifying Party.*"

"Okay Steve?" she asked, tilting her head like a gentle puppy dog.

"So far so good. Maybe at this rate we'll be done before lunch. There's only another five and a half pages to go," I quipped sarcastically, knowing at the present rate we'd never finish at anything close to lunch.

"*6.(b)* *Licensor (that's me) shall have the right but not the obligation to initiate an action to enforce the Licensed Patent. Any such enforcement shall be at the expense of the Licensor, and all damages awarded as a result of such action shall be for the Licensors account.*"

Well that looked good enough to me. Because to tell the truth, I wasn't planning on suing anybody for infringement anyway. To mount a defense against any such interloper would be a joke for someone in my position, requiring liquid assets of millions of dollars just to prepare for such a battle.

At the time, I only had about ten grand in the bank, so the prospect of making money from a high drama conducted in a court room was out of the question and so was getting involved with the appeals process that could easily span well over a decade. Going to court to obtain justice or to make a day's pay was at the bottom of my list of things to do. I can assure you, I didn't have any preconceived notions that I would be defending my patent, not now and not later. Besides, in truth, I was in the process of assigning all control of this enterprise over to them, my destiny included! From where I stood it would have been impossible from a financial standpoint to enforce my patent single-handedly against an infringer. My liquid assets precluded such a maneuver against a foe that could mount a multi-million-dollar patent trial. Anyhow, just the prospect of facing that sort of onslaught was reason enough to justify me teaming up with the big boys in the first place! As far as I was concerned, protection was a very important aspect of this licensing deal!

The remainder of page four included several more lines, that dealt with the formalities of how and under what conditions I could personally bring suit, if I decided to do so on my own. I just went along for the ride, as Dianne read the rest of the legal mumbo jumbo, the whole time believing in my heart that I would never have to exercise that option. What it really boiled down to, was this... I was banking on the fact there wasn't a company stupid enough to infringe against a product made by AlliedSignal. 'After all, who would want to face them in court?' I certainly wouldn't want to!

Moving right along now, we had made it to the top of page five, nearly the midway point in the contract. By now, the morning's events had sapped a good deal of my energy thus far, 'only a little further, then perhaps Kevin would call a break, it was well after eleven.' I really had quittin' time on my mind.

I resisted the urge of wondering off to somewhere pleasant, killing any fanciful moment that I was now planted under a large tree in green meadow, looking up at the blue sky. Oh, how I fought the allure of a peaceful daydream, after all, it looked like things were going to work out for themselves. I could feel my faculties giving ground to my tired body, as I sat there unsuspectingly, like a stupid frog, about to be boiled, as she read, *"that AlliedSignal shall have the right to credit against future royalty payments due (the Inventor) under Section **3.(b)** and Section **3(c)**, above, an equal amount to fifty percent (50%) of the expenses incurred by AlliedSignal in the enforcement of the Licensed Patent."*

'What!!!' I exclaimed to myself. I must not of heard her right! But I knew I had, as those words began to twist, like a knife in middle of my back. Beginning to hyperventilate, I desperately called my mind into subjection with everything I had. It was no time for blue sky. Nor was it time for emotion, as I forced myself to reread what she had so casually cited.

By now I wasn't listening to a word she was saying, as I submerged deep into my own world trying to cipher if there was some sort of mistake! I didn't rightly know how I was going to react to such a blatantly greedy and overreaching caveat!

I read on ahead, just to make sure I didn't misunderstand what I was seeing, so I continued reading a bit further. *"With respect to any action initiated by AlliedSignal, damages and costs awarded pursuant to any such action shall be to the sole and exclusive benefit of Allied Signal."*

'Those greedy bastards…,' I screamed, from deep within.

'Oh my God, I was right!' It didn't take much to see though their legalese, even with my lightning fast mind. If they sued, they wanted me to be part and parcel of their prosecution strategy, and the big-hearted fellows were going to pay for my expenses such as food, travel and logging. Then for my reward they only wanted fifty percent of my future royalties in exchange for the favor. 'Oh, how nice of them to return the favor!'

'So why was this outfit acting with such blatant disregard towards a business partner who had done nothing but help them along over the last sixteen months?' I cried in agony, deep from within.

'Were they really just another faceless and heartless corporation?! You know, the ones we see on the TV news all of the time. The kind of company that we, the public, constantly warn each other about?' I was being left no other choice, but to believe they were in fact showing their true colors now. Unfortunately, by this time, I had handed over my entire plan to them. Regrettably, it was coming down to the money…, the greed of a dime!

'Was that any way to treat a business partner who lives in a forty-year-old ranch house and drives a striped Dodge Caravan?' I didn't think so. The last line of that clause made it crystal clear, as they jammed the point home. I hurried on, to read the last line… *"In any action in which AlliedSignal requests the assistance of the Licensor, (that's me again, the inventor), Licensor shall assist AlliedSignal, entirely at AlliedSignal's expense."*

That was it, the lamenting in silence was over, and I blew! "Who the heck wrote that piece of nonsense Dianne! Was it you?" I said accusingly. Right then if I could of, I would have reached over across the table and strangled her. And believe me, if there wasn't a God in Heaven, or a jail cell with my name on it waiting for me, I would have.

"Really now! What kind of a fool do you guys take me for! I've been real good about everything so far! And, so that's what you do to me!"

My eyes were fixed on Kevin, wishing for x-ray vision so that I could read his heart. I didn't need to bother with Dianne's, for I was quite certain I already knew the contents of hers. For the moment, the only real option I had besides getting up, was to plead for sanity. No amount of screaming could have fixed the lunacy presented before me!

"Hey, don't look at me Buddy!" squawking guiltily, knowing full well the Company's intent. "I sure as heck didn't write this, that much I can vouch for! It was at least somewhat reassuring that my friend siting across the table from me had enough honor to recognize the absurdity of the Company's greed.

"Well, what do you think about it Kev?" still unable to leave it alone. The moment required the answer to come from him. I just had to know where he stood after all we had been through together.

"Well?" he said, taking a deep breath, "What do I really think? I think someone is out of their friggin' mind! he cried. "Expecting that you give up half of your lousy dime so that you can help bankroll AlliedSignal in a patent lawsuit. The very thought of it boggles the mind. That's what I think!"

Dianne looked on in horror, transfixed as she beheld Kevin doing the right thing. By her reckoning, his Friday departure had already gotten to him.

Turning just in time, I caught her disingenuous spirit change colors faster than a cuttlefish on a coral reef. In a split second, her look of disgust aimed at him, suddenly changed to, 'may I be of service to you' as she refocused her sights on me, knowing she was more or less gonna have to go it alone from here on out.

But it was way late for that trick, as I saw right through her front. "Dianne, this is unacceptable, I said calmly. I'll tell you what, right now, I won't be going into business with a Company that is so overreaching as yours."

Un-flapped, she as much as looked at me and said, 'the ball is still in your court Mr.'

'So it was, so it was,' I thought. "Kevin, I've had just about enough. I think I'm out of here my friend. I never had a chance to tell you this, and I was going to this morning, but due to everything that was going on, I didn't have an opportunity..."

"What was going on?" she interrupted, as the blood began to drain out of her face. I guess for the first time now, she must of been on to the fact that I knew he'd be leaving Friday. It was etched across her round face.

Ignoring her, I went right on with my little secret, "So..., you can take this for what it's worth, but my contact at Wix called me yesterday. And he said they finally wanted to meet with me. I guess he was serious too, because let me tell you something, Dick has never reached out like this before on anything! As a matter of fact, I probably hadn't spoken with him about my patent in nearly a year!"

Mumbling under my breath, 'those damn fools, it sure took them long enough to decide and call me, and what timing!'

"Come on now Steve," she sniped. "Do you really think I was born yesterday to go for something like that?"

"Nope. No, I don't at all. Far from it. Just like it isn't like me…, to make something like this up," as I slid my chair up to the table.

"Kevin! Kevin! He's leaving! What are you going to do?" she said, in an absolute panic.

"He's a big boy, it's not like I'm gonna tackle him, Dianne."

"You wanna know what I told him when he called, Kev?"

"As a matter of fact I do, Buddy. What did he say? his head cocked to one side, as if that was going to help him to figure out my next move.

Truly on my way out the door, I said with a heavy heart, "I told him that I had given Fram my word of honor. And that I was going to cut the covenant with them tomorrow. That's what I told him. And look at the crap your outfit's pulling. You guys ought to be ashamed of yourselves! "Kev, I'm gonna split now, so I can beat the traffic home. Thanks for everything. I know you tried your best. You were just out manned and out gunned on this one.

"And hey, there's no need to go out for lunch," I said, doing my best to choke back my aching heart. I was scarcely able to believe my own ears as the words began to register as I began to walk away from my dream.

Nearly screaming she pleaded, "Kevin don't let him run out!"

"Hey, Dianne, it's not up to me, I think you know that," as I made it for the door, briefcase in hand.

"Steve, do me a favor, would you? Go and wait out in the hall and give us a moment, would you?" he said, trying to calm her…, taking control.

I couldn't hear anything of what they were saying, as I waited out in the hall. All I knew was that this morning had turned out to be a disaster in almost every conceivable way. I was numb, as I shielded the windows to my soul from the occasional passersby in the hallway. I didn't hold it against them as they stared at the broken man who was leaning against the wall. I was terribly lost as I contemplated my next move.

The Wix thing was true, as my thoughts quickly headed that way. Dick Dye had called me only the day before, around noon time. After I finished hearing what he had to say, I was flattered just the same, but I didn't want to go with Wix! I wanted to go it with Fram! Yet the situation I found myself in, didn't bode well for reaching an agreement anytime soon. Only a desperate fool would of acquiesced to their audacious demands.

Suddenly, they came out of the room, Dianne turned sharply and headed down the hall in a huff, never bothering for even a second to look my way. On the flip side, there was Kevin. With sincere face in hand, he didn't hesitate to come looking for me. "I believe I have it all worked out now Buddy," putting his arm around my neck. "Let's say we go and grab a soda."

I looked over at him and smiled, he was easy to forgive. "I was leaving; you know…"

"Hey… You don't have to tell me. But it's over now. She's gonna get that part of the contract removed. And she's gonna get the rest of the contract straightened out as well. …And I warned her, that you'd never sign something like that. Anyway, as far as I'm concerned, you shouldn't have to sign anything like that anyway."

We walked down the hallway and grabbed a soda, heading down the stairs for the picnic table out back. Sitting down, he volunteered, "Do you know what happened up there when we were in the room?"

"No, I don't. How could I?"

"To begin with, she had no idea that you knew that I was leaving, at least not until you mentioned that thing about 'the goings on this morning.' Man, I'll tell you, she really freaked out about that one! You weren't supposed to know. Everybody around here thought you might not of signed, if you found out beforehand that I was leaving…, especially her! You wouldn't believe what she said to me up there, once she knew you had found out. All I can say it's a darn good thing she's a woman, 'cause I sure wouldn't of taken that sort of abuse from a guy."

"Hey Kev, you can skip the details for now, if you don't mind, but just make sure Jodi doesn't catch any heat because of it, because you're the only one who knows how I found out. Besides, it wasn't her fault anyway. Maybe she wasn't in tune to the sneaky tactics you guys were employing here.

"You know Kev, I gotta tell ya something, you guys are a bunch of sneaky bastards. I just want you to know that, okay?"

"Well…," he said.

Before he got a chance to pick up a head of steam, I walked on him before he had a chance to say anything. "So, you guys were afraid I wouldn't sign, 'cause you were leaving, huh? So, I was going to bail on my dream, just like that? What a bunch of friggin babies you are! I guess somebody's been sucking at the corporate tit for too long…, seems like to me. Maybe what I'm seeing, is that nobody around here can even begin to fathom the passion it requires to motivate an average slob like myself to make it to the pinnacle of this mountain."

Not quite finished, I offered, "So what! It doesn't matter anyway. I'm still gonna go into business with you guys as long as that contract is something I can live with!" No matter how much I may have tried, it was nearly impossible to extinguish the dream.

"Good," he said not attempting a rebuttal. "Let's finish our sodas, then I'll go and get her, so we can wrap this thing up, then when it's all over we can go out and grab a beer."

"Yeah… I could sure use one about now myself."

Kevin had left me safely behind to wait it out in the conference room, as he went and looked for Dianne. I just stood there leaning on the window ledge, starring out at the blue sky, wondering what lie ahead.

Oh, perhaps I could have known the answer to that question easily enough, because my copy of the contract lay where I had left it when I had gotten up, still open to page five. As for right now, I couldn't be bothered to leap ahead and read on, I wasn't feeling that ambitious. Besides, I didn't want to get worked up and waste what energy I had remaining by getting aggravated all by myself.

From here on out, I just wanted things to be fair, if that were at all possible. Somehow, I guess due to my own naïveté, I had seriously miscalculated that this would ever be happening to me.

'I know it sounds crazy Lord, but I'm doing the best I can. And I'm realizing now, that it's a good possibility that I had put my trust in the wrong places. And if that's the case, I'm sorry for that, believe me. And I also know, that if I hadn't heard it for myself, I wouldn't have believed it… But you told me, didn't you? You know… That very first time, when you told me that "You wouldn't have allowed me to get this far, only to meet up with failure!" Well I'm telling you Jesus, I sure hope I heard you right!'

After about ten minutes or so they came prancing into the room, fresh as two daisies.

"Shall we begin again," she smiled, as I dodged her intended barb.

"Sure," I said, intending on keeping things simple.

Looking innocently over at Kevin, she eased back into it, "So, where were we?" as much to insinuate that I was the one who had caused the disturbance.

Before he had a chance to speak I answered her question, "We're in the middle of page five, section 7, as I began reading it to her:

7. MAINTAINING PATENTS

*"**7.(a)** Licensor shall maintain active and enforceable the Licensed Patent."*

'Simple enough,' I thought. 'Just something else I'll bet they want me to pay for.'

I was amazed at the contradiction. In section **6.(b)**, there was no doubt, the Company was out to gut me. Now in this section in true schizoid fashion, they were willing to entrust me with the responsibility of maintaining the patents anniversary fees, crucial for the enforcement of the patent. 'I didn't get it, was this just another money saving measure on their part?' I was totally befuddled. Nearly every time in a deal such as this, the inventor or patent holder assigns over his patent rights. I was going to consult my attorney, but I couldn't resist testing the depths of her stupidity.

"What do you say Dianne?" I began, "Those licensing fees are going to add up over the course of the patent. I'm not complaining, but they are gonna amount somewhere in the neighborhood of several grand. Don't you think the Company could be a sport about it, and pick up the tab?"

"I can't say Steve; I'll have to check on it for you. How does that sound?"

"Okay I guess," knowing I had just made it look like I had conceded on another point.

Yet, I couldn't help but think about all of those situations that I sweated out while at someone's dining room table, especially when it came time to make presentation and negotiate the money. My experience in real estate up until now had taught me well, 'greed rules.' And I had innumerable deals under my belt to validate that fact. It seemed clear, at least to me, that most people weren't able to let go of their precious money without a fight. I vowed to never let that be the guiding force in my life, and especially not here with Fram. So far, that held true…, and that left me with a sense of pride.

Yet I still couldn't shut it off, reflecting on many a real estate deal where either one or both parties were millionaires. It was impossible to forget, that those folks with the big bucks would absolutely claw each other's eyes out for a lot less than that maintenance fee I left back there on the table. And trust me, those types of people made no bones about it while doing so. After all the years of catering to those types, I was still unable to figure out how they always seemed to come out with the deal having gone their way!

Before I had a chance, the axiom about 'the rich getting richer and the poor getting poorer,' came flashing across my screen as if to incite me further. I paid it no heed, letting it pass on by, knowing I had to double back and re-enter the fray.

"Hey Dianne, not to beat a dead horse, but on another note, Kevin told me that you are going to strike that part in *section six*. You know, the section concerning my giving back fifty percent of my royalties if Fram should have to defend the patent."

She wasn't quick to respond, like she was suffering from amnesia. "What?" she said.

Trying to keep a rein on my ire, when it came to her incessant game playing, I raised my voice a little, saying, "I want your word on it Dianne. Right here and right now!"

"Oh, you mean that section? Yeah, sure."

"You heard it Kev," I said sharply, meeting him square in the face. "I expect you to back me up no matter what it takes, and wherever you might be. And you know what I mean." He got the message loud and clear as the look I sent his way telegraphed my sentiments.

As we moved on to the next section, I still couldn't let go of the fact that somehow, he was more than a little bit responsible for this charade.

8. PAYMENTS

"*8.(a)* *All payments which shall become due under any provision of this Agreement shall be made by AlliedSignal to Licensor, (that's me) without discount or offset, in lawful money of the United States to the Licensor; or such bank or other location that Licensor may designate....*"

Again, this clause appeared acceptable to my untrained legal mind. Maybe I should of been paying more careful attention to the phrase *"without discount or offset"*, but I wasn't. As it would turn out, those words which were intended to be followed by the Company, would prove to be only a hollow promise. I had no way of telling the future, but in the offing, those words would fall flat. Another promise yet to be broken by the big boys.

"*8.(b)* *Within ninety (90) days after the end of each Reporting Period AlliedSignal shall render to Licensor an Accounting statement showing the quantities of Licensed Products made in the U.S. during the Reporting Period, the amount of royalties payable to Licensor (that's me) and, at the same time, AlliedSignal shall pay to Licensor the royalties shown by the report to be due.*"

"Hey, Dianne! Did you forget what you told me at the airport?" I said, once again, trying not to lose my cool.

"What do you mean Steve?" If she batted her eyelids anymore, I was afraid she'd get a migraine and we'd have to stop.

"What do I mean?" repeating myself again for both their sakes. Suddenly, the warning from the old man came hurtling through my mind, "Watch those bums, don't let 'em take your kindness for weakness." Those words of Patti's dad reminded me of Jimmy Cagney playing a vintage boxing coach as they began to stir the pot.

In a moment that seemed frozen in time, I ran down the situation. 'She couldn't of possibly of proof read this contract with any degree of accuracy before our meeting.' That was evident, even to my unskilled eye. Once again, I was embroiled in that interminable struggle from within, perplexed as to how I was going to straighten out this endless mess. For God's Almighty's sake it was like the dreaded Y2K bug! It seemed to be built into this thing, layer upon layer. It seemed that the further we went into the contract, the more screwed up it got!

"What I mean Dianne, is that you got it right on the one hand, where it says *"made"* but on the other hand, you have it wrong…, real wrong. I'd like to ask you a straight forward question. Where the heck is Canada?

"Now you specifically told me that Canada was a throw in for crying out loud! So what is it Dianne, could you please give me an explanation? Is Canada a throw in, or not? Or were you speaking out of turn that day at the airport and now it's too late and you just can't admit that you gave me something you weren't authorized to give? Tell me... Does the Company want to give me Canada, or not?"

Kevin just sat there bracing himself, no doubt as another round of game playing was about to begin. It was becoming evident that the whole scene was beginning to wear on him as well. Not by any means was I being obstinate, just going after what little which had already been promised me beforehand. Studying his tired face, I wondered what he'd be saying, if he could.

Dianne broke the silence with a nervous yawn, "I don't know why it's not in there Steve?" deflecting any hint of responsibility.

I replied, driving my point home once again, "Well it doesn't seem to appear in the contract so far, you wanna let me in on the secret? Let me ask Diane, is it gonna show up before we get to the end, or are you going to just keep me guessing?"

"I'm not exactly sure Steve?"

Not wanting to subject myself any further to her patronizing attitude, I just politely directed her to write it down on that yellow pad of hers, making sure that it was something else that needed fixing. I can recall sitting there while she scribbled something down on the pad.

For just a moment, please indulge me in a brief object lesson here. Even a lowly Real Estate agent selling houses in the state of New Jersey would have been light years more mindful of disclosure and entrapment than how this Company was conducting itself. And if I hadn't experienced it firsthand myself, I certainly wouldn't of believed it. At any rate, it was blowing my mind!

'How could Allied, so casually have allowed a couple of company employees to negotiate with a first-time inventor such as myself, alone and unmonitored! The Company's disregard as to the magnitude of the document placed before me for consideration was again mind boggling. And I would like to make something abundantly clear. AlliedSignal fully intended for me to agree and sign that contract exactly the way it had been presented. I was more aghast over that than words could ever describe!

'For their own protection they should have at least of had a lawyer present to satisfy the requirements of fair disclosure, wouldn't you of thought?' Furthermore, they should have vehemently insisted that I have council present to review such a document, or at the very minimum have me sign a waiver, stating I opted to waive that right. That's the very least we do in Jersey, when it comes to selling a house!!!

Let me tell you something. If I ever practiced real estate like that, my humble little license would of been yanked long ago, and I would of been on the receiving end of a law suit.

With that behind us we made it to the top of page six:

"**8.(c)** *Acceptance by Licensor (that's me), of any payment rendered hereunder, whether or not the amount thereof shall be in dispute, shall not constitute acceptance of the amount or schedules on which such payment is based; provided, however, that the correctness of any such payment shall be conclusively presumed unless questioned within one year (1) year from the date of receipt thereof.*"

Now for some reason I didn't understand the full meaning of that section, (I wonder why). In the midst of that, I started getting a panic attack, because it was incumbent upon me to ask Dianne to spell it out, and after all I had been through I was feeling a bit gun shy. I could feel myself hesitating to reach out for her help, sort of like one of the three pigs asking the wolf if he wouldn't mind lending a hand. Believe me, one of last things I needed was for my motives to be misconstrued and precipitate another needless mind game session.

Before I had an opportunity to check myself, I blurted out, "Hey Dianne, help me out here, would you please? I really don't follow the meaning of that section."

For a moment she stared at the contract, while I pensively glanced over in Kevin's direction, making sure he still sat guard. Catching my roving eye, he flipped me a reassuring smile, as if to say, 'we're almost through.'

Picking her head up from the paper she asked, "Did you read on ahead to number 9 per chance? Where it says, **_9. Books_**."

I tried not to give her the impression that she was expecting a lot out of me, so I answered, "No, why?"

"Well, let's just read this section, it kinda goes with **_8.(c)_**, maybe it will clear up your question after I read it to you."

"*__9.(a)__ AlliedSignal shall keep adequate records in sufficient detail to enable the royalties payable by AlliedSignal hereunder to be determined, and shall permit said records to be inspected, at Licensor's expense, at any time during regular business hours by an independent auditor appointed by Licensor for this purpose and not objectionable to AlliedSignal, who shall report to Licensor the quantities of Licensed Product made in the US and the amount of the royalties payable hereunder. However, AlliedSignal shall not be obligated to retain said records longer than one (1) year after the receipt by Licensor of such payment unless the amount of the payment is disputed. In the event the auditor determines that additional royalties are due Licensor, Allied Signal shall, within thirty days of receipt by AlliedSignal of a copy of such auditor's determination, pay to Licensor all additional royalties due him.*"

This time Kevin broke in, "Steve I'm not exactly sure, but **_8.(c)_** appears to go along the same lines as this section number **_9.(a)_**. That you can check the books. You know…, just in case we make a mistake or something and short you."

Before he had a chance to elaborate, this shot raced across my screen, 'wouldn't that be par for the course.'

Rounding out his assurance he then added, "I guess it's also saying that just because you accepted payment, Allied can't hold you to an inaccurate count, is all."

Dianne looked over at him with this big smile, "Very good Kevin. Very good!"

"Okay, that sounds understandable, I guess." 'How comforting,' I mused sarcastically to myself. "But I'm gonna have my attorney spell it out for me just the same if you don't mind. Just as soon as I can fax this agreement to him along with the proposed changes."

"That sounds fine Steve," Kevin volunteered.

Dianne was all smiles, now treating us to, "It's so nice, now that we are agreeing. Don't you think! Let's have a look at the bottom of page six:

10. Term and Termination, shall we? Beginning to read:

"**_10.(a)_** *The term of this Agreement shall commence on the Effective Date and, unless sooner terminated as provided in this Section 10,* **_shall continue in force until the date of expiration of the Licensed Patent._**"

194

There it was! There had never of been any question in my mind concerning that fact! I was entering into this relationship for the long haul, the life of my patent, of which I still had seventeen years left on the clock. Despite all the curves that Allied had thrown at me thus far, it had never ever occurred to me that they would of played games with regard to the duration of our contract and I was comforted by seeing it in writing that they hadn't! I cannot stress it enough, that was the one issue that I believed that they would have never be tampered with. Little did I know what future plans they held out for me, just a little on down the road apiece.

"That's simple enough," I said happily.

"Good Steve, I'm glad you're ok with that as well," she offered.

"Yes, I am happy. But don't get me wrong Dianne, I was never in this thing for anything less than the life of my patent! Never!"

"I'm sure," she said, glossing over the import of my declaration. "May I read on?"

"Please do."

"Okay…"

"**_10.(b)_** *This Agreement may be terminated by Licensor at any time by giving not less than sixty (60) days prior written notice of termination if: (i) AlliedSignal fails to make payment due under this agreement when due or fails to perform any material obligation hereunder when due and such nonpayment and/or failure continues for sixty days after receipt of notice from Licensor, except as otherwise provided under Section 3. (c) above. (ii) AlliedSignal is dissolved or becomes bankrupt or insolvent, or makes any assignment for the benefit of creditors, or if a trustee or receiver of its property is appointed, or (iii) if AlliedSignal takes or is subjected to any other action based upon its inability to meet its financial obligations. In the event of such termination, all rights and licenses granted AlliedSignal hereunder shall cease and terminate.*"

'Wow that was a lot!' And at the time, that was about all that was registering. Thinking, 'sure glad I have an attorney capable of weeding through all these run-on sentences.'

She was still motoring as she launched into "**_10.(c)_** *This agreement may be terminated by AlliedSignal at any time by giving not less than sixty days (60) days prior written notice of termination. No termination by AlliedSignal under this Section **10.(c)** shall relieve AlliedSignal of its obligation to make all payments due to Licensor resulting from activities conducted by AlliedSignal on or before the date of termination.*"

After she finished reading, I picked up my head off the paper and just thought to myself, 'what a way to start off a relationship?' I knew this was business and that's how business is conducted, but nonetheless, I couldn't let the irony of it all go unnoticed. 'What a shame to put forth all this effort planning our amicable breakup, and to think, before a single filter ever rolled off the line!' Though I kept these sentiments to myself, she must a picked up on them, because I wasn't too good at hiding the wrinkles etched upon my brow.

"Hey Steve, I can almost read what you're thinking," she offered, in a rarefied moment. "This language has to be in here. It's for both of our protection, surely you can see that much? Can't you?" she said, attempting to sound empathetic. But by now I knew her heart, those words were motivated more out of justification than anything else.

"Yes, I can Dianne. Of course, I can. But it just seems so negative to be talking about a breakup or defeat before we even get started, don't you? We aren't even out of the gate, and yet we gotta cover our backsides with this prenuptial for God's sake. It just sickens me to look at things this way after all I've sacrificed to get this far."

That little cry of sanity was apparently more than she wanted to hear form this bleeding heart on the way to becoming a millionaire, so interrupting me, she rather coolly interjected, "So do you mind if I read on?"

"No, not at all. I hope the rest of what you are going to read is boiler plate, because I've just about had about my fill."

"Oh, I think you're gonna be granted your wish, just hang in there a little while longer," she said, now wanting to get it over about as badly as me.

"**_10.(d)_** *During the period of one (1) year commencing on the date of termination of this Agreement, AlliedSignal may, subject to the payment to the Licensor of the running royalty amount due to it in accordance with Section 3.(b), above sell Licensed Product which it had on hand as of the date of termination.*"

Foggily, I looked over at Kevin.

"You don't get it, do ya Stevie?"

"Yes. Well…, sort of."

Then he began to explain it to me. "Dianne…, correct me if I am wrong, but it just says to me that Allied has up to one year after termination of our contract to get rid of any filters it has unsold in inventory. And of course, during that liquidation period, Steve, they are obligated to pay you your royalty."

Quickly before I had a chance to speak he added, "But I wouldn't worry about that, because that ain't going to happen man!" he said, trying to reassure me before I even had time to consider that one.

"I would hope not Kev. Besides, in this day in age of 'just in time manufacturing and distribution,' I can't see how they would ever accumulate that big of an inventory anyway." Looking back, I'm sure I said this out loud as I tried to reason away the advent of such a perishable outcome.

"You're right Steve, we don't store lots of inventory. It's not like we're in the business of selling groceries around here." Thinking to myself, 'perhaps I might of been better off if they had.'

Dianne was returning to her former self as she glared at both of us, "Shall we move on gentlemen?"

Kevin winked at me, as he whispered over, "We're almost done."

"Okay then, as she began to lead us down the home stretch, reading aloud…

11. FORCE MAJEURE : 11.(a) *If either Party is rendered unable, wholly or in part, to carry out any of its duties or obligations under this Agreement by reason of (i) act of God or public enemy, fire or explosion, perils of sea, flood, drought, war riot, sabotage, embargo or (ii) without limiting the foregoing circumstances, any circumstances of like or different character beyond the reasonable control of the party so failing; or (iii) inadequacy or shortage or failure of supply of materials or equipment, breakdowns, labor trouble from whatever cause arising and whether or not the demands of the employees involved are reasonable and within said Party's power to concede; or (iv) compliance by either Party with any order, action , failure to act, direction or request of any governmental officer, department, agency, authority or committee thereof, and (v) whether in any case the circumstance now exists or hereafter arises, such Party shall forthwith give written notice thereof to the other Party (such notice briefly to describe the circumstances causing such inability),* *and, thereupon, to the extent that the party giving such notice is unable to perform such duty or obligation shall be suspended during, but no longer than the continuance of such circumstances."*

She lifted her head and directly inquired if I had understood what she had just read.

"Yes, I do understand it fully," I said, as a myriad of insults began to up well inside of me.

My casual response temporarily sent shock waves through her, as she must of thought, 'surely he must have given up altogether by now!'

With great haste, she flew to get down to the middle of page eight, before I could create yet another disturbance. As she proceeded to announce, *"Section **12 Assignability**,"* her tone belied the fact that my behavior had indeed left her dumfounded. Trust me, my sitting there like a sheep before its sheerer was throwing her for an awful loop.

"Assignability," she said, exhaling deeply in a vain attempt to cover up a sigh from the strain. "This is rather straight forward here," she began. *"We have in **12 (a)** the following: Either Party shall have the right to assign this agreement to any Affiliate and/or Third Party."*

Again, I sat there in silence, not stirring a bit, at least not outwardly. Inside however, was quite another story, there was a cauldron that was about to bubble over as I wrestled with the principal of the whole thing.

'Should I even bother to open my mouth?' I wondered. I was so mentally exhausted, I wasn't sure if it was worth it, wishing this was all a bad dream. But the probing gaze of her eyes as they tried their darndest to figure out where I stood, served to let me know that I was truly in present time.

As was often the case, the horse was out of the barn before I had a chance to properly coral my heartfelt intentions. They were already on their way out, like finely tuned projectiles. "You know guys…, back there at number eleven; Force Majeure? I realize it's standard insurance company lingo, well not exactly, but darn close…"

Kevin's eyes began to roll in the back of his head, picking up on my intonation, he could sure enough see that I was about to mount a soapbox. He could just see it coming.

"Here, I'm going into business with you guys, and at this very moment, we are exchanging our words of honor, right?" as I began to ease out.

I couldn't help but to glance over at Dianne, as she looked on intently. Believe me, she didn't have the foggiest notion of where I was about to take this one.

"Now the Company under *section twelve*, just ran through an entire litany of how they might fail, by naming every condition under the sun of things beyond their control. And I certainly agree! We all live in a dangerous world here. And as we all know, there are many things that could happen outside this Company's control. But the way I see it, at this juncture I am more concerned about the things that might pop up that are directly within the company's control, for instance; like the success of this project! So at this time, I think it only fair that we insert the marketing and business plans, as an addendum to this section. Oh, let's identify it as the 'Company's promise to perform,' or something to that effect.

"What do you say to that?"

Oh! If there was only a fly on the wall to record both of their simultaneous sputtering. Terrified! As if she had something to hide, she was the first to speak. "We can never agree to anything like that!"

"And so why not?" I asked, calmly. "Performance clauses are routinely inserted into all kinds of contracts. I'll bet Larry Bossidy has got all sorts of performance clauses in his contract pertaining to his compensation, relative to this Company's performance."

"Oh, I'll bet he does too, Steve. But you ain't Larry here," Kevin rumbled. "They'll never agree to put our business plan into the body of this contract. Never! So, you might as well just forget about the fact you ever asked for it!"

Now suddenly, I was lost! Because at least in my mind, that wasn't an outlandish request on my part, since it's done all the time. Once again, that nagging feeling of uneasiness began to arise within me, as to what was this outfit was hiding from. I still couldn't figure what they seemed so afraid of? You would of thought that they would of been proud to state their objective right from the get go, then follow through on it! Kinda like what I had been doing all along! But they weren't, and this cowardice on their part was a huge red flag, I shoulda heeded!

Still in a quandary, I asked, "But why not Kev?"

"Because I know how they are Steve! They just won't." Clearly, he wasn't about to elaborate any further. "It's not like they aren't going to perform, so why worry about it. Okay?" He was pleading with me now, doing his darndest to get me as far off that subject as possible.

Not able to let it rest, I grumbled, "Well I'm going to ask my attorney about that one, anyway. I wouldn't mind a little bit of added protection. You can be sure of that."

"Are you finished Steve?" as she prodded me to move along. We were nearly done, and she could smell it.

"No. I'm not, thanks. I have a couple more issues that I'd like to put on the table before we move on."

"You do? And what might that be?" she inquired.

"I would like to say something to you both in reference to that *"Act of God"* clause.

"God happens to be my friend, and the Bible which is His personal word for my life, clearly states, that He is for me and not against me! And let me tell you something else. In my heart of hearts, that's the very reason why I have made it this far anyway…, because of God. So, as you can see, I'm not too thrilled at the prospect of entering into a business agreement with anybody who is so patently willing to attribute all matter of catastrophes to His doing.

"You know… God ain't in the business of disaster.

"And for what it's worth, I'd like to say something else, I know quite a bit about Him, and I have to tell you, He doesn't operate like that. No, to the contrary. He is the Lord of blessings.

"In good conscience, I can't allow myself to exchange my blessings for the curse you just read to me a moment ago. Besides, from what I've experienced so far with my dealings with this Company, I'll be needing all that the Lord has to offer to make this union of ours work out. So, whether you understand it or not, Jesus is my business partner and I'm not about to offend Him by having His Father referred to like that in this contract."

Dead silence fell over the both of them as the social protocols I just violated came screaming across my screen from every conceivable direction. 'You have really done it now big mouth! What are you crazy? You can't bring God into a business deal like this you fool! What'll they think?'

I just waited. Once again, I was just playing the game the only way I knew how, flat out. Besides, I had just about all I could stomach from this outfit anyway. By now, I had been worn pretty thin from all their slick maneuvers and it was rather apparent by the looks of this contract that the big boys from Allied Automotive had now stepped in. 'What did they care about Steve Moor, they didn't know me from Adam. And they could have cared less!

There was no mistaking it, the contract set before me had already been authored by those guys. The windage of their sights had already been factored in, so that Fram might now hit their mark, but at who's expense?!

Well it was obvious…, mine of course!

Temporarily, I was moved to a place I had never considered. To a point nearly beyond caring. Suddenly all of those thousands upon thousands of hours I had invested over the last ten years came rushing in on me. The endless dealings with the Patent Office. The untold hours which had become the days and the years that I had spent crafting this piece. Until at last, that fateful day back in October of 94' had finally arrived; a day in which I could finally be heard! Oh, the incredible amount of shepherding involved to sell this darn thing! Really now, if you could only know about the time, the effort and the incredible expense of energy that went into my arrival at this point. You would think it rather insane…!

But I have to level with all of you, right here and right now! The real insanity of it all, was that never in my wildest dreams was I prepared for such a fleecing! My entire being had been invested in the battle of swimming upstream, and not spent on scheming how to keep my business partner from squeezing me to death!!! And it was that ill-preparedness on my part, which left me with nothing more to do, than to just sit there and stare down the gapping barrel of this one-sided business contract. A contract which had been preordained to suit the big boy's objectives, while paying little attention to mine.

Kevin began to stir in his seat, as he shifted his body towards Dianne, "You know Dianne he does have a point there. "If you think about it, why would God be up there somewhere, toying with us like that? You would think that he had better things to do than that. Besides, if He was responsible for all of those horrible things, it would make Him some sort of a maniacal being. Even with my limited knowledge of that sort of stuff, I have a hard time subscribing to that."

An irresistible smile broke across my face, as I witnessed the reality of the Lord as He upheld His own good name, indifferent to circumstances. Kevin's defense caught me totally off guard, and momentarily I was whisked away to that rock pile on a cold wind driven beach in the dead of winter, where ten years hence, I had made a covenant with the Lord. A pledge that we would go into this filter business together, just He and I. It was an oath I sorely wanted to keep this day. I knew in my very core the Lord Jesus wanted to be involved with my business dealings with Allied. I just knew it! He wanted to be in a position to bless the both of us beyond our wildest dreams. But how could I possibly get that over to them? They seemed to be resisting His blessing at every turn of the page!

"So, what do you want me to do about that request Kevin?" she asked, stunned by his affirmation. "What do you expect me to do?" she pleaded.

"Just write. Put it down on that yellow pad of yours along with the other revisions." I was pleased that there was a certain finality in his tone. I was so happy for him, as the little bit of God that I brought to the process began to work on his soul.

On the other hand, she couldn't let it be, "What about legal? she wailed. I guessed the very thought of mentioning God and business in the same sentence was enough to provoke her to lament, "What are they going to say?!"

Annoyed, he offered, "I don't know what they are going to say? Maybe someone over there for the first time since King George, might think about how stupid that language really sounds. And maybe Dianne…, just maybe, they'll decide to change it!" Tired, he just huffed, as he rubbed his eyes, muttering to himself, "I don't know…"

Rejuvenated, from my sermonette, I chimed in during the momentary lull, "And one more thing Dianne… while you have that yellow pad of yours handy. I took the liberty of reading on while you and Kevin were discussing the 'Act of God' clause.

"You know; I don't see it mentioned anywhere in here that my patent number is to be printed on either the filter nor the box. The whole essence of patent protection is to mark the item with the patent number. The mark tells a would-be infringer that the item is exclusively protected under the law. What do you think?"

I caught her fishing for an intelligent excuse, for which there really wasn't any. All she could do was lift her head from the pad and bat her eyelids.

Not giving her a moment more, "Of course it should be on the damn can, as well as the packaging," he bellowed. "I don't understand it?" he chimed in with a worried look on his face. I knew instantly, it was a look that he wished I hadn't of picked up on. "So, what's the matter with those people anyway? Steve here, seems to know what's proper. So how come they don't? So, do me a favor Dianne, would you? Please put that item down on that pad of yours, along with the other stuff."

She didn't even attempt to override his fury at such an oversight. The very notion of launching this filter without emblazoning my patent number on the product was enough to get the vein on the side of his neck popping. I just smiled to myself, glad his sense of fairness hadn't taken its leave prematurely.

The contract without end, finally concluded on the bottom of page ten. And as far as I was concerned, we hadn't gotten there a minute too soon. We had just finished wading through the last couple of pages, of which I was relatively confident would turn out to be nothing more than just the standard lingo. 'Besides,' I kept reassuring myself, 'I had a patent attorney from D.C. lined up, who seemed more than capable of reviewing this document for me. Surely, there wasn't going to be any problem in reviewing the contract in light of the agreed upon changes?' 'Or would there be?

'Of course not!' I told myself. 'We had agreed, didn't we? And besides, didn't she have the authority to agree, or not to agree anyway? After all, wasn't she always flaunting her power?!'

It was after one thirty in the afternoon now. I had finally arrived at the end of the road, ten long pages later and after a grueling four-hour session with all the trimmings. Needless to say, I was exhausted and worn out from nerves. Yet, I was relieved, as I reflected upon the fact that I had just made my way through such a document, alone no less! A document which to my absolute disappointment, had proved to be anything but friendly.

But it was time now to snap out of my sullen mood. So, the best I knew how, I began to pump my soul with the joyful expectations of the future. After all, it was going to be through this agreed upon and revised version of the contract I now intended to provide for both me and my family.

Upon the conclusion of our little gathering, as if on cue, Kevin excused himself, falling back towards his office. "I got a few things to straighten out before I can take off, so I'll be in my office. When you're done here Stevie, come on down, okay?"

"Yeah sure Kev, you can count on it. But give me a few minutes, 'cause I gotta give Dianne my attorneys name and number and wanna get a photocopy of all her notes regarding the changes, so we can all be on the page."

"Good! So why don't you stop on by when you're done, and we'll head out and grab a bite," he said, releasing himself from the doorpost.

Naturally, I thought nothing of his leaving, knowing that his services were no longer required, as he left Dianne and I to ourselves. It was gonna be up to us now. All that remained, was to establish the ground rules and most importantly, the lines of communication.

Just so you know, I had brought my own legal pad and was taking copious notes the entire time, citing all of the agreed upon changes. However, I wanted Diane's changes made by her own hand so that there could be no dispute. I know that I might appear to be a little stupid…, but I'm really not.

I took the opportunity to start us off. So, pulling her aside, I drew out a piece of paper and said, "Dianne, as I made mention earlier, the contract that Allied presented to me this morning is not what I have agreed to…, correct?" searching her face for a response.

Lifting her head, she stared off to the side, as her arms crisscrossed her chest, bracing her gear. After a faint moan, she shook her head in the affirmative and mumbled me a faint, "Yes." It was all so curious, almost as if she had been taken down in some sort of defeat.

'Hardly the case,' I thought. Yet I couldn't shield my eyes from the pain locked up inside her tortured soul. And to be honest about it, that was the aspect of her personality that absolutely frightened me. It was that unbridled tempest inside of her, that motivated me to put as much distance as possible between her and me as possible.

"So, Dianne, here's my attorney's name and phone number," I said, handing it to her. "He's an intellectual property attorney from the firm of Staas and Halsey, out of Washington DC and he'll be representing me from now on. And if you don't mind, I want to be kept out of any further communications, everything goes through my lawyer now. Okay?"

It certainly wasn't my intention, but those words caused a mini eruption, "What do you mean by that Steve?! You sell houses for a living, don't you?!" she snarled, apparently not ready to let me go.

I wasn't near enough in tune, but it was etched all across her face, except I refused to read it. This game wasn't over between us until she said it was.

For a moment there, I wrestled to get my bearings, before speaking, her response had definitely thrown me a curve. "Well yes… I'm aware that I sell real estate for a living, but may I ask what that has to do with anything?"

It was amazing. I could actually watch her gears spin, as she began plotting, motivated by what, I don't know…

"Oh nothing… I just thought you were going to use one of those attorneys down where you live. That's all. You know… One of those guys that handles the real estate matters for you," she said, sporting a conniving smile.

All I could do was look at her like a bleating calf in the middle of a hail storm, as I let it slip out, "For God's sake Dianne! Get real about this thing here! I'm about to go into business with you guys and you expect that I'm that much of a clam digger to rely upon a guy that does real estate closings!

"No way! I can assure you that I have already found my lawyer. My guy will be calling Gus, just as soon as we rework this contract to reflect everything that we've all just agreed to. Okay?"

Just then Peter stuck his head into the room, it was rather obvious that he hadn't sashayed on by out of pure coincidence either. No, I gathered he showed up just in time to pick up the baton that Kevin had so neatly handed off, but not before getting a whiff of our heated exchange. The expression on his face belied the fact that he was just as glad for having sat this one out, as he scrunched his eyebrows.

"So how did it go, guys?" he asked, in jovial tone. I figured he was relieved that Dianne and I hadn't killed each other, at least not on his watch.

"Oh, it went just fine Peter," she beamed, clutching her prized cache to her chest.

Turning to me, "And Steve… What about you?" he asked, truly pleased.

Pausing for a moment, I determined to quell the plethora of emotions that were still rolling around inside of me, before I spoke.

Really, Peter hadn't a clue of what had just transpired over the course of the last four hours. As far as I could tell, at this juncture he was pretty far removed from what I had actually endured in the pursuit of this friendly business deal. So, he just stared at me, with a pleasant smile, waiting for me to confirm my allegiance with perhaps an endearing toast of some kind.

"I'm on board Pete. I've agreed to this contract in principal, although there are several major, major changes that I feel must be adhered to. And we've agreed to them all! Right Dianne?"

I wanted to pin her down right then and there, in front of my new witness…, a guy who would hopefully be sticking around for a while. Lifting her head from the clutch of papers she smiled, her mind way off somewhere else, "Hum…, why yes of course."

"So we are in agreement," I said, one more time, just to make sure.

"Oh yes Steve!" deliberately releasing her grip from her prize clutch, just enough so that she could playfully brush me on the wrist, as if to say, 'you doubting Thomas.'

Not skipping a beat, I continued, "I might also add that there were several key issues that were either missing, or clauses inserted that I can't live with Pete," I said gazing into his face. His smile had long since gone. The look was reminiscent of that morning back in April, when I pressed him about the installed sales market in his office, and how his mood back then, had changed on a dime.

No matter how hard I tried, I was still unable to put the whole day's experience behind me. Up until this point, I hadn't been able to shake that 'beyond caring' mode, as I continued on. "Overall, I guess we have this agreement fairly well hammered out. Now it's just up to the attorneys to agree upon the language." What I really wanted to say to him, 'was what we really needed, was two separate sets of attorneys in here today to have battled this thing out!'

"Good!" he replied, his smile returning, as he started to turn for the door, signaling we were through. However, I wasn't quite finished yet. I quickly came up from behind and corralled the both of them in the opening of the doorway. My eyes beheld their faces, as I dredged up my innermost sentiments, "Like I told you Pete, I'm on board, but..." I said, moving in a little closer.

I wasn't exactly sure of the origin of what I was about to say and one thing for certain, never in my wildest dreams had I practiced for this one. All I knew was that my heart wrenched, as it welled up from deep with inside of me. What had to be said, had to be said to the both of them, right then. There was no way I could shake this mandate!

"I'd like both you and Dianne to understand something. And whatever you do, please don't think that I'm like some sea turtle, who happened to climb up on a beach to lay her eggs. And when she's finished, then swims away, never to see her hatchlings. 'Cause that's not me," as I gazed into both of their frozen faces.

It didn't take much for Peter to offer me a strained, "Of course not Steve." He was no dummy and I was more than certain he had a fair idea of all that I had witnessed during my sixteen-month sojourn through the Allied odyssey. More than anything else, I wanted to impart to my new handler, that I was as serious as a New York City heart attack and to what lengths I'd go to ensure that we had a success on our hands.

"So please, don't think for a single moment that I am going away either, just because I signed a contract. That's all the more reason why I am not." At that moment, I relinquished control of my baby into their care, gazing into their faces as I did. I fidgeted with my hands tucked safely away in my pockets looking, looking for the proper words to sum up the entire ordeal I had somehow allowed them to put me through.

For some reason, all at once I began to grasp hold of the magnitude of the stakes…

Just so you know, there was never going to be a contract between us that would be mighty enough to prevent them from destroying my life, if they had a mind to. Allied wasn't in the practice of giving out any iron clad contracts with their business partners, least of all with a little guy like myself.

Right about then, I could tell that I was on the receiving end of that policy. Seeing that it would have been an utter pipe dream for me to of believed anything after the demonstration thus far. So, I did the only thing I knew to do. I asked them a question point blank...

"If you guys blow this one, will you at least lose your jobs?" wanting to make sure at the very least, the both of them had a vested interest in my enterprise.

They just looked at each other horrified, like I had become rabid for no good cause. But that wasn't how I saw things. Because if I could bank on anything at all, it wouldn't take long for all the people involved in this enterprise to come up with acute memory loss in the event this project crashed and burned! And that of course would leave me out in the cold…, all by myself.

At that moment Peter replied for the both of them, still in shock, "Why yes! Of course, we would! Steve, we're behind this thing one hundred percent!"

"Good then!" rang my hollow reply, as some of the poison rolled off my lips.

"Because I would just like say something to the both of you… If Fram wets the bed on this one, I can only promise you one thing, I will be your worst nightmare!"

Right then I turned directly towards Dianne. For a change, she was in my sights not the other way around. "Remember Dianne… Like I told you at the airport, this ain't just business with me, it's personal!"

CHAPTER 11
THE LONG HOT SUMMER

It was nearly three o'clock as I glanced, down at my watch. Picking up on it, "I guess you better be going, or you'll never make it home through all that traffic."

I just looked at him and gently sighed, "Oh you can forget about that, Kev. If I had any plans on avoiding the traffic, I would have left here a good three hours ago."

He began to look towards the door, as I finished the last of my iced tea. "You know, I used to run this section of I-95 a lot," rattling the cubes around in my glass. "Besides, coming up here wasn't about beating the traffic home anyway," I smiled.

All he could do was muster a feigned chuckle, at the simple truth of what I had just said.

"Sorry man, I forgot. You used to be a truck driver or something, right?" he irreverently quipped.

I just smiled at his snide attempt at humoring me. Thinking… After the festivities of this day, the drive home would be a welcomed obstacle by any stretch of the imagination. As for the traffic, I didn't give it a second thought, knowing that I'd be driving smack dab into the middle of a parking lot by the time I hit rush hour in southern Connecticut. At any rate, it was already a foregone conclusion that my five-hour ride home was beginning to look more like eight.

Just the same, after the events of this day, I was rather looking forward to the drive home. 'It would be more therapeutic than anything else,' I mused. And perhaps like a good tonic, it would help me to unravel what had taken place during the unbelievable turn of events.

As it turned out, Kevin and I never got the chance to drink that beer we had always been talking about. And after today, when we both went our separate ways, it was nearly certain we'd never get the chance again.

"Hey Steve, I'm gonna split from right here, okay?" as he played with his straw, staring into the empty glass. At long last our humble celebratory drink had come and gone without much fanfare, and now the moment which I had dreaded was upon me, it was parting time. Intuitively we both knew there wasn't much cause to linger on any further, our genial exchange had run its course.

I still loved him. I realize that doesn't sound macho, but I did. And in some strange way, I owed him. My head sought to plow under the torrent of emotions that wanted to take charge, as I searched for a proper way to say good bye. Despite what I thought about him, much good, and yes, some bad, there was no getting around it. 'Cause if he hadn't of picked up the phone on that fateful day, there never would of been any hint of deal between Fram and Stephen Moor.

Yet on the other hand, there was a part of me that wanted to curse him as well. A part of me that insisted, he had been part of the betrayal.

"Will I ever be able to talk with you again? Because I want to, if you don't mind?"

"Yeah, sure," he said, keeping his emotions in check as we headed for the cars.

"Well how are we gonna do that? You're moving to Chicago and you don't even have a house out there yet," as my mind began getting tangled up in the logistics of it all, afraid we might lose contact forever.

"Don't worry about it, okay Buddy? I'll call you as soon as I'm settled. And if you need to get in touch with me sooner, call Jodi. She'll know how to get a hold of me.

Hey look! I know that you're the inventor and everything, but this filter is every bit as much my baby now as it is yours. And you can mark my words on it Stevie, I'll be watching it!"

Alone at last, I strapped myself into the Dodge Caravan and headed south, down the highway, on my way to leaving Rumford far behind. As I sped away, the big city began to disappear into the rear-view mirror and along with it, all the nastiness of the whole affair.

Looking at a long ride home, I automatically reached for the trusty radio and flicked it on, attempting to drown myself in some music. The last thing I wanted, was any further reminding that this had been the longest haul of my life. So, I purposed in my heart that if I was going to dwell on anything during the ride home, it would have to be the positive.

Every now and then, while trying to hunt up another good song, I'd work the knob on that thing in the vain attempt of keeping my expectations afloat. Occasionally, as I fussed with the radio, I'd glance down and catch a glimpse of my Bible, that happened to be lying there on the passenger's seat beside me. It seemed as if those pages just stared up at me, begging a response.

'My mind has got to be playing tricks on me,' I thought, not wanting to pay them any heed. I was just as content to ignore their message and make it for home, as I tried to lose myself further in the music. And I'd have to confess, it worked for a good long while.

I'm not sure, possibly I was in the midst of working some things through in my mind. I don't know, but somehow, I was able to put my hurts aside long enough for the realization to finally hit me. 'The victory!'

It started to sink in, I had made it after all these years! It was within my grasp now! The moment I had pursued with such reckless abandon. It was so close that I could almost taste it! It was actually going to happen! My Dream, it was coming true! Oh, not like I had envisioned it of course, no..., not at all. But nonetheless, there was no denying it, at least it was coming true!

Then it hit me. Realizing what I should of been doing the moment I got into the car. I had neglected to thank Him! Immediately I began to thank and praise Him for being so faithful in upholding His word, to me! As a matter of fact, I was certain that He was in the very process of gift wrapping the desire of my heart, but my spiritual eyes at the time had been so clouded back there, in the midst of all that chaos.

Only moments after readjusting my perspective was I treated to this most incredible experience… I would call it a force and could only describe it as nothing short of pure joy, as it came all over me. Indeed, it overtook me. Wanting to be alone in His presence, I reached for the radio and turned it off. I tell you, my physical body was nearly consumed by the triumph of it all. I knew beyond any doubt; the victory was something preordained of the Lord.

Finally, the ten long years of standing firm under all sorts of circumstances only served to reinforce what I already knew. What I was now becoming a part of, was in large measure a product of my faith at work.

Once again, I glanced down at my Bible, but this time on purpose. A smile broke across my face, as I thought about the debt of gratitude I owed that Book, for all the many life changing messages I had gleaned His word.

It had been some fifteen years ago, that God had finally been introduced to me in a personal and meaningful way. And looking back on it, it had to of been around this time frame when I slowly began to build me a framework from within…

I guess the best way to describe it would be like building a bridge that would be capable of linking up God and myself, connected by this blueprint that He refers to as Faith. I am not being melodramatic, but it was this blueprint of faith that had made the way possible for me to go into business with the largest filter company on the face of globe. It was every bit as much my faith, as it was my brute determination.

The miles faded away as the gentle hills of the New England coast line flowed towards the Jersey flatlands. I was driving hard, doing my best to make it home to Patti and the kids knowing that I wasn't going to make it home before I'd find them in their beds fast asleep.

The precious interlude with the Lord had long since faded, and the reality that I had become part of a pack that was now hurtling along at sixty-five seemed all too quick of a reminder. Still a long ways from home, exhaustion was gaining on me, as I battled just to keep my eyes open.

'I should of pulled over an hour ago, I can't go on much further,' I told myself, my hands white knuckled with tension as my body grudgingly wrestled the onslaught of fatigue.

Hemmed in on all sides by the massive flow, the stakes began mounting quickly, leaving me no choice but to stop playing games with the deadly marauder of sleep, which now stood between me and getting home in one piece.

With the battle lost, I pulled off at the next rest stop, and found a spot in the corner of the lot where I could collapse. Climbing over the rear seats, I sprawled out in the cargo area, exhausted, putting aside all hopes of making it home in time to be greeted.

Next morning, the first of June, found me back at my post in the real estate office, taking advantage of the early morning calm, as I worked my way through most of what had piled up during the last couple of days. Out front, I could hear Norma, coming through the door, as I punched in the last few numbers on the fax machine. It was getting late, as I glanced down at my watch only a few minutes before nine. 'Better hurry, just a few precious moments of quiet left before my shift would begin', as the fax machines began talking to each other.

Waltzing by to hang up her sweater, she teased, "How was your trip darling?"

"Oh it was fine, Normie. Just fine," as I stared at the machine, waiting for it to print me out a confirmation.

"So how'd it go? Tell me? She was there, wasn't she?" not able to resist a sarcastic dig.

Rather melodramatically, I replied, "Yup… She sure as heck was there all right," as my confirmation starting to come through.

"Steve! Would you stop looking at that stupid machine. It's not going to work any faster by you hovering over it," wanting me to pay attention to her.

Then all of a sudden it must of dawned on her. "What have we here? Are you sending your contract off to the attorney by chance?"

Looking away from the machine I turned to meet her smiling face. She wasn't the least bit nosy, this consummate keeper of clandestine deals. The last thing she'd of been looking for was another secret to safeguard, she already had enough of those. No, I knew her too well. If anything, she was proud of me, like a son.

Playfully I replied, "I just faxed my attorney a copy of the contract, with copies of all the changes. I'll try to reach him a little latter, so we can get this review going. You know, so I can be on my way out of here, if you know what I mean!"

"That's good, Stevie. So, I guess you did okay for yourself, huh!" she said, ribbing me again. "That's real good. At least it looks like Dianne kept you in one piece for me," laughing, as she took a drag off of her cigarette. "Yeah, I came through in one piece all right, but it was some tough sledding Norma, I can tell you that much," as I drew a deep sigh not wanting to go there.

Pleading, "Well you're going to tell me, aren't you?" I knew that I had already teased her far enough to get her motor going, but before I could launch into the first detail, the darn phone started. I grabbed one of the lines while she grabbed the other. It just so happened that I was greeted by the other agent that was scheduled to share the shift with me, calling just to let me know that an unscheduled appointment had come up, and she'd be a couple of hours late.

There was no doubt, that the work day had begun in earnest. Norma feigned a groan, as she whisked past me on the way to her desk out front, no doubt doing a favor for someone. As for me, there was no other proof required. I had landed hard, back into reality, as the phones lines lit up in the shorthanded office.

During the busy morning my mind inexorably would drift back to the blurry events of yesterday still looking for some clear-cut answers and finding none. So, from time to time, as the different scenarios would pop up, I would have to remind myself, 'what was done, was done.' Besides, it was in the hands of the two attorneys now, I kept reminding myself, shooing away the gremlins that might of suggested otherwise.

If I had any intentions of keeping my sanity, I had better believe that the review process ahead of me was going to be nothing more than routine. I had to be optimistic. 'At the outside, how long could it take both attorneys to ratify the agreement. What…, a couple a few weeks? Certainly, before the Fourth of July.'

Just the sweet thought of it being over caused me to lean way back in my chair and draw a deep sigh of relief.

On the surface, the situation couldn't have been better as my lawyer hit the ground running with the faxed contract and changes in hand. The moment held great anticipation, at least from my vantage point, as he began to clear the decks in preparation for the work ahead.

By this time, I was justifiably worn out from the long haul and was more than eager to pass along the torch of responsibility to someone else, leaving the weightier matters to him. Just the very notion of being able to sit this one out, while someone other than myself took care of the contractual responsibilities seemed nearly too good to be true. Overjoyed by the sheer relief of it all, I cascaded back to reflect upon the circumstances which had caused our paths to cross…

───────────────

Probably the first time I ever spoke to Bill, was a good year or so ago. At a point when things between Fram and I were beginning to hold some real promise. I reckoned it was around the time I had sent the six independent test studies off to Fram, so the engineering department could make a determination whether my patent merited any further investigation or not. Optimistic, though guarded, I couldn't discount the fact that the process was farther along now than ever before, so I began poking around for an attorney. Hope was running strong, and just maybe with Kevin's help we'd be going into business someday.

But I was facing a dilemma, because it had been at least a couple of years since I last engaged an attorney concerning anything to do with my patent, and I wasn't exactly sure where to begin. Oh, I could have consulted the law journal or the bar association, but to me, they were just a bunch of names, and that's not how I envisioned finding someone to entrust my life's work to. What I was really looking for was a warm-blooded reference for this job. And at the moment, all I could think of, was that it was high time that I get it gear, and line somebody up in a hurry. Just in case!

The question was, 'where would I turn?'

Then it hit me. It was right under my nose. The most logical place to turn to would be my old friend, Dick Dye. I was certain he was always doing this sort of stuff, 'he'd know how to advise me.'

Without any hesitation, he recommended that I check out the same outfit he used, the Washington based firm of Staas and Halsey, a mid-sized practice of about twenty attorneys who specialized in nothing but intellectual property law.

And I'll never forget how he put it, as he proceeded to give Bill Herbert his blessing. "Bill's a good guy and a straight shooter, he knows about the automotive business, and you'll need that. I've used him before on a couple of matters and he's done real well for me. He's a real good bet.

I've also used the firms senior partner, Jack Staas, rather extensively and let me tell you boy, he's top's, but I don't think the situation you're in warrants that sort a gun. And to be honest with you Steve, you wouldn't want to pay his hourly. I'm sure Bill's gotta be over a couple of hundred bucks an hour as it is, and Jack's way over that," he said thinking out loud, mindful that his young protégé would be on a very limited budget.

Just like it was yesterday, I can recall his parting words, as he was about to hang up the phone, "Don't worry about a thing Steve, this guy's the one. I promise! Bill will take good care of you, just make sure to let him know that I sent ya." Click.

Those parting words of Dick's, ran through my head now. Though it was nearly a year later, as I began to deal with Bill for the first time in earnest. It was the morning of June 2nd.

Oh, I had casually spoken with him on an occasion or two before, but I was on the meter now, his meter, as it began to tick away at my small nest egg.

"Bill, I'm not trying to be cheap, nothing like that, so please don't take it that way, but how much do you charge an hour?"

Matter of fact like, he replied, "The going rate is two hundred and twenty-five dollars an hour for my services, Steve. Is that all right with you?"

"Yeah sure," I said. "It is, what it is. I just wanted to make sure, I'm not bottom fishing here. What I need is a good lawyer, and as you're aware, Dick Dye who's a friend of mine, recommended you highly. Of course, you know Dick Dye…"

"Oh yes, sure I do," chuckling a bit. "I've known Dick several years now, and I've helped him on a few matters," he offered obligingly.

"You're laughing at Dick, that's a good sign? Right?"

"Oh yes of course! "He's just a piece of work, is all."

I felt it safe and began to chuckle along with him, agreeing, "I hear you on that one."

Changing the subject, "Bill..., I've been selling real estate for the last eight years, so I think I know how I want this thing to go, if you don't mind. Would you object if I laid things out?"

"No, not at all. Go right ahead." For an attorney, he wasn't the least bit threatened that I had my own ideas as to how I wanted things to go.

"It's was just that during my real estate career, I'd been exposed to a lot of needless saber rattling done by attorneys, and in my estimation, it just made things so much worse for the client. And I guess since I am hiring you to represent me, I prefer things don't turn out that way, if you know what I mean? I really don't know any other way to put it."

"As a matter of fact Steve, I agree with you, and that's just fine by me. I realize that unfortunately sometimes things can get a little bit nasty, but that's really not how I prefer to do things myself."

"Great, that's what I was hoping! All I really want, is for you to be able to handle this contract between Allied and myself as speedily as possible and with a minimal amount of hassle."

"That sounds fine by me Steve, and by the looks of things, we shouldn't have too much of a problem here," he offered optimistically.

I shot back almost reflexively, "So, did you get a chance to look at my contract yet?" Wondering if he was referring to the same document that I had already become aquatinted with?

With memories still fresh, I wasn't about ready for somebody to try and convince me what I had experienced just two days prior was a mirage or something, even if it was my very own attorney!

"Oh I gave it a quick look over, but I haven't studied it by any means. What I meant to say was, that from my initial impression, things seem to be fairly in order." he said, picking up on my tone right away.

I realized that he was just doing his job, as he reached out to gather hold of the reigns. It was far too early in the game to even entertain the possibility of bringing him up to speed. Dear Lord, it was bad enough that I couldn't fathom the circumstances yet myself! 'So how could I expect some stranger to read into all I had been through, just because he happened to be in receipt of my contract?' There was simply no way!

Besides, now certainly wasn't the time to enlighten him anyway. And for what it was worth, I truly hoped that I would never have to, because it would wind up being one very, very expensive catharsis.

It was supper time on the evening of Monday June the 5th, I was in my kitchen and strangely enough, I found myself on the phone, and to of all places… Southfield, Michigan. They had come calling on me, under the auspices of a very disturbing inquiry.

We had put nearly five days behind us since our meeting when apparently, Ms. Dianne had dropped off Allied's radar screen. During my conversation with Mr. Hampilos' office that evening, it was revealed to me that for some unknown reason, Dianne had neglected to pass along my attorney's name and number to his office. So consequently, Hampilos came looking for me, expecting that I might be able to fill in that missing blanks for them.

Now that got me to thinking, 'was this just another slip-up on her part, or merely a coincidence in light of what occurred the other day?' I wasn't quite sure, but I wouldn't have taken odds against it.

As I hung the phone back on the wall, I couldn't help but wonder 'why Mr. Hampilos was taking such a strong interest in who my attorney might be all of a sudden?' In a weird way, I was kind of puzzled, since the legal department hadn't demonstrated any real concern over the fact that we had been left unchaperoned all this while. That was unless Dianne had their blessing to practice law!

One thing for sure, the situation like so many others before it, had left me flabbergasted. I had to remind myself once again that I was dealing with the biggest company of its kind on the face of the globe and that they knew what they were doing. I began to wonder, 'how a woman as incompetent as Ms. Newman could have ever escaped the watchful eye of AlliedSignal. How was it possible for Dianne to have not only escaped Allied's brutal downsizing, but still remain in her highly visible position as the Head of Strategic Planning and Worldwide Development for the Fram Corporation?' Those couple of questions certainly kept gnawing at me.

Allow me to put things in proper perspective…, Southfield was an acronym for AlliedSignal's Automotive corporate nerve center, and Gus Hampilos, was their Chief Intellectual Property attorney as well as AlliedSignal's Associate General Counsel. In layman's terms, he was not only in charge of guarding their four-billion-dollar automotive business unit, but he was generally in charge of the entire shooting match as well.

So if you don't mind, let me ask a stupid question… 'How could some itinerant backyard inventor be expected to handle a contract drawn by such a talent? Then expected to be treated fairly by his conjuring?' …Well, you already know the answer to that one.

Here's another flashback… After our negotiations that fateful day, Diane was having an absolute out of body tantrum, for me to not only agree, but to sign the agreement as was first presented!

Over the course of the next several days, Bill and I worked closely together as we took Allied's version of the contract apart, line by line and began fine tuning it. The man was methodical, as he made all of the necessary changes to the contract, and I must testify, he did so in accordance with all of my instructions. Every single one of the major adjustments to that contract were based solely upon what Kevin, Dianne and I had agreed upon during the May 31st meeting.

Oh, and I guess I was right after all, because after careful examination of the document, Bill ended up changing some of the other language that I suspected was in there all along. You know, the stuff put in there by Allied's legal department, the kind of verbiage not expressly put in there for my benefit. The lack of fair dealing on their part, was beyond glaring for a trained legal eye.

So, by the late afternoon of June 8th, Bill sent me off a 26-page faxed document sighting the many changes to the contract, while at the same time posing many more important questions yet to be discussed. At this time, I want to tell you something, his service and dedication to my matter was flattering, and I was in total amazement as to the ground we had covered in the span of only a few days. Naturally with everything going so smoothly, I couldn't help but be filled with a spirit of anticipation. According to Mr. Herbert, we would have this matter wrapped up in the next couple of weeks!

'And why not?' I had an attorney that was cooperative and from my experience was working at warp speed. Please keep this in mind, I wasn't wearing rose colored glasses here, just because I dared to view the ongoing process so optimistically.

I want to get this over to you somehow. I cannot emphasize enough that I truly believed that everything was going to be all right! At long last I was safe, having a trusted attorney at my side, to use not only as a sounding board, but as a witness if need be. Though I was glad for the backup, I wasn't really intent on using him for that, since this wasn't between Dianne and I anymore.

'We were both supposed to be out of the picture, remember?'

So at least as far as I was concerned, there wasn't any earthly reason why this contract shouldn't have been ratified in short order, notwithstanding some minor changes, I knew Hampilos would invariably insist upon.

I was beyond thankful that Bill Herbert was on my payroll, and it was going to be his job to institute the specific changes that the three of us had agreed upon that day in the room. And believe me that's what I intended on sticking to!

As we worked our way through this twisted amalgam of contract and patent law, I began posing ever more questions to him. As he began unraveling the true meaning of the deal, I couldn't help but feeling so stupid. He went to great lengths to enlighten me as to what the language actually meant. He took great pains to ensure that I not only understood the language, but the ramifications of the law that would be sighted to interpret our relationship under the contract in the event we ended up in court against each other.

The legal posturing hidden behind the guise that this was a straight business contract was downright depressing! Then throw in the fact that Allied had intended for me to sign this document upfront and without the proper representation was absolutely off the scale! The waters beneath this contractual process ran quite deep, making my real estate dealings seem like I was playing in a sandbox.

'So in light of all the complexities, what if I suffered a weak moment and thought that my attorney could make a play and get something extra I hadn't already bargained for? Like for example, get me more money for a sign on bonus?'

Well..., I just couldn't of allowed that. Going down that path wasn't an option, no matter how tempting the appeal, because my word had already been given that day to both Kevin and Dianne. We had a deal, and I had a copy of her changes!

'But why not try? What harm could come of it? I could have always backed off if they made an issue of it..., couldn't I? And if he was such a good lawyer, perhaps he could strike a better deal somewhere along the line. This was just a game, wasn't it?'

I shouldn't have to remind you of this, but I had already given my word! Besides, if I knew anything at all about the human condition, I knew that greed always exacted a terrible price!

And as a consequence, if I gone for the bait, though tempting as it might have been, I would of been guilty of what they had already set out to do to me. Besides, a stupid move like that, would have precipitated the wrath of a legal team backed by fourteen billion hard dollars to come tumbling upon me!

So, let me tell ya what happened... I want to set the stage for what was about to befall me.

I can still remember holding fast, as the heat of summer began to bear down, it was sometime late afternoon, Wednesday, June 14th and Bill had just sent our revised version of the contract over to Allied Automotive's patent council Mr. Gus Hampilos. There was nothing more for me to do, but to sit back and wait patiently for them to approve the contract as amended. I was confident we had a deal, and to be candid about it, after having demonstrated such good faith during the entire relationship, it would only have been fair that I wound up with one. Even my lawyer's cover letter to Mr. Hampilos reflected a spirit of respect and cooperation, ever mindful of my mantra, of 'no saber rattling!'

Yet despite the fact that we had conducted ourselves above board, I still wasn't spared from the torment of nagging doubt that would attack me from time to time. More than I would like to admit, I would be haunted by, 'did she in fact do her job this time? Did she send those changes along to Hampilos after our meeting like she had promised? And if she had, how come Hampilos' office was calling on my kitchen phone, lookin' for my attorney's information?'

One things for sure, if those changes of hers weren't sitting in front of Hampilos when our revised version arrived, let's just say that our version of the contract would have appeared more like a declaration of war than anything else!

I also realized, that if we heard anything back from Allied by following week, I should consider myself lucky, because there was no way in God's green earth that Allied was going to work on this matter with the same urgency as my attorney. It was just an educated guess, based upon lots of past experience watching lawyers drag out the simplest of things.

As for my attorney, I gotta say, Dick Dye's recommendation was proving out to be right on the money. It was a pleasure to behold, as I watched Bill dig into my case the moment he received it. He chose to direct his energies towards my time sensitive circumstances, jumping headlong into my case well in advance of sending out his retainer agreement.

So, when I tell you, we not only did Allied's job and rewrote the contract the way it should of been presented to me in the first place, we did it in record time. And I am not exaggerating! And like I said, there wasn't a single change put forth which might have compromised their position whatsoever.

All that was left for them to do, was to review it and sign it!

But as fate would have it, that's not what happened…

I can remember calling my attorney's office around mid-morning on Wednesday June 21st and getting Bill on the phone. I wanted to know if he had heard anything back yet, except what he was about to tell me, I wasn't exactly prepared for.

"Uh Steve, as a matter of fact I did hear back from Allied just a little while ago. I was just about to pick up the phone and give you a call."

My Lord, it was all over his tone! Something had gone disastrously wrong, I could just sense it, as I squeezed the phone, wanting to turn it to powder. He was acting the cool oncologist on the other end of the line, about to tell me I had cancer, and it ain't lookin so good. I tried to keep it together as I cried within myself, 'Oh Jesus, no!'

"Dianne's back," he said, sounding rather befuddled. Of course, he was lost! Up until this point there was absolutely no need to have filled him as to all I had been through! He didn't have the foggiest idea in the world what he was reporting to me by saying, "Dianne's back."

Immediately I tried to calm myself, groping for something intelligent to say. "At least they didn't say we didn't have a deal, right?"

There was a long pause before he spoke, he seemed to weigh every word before speaking, "Well, that's not true either, Steve", he said giving me the news.

I took a quick look around my office, as I replayed his words, not wanting any of my colleagues to witness my world implode.

"Bill! Would ya please! I can't take your deliberate speech. Cut to the chase man, I'm gonna black out here, if you don't hurry up and tell me."

"Okay… This is what happened. Dianne called me this morning and told me that this contractual matter was directly between you and her. I have to be honest with you Steve, I really had a difficult time under-standing exactly what she was saying. She seemed to be quite emotional about it for some reason. The only thing I really got out of her was this, apparently, she feels that what is going on, shouldn't concern us attorneys at this point."

Uncontrollably, I screamed into the phone, "Bill…! I'm lost here, you gotta help me out! I don't understand? I hired you to represent me in this matter! That's your job man! You're my fiduciary, even I know what the meaning of that word is from selling real estate!

"You're supposed to be representing me now, and I made that clear to her right after we were done with the meeting. Please, correct me if I'm wrong, but didn't I tell you from the beginning that I didn't want to be personally involved in any further negotiations with Allied!

"Well? Didn't I?" wondering if I had suddenly lost my mind all together?

"Now Steve…, I remember exactly what you told me. It's just that she feels that these various points that we have brought up in the contract are still business decisions that only directly concern you and her. Steve," he said trying to reassure me, "I'm sure we'll work this out…"

At that point, out of sheer frustration I nearly jumped down his throat. "But we had agreed on all of those points I tell you, or I never would have allowed you to put them in there in the first place!"

"I know, I know," as he began to pick up where he had left off, "But I just want you to know for the record, that she feels quite strongly at this time that if there is any unfinished business, it's between you both. I would like to be clear about that okay?"

"Yeah sure," I said, lost for any more words.

"I realize that this seems highly unusual to you, but Dianne feels that this contractual procedure doesn't concern the attorneys at this time. And oh…. Steve, she wants you to give her a call…"

'What could I say?!'

I got an attorney here, a real one. Not just some flunky I picked out of the yellow pages whose trying his best to convey to me that some crazy woman has got both he and this other well-heeled lawyer hog-tied.

I couldn't figure it! 'What was I supposed to do now, remove him from my case? Should I have dismissed him on the spot and went for the big gun, Jack Staas?' I didn't know what to do, I was so confused, and I didn't see any point in dumping Bill. Besides, I felt comfortable working with him darn it, and besides…, I didn't particularly want to change horses in the middle of the race anyway. Oh, it was so ridiculous! But my God, 'what in the world was happening?' I didn't have a clue.

Right then, a myriad of thoughts concerning my situation came flooding in as I began to survey the damage…

I still had to walk softly here and not carry a big stick. And let me tell you something, this whole ordeal was never about carrying a big stick. So, if I may, allow me to give you a smattering of what I was still having to juggle, then perhaps you might be able to tell me if I should of been picking up any big sticks or not.

Just for spite if you can believe it…, a prototype still hadn't come forth yet from the engineering department. Yes, that's true, despite the fact that Fram had projected a finished goods date of June

15th! So just to add insult to injury, I was still in the midst of coddling a very confused project engineer.

Then there was Peter Ross. To my chagrin, he was a far too detached from the project to ever build a bond between us, and especially now with Kevin gone he showed no real desire to do that anyway. And if I might say, it didn't require a soothsayer to figure out that he was much too harried for me to even consider that a possibility. So, from where I stood, it was pretty much a foregone conclusion that I wouldn't be taking the pulse of the marketing end of things anytime soon. And the way things looked, quite possibly ever!

Then there was that one small item which had stuck in my craw from the very day I had made her acquaintance. 'So, who was going to keep Dianne in check now that Kevin was gone, Peter?' I didn't think so, 'cause Peter didn't exude the required strength to do so!

'How about Hampilos, the seasoned attorney from Allied Automotive's legal department? The associate general counsel of the entire Company for God's sake! Well, at the moment, he seemed incapable of applying the brakes to this runaway train, which just so happened to have my name written all over it.

Nope, she was back again! But this time with a vengeance, already operating outside of everyone's control!

'I had just been advised to call her, remember?'

Apparently, my choice of legal counsel had made her absolutely catatonic! And judging by the way things were looking, it kinda made me wonder if I should have even of bothered to hire an attorney in the first place, since this outfit didn't appear to wanna let me use the one I had picked anyway!

Certainly, I had no clear way of seeing how things were about to unfold, I wasn't a clairvoyant by any stretch, just running on my best laid plans and some famous last words of Kevin's, "Don't worry Steve, it's in the pipeline now, even they can't screw it up!" But judging by the magnitude of this dilemma, those words seemed to only grow paler by the moment.

Eerily, it appeared that my guy was on a trajectory of being rendered down to about the effectiveness of a little league coach.

'So late in the morning of June 21st, I found myself left no option, as I picked up the needle I had so proudly walked away from and jammed it squarely back into the middle of my vein…, I called Dianne!

My heart was pumping out of control as I gave the operator my calling card number. "Yes operator, Rumford Rhode Island please." It was ringing, and I hoped one of her secretaries, wouldn't grab it, 'cause I wanted to get this conversation over with as soon as possible.

After a couple rings, a pleasant voice on the other end of the line greeted me with a friendly, "Good morning, Dianne Newman."

"Hi Dianne, it's Steven Moor," forcing it out, in hopes she wouldn't latch on to the nervous quiver in my tone. "I was just talking with my attorney, Mr. Herbert and he said you guys had been talking. He told me that I needed to give you a call, so here I am."

"Oh Steve, I'm so glad you called. I was beginning to miss you!" she chirped, madly back into the phone. "So, do you have a moment?"

"Yes of course I do. But can I ask you something?"

"Why of course go right ahead," she offered, nearly drunk over my pain. "What's this all about Dianne?" realizing that I was completely at her mercy once again.

"Why it's about our contract Steve," careful not to divulge her motives.

'Of course, it was about our contract, any fool knew that!' The oppressive anxiety that had left me numb for the past hour had suddenly gone, and in its place, rose up some pretty white-hot indignation. I felt as if I was a caged rat, about to be drowned, just for sport!

"I realize it's about the contract Dianne," never giving her the chance to test me. "So why don't you just tell me what this is all about. 'Cause frankly, I don't know what is going on here. I hired a lawyer to handle this for me, remember?"

But that wasn't about to sway her. I could sense that she was still intent on working her magic as she attempted to mother me with guilt, doing her level best to make me feel as if I had done something wrong. "I know you have a lawyer Steve, we've spoken. And I'd have to say, he's quite a gentleman."

"Yes I know, but that's not why I hired him! I hired him for the expressed purpose of talking to you guys! 'Because I'm finished negotiating with you, remember?!"

"Just relax a moment Steve, and take a deep breath now," she said patronizing me. "I believe that we might just have a slight difference of opinion as to how things should be worked out here, that's all. And so, if you don't mind, I'd like to try and explain."

Doing my best, I just shut my mouth for the moment and took it all in as she laid the incredible nightmare out for me. "It's really not such a big deal after all, Steve. But for the moment, all I can say to you is that I'm not prepared to allow the attorneys to handle this matter yet.

"You see Steve, as I explained to Mr. Herbert, we still have some unfinished business here that directly affects the Company for which I am directly responsible. So as you can see, it really doesn't concern either attorney at this time."

"Well, then let me ask you something Dianne. Then if what you are saying is true, and this matter directly effects the Company, then what happened to everything we had agreed upon in the room with Kevin?" I asked, wanting to reach through the phone and choke her.

"Oh well…, that? Well… I seem to have a problem, I just don't recall agreeing to all that?" she said, caustically dismissing the foundation of my argument. Right before my eyes, she morphed back into vintage Dianne.

"So… Maybe you don't, but I sure do! And I'm sure Kevin would as well," continuing to plead my case to a deaf ear and a blind eye.

Tiring of my objections, she pulled out all the stops, "Steve, you know as well as I, that Kevin is no longer associated with this Company anymore."

Well I just lost it over that one. Restraining myself, I tore into her as politely as I could, fearing she'd hang up on me if I did otherwise. "What the heck are you talking about here Dianne? We had an agreement! You're not about to tell me that what we had agreed to the last time we had met was just some figment of my imagination, are you?!

"Let me ask you something. Why did I bother to hire an attorney and have him spend two weeks reworking this contract in the first place? Because I have nothing better to do?"

"I don't know, Steve? So why did you hire one? Why couldn't you have just been satisfied with what we had initially given you? It was certainly fair enough….

Really now, what could of I said to that one? My mind had just gone tilt!

Not bothering to dignify that question, I started in… "And look at you now! You are summarily going back on everything we had agreed to on May 31st. It's incredible! It's not only incredible, it's inconceivable to my way of thinking!

"So Dianne, why don't you just tell me. Don't be afraid, 'cause I'm sure that I already know. It has got to be the lousy dime, right? It must really be galling you guys that you have agreed to pay me a lousy stinking dime! What you really want, is to have this whole thing for free. You ought to be ashamed of yourselves!"

There was dead silence on the other end of the phone, as I spun around in my chair, making sure that no one in the office could see me coming unglued.

"You know Steve you're being totally unfair about this whole thing and I don't have to subject myself to this kind of treatment!" she said, throwing out an ultimatum.

"Well, I'll tell you what Dianne, I prefer not to talk with you any further concerning this matter. You can talk with my attorney now, because that's what I have one for. Have a good day." Click."

Driven by desperation I began to reach out for him... The calendar clearly pointed out that it was already the 24th of June. I started trying him sometime that morning but didn't hit pay dirt until later that afternoon. Though I had never been granted clearance to do so before, I had to call this fiercely private family man at home. And to complicate matters, it was a Saturday afternoon, and I was no doubt cutting in on his wife and baby.

Much to my delight, upon hearing my voice, he was like a little kid gushing with excitement as he greeted me. I could only have wished that I could have left him the way that I found him, but by the time our little chat was over, I wasn't sure who was more ill, him or I.

We were friends. And like myself, he had put his life's blood into this project. Of course, he was glad for the call. Intuitively, I just knew that he would be genuinely concerned how things were shaking out for both me and the project alike. So, just because a career move had dictated he pull himself away from both the Company and the project that he loved, he wasn't about to turn his back on them both, and completely walk away. And most of all, I was grateful that he hadn't walked away from me.

"Hey Kev, I hope I didn't call you at a bad time?" I asked, sheepishly.

"No, absolutely not! As a matter of fact, Stevie, it's a real good time. What's happening?"

'Well at least his circumstances hadn't seemed to of affected him,' I thought. It was the same O'l Kevin, still chargin'.

"So Steve, tell me my man, what's going on?" he asked with a self-satisfied air of contentment. "So, do you have a signed deal yet?" he asked excitedly, assuming that minor detail had already been dispatched with.

I took a hard swallow, hating to break the news. Oh, how I wished he could have helped me, but deep down inside I knew that he couldn't.

I was on a fact-finding mission as much as anything else, hoping to glean something, anything which might help my plight. Or more like, I was just glad that he would be around for a moment, 'cause all I really wanted now was for someone to hold my hand and tell me that everything was going to be all right.

"Kev, you aren't gonna believe this at all man, but we haven't agreed on a damn thing yet. As a matter of fact, I'm terrified that this thing might blow up in my face if I'm not careful."

Horrified, he jumped in, not giving me a chance. "What the heck are you talking about! We had a deal! What, are they crazy?" The phone went dead for a while, as we both tried to make sense of it in the silence.

I was the first one to speak. "Kev would they ever try to steal it from me?"

"No way man. No way at all! This is AlliedSignal we're talking about here. They don't do stuff like that, and besides Steve, you got a patent and all the rest of the stuff you brought them. They'd be crazy!"

Just because he left the Company, nobody could call Kevin Gill a turncoat. Oh, I'm sure he had endured his share of scrapes and bruises during his tenure serving the great behemoth, but he wasn't about to badmouth them, just because he moved on with his life. Mr. Gill wasn't prone to sour grapes.

"I hear what you're saying Kev, and that's what I want to believe, but I get this really strange taste in my mouth that they would be just as glad if I wasn't tagging along for the ride. If you know what I mean?" I said, pressing the issue.

"Well, now that you put it that way, I'll tell you a little something. But I'll forever deny it…, you got me?"

"Yeah sure, tell me!" I said, begging.

"One day I was having a conversation with this guy in my office, and we happened to be talking about the filter and somehow you came up. Oh, not you personally, but you the inventor type. Anyway, this guy asked me and I'm sure that he was just fishin'… You know…, real innocent like, as he leans over and asks, he says, "What would this guy do if we ever stole this idea from him, what's he really like anyway?"

"Wait a minute Kev, how long ago did this happen?!" I just hoped that what he was sharing with me would fill in some of the missing blanks and perhaps account for motivation behind some of Dianne's actions.

Already as if reading my mind, he balked, knowing where I wanted to go with this one, "It doesn't matter Steve, it was a long time ago, long before you ever went into contract with them. Okay?

"Besides, this guy was just being a smart ass. I guess he was just trying to figure out what it must take to drive someone like you to accomplish what you've done. That's all. So, let me finish now, would you?" he said, back to his gruff old self.

"So, do you wanna know what I told him?"

"Yeas, sure I do!"

I told him first off that you were crazy and that was just for openers. Then I told him that if this Company had any thoughts of rollin' you, it would be a tactical error they'd end up deeply regretting. Then I just told him that you were the closest thing to a wolverine with scruples that I'd ever met, and that if they really wanted to steal it, they'd better plan on having you killed first. That's all!"

Friday morning rolled around, and I had put nearly a week behind me since I had sent out the distress call to Kevin. I was beginning to feel more like a dish rag, than an inventor on the brink of great success. The days and weeks ate into my soul as the writing on the wall began to reveal that the shell game between Dianne and I was catapulting towards a meltdown.

For the first time in a very long while, I had become disillusioned nearly to the point of regret, wondering how I had ever allowed myself to pursue the beckoning 'siren of success'. However, that being what it was, the object lesson of 'how to negotiate successfully with a Fortune 38 Company and to live to tell about it' wore on into its second full month, mattered little how I felt.

'So, was this my payback for daring to follow a dream which held the promise that perhaps maybe someday I could be a part of something bigger than myself?' I wondered. 'Cause at this point, I certainly wasn't basking in any afterglow of success here. It seemed just as the heat of summer cranked up, so did the volume of the maniacal game I was now inexorably a prisoner of.

Somehow without so much as a foreshadowing, I found myself cast into the ring facing this behemoth who sought to come against me with this incredulous double speak. And by the looks of things, although their word had already been given, amnesia had gotten the better of them, creating a pain in me that was so intense, it took all I had to keep from running away and hiding. And so it went…

Later that morning a fax came hurtling my way, no doubt only a precursor to as to how I was about to celebrate the Fourth of July festivities, which happened to be only four days in the offing. By the looks of it, the fax wasn't just intended to be a warning shot across my bow either. No, it was fired off in full blown retaliation for having spent the last couple of weeks trying to wrestle out of her what had already been promised!

Sadly enough, by this time the unfathomable happened. Dianne had effectively precluded my attorney from speaking directly with either Mr. Hampilos or even herself! Instead, she insisted that she and I carry out the negotiations between us first, 'under the guise of business' of course. As a result of that tactic, I had lost my first line of defense and had been all but forced to re-negotiate with her the key issues of my contract all over again! For right now, all I could do was wait, as she left me to twist in the wind while she passed judgment upon my revisions.

Naturally she felt it best that I just accept all of her proposals uncontested. But at this juncture I still fought vigorously for what was already mine. So, in keeping with the bizarre protocol she had hatched, I didn't have any real choice other than to run back to Bill every time we spoke and have him coach me, as she upped the ante. For his part, Bill would then counsel me, often times in great detail as to what might befall me legally, if I should accept her offerings at face value.

And please allow me to make what was going on crystal clear. This wasn't about some bizarre need I had to play tit for tat!

No! What this was about, was making a quiver full of irrevocable decisions that would affect me and my family for the rest of our lives. We were working, albeit struggling; toward a contract that once ratified, would be etched in stone! These decisions had to be arrived upon based on the facts and not something as fickle as how I might of been feeling at the time!

And to this day, I still contend those facts were given me by someone whom I still consider to be an expert in the field, by an individual who dispensed his counsel grounded in contract and intellectual property law. Nothing else!

It didn't matter whether I liked what he was telling me or not. That was never the issue. What became the heart of my decision-making process had to do with the immutable reality of the law and how it would affect my future life!

So now, with that said, let's take a closer look at what she had not only reneged on, but what she in fact put me through.

And if I might add one last thing, it wasn't in the pipeline, not by any stretch of the imagination, because the engineers were still wetting the bed!

June 30th, 1995

Dear Steve,

As agreed, I am forwarding a second revised draft of the Licensing Agreement which contains AlliedSignal's response to the changes previously proposed and forwarded to us by your attorney on June 14th.

Our comments about the proposed changes are listed below, using the reference numbers from the version sent us by Mr. Herbert:"

Just to bring you up to speed, the introduction clearly points out that this is the second revised draft. The first draft being mine, was sent out on the 14th of June and now some two weeks later, Dianne in keeping with the rules of engagement, faxes me and not my attorney her first written revisions of the contract!

Now what is conspicuously absent in the tone of the letter, was that she and I had been virtually at each other's throats for the last ten days playing this incredible game of, 'he said she said.' You know, the insane game based upon the premise of who's better at lying.

Just so you know, she cranked up Allied's contractual machine once again and re-introduced twenty-three points of consideration that we had already settled that day with Kevin! For brevities sake, I am only going to focus on the issues that I considered of paramount importance to me.

"***1.(h)*** *We have not agreed to separate light, medium and heavy truck application."*

Well we all knew that there was a vast difference between the automotive market as opposed the heavy-duty truck market. And we had agreed that I would be compensated accordingly in the room on May the 31st. So just to be fair, I want to show you how Mr. Herbert prepared our ***1.(h)*** to have evoked such a response from Dianne. To start with, Mr. Herbert never mentioned "medium duty" nor did I. The market had always been broken down into light duty versus heavy-duty.

His ***1.(h)*** read as follows: <u>"Light Duty Market" shall mean the gasoline engine automobile light truck market only."</u>

Dianne goes on to say *in **2(a)**, under the GRANT: "…No distinction should be made regarding light vs. heavy-duty applications."*

That should plainly spell out that what we had agreed upon that day as distinguishing the two classes of filters was out the window now, as far as she was concerned!

With regard to my fifty-thousand-dollar up-front payment, well that was still intact but look what she had done about paying me in ten days like we had agreed to…

"***3.(a)*** *We propose compromising at 90 days".*

Of course, she had capitulated on the original one hundred twenty days they initially wanted me to wait for the up-front money, but it was still a far cry from the ten days for which the three of us had all agreed upon!

Oh, and here's one she seemed to derive a special pleasure beating to death. The *Canadian issue*. And albeit, I have to admit, I was a stickler about her honoring that one to the bitter end. I considered this issue to be something I'd be willing to go down in flames on.

'And what made you especially feel that way?' Well, I just firmly believed that if she never intended on giving it to me from the beginning, then she should have been responsible enough to have never of offered it to me back there at the airport in the first place. And don't get me wrong either, 'cause if she had come to me at some point and provided me a reasonable explanation why she had to make a retraction, I would have backed off in a heartbeat. But that's not how she chose to handle this. Here's how the double speak game started off on this one…

"***3.(b)*** *We agree to royalties on that we sell in the US and what we make outside the U.S. but sell into the US.* You have no patent position outside of the U.S."

First off, no one knew better than I! No one had to tell me that I didn't have patent coverage outside of the US! And I can remember vividly that during our very first meeting back in October of 94', that I was quick to inform Dianne of that minor detail; only to make mention of it for the second time at our little meeting at Newark International in March of 95'. Then incredibly enough, she called me at work as recently as May, only to rehash it over the phone for yet a third time!

I don't profess being a mind reader here, 'but was I missing something?'

'…But yet, Canada was still supposed to be a throw in! Remember?!'

Now take a close look at my attorneys version *of* "***3.(b)*** *In addition, AlliedSignal shall pay Licensor an earned royalty, for each Reporting Period, of (**i**) ten cents ($0.10) per Licensed Product (made) <u>sold by Allied Signal its affiliates and licensees in the U.S. and Canada, regardless of origin of manufacture and (ii) five cents (0.05) per Licensed Product sold by Allied Signal, its affiliates and licensees, outside the United States and Canada, regardless of origin of manufacture during each Reporting Period.</u>"

Well I guess it didn't much matter that we had already agreed upon the proper language nearly a month ago with Kevin, notwithstanding the fact I was to be compensated five cents for every filter sold outside the U.S. and Canada. Upon further inspection of her rework of ***3(b)***, any mention of Canada was conspicuously absent!

So, once again out of fairness, I'd like to restate her rational as to why the Company would so generously compensate me for ***any*** *filter sold in Canada*, even though I wasn't afforded any patent protection outside of the United States. According to Dianne, at the time in which we spoke, in March of 1995, "AlliedSignal did not have in place an accounting system capable of differentiating the sales which occurred between the two countries when it came down to tracking Fram oil filter sales!"

The Canadian market was my real bone of contention, 'cause like I told her at the airport, the rest of the world didn't really interest me although in the meeting with Kevin, she insisted that I take it! However, the language they were employing with regard to Canada, was far too ambiguous for me to settle on.

'Remember I told you that my attorney found language in that contract that I couldn't have hoped to of understood?'

Well…, here's one we asked for, so perhaps you might be able to decide if it was too overreaching on my part or not.

We asked that AlliedSignal would use its ***"Best Efforts"***, instead of what they had included in the original contract which read, ***"Reasonable Efforts"***. At least according to Bill, the courts put a much greater premium on a company's performance when viewed in light of the ***"Best Efforts"*** clause, as opposed to a company stating that they will only commit to ***"Reasonable Efforts"***. Especially, when it comes down to the marketing of a product. So, I went along with him on that one. It only made sense if you think about it.

Which led me to ask myself this question, 'how could the most advanced filter company in the world, who hadn't done anything this innovative in the last twenty years embark upon a billion-dollar market with only *"Reasonable Efforts"* on their minds?!!'

No! Under the circumstances I opted for the added protection of *"Best Efforts"* and became rather insistent upon that point.

'And then again, how could I have settled for anything less after all the internal shenanigans I had witnessed thus far, including the ones still going on around me?'

Simply put, I couldn't have!

But it didn't seem to matter anyway. I could have used all the rational in the world, but there was gonna be no changing her position. Her reply was as follows:

"3.(c) We will agree to use "Reasonable Efforts."

I can tell you that she went a little off the wall about the compensation part, *"3.(d) We had agreed to 50K, 75K, and 100K respectively for the first three years, and not 100K per year. Your request for $100,000 per year guarantee is a major change, and we find it unacceptable."*

Just so you know, Bill wasn't pulling the "reasonable/best efforts" clause out of his drawers. During my research of case law, "best efforts" actually set the standard of performance. "Reasonable efforts", signified nothing and only cowards and companies destined to fail used it to represent their level of performance.

Now let me point something out here. Notice she refers to this as a major change, although for argument sake, I'm telling you that it was already agreed upon that day with Kevin that my compensation would be bumped up. But that aside for a moment, nothing else contained in this fax revision was referred to as a major change, 'and why not?'

Because, I'll tell you why. Aside from the fact that these changes had already had been agreed to, simply stated they weren't major changes to start with! They weren't a threat to Allied's exposure. And that would have been true even if we hadn't already reached a consensus on these points! And I'm telling you we had!

So, in hopes of reaching an agreement, and in the true spirit of compromise, I soon backed off on the issue of compensation. Because, like I had informed both Kevin and Dianne on that fateful day, I was never in this pursuit for a lousy couple hundred grand. I was in this full bore, to earn multiple millions!

As for exposure, I certainly was taking the greater risk by entrusting Fram to fulfill its duties to perform its job, certainly not the other way around. Furthermore, I unequivocally swear that the insurance policy Allied disclosed to me that morning was a complete and total shock. It had never been mentioned in any vein or eluded to before that morning!

So, if anybody is inclined to remember, that was enough to prompt me to leave them with a little promise of my own. That's if you can remember…

"4.(a) We would expect you to warranty that you own the patent and that you have no knowledge of information that could impact the validity or enforceability of the patent. However, if there are other limits you wish to place on your liability, we are open to proposals."

You know... When I had read this part of the contract for the first time I really didn't have a problem stating that I was the owner of the patent. To me that was overly simplistic, because it happened to be true. And really, I didn't have a problem warranting that I had not knowingly or unknowingly infringed on someone else's patent either, because it seemed like the United States Patent Office was capable of knowing whether or not I was plagiarizing someone else's idea when they had scrutinized my application.

So, let me pose this question to you, 'if Dianne had been doing her job all along like she had been supposed to been doing, then how come my ownership as well as the validity of my patent was now being addressed in the body of this contract? And at the very least, shouldn't she, or Allied's massive legal staff answered these questions to their satisfaction during our pre-licensing period?' They only had nine months from October of 94' to have me attest to that!!!

'So how fair could it of been to wait for the last minute and ask an inventor to go along with their request now, as put forth in the contract?' And what in God's name did they mean by asking me such a stupid question like, "However if there are other limits you wish to place on your liability, we are open to proposals."

Hopefully you can see that by them not doing their jobs ahead of time, it not only complicated the contract, but made it nearly impossible for me to sign the document in light of my attorney's advice! And that's not withstanding the fact that they were hell-bent from the get go on me singing the contract as originally presented!

So, let me ask another question, if I might? 'Who in their right mind would sign a contract this complex and this weighty without legal counsel and without the appropriate changes being made?'

'Do you think Larry Bossidy the CEO would have signed such a document on his own? Or, do you think even Allied's Chief General Counsel Mr. Peter Kriendler would have done so before attaining the proper advice?' Surely, you must have heard the adage, "that a lawyer who represents himself is a fool!"'

'So why all of a sudden would I be expected to do something they wouldn't do?'

Now keeping this in mind, I don't want you to lose sight of the fact that this was a ten-page contract and there happened to have been at least twenty-two other points that needed careful looking after!

'And why do you suppose they would want to treat a business partner that was doing his best to turn them onto a billion dollar per year enterprise that way?' I have to be honest with you, it didn't make sense, they couldn't be that criminal, or were they?!

Just so you know, one of the very first moves played by an intellectual property robber when it comes to stealing someone else's patent, is to inform the owner that their patent *may be* invalid. It was evident, that AlliedSignal was telegraphing what I could expect if I didn't come their way!

So for illustration sake, why don't we take a look at my attorney's thoughts on the matter. I believe the twenty-six-page fax that he sent to me at six p.m. on the evening of June 8th, will prove a rather fine illustration.

First off, I would like to call your attention to the fact that Bill was working late, attending to my file. As I made mention of earlier, his level of service and dedication to my cause was admirable. And now if you would, please notice the tone in his analysis. There is a total absence of game playing in his conveyance, just stating my position in light of the reality of the law.

So if you don't mind, indulge me as I quote, *"You don't want to make any representations or warranties, such as the validity of your patent or non-infringement of others' rights if a product is made under your patent. Such representations or warranties would give Allied a contractual ground to void the agreement and possibly seek damages against you."* Holy...!

Gee that sounds more like a set up than good faith doesn't it you'? *"We have beefed up this section so that you also won't be making any representations about the patent, such as validity, and have made an effort to prevent you from being held liable for product liability claims (new section **4 (c)**."*

'Intelligent, evenhanded analysis, don't you think?'

Well, I can assure you, it followed suit consistently throughout his entire analysis of the contract. And you know something, that's all I ever intended for Bill Herbert to do for me from the beginning. Just analyze the contract and make the appropriate adjustments in light of what we had already agreed upon and do so in light of what could only be interpreted as fair to both parties!

So let me ask you, 'how could of my evenhanded and non-contentious attorney possibly have been barred from acting directly as my representative against my wishes?'

Please don't be stunned, because any fool could see that Diane wasn't the captain of the ship, she was just steering it. Gus Hampilos was the admiral here, having this stupidly blind fixer do his handiwork! Let's be honest here, AlliedSignal did not want a lawyer to represent me.

So…, for the last time, I must beg this question. 'I want to know how the AlliedSignal Corporation with fourteen billion dollars per year in gross revenue and with a fleet of attorneys at their disposal, expected some clam digger from Jersey to be locked up in a room for several hours and then figure out the real meaning of something like this, then sign it!

Here's what they presented me to sign:

"4, No representations or Warranties"

4.(a) *Licensor makes no representations or warranties, express or implied, that the exploitation by AlliedSignal of Licensed Patent does not infringe any patent right or other proprietary right or alleged right of any third party.*

4.(b) *LICENSOR MAKES NO REPRESENTATION OR WARRANTY, EXPRESS OR IMPLIED, REGARDING THE MERCHANTABILITY OF LICENSED PRODUCTS NOR THE FITNESS THEREOF FOR ANY PARTICULAR PURPOSE."* [the bold type and the capitals was just the way that they presented it to me in the contract].

As you can see, to the unschooled, this clause as presented wasn't nearly as benevolent as it might have appeared, at least not according to my attorney's analysis.

We are nearly though here, so hang on. I'm about to share with you a real sticking point and what very might of well precipitated Allied's fury to of come upon me!

'Remember back to the previous chapter, when I was lamenting over the fact that Allied wanted me to kick in half of my "*future royalty payments*", should they become embroiled in a patent law suit, in effect making me a partner in their legal defense fund?'

Well in addition to that requirement, I would also like to remind you that if they were successful in winning such a judgment, they were entitled to *all* of the settlement money despite my kicking in the fifty percent of my earned royalties to help fund such an endeavor.

'So what's my point?' My point was that Allied was hell-bent on keeping that clause intact in the contract, the way it had initially presented me!

Oh, there was no doubt about it, I was frosted over that one! And just the same, I can assure you that O'l Bill and I kicked that one around a good five-hundred dollars' worth at least.

"Steve," he said. "You know this leaves you highly exposed here, you know, that don't you?"

"Of course, I do Bill! Why, I can remember nearly going through the roof the first time I ever saw it. As a matter of fact, just like I originally mentioned, I told Dianne to strike that clause from the contract.

"Remember I even told you that I got up and walked out of the meeting over that one? And now you're telling me they're inflexible on that point! I just don't know how I can handle that one Bill, I really don't."

Right away, he attempted to make me feel that it wasn't the end of the world. I'll tell you, he was pretty good at that, despite the fact he most certainly didn't agree with what they wanted to saddle me with. But from his experience, I guess, he didn't see the value of starting a war over it, like another attorney easily would.

No, he realized how the law viewed it and he certainly wasn't about to minimize how I viewed it either, but importantly enough, he was able to look at it from a purely realistic side, just in case a compromise wasn't coming my way.

"Hey Steve, Allied's a very powerful company, aren't they?" he asked, playing the devil's advocate.

"Why sure they are Bill. You know that!" I replied.

"And from what you have told me, Fram is the largest filter company in North America, if not the world correct?" he probed.

Puzzled now, I asked, "What are you driving at Bill?"

"Well let's just suppose Allied isn't going to change their stance on this clause, the one we've been kicking about, the infringement suit liability clause. So, let me ask you Steve, what are the chances of somebody actually trying to infringe on AlliedSignal anyway. Do you know?"

I knew what he was doing. He was feeling me out to see if I'd consider dropping my hard line on that lawsuit stuff.

"And do you think any of the players out there in the filter business would be foolish enough to infringe on Allied?" using his best rational.

"As a matter of fact, Bill, I don't think they would. And I see what you're driving at besides," I told him. "But I have to be honest with you right up front, at this time I don't feel like folding on that one, like some beach chair, either. It is a matter of principal now for me."

I couldn't help it, but it was enough to make me rant a little bit. 'What the heck', I thought, 'the guy was making $225 an hour and for that kind of money, he could endure a little of my anguish.'

"You know Bill; they still have a heck of a nerve asking me to be a participant in the first place. Secondly, I just have this incredibly hard time overlooking their incredible greed, since they don't even mention that they'd reimburse me for my participation in such an expensive law suit. But what really irks me, is that Dianne was supposed to of stricken that part from the contract I tell ya!"

"If anything, Steve, I'm sure you're more than capable of recalling what you've already agreed upon. And by your own account, Kevin's no longer employed by Fram and Dianne has suddenly developed some sort of a memory problem. I know that's terrible, but all I'm telling you is that this situation might create some sort problem for you either way. You may get hurt if you accept it as proposed, or they might really play hardball with you if you continue to reject it. I don't like this Steve; I just don't like this one bit at all!"

"Yeah, I know Bill, believe me! I happen to be on page six of the fax you sent me."

"Which fax are you referring, there's been a few already?"

I replied, "I'm sorry, the one you faxed me on June 8th. I'm looking at your last paragraph you wrote on the bottom of the page 6. I even have it highlighted."

Interrupting me, he said, "Can you read it back to me, or is it something I should run back to the file for?"

"No, no. I can read it to you, it's so straight forward you'd need help to misunderstand it. *Unfortunately, the proposal also indicates that* **"any expenses incurred by Allied in enforcing the patent will be charged against royalties."'**

After I got done quoting the infringement clause, he then went on to enlighten me about its insidious implication, "Since the cost of a patent lawsuit can easily eclipse a million dollars, this charge back could wipe out any of your royalties. And here's something else, even though Allied gets to charge back the costs to you, Allied is the sole beneficiary of any damages. Now here's what that means Steve... Allied gets you to pay for the litigation, but gets to keep the spoils of victory, if any."

I trust that by now, the picture should be crystal clear. Bill with his vast experience already sensed that they were going to take a hard line on this one. As for me, well I was getting that sick feeling in the pit of my stomach that I was going to be forced to live with this edict whether I liked it or not.

Justification on my part accounted for nothing...

Now here's a little something that seems to be as telling, as it is remarkable. Remember I made it a point at the meeting with Kevin and Dianne that I wanted my patent number both on the can and the packaging. Naturally at the time, I didn't know the legal bulwark that would prop up my contention, but I did know one thing, I knew that somehow it was important that my patent number be on the filter. So, Bill added a whole new number eleven... **"11. MARKING REQUIREMENT"**

"Licensee shall apply to all Licensed Products the following notice: U.S. Patent No. 5,209,842".

And just so you might understand where Bill was coming from, he referred to the addition of this language as standard boiler plate. Now here's the point. If the product offered for sale in the open marketplace has been granted a patent and it hasn't been marked, when it comes time to defend the patent against a would-be infringer, it becomes more difficult to do so under the law.

You see in layman's terms; Bill had put it to me one day like this. "A patent is sort of like a flashing caution light, warning all would be infringers that this product is registered with the United States Patent Office. If the product is so marked, then the would-be infringer is considered warned, but in addition to that, a marked product also helps the manufacturer to calculate damages as well. This is done by keeping track of the items produced from the time in which an infringer has been formally cited by the manufacturer."

"Pretty simple, it makes sense," I told him.

'So, based on this rational, it would only be a natural consequence that AlliedSignal would have wanted their new Fram oil filter marked with a patent number, now wouldn't you of thought? But then again, how come it was never part of their original contract?'

Sort of mystifying don't you think, in light of their pursuit of wanting me to warrant the goods I was about to transfer over? Call me paranoid, but somehow, I was getting this curious vibe that they were actually afraid that I was in the process of defrauding them! And really now, for the Lord Almighty's sake, it was the same patent I had presented to them from the beginning, over a year and a half ago!

What was really going on, was it that AlliedSignal by some genius had forgotten to do their homework over the course of the last seventeen months and had waited until now to start scrutinizing my patent. And believe me, in their haste to catch up, they hadn't even considered for one minute how I might of reacted when it came time for them to cram these damning clauses down my throat to sign!

Thank God Dianne's response was as follows…

"**11**. We accept, subject to not being restricted as to the exact legend or location we must use."

As you can clearly see, Dianne accepted the marking requirement, but with a caveat. And without fail, there always happened to of been a caveat!

Nonetheless though, I was elated! My patent number was now going to appear on every filter and on every box! All the legalism aside, this was the next best thing to signing each one personally! Just the mere thought that my patent number would be affixed to every Fram filter sold throughout the land went a long way in propping up my dream!

Here's a new twist. I think it's only appropriate that her parting words should set the stage for the next escapade.

"We look forward to meeting with you and Mr. Herbert for further discussions of the License Agreement. Due to flight times, I suggest that we set the meeting for 10 AM on Friday, July 7 at the office of Stass & Halsey, 700 Eleventh Street, Washington, DC."

Before I even attempt an explanation, I have to make one last point crystal clear. The letter was signed, "Dianne Z. Newman; Director, Business Planning & Development", with the following carbon copy: "G. Hampilos with attachment, S. Mishal without attachment, and P. Ross without attachment."

I hope that this little gem will begin to give you a better glimpse as to what had been actually going on during the course of these last ten days. And by any estimation, other than perhaps Dianne's, things had gotten way out of control…

There could be no more doubt. Dianne was indeed orchestrating the event, her signature at the bottom of the page was proof enough for me. The fifteen-page fax addressed to me in of itself was telling, but the carbon copy was downright incriminating. She had truly emerged as the fixer…

Please notice that Peter Ross had been included in the line of communication, although not fully, since his correspondence was minus the attachment, [in this case the attachment was a copy of my contract]. So if I ever came to him for help he'd by clueless. And to my amazement, there was still a major officer of the company whom she had neglected to carbon copy, her boss! None other than John Corey, the President of Fram!

'And how could that of possibly been, especially in light of the fact that Fram was about to embark upon one of the greatest leaps in oil filtration technology?' Nothing like this had ever been attempted on this scale before by any of the leaders in the history of this field. And to think, how she was conducting herself! It was all about to go down on Mr. Corey's watch and he was clueless!!!

So now in the midst of an agreement that she had totally fouled up, Dianne is taking it upon herself to broker a meeting to re-negotiate the contract, but this time in Washington! I thought that we had already done this before in Rhode Island a month ago!

At first blush, her proposal appears to be quite forthcoming, but in reality, it was just another carefully laid snare as it spawned yet another major dilemma for me to contemplate.

Clearly, once assembled we would start any talks from the basis of this most recent fax, and in my mind, that was just so unfair, I couldn't stand it! I was under no delusion that any meeting with her at my attorney's office was about to rectify the fact that she had already lied profusely and had already built a neat facade around it.

No…! The more I considered the invite, the more I realized that this meeting was about her coming up here and creating just another shit show before her barbecue grill barely had time to cool off from the Fourth of July holiday.

Call me stubborn, but I wasn't buying it! This trip was more about power than anything else and I was the last one to cater to her misplaced desire to journey on down to the Capital so that she might tend to the Company's business.

As for me it was quite something else. Any meeting at this point would be at my expense, and to meet once again over something Fram had already agree on… Well that would just serve to make me out a liar! So, I guess you could say I wasn't about to help reinforce the fable. I just wasn't able to subject myself to sit in a room, certainly not after I had been lied to, only to give back everything that was already agreed upon! 'Cause seriously, if I had a mind to play the part of the liar come clean, I could have just as easily done that at any time over the telephone and wrapped this thing up in a heartbeat!

Interestingly enough, when I first approached Bill concerning his fee, I asked him right up front how much it was going to cost me, so that there wouldn't be any surprises along the way. He came back and told me that in round numbers as long as things went smoothly it would be about two grand, and at the outside, maybe twenty-five hundred. I certainly didn't have a problem with that, because at the time we were having this conversation, that fee seemed extremely reasonable for what lie ahead.

But now, meeting or no meeting, we were fast approaching the twenty-five hundred mark and my wife, and I had less than ten grand in the bank! Patti had just finished up school for the summer break and we had already long since spent her last paycheck. And she wasn't gonna see another one until she reported back to school in September.

And as for myself. Well my commissions fluctuated like the weather during hurricane season, and there weren't any closing checks on the horizon.

No matter…, we had been together long enough to know how to live with that, so there wasn't any cause for panic. We'd make it through this summer like we had done every summer before, except for one minor detail, we had only budgeted a certain portion of our savings to pay for Mr. Herbert's services and I was in the middle of a sales slump with no rich uncle to turn to.

After hapless 4th of July and much deliberation, Patti and I decided that in light of all the road blocks that Dianne had thrown in front of us in the past, our chances of receiving fair treatment under her system wasn't going to be in the cards. Unfortunately, due to all of the game playing which had gone on, we declined the invitation, not wanting to endure any further debt. Just the thought of paying his fee for the day, with all the miscellaneous trimmings would have cut things far too close to the bone for either Patti or I to of been comfortable with.

But hey, wait a minute! We would of gladly of paid for the day! And perhaps twice as much, if not for one minor detail!

So, when it came down to actually pulling the trigger, not even Bill Herbert was sure if the meeting was worth the additional time and expense considering the way things had been going!

As a matter of fact, by this time I was beginning to sense that even Bill wasn't certain if there was ever gonna be a meeting of the minds. Allied was very far afield now. They moved closer and closer toward law suit territory, led by none other than Diane the fixer.

CHAPTER 12
THE INDEFENSIBLE LIE

Independence Day had come and gone, and I must admit, I was feeling more like a prisoner than a freeman. Still held captive by the likes of something which I had never dreamt possible.

By any stretch of the imagination, the filters' head should of at least been crowning by now, making its way through the pipeline and out into the world. But that was far from the case. Disturbingly enough, nobody from the Company seemed to be overly concerned about it, least of all, the engineering department.

I received a phone call that warm July day, and it would be from Gary, piped into my kitchen. As fate would have it, the call arrived the very afternoon I was supposed to be down in Washington, DC meeting with Dianne. And to think, the irony of it all, it was July 7th, exactly ten months to the very day I had agreed to go into business with Fram.

So, take a look where I found myself. Ring, ring… "Hello?"

"Steve!? It's Gary. How ya doing?"

"Fine Gary, and you?"

"Okay, I guess? I have a couple of questions for you if you don't mind?"

By now his queried calls made me feel helpless, despite his pleasant tone coming over the wire. I couldn't help as to wonder, what he could possibly be stuck on now? I had given him every bit of information months ago, but by the way things had been turning out, anything was possible.

"So, what's on your mind Gary?" I replied, knowing he wasn't just paying me a social call.

"Oh, I have a few questions for you concerning Slick 50, nothing much." Then chuckling, "By the way Steve, how are you and your girlfriend making out?"

I was puzzled, not having any idea what he was referring to. "What do you mean by that?" Repeating back to him the part about the girl friend.

Sensing that he stuck his foot in his mouth, he attempted to back pedal. "I was just kidding ya Steve, it was a little joke is all. But it's all over the place…"

Alarmed, I asked, "What's all over the place? I don't follow you?" I said, completely sidetracked about the information he had come looking for.

"I shouldn't be saying this, and really, I'm not making light of it, but it's all over the place," he repeated. "You know… That you and Dianne are at each other's throats, if you catch my drift?" There was a twinge of 'shame on you' hidden in his tone and I felt that was an awful cheap shot, considering I had made every effort to conduct myself with honor.

As the anger rose up inside, I made it a point to grab hold of myself before I said something I might regret later. "So, let me ask you something Gary, and be honest," I said, masking my anger. "You and I have been working together since December, right?"

"Why yeah."

"Let's see, that's about seven months by my counting. So why don't you tell me right here and now, if I've ever conducted myself in a manner other than being honest and decent. Go ahead, be truthful about it, don't back off."

"No…, no! Don't take it personally Steve. I was just ribbing you, it really doesn't have anything to do with you. She does this sort of thing to everybody! It's just her man! This is just what she does. All of us around here know it, we all kinda sit back and laugh at her."

"Well that's all well and good, but she's taken something which was so straight forward and now she's in the process of destroying my life! So, how can that be so funny!?"

"I'm sorry Steve. I really didn't know to what extremes she's been putting you through!"

Jumping down his throat a little, I said, "That's right, you don't have a clue, believe me Mr.! So, while we're on the subject of Dianne, why don't you let me ask you something. Who's gonna help me deal with her, now that Kevin's gone? Are you?"

Ah… ah, he began sputtering, "I can't... You know that!" Perhaps for the very first time, he was tasting a sample of what I had been going through on the other end.

Thinking out loud, I offered, "I don't know Peter very well at all, and I don't think it's appropriate to go crying' to him even though he's the Vice President of Marketing for God's sake! As a matter of fact, Gary, where does it state that just because I'm doing business with you guys that I should be crying at all?!"

Right about then, I began to unload, "Perhaps you're not aware that Allied's Chief Automotive patent lawyer is dancing 'round her even as we speak! Well, are you? And Gary…, you wanna know something? I've never seen anything like this before in my life, …really! So tell me, what does she have on everybody around here that gives her a license to act with such immunity?"

He couldn't answer it of course; he didn't have a clue. No one around there seemed to!

About the only option I hadn't explored yet, was going to John Corey the President of Fram concerning this situation. But after careful consideration I decided against it, concerned that it might be too a high profile move on my part. After all, she worked for him and there wasn't any guarantee that it wouldn't of backfired on me. So, I just ruled it out.

In the spirit of peace, I decided it was best to back off, by putting an end to our little conversation. At least in my mind, I realized that it would be far more profitable in the long run if I dealt with the situation concerning her by myself. And by now, it had become quite evident that I didn't need anyone telling me that I'd have to fend for myself against Dianne, that had become quite clear. Just like it was obvious that at this late date, Gary still needed my help on something or he wouldn't have been calling me.

The fate of this project still weighed in the balance…, his balance. He was the key, 'cause if I didn't assist him, we'd have nothing to go to market with, and that would just make all of this meaningless nonsense, all the more meaningless. For lack of a better description, the filter was still jammed in his pipeline and I was the only one capable of pulling it out, because surely, he wasn't.

"So Gary, let's just forget about Dianne, okay? Let's just drop it. So, why'd you call me anyway? What can I do to help?"

Relieved that I let it drop, I caught him off balance, "Okay, let me think here for a moment. Yeah sure, I got it. I have a newer version of Slick 50's packaging here and they mention something about a ball on cylinder test. I don't quite understand what they are referring to. It's a test I'm not quite familiar with. Do you know anything about it?"

"Hum…" I thought long and hard to come up with an answer that would make sense, but I couldn't. I caught myself moaning inside, 'like I really needed this now on top of everything else that was going off around me.' At the moment, I really wasn't feeling much like the 'Shell answer man'!

'What in God's name was he doing? Calling me up to check on something an automotive engineer in a white lab coat should a known! The seconds ticked off like hours, and I could feel the vein that ran across my temple, thumping against the phone. I strained to come up with a plausible reply. All I knew was that for some reason he needed it, or he wouldn't have gone through the trouble of calling me. It had to of been important!

I tried to buy a little more time before pleading ignorance. "So Gary, what do you need that for?" having a good idea what was driving him.

"Oh, we're trying to substantiate our claims here for this filters performance, just in case someone wants to challenge its viability."

Not being able to resist, I chimed, "Haven't you guys conducted any tests on this stuff yet?"

"No…, not really. We really didn't have to. We're using the same basic formulation that's in Slick 50 and they've already done all the testing for us. We're just going off of what they've already done," he said, like the cat that swallowed the canary.

"Yes, I know. That's exactly why disclosed to you under PIA the existence of Acheson Colloids and SLA1612 in the first place. Because, I had already figured this out, remember?"

Switching topics, "By the way Gar, how are you guys coming along with the filter? Are you done with the delivery system yet?" I asked, baiting him.

"Na… Not quite, but almost. We just have a couple of more bugs to work out and then we should be there."

Holding my breath, "So you don't see any real problems, do you?" Realizing that another major delay might have pushed the project over the edge at this point. I was certain Dianne knew of this engineering morass and was skillfully using this situation for her own advantage. Actually, my sixth sense was letting me know that she was painting me into a corner with it!

"Na…, you should be okay," he offered, totally oblivious to the storm of great consequence he had spawned.

I thought now would be about as good of a time as any, to let him know that I didn't have the answer he came a calling for. "Hey Gary, you have a copy of that SAE report, don't you? The one conducted by Southwest Labs? You know, the Slick 50 study? Because I already gave you a copy and that details everything you need to know. And if you don't, I'll make you a photocopy and send you another," I said offering to prop him up once again.

"You don't have to bother Steve, I still have the one you sent me."

"So, let me ask you something, don't they detail in the report what you are trying to figure out? Because, I have to be honest with you Gary, I'm not familiar with the ball on cylinder test myself."

"I didn't think you'd be familiar, but I thought it might of been worth a try. So, Steve, can I ask you to do me a favor?"

In the wake of his calm inquiry, I snapped back, "Yeah sure, fire away."

"Would you mind giving Slick 50 a call and see if you can find out what the actual industry standard for that test is?"

I was horrified… I swallowed hard, as his request began to register. What he was asking me to do was something I felt very uncomfortable with. In all my years of research, I had never called Slick

50 looking for information of any kind, and I didn't think now was an appropriate time to start. At least as far as I was concerned, the day I filed my Teflon treated oil filter patent and gathered my trade secrets, was the day I had decided to knock them off the hill. And to my way of thinking, it would of been rather stupid of me to have called them for anything, except an alliance!

Accordingly, it was dicey enough that Fram had decided that they were going to use the same formula as Slick 50, and not what I had originally specified in my patent. But that was now their choice! However, this trade secret of mine was the last bullet in my gun, and it was something I'd end up force feeding the Fram engineers, in order to keep them from going down in flames.

So, as you might of expected, I felt a tad bit uncomfortable when Fram's lead engineer asked me to call the standard bearer of the industry to see if they wouldn't mind sharing a little secret something with me.

The utter nerve?! Asking me to go directly to Slick 50 ask them to divulge some highly prized technical information that may of cost them a tidy sum to develop, just so that my business partner and I could use it to our advantage and slit their throats with it. I don't know, but the sheer audacity of the request left me kind of numb.

And just one last thing, had I called Slick 50 and asked…, they would of slammed the phone down on me.

So, I flat out told Gary that I couldn't possibly go snooping around and call up Slick 50 and ask them for something like that. Besides, I didn't do stuff like that. I didn't do it before I went into business with Fram, and I certainly wasn't about to start it now. I just ended up telling the lead engineer the obvious. He needed to call the Society of Automotive Engineers in Lansdale, Pa. or the Society of Tribologists and Lubricating Engineers out of Illinois to get the answer to those simple questions himself. How friggin' lazy!

Just so you know, through some rather fantastic pre-internet detective work, I found out directly from Dupont, that Acheson Colloids out of Port Huron, Michigan made a product known as Acheson Colloids SLA1612. This material was the heart and soul of Slick 50's Teflon oil additive. I brought this to AlliedSignal/Fram as my *trade secret* and I disclosed it under two separate trade secret agreements, followed up by at least two or three certified letters stating as much.

And one last thing, the shelves of my basements furnace room were still littered with all the correspondence and test studies from both SAE & STLE. There would of never of been an October presentation if hadn't of done my homework. But somehow, even though he was being paid the big bucks, he couldn't quite do his.

It was all coming back to me now. Like the time I had mentioned to Kevin that the engineering department should a been sufficiently motivated to gather up enough test studies to substantiate the validity of my patent. I can still remember being dumbstruck that Fram wasn't interested in tasking a junior engineer to do the leg work then, and it seemed like things hadn't changed much now.

So, on the eve of our supposed launch, I found the lead project engineer asking me to call the competition for some last-minute help in substantiating our new Teflon oil filters claims! Apparently, he wanted it so bad, he faxed me a complete copy of the box along with this note:

"Steve, following is new packaging of Slick 50 product. As we discussed on the phone I need to find out what the actual industry standard number is for the Ball on cylinder test (ASTM #, SAE #). Slick 50 shows wear comparison vs. different products. All Slick 50 mentions is it's "Industry

Recognized". The reference I have on this test is for Fuel Lubricity. Would you please contact Slick 50 and find this out?"

The incessant war of words dragged on, and I gotta say one thing about it, at least it was consistent. My daily routine at this point seemed to revolve more and more around making those ever-important calls throughout the day, to someone…., anyone who might hear. Anyone who might bring us closer to an agreement. Yet no matter what I tried, Dianne was holding firm on her retracted promises, having a pit-bull like grip when it came to relinquishing hold of her controlling lies.

Oh, how I tried! Trying from every imaginable angle to free myself from direct contact with the negotiations, but to no avail. As I lamented earlier, this bizarre protocol dictated that all communications about the licensing agreement come directly through me first. So why don't you come a little closer and take a peek into the boiling pot?

It was Monday morning, the 10th of July, and I woke up that morning with a mission in mind, placing a call to Dianne's secretary. Fortunately for me, I grabbed her just before she was about to make her way for a much-needed Monday morning refill.

"Good morning, Jackie Stevenson. May I help you?"

"Hey Jackie, it's Steve Moor. How are today?" asking, like everything in the world was going my way.

"Hey Mr. Moor, I mean Steve! I'm doing fine today. I hope you're doing the same," she said, genuinely happy to hear my voice. Now Jackie was a class act and I was taken by her kindness from the first moment I ever spoke with her. I could see she was still having a time letting go of that Mr. stuff, though I had admonished her long ago to please dispatch with the formalities.

"So Jackie, I guess by now you must have figured out that I just couldn't bring myself to meet with your boss on Friday," unable to disguise my heartfelt exasperation.

Though Jackie's loyalties to both the Company as well as Dianne were unquestionable, that didn't seem to diminish her ability to perceive what was happening to this young inventor that she privately held out so much hope for. There was little she could do, but take to it in, as the big truck dragged me down the road like some rag doll stuck under its bumper.

"I'm sorry things had turned out that way for you Steve. I was really hoping that by now things would have worked out for you," trying her best to console me.

Pulling herself away from my circumstances she shot back all business, "I'm really glad you called anyway!" As if she nearly forgot something important. "You're supposed to call Mr. Hampilos' office right away!" she said in an awed tone. "Something about you need to look over the revised contract? Dianne mentioned something about it to me on Friday before she left. Actually, I was about to call you in a little while!

"Of course, I don't know any of the details about it Steve, but I can give you his number if you'd like?" Then in a moment of self-recrimination, she added "And even if I did know the particulars, I'm afraid I wouldn't be able to understand them anyway."

"Don't feel bad about that Jackie, you're not too far off about that one. I can barely understand what the heck they are putting in there myself," I said, letting her know that I didn't take her for just some secretary. "And thanks Jackie, but I don't need his number. I've got it. We've already been in touch."

She just gave me a hollow, "Oh I see," and left it at that.

Thinking to myself, 'who was this guy that even Dianne's secretary was so taken aback with, anyway?' It wasn't like my lawyer ever mentioned that this guy was such a big deal or something, because if he'd a known, surely, he would have told me so. And as for Dianne, well you couldn't necessarily go by her. 'Cause judging by her attitude, he didn't seem to be much more than a garden variety staff attorney. Anyway, I didn't pay that much attention to it at the time, if you know what I mean?

It was already beyond the point of incredulity as she happened to be leading him around.

Suddenly, while in the midst of my unceasing quest for clues, this bit of information popped into my head. Going back quite some time ago... I mean many months, when things were still so fresh and new, when I was still in such awe of this shinny corporation... I'm talking about the days when my rose-colored glasses were truly rosy. Someone in the know, told it to me this way, confiding, "Steve, Dianne goes through secretaries like a chainsaw through twigs. There hasn't been a single secretary who's been able last with her for very long before quitting. Until one day, one of the geniuses upstairs figured out she couldn't tear up five of them at once!"

'Do you know how naïve my response was when I learned that Dianne required an entire pool to attend to her needs?' Well, I'm embarrassed to admit it, but I just laughed it off. How was that for lack of judgment on my part!

Once again Jackie interjected, "You know Steve, since you guys decided not to meet this past Friday in Washington, she decided to head up to Vermont with her husband for a vacation. She'll be back by the end of the week or so."

Before I had any chance to question her further, she seemed to of been reading my mind. "Oh..., and Steve, it's not like she goes anywhere without checking in for her messages either, it doesn't matter whether she's on vacation or not. So, don't hesitate to leave a message for her, because I'll make sure she gets it!

"Oh, and one last thing. She reminded me that she was bringing along her cell phone, so I guess there's no doubt that you'll be hearing from her."

After catching my breath, I jumped on the phone to Southfield. Much to my astonishment, I was put through to Mr. Hampilos. "Good morning Mr. Moor, rang his voice, no doubt reverberating off his king sized mahogany desk.

"Hello Mr. Hampilos," I shot back cordially, foolishly fantasizing that he would see that I was a nice man and stop the speeding merry-go-round, so I could jump off without getting pummeled to death. "I just got off the phone with Dianne's office, and I was asked by her secretary to give you a call, sir."

"Thank you, Mr. Moor," came his no-nonsense reply. Apparently, there was no basis for my ridiculous fantasy.

"Please, call me Steve," I offered in a vain attempt to cut the formality. It didn't matter anyway, because, somehow, I had already gotten the feeling that this conversation was going to be short lived. Still, I thought it best at least to try. After all, were we on the same side!

Oh..., well not exactly! Of course, he represented them. Any fool could have told me! But just the same, we were on the brink of forming an alliance, and if it hadn't been for Dianne, there wouldn't have been a bruised feeling amongst us. While we spoke, at least there was one thing of which I could be sure. I had long since proven at least to myself, that I was more than capable of forgiving the Company's sloppy insults to the business at hand.

"Okay Steve…" I am in the midst of going over some last-minute changes to this agreement and I should have it out to you by early this afternoon. As you know, Dianne is out of town for the next several days," he offered coldly, making me feel as if I was truly the enemy.

"Yes sir, I know," as my heart began to pound. Oh, how I wanted to tell him that all this going back and forth, all this perceived obstinance on my part was because of her, and not me! But he didn't have time for that bit of nonsense, I could just feel it. 'Besides, how was he gonna believe me anyway?' This odyssey had already taken us well beyond the point of fiction.

'Don't kid yourself,' I struggled to keep my mouth shut. Thinking, 'this guy's already been prepped that I was some sort of pesky mosquito flying around his Company, just waiting to be swatted.'

I couldn't help but be saddened by it all, and my heart felt like wax, as I held my tongue. The conversation came to an abrupt halt and the phone went click.

It wasn't until much later that morning, when I finally made it back to the office, my mind still whirling in a million directions. For the moment though, I was more preoccupied about feeding my family, as I readied to draw up a contract for the clients I had just left off for lunch. Slipping through the front door of the office, I brandished a hurried smile Norma's way, working my way past her desk. Seeing that I was all business, she shot up from her chair and grabbed my hand and stuck a message slip in it. Then in a motherly tone said, "You'd better drop what you're doing and call her. I have a feeling this is important!" Glancing down at the number, I knew that if area codes could only speak… It was Southfield!

Gus's secretary, Mary had come calling for me about an hour ago. Evidently when she had called, Norma told her that I was out of the office with clients. What she didn't know, was that I was out on the road with a scheduled appointment, trying to close a sale. No matter how much I may have wanted to, it wasn't like I could just hang around the house waiting for Allied to make the phone to ring. Even the most flexible flex time doesn't work that way. After all, I had a wife and family to support, which meant that I still had a real estate career to maintain.

Upon calling her back, she told me that I could expect a fax to arrive sometime after lunch. So, as I busied myself, preparing the contract of sale, I tried not to dwell on the impending arrival of the contract of my life. How I hoped we could agree! Half watching for any sign, I prayed with my whole heart and soul that the madness would soon be over.

Through it all, I had my faith firmly planted on the line, believing! I was banking that this revised contract would bring me the closure I so desperately desired. Let me say something here. I fought this storm with every fiber I had. Not only did I endeavor to do everything I knew to do in the natural realm to make this thing succeed, but I used every bit of spiritual weaponry I had as well. I'm telling ya, I was running headlong at this storm with everything I possessed!

As I passed the fax machine on the way to the water cooler, I could see my destiny coming over the wire. Allied's second full revision of the contract in the form of a fourteen-page fax was being sent this time via Mr. Hampilos' office. It was making its way to me…

"Mr. Moor.

At Diane Newman's request, attached is a revised draft License Agreement incorporating concepts, which I understand, she has discussed with you. Please understand this Agreement is subject to review and approval by AlliedSignal Senior Management.

Diane will be in contact with you.

Gus T. Hampilos

Assistant General Counsel

Chief Patent Counsel-Automotive"

After finishing his cover letter, I couldn't help but think to myself, 'not too shabby for somebody pleading to be left out of the loop, aye Steve?!' Never in my wildest dreams would I of believed that Allied's Chief Automotive Patent Counsel would be communicating directly to me instead of with my lawyer!

'My God man, take another look at his credentials!' I told myself, 'cause if you're reading this right, this guy is the second highest ranking lawyer atop this mighty corporation!

And if any doubts remained as to why he was faxing this document directly to me at my real estate office instead of my attorney's office like he should have, well let's just say, it was a tip-off that something afoul was afoot!

Finding a quiet spot amidst the office supplies, I hunkered down and lost myself for a good half hour. I did the best I could, making notes for Bill, as I scrutinized the thirteen pager, now up for consideration.

After all was said and done, my body nearly went limp from the crushing disappointment. This document was nothing more than a feigned attempt at living up to what had already been promised me back in May. As it turned out, I had gained very little ground from where Dianne and I had left off from her last version. In a fleeting moment of weakness, with Hope nearly running out, I entertained another rare moment, quitting!

Suddenly it began to dawn on me, as I looked down at this stack of papers that I was holding in my hands. This supposed contract more resembled the terms and conditions by which this five-billion-dollar business unit intended on acquiring my property. Nothing more! And I hated it!

As I began to ponder this armistice, a really nasty thought began to attack me. By now, Dianne had to be cruising around in the heart of New England taking in the magnificent scenery at her leisure. And as for me, I was left here stranded; only to suffer through the process which she had conjured up for me to endure.

Keeping my notes close at hand, I forwarded my copy of the contract off to Bill. There was nothing I could do but be patient as I awaited his analysis. The waiting part of this game was incredible, and it exacted a great price, as I willingly gave away some of the most productive and precious moments of my life, …waiting.

Late in the afternoon, driven by desire to make sense of it all, I wagered a call, hoping we could talk. Thank God, at least for my sake, by the time I caught up with him he was already up to speed on this revision. So, for the next hour, we went about fleshing out my next move.

I have to tell you; by this time, it was becoming more difficult as we dissected the remaining language which still kept us at loggerheads. It was apparent, we were now working our way amongst the provisions which Allied held sacrosanct. Bill didn't even have to whisper, there wasn't much flexibility left in their position. No matter how much I tried, I couldn't help myself from feeling hostile towards their motives. Their arrogance still dictated that I hold the bag!

So, here's where we stood after enduring forty straight days of this raging storm…

*They had finally agreed to pay me twenty cents for the sale of each heavy-duty oil filter, although under **"DEFINITIONS"**, it read… "*1.(b) Licensed Products shall mean all products within the scope of any one or more claims <u>of the Licensed Patent, excluding Licensed Heavy-duty Products.</u>*"

Now as a layman, I couldn't quite figure out how they excluded licensed heavy-duty products under this section of the definition, yet somehow, they were going to manage to pay me twenty cents for each heavy-duty filter sold. However, hidden within that clause, even though it wasn't spelled out, I wasn't going to be paid a nickel for anything sold elsewhere, except it be sold in the U.S. or Canada. Something I had already made clear to Diane months ago back at the airport.

*Allied was now going to pay the 50K signing fee in thirty days, a far cry from their original offer of one hundred and twenty days. Yet, not nearly the ten days we had agreed upon that day in the room with Kevin.

*The word game concerning Canada was still alive and well. They just couldn't bring themselves to put in there made in Canada like she initially said they would. At this stage of the talks, I was still maddened by all the double speak concerning this issue and insisted upon what we had all agreed to.

*They still insisted upon "Reasonable Efforts"! I guess "Best Efforts" was just going to be too much of a stretch for the largest filter manufacturer on the planet. Bill warned me in advance that it looked like we were going to have to settle on that level of performance. Of course, I was very disappointed, because I certainly expected more out of them than that!

*Concerning the minimum guarantee of 50K for the 1st year, 75K for the 2nd, and 100K for 3rd for which I referred to earlier as the insurance policy, well, they were vehement about sticking to their original offer. In turn, I had dropped that whole pursuit awhile back, but here's something of interest, that I'd like to note. If the royalties earned after the first three years did not equal or exceed the sum 225K, then the license would revert to a *nonexclusive license* to them, and therefore control would revert back to me.

So, what did that mean exactly? That simply meant that for $275,000 or less, they had taken an option on testing a Billion-dollar a year repeatable market where, I would bear most of the risk. The $275 grand was their insurance policy, and that was all they'd be risking. And if they failed, they could hand back partial control to me. Partial control being, they still had chiseled in stone that they'd be granted a nonexclusive license to sell their product.

But here's the catch, by doing so they would have destroyed a pristine and viable opportunity in the process, making it impossible for me to interest another player in taking on a license, nonexclusive or otherwise, since the biggest player of them all had already failed at the game. As far as I was concerned, it was like exchanging clean linens, for soiled ones.

*The whole thing about me helping bank roll a patent infringement law suit was still embodied in the contract, in nearly the original language they had initially set forth. Even though an infringement suit was a long shot, at this stage in the game I was still willing to fight to the death to have it removed from the contract!

*As I made mention to earlier, Allied was still in agreement to mark the product with my patent number. Now again, I ask you to keep that little tidbit in mind.

Well, that was about it! It was enough to keep my attorney on the payroll for nearly the next two months. And certainly, enough to keep me fighting for what I believed already belonged to me!

The next morning, I awoke before the dawn broke. I hated to admit it, but I was scared! This situation had now developed a life of its own, as it hurtled out of control! I needed to share my hopes, and more importantly my fears with someone this morning, and Patti just wouldn't do. Anyway, she'd been through enough of this cruel odyssey. Besides, I wasn't so weak that I was about to steal this peaceful moment from her, as she lie there fast asleep. I was the one who needed to slip out, not her! It would have been beyond selfish to have her greet the new day, the way I had been prompted to greet mine.

I loved my wife dearly, and though I shared with her the innermost workings of my heart, I was compelled to shield her from what was happening to me. It wasn't that I was being especially brave, I was just trying to protect my best friend from the pain.

I headed for the trusty rock pile that jutted out into the sea. Finding a dry place to sit, I nursed a cup of hot coffee and waited in silence for the sun to make her way up out of the Atlantic. I was burdened down, dogged by those ever-persistent trio of demons, which now, more than ever, sought me out with malicious intent. I knew them as, Fear, Doubt and Unbelief, but this time they brought along a favored companion… Death.

Before I could get down to any serious prayer, I had to work my way through the jumbled thoughts that fueled the raging battle inside my head.

My thoughts turned toward Bill, as I evaluated his performance from every possible angle. 'And my conclusion?' Well, I was satisfied, more than satisfied. Perhaps in this day and age, that might sound a bit odd, but it wasn't my habit to go running around looking for someone to blame, cause my life happened to be spinning out of control. What I really needed, was someone I could lean on. A counselor perhaps, someone whom I could place my trust in to do a job for me, and I'll tell ya, I got what I bargained for in Mr. Herbert.

I reasoned, it was only right that I judge Bill in light of the situation we found ourselves. Though he gave me good counsel, he could only dispense his advice as the situation unfolded. It manifested for him the same way that it did for me, moment by moment. I knew that he was doing his best to represent me, but even a fool by now could have seen that he was precluded from doing his duty! 'Crazy huh?' But that's exactly what was going on!

Just in case you might of forgotten, I was fairly confident from the onset about his lawyering abilities, yet no one had ever warned me that I'd be needing a magician to oversee this simple contractual matter.

'And if that wasn't the case, then how do you explain Mr. Hampilos' professional conduct?' I couldn't very well point a finger at my attorney after witnessing how this man who wielded considerable power, was allowing Dianne to play the role of a crime scene cleaner.

So, I looked to the Lord for guidance. There was no pretending, I was lost, and I knew it. I didn't go looking for Him that morning seeking fame nor fortune, nor even victory, but rather, His direction and peace amidst the violent storm I had become a prisoner of.

It didn't seem like my prayers were getting heard. "Sweet Jesus, my Friend, my Father, my Love… I'm getting pummeled down here, where are you? I need your help," I called, as the tears ran off my face tumbling down and mingling with sea.

No matter how hard I tried, I didn't hear Him that morning. The only thing I had to go on was something He had imparted, what seemed like an eternity ago. "I didn't let you come this far to fail, my dear Stephen."

'You know something?' He was right. After all, He was God. I left there that morning strengthened, realizing that quitting wasn't an option I could consider!

What may not be entirely clear to you as of yet, is this… Allied had the power to rip this thing out of my hands at any moment of their choosing. I knew it…, they most certainly knew it, and of course Bill knew it. And if they chose that option, it wasn't like I could call the police, my congressman or the Patent Office. You see once this particular pair of dice gets thrown, the only arbiter, is a law suit in Federal Court.

Having been left no other choice, I reluctantly decided to get Peter Ross involved. There wasn't going to be any new avenues opening up, which even remotely promised to remove me from having any further dialog with her. I was beyond desperate!

About a week ago, I gotten up enough nerve to get him on the phone in an attempt to bring him up to speed as to what was actually going on…

"Pete, I hate doing this, and I absolutely understand you're jammed, but I really need your help, or I wouldn't be calling you, but I really got a problem here. I have nobody else to turn to," I told him. And it sure wasn't like I had been calling him every day either, 'cause by my count, I hadn't spoken with him in over a month.

There was no doubt Ross was working shorthanded. And believe me, Fram wouldn't be finding a suitable replacement for his workaholic subordinate in the form of Mr. Gill, anytime soon. That was for sure. Then there was still the slot above him; Jack McGrath's old job which had been left gaping wide open for the last six months. Despite the fact that Peter was my new handler, the last thing I wanted to do was to come crying to this guy who was already in over his head.

Think about it, his right arm had been cut off! And as if the agony of losing Kevin wasn't enough for him to bear, he obviously wasn't the heir apparent for Jack's old job either or he would have already of moved into his office. What a kick in the teeth! I'm not making any excuses for him, not by a long shot, but the guy under those circumstances wouldn't be playing at the top of his game. By now I viewed Peter as some sort of lame duck. The way he was handling Dianne was a total embarrassment, and just reinforced what I was witnessing.

Just so you know, I would find out much later on down the road why Kevin left Fram. Turns out, Kev wrote a rather telling letter to Bossidy, detailing how the Fram brand name, as well as the Division was in serious trouble. He came right out and asked Bossidy for Jack McGrath's now vacant position; Senior VP of Marketing. He got some lip service out of the boss, but he didn't get the job, so he quit, and I might add, justifiably so! There was no doubt at least in my mind, that he deserved to be catapulted ahead of Peter Ross. Kevin was the only sailor on board capable of steering this now rudderless ship.

"Of course, Steve. What's on your mind? I'll try and help you anyway I'm able," he offered politely.

"Well, without getting crazy about it Pete, since Kevin has left, I feel that Dianne has taken it upon herself to take me to the cleaners. And at least to me, it seems like no one around here is watching the store. The contract that we supposedly had agreed upon back in May has been gutted. And for the last month, I've been saddled fighting with her for something which should have already been mine!

"Not to change the subject or anything, but do you by chance remember what I told you that afternoon? You know, when I spoke with the both of you in doorway of the conference room after we had all agreed?"

Stammering a bit, he came back, "Well not exactly Steve? It was a while ago, and you said a few things there, if I can remember correctly."

I couldn't miss the opportunity to admonish myself, 'see what I told you about selective memory loss.' The last thing I needed to do was to quote him what I said back there about the sea turtle and her abandoned eggs.

"So, what seems to be the problem?" he said, real coy like, knowing darn well what the problem was. Everyone around there seemed to know what the problem was, long before O'l starry eyed ever arrived on the scene.

"You see Peter, that day when I had left the both of you, I specifically recited the fact that we had an agreement in principal. And I did that on purpose, you know. I did it because Kevin was the only witness I could count on, up until that point besides myself. He was the only one that could vouch for what had gone on in that room, and by that time, I was already aware that he was leaving the Company.

"I shouldn't have to spell this out for you, but I will… You took his spot. You became my witness that day.

"I know you're a busy guy, and have a major business unit to run, but I really need your help now! Besides, it ain't every day you buy some guys patent and launch a new product from it either!"

Unfortunately, my gut instincts were correct, as he let the opportunity for a fact-finding mission slip on by. "So, what exactly is going on Steve?" Probing just enough to make it seem like he was interested in my plight.

Here we go, I thought. "Look we had already agreed that there was to be distinction between the automotive business and the heavy-duty. And don't ask me how, but she's gone back on her word."

"Okay Steve, I hear what you're saying," he said, not wanting to commit himself.

Instinctively, I broke into a logical explanation for my position, as he sat there on the other end of the line, listening in silence.

I could tell this was just what he needed, getting involved, I mean. As the truth of the matter came streaming out of my heart, I couldn't help but think to myself sarcastically, 'I feel like some kid here, tattling on the playground bully.'

"Steve, I already thought we went over this ground," he began, rather authoritatively.

Stunned, "I don't follow you Pete, what ground are we talking about?"

"We don't do a huge volume in heavy-duty. You already know that."

"Of course, I know that, but it's based on the sheer principal of what we had already agreed upon! Isn't it already obvious, that I already know that you don't do anything to speak of in installed sales either. But hear me… I'm still going into business with you guys despite the fact that your present market share is shrinking, even as we speak! So why would a smart guy like myself be going into business knowing all that?

"Well let me answer it for you. It's called upside potential for future growth! And it's all wrapped up in the Double Guard Pete, you just wait and see! If you guys market this thing the way I know you can, I'll reap the rewards of both the markets you have presently walked away from. Now that's what I'm, banking on! Because let me tell you flat out, my future sure ain't riding on that fifty-grand sign on fee. I can tell you that for sure!

"All I can tell you, is that my hopes are riding on the fact that you guys are able to perform!" I said, putting the burden of performance strictly upon his Fram shoulders.

Barely pausing for a breath, I stuck this in, "So how fair would it be to deny me any future compensation based upon the good faith that I'm willing to place in your Company right now?

"I don't get it Pete! I really don't get it? I'm betting the farm on you people and yet I'm still being squeezed. How much is enough, for you guys? Huh?"

Since he was doing more listening than talking, I just decided to keep on going, as I ran down the next point, "Canada." And then the next one, "The law suit partnership." I then concluded my list of grievances with a personal touch, just for him, "Best efforts"!

I can assure you, he got my message about all the remaining sticking points of the contract, but his reaction to it, left me all but puzzled. Only time would tell whether he was willing to do the right thing, or if he was just gonna pay me lip service. I didn't know him near well enough to make a true determination as of yet.

One thing for sure, I didn't require much coaching to know our little exchange was over. "Okay Steve, are you satisfied that you've expressed all your concerns?" coming back, like he had places to go, and things to see.

"Yes, that's it Peter. I really appreciate your listening to me this morning. So, if you can help straighten this out for me, we can all get on with the launch."

Today's call to Peter, I hoped was going to be different. I wanted to take advantage of the fact that Dianne was still going to remain a moving target in New England for the rest of the week. It was my plan to get something fruitful accomplished before her return. Today was only Tuesday, so if we hustled, maybe we could accomplish something. Before weeks' end, I'd log no less than eight more calls into Peter Ross.

Fortunately for me, I got him on my second attempt, around nine thirty. "Good morning Peter Ross," as my call went directly through to his office.

"Hey Pete! It's Steve Moor. How are you today?"

"Oh, good Steve. What's up?"

"Well I just want to let you know that I just received Dianne's second full revision of the contract."

Without hesitation he jumped in. "You did? How'd you get that! I mean when did that arrive?" I knew he had to think about that one for a moment, after all she was on vacation.

I could see where he was coming from, so I filled in the blanks for him. "Mr. Hampilos and I have been in touch and he sent it to me," I said, matter of factly.

"Oh…, oh, I see. And…?"

"First off, she finally agreed to make a separate distinction for the heavy-duty class and pay me accordingly and I have nobody to thank, but you for that," I said, truly appreciative.

"Good Steve. I'm glad that I could be of some help. There is certainly a distinction between the two product categories and it would only be fair to compensate you accordingly," he offered, like a gentleman.

"Why thank you Peter. I thank you again for your honesty on that one."

"So, how'd you make out on those other points we were discussing? What were they…?" as he stopped to think for a moment. "Wasn't it Canada, and something else you were mentioning, I believe 'Best Efforts'?"

"You got it Pete. That was it pretty much it in a nutshell, except you forgot one thing?"

"And what was that Steve?"

"The clause about my being a paying customer for any would-be patent infringement law suit that Fram might get into. That's all!"

"Oh, I'm sorry Steve, I forgot about that one. So, how'd you do?"

"To put it mildly Pete, I struck out." For a time, the both of us held our peace in the anguished silence. Feeling that it was incumbent for me to speak, I offered, "Now it looks like I'm gonna have to beat this thing to death some more, once she gets back. And frankly Pete, I'm dreading it!

"She's hasn't allowed my lawyer to represent me like he's been hired to!" holding myself back from an all-out explosion. Then in a moment of passion, I capitulated and threw myself on my sword. "So, Pete, can't you take her spot? Can't I just reason theses remaining points out with you?

"I mean look! Look how calm and rational we're getting along. This is how it should of been from the very onset. Won't ya please try and help me?"

Now I was begging…, something I loathed. This situation had reduced me to begging and I felt so darn cheap.

Swallowing my shame, there was nothing I could do, but wait for his response.

"I can't say for sure Steve. It's really not my job to be doing that," came his noncommittal reply I'd been dreading. Offering in a fatalistic tone, "Steve, try and understand that it wouldn't look too good for all of us, if I got involved now." My heart just sank…

In the pain and confusion, I snapped back without hesitation, "You know Pete, I've heard that line a while ago, outa Kevin."

"I'm sure you have Steve. But unfortunately, I have to tell you the same thing he did. I'll try, but that's all I can tell ya. What you're asking for, is a lot easier said than done. You hear me, don't you?" saying it more out of guilt than if he was letting me in on some big secret.

"See what you can get accomplished this week with her, okay? And if things look like they're getting a little bit too intense, well…, I'll just have to see what can be done about it then."

Catching me off guard completely, he changed his tone as if this madness had suddenly disappeared. "Hey! It looks like you're almost on your way, mister! You've come this far, so why don't you try and hang in there?"

I soon realized that no amount calling was about to change anything, whether it be to Washington, Rumford or Southfield. Plain and simple, Dianne's absence meant that the negotiations came to a grinding halt, and with that, so were any plans of my moving forward without her!

As the mornings madness continued, I found myself dialing for dollars, as I place a call to Bill Herbert. "Steve, I just got off the phone with Dianne a little while ago," he offered calmly. "She wants to go over a few things with you, all right?"

You wouldn't believe how happy it made me feel to hear him say that to me. It was the last thing I expected, when he picked up the phone.

"So, Bill, what did you guys talk about anyway?" I asked, half holding my breath, hoping…, hoping.

"Well, we discussed the language of the Canadian issue."

Jumping in, I interrupted him before he could even chance an explanation. Catching myself, I apologized, "I'm sorry Bill, it's just that I'm so torqued up. I'm sorry, I'll keep my mouth shut until you're done. I promise."

In a fatherly tone, he was quick to console me. "That's all right Steve. I can only imagine how you must be feeling right about now. I realize this is a big deal for you."

"Thanks for your understanding Bill, I appreciate that. Please go on."

"As I said before, we have been discussing the Canadian issue and frankly I have to tell you that I'm amazed. I'm still having quite a difficult time getting her to agree to the exact language. I really can't figure out what her problem is? All we want, is for them to compensate you for any filter that's produced in Canada or sold in Canada or in the United States. Now really, what is so complicated about that?" he said, in a rare visceral moment.

"You know Steve, it's only fair they give it us, since they've already disclosed to us that they have a manufacturing plant up there and that it's only a matter of time before they might end up producing some of your product at that facility. And based upon both of our conversations with Dianne, we already know that they don't make a clear distinction as to what they sell between the two countries already. In my opinion, it would be a shame to give them any loophole to cut you out of that portion of the royalties, especially since she's already offered it you."

"I know Bill. That's exactly how I feel about it, and I don't feel like caving in on that one. I just don't.

"So, what else did you guys discuss?"

"As you might of expected, we discussed Allied's use of the language, "Reasonable Efforts", as opposed to what we wanted to see used, that of course being "Best Efforts"." I noticed his tone sounding more ominous than I could ever recall concerning that issue.

"So, what about that one Bill? What would happen if I soften on that one? We've been going at this for nearly forty-five days and I just want this thing over with now."

"I know exactly what you mean Steve. I never dreamt it would of dragged on like this…, never! But here's what you're looking at. Allow me to play devil's advocate here a moment. Do you feel secure in the fact that they've agreed to pay you fifty thousand dollars up front?"

"No…, a thousand times no! You already know that Bill. I shoulda been paid at least a million dollars to sign!"

"Okay. Now hold on there a bit. Now as you've stated time and time again, Allied's the unequivocal leader in this field the world over, right?"

"Why yeah, so?"

"So how would this sound Steve, I mean for somebody like them agreeing to limit their promotion of this product to "Reasonable Efforts"? Now wait a minute before you say anything here! I mean in Federal Court, in front of a judge, or in front of a jury of your peers. You know in the very real event that you might have to take them to court for non-performance?"

"I'm not saying that this is going to happen…, but Steve, I wouldn't be guiding you properly if I didn't tell you that shouldn't be ruled out as a possibility. I've certainly seen it many times before in my experience with these big manufactures, you know."

"Well…, I guess that doesn't seem too good, right?" I shot back.

"Precisely my point Steve. Let me explain something to you. I'm not sure if you are aware of this or not, but what is contained in this contract supersedes everything that's ever been promised to you. Do you realize that? Because, it's of supreme importance here?"

"No not really," I said totally ignorant of what he was about to say.

"Well then, let me explain it to you. That means that this contract takes precedent over whatever has either been said, or whatever has been put in writing to you before. Do you realize that?" he said, not mincing any words.

"I see! So that's why when I had asked both Kevin and Dianne to put the Company's business plan into my contract that day, they both flatly told me that it would be totally out of the question."

"Why yes Steve, of course. To of had your business plan inserted as part of the contract would have been excellent protection, so long as you had approved of the Company's business plan.

"Now look Steve, I'm not trying to scare you. But whatever is not written into this contract, may be impossible to introduce as evidence into a court of law later on. Specifically, I am referring to any of those conversations you may of had with Kevin or Peter or anybody else concerning the Company's promise to market your product adequately."

"Hey Bill, I'm no lawyer, but that sounds crazy. I never heard of any such stupid thing," I said, unable to believe what I was hearing. "So, what about the marketing and business plan that I'm holding of theirs? What about all of the promises and the inducements they had given me to go along with them once they had shown an interest?"

"Now Steve, listen to me carefully here. There's a little something in the law which you may not have understand too clearly. The law refers to it as parole evidence. In which case, may in fact, cover a great deal of the material we've been discussing. However, generally, it's not admissible in court."

"Are you serious? I can't believe what your telling me!" I went numb.

"As a matter of fact, I am! Why do you think I'm taking the time to explain all of this to you? Don't think for a second that Allied in their nice little way hasn't already considered what I've already told you. I'm sure they're prepared to play this one out to the end! So what I am saying to you is this, if this partnership fails because of them, and more specifically due to their inability to market this item properly, are you willing to be satisfied with the fifty grand up-front and the two hundred twenty-five thousand dollars the contract guarantees you over the next three years? Because that's all they are risking at the moment!"

"Ah no! Of course, not Bill, you know that!"

"I didn't think so, but that could very well become a reality if they still insist upon being held to the standard of 'Reasonable Efforts'." Then he added, "And oh… I'm sure that you also realize, if that be the case, you would get your patent back."

"Yeah sure Bill, that sounds reassuring! Like my patent would really be worth anything after the largest filter company on the face of the planet screwed things up and contaminated the market. There are only four players here in the states remember? Who in their right mind would pick it up from me after Fram failed with it?"

"Hum, I don't know?" he said. Maybe Purolator?"

At this point, I just laughed at him. It was all I could do offering, "You better stick to lawyering Bill," I said, teasing him for suggesting something as ludicrous at that. "Na…, if Fram screws this thing up, they can keep my patent," I suggested angrily. "Because nobody else would touch it."

"Why Steve…? Come on now, it would still be worth something, wouldn't it?"

Just trust me Bill, it would have been rendered soiled goods by time they get done messing with it.

"So, what else did you guys talk about?" I said, wanting to get off of that heartbreak.

"Well, we started to talk about your exposure under their proposed language concerning a patent infringement suit, but she started breaking up. I could tell she was on her cell phone the whole time. What she did manage to say before we got cut off was, that she'd be calling you sometime this afternoon at home.

"Ring, ring, ring." I had sought refuge behind the closed door of my bedroom when the phone began to ring. I don't know how long I had been lying there, but it had to of been at least a couple of hours anyway.

Outside my window, I could hear Patti and the kids out in the backyard, still frolicking in our above ground pool, yet I was worlds away, removed from their innocence and love. Like some patient with a terminal disease, I just lay there hapless, nearly resigned that the world was about to pass me on by. I was alone, terribly alone. I was praying, but I had little faith left in the tank. At least in my mind…, I was already a walking dead man.

After getting off the phone with Bill earlier that morning, I can remember telling Patti that I was tired, and that I needed to take a nap. As the battle progressed, the need for these 'naps' became more and more frequent.

"Are you sure honey? It's such a beautiful sunny day out here, and the kids would love to play with you in the pool," she said, trying to free me from the morass the best way she knew how. Patti was no dummy; she knew what was going on. She just respected the fact, that like a wounded animal, I was better off left alone, until I could heal.

"No thanks Pat, I'm exhausted. I gotta lie down Baby, you play with them. Listen, here's the portable phone, if it rings, please pick it up. Bill says that Dianne should be calling me sometime later this afternoon. Okay Honey?"

"Yeah sure," she said, sadly. "You go inside and take a rest and maybe tonight we can go up to the boardwalk like a family. I have loads of tickets left over from last year and we haven't been up there yet all summer yet. It would be nice to put Jackie on some rides!" unable to restrain herself from letting me know that this process had wounded her as well.

I knew she had me dead to rights, but she was too much of a friend to really make an issue out of my broken condition. There was no better team player than my wife, and I knew it.

"We will Pat, I promise ya honey," I said, drawing a feeble breath.

Pulling the slider shut, I effectively shielded my little brood from the crushing vortex that was now eating me alive, from the inside out. I could only have wished, that it would be that easy. Truly in a much deeper sense, I hated myself for all that was going on.

Though she was my eternal soulmate, I was compelled now more than ever, to do something I hadn't ever done during the entire course of our ten-year relationship, I was shutting her out, and I was guilty of doing it on purpose. I couldn't bear to share with her the details of what was actually going on…

For what! So, I could break her heart as well! No, I didn't think so. A move like that would have only ruined her remaining days of the precious summer, a season when she was truly free to mother the two babies she loved more than life.

I might of been at my weakest moment of my entire life, but weakness didn't have to spill over into selfishness, at least not in my book.

The more I wrestled with the situation, the more perplexed I had become. The negotiation process…, no, the entire ordeal had drained me to the point in which my body felt lifeless. Nerves had robbed my once virile frame of nearly all its energy.

On the one hand, I was ready to fold, and the lure of big money had long ago begun to lose its luster for me. I had endured just about all I could stand. Then on the other hand, Bills words seemed to be ever present, as if placed there to haunt me.

Bill Herbert by nature was gentleman's lawyer, non-confronting, non-litigious. There was no doubt why he and I meshed so well, he was in many ways, a man after my own heart.

But wait a minute, as I jumped out of bed knowing good and well who was going to be on the other end of the line. Moving past the slider I stole a glimpse of my most precious commodity out there in the back yard, all of them playing without a care. Yet none of them having the vaguest idea of just how much of their future Daddy held in the palm of his hand.

As I reached for the phone, Bill's very cut and dry legal advice burned away the chaff that cluttered my confused mind. I wasn't about to give into Dianne, to Allied, nor to anybody else for that matter. I guess right then and there I decided it would be better to crash and burn before I'd do anything like that.

Picking up the ringing phone I put the receiver to my ear and for a moment, all I heard was screaming going on… "I thought I told you how I wanted you to park this car!" It was a woman's voice and I was having a hard time figuring out what was going on, as these whooshing sounds came over the phone. Was it a bad connection? Or did I have a solicitor on the other end gone mad. Whoever it was, she was still yelling at this person. All the while thinking, 'I ran into the kitchen for this?'

"I told you not to pull in head first! I have to grab something out of the back. I thought I told you to back it in!"

"Hello…, hello. Who's this?" I called out, seemingly about as lost as the caller. Beginning to lose my patience for this misplaced communication, I headed for the phone hanging on the wall, ready to cut this screaming marauder off.

"Hello Steve…" I was shocked, after all it was for me! Wondering? "Hello Steve?"

"Yes, this is Steve Moor, who's this?" I asked, still very much in the dark.

"It's Dianne Newman. I'm on my cell phone, can you hear me all right?" At that moment I had to laugh, she sounded like a lost astronaut trying to reach mission control.

"Yeah sure Dianne, I think I can. Say, what's all that yelling about? And that whizzing sound I hear in the background?"

Oh, we're on our way to a wedding in upstate New York and we've just pulled into a rest area for a couple of minutes, so I could give you a call. There's not too many towers up here so this phone doesn't work too well at all when you're moving along. You know they really have a long way to go with this technology," pleased to cast a rock at the phone company.

"So, what was all that screaming about, when I first picked up the phone? Is everything all right?"

"Yeah sure, everything's just fine. I was just yelling at my husband. He was supposed to be parking the car, but he missed the space I wanted, then he put the car in the wrong way.

"So, did Bill Herbert tell you that we spoke this morning?" as she turned her attention toward business.

"As a matter of fact, he did Dianne. I spoke with him at length about your call."

"And… So, I guess there was no problem in you receiving the contract from Gus, either, huh?"

"No Dianne. Of course not. I've had it since Monday afternoon, and today's already Thursday. I've read it, Bill's read it. So why are you asking me all that?" unable to make the connection.

"Oh, it's nothing really. I was just making sure all was well. Is there anything you'd like to discuss at the moment?" asking me like she had nothing better to do on holiday.

"Yes. There are a few things that need to be ironed out before I can agree to this contract Dianne." I could feel the force of hate curdling through my veins as her stupid and insensitive line of questioning rolled off her lips; seemingly sent my way to satisfy a sudden yen she had to berate someone other than her husband.

"Well you already talked with Bill this morning, I'm certain he communicated my position, Dianne." I offered, trying to mask my charged-up emotions, concerning the long-overworked details.

"As a matter of fact, he did Steve," she offered sweetly. 'Good', I thought. 'At least I hadn't gotten her beyond that point yet, but I knew that it would be only a matter of time.'

"So, Dianne, why don't you just continue to talk with him about it okay? Like I've been trying to tell you all along, he's my lawyer. He knows what I want. He knows what's best for me, and he knows what I'll agree to. So why do you and I have to still be hashing this stuff out over and over?" begging for her to cut me loose.

Her reply belied the full sea turn in her demeanor and I could only imagine what was waiting on me. "Because this doesn't concern the lawyers yet. I thought I had already made myself clear about that!" she said angrily. "So, do you want to discuss anything?" she yelled into the whooshing phone.

"Well if we have to," I offered, "Let's start with Canada. Why can't we seem to get the language straight on that one?"

"How so Steve?" she asked, assuming her posture of playing the dumb negotiator.

"The proper language Dianne, '….is made in Canada or sold in Canada or sold in the United States.' Let me ask you something. Since you've already volunteered to give me all the Canadian business, why are you having such a difficult time of putting it into the proper language? We've only been at this now for over forty-five days!"

She then gave me a rather deflated, "I'll consider it." I thought I had finally hit pay dirt, she was going to give it to me, after all, today was going to be the day she would finally cut me loose!

So, all happy and high-toned, I came back to her with this big smile which by now could have knocked her over. "So, Dianne, does that mean we are in agreement?" I asked, holding my breath, all the while thinking to myself, thinking, 'if we knock this one off, there'd only be two more issues to handle!' Please Lord…, please!

"No, it doesn't Steve. It just means that I'll think about it."

It didn't take much for me to see that my captor wasn't about to relinquish her grip on my affairs anytime soon!

Dianne was truly a marvel, shutting me down effortlessly. Assuredly, it mattered little to her from where she dispensed her judgment, whether it be from the front seat of her car stationed at some far and away outpost such as a rest area, or from her little cubicle back in Rumford.

Not about to give up after that episode, I proceeded to dust myself off, reregistering several more calls into Peter before her return. All with the same result, nothing. In plain language, there wasn't a man amongst us that could deter this Babylonian princess from her despotic mission. Apparently, she had determined the course we were to follow long ago. She was truly Allied's fixer.

One of my many cries for help during this particularly grueling session went out to Kevin. And it was during one such heated bout of therapy that he shared something very unexpected with me. Something that rocked the very foundation of my world.

"You know Kev; I can't figure out her motives for doing this to me? I can't help but feel that what she is doing to me is motivated by something personal. Is it because she knew that we were both close, and now you're gone? It's because you've left, right?

"Because I'll tell ya man, it's as if someone has set her free to run all over my hide. What's the deal, I can't figure it out?

"And Kev…, is the Company behind it, because I think they are?"

Something happened to him, I don't know, but the dead silence was no hindrance as it made its way over the phone. It was as if the blood in his veins had suddenly turned to ice, offering, "Nice try, but I'll take odds that it's none of the above."

Just so you know, Kevin desperately clung to the belief that his beloved Company was honest and ethical. At this point, he wouldn't allow himself to consider otherwise, since everything he stood for was at stake. He would continue to cling to this rational for quite some time. However, once I sued Honeywell and deposed him…, let's just say, that's when he got a good dose of reality.

Swallowing hard, I got up the courage to ask him what this was all about. I knew if any human being possessed an honest answer as to what might be at the root of my dilemma, he'd top the list.

Unable to wait for him to tell me, I couldn't resist proffering a conspiratorial hunch. "It's them, right? They've put her up to it!" I said, trying my best to lead him with the obvious.

"Maybe Steve, but I doubt it. Oh, not that I wouldn't put anything past those boys back there, 'cause let me tell ya something Stevie; they've been known to play a pretty mean game of hardball. But ya know, I really can't say for sure if they're pulling all of the strings on this one," he offered with an uneasy finality. "I don't think it's that cut and dry. I wish it was," he mumbled to himself, deep in thought.

Coming back like a little kid, asking for his big brother's reassurance, I pressed, "You don't think so, huh?"

"Nope. I don't.

"Now let me ask you something Steve. Can you remember back to the time when you first spoke with me. I mean the very first call you ever made to Fram concerning this patent. When the heck was that anyway, man? You've got a better memory for these things then I'll ever have."

'Where in God's name was he going with this one?' I wondered.

"It was early January '94 Kev. Early January '94," I said, repeating it to myself, just to make sure.

"Well can you remember who you asked for when you had called that day?"

"Yeah sure. I didn't know who to ask for, that much I can tell you. I certainly didn't ask for you; I didn't know who Kevin Gill was. The operator was the one who put me through to you. Why?"

"Precisely my good man, precisely! You may of not have realized this, but your call shoulda been directed to her that day and not to me! Are you starting to see what happened?!"

"No, not exactly Kev, I'm a little slow here, so you're gonna have to spell it out for me if you don't mind. Okay?"

"All right Stevie, it goes something like this. She's the Head of Strategic Planning and Worldwide Development for Fram, you at least got that much? Right?"

Still lost, I could only muster, "Yeah so?" seeing that he was about to make the most out of unraveling this riddle.

"Okay, so let me spell it out for you my good man. The call that you made that day was supposed to go to her! Get it!" I could sense that if he could have come through the phone and whacked me for being so dense, he would have.

"Na...! You're crazy, Kev. I thought I was on a fishing expedition, but you..."

"Now just shut your mouth here a bit, and listen to me for second here buddy boy, after all, you're the one looking for help here, not the other way around, remember?"

"Sorry Kev."

"It's all right, it's all right. You know Steve, I feel terrible about this mess. I don't mean to be so darn short with you, but just watching what they're doing to you is killing me! I mean it, damn it! If I could have only of known what they were about to do to you, I would have never let you get this far, believe me! You know Steve, I can't help but feel partly responsible for all of this." I could see that he was having a difficult time ridding his hands of some of my blood.

"Kev, I appreciate all that, but please don't get side tracked here. I just gotta know! Like I already told you a hundred times, you did your best. You left 'cause you had to..., and besides, I don't blame you for what's gone on. You're not capable of doing this sort of thing to someone."

"Thanks Steve. Coming from you, that means an awful lot to me."

Pulling himself together, he began to close the loop. "You know, that day when your call came in, she was out of the office traveling. By rights, she was supposed to be the one who fields calls like yours, but since she was gonna be out of town for a while, the operator sent you over to me. Innocent enough, aye? And let me put it to this way Steve, I didn't know you from a hole in the wall, you were just a voice on the other end of the line. As a matter of fact, you could of been a nut or something.

For God's sake, you could have been Larry Bossidy's nephew for all I knew, just checking in to see if I was capable of doing the right thing. I didn't know, so of course I took the time to hear what you had to say!

"But Steve you got to understand something here. After speaking with you, after feeling your passion and sensing your mission, your incredible determination, well, I just couldn't turn it over to her."

Then caught up in a moment of deep introspection, he confessed loud enough for me to hear, "It didn't matter any way, it wasn't like I was breaking any company policy or stealing anything, what the heck, there was nothing to steal anyway!"

"Kev don't get me wrong, because I'm flattered, but why didn't you turn me over to her when she got back?"

"You wanna know why do ya! Well, because she would of flat out screwed this thing up beyond recognition. That's why! And do ya know what would have happened to you?" he asked angrily.

"Well…, you my friend, would of wound up in the trash can. So that's why I decided to handle you! Besides, if you think about it, I was only doing my job by covering for her," he said unapologetically.

"Hey Steve! Do you actually know what her job is?" he offered with honest disdain.

"No. What?"

"Well, to put it in a nutshell, it's her responsibility to chart the direction Fram will take on a yearly basis, you know, similar to how the Russians have their five-year plan to get stuff done? Well Fram does the same thing, except Dianne's in charge of charting the course so to speak, one year at a time. And let me tell you something, this gal is really lost for ideas.

"As a matter of fact, if you ask me, so is the whole damn outfit. I think last year's big accomplishment was an air freshener to hang off your mirror," he said, sneering. Then as if to add insult to injury, he added, "How'd ya fancy that for innovation, from the leader in oil filtration? You know Steve, it's actually one of this woman's main functions to come up with marketing plans for us to follow! But all we seem to do, is go over the same old ground, forever trying to find new ways to make chicken salad out of chicken manure.

"So, when you hit me with your idea, what was I supposed to do with it? Sit on it! Sorry man, I'm not the type, because as we both know, these things just don't happen all by themselves! Now am I right? You know darn well that I am! Like I already told you Steve, your timing couldn't of been better, because trust me, there's are a ton of huge retailers out there just salivating for this thing. I know, because I was the one who had been talking with them, not her! They had just been waiting for something like this to come down the pike. And you wanna know something, I just wasn't about to let her blow it, 'cause she sure as heck would have!

"Anyway, I want to make something perfectly clear to you. If you guys had spoken and she gave you a thumbs down, do realize what would of happened to you and your little idea, Mister?"

In shock, and nearly lock jawed, I came back, "No… what?"

"First of all, I probably wouldn't have ever known about it. And secondly if I had, well let's just say that it wouldn't have been looked upon too favorably for me to go traipsing through her garbage can going over her discarded ideas."

Finally, it all began to register! "So, let me ask you something Kev, did this ever cause a commotion between the two of you?"

I tried to visualize him leaning back in his chair, with that big smile of his, as he let out a sinister laugh. "Na, I was too smart for that Stevie. Besides, she was so darn busy doing her own thing, that by the time she ever caught wind of it, I was already way too far down the road.

"Anyway, what could she of done? And like I already told you, it was no big deal anyway. I'm sure knowing her the way I do, that she was probably just as glad. It was just one less thing to worry her overworked mind."

"So, Kevin, then why'd you bring all of this up? I still don't get it?"

"Well, because as I told you, I've already done all the work, and any dummy can see that this thing is going to be a huge success. Now I'm going to tell you something Steve, and I hope that I'm wrong, but I'm sure I'm not, because I know her. What she's doing is just making sure that she gets her signature on it somewhere…, anywhere. Do ya get it?"

My heart bottomed out in the pit of my stomach, "I'm afraid I do!" Then in a loud voice, I cried out, "My God, the contract!"

"You got it baby! She's gonna bring home this slab of bloody bacon for somebody, and for whom I'm not certain. But this woman won't be denied! I'm telling ya! And I don't know how I can help you out at this point either. It's not like I work for the Company any longer. Besides, you've virtually gotten everybody under the sun already involved at this point. Who you gonna go to next? Corey?

"And Steve, by the way, don't be too quick to take me up on that one either, because he's her direct boss and who do you think he's gonna side with, some outsider like yourself? It's highly doubtful. She's too much of a fixture around there.

"Stevie, I'm really sorry. I feel terrible about all this mess! What you're lookin' at here partner, is a runaway train!"

For spite, the garbled transmission from the rest area kept playing itself over and over in my head. Nearly a week had passed since our last communiqué, and I was beginning to wonder if she had once again had dropped off the radar screen. In as much as I may of not wanted to, I was compelled to reach out for her. That's if I had any hopes of putting an end to this madness, which by my count was now entering its fiftieth day.

The phone was ringing on the other end, as I held my breath, wondering if she'd be in. More importantly, I wondered what kind of mood would be in control of her this time. An involuntary shiver ran through my body as she picked up.

'So much for Jackie picking up,' I thought, regretting that I'd have to do without her pleasantries before this session would begin.

"Hello," came an extremely harried Dianne Newman.

If at all possible, I wanted to know straight away which one of her several personalities we might be dealing with this day. So, I replied all cheery like, "Hi Dianne, it's Steve Moor. How are you today?"

"Oh I'm fine Steve, how are you?" came back her stiff reply.

'Not enough to go on,' I reasoned.

Fumbling for the right words, I just decided that it would be best that I approach this well rested maven as directly as possible, "I guess I'm okay. Say, I just figured today would be a good day to give you a call. I let a few extra days go by, hoping that would give you a chance to catch up after your vacation.

"By the way, how was your vacation?"

"It was all right, but it's sure good to be back at work."

'Oh boy. After a reply like that, I wasn't sure how to approach her at all. 'Should I go for it like a man, or should I try and pacify her?'

'No darn it!' I reasoned, 'that tack up till now had gotten me some pretty poor results, any fool could have seen that much. Na, I wanted to end this madness today! Standing there by the phone with folded my arms, I chose to not to let her diehard response weaken my resolve. There was still a good month of summer left, and I had decided that I wasn't about to spend the rest of that time living out some tortured existence that this lunatic had conjured up; just because she was hunting brownie points for someone higher up the food chain.

"You know Dianne, I'd like to try and wrap this thing up now. We've gone 'round enough. Anyway, there ain't no reason on God's green earth why we can't do so now…, today! The way I see it, we just have a few straight forward matters left to concern ourselves with, and what we need to do shouldn't take very long."

There was momentary silence on the other end. I knew that she would need some time to digest that one. As usual, she came back with another evasive response, put out there to test my mettle. "And may I ask what do you see as being so straight forward Steve? And besides, what could possibly be so simplistic, to think that we could wrap up during this telephone call?" It was obvious that she wasn't about to let me go. No, I could see that she was intent on carrying on this twisted association of ours throughout eternity and at the very least the rest of the summer.

She was dug in hard, that was obvious, but I wanted this over and today! My wife and two babies were out back, frolicking in the pool while daddy was betrothed to this diabolical process which had more or less become my master these days. I hated being separated from them, and I hated what Allied was doing to me!

'And all for what, so that we could go into business after this was all over and pretend that we had gotten along like the family?' To say the least, I was doubtful.

'Nope. Not this time Dianne,' I thought. "We're moving on with this today!" I told her, as I launched into the 'Canadian issue.' "That should be simple enough," I started out. "Besides, it sounded like you were about to approve it anyway. You know, when you called me from the rest area last week. I don't seem to understand what the big deal is all about on your end Dianne? I really don't."

"Well, I wouldn't expect that you would be able to anyway Steve," she quipped, quick to show her ire.

Not wanting to start, I chose to ignore the jab and move on. "Then there is the issue of the 'Best Efforts', and the 'law suit liability' clause to work out. Let's just say we deal with these three issues and be done with it today, all right Dianne?"

So, in a futile attempt to read her mind, I offered, "Yeah, yeah. I know there's still some legal language yet to be haggled over, but the attorneys can do that once we've agreed.

"So what ya say Dianne? Why not end this today? Huh?" I asked, wanting to scream at the top of my lungs. 'Enough!'

There was dead silence for a moment. 'That was a good thing, right?' I hoped. 'It had to of been! She would have been down my throat already, riffling through my contact if it wasn't. It must have finally of sunk in! She was finally gonna deal! Thank you, Lord for answering my prayers!'

Breaking the silence, "Steve, what you are asking for is not possible at this time. Allied has decided to go on without you. We feel that we no longer have any further contractual obligations towards you!"

Before I could muster a scream of protest, she was off and running. So quick, so very quick to justify the newly proclaimed edict!

Having been given no other choice, I listened on in horror. I just shut my mouth, listening to the rest of what she had to say. "…The engineering department has informed us that they are now capable of manufacturing this filter outside the scope of your patent, and that of course means that we are not obligated to pay you anything for it."

'Oh God… Oh my God?!!' That's all that kept running through my mind. I was numb, I was so numb that I couldn't even feel myself. Oh, how my heart was cut. Those bungling engineers! The very same bunch that I had been so deliberate in covering up for all this time. And look at 'em now, ten months later, they seemed all so eager to cover their backsides after finally getting it together. 'And at who's expense?'

I felt the pangs of death coming upon me, but so great was my rage, it repelled that gray horseman. I marveled at the collective memory loss, watching as this huge nameless, faceless corporation made its move. Truly a study in 'situational ethics,' at its very slickest.

I took it all in, as the very engineers I refused to drop a dime on, aided and abetted the theft of my trade secrets! Their betrayal had spared no expense.

By now my shell of a frame was hunched over as I struggled to keep the phone to my ear. Despite the pain, I dare not miss a whisper, as the onslaught of disaster kept coming over the line. "…and Steve, this is something you might like to know. Gus has brought it to my attention that you have plagiarized somebody else's patent!" This time she was barely able to disguise the victory in her voice.

All I could think of was, that Kevin had been right. She had done what she had set out to do! Her signature was now emblazoned all over my life's work and she had the bloody slab of bacon under her arm. I just didn't know whose feet she was going to lay it at!

"I can't take what you're saying to me, Dianne. Put me through to Peter Ross. I can't bear talking with you for another moment.

Amazingly, she whimpered, like I hurt her feelings or something.

"Okay Steve, if that's how you feel about it." "I'll try and reach him for you, but you better hold on, it might take a few moments to get a hold of him."

'Yeah right,' I thought, 'you mean that you guys need a few minutes to get your stories straight.' As I sat on the phone waiting, I could hear my little crew out back laughing and screaming enjoying every minute, now that their mommy was home. Amidst their joyous cries, my soul wretched in anguish, as I ran over in my head all of what Dianne had just so callously said. 'Dear God, if she had only kept to her word from the beginning, this would have never of been happening.'

I was terrified, fearing that all was lost and that it was too late. The killer whale had finally tired of playing with the seal pup, it was now time to eat it.

"Hello, Peter Ross." My mind stopped reeling long enough for me to get off, "Peter, it's Steve Moor. I just got off the phone with Dianne."

His calm reply came back, "I know you did Steve. She told me all about it, and she told me what you said."

"Hey Peter, what are you supposed to mean by that." I shot back, unable to corral my anger.

"Well Steve, she was just a little bit upset that you told her you didn't want to talk with her any longer. That's all."

"Give me a break Pete, you know good and well what she's capable of! And why you're choosing to defend her, I'll never know? But if you can remember, I've been asking not to talk with her for the last six months now!

"So, what do you think about what you and I had just talked about all last week? That I couldn't take her any longer, right? So now if she's upset that I don't want to talk with her any further, than that's just too damn bad. I just regret that I didn't stick to my guns a long time ago.

"And what about me Pete? Why don't you forget about her bruised little feelings for a moment and think about what you guys have just done to me!

"For God's sake man, I brought you guys this entire project and now you're telling me that you don't owe me anything after seventeen months. No way! I'm not about to accept that. I can't, and I won't. I'm not threatening you…"

At that point, he rather abruptly barged in. Apparently, my reaction to the grand larceny had gotten his Irish was up. "Steve, it would be best for all parties involved if you didn't threaten anyone here. Okay?"

"But you didn't let me finish Pete! I'm not threatening anyone. I'm just gonna point into left field just like the Babe did, and make you guys a promise, that's all."

"And what that might be Steve? Your promise? And what's that supposed to mean anyway?"

"Just that I'll be coming at ya full bore!"

"What do you mean by that Steve? I don't get it."

"That's all I can say for now, but I promise you one thing, I'm coming." As I told him for a second time. Quite frankly, he didn't get it, and subsequently no one else there would either.

"Listen Pete, you guys are attempting to steal this thing from me, and everyone around here knows it, and I'm not about to lie down and let you do it.

"Now before you answer, I want you to do something. Put yourself in my position. Go on…, go ahead. Think about what I must be going through at this moment. After all this time has gone by and after giving you guys the entire business plan, including the inner workings of both of my patents and my trade secrets!" Remember Mister, I'm the one who brought you guys to the dance! And without me… there wouldn't even be a dance."

There was an incredibly long silence as I waited him out. His response would give me a good idea what kind of human being I was about to deal with. 'Cause up till now, I more or less knew him as a passing ship in the night. Looking back, Peter Ross was the only person standing between me and a courtroom. Realistically speaking, the higher up this traveled in the organization, the further removed they would of been from my situation; and the more likely they would have been predisposed to squash me like a bug.

And besides, it was rather obvious that Dianne was at least getting some, if not all of her marching orders from Hampilos, and like I had mentioned earlier, he was already very far up the food chain at Allied. I can tell ya for a fact, Hampilos didn't have a clue how pivotal my contributions were. And by corporate standards he probably didn't give a damn either. But here's where O'l Gus missed it. Protocol or not, for him to accuse me of plagiarism only served to prove that this guy was now stumbling along in the dark, along with the others. With a statement like that, I was convinced now more than ever, he didn't have the foggiest idea as to all of my contributions to date. And frankly at this point, he couldn't of cared less. Due to his warped sense of corporate greed, he was just doing his job, by going on the attack and trying to steal my intellectual property!

'So, who was gonna come to my aid, and fill in all the blanks for him now? The engineers, Dianne, the tattered marketing team, the graphic arts department, the secretaries? Who?'

For what it's worth, I didn't have some hero waiting in the wings to pluck me from this disaster. All the marbles were riding on the fact that maybe, just maybe, Peter Ross knew enough how to do the right thing. And I wasn't the least bit sure, because as far as I could tell, he was rather spineless.

That session left me dazed and confused, so after I dropped off the phone with Peter, I just sat there with my head in my hands groping for options, lost, so very, very lost.

It didn't take a genius to figure out that I wasn't gonna get anywhere if I just sat there all wrapped up in myself.

'What should I have done? Should I run outside into the brilliant sunlight and unload on my unsuspecting wife?

'Should I of told her that the dreams we had woven into the fabric of our union during the course of the last ten years had just been irretrievably lost? Or should I of immediately hopped on the phone to Bill and inform him that the big disaster we had been tiptoeing around just struck?'

My options at this point were infinite. Yet to my way of thinking, anything that I might a done at that point would of absolutely been futile in light of what I was facing. All except one... I fought to bring the raging storm that was swirling around inside of me under submission and it required everything I owned to do so.

"Lord Jesus…" I started out. "I really need your help here. I guess just like Job, what I had feared the most, has now come upon me!!!

"Dearest Jesus, is this how the odyssey was meant to end? Because, I will not accept it!

"I heard what they all said. They both accused me of being a plagiarizer, and therefore in their eyes, I must now be some kind of a liar and a cheat. But you Lord, you alone can read my heart. You alone know if I intended to defraud them from the very beginning or not. You know the truth, and so do I Lord! So, Lord, if you want me to pack up my gear and call it quits, you just say the word, and I'll do it in a heartbeat. But you will have to tell me and must be able to hear it!

"This filter thing was your idea from the beginning. You gave it to me that day on the beach and since then I've done the very best I could with it under the circumstances. There was no way I could have read their hearts, unless you had revealed it to me. And if you did, I surely must have missed it along the line somewhere. And please! Please don't think that I'm dropping out here, 'because I don't want to, because there's still plenty of fight left in me. Oh, and please don't think that I'm conveniently trying to give it back to you, because it looks like a failure, because I'm not!

"So, I'm gonna just sit here for a while, and try to hear from you."

Before I knew what was going on, I was running down the hallway to my bedroom. Pushing the door aside, I jumped up onto the middle of my bed, and began flipping through my Bible.

'Where did I read that before? I know that's what He's telling me. I just know it! But I've got to find it first!'

It took me a good little bit, but I finally found what I had come looking for. There it was in plain sight, as if it was written just to me! My heart soared higher and higher as I read my Heavenly Father's personal guarantee!

"And I will rebuke the Devourer for your sake. So that he shall not destroy the fruit of your ground. Nor shall your vine cast its fruit before its time in the field, says the Lord of Hosts." Malachi 3:11."

So, there it was in black and white. The cornerstone of a promise. A promise that He had given me long ago, and during another time of trouble. A promise, "That He wouldn't allow me to get this far only to meet up with failure."

I ran outside and pulled up a lawn chair next to Patti. "Hi honey! How'd it go with Dianne? Did you get a chance to speak with her yet? she asked smiling.

After what I had just been through, I should of been leaking out of every pore, but thankfully I wasn't. That in itself was a miracle! And let me tell you, if there was something to detect, rest assured, Patti was capable of detecting it.

'You know, I thought to myself, 'this God of mine truly does work in every way. 'Because without His providence over my life, I would have surely crumbled under the strain of this madness, certainly after this one!'

"Pat… I have something to tell you. On the surface it doesn't sound too good at all, but it's gonna work out. I promise you Honey."

"What is it Steve?" she said, her beautiful smile now replaced by a vacant stare. I don't know, it had to of been my tone, because I could see the panic wanting to set in all over her face.

"Now listen to me carefully. I've already talked it over with the Lord, and I'm telling you, it'll be okay. But what we need to do now is to stand firm in our faith as a couple, and not waiver. Okay?" I said, doing my best not to sound like the world was coming to an end.

"Okay Honey, I'm with you. So, what did she tell you? Something ridiculous I'll bet," she said, with a sarcastic twinge wanting to make light of it. "I'll bet it was something stupid, like you don't have a patent?"

Throughout these long ten years she had stuck closer to me than a friend, and when it came to this odyssey, we could nearly communicate telepathically.

"Well Pat…, I hate to tell you this Honey, but in so many words that's about what she has just got done telling me."

Slapping her hand down on the tops of her thighs, her eyes began to instantly well up with tears the size of quarters. "I'm so sorry for you Honey. I'm so sorry…" as she began to give into the pain and gently sob.

Grabbing her hand, I gave it a squeeze, as I held onto it tightly, gazing into her big brown eyes. "I told you Pat, it ain't over, till it's over. That's how you must play the game Baby," I decreed, doing my best to rescue her.

"I know Steve. But it's just that this thing has been going on forever and I'm a little tired is all. I'm sorry Sweetie, please forgive me, I'm all right. But how are you holding up? I don't know how you can just keep on going?" she said, wiping her tears with the back of her hand. As she did, the late afternoon sun seemed to radiate off her wedding bands bringing to mind one of the many reasons why I loved her so much. For her strength, for her love, for her loyalty.

We talked a while longer as the kids splashed in the baby pool, oblivious to the life and death struggle that was playing out in front of their mommy and daddy. After we finished praying together, I shot up from my chair and without warning, headed for the door.

"Hey, where you going?" she called out.

"To call Bill, where else?" I replied, smiling at her.

Bill Herbert didn't have an aversion about working past five o'clock, I can tell you that much. Most days he didn't leave the office until well after seven. And if there was ever a time I needed to speak with him, that afternoon would have qualified. It was getting to be quittin' time around most law offices, but I had long since been entrusted with Bill's private number. As the phone rang on the other end, he picked up on the second ring… "Hello."

"Bill… It's Steve!"

"Oh, hi Steve. What can I do for you?"

"Bill, I really need to talk with you! Do you have time? Because I really need to speak with you. It's an emergency." 'This running back and forth to him was becoming ridiculous,' I thought. It made me feel more like some unstable nut job who couldn't make a decision in life, without calling his shrink every five minutes for advice.

"Sure Steve, what's on your mind? I was just finishing up on some paperwork. That was all. So, tell me, what's our friend Dianne up to now?" he said, employing about as much humor as his ivy league persona would allow.

"Bill, I don't know where to start? I don't know how I'm supposed to tell you this? But I just got off the phone with Peter Ross and he told me that my patent was no good and that Allied was going on without me!" On the other end, I could almost hear an audible thud, as the news slammed into him broadside.

"Steve, if you don't mind. Could you please repeat yourself again, one more time? I want to be perfectly clear about what you have just said." There was no doubt in my mind, even this cool cucumber was caught off guard and now trapped between the ropes.

"You heard me right the first time Bill. They said that my patent was no good, and that they didn't feel any contractual obligation towards me, and that they were going to proceed with everything I had given them. Oh…, and with one exception of course, they made it quite clear that they were gonna go on without me!"

"Hmm… That's what I thought you said. But I just had to make sure."

Not able to wait, I jumped in despite the fact that he was going to be needing more than a moment to think this one over! "So, what can we do? "They can't do this and get away with it, can they Bill?

I've been dealing with them for almost two years now! And they've had plenty of time to go over my patent! Why didn't they tell me right up front that my patent was no good, if that was the case?

"Why did they wait until now, to ever pull a stunt like that? Can they legally do this to somebody like me?"

"Well yes and no, Steve. Yes, they can do this. Unfortunately, that's the way many of these big companies operate. It's often times the way they do business."

"Get outa' here! What your telling me is insane! I have a patent here! What about the U.S. Patent Office? What good is having a lousy patent anyway then?"

"I'm afraid that the way the system is set up Steve, at the moment that really doesn't mean too much…, your patent I mean. You know…, this sort of stuff goes on a lot more than you might want to realize."

I was horrified at his cool response. 'Where did this come from?' I wondered. It was certainly the first time I was ever hearing something like this before! Suddenly I got this bizarre feeling that I was in a game that I wasn't qualified to be playing. But that was a ridiculous thought darn it! This is America, the land that nurtures things like entrepreneurialism and capitalism!

Yeah… sure, I knew that I was playing Russian Roulette as far as getting them ticked off at me, I was already well aware of that. And I was also firmly aware of the fact that if had tried their patience sufficiently, I'd be met with an ultimatum, except the ultimatum that I was expecting, was something more like that of the 'take it or leave it' variety. At least that's what I had been expecting. Never in my wildest nightmares did I expect them to tell me at the twelfth hour that my patent was no good! And I gotta be honest with you, just like some of the other areas I trusted them on, this move was so far out in left field, I had never even seen it coming!

And yet I make no apologies for pushing like I had. I really didn't care how big they might have been; I was still fighting for what had already been promised me!

Apparently, no one had bothered to warn me, not even Bill, that they could skip that little formality, and go directly to extortion. Somehow, the powers to be over at Allied saw fit to inform me that after eighteen months of knowing each other's business, my patent was no longer worth the paper the Patent Office had bothered to print it on! Yet unbelievably, by the same token, someone had forgotten to remind those bastards about their obligations to me under both the proprietary information agreement and the test marketing agreement where I had shared my deepest trade secrets.

But for the moment, none of that mattered at all. I mean my rights, the intellectual property laws, the whole ball of wax. None of it meant squat! Everything was annulled and disavowed, all because it had suddenly become convenient for them to discard me like an unwanted mistress. So that's how it really was, I was clearly in heat attack country!

"So, what do you mean Bill?"

"Let me explain something to you Steven. A patent for all intended purposes is like a stop sign. It's bright and it's red; alerting everyone who sees it, that they must stop.

"But does everybody stop when they see a stop sign, Steve? No of course not. So, in many ways, a patent is just like a stop sign. Its job is to tell all would be infringers to stop or consider the consequences.

"But do all would-be infringers stop? Well, of course not! And that is what patent court, Federal lawsuits and the legal system is all about."

As numb as I was, I had no problem grasping the simple object lesson. "So, you mean to tell me that a person really doesn't know how strong his patent is until it's challenged, and they wind up in court?"

"In so many words, you're about right."

"Wait a minute Bill," I said groping at straws. "After I received this patent, I brought it to another attorney not even familiar with my file so that he could independently evaluate the strength of my patent. And I did that purposely, before I even started marketing it, so I knew how much stock to put in it."

"Fine Steve. That's all well and good, and you should be commended for having the foresight to have done so. So tell me, what did he have to say after he reviewed your patent? I'm assuming that he was a registered patent attorney of course."

"Of course, he was" I shot back. "And from what I was told, a pretty good one at that. Anyway, after his review, he said that my patent was strong. So after that assessment, I went about my merry way trying to find an interested partner.

"Do you want me to fax you his opinion Bill, because I'd be happy to?" hoping that might give me some leverage.

"I'm afraid that wouldn't help us much at this point Steve. At the very least, I would need to see your patent application, including your entire prosecution file to make a proper determination for myself, as to how strong your patent might be. I would have to study your entire wrapper file, in order to come to any worthy conclusion."

"Okay then. I'll root through my files and pack what you need and send it up to you. I'll send it Fed Ex to you in the morning," trying to offer him every angle to avert this disaster.

"Not so quick Steve!"

"Why not Bill?" I asked, truly put off.

"Because for one thing, it would unfortunately be very costly for me to review that much documentation and I'd only wind up with part of the picture."

"How so?"

"Well, I would also have to study your entire document file that you've generated from Allied, and of course that would only run into much more money for you."

"Look Bill, my finances at this point are really tight, but I'd be willing." My bank account at best had seven grand left. I'd already paid him five grand and could tell that his monthly statements were gonna start rolling in like clockwork. Who knew where his tab was going to end up before this thing was over. At this rate, the sky seemed to be the limit.

Interjecting before I could take it any further, "Steve we're talking ten to fifteen thousand dollars here. And I still can't guarantee that it would be enough to stop them. Frankly Steve, under the present circumstances, I really don't see how I would even have the time to go through your paperwork. Because if you ask me, it already looks like that they've already made up their mind as to what they're about to do."

Driven by the hard-cold facts, I mentioned the S-- word for the very first time in my life. "So I'll sue them," I shouted into the phone unrestrained, hoping that would stop their barbaric onslaught.

"Wait a minute Steve, just try and relax. You may have an option or two available before you start considering that one. You just don't rush into these types of law suits headlong, they're very complicated, very time consuming, and extremely costly."

"I'm sure they are," as I ignored his warning. So would you represent me?" I asked, not wanting to let a moment get by, before I began to plead my case in front of him.

"In as much as already told you so, I wouldn't even begin to take on this kind of a risk without all the facts in front of me. And that would include a thorough review of every piece of paper you have. Then it would have to be put in front of the firm for a vote as well. Steve I'm not trying to upset you any more than you are, but what you're looking at is an incredible task, to take on somebody like AlliedSignal."

"So anyway, humor me Bill, 'cause I just got to know, what would it take to sue those bastards?"

"Oh, about two million dollars and about five years of your life. Then there is always the very real possibility of an appeal which would amount to going through the same thing all over again."

"So, I guess you guys don't take many of these cases on a contingency basis, do you?" I said, realizing that the possibility of a law suit was beginning to sound more like a pipe dream than anything else.

"No, we don't," came his somber reply.

"Then what about all these law suits I see flying around all over the place, about nothin'. How come all of a sudden when I decide to sue, the odds seem to be so insurmountable? Why is that Bill, can you please tell me?"

"Now let me explain something to you Steve. This isn't like a liability suit, where someone is going up against an insurance company or like some fool lawyer is trying to drum up business. Patent law is extremely complex and you're looking to take on a giant on top of it."

"So, what about a contingency?"

"That's an incredible long shot Steve. We take on so very few of those types of cases. And of course, they have to be better than air tight for us to suffer that much exposure. You'll find that most firms, especially patent litigation firms don't do contingency work unless they are in possession of a smoking gun."

"I guess what you're telling me Bill, is that I don't have one of those either."

"Sorry Steve, I just don't see one. Unless you're willing to pay me a lot of money to find that out. But I don't think you can afford to do that. And I'm afraid by now, they already know that as well.

"But why don't you think about it. I'm sure at this point they're calling your bluff while at the same time showing you their intention. Maybe with a little luck, we might be able to salvage something of an agreement here. I really don't know. Unfortunately, it looks like a pretty good long shot at the moment.

"Look…, let me spell it out for you…, here are your options. You can sign, that's of course if they will still let you. Or you don't have to sign, in which case you might consider going to court in light of what I just told you. But whatever you decide Steve, you must move rather quickly, because if this matter goes any higher within the company, like to the level of the chief general counsel of Allied… Well, then there's darn good chance all bets are off. Trust me, if it makes it to that level, and nobody is promising that it hasn't gone that high already, they'll more than likely opt to run you over. Okay?

"So, I want you to talk this over with Patti, then give me a call as soon as you can, because we have to move very quickly."

"I got ya Bill."

"I'm not finished yet," he said.

"All right, go on."

"Nobody here is telling you that you have to sign anything either. I want to be perfectly clear about that. Do you understand me?"

"Yes sir. I understand you loud and clear."

"Just keep in mind you can let them do what they are going to do. Which of course as you said, is to go on without you. And if they do, well at that time you can decide if in fact you want to pursue it further."

That afternoon right in front of my eyes, my friend and my confident turned stone cold. No different than an oncologist pulling someone into the office, to break the news. And let me tell you something, I felt like a patient more than anything else.

So as you could see, I was asking, but he sure wasn't offering. And you know something, I really couldn't blame him, he was right. As much as it hurt him to tell me, at least he was being honest about it. All this poor guy was going off of was a very muddy contract, because at the moment he was file-less.

It was going to be up to me to try and find a way to negotiate my way out of these monstrous jaws!

The following day was July 20th, and I was still reeling from my very own version of Pearl Harbor. Somehow, I got Peter Ross on the phone, and as usual, I had a strategy in place. I was going to compromise now, I had to. I was hoping to be spared just enough, to straighten out the details later…, that's if there was going to be a later, and so far, only God knew the answer to that one. At this point I was banking on the prospect that Peter had some sort of a conscience, and that he was going to be a man enough to stand in the gap for me, a virtual stranger…, and do the right thing. I also hoped that he was perceptive enough to realize that he was also dealing with a warrior of sorts, the kind not easily dispatched with. So I let it all hang out…

"Peter, like I told you yesterday, you just can't take this away from me and not expect a fight. It'll cost me everything, but I'm prepared to go down in flames, and in the process, I'm gonna drop out of the sky and make a gaping hole in your deck someday!"

"All right Steve. Don't you think I already know that? And believe me that's the last thing either I or Allied wants happening right about now! We don't want this thing to get out of hand. So why don't you hear me out, because this is what we are prepared to do…"

Then he started off, "Since we both understand that we are now proceeding to make this filter outside the scope of your patent we can't possibly be expected to pay you for the full duration of it." I just listened as my heart went limp and it certainly wasn't the time to start pointing a disparaging finger at the engineers either. The water was well over that dam, having had let that opportunity in the name of peace go by the wayside long ago. I'm telling ya, it was an issue that I'd have to keep my big mouth shut about if I had any hopes of pulling this thing off.

So, my response was to the point, "I understand."

"Okay good. Now that we have that settled," he said, leading me toward a brutal armistice.

I couldn't restrain myself from jumping in, "So what about everything else I gave you, like the marketing plan? And Pete, let's not kid each other, you guys are still going to make a Teflon treated oil filter anyway, aren't ya?"

"Why yes, of course we are still going to make a Teflon treated oil filter?" he replied, puzzled.

"Well I just wanted to make it clear before you go any further that I have the only Teflon treated oil filter patent granted in the world. And one other thing…, I'm sure that you are not aware of it, but the fact still remains that my claims, which happens to be the benchmark of this patent clearly mentions the fact that this patent is what it claims to be. A Teflon treated oil filter! Teflon is still the main novel idea, not some peanut butter filling. And while we're on the subject, do me a favor, would you? Who was this other inventor, that Hampilos says I plagiarized?"

On the other end there was nothing but silence, then the stirrings of life. "Uh…, ugh, McCreedy, I think he said. McCreedy. Does that sound right to you?"

"Yes, it does Pete! And not for nothing, Mr. McCreedy is sighted by the Patent Office as prior art to my patent."

"Well, I wouldn't know what that's supposed to mean Steve."

"Of course, you wouldn't. Why would you unless you were familiar with the process? So, let me spell it out for you. That means his patent has been referenced with regard to my new application. Don't you get it? He's cited like a footnote in a bibliography! And who did the citing here? The United States Patent Office! So, let me ask you something Pete, if I may? How could I of plagiarized his work?!"

"I…., I don't know? Now that you put it that way. But anyway Steve, that's between you and Mr. Hampilos now. And before you go any further, let me give you a bit of advice. If I were you, I'd keep my mouth shut for the time being. Okay?"

"I hear you Pete. It's just that I think you're a pretty smart guy and I just thought you ought to know what has really going on here. That's all…, 'cause however you want to slice it, Allied would be dead in the water without my trade secrets! And in case you need reminding, I've already signed two separate trade secret agreements!"

Then out of the blue Peter threw it on the table, "Two years." Never in my deepest paranoia would I of dreamt of giving my baby away for a two-year contract!"

"Hey Pete! I'll face you guys in court before I let that happen. Okay? So, if you don't mind, I think I'll take my chances with a judge and jury as to whether we're talking about a Teflon treated oil filter here or not. Or if I can be found guilty of plagiarizing someone else's patent trumped up by a Fortune Fifty's chief patent attorney, which happens to be asinine enough, to be citing my own prior art against me! Oh, and here's something that really bugs me!"

"And what's that Steve?"

"This little act that you guys are pulling on me at the twelfth hour. It ain't Kosher Peter! It just ain't Kosher!"

I don't know what came over me, but before I knew it, I began cutting my own deal…

"Look, the bottom line is that I want at least ten years. Okay? I'm not happy about it, but I'll settle for ten."

"Gee Steve that's an awful long time. Don't you think? How about three?"

"Pete my position is the same as before. I'll see you guys in court."

It didn't take a rocket scientist to figure out that we were worlds apart, just like Dianne and I had been over the upfront money. 'These rotten people always seemed to want something for nothing,' I thought. Just feeling him out, "Maybe seven."

"Hmm… Still too much Steve. But you're getting closer."

"Hey Pete if you don't mind…, I already know that you have your marching orders, so why don't you just cut to the chase and tell me. Okay? My patent is good for seventeen years as far as I know, so why don't you tell me how long of a contract Allied is willing to offer me."

"Five years Steve."

"Wow…, that's a hellava discount don't ya say Pete? All because Dianne's a pathological liar and backed me so far into a corner that I got some muckety-muck upstairs ticked off."

"How about seven?" I asked again, just to make sure.

"Steve! Now you've already asked me, and I told you! It's five years, take it or leave it."

"Gee that sounds pretty final, Pete."

"Believe me it is! I put my butt on the line to get even that much for you. Believe me when I tell you."

I had to think it out for a moment. True it was an all-out disaster, but at least it was something I could work with. I mean I could always go back to the Company later on and point out the errors of their ways and fix this thing, right? 'I mean after the ink was dry, I could go to Bossidy and tell him what I had suffered at the hands of his employee's.

'Couldn't I? I mean, he'd want to know, wouldn't he?' After all he was promoting himself all over the globe to be such a stand-up guy.

I was sure I could make it work! So, I chose to take Peter up on his measly offer. Immediately the self-kept proviso in me began to burn. Larry here I come!

Don't ask me how, but I somehow felt relieved. The cancer that the doctor had warned me about, the one that was supposed to kill me, suddenly went into remission. "Okay Pete. It's acceptable. I'll take the five years that the Company is offering."

"Not so fast Steve. It's still not that quite simple. We still have one more major hurdle to cross before it can be over for you."

Exhausted… "And so, what's that Pete?" Enough never seemed to be enough for this outfit, as I fought on with the remaining power I had left.

"We are going to require a new threshold concerning the performance of this product. You and I, right now, must come to some agreeable terms as to performance," he added, showing me that he was still holding all of the cards.

As bruised and as beaten as I was, there was never any doubt as to the appeal this filter would have on the public. However, before we could go any further, I needed to let them get on with the theft they so badly wanted to perpetrate. And if I wasn't cooperative, this filter would never make it into the marketplace and have a life of its own.

Despite what they had tried to put me through, I never had any doubts that this filter would be anything less than well received by the consumer. So once again, I raised the bar that both the Double Guard and I would be required to clear.

"Okay Pete. Base it on your net receipts. Go ahead pick a number."

"Na…, we can't do that Steve."

"And why not?"

"It has to do with accounting. It would become much too messy to track its performance that way." He began thinking, I could hear him thinking out loud. There was no doubt, he was stumped, and I had to do something quickly. But what? I was no accountant!

Here's where my undying belief in my baby came through. "Forget all that Pete, scratch it. I'll make it simple for you, five hundred thousand units per year! If you guys don't sell a lousy five hundred thousand units per year, you can keep the damn thing. How's that sound? 'Cause if I don't make a paltry fifty grand a year off this filter, I may as well get a job shoveling out barns for a living. And correct me if I'm wrong, but I can already smell it. You guys are out to own this thing right out from under me! Lock stock and barrel!"

He ignored most of what I said and frankly who could of blamed him. He was just acting as the interim bag man for the industrial giant.

I was onto their game. Beyond a shadow of a doubt, I knew what was going down, but there wasn't a whole heck of a lot a guy in my position could do about it.

Later that afternoon a fax came streaming into my real estate office. By their clock it was fifteen hundred hours, by mine, it was three o'clock in the afternoon. It seemed that from the get go, we couldn't even agree upon how to go about telling time. That aside, we were all but in agreement now. I had surrendered my God given right to disagree with them any longer, and their extortion complete.

Emblazoned across the top, the cover sheet proudly declared, "*From Administration*." The sender of the communiqué, but of course, was none other than Dianne Newman. It was still very much her assignment to dispatch with me, not Peter's. And the message, well there really wasn't any further need to elaborate at this point. In her own hand, left circled in the middle of the page read, "*Personal and Confidential*," with a star next to it for emphasis, no less.

Page two was conspicuously absent of any of the legal jargon that had helped to create this mess. In its utter simplicity, page two read as follows:

AGREEMENT WITH STEPHEN MOOR
Initial Payment: *$50,000 (within 30 days of signing Agreement)* **Year One:**
*$ .10/Filter   U.S. and Canada   PC/LT *(passenger car and light truck)*
$ .20/Filter   U.S. and Canada   Heavy-duty **Minimum Guarantee: $50,000**
Year Two:
$ .10/Filter   U.S. and Canada   PC/LT
$ .20/Filter   U.S. and Canada   Heavy-duty **Minimum Guarantee: $50,000**
Year Three:
If Year Two Volume > (greater than) 500K Units:
$.10/Filter   U.S. and Canada   PC/LT
$ .20/Filter   U.S. and Canada   Heavy-duty
***No Minimum Guarantee**
If Year Two Volume < (less than) 500K Units: No Royalty Payments.
Year Four:
If Year Three Volume > (greater than) 500K Units:
$.10/Filter   U.S. and Canada   PC/LT
$.20/Filter   U.S. and Canada   Heavy-duty
***No Minimum Guarantee**
If Year Three Volume < (less than) 500K Units: No Royalty Payments.
Year Five:
If Year Four Volume > (greater than) 500 K Units:
$.10/Filter   U.S. and Canada   PC/LT
$.20/Filter   U.S. and Canada   Heavy-duty
***No Minimum Guarantee**
If Year Four Volume < (less than) 500K Units: No Royalty Payments.
In all cases, payments are complete following Year five

So there it was, the backbone from which the fourth revision of the contract would be drawn, Allied style. I guess there was a lot more to that old expression than I ever dreamt. "Three strikes and you're out!"

As you can see the original insurance policy which had guaranteed me two hundred and twenty-five thousand dollars, had now been conveniently reduced to one hundred thousand dollars. Sign on fee and all!

The 17-year life of the agreement which had never been in question. Well, as you can see, had been summarily reduced to five years. Something I would of never considered for the life of me.

The patent, the intellectual property and all, would automatically revert back to Allied's complete ownership after the second year, in the event that sales slipped below the 500,000-unit mark and most definitely become theirs, on September 1st, 2001. A vast difference between the last version, which stated that if the Company failed to perform on any number of grounds, the patent would revert back to its rightful owner. Me!

Now here's something to keep in mind. Remember the raging battle between "Reasonable Efforts" and "Best Efforts"? Well of course I lost that one too! "Reasonable Efforts" prevailed. 'And gee, based upon everything I had witnessed thus far, I was left to ponder what kind of performance lie ahead come marketing time under this new watered-down standard.

And remember when both Kevin and Dianne had both balked the day I had asked them about putting the Company's marketing plan into the contract?' Well, all I can say was that I was now on the receiving end of that little setup as well!

'So let me ask you all something. Would you ever agree to let a plumber into your home to fix a broken toilet based upon "Reasonable Efforts"?' I didn't think so.

Puzzling enough, I was still referred to as the inventor in the fourth version of the contract and this contract was still being referred to as a patent licensing agreement! Yet, the filter itself, as well as the packaging, would now be devoid of my patent number! It was beyond bizarre, because Hampilos' last version of the contract had clearly set forth the fact that every item was to be marked with the patents identification number. Now suddenly, that had disappeared in thin air!

'And remember the patent lawsuit thing?' You know, the section where Allied deemed it only fair that I be an equal participant in any future patent litigation. Well, that was still left in there; unaltered and in pristine condition!

Oh, would you like to view something that had gone full circle? I mean from the sublime, to the utterly ridiculous. Remember the Canadian issue in which I had fought so hard?' Well, after all this time, it suddenly appeared! I mean, it not only appeared, but it showed up in the very language in which I had been insisting upon all along! Small wonder, ha?

And the price?

It only brought the wrath of Khan down upon me, but at least I got what had initially been promised me. Now that was good for a laugh.

Needless to say, my days of talking with Dianne were not over. Peter insisted that we kiss and make up. So we did. We talked through the rest of July and if you can believe it, the whole month of August as well!

'Why?'

Because she insisted it be that way! That's still what it required to firm up the contract. It would wind up taking the next forty days for the language to get straightened out and along with it, another five grand in attorney's fees that I didn't have.

And before this little exercise would be concluded, Mr. Herbert's services would climb over the ten-grand mark! And you know, I really couldn't figure out this could of ever happened in the first place. It wasn't like I had ever said anything that would have made Dianne wanna hold a grudge?

'Oh, wait a minute!' Now that I think of it. At the point in which Peter and I were going over the final touches, concerning the five-year contract, he kinda said something that caught my attention.

"You know Steve, I realize that you blame Dianne for what's gone on here, but I feel it's only right that I defend her. I hope that you realize that the upper brass, feels that it is truly overstepping our responsibility as a Company to pay you a dime. I want you to know something, Dianne really went to bat for you and put herself on the line."

To which I said, "I can appreciate your point of view Pete. But unfortunately, I see it completely different."

"How so?"

"I see it like this. Dianne was like a little kid playing with matches next to my house. Then by her own doing, happened to light my house on fire. So, after she sees my house going up in flames, she runs next door to get a hose, hoping to put out the little fire she's started. But upon her return, she finds out that, the house is fully engulfed. She's too late, the house is toast. That's more or less how I see it Pete. Sorry!"

True to form, Gary the lead engineer was still running behind schedule. He really wouldn't be up to speed until that September. My instincts of not wanting to rock the engineering boat too much were right on the money, because if I had, the engineering department would have certainly suffered a miscarriage and we would of both wound up in the dumpster long ago.

Please don't dare underestimate what the mighty 'Signal had put me through during the month of August, because it was a waiting game like none I had ever played. It had become a game orchestrated out of the pit of hell. Just because we had agreed upon an abbreviated contract didn't mean a thing Baby! Because both parties have to sign a contract to make it binding.

Oh… and excuse me, that strictly depends on what bar you drink at, because there's seems to be a significant divergence of opinions on that little detail as well; depending upon which lawyer you might ask.

And another thing. You can just forget about all that legal stuff like intention, verbal agreement, promissory estoppel, promise of specific performance and the like.

At this time, I would like to leave you with the kicker…

"Steve there is one small item that has to be completed before my boss John Cory can sign off on the final contract." The time frame, being the early part of the third week in August.

"Okay Dianne, what's that?"

"Gary's going to ship some of these filters cross country in about a week or so, to California and back." she said, trying to act deeply concerned about the would-be outcome.

"Okay that sounds fine Dianne. So, what's the big deal?" I asked, like I really had control over anything they might do at this point.

"Well I just have to warn you Steve, it gets pretty darn hot in those trailers during the summertime, you know."

"I follow you so far Dianne, but what's that got to do with anything?" Oh, don't kid yourself, I already had a pretty good idea of what she was up to. I wasn't that naïve!

"If any of those filters leak Steve…, all bets are off!" True to form, she still got a rise out of a good twist of the knife.

"Okay Dianne, that's only fair. But the filters are supposed to packed tapping plate to the sky and they're supposed to be sealed with a cap on the end. Aren't they? So, I don't understand what the fuss is all about?"

"Well I wouldn't know all about that Steve. I just know that if that case of filters comes back here leaking, Mr. Cory will not be signing any contract with you." Click…

Believe me when I tell you, though things were supposedly on their way toward being settled, I wasn't banking on anything. Bill forever the metered coach, was still warning me that there wasn't any guarantee that they'd sign. "Steve, I know that you're a prayin' man. So, at this point, all I can tell you, is that you better not stop. If this situation reaches Peter Kreindler and I'm not saying that it already hasn't… But let me make one thing extremely clear to you, if Kriendler has a mind to, he can squash this deal in a heartbeat, since he's Bossidy's Chief General Counsel."

So, on it went. Another full forty days of torture!

———————————

Whew…. After reading those last few chapters, I'm sure anybody in their right mind, must surely have more questions than answers. Following that white-knuckler of a licensing negotiation, you just got to be wondering… How the heck did two smart guys like you and Bill ever allow this madness to escalate to such a psychotic level?

So instead of running from an explanation…, I'd like to share my ten-point reality checklist with you.

First… when I started negotiations with AlliedSignal/Fram I had less than ten grand to my name, and that's a very paltry sum to take on an uncharted enterprise such as this. So right off the bat, I couldn't afford to have a high-priced lawyer at my side.

Second… my relationship with Fram was contentious, there's no denying that. To complicate matters, I'm guilty of inventor-shaming a Fortune 38 Company, of innovating a business unit they never had any intentions of doing. At the time of my arrival, and unbeknownst to me, their business plan was to sell that laggard Division and get the heck outa the business altogether. But of course, they never shared that little tidbit with me before we started our courtship. So how could I of known?

Looking back, my relentless drives toward the goal line may have caused things to come around and boomerang on me more than it might have. But let's keep things in perspective, I was negotiating a licensing agreement, we didn't need to be lovers to make this thing work. Just the same, I was never supposed to be painted into a corner, and wind up selling my soul to the devil either. In the end, the Company was both cowardly and dishonest…, and you can't very well defend against dishonesty, no matter how hard you may try.

Third… as laid out, Dianne was a liar and a manipulator of the highest order. Everything she had ever said or agreed upon was at best was reneged upon or outright pulled back. It is impossible to conduct an 'arm's length' negotiation under those perilous conditions. And I don't care how great a negotiator you may think you are.

Fourth… I was negotiating from position of weakness…, not from strength. I was a sole inventor, left to bargain with a Fortune 38 Company behind closed doors. No witnesses… and they always had home field advantage. I'm guilty as charged, for being way too trusting and especially for not having a lawyer present at all times…, regardless of the financial cost!

Fifth… their versions of the contract screamed that they were setting me up like a pigeon. Their mission from the onset, was to go behind my back…, to not only control my IP, but to outright steal it. Bill and I didn't even have a chance to settle in, before we'd be locked into an all-out chess match where every one of my agreed upon contractual interests had been clawed back by Allied. We were in a race against time to reclaim as many broken promises as possible. The trick was…, we had to walk a very fine line, because pushing Allied too hard, would result in disaster. One wrong move, and they'd throw down the gauntlet, and walk off with all of my marbles.

Sixth… Bill was hired, because he was a patent prosecution attorney and very skilled in the art of understanding licensing agreements. His strength was in the field of filing and analyzing patents. His world of expertise was limited to the practice of Intellectual Property law, he was by no means a court room litigator. His expertise was understanding patents and how they work, then to be able to apply the appropriate laws. It was also his prevue, to examine the whole ball of wax that we were dealing with, through his extensive knowledge of contract law. On this scale, not only was he qualified, but in my estimation, he did a fine job. 'Was he aggressive?' Absolutely not! I didn't choose him on that basis. From the onset, I was smart enough to know that I was playing a flute to a cobra.

Seventh… if I had wanted an aggressive attorney, I would have hired a balls to the wall Intellectual Property litigator from the very beginning. And I'm sure that I may have gotten entirely different result…, and quite possibly, not for the better. Something to note…, should you ever find yourself in a life and death legal contest, it's not always expedient to change horses mid race…, besides, it's much easier said than done. My advice, is to pick the best horse you can find, then to ride it carefully.

Eighth… if I had hired a fearless killer of a litigator, in my estimation he would have tipped the power balance. There's no doubt, I would have put myself much deeper into lawsuit country, had I of gone with that choice. Allied made it more than clear that I'd have to live with their initial version of the contract, or "they'd go on without me," just like they had threatened. Here's the catch-22. Up until this point, they hadn't committed any crimes as of yet. Obviously…, they were strong-arming me…, but I couldn't sue them for that! At this point in time, we didn't have signed a contract for them to violate, and I didn't have any proof of them misappropriating my trade secrets either! You cannot file a real lawsuit based upon something as flimsy as your feelings. In 'big boy's world', you'd be facing a Rule 11 for doing so! That means, if you file a frivolous case in Federal Court, you are responsible for paying your opponent's legal fees!

Ninth… just for arguments sake, let's assume that I had a bonafide lawsuit during this timeframe. 'Would this fearless litigator defend me in court for a 50% to 75% contingency cut of the prize? Would he stick around for the next 10 to 15 years to see me through the Appeals Court process? Or… would he be like everyone else that I auditioned for, and require a two-million-dollar retainer…, just so he could he could get started? In the end, would this litigator be man-enough or qualified-enough to take on a Fortune 38?' Now I'm speaking strictly on experience here, since I can. I've interviewed dozens upon dozens of the top attorneys in America in this field and for this very task…, and you know what, despite their reputations…, I found most of them lacking.

Tenth… Allied's revised contracts, were telegraphing, even to a blind man what their intended plan was…, well before the seventh version of our licensing agreement was ever ratified. At the time, my only choice was to either sign it or to back out and wait for them to start selling my stuff without me. Then… once I caught them red-handed, I could file a law suit against a Fortune 38 Company, which would guarantee me a ten to fifteen-year legal battle. Every Federal Court case of this magnitude ends up in an appeal.

Other than that, the only other choice left…, would be to remain a silent spectator on the sidelines and watch them illegally run with my baby. To me that option was totally out of the question as well.

My choice at the time was to avoid all those many unpleasantries and play ball with them no matter how hard they made it for me to swallow. To this day, I accept total responsibility for deciding to play ball with them.

The long hot summer had run its course; it was finally over. It was now September 1st, and I had just put my signature to an armistice of sorts. And believe me, by the time it was all over, I was eternally grateful that there was still a vestige of a contract left for me to sign.

So incredibly, after ninety-two punishing days, the massive business partner that I longed to trust, and the Company I so yearned to share a glorious legacy with, had nearly destroyed me in the process.

'And over what,' you might ask?

Well, it took me a long while to piece it all together, but when the dust had finally settled, I awoke to what had been driving them from the onset.... The Greed of a Dime.

PROLOGUE

By this point in the journey, I had taken on the visage of a hapless fly, floating in the middle of some toilet bowl, overflowing with Allied's unfathomable incompetence and corruption. You see, once you get deep enough inside, you get a real sense that it's just a matter of time, before someone daring enough, is going to flex their muscle and flush. As the rushing water forms a swirling vortex, there can be little doubt that you're in for the ride…, the Nantucket sleighride that's about to carry you deep into the bowels…

The canary in the coal mine, had already let me know that the brutal three-month licensing negotiations was only a foreshadow of what still lie ahead.

Make no mistake, I could have gotten off of this merry-go-round at any point of my choosing…, there's absolutely no quibble about that. I could have jumped off at the very beginning, if I had so chosen. But here's the dilemma… By my calculation, nine out of ten inventors or visionaries with very valuable ideas will get attacked. As you've witnessed, it's not so much a matter of when…, but it's more about, by whom and by what means. You see, if I bailed on this journey at any point with Fram, all I needed to do, was to sit back and watch. Because, as sure as the sun rises, AlliedSignal/Honeywell would have been out there in the marketplace, selling my product as pretty as you please… in Walmart, and everywhere else without my consent. So hang tight, they're just about ready to prove it!

During the intense preparation for my lawsuit, I immersed myself in the study of case law. I came across many cases where many an inventor shared his trade secrets for a valuable product, and in every instance, the Company or the receiving party, broke the law by stealing, then capitalizing on the inventor's trade secrets. The result was always the same, within a year or so of disclosure, that identical item would end up being offered for sale under that Company's moniker…, minus the inventor of course.

It's sort of ironic, but my search never led me to a single case, where the inventor was the one who violated these agreements! 'Was it because, we inventors tend to be more virtuous?' Of course, not…, we're just smart enough to realize, that if we contemplated doing something that stupid, we'd be run over by a speeding freight train.

So…, if I wanted to stop them, I definitely had options… 'I could sue them now…, or I could sue them later.'

My choice however, was to never sue them at all… Besides, who sues a Fortune 38 Company all by themselves? As Kevin once said, perhaps, "only a madman." But then again, they were building a compelling case for me to do so. They taunted me. The more I pleaded with them for sanity, the deeper they shoved the cattle prod up my backside. Until one day…, while Pat, I and the kids were taking a leisurely stroll through Wally World, I came across something rather unsettling. It was that evening, when I first saw AlliedSignal's patent numbers on the Double Guard packaging. Not mine…? Shortly thereafter, they would launch the Fram TRT, a clone of my additive treated oil filter…, again, emblazoned with their patent numbers…, not mine. Another violation of both my patent, my licensing agreement and my trade secrets.

You see, Allied/Honeywell made a fatal miscalculation by filing those two patents and not enjoining me as the rightful co-inventor, as the law mandates. They built both of those patented products using all of my trade secrets. In their greedy haste to screw me, their brilliant law team led by Gus Hampilos overlooked a glaring detail. My test marketing agreement/trade secret agreement would live on for yet another precious few years after the signing of the licensing agreement! This kingpin of an agreement, was not extinguished by the Force Majeure clause contained in the licensing agreement as they had incorrectly assumed! This opened the Pandora's box from which I launched a nine-count complaint against them in Federal Court.

As you may recall… I came a calling on them with two patents, they were both bench mark citations, backed up by a truckload of trade secrets. I was a college educated over the road truck driver, a back-yard inventor…, a total industry outsider. I was a sole inventor who dreamt up my dreams alone…, and I carried my IP onto the raging battlefield of business, where I gave it my best shot to sell them both my manufacturing and marketing plans.

When I first called on Fram, not a single one of their dozens of filter engineers could lay claim to a single oil filter patent, and now they were in the midst of building a cottage industry, racking up record numbers of oil filter patents based upon my IP. Please note, the ink wasn't barely dry on our licensing agreement before they begin their march toward filing the most oil filter related patents in the history of their Company…, and I didn't have clue.

In case you might be wondering, during this timeframe, there was no internet to keep a watchful eye on anybody, so you could forget about that. In addition, unlike our present-day laws, the USPTO kept every patent application a total secret back then. So in effect, I couldn't possibly know what they were up to, unless I took an insane calculated risk, and filed a law suit to find out what they'd been up to.

Just so you know, the way our legal system works, under the Discovery process, I wouldn't be able to get that proof for some two…, possibly three years later.

So, suing them of course, would be totally out of the question, it would be nothing short of sheer madness. And I did everything possible to avert that.

Here's a teaching moment… In the event you ever obtain a valuable patent or develop a valuable quiver of IP…, and you go into business with a producer/manufacturer, they will not be able to give life to your widget unless you bear your very soul, and that means you must share your trade secrets with them. Trust me…, in nine out of ten cases they simply won't be innovative enough to pull off what you did so easily in your garage. The double-edged sword, is that you will not have only teach them the secrets behind your creations, but due to the process being undertaken, you will directly be responsible for teaching them how to reverse engineer around everything that you've shared with them. It's an oxymoron of sorts…, nonetheless it's true.

'But isn't that what nondisclosure agreements and all matter of trade secret agreements are for…, to protect the inventor? Isn't that's what the US Code, Patent Law, Contract Law and the Uniform Trade Secrets Act, are supposed to prevent?' Well…, supposedly yes.

However, despite all those many assurances, only a very green inventor would be so blind as to place their trust in those virtuous promises…, I know I did… so be wary grasshopper.

This leads me to the following… Many years after this book was written, I successfully emerged from the fight of my life that had just played out in Federal Court. After the dust finally settled, I had plenty to think about, regarding those many assurances…, of which, I had so blindly placed my trust in. So, after giving it careful consideration, I was determined to reverse engineer what this alien abduction had been all about. My catharsis, was to sit down and to write *The World Class Inventors Handbook*. The book is a compilation of hard fought lessons based upon my many experiences, and it's presented against the backdrop of one of the most complex intellectual property lawsuits imaginable. It is the definitive book for all modern-day inventors, product developers, market makers and entrepreneurs.

The goal is to teach anyone how to go about to the inventing process the right way…, beginning from the moment the idea first arrives.

The mission…, to systematically teach any would-be inventor how to look way out over the horizon, in order to guard against the various dangers that will certainly pop up along the way.

In essence, it's the art of how to take those many assurances, and make them work for you, as you journey along the inventor's path. If you're dreaming about developing a product that you want to commercialize and take public for your own profit…, it's required reading.

There's still way more come… However, I can't resist sharing this little lawsuit ditty with you before continuing on. As previously mentioned in the Preface, I ended up taking the deposition of seven individuals. I took the deposition of Diane Newman, Kevin Gill and Peter Ross and now you know why.

I took the deposition of my friend, Dick Dye, the ex. Chief engineer of Purolator. He would do nicely from the vantage point of illuminating things from an expert's point of view. And before Dick would finish, he would thrust his sword into the ground and vouch for both my authorship and expertise in this field.

I took Gary Bilski's deposition, Fram's lead project engineer who went from not having a single oil filter patent, to now being the proud owner of over a dozen, all of which genisised from my IP. Telling…, doesn't even begin to describe what I got out of him.

I took Gus Hampilos' deposition just for kicks, and I'll be glad to share a couple of interesting tidbits with you. Gus after all, was the Chief Intellectual Property lawyer for Allied/Signal Automotive and the associate general counsel for the Company, and of course, he was the mastermind behind their lopsided licensing agreement and much of what befell me. I was intrigued as to what he'd have to say, but I was smart enough to know that he'd be tighter lipped than any sea clam that I'd knocked into. But, yet I owed it to him…

His deposition was defended by a young lawyer…, an up and coming superstar of sorts. He graduated number one in his class from Columbia, and Maga Cume Laude from Harvard law school. As I recall, they both seemed to be enjoying themselves that day, as this non-lawyer had the unmitigated gall to question such a big shot lawyer defended by a Harvard trained attorney.

Now David Brafman, was tasked among other things, to follow me around the eastern half of the United States, as I tried my hand at conducting depositions. Before our little contest would conclude,

I would prove to be a bit more than just a worthy opponent. Before long, he would part ways with his law firm and Honeywell in their infinite wisdom would end up hiring him to be my shadow agent. Since he had already read *The Greed of a Dime,* he was well on his way toward developing an award-winning trial notebook on me for later use. There was even a rumor was going 'round…, that he knew me better than I knew myself.

As this lawsuit of mine began to pick up a head of steam, it began to reverberate throughout their legal department. That's when Honeywell would go on and replace the Manhattan based law firm from which Brafman once hailed. Their next strategic move, was to hire the ultra-connected Newark law firm, that had the innermost workings of the Newark Federal Courthouse tattooed on the inside of their eyelids. Coincidentally, I went through five separate judge changes, so you can just imagine how Honeywell was settin' up the chessboard! Honeywell was in kill mode now. Before long, they would place a call to the bullpen, and bring in their closer…, Kirkland & Ellis, the ninth largest law firm on the planet.

When I deposed Hampilos, he was the CEO of Engelhard Corporation. For kicks, you may want to look up this merry cast of characters.

The last deposition on my seven-man roster, was that of Robert Franklyn Voight. A humble fella…, an unwitting a straw man that Allied put on a patent, that perhaps…, they shouldn't have. Never in their wildest imagination, did they ever expect that one day I'd turn up, with over twenty pages of typewritten questions to ask him. You see…, Mr. Voight was a janitor at the Fram filter plant in Indiana. And after decades of service, the plant engineer decided to enjoin him on an oil filter patent as a retirement gift. It was a touching gesture, and I'm sure it was a nice addition to the hat and wind-breaker ensemble they had already bestowed him for his many years of dedicated service.

At bare minimum, and under every imaginable Intellectual Property law on the books, I should have at the very least, been the rightful co-inventor of this patent. Although, let me tell you, it was worth it all to have Mr. Voight tell me firsthand and under oath, how he wound up being the co-inventor.

With that, the stage has been set for the Second Act…

Come…, come finish out this leg of the journey. I can only refer to this, as the Aftermath.

I guarantee that the chaplets to follow, are going to fly off the pages! I realize, that it's never wise to over-promise, but I have to clue you, this next phase is more psychotically intriguing then the first! By the time this journey concludes, you'll come away knowing why I did that little something, that I had vowed never to do. You will no doubt be astounded, as to who I would bump into along the way, and what new madness would yet to be uncovered. As they say, "truth is stranger than fiction," here's hoping you'll see it too.

CHAPTER 13
THE AFTERMATH

At last, I was at peace. The buffeting storm which had swallowed up my life, had finally blown itself out. Indeed, I had made it! I had without reservation proved it to myself and to all who cared to notice. I had paddled out through the huge breakers that most people could only dream about. I had made it through that maze of killer riptides, the ones noted for pulling a man apart. The kind that can pull you under, and never let you go.

And to think of it, I was privileged enough to have wrangled out from this untamable torrent…, my life. For the moment, at least for this round, I had beaten the sea, as I sat upon my board. Poised, about ready to mount the crest of the biggest darn wave of my life. I was just so appreciative to have survived the whole ordeal, as I drew in a giant sigh of thanksgiving.

Remembering at one such point, when things had become so desperate, Bill could only offer me these feeble words of encouragement. "If they sign Steve, let me assure you of something, you better consider yourself a very lucky man indeed, because you will have pulled off a major coup here!"

Well they did sign! And as best as I could tell, John Cory, the President of the Fram Filter Division, ratified our contract on September 1st, 1995.

I was a shade over thirty-seven years old, and had just beaten some pretty incredible odds, N.I.H. and all. I considered myself blessed. The feat was absolutely Jordanesque, though I'll be the first to admit it, I ain't no Michael.

Ten long years had passed since my Dad's passing, and I still couldn't get over how much I missed him. I only wished he could have been here now, for this moment, to witness the unfolding of my life's dream. There was so much to be proud of! And it was a crying shame, because I still firmly clung to the belief that I had finally developed the tools and the wisdom to of reached him.

Well it was obvious, I'd never get the chance.

I would like to set the record straight before we go on any further, and now would be an excellent time to do so. I made a supreme effort to forgive both Dianne and the merry cast of characters that had left their mark on my property. The very same ones who didn't hesitate staking out claims, where they had absolutely no right to do so. I didn't even begrudge Allied for the theft which they had perpetrated. But please, don't think that I'm a fool, nor am I going to put on here like a pious individual loading up on self-humility either. Because stealing is stealing, and that's exactly what they had done!

But if I chose to forgive 'em, well, that would have to be my personal decision and not anyone else's. And let me tell you something, I was determined to forgive them. So that's exactly what I started out to do…

What was done to me, was done. It was over. Yeah, I realize that they had beaten the sap outa me. And yeah, I knew most of them didn't deserve to be working on my project, but that was life. It was no time to be sour grapes. And as usual, I was already on to my next plan.

I still very much knew my place without having to be told.

'If you want something bad enough, you've gotta charge it with reckless abandon.'

One last shameless surfing shot.   summer of '13.   photo Jackie Moor

The old man drivin' hard following a late summer's tropical depression.
I was 55 that summer.
Started surfing back in August of '69, been at it now for 50 years.
Riding various Harbour long boards for the past 25 years.

The glory days are now passing quickly in the rear-view mirror.

CHAPTER 14
THE ROLL OUT

With all that said, on August 28th, I fired off a brief note of thanks to Dianne and sent along the set of original contracts bearing my signature to her attention. Though I wanted to forgive her, I couldn't help but shiver, as I began to pound out on my mother-in-law's IBM Selectric; "Thank you for all your help." It was the only way. We had to be genial, she wasn't going anywhere, and as far as I could tell, neither was I.

Remember the part about the sea turtle? Well I meant it. With every fiber of my being! There was a roll-out to be watching!

Just so that we're on the same page, a roll-out is synonymous with what a company might refer to as the launch of any new product. A rollout, mind you, can only happen once. The event is akin to throwing a ball room gala, perhaps for the coming out of child, who's come of age. Announcing to the world with all the fanfare and the like, that this child is worthy to burst upon the scene. At least that's what a roll-out is in my mind.

Before we go any further let's have a closer look at exactly who was going to throw this party, and for whom it was being thrown; including the invited guests. First off, let's take a brief overview of Mommy and Daddy's intentions. In this new age of political correctness; capitalists as well as others these days are wrapping themselves in their own tailor-made mantra, something referred to as a **Mission Statement.** I'd like to introduce you to Allied's:

"We are a leading global supplier of original equipment and aftermarket products to the Automotive, Truck and Off Highway Industries. Our mission is to satisfy ever-increasing customer needs through continuous improvement in quality, cost, technology and services, thereby enhancing profits and shareholder value."

As is often the case, the Mission Statement is followed by an interesting group of proclamations, in this case referred to as a **Vision of Values and Guiding Principles.** I'm compelled to put before you the following… If adhered to, truly awesome. If not, then it's just a bunch of double speak and hypocritical pontification, meant to impress the unsuspecting ideologue and potential share holder.

*"**People** are our most important resource- We will create an environment throughout the organization that provides for development, encourages excellence and involvement and rewards employee performance.*

***Global Teamwork** is fundamental to our success. Cooperation and teamwork in all activities, within and between business units, across functional disciplines, with customers, suppliers, and the communities in which we do business, are essential.*

***Quality** is foremost in all of our business activity. Continuous quality improvement is essential to customer satisfaction and our ongoing success.*

***Continuous Improvement** is a way of life and is a never-ending process. Success requires that all of us, every day, work to increase the effectiveness of what we do to provide better products, processes and services.*

*We will be a **Responsible Corporate Citizen** to all our constituencies including employees, customers, suppliers and communities. We will respect the environment and the health and safety of* *our employees. We will conduct ourselves responsibly maintaining a high level of* **Ethics** *and* **Integrity in** *all of our business activities."*

Well, you get the idea. Surely, at least in the beginning of our relationship, that's what I believed I could look forward to experiencing. At this point in time, I was still searching for my spot amongst the shiny proclamations of the Company, determined now more than ever to find it!

Let's take a quick peek at exactly who was about to throw this gala event: AlliedSignal Automotive Aftermarket Division. Just to get it straight, Allied Automotive was a fully diversified self-proclaimed leader in the one hundred-billion-dollar automotive aftermarket. At the close of 1995, their sales topped the five and a half billion-dollar mark. Familiar products brandishing their name in this field are none other than Fram filters; oil, air and gas; Autolite spark plugs and ignition systems; Bendix brake products and systems and Garrett turbo chargers. All this information I'm about to present, comes from their own very well-prepared publication put together specifically for the debut of the Double Guard!

Again, in their words, not mine: *"One of the world's largest and best positioned independent suppliers to the international automotive industry. A worldwide technical leader, AlliedSignal Automotive has more than 80 manufacturing plants in 15 countries; an international network of 26 research, development and engineering centers; more than 30,000 employees worldwide. It also markets its products in more than 100 countries through original equipment and aftermarket networks."*

In 1994, the parent company **AlliedSignal, ranked 38th on the Fortune 500 list**, headed by none other than CEO Lawrence A. Bossidy, a noted stickler for all-round perfection. In 1995, the Company enjoyed sales topping 14 billion dollars.

So at this time, it's only fair that I provide you with a list of their principal business areas: Aerospace, Aerospace and Equipment Systems; AlliedSignal Engines, Commercial Avionics Systems, Government Electronic Systems; Automotive, Automotive Aftermarket, Braking Systems, Engine Components, Safety Restraint Systems; Engineered Materials, Fibers, Laminate Systems, Performance Materials, Plastics and Fluorine Products.

On any given day, the Company employs 83,500 people; of which the Engineered Materials Division employs 13,000. The Automotive Division as previously mentioned, 30,000; and the Aerospace Division 38,700. They own, or operate some 383 facilities across the globe, spanning 40 countries.

Just so you know, by their own admission, Allied was a world leader in both Plastics and Fluorine products. What's not spelled out, was they were specialists in the research and sale of fluorinated hydrocarbons, and PTFE was one of those products, something that most people identify as Teflon.

'Remember all the resistance heaped upon me at various times by both Diane Newman and Ron Rohrback the PhD regarding this subject? Now might be a good time to ask…, was it real, imagined or plain 'ol incompetence?' I'll leave that one for you to decide.

Coincidently, Mr. Rohrback didn't have a single oil filter patent to his name when we had first met. However, after our time together, he wound up with many. Hum…, I know.

I guess by now; you have a fairly good handle on who the adopted parents of my new filter had represented themselves to be. However, before we begin to run along, I think it's only just that you get a deeper insight as to who's honor the Roll Out was to be held.

*"Rumford, RI (February 1, 1996) -- AlliedSignal Automotive Aftermarket today unveiled the **most significant oil filter innovation in automotive history** – the new Fram Double Guard engine protection system. Fram Double Guard with DuPont Teflon PTFE additive is the only product of its kind that does the job of an oil filter and additive in one."*

"For the first time, Fram Double Guard offers consumers two leading friction-fighting technologies combined in one engine protection system," said Paul Coccari, AlliedSignal's manager, filter product marketing..."

It was the confirmation I had been looking for. AlliedSignal was announcing to the world that my invention was truly a high watermark for the oil filter industry, just like I knew it would be all along!

But now it's only proper you meet the guests, since no coming-out party would be complete without guests, you know. You see, Allied eventually commissioned a study, and had come up with some pretty incredible findings. Permit me to share with you some information given directly to their retailers:

*"AlliedSignal, the recognized leader in the filter industry, is once again setting the industry standard with the new Fram Double Guard engine protection system - **the most significant oil filter innovation in history.** Fram Double Guard filters provide double defense against dirt and wear - for substantially less than the cost of leading bottled additives plus a filter purchased separately.*

Better protection for your customers, better profits for you.

Fram Double Guard will help you in two ways. Your customers will get a better product, while you received increased profits with every sale. Initial research indicates wide consumer acceptance of the Fram Double Guard concept:

Concept appeals to both additive users and non-users.

Purchase intent is very high - 84% among non-additive users and 87% among additive users.

Almost 7 out of 10 respondents rated the concept as being excellent or very good.

About 90% of the respondents said that Fram Double Guard was equal to or better than Slick-50 or STP.

70% strongly agreed that Fram Double Guard is a convenient way to add an additive and that it would help protect their engines during start-up.

Consumers even liked the overall look of the new product and pack-age design.

Comments included "sleek" "modern" "different" and "stands out from the rest of the pack."

In 1995, the top 100 automotive chains had amassed nearly 10,000 stores between them. And that didn't even begin to touch the giant retailers of the world, such as Kmart, Target and the granddaddy of them all; Walmart with nearly 2000 locations!

In 1995 there had to of been close to 20,000 points of retail filter distribution in the United States alone, in which Fram was either already a player, or easily could have been, if they had so desired! Please keep in mind I'm not including gas stations nor installed sales sites of any kind. Just points of retail! We'll get to installed sales later, you can count on it!

But as we prepare to take this incredible voyage, I do want you to remember something. Remember, their own words:

'The biggest and best independent supplier in the world.'

Oh…! I almost forgot the most important guests of all… You!

Don't forget about yourselves! Because this Roll-Out wasn't intended solely for the retailers benefit alone. Ah no!

In all honesty, it was orchestrated for you, the consumer! The service driven, the new and improved crazed, free spending American! It had always been my intention to go after the ever growing 400,000,000 million oil filters sold throughout the United States every year! That was impetus that drove me from the beginning, and the force that would continue to drive me, to do what I had to do.

I let at least a couple of weeks pass, before I started calling on the Company once again. The contract of course had long been signed, and I had the Roll-Out gently playing on my mind. It didn't take me very long to figure it out, but Peter was much too busy to bother with me now. Actually, upon his request, he asked me to give this fella, Paul Coccari a call.

So, I did as he wished, and started calling this new guy. At least he was new to me, I had only met him once before, and then only briefly. I can tell ya that he certainly wasn't at any of the three meetings I had ever attended at Fram's headquarters, and he wasn't some new hire either.

'But do you know what his position was now?' None other than the new product manager for Fram! It had befallen him to pick up where Kevin had left off?!

By now, the nature of my calling was simple, more accurately, focused. "So, are you guys almost ready for the 'Show'?" I asked him, early one day. Before I could even prepare myself, he flatly replied, "We're not going to the show this year. I mean Fram's going, but the Double Guard won't be going along this year."

Beyond shocked, I asked him why, and his answer was rather simple, "Because we're not ready." There would be next year, but the Double Guard wasn't gonna make it to the launch for 1995!

'Why?'

'What about the all the promises Jack McGrath made to me that day in the room full of high ranking employees?' I thought. You know when he promised me that Fram was prepared to back this concept the hilt, and that they wouldn't drop the ball!

Unfortunately for me, Jack was gone. Because I would have called him on it. And believe me, if Jack had been around. Well..., I believe in my gut that things from the very beginning woulda been different. Much different.

'So, what about everything Kevin had said?' Oftentimes when we talked, our conversation focused on the Show, the Show, the Show. As a matter of fact, it was common knowledge that AlliedSignal was going to take me as their honored guest to SEMA; the 1995 Automotive Aftermarket Show that fall in Las Vegas. Not only did it come out of Kevin's mouth, but Mr. Ross', the Vice President of Marketing for Fram as well!

So now look what's happening here. I have Peter Ross telling me to speak to some flunky that's not even qualified to carry Kevin's briefcase, and this guy blurts out on our first date that we ain't going to no show! I'm telling ya, he did so with about as much concern as it takes to cut the grass!

'And you want to know what really frosted me?'

No one dared say anything about missing the Show until after the ink was dry upon the contract. It had never even been eluded to before!

'Where had the commitment to "Reasonable Efforts" gone to so quickly,' I wondered?

But instead of logging an immediate protest, I kept my cool and my mouth shut like a good little trooper; all the while letting the inexperienced hand, dig his grave a little deeper.

"So, when are you gonna hit the market with my new filter, Paul?"

"I don't know exactly. Hopefully, sometime around the end of December, I imagine."

Let's see, I approached Kevin in the beginning of January of 1994. Unveiled my idea to the upper management of Fram in early October of 94', and now it was nearly October once again, except it was 1995. I gotta quote Larry's own words here, if for nothing else, for effect...

"Speed... We focus on speed for competitive advantage. We simplify processes and compress cycle time."

Allied was in possession of my idea for one year and a half! I sure didn't witness any *"compression of cycle time,"* certainly when it came down to sticking some Teflon in a metal can and painting it black! They had a full year to get this thing ramped up for the show!

Hey...! Don't think that I'm being inflexible either. Just go back and look over the stuff this outfit routinely builds! Well, if they couldn't figure out how to put some lousy Teflon inside of an oil filter in one years' time...

Well, it was too late now. I was once again getting that sick feeling that I must of picked the wrong horse to ride in this race!

I was in receipt of my fifty grand. Somehow after all her vein attempts to delay its arrival, it happened to have found its way to me in a little over two weeks. With that little detail out of the way, I began initiating my phone campaign of calling on the Company once again in earnest.

At this time Patti and I didn't dare quit our jobs, nor were we about to. To be honest, we weren't sure if we could trust Allied' to leave our jobs..., ever! Besides, it was already September, and if Patti had hoped for a leave of absence, the papers should of been submitted to her administration way back in early May.

So, there we were. Her in dire need of a sabbatical, and me still toughing it out as a real estate agent. Certainly, by now I had earned the right to look upon myself as a world class inventor, yet the situation had even striped me even of that honor.

Unfortunately, as my relationship with Paul grew, so did the setbacks. Let me explain. As I mentioned earlier, the unveiling at the show was but a memory now and the roll-out date for the major retailers kept getting pushed further and further back. The November/ December time frame had been growing like some unstoppable cancer upon my five- year contract! Over the course of the next several calls, the cancer grew until I was being told that I could expect the filter to show up in stores sometime around March/April 1996!!!

Now I'd like to say something. I was still under the conviction that Kevin was an honest and decent man.

...Of course, I had maintained close contact with him! I treasured his forthright and insightful analysis concerning the whole ordeal, so allow me to explain the facts of life, concerning automotive retailing these days.

There is a little something called a planogram. It's a fancy word for a product display, but its oh so much more than that. Simply put, it's often times a retailer's first and last chance of landing a browsing customer. Kinda like a Venus fly trap, if you know how that one works.

Anyway, as far as Fram was accustomed to doing things, planogram changes occurred only once per selling year and were rigidly initiated at the same time every year, in late December, early January. And believe me, that doesn't just happen mindlessly, it's done for a very specific reason. For one thing, it's a matter of cold hard timing, and several factors are at work here. Remember, you have to have an accurate picture of the consumer. They've been walking the aisles in that first quarter right after Christmas, it's cold and gray outside, and to complicate matters, they're low on cash. Most of the country is in deep winter and who feels like changing their oil, or working on an automobile in the cold and snow?

Let me point something out to you, the automotive retailers are well aware of the fact that there's a lot of pent up buying power walking around those automotive aisles. So as this unsuspecting consumer stalks the items that have already been subliminally planted in their heads…, well, once the rites of spring catch hold of em', he's a buyer.

Don't kid yourself, the retailers know long before you do, that Spring's right around the corner.

'Did you ever wonder why bathing suit catalogs begin to arrive at our homes in the dead of winter?'

Obviously, the retailers must be aware of something the masses are not attuned to. They can predict and with accuracy, that when the snow begins to melt in the second quarter and the rites of spring begin to take hold of every automobile loving soul, these kinds of products fly off the shelves. The second quarter is typically the best quarter for automotive aftermarket retailing.

So, here's what I found a bit strange. Despite all Larry's pontification about how streamlined his Company was, little O'l me was there to witness firsthand his five-billion-dollar division bungle through the most crucial aspect of any new product launch. The Roll-Out!

Fram's entire stable of loyal retailers wouldn't have the Double Guard in their planograms for the upcoming planogram change! My God, it was shaping up to be a full-blown disaster! The missed Show, and now the missed planogram changes! And to top it off, a launch which promised to be at least six months behind schedule!

I can tell ya, Patti wasn't about to leave her job, and neither was I!

From my vantage point it was ludicrous to try and explain away the mistakes that were being made. The only comfort I had, was in the knowing that this experiment now 'gone mad', was not the product of just a convenient few. It was now out in the wide open, for all to see! The blood was going to be on everybody's hands this time. And let me assure you, before it was done, Larry hands would be dripping from it as well!

CHAPTER 15
I'M GONNA BLOW THE BRIDGE!

Finally, I could take it no longer. Sometime around mid-October, I called, looking for Peter. What I really wanted, was a little reassurance. What I ended up with, was anything but.

I'll be the first to admit, I did my best, probing him for answers and all I wanted, was for him to corroborate all that the new man had been feeding me for the last month or so. Quite innocently, I hit him with this one liner during our hurried conversation. "So, I guess you guys are going to miss the show, huh?"

"Yeah, it certainly looks that way Steve," came his reply.

Trying to make myself feel better, I offered, "It's no big deal, I guess. You guys are going to be there next year anyway. It's only a trade show, right? It's no biggie."

What he was about to tell me, nearly dropped me in my tracks. "I'm afraid you're wrong about that Steve."

"How so?" I asked, not having the slightest idea about the importance of this highly touted trade show. You see, as informed as I might of been, there was certainly more to this clandestine automotive world than I could ever know. I was learning as we went along, kinda like a giant paint by numbers game. As a matter of fact, I may as well level with you now. You know all that stuff I just rattled off back there, concerning the Company's size and greatness? Well, when I was dealing with them, all I really knew about 'em, was that they were very big and very strong. I certainly wasn't up to speed on them, like I am today and to be honest with you, I still don't know exactly who they are!

Oh…, and another thing. That Mission Statement of theirs, along with the rest of that diatribe… Well, now that I think about it, I do remember seeing a couple of laminated copies pasted on the wall in the foyer when I came up to see Kevin at Fram.

Of course, I read 'em! I just didn't pay much attention to them at the time. It wasn't like somebody pushed an autographed copy under my nose and proclaimed, we swear to you Mr. Moor, we will uphold these precepts.

So I'm guilty, big deal! Like a fool, I trusted them. Mission Statement or not, I went into this thing expecting nothing less than the best outa my new business partner.

So, let me get on with the rest of the story and I'll end up showing you how important those plaques were.

"Steve, it really is a big deal. It's a very big deal! This show happens only once a year, and every vendor worth his salt is going to be there. And we're gonna be there as well. I'm just afraid that the Double Guard won't be. It'll have to wait until next year's show."

I politely, got the heck off the phone. The clam digger in me had just about enough. Oh, the insensitivity! Beyond that, the utter stupidity of telling me something as damning as that. He shared it with me all right, and what he said rolled off his tongue as smoothly as the water off a duck's back.

Maybe it was that same day, I'm not exactly sure, but it was close enough. I called Paul Coccari back one last time to pin him down when my filter would make its way onto the retailers' shelves. The answer came back rather brusquely, as if suddenly I had become a pest, instead of a partner. "We'll have it out sometime late in the second quarter," he said.

"How late?" my guts wanting to explode.

"I don't know…? But it is a fair guess to say May/June sometime."

When I had finished talking to those two clowns, it was over. I was red lining.

Now I want you to keep in mind something. I still fully expected to make several million dollars off of this abbreviated run on Broadway. Certainly not the thirty million that I rightfully should have, but still enough that neither my wife or myself, would ever have to work another day in our lives if we chose not to.

'But after what I was experiencing, how was that gonna be possible now?'

I didn't exactly know! I wasn't sure which was worse, missing the show and planogram dates, or the theft of another additional six months off of my contract!

All I knew, was that I was about to do something that I had never done in my entire life…, break rank! You remember that hollow threat I made back there several times. "The one that if I had to, I'd go to Bossidy." Well, it wasn't so hollow of threat after all!

One morning around mid-October; a Tuesday I believe, only couple of weeks before the show, I called looking for Larry. Before I knew it, I found myself talking to one of his lovely secretaries early that morning, around eighth thirty. When the main switchboard put me through, I was in utter amazement at how accessible his office was.

With great fear and trepidation, I introduced myself and slowly began pouring my heart out to this young lady on the other end of the line.

I was no fool. Sure, I could hope, but even I knew that it would take a miracle to get piped into the boss's office. Nonetheless, I gave it my very best shot, as I passionately attempted to latch onto his secretary's heart…, hoping. Hoping to be rewarded with an audience with her boss. She listened intently, as I began. "I really hate doing this, but I have to… Mr. Bossidy has got to know what is going on. I've never in my life have gone over anybody's head before, but they're ruining my filter. Just tell Mr. Bossidy that I have to speak with him about it. Tell him that the inventor of the Double Guard oil filter is calling and let him know that Fram is about to blow a billion dollar a year opportunity and that they're gonna miss the trade show in Vegas! Please tell him that I regret this call but tell him I've been forced into this situation and unfortunately, I'm gonna blow the bridge!"

Her reply was as sweet, as it was comforting. "I'm sorry that this is happening to you Mr. Moor. Sometimes things can get out of hand in such a big Company as ours. It's too bad what's happening to you. But I understand. Please don't feel bad about your calling, sometimes you just have to do what you have to do."

Hoping I had made the cut, in my naïve and frightened mind, I prepared myself as best I could before she'd put me through to her boss. My heart was in my throat as I prepared to speak with the all-knowing and all-understanding captain on the bridge.

After a bit, she came back to phone, this time with a bit of sadness in her voice. "I'm sorry Mr. Moor, but Mr. Bossidy is out of his office at the moment, but I promise you, that he'll get your message." Her voice belied the fact he was in…., I could just sense it. Nonetheless, he wasn't about to make himself available to me.

CHAPTER 16
A FEIGNED CALL FROM THE CHIEF

That same morning after calling Bossidy's office, I ran out the door and headed for the office. As I drove to work, I considered what I had just done. The thought of going over everybody's head directly to the CEO frightened me, but I guess it didn't matter.

I was in that mode again. All or nothing! If the filter was truly as great as I believed, then it would rise or fall on its own merits, and that despite Allied's ineptitude's, especially now that I had gotten the boss involved.

'Remember how I thought it best not to go the President of Fram during my torture session with the ice maiden, dreading a move like that could have backfired on me?' Well just multiply that a thousand times, except that this time, there could be no backing off. I had stepped way over the line. I was prepared to expose the whole lot of them!

Oh..., and one last thing before I move along. Remember all that stuff I eluded to back there..., about how great the filter was? You know, *"the most significant oil filter innovation in history."* Well I actually would see that material in print much later, so I really didn't have an accurate picture how the Company actually viewed when I put in that call to Larry! In fact, up to this point, nobody had even whispered such a thing to me, and nor did I ever come across anything like that in print yet.

When I returned home from the office that afternoon, nothing much was unusual as I greeted Mary Beth at the front door. It was her day to baby-sit the kids. We had a beautiful thing going Patti and me. We were blessed to be able to split the load of caring for the kids between her parents who lived across the street from us and Mary Beth who lived just around the block. And like always, she'd tell me how Matt was getting on, and perhaps any phone calls she had intercepted before my machine picked up.

"Steve a Mr. Barter called you. He called right after you left. I don't know, sometime around nineish."

"Did he leave his first name?" I asked, puzzled not having any idea who he was.

"No, he didn't. He just said that he was Mr. Barter from AlliedSignal. That's all he said."

Now I was really lost. I didn't have the vaguest idea who this guy might of been. "Are you sure M.B? You mean to tell me that he didn't leave a number?" Truly stumped.

I could tell my line of questioning was making her feel uneasy, like she broke the kid or something. "No Steve, really. Believe me he didn't. He just gave me his name, Mr. Barter."

I ran down to my basement and began rooting through the mounds of papers strewn about the furnace room, still left in unorganized heaps, like so many rotting corpses from the battlefield.

There it was! The Company's 1994 annual report. Thinking to myself, 'if this guy was anybody, I'd be sure to find his picture in here somewhere.

My first reaction was, My God! Larry got my message after all! There he was, bigger than life, John W. Barter, Executive Vice President; AlliedSignal Automotive! Oops! I didn't even realize that the unidentified caller existed! At the time, I was so angry I hadn't even given it a second thought to reach out for him. Besides, it was Bossidy I needed to speak with anyway, especially in light of all the goings on.

As I stared at Barter's face, I began to feel terrible that the situation had possessed me to the point of jumping ranks and going over his head. But the longer I stared at the group photo, the angrier I became as the nasty reality of the whole fiasco began to rise up inside of me.

Then it hit me, this man was responsible for the launch of a very unique oil filter. Certainly, a once in a lifetime deal for me, and more than likely, a first for him as well.

There was little doubt, I'd be calling him back. As far as I was concerned, he wasn't about to get away with anything. I could only wonder if he realized what the crew was doing onboard his watch!

I remember letting that day go by, before I called him. It was a Wednesday morning before work, and I had gotten myself psyched-up enough to pick up the phone and call him. And I came up empty handed, well..., not exactly.

"Good morning, Mr. Barters office." Came a pleasant voice.

In all fairness… AlliedSignal's secretarial staff, seemed to have been the nicest, friendliest bunch of well-trained personal assistants I had ever encountered anywhere. 'If only their bosses could have followed their lead, I surely wouldn't have been in this situation,' I mused.

Anyway, after a brief introduction, the nice lady informed me that Mr. Barter was out of the office, but that he had been expecting my call. So, after conferring with his diary, she asked me if I wouldn't mind calling him back on Friday morning at 8:00 AM, October the 20th for a telephone conference. To which I said okay.

I called promptly at 8:00 but he was unavailable, and she asked if I didn't mind waiting a few minutes until he could return the call. Of course, I agreed.

And let me tell you something, as that fifteen minutes began to work me over, so did my suspicions. By time he called back, they burned out of control like wild fire!

"Hello, this is John Barter. Is Steven Moor in?"

The first thing out of the box, he asked me if it would be all right to put me on speaker phone. Say no more..., it was so smooth..., real smooth. I knew to my very core we weren't alone, and quite possibly, we could of been making a recording here. So quite naturally, I endeavored to be on my best behavior.

I got to tell ya though, at first blush he seemed quite cordial and obliging, as I unloaded on him.

'Let's see, what did I tell him? What sort of ground did we cover?' I guess just the usual. Stuff like Fram was gonna miss the big trade show that only comes around once a year. A June Roll-Out, instead of the November one I had been promised for the last year and a half. The missed planogram changes for December/January 1995. The abysmal lack of communication, especially now that my contract had been signed. Six months lopped off my contract without so much as a, 'we'll make good for it.'

I told him that the retail price for the filter was way too high. That much I had already found out from Peter. The filter was going to be offered at $10.94. I didn't hesitate at this point to express my utter dismay concerning the price. I told him right up front that the retail price was way out of line, that it should been more like seven to seven fifty. I didn't hold anything back. I can remember referring to AlliedSignal as a bunch of greedy bean counters! By the way, that was one of the very few times during our conversation in which he spoke up and defended the Company's game plan.

I went on to tell him about the inefficiencies during the birthing process. I mentioned that I wanted to tell him about everything I had experienced, telling him that I had gone deeper inside his Company than any high-priced consultant they could ever hope to find!

I mentioned Dianne, and what I had suffered at her hands. I accused the Company of stealing from me… I'm sure I used the word extortion! Lastly, I told him that I wanted to go over my contract quietly and peaceably, that I wanted to address what had gone on with me and receive a revised contract.

He feigned ignorance of course. Especially on the point concerning the contract, saying he couldn't speak to that, because he didn't know anything about such a matter.

Just so you know, Gus Hampilos, had in all probability had a corner office next to his. 'Who was he bull-shitting?' Gus was the Chief Intellectual Property Counsel for the Automotive Unit and the Associate General Counsel for AlliedSignal. Gus wrote the contract to acquire the *"most significant innovation in oil filter in history."* 'So you mean to tell me Barter didn't know?' Was I supposed to believe that Gus's office was in the basement like the quaint portrayal in *A Civil Action*? I doubt it.

And last but not least, I told him that I had enough dirt on the Company that I could put a Wall Street Journal reporter up in my finished basement for one week before I'd run out of material for him. I warned him that I could feed a good reporter enough story, that I would own the front page of that paper for a week! Not wanting to sound overly dramatic, but I did make it quite clear to him that I had enough on them to send the Company's stock price into the toilet.

Upon the conclusion of my little talk, well…, I had made it quite explicit. I was done talking with anybody from Fram. Telling him that I would talk with him, and of course, anyone he deemed I should communicate with, but that I didn't want to talk with either Peter Ross or Paul Coccari any further.

'You wanna know what he said?'

He said, "Give me some time to get to the bottom of this. You have my word that I will. I promise you that either I, or my trusted associate Steve Price will be calling you back shortly."

'Would you like to know when he called me back?'…

CHAPTER 17
WHO THREW GASOLINE ON THE FIRE?

The Show was less than two weeks away, it was now mid-October of 95'.

You know, the Lord is funny. I mean He's great! Never let yourself believe for a moment that He's not in loving charge of your destiny. I mean, that's if you're in the game…, and Baby, I was most definitely in the game!

I had never planned it that that way, but I ended up calling Larry's office just in time to call his bluff. Because if he was interested in the project's success, I had certainly put myself in a position to find out! And I have to tell you, not in a million years I did plan it that way. It just happened!

I don't know when it started, Tuesday or Wednesday perhaps…, but suddenly, I began receiving a barrage of phone calls from Peter Ross. From the Show no less! Like I told you, Kevin had called me only few times during our love affair, but Peter! He had never called me outa' the blue. The thought of him calling served only to reinforce the fact that my call to Bossidy was in the process of vaporizing the poor guy. He was a desperate cowboy all right, as he began leaving impassioned distress calls for me at both my home and office. Unfortunately for him, it just so happened that I was a moving target that day, but I can tell you one thing, he caught up with me that evening after supper.

Sure enough, he started off calm and polite, but it didn't last very long before he came unglued at every joint! He was half screaming, half crying. There was little doubt, his backside was in a sling!

"You wanted attention! Huh Mister?! Is that what you wanted?! Well you got it!!! You really got it…, 'cause let me tell you something! You really threw gasoline on the fire this time!"

'I guessed someone had called him, don't you think?'

I never wanted it to go down this way, but I was through playing games with all of these children. He had plenty of chances to help me, but he had long since passed on 'em. I knew full well that his job was at stake and I hated to see him hurt, but after his performance I guessed he had whatever was coming. It was now his turn to twist in the wind a while. I had already been doing more than my share of that!

"This phone call to Bossidy… Do you have any idea what it could mean to you? I'll tell you what! They're all looking at this thing real closely now! And if this filter so much as coughs, it's all over for you Mister. Do you hear me?!"

"Well that's okay," I told him. "You bastards painted me into a corner and it doesn't matter at all now to me Pete. It's all or nothin' for me. If this filter is what I know it is, it will truly fly. And if I just conned you guys, well…, then it's gonna just crash and burn. What else can I tell ya? As far as I'm concerned, you guys have already failed."

I don't know what moved him to play his hand so openly, he had never done anything like that before? I guessed that the desire to come through the phone line and wring my neck had gotten the better of him.

"Do you have any idea what I've been doing all day for you? Do you have any idea at all?"

"Nope."

"Well let me tell you something Mister, I've been showing this filter to our biggest and best customers in private all day long, behind the booth and up in my room. …anywhere I possibly could.

And do you have any idea what their response has been so far? Do you know? Do you really want to know!" '"Get it to us as fast as you can!!!"'

CHAPTER 18
THE GRAND THEFT

Over the course of the next several months I had precious little contact with the Company, it was as if there had never been a patent, a contract, nor an oil filter. There seemed to of been an all-out communication blackout on the part of the Company towards me.

Of course, right after it was over, I made it a point to apologized to both Peter and Paul for doing what had to be done. Blown bridge or not, these guys didn't seem too capable of straightening out the business at hand despite the previous object lessons. Allow me to demonstrate.

I can remember it like yesterday, it was around the time of our wedding anniversary, so Patti tells me. Walking around one day, there it was, she saw it! In all its splendor, it had arrived, there simply wasn't anything like it! The Graphic artist Geoffrey Skog had outdone himself for sure. The black beauty had finally arrived, available for sale in one of the finest retail venues in the world. Walmart!

A few people who knew, and cared enough, began calling us. They were hearing radio spots. Some saw the television commercial, while others saw the full page adds in popular magazines. My God in Heaven, it was out! The Company was doing something they normally wouldn't have even considered, a mid-year roll-out! The shelves were stocked, 24 models in all were now being offered to the buying public. 'Better late than never,' I thought. I just wished they weren't being so greedy, offering it for $9.97. 'Oh, what the heck I figured, things by now were so far out of my control, I'd need a fleet of attorneys to coral this monster…, just wanting to let things be. I did my best to console myself and revel in the fact that my creation was alive!

Anyway, it was up to the public now, and of course Fram's marketing prowess, to let me know if I was all wet or not. You know self-deluded, blinded by one's creation, self-deceived and the like.

Before the month of May was out, something which had never occurred in the history of oil filter sales began happening…!

It was happening in stores packed with customers. It was happening deep into the night, when only the night owls prowled the isles. There was a myriad of techniques employed. It just couldn't be stopped! The sophisticated surveillance systems were no match for the consumer turned thief. Even the threat of a police record was no deterrent! The Double Guard was being stolen! Pilfered, as it was clandestinely switched into other less expensive filter boxes. And it was happening nearly as fast as the product hit the shelves! Of course, I didn't have a clue what was happening, only having visited the shrine perhaps a time or two, on a routine detour to the fishing department.

"Steve, Steve, you've got to get to Walmart!" Came the voice over the other end of the line. It was Joanne, a top real estate lady from my office, who over time had grown to become a staunch supporter of my quest. "Steve…, it's terrible! You have to get down there right away; the people are stealing your filter! They're ripping the boxes apart and making a mess of your display. You've just gotta get down there and do something about it. I told the manager that you were the inventor, and that I'd send you on by!"

When I arrived and greeted the display, it was obvious. She was right. It was pretty well manhandled. I sought out the manager and we had a long talk. We put our heads together and came up with some pretty good cost-effective ways to handle this situation.

It was now time to call Peter Ross and fill him in. As for Paul, after apologizing to him, I felt it a waste of time to ever bother with him again.

First thing out of the box, Peter began to systematically down play the whole thing. "We're on top of it," he said. Assuring me that undoubtedly Walmart was purely over reacting to a very tiny problem.

Boy…, as a senior marketing executive, this guy did a heck of a lot of back peddling in the wake of this oncoming marketing fiasco! "You know how these guys at Walmart are, Steve. They're just making a big deal out of nothing. This outfit is just a big pain in the ass, they really don't have any idea what they're doing. They are making much to do about nothing, because they can't manage their own inventory."

'Well let's just see about that,' cringing at the thought of yet another chapter ready to unfold.

'Wanna know who was minding the shelves at this high-volume Walmart in Brick, NJ?'

An Italian immigrant named Giuseppe! A most likable fella, barely in his twenties, who like millions before him, sought out his opportunity in this land of ours. As far as his thick accent and diction was concerned, I could have cared less. His broken English didn't mask what he instinctively knew what was happening to his shelves. This boy was sharp enough, and he was up for the job at hand, and most of all, he cared! No store manager in his right mind would have given him the job, if he couldn't of handled it.

Over the course of the next few visits, he shared with me the bizarre lengths in which the filter thieves had been mounting their assault. I asked him if he had the opportunity of talking with the salespeople from Fram. He said he hadn't, 'cause there wasn't anybody showing up to talk with! You see, Allied/Fram farmed out this very important responsibility to a service that handled many of other of the stores displays found in Walmart. From what I could gather, this outfit did it all, from automotive to housewares. 'What did they know about automotive and especially how to launch the newest oil filter in thirty years?

'Wait just a minute! Where was this mighty sales force I had been told about so often?

'Fram had a sales force, didn't they? They were supposed to be managing the displays, weren't they?'

After what I was seeing, I didn't rightly know the answer to that one?

Shame on you Fram! Once again 'you get what you pay for'. Isn't that what you had been telling the American consumer for the last twenty-five years… "You can pay me now, or you can pay me later."

I guess nobody wanted to take me seriously, except the impressionable young Italian immigrant. After all, the both of us didn't seem to have much of a problem figuring out, how to fix this thing.

Oh…, and while we're on that subject. 'Would you like to know when Mr. Barter called me back?' Well, let's put it this way, I finally called his office back some forty-five days after we had talked. And his response…

Neither he, nor his protégé Mr. Steven Price, would even come to the phone and talk with me!

So you see, that had become a complete mystery as well. Because as the story goes, the morning after I got off the phone with Mr. Barter, I was told that he immediately called the west coast and got Mr. Price out of bed, summoning him back from California to put him in charge of the situation. And I mean the whole situation. In December of 95', shortly after my conversation with Barter; Mr. Corey, the President of Fram, was fired. And guess who took his spot? You guessed it, Mr. Price.

On a more personal note. Let me ask, 'are you in the habit of being slow with a pat on the back to another deserving person?'

Well don't be! First off..., it's not nice. Second, if you're in business, it'll prove costly later. Case in point. I gave Mr. Skog my deepest heartfelt congratulations for the spectacular feat he had performed on the Double Guard box and graphics, the last time I had seen him in Rhode Island. Now keep in mind, it had to have been at least six months since I had seen the man. His work in my critical view, was nothing short of superlative and I let him know that, both barrels.

Around late October of 95' these unsolicited packages from Federal Express started showing up at my doorstep one day, and from guess who? Mr. Skog! I received a full accompaniment of handouts, and posters. The most beautiful mechanic mats you ever laid eyes on and a marketing video which included the commercial. Soon a cardboard display stand followed, designed to be placed in the front of the store, meant for holding samples of the product. And the list went on.

Thank God, I befriended this man, because it had paid off in spades! As it turned out, he along with Jackie, were the only two people ever to send me any evidence that I had been a member of the team. It never came from the marketing team nor anyone else!

And another salute goes out to Karen Borger. Remember the lady in charge of the commercial? I'd put that spot up against anyone's, it was Cleo material in my mind. Perhaps if the commercial had been played long enough, she woulda been a contender.

And one last thing about the box. The next time you want to send something to an outside agency to get done, and you have good capable people on staff to handle it, well shame on you! Let your own staff members have a go at it first, they'll be up to it.

As the story goes, Mr. Geoffrey Skoog saved the Company a good chunk of change for his work on the box by keeping it in house. Way to go Geoffrey!

Oh..., and I almost forgot... It was worth it all, because in the end, I finally got my stupid hat. You know, the one that those two jackasses were beating to death the marketing strategy meeting!

CHAPTER 19
IT'S... WAIT AND SEE TIME

June of 96', the filter arrives in Pep Boys! Ranked number six in total dollar volume, I'm comforted to know that the giant automotive retailer will give the Double Guard, its rightful place amongst its lineup. Pep Boys in the auto trade, is referred to as a "red front" store, meaning they are strictly an automotive retailer.

Nothing against Walmart and it's 2000 stores, but Walmart is in another class, they're a mass merchant. It just stands to reason, there had to be vast differences between their respective approaches to this business. Right? At least I would have thought so, wouldn't you?

To say the least, Pep boys is on the cutting edge of the highly competitive automotive aftermarket business, and it's nearly two-billion-dollar revenue stream should be proof enough.

Just so you know, Pep Boys operates some 600 stores and over 5000 service bays and that means that they have over ten times more service bays than anyone else in the business! So please keep that in mind, it will become an important piece to the puzzle later on.

'Was the theft just my imagination?' I doubt it. I had checked it out myself. The theft was so pervasive that it had even worked its way into the hearts of the buyers that frequented Pep Boys!

And once again, I still found myself asking if Fram had a sales force in place, because their assurances meant little or nothing to me by now. So, after several occasions of pretending that I was a prospective Double Guard customer, I had arrived at a very different conclusion. As it turns out, the responses offered while visiting a few Pep Boys in my area, quickly saddened my heart. The sales people didn't have a clue as to what the heck they were selling.

Just like in Walmart, the product came in on a Monday, and found its way onto the shelves by Tuesday. And as God is my witness, by some miracle, the filter began to sell immediately, all by itself with no apparent support!

Now, I could only have wished that I owned a patent on that one! The formula for an inanimate object that's able to grab the consumer's wallet and sell itself! I was told stuff by the sales people at Pep Boys, that wasn't fit to print regarding the lack of support they got from Allied Automotive.

I was getting another one of those flashbacks, as I stared into the clerk's face.

The Atlanta Grand Nationals, you know, the National Hot Rod Association event that Fram sponsors in April, the last eight years running..., that one!

'Well, remember the hat? Remember the two senior field reps at the marketing meeting a year ago, as they made love to that silly hat?'

Like I told you, Fram made me a hat too! And they were giving it away at the 1996 Fram Grand Nationals down in Atlanta that April. They had a huge balloon type filter made in the image and likeness of the Double Guard! They had a plaque of the Double Guard, garnishing the base of the starters Christmas tree! There were posters and banners all down the length of the track, placed in strategic places for the cameras to lock onto. It was awesome! And just imagine, just like the trade show in Vegas, I was supposed to be their invited guest as well. But somehow, they must have forgot about the invite.

Even so, I woulda gone down on my own dime, but I wasn't a part of the team any longer.

'And knowing people the way I do, who could a blamed them? After all, I had blown the bridge, but yet, through sheer incompetence, they continued to slowly but surely destroy my dream.

I sat home and taped The Fram Atlanta Grand Nationals on ESPN one afternoon and you know what I caught? I caught the race car driver they had sponsored for this event. His beautiful long black dragster took on the aura of Double Guard gone missile.

I can remember that he was rather distraught, that he hadn't made it to the qualifying rounds. According to this racer, he might of done better for the team, if only he had gotten more notice that he was going to be sponsored by AlliedSignal for the race. I can recall him saying that he had received about ten days' notice to prepare for such an event, and that it was impossibility as far as he was concerned!

Allied's bloated arrogance, and inattention to detail was beginning to show up now, in the funniest of places.

CHAPTER 20
SURPRISE, SURPRISE…, SURPRISE!

Meantime Patti and I were committed. Maybe we shoulda been committed elsewhere, to an asylum perhaps, but I'm talking about another type of committed. Please allow me to backtrack for a moment here.

After I signed my contract in September of 95', out of sheer jubilation, we had agreed that Patti would take the upcoming year off; meaning the following school year starting in September 1996. It was by far, the greatest gift I could of given her, having her home with the two kids for a full year.

Keep in mind that she filed the paperwork for her sabbatical right after I signed the contract; pre-show, pre-planogram, pre-rollout, in early October of 95'. We both felt that her taking off was a conservative move, she didn't burn any bridges, nothing like telling your boss to take your job and… None of that! Only an idiot with eighteen years of service teaching school would have done something like that! Or somebody who already had the money, and we certainly didn't, unless you call fifty grand the money.

I knew from previous conversations with Kevin, that our projected income in 1996 would more than eclipse anything the both of us had ever earned before. So in May of 96,' I decided to join my wife, entering the world of semi-retirement. And believe me, if you've never tried it at thirty-eight years old, you should!

Of course, we were nervous about the sloppy Roll-Out and the happenings both in Walmart and Pep Boys, but we still trusted that things could only get better, not worse. We were in business with AlliedSignal, remember?

I'm not sure of the exact timing, but they tell me that somewhere around May/June of 1996, the chief engineer, Mr. Anthony Coronia retired. The man who opposed the idea of the Teflon treated oil filter to begin with. The man who vehemently protected the noble concept of "not invented here!" The kind gentleman who had wagered so gallantly against both my patents, was now just a memory!

I'm just throwing that in to illustrate something for which none of us mortals can control, certainly not with any degree of assuredness, it is something called 'timing'.

Oh, my travels would have been so much easier without his earlier intervention. 'Or would they of been?'

I had been waiting patiently to press the issue about my contract and all that I had been subjected to, but as you can see, my initial attempts with Mr. Barter got me nowhere, and it didn't take a rocket scientist to realize that an explanation for "incompetent efforts," wasn't coming anytime soon either. Along those same lines, it didn't appear that first six months that the Company had already blown would ever be returned to me anytime soon either, that was unless I made an issue about that as well.

And please let us be clear about this six-month thing. It wasn't the six months from the time in which I signed the contract. Despite all I had been put through, I wasn't prepared to be that trite! The six months that I was talking about started from the end of November 1995. That's when Kevin told me that the filters would initially start being shipped, and that's exactly when I expected performance!

And there was another thing which prevented me in all good conscience from opening up that can of worms relating to my contract, Dianne! As long as she was on the Company's payroll, I can assure you, if I broached the issue, all hell would of broken out! So, in the spirit of peace, I didn't press the issue the least little bit after Barter had reneged on his promise to help.

'But guess what happened?' As sure as there's a God above, the mighty Signal fired Dianne in July of that summer of '96!

'Dear God, Lord Almighty! 'How was that for timing?'

My only explanation for the whole thing…, it was just my unfortunate fate to of dealt with her.

Now keep in mind she was fired! A fifty-year-old woman pressing up flat against "The Glass Ceiling," in a politically correct world and in a politically correct Company no less! Fired!!!

Silently I began to plan my vindication.

CHAPTER 21
WILL YOU REMEMBER ME IN SEPTEMBER?

It was around September of '96 and I began to call Peter Ross with greater and greater frequency. While the theft still continued unabated in both Walmart and Pep Boys, we rarely discussed it. I could only have guessed that as far as he was concerned, the thefts were a non-event. On the other end of the spectrum, my filter had never made its debut in some of the most obvious of places, like The New Big Kmart for example. The one that Bob Hope keeps telling us about!

I was flying blind now. I knew what it cost them to make a filter. I knew what their profit margins were, and what was required of their vendors to sell the product, but somehow, I couldn't wrangle out of them who was actually selling the product. Suddenly all that stuff had become top secret. All I could do was drop into the local shops and talk with proprietors and walk the aisles of the major retailers that weren't carrying the Double Guard and come up with my own conclusions as to what might be happening.

Though Fram was a featured vendor in Kmart, the Double Guard was nowhere to be found there, and subsequently never would! Nor was the Double Guard to be found in Strauss Discount Auto, a noted retailer in the north east, certainly ranked amongst the top twenty-five. As a matter of fact, 'do you all remember the salesman I had met from Jersey, while at the marketing meeting in April of 95'? You know, one of the salesmen falling all over Grand Nationals hat?'

Now I realize what I'm about to tell you, might sound a tad bit odd, but Fram already did a huge business with Strauss Auto. And for his part, Mr. Taverna with over twenty years' experience working for Fram, had personally serviced that account. The only thing was, he had never been successful in getting this top-ranked auto parts chain to carry my filter.

'Sounds kinda funny, don't it?'

I mean me, a total industry outsider, able to sell Fram an oil filter, and all the while they seemed incapable of selling this same filter themselves to their established customer base!

Nonetheless it's true. And to this day, neither Strauss Auto, nor Kmart has ever carried the Double Guard oil filter line!

It was now the fall of 96', Peter was going to the Show once again in Vegas, and this time, so was Double Guard. It was to be featured as the headliner for AlliedSignal Automotive this time around! Same old story, I wasn't invited. It seemed to me, that the wounds I had inflicted on the marketing team, were still running about as deep as their incompetence. So, I settled for the prospect of him taking a couple of snapshots of their booth for me instead.

To back track a little here… Located on the very last page of Allied's first quarter report to the shareholders for 1996; under Automotive, I'm compelled to quote…

"…net income rose 16% to $72 million from $62 million, as sales grew to $1.5 from $1.4 billion, (this is per quarter folks). Sales increased due to higher volumes of vehicles in Europe equipped with AlliedSignal turbochargers and airbags, and strong sales of the new Fram Double Guard oil filter."

In that same vein, Peter Ross had already assured me that Double Guard was going to be featured in this year's upcoming Annual Report for 1996! My expectations would have been met if my goals had been based solely upon these two watershed events. In my mind, to have your invention featured in a Fortune 38's annual report and then to have it headline the largest trade show in the world was tantamount to wining your own Oscar!

Yet the honeymoon, if you could call it one, was drawing quickly to a close. Little did I realize, that hidden just beneath the jubilant waters of the Company's glowing reports and fanfare, was something quite sinister lurking about.

CHAPTER 22
I'LL MEET YOU AFTER THE SHOW

So, I kept calling…, kept pushing…, until finally I had fought my way back upstream, back to the O'l spawning grounds in Rumford R.I. It was December 12th, 1996 and we had come full circle.

My recall is nothing less than vivid. We were both to have lunch…

Hey! 'Did you ever have something going on in your life that was big enough to compel you to drive eleven or twelve hours just to have lunch with somebody?'

Along the way in Connecticut, I had stopped for a quick something I could eat in the car for breakfast. As soon as the lady at the counter handed me the bag, I suddenly lost all desire to eat. There it was in plain sight, splattered all over the bag, McDonald's had become NASCAR approved. I wasn't exactly sure what that meant. All I really knew, was that only a few weeks ago Peter Ross had told me that somehow that designation had already been offered to Fram first and that if Fram didn't pick it up, McDonald's was next in line. As I pulled my Egg McMuffin out the bag, I threw the bag onto the floor in a crumpled ball, so I wouldn't have to be reminded about, yet another opportunity lost!

I had arrived early and strolled about the foyer, glancing at the Mission and Vision and Values Statements as they hung prominently on the cold thickly painted walls of the austere headquarters. Grabbing a copy of the Fram's phone list, I ran through it quickly just to make sure, before folding it up and storing it safely away in my jacket pocket for future reference. Sure enough, Steven Price's name was on the list now, proof that he had indeed replaced Mr. John Cory, the fallen President of Fram. Hurriedly I scanned the N's looking for her name just in case, though it had been eradicated from the roster, I still couldn't believe it, but it was true! Dianne had become nothing more than just a bad memory.

'Who had taken her place,' I wondered?

Suddenly my eyes peered through the glass security wall, and there it stood. Just like when you were back in high school. The trophy case, strategically placed in the gallery. There to greet every visitor who might happen upon the campus. After a bit of scrutiny, something obvious was missing, albeit perhaps forgotten?

Okay then, it just might have been overlooked! Quite possibly the night janitor had forgotten to stick it in there one lonely night while dusting, but the Double Guard was nowhere to be found amongst the other trophies in the case! There were oil filters, air cleaners, gas filters, spark plugs and wires; a virtual cornucopia of aftermarket products, but no black beauty!

I had a good idea that Pete was doing me a favor by having lunch with me, but not being brought up to his office beforehand began to arouse my suspicions. So, you might imagine after watching him fly through the foyer like a bat out of a bell tower, leather bombers jacket trailing behind, only served to confirm my instincts.

Anyway, it didn't matter… I had to talk with him.

We talked about this year's Show and he informed me that Fram had picked up very few new Double Guard customers at this event, ever so quick to remind me that most of the customers on board had been already cultivated at last years "non-event." So, in reference to that almighty trend line, which is supposed to be forever upward or else, well let's just say it didn't appear to be so upward.

Then we talked about Walmart, and about the theft as well as the returns. Oh, I almost forgot to tell you this! But Mr. Walton and his fellow Walmarter's kicked AlliedSignal out of their 2100 locations! It went something like this. "Oh, it's a good selling product all right, but it's just creating too much havoc for us. So, don't bring the product back here for sale until you put it in tamperproof packaging!!!"

Let me ask you, 'do you think I was vindicated when that occurred?'

Na..., of course not! Pete's stock reply was that "Walmart was still a pain in the ass and that they were a bunch of crybabies and that it was hardly worth all the trouble for Fram to deal with 'em." Yet, according to AlliedSignal's cyphering, they were doing around sixty million dollars a year with those pains in the ass.

By the same token, Walmart had asked Fram to withdraw the product due to inordinate amount of theft and loss of inventory control around the end of October. Again, the year was 1996 this occurred approximately six months after the filter had made its initial debut in the Walmart chain.

Just so you know, and to be redundant... approximately 750,000 thousand Double Guard would be stolen out a Walmart during its initial roll-out. 'How do I know?' Simple. They withheld my royalties a dime a copy for every black beauty that went missing.

We discussed manufacturing as well. Gary at one point told me that the Company had one plant cranked up, three shifts a day making these things. And 'you wanna know something, maybe that was true!'

'Because Peter told me that afternoon over lunch that the Company was making these filters by hand, one at a time!

Dear Jesus! 'What about a putting a little investment into the manufacturing lines? What about all that Economics 101 gibberish, about ramp up time and opportunity costs! They were still making' the filter by hand for God's sake, treating the 2.4 million units like they had sold in last nine months as if they were nothing more than prototypes!

'Why?'

The answer came back to me that day over my burger and fries. "The Company wasn't committed enough to build a manufacturing line yet," as Mr. Ross put it.

Nearly in the same mouthful he offered me a ray of hope, "We're working on getting the NAPA account you know." He didn't have to tell me about number two rated NAPA, I already knew they did a hundred million dollars a year worth of filter sales each year with Wix. And on the que-tee, I was already in the know, that this billion-dollar retailer was in hot pursuit of upgrading their filter lineup as well..., except one for thing was missing for them..., the concept from which to launch out from.

It was quite simple. NAPA carried a silver series and a gold series line of filters already. What was missing, was the platinum line, for which they had no suitable 'new and improved'.

Just figure it out, 'where would a premium Teflon filter fit in?'

Installed sales had come up. If you know me by now, it would have to. And before long, Peter would let me in on a little secret... A secret he would have been much better off keeping to himself.

"…We did a test study out in the mid-west you know. I believe in the Kansas City area, not too long back. We hooked up with this guy who owned 5 Jiffy Lube sites, and I gotta tell you Steve, the results had come back pretty disappointing," as he began to let me in on the dismal results of their field trial.

Immediately I could feel my heart headin' south, as he worked his way through what he must have believed was a plausible explanation for it all. Yet, as much as I tried, I just couldn't accept what I was hearing. No darn it! Not only was it improbable, it was downright impossible!

'What about the previous study which boasted that this product scored an 84% overall acceptance level with the consumer?' I had to wonder. 'Or was that just something that the Company had made up to peddle to their major accounts?' I couldn't be sure, because by this point in our association, I had virtually been reduced to the status of a bag lady when it came down to the Company sharing its ongoing marketing strategy with me.

So, when I had put it out there for him, I had to be extra careful. "Why Pete? I don't understand it?"

"Oh, I don't know exactly what went on, but I did hear that the guy who owns the facilities out there had been against anything to do with additives ever since he was old enough to have an opinion about 'em. All I was told, was that the test hadn't gone very well for ya Steve."

"What exactly do you mean Pete? I don't get it?" As the long-forgotten precepts of Clinical Analysis 101, began racing through my head.

He was gonna tell me more, of that much I was sure. I just had to wait for him to launch into his burger. And as I waited on him, my expensive college education flashed before my eyes! As incredible as it may have seemed, someone in their operation had failed to alert them of this minor glitch. Fram's field test had been skewed from the beginning! At least I had come away from my college education remembering that much, recalling the benefits of conducting a properly run double blind study!

Pausing a moment, he took another bite full, then offered these words of wisdom. "Steve, they're just too busy selling other products, like antifreeze, air fresheners and even stuff like Slick 50 at those places. They must have at least twenty other items to be selling. It's just not worth the hassle for them to be selling another oil filter."

"Hey, wait a minute Pete!" I told him. "These guys are in business to sell one primary thing, an oil change! That's why they are promoting brand recognizable oils like Castrol, Valvoline, Quaker State or Pennzoil. For God's sake Peter, why do you think Pennzoil owns Jiffy Lube anyway?

"We both know that when a consumer drives into a Jiffy lube they do not…, I repeat, do not have a choice of either choosing their brand of oil or their filter. They get a bare bones version of Purolator's Group Seven, made for Heritage Automotive! As a matter of fact, I don't know of a single installed sales operation in the country that offers the consumer a choice, when it comes down to picking an oil filter!

"You mean to tell me that if a customer came into an installed sales site with the proper advertising and support, such as a couple of posters and perhaps a banner or two, that consumer wouldn't opt to strap on the newest offering by the preeminent filter manufacture in the world?! And that would be just the beginning!

"Because, before the customer would ever get out of the bay, that very same consumer would leave knowing they could look forward to enjoying better fuel economy, less engine wear and better performance. All because they made the choice of installing a new Fram Double Guard oil filter!

"Get out of here! People don't drive into these places just to pick up the newest offering in air fresheners and get their anti-freeze checked. Americans love their cars man! Just look at the way they are devouring sport utility's, 4x4's, and sports cars at such an unprecedented rate. These people are especially mindful of their oil and filter combination!

"Hey Pete…, I really don't get it. It seems to me, that I believe in your trademark more than you guys do!"

I just shut my mouth. Apparently, it was all for naught. I hadn't convinced him and if I hadn't tried to do so myself, I wouldn't have believed it. In a nutshell, the way he saw it, the whole darn thing was just too complicated for his marketing team to attempt.

Then out of sheer exasperation, I cried, "What about Prestone?!"

"What about 'em Steve?" came his sedate reply as he played with his fries.

"Well you guys are in the process of acquiring them aren't ya? And they sell anti-freeze and any number of items that can be found in nearly every installed sales site across the country!"

The thought had never even crossed his mind, I'll bet ya. I mean the very reason why Allied Automotive had acquired Prestone was just so that they could expand into the more lucrative consumer products segment of the business and become a powerhouse in that venue. The very same market that my filter was tailor made for.

The invite was there, so was all the infrastructure anyone could of hoped for! They could have hopped on Prestone's coat tails at will and ridden into any installed venue they wanted to. All for one minor detail…, lack of vision!

I also talked heavy-duty as well, and that issue was all but dead. The Company felt that market wasn't worth the effort until the sales from the automotive sector had picked up substantially. So, I guessed all that fighting over my heavy-duty royalty with Dianne had all been for naught. Peter had made it clear in a very nice way, that Allied for all intended purposes, was gonna shelve that aspect of my patent and it would never see the light of day. As of this writing, Fram has held true to their word. No heavy-duty filter has ever rolled off any one of their lines for retail distribution, despite their many incredible connections into that lucrative market as well.

After about an hour and a half, we had just about touched all the bases as far as marketing was concerned. And when our little discussion had concluded I brought up the topic of the theft in Walmart. Right away I could see that it was a sore spot with him.

"Ah… I don't know what those guy's problem over there is. Walmart is just such a pain in the ass to deal with. Believe me, they are a lot more trouble than they are worth. Like I've been telling you over the phone the last couple of times you've asked, the theft has been nil Steve."

"How nil Pete. I'd really like to know!"

"I don't remember exactly, but its small. Maybe one… two percent. Certainly, under two percent," he said rather annoyed.

I didn't want to press him, but I had to. "So, if the theft is so small, then how come they kicked you guys out in less than six months! And it was due to the theft, right!" I said, deciding to make an issue out of it.

"Look it Steve... these guys just can't manage their own inventory system is all…, and they need someone to blame it on. Okay? I just wish we could exit those mass merchant accounts and concentrate our efforts on the specialty retailers. They create a lot less headaches for us."

"So, Pete… When do you think I'll be getting back into Walmart? Double Guard's been kicked out since October and it'll be January in a couple of weeks…"

Right about then, all I could hear was the death rattle for my beloved Double Guard. Not unlike a loving mother, who knows intuitively all there is to know about her baby, I too realized that it would be only a very short while before I'd start to witness the irreversible death of my baby.

As he made his move to get up from the table, signaling we had about finished, I leaned over and made a move of my own, it had been building inside of me for well over a year. As best as I could tell, the Walmart fiasco along with all the other nonsense for which I had endured, pushed me over the edge.

Meeting him head on, I told him that I wasn't satisfied with my contract, and all that had been done to me. The pronouncement caught him off guard as I invariably knew it would. Undoubtedly, he was under the impression that all my objections up until this juncture had been sufficiently aired. I left him no recourse, but to settle back down in his seat and hear me out as he began to ask me, "How so Steve?" giving me this incredulous look, as if I was insane or something.

Look or no look, I forged on and hit him with the weightier aspects of my complaint. And I'd have to say that I hadn't been under way very long, before he rose up from his seat, reminding me of the obvious. That I had signed a contract!

'And you know something?' He was absolutely right in saying so. I have no problem admitting to that minor detail. In fact, I've been told by the best of them, that I did indeed sign a legally binding contract.

But between you and I, that stock objection didn't quite cut it after all I had been put through. I was in no mood then, nor am I of a mind now, to back off my quest for justice, contract or no bogus contract!

So just for kicks, I asked him if the Company was behind my filter.

"Of course, it is! Why?" he asked.

"Oh nothing," I replied. I just didn't see it in the trophy case is all. And I though it rather odd, since my contract has been in force now for almost a year and a half, and everything else you guys make happens to be in there."

His response was not what I wanted to hear, though as you can imagine, fairly standard. "I never really took notice of it before. I…, I don't know why? I'll have to have somebody take care of it, it's not my job.

"Of course, we're' behind it! I have it tattooed under my eyelids, I see it when I go to bed at night."

How sick this thing had become? I had gone full circle and gone straight to hell. Now my energies were to be focused on justice and nothing else. There was nothing left to fix, it was nearly lying there in pieces.

As we made our way to the parking lot outside, the litany which I had begun back at the table, followed us through the parking lot, and all the way back to Farm's headquarters. And it was there, on that cold December afternoon, that I made him a Christmas Promise. I warned him, that for the first time, I was going to reluctantly take my gloves off. I made it clear to him that I was now going to mount a one-man campaign to seek out justice. I told him that in the name of fairness, I was coming at them, and that I felt it best that the entire outfit knew I was coming. And that I had no compunction about going to Larry and beyond this time."

He was scared, but he did his best not to show it. If he had picked up on anything about me, it would have been that I was stickler about keeping promises.

Out there in the parking lot he told me about the new man who had taken Dianne's place, Richard Bjelde; a lawyer. And from what I'd been told, he was the first staff attorney Fram had ever brought on board, since the division's humble beginnings.

"Too bad Rick wasn't on board when you were negotiating your contract, huh Steve?" he offered sheepishly, trying to make light of my plight after the fact. Rick's been with us a while now, and I think he's a pretty good guy for you to talk with. So, if you're that upset Steve, let's go march upstairs to the second floor and meet this guy. Come on, let's go right now. I'm willing to do that much for you."

"Nah. I appreciate the offer Pete, but I'd feel kinda funny barging into this guy's office without a proper introduction. So, if you don't mind, when you go back upstairs, why don't you go and have a little chat with him and bring him up to speed on things. Then have this guy call me. That would be the proper thing to do now, don't you think?"

CHAPTER 23
A CHRISTMAS PROMISE

It took some doing, but it had been arranged, I drove to Rumford for my luncheon date with Mr. Bjelde. It was now January 20th, 1997. 'Remember me saying that I never wanted to study for this stuff ever again?" Well I was about to meet face to face with Fram's new General Counsel and I didn't have the foggiest line on who the man was, not like it really woulda mattered at this point anyway. Besides, I wasn't too good at sizing people up over the phone and there had already been quite a bit of maneuvering done by both sides in preparation for this auspicious meeting.

Initially when I first spoke with him, he wanted to tackle this situation strictly over the phone. He was of the mind that it could be accomplished in fifteen minutes or less. Of course, me being a face to face player, I declined. Telling him that I would need at least two hours in person.

To which he replied, "That he'd never given anybody two hours' time, ever before in his life, and that he wasn't about to start with me."

I had been glued to the trophy case, my heart sick. Above it, read a cheery banner, "AlliedSignal welcomes Prestone Products Company." It seemed that Allied Automotive had just acquired the premiere anti-freeze maker from Darien, Connecticut for a cool $550 million. The ink wasn't even dry on the contract, and yet all their stuff was in there, already sittin' in the case.

Angrily, I mused to myself, 'Peter must not of heard a damn word I said...' The case was still conspicuously absent of any sign of The Double Guard!

I began to berate myself, 'you see what happens when you give something like this away so cheap..., there can be no respect! It didn't take much for me to realize that Prestone could be our stepping stone into the installed sales market! They sell their anti-freeze just about everywhere, including supermarkets.' But I didn't have supermarkets on my mind, just the 1,500 Jiffy Lube sites, and the 400 new Sears locations they just added to their already prominent roster of locations!

Suddenly, the glass security doors burst wide open. For all I knew, I was about to get run over!

He had a European flare; sophisticated, sporting a pair of tortoise shell spectacles with his face neatly framed within a handsome beard.

The look... Well accented with a colorful yellow silk scarf to ward off the New England cold, wrapped in an ankle length blue cashmere coat.

He was pretty all right, but I wasn't up here for a fashion show... And so it went.

First order of business, where to eat, as he climbed aboard my black Chevy Suburban. Though I had traded up from the Dodge Caravan I used to drive, it was still a far cry from the Kenworth I'd been dreaming about. We small talked in the car, I was good at that. Small talk had been instrumental in filling in the many questions left unanswered thus far, so I fired up the conversation pit, as we drove along.

He had previously worked for a major law firm out of the Windy City, and by every indication he was as well heeled, as he was schooled. After doing a several year stint over in Germany for a large communications conglomerate, he was fresh back in the States when I got him. I could only marvel at the coincidence, him landing on Dianne Newman's old square.

We pulled into his favorite restaurant, but they were closed. I supposed that he was 'a show me' sort of guy, 'cause he got out of my car and walked nearly around the entire perimeter of the restaurant before he got the message that they were really closed on Mondays.

We then drove down the road a piece and landed at a pizza joint, but it wasn't quite up to his standards, so we shoved off once again, landing at our third eatery. Thank God it was a place we could finally sit down and talk. I couldn't help but remark to myself, 'he had already mentioned that he was only gonna give me an hour and fifteen and we had just eaten up nearly half an hour of that time, trying to satisfy his dining requirements.

As always, when you go to lunch with these types, eating is usually the main priority on their agenda, not the fact that I had driven five and a half hours one way to meet with them.

While his food was on order, I jumped into my treatise, not about to let another unproductive moment get by us. I had already decided to skip lunch, which had already kinda thrown him for a loop, but there was entirely too much for me to tell him about, and not enough time for all that chewin' and swallowing!

As I picked up the tempo, he reached for his thin leather satchel and pulled out a yellow pad and began to write. In the middle of his writing, I grabbed his hand, just in time to meet his astonished gaze. "Rick, I know you're a lawyer, and I realize that you're supposed to take notes, but I want to ask you to do me a favor…"

Half offended and half alarmed that I had the nerve to invade his space, he asked, "And what's that?!"

"If you don't mind, I got a heck of a lot of ground to cover here, and I'd appreciate it, if you could just sit back, enjoy your lunch and listen to what I have to say."

"Really," came his stunned reply.

"Yes…, really. Let me ask you something, do you have a file on my case?"

"Ah…, ah…, no," he said, not fathoming the depth of my query.

"I didn't think so. So, this is what I'd like to propose, if you don't mind. You just listen. Ah…, you can write if you really have to, but after this is all over today, I'm gonna go home and prepare you a timeline of the events. It's just that I don't see any need for us doing it twice. 'Cause, let me tell you something for certain, I have a file!"

With that, he put down his pen and laid it on the pad, giving me an impish smile. "Okay, if you want to do all the work, I'm all ears. So, what do ya have to say?"

After the conclusion of our little two and half hour session that afternoon I walked out feeling somewhat relieved. Without a moment to spare, I had somehow managed to put all the gory details into perspective for this now overwhelmed attorney. Suddenly, his appearance didn't appear as crisp as when we had first bumped into each other in the lobby. I'll be the first one to admit it, but I did throw a bomb at him, as I discussed the failed marketing plan regarding "Reasonable Efforts", and I most certainly got my licks in, concerning the Company's unethical tactics and the games the hire-ups had allowed Dianne to play with my contract. As for the finale, I let Mr. Bjelde know that the Company had been holding a percentage of my royalties back ever since the theft problem in Walmart had exploded.

Now I wouldn't want to be accused of being melodramatic here, but I'd call getting kicked out of Walmart due to the clamor of one's customer base, driven to the brink of stealing, an explosion of sorts. 'Now wouldn't you?'

With all that to digest, Mr. Bjelde made me a flat out promise that he would certainly take a good hard look at all which I had presented him, with an open mind of course. Additionally, he looked forward to whatever I could provide him that might substantiate my claims.

'Yes,' I reassured myself, 'I was more than satisfied with the outcome of our exchange, looking forward with great anticipation for him to handle my circumstances honorably and equitably.

Now I want you to be mindful of something here. As we sat there that day, Fram had not brought the Double Guard back into Walmart as of yet, and I was undoubtedly going to be out any of those potential sales for at least a quarter, if not two! So just keep this in mind, because no one from the Company was offering to make me whole concerning that score either! And you know something, I could have forced myself to have lived with that fact, that's if the rest of the machine had been up and running. But of course, it wasn't!!!

Installed sales was a joke, and at least to my way of thinking, for all intentions had already gone the way of Heavy-duty. "Shelved!" Yet another market never to be tapped! From what I could tell, my filter was only being offered in possibly five separate chain operations, and not the hundreds of separate chains promised me from the onset!!!

Not for a moment did I pretend to be playing lawyer with this guy, as I laid out my case before him. Heck, if I wanted to play that game, rest assured I woulda become one of them for real.

So, this is what I did. On February 6th, I sent him a cover letter and a twelve-page type written timeline with sixteen corroborating exhibits; accompanied the pertinent documentation. Let me tell you something! I guarantee that it if anything at all, it was a concise presentation of the facts. But that game would only hold true, if he had an open mind. Conversely, if he didn't, well then, even the most mediocre lawyer is capable of disavowing any set of facts, no matter how immutable the truth presented might be.

Let's see how he handled my plea for justice, corporate style

CHAPTER 24
NOTHING HAPPENS BY CHANCE

I can remember preparing what would amount to be the beginnings of a law brief for this man. My mind was going in a million directions, as I sifted through the various piles of documentation which still commandeered my furnace room. It would take me at least the next few hours, but I was determined to organize this material in a systematic fashion. I had to! My very future was going to depend upon this precious mess of a paper trail. And let's face it, I was on to bigger game now, and it may as well be in order.

———————————

During the clean-up effort, my mind slipped back to this past fall. I had been fishing the beach early one Sunday morning, long before the dawn broke. It was striper season of course, and thankfully, the sand eels were abundant in a magical place where the waves lap onto the beach…, better known as the wash.

It had to of been November, I can remember that the thin cotton gloves were hardly a match for the stinging cold of the black dawn. I couldn't wait for the sun to come up, so I could at least warm my already stinging fingers.

This day there were no waves to contend with, but the tide was in heavy, so wading the bar was out of the question. And that was okay too, because just before that faintest hit of pink light filled the sky, they started boiling all over the place like trout in a mill pond. Just as the majestic light started to fill the sky, you know…, that kinda light which only God could have manufactured, the fish began to hit my imitation rubber eel. If you had any designs on catching these fish, you better know how to match the hatch, or your efforts would truly be in vain.

It was getting to be near quittin' time, and the fish were beginning to shut off with the presence of the rising sun. Maybe it was eight o'clock and I was about ready to head for church when these two guys came down the stairs and invaded my private haunt.

Surely, it was time go now! But I couldn't. I'm telling ya, these two guys were so lost. I just had to stay awhile longer and watch. First off, they were both so heavily overdressed, it was comical as they rolled down the stairs looking like a couple of lost Michelin Tire Guys. They were wearing these brand new gleaming white boots that came up to their shins, not much protection against a cold pounding ocean, and those white latex gloves…, a look straight out of a Three Mile Island nuclear cleanup. But here's the part that really got me. The tall one was barking out orders to the short one as they carried their oversized poles and their glistening sanitized five-gallon buckets onto the beach. For a moment there, I feared it might be Rodney Dangerfield and his caddie doing a shoot on the Mantoloking beachfront.

I kept on a fishing, and the fish kept on hittin', so I kept on unhooking them, throwing them one by one, back into the sea. Meanwhile, the taller one of the two, like a brazen gull, kept creeping his way towards me. To the point, if he had come any closer, he would have pushed me out of my little spot. I'm telling ya, nobody was on the beach that morning except for us three, and he was making his way on top of me!

Apparently, his oversized plug meant for catching the big one wasn't doing the trick for him and apparently, my catching ability was looking more and more like I had an eighth-degree black belt. So, by the time he was atop of me, there was little doubt that he barely knew what end of the pole to cast.

'Darn this guy was obnoxious,' thinking, as he violated my space. In less than five minutes time, he had managed to brake nearly every rule of surf fishing etiquette.

'Who was this joker anyway? And what right did he have fishing in front of these million-dollar oceanfront's, putting a crimp on this master's session?' I wondered.

At that very moment, I had a choice to exercise. Love the poor fool and teach him a trick or two, so that he might experience the joy of hooking up or curse him under my breath and leave 'em flat like any self-respecting stripe bass fisherman would have done.

I chose to love him. It comes natural for me; I love to teach. And I guess I'll have to admit, I'm a sucker for a poor face as well.

'You wanna know who that poor slob was?' That pushy 'so and so' from North Jersey, who came down this morning just to invade my privacy…

Back over the dune a ways, was a splendid row of homes on the Bayfront, and just like the Oceanfront's, they start off at around a million bucks. Remember, that's mid 90's money. Today it can be well past the several million-dollar mark.

And all that real estate does, day in and day out, is go up in value. Mr. Pushy, just happened to have owned one, though you would have never of guessed it. I knew the house well; it was a real beaut.

They say, teach a man to fish, and you'll make a friend for life. Well we got know each other all right. Me and this auto parts warehouse stocking distributor, referred to in the trade as a WD. He happened to have owned one of the largest business of its kind on the east coast. 'What a coincidence eh?'

And you know what, before I left him that morning, he would have a little something to teach me as well. Like how a one of the largest 'warehouse distributors' goes about selling oil filters for a living.

As the story goes…, one day two Fram field salesmen came a calling on my new friend, who by now insisted that I call him Uncle John. And as you might expect, they offered to take him out to lunch. In the process of turning down their invitation, my new-found friend asked them about The Double Guard oil filter. Now keep in mind that when he had popped the question, the filter hadn't been out, not yet six months. And Uncle John hadn't anticipated, that its inventor was about to become his fishing instructor either.

So…. 'Do you have any idea what these two salesmen told this high volume, high roller, worth wooing?'

When Uncle John asked them about stocking their new filter, "They simply told him not to bother with it, because it was dog, and that the Company wasn't behind it! And surely, it wouldn't be too long before it would fade out." That was their sales pitch to one of the most successful WD's in the business.

I was most appreciative that nothing in life doesn't just happen by chance! And I was especially glad to find out first hand that Fram had a sales team that wasn't backing my product! Because, out of all this madness, I couldn't very well blame myself for all I had been witnessing. The last thing I needed, was to believe that I was either self-deluded or crazy…. Ha.

CHAPTER 25
DO THESE GUY'S EVER RETURN CALLS?

You know it was funny, but these guys never seemed in much of a hurry to call me back. Three full weeks had lapsed before I'd be afforded the chance to catch up with Mr. Bjelde. And believe me, it wasn't for lack of trying on my part either, I must have called him a dozen times. Finally, after all my efforts, I was about to be rewarded with a labored exchange which would last maybe ten minutes.

It was the afternoon of March 3rd, and the fella in whom I had misguidedly placed my faith in, had turned stone cold. Dispatching with formality, I got right to the point. By the same token, he was quick to inform me that he hadn't bothered to read my documents as of yet!

Damn! I just knew that my initial impression of him was correct! And as it would turn out, the striped bass I was accustomed to catching, had warmer blood running through their veins than he did. First thing out of the box went a little something like this, "You signed a contract, and nobody put a gun to your head. You're gonna have to prove duress, and you have a long way to go on that one."

Now I would like to inform you of something. More often than not, this fraternal order of starched shirts, will settle for nothing less than a loaded gun pointed someone's head before they'll even consider an allegation of duress.

'Well, have any of you gone into a business deal lately, where your business partner has literally pointed a loaded gun at your head?'

I didn't think so, unless you're do business regularly with some drug dealer.

He talked to the engineers, he told me.

Well so did I. Except my big mistake, was that I didn't rat them out in while they were bungling my project.

He said, "I shouldn't have been intimidated by a five-foot-tall, fifty-year-old woman…."

I told him he didn't have any idea about for whom he was making excuses. 'But he knew better than that, after all, who was he trying to kid?' I guess he must have forgotten his own words over lunch that day. Perhaps it was in a moment of levity, but I saw it more like in a moment of weakness, as he began to share the obvious with me… "You know, Fram has hired me specifically to clean up the mess which Dianne's created and that the job required nothing less than a full-time lawyer to do it. Right now, my desk is piled so high with her files, I figure it will take me a year or so before I can dig out from under what she's created!"

'And if that was not so? Then why was he so quick to allow me to supply him with a written account?'

Because God only knew where my file was. That's why!

I had to laugh! This fella whom I had already seen through, was now trying to sell me that Dianne, "Had a good track record, and a fine reputation," after telling me otherwise over a salad with boiled ham in it.

I guess he must have forgotten that's why she gotten herself fired last July, and that's why he was sorting through the massive pile on his desk.

Don't think for a single moment that I was about to absolve the Company for all of its many flaws, because I wasn't. And don't for a second, think that I was about to allow them an opportunity to dump it all in Dianne's lap either. There's little doubt that I had ended up being one of her many casualties, and that was certainly apparent. But remember, her performance was nothing more than symptomatic of the entire Company's handling of my situation from start. And besides, as already demonstrated she wasn't acting merely on her own, she had handler's way on up the food chain.

As might of been expected, we went round and round until it had become futile. And it wasn't very long before he volunteered that he had in fact done the worst thing possible with my case besides not reading it. He admitted handing my stuff off to some patent attorney within the Company! Making this whole thing once again a patent issue, something that it never was!

Sure, I was open to discuss the finer aspects of situation to see if this was indeed a patent issue, but much later on down the road. For now, all I was concerned about was that Allied had a contract which clearly stated they would employ "Reasonable Efforts" to market my filter and as far as I was concerned they were in breach of a contract for which *they* had signed! That issue alone, was enough for me to base a law suit upon, allowing me to open up a whole can of worms for them!

He was dancing now! Quick to remind me that I had the benefit of an attorney on my team back then. I guess he said that just to remind me... That in case if I felt so inclined, I could focus the blame Bill Herbert's way.

Just before our chat ended, he left me with a bit of assurance, telling me that "I shouldn't be getting so worked up and taking this call so serious, after all this wasn't a 'fuck you call'."

I wasn't quite sure what he had meant by that illustration, and I figured it couldn't have been one anyway, 'cause I had been the fool who had called him in the first place and not the other way around.'

Oh…, and one last thing. At the end of the month he would be heading off to Germany on some business. I don't know what came over him, perhaps he might a been feeling a little bit guilty after speaking to me that way, so he made me yet another hollow promise.

"I'll lug your papers with me on the plane to Germany and I'll try and read them. I would like to see your point, but I probably won't."

CHAPTER 26
BETRAYAL AT THE BEACH

Any fool could see that Fram's lawyer wasn't about to make my phone ring anytime soon. It was way passed "late," as we were quickly approaching the end of April. Now keep in mind that even after his return from The Rhineland, Fram's lawyer, Rick Bjelde, chose not to acknowledge any of my calls, leaving me no other choice in the matter. Once again, it was time for me to formulate yet another plan and kick it up another notch.

The little burb in which I was so familiar, held a sizable bevy of movers and shakers in the world of the moneyed class. And it just so happened, that nothing much had changed around these parts since my childhood, as the timeless Atlantic Ocean still drew vacationers like flies. And true to form, the miles of private beach still remained mostly the exclusive domain of the landed gentry, who would come and stake solid claim to it for the magical ten weeks out of every year.

As my fate would have it, the Vice President of Human Resources and Communications for AlliedSignal had been drawn to this ambiance himself, summering just a stone's throw from the doorstep of the blue Atlantic. Though I had been aware that he owned a getaway here for years, I never paid much attention to it, that was at least until I had my fill of Mr. Bjelde blowing me off for the past four months!

As God would have it, this Vice President was just a simple phone call away. You see, a lovely lady in my office with whom I was close, had sold Mr. Redlinger this home several years back, and as was often the case, the two of them remained in touch and had become friends. The both of them even belonged to the prestigious Bay Head Yacht Club together, and if I'm not mistaken, I believe she even sponsored his membership into this elite clique of sailors and tennis players. So, as you might of expected, it was nothing at all for her to make the intro.

It happened all so quickly…

One bright morning I walked into the real estate office and asked her if she wouldn't mind doing me a little favor. It was the third Saturday in April of 97'.

Her reply was so predictable, "Sure Steveo! Anything to help, if I can…"

Well, that's about all it took. Before I knew it, I had an appointment to keep with one of Larry's right-hand men. I was all blue jeans that day; shirt, pants and jacket, sporting a favorite pair of beat up leather deck shoes that shoulda been retired a season ago. To top it off, I hadn't shaved yet that morning and I was lookin' rather scruffy, but it was no time to run home and hop in the shower, the meeting was on!

All of a sudden, he was expecting me! Though I bemoaned the fact that I looked like a slob, Tina would have no part of it, spurring me on, insisting that Don was a regular guy. I had no choice, but to go as I was.

When I pulled up in front of his home, he was in his garage, busy puttering on a vintage green Aston Martin rag top. To put it mildly, I was pretty nervous, but thankfully I was no stranger when it came to dealing with people of his lofty social status. My humble real estate career had more than prepared me for moments like this, but that wasn't exactly what was bugging me as I pulled my black Suburban alongside the curb, making my way onto his turf.

I was so nervous, as I grabbed for his hand, realizing he looked exactly like the guy pictured to left of Larry in the Annual Report! This by far was the closest I had ever gotten to the flame and all I could do was pray that I didn't get my little wings singed off for all the trouble!

We small talked a good fifteen minutes or so as I did my best to break the ice, all the while wrestling how I could discreetly bring this unseemly matter up to him. Then there was an interruption, something unforeseen! Another visitor had moseyed up the driveway, I could tell immediately it was a friend of his. I was sensing our genial visit might be short lived and I'd never get my chance! I had to think, and think fast, as the man I recognized to be the owner of Western Termite Corporation strolled up the pebbled drive.

Before the gentleman reached us, I blurted out, "Look Mr. Redlinger, I know it's the week-end and I'm kinda barging in here, but there is something of great importance I must share with you. It has to do with the Double Guard oil filter and your Company. I have to tell you about what's been going on, and I really need your help! If you don't mind sir, take as long as you need with your friend, and I'll just wait around the corner until you're through, if you don't mind?"

He didn't need much help to figure out my intensity, so without skipping a beat, he kindly introduced me to his friend as, "The nice young man affiliated with his Company, the inventor of our new Double Guard oil filter line;" thereby allowing me an opportunity for a graceful exit.

Please permit me this small illustration which might serve to demonstrate just how vast a difference there was between our two worlds. Immediately their conversation centered around a planned golf outing down in Augusta, Georgia sometime the following week. Tiger Woods had just picked up his first green jacket there in the P G A Masters and the civilized world was still reeling from Tiger-Mania. It sure as heck didn't take a genius to figure out that only the most privileged of the faithful, could ever hope to play that course on the heels of such an epic event.

Once that piece of business had been tended to, the talk quickly turned to the car, and where his friend, the pest control magnate might find one just like it. This car, just like the high-profile golf outing carried its own mystique as well. It would require a trip to a private loft in a trendy section of the East Village of New York City if the gentleman had any desire to preview the vintage autos for himself.

Anyway, I had caught all this, in the time in which it took me to turn around and walk down the driveway. 'He was entitled to his life,' I mused, 'and I was certainly entitled to mine!' All I had to do was figure out how I was going to break all of this to him.

It wasn't long before I found myself back in the garage once again. He was all ears this time, as I began to recount the low points of my relationship with his beloved Company. As my tale of woe unfolded, I couldn't help but marvel that I was in fact able to approach this incredibly powerful officer of one of the largest companies on the face of the earth. To say the least, I was truly in awe of the moment and how such an important man like him thought it nothing to put me at ease during such a difficult moment. If I was ever blowing the bridge for the second time, now would certainly qualify as that moment! My presentation was flawless as it flowed out of me like a river in a springtime rain, as I proceeded to rattle off the names, dates and players. Nothing was spared! Everything was fodder this time!

Never for a single moment did I take my eyes off the power this man wielded within the Company either, as I willingly placed my fate directly into his care. I had decided from the moment I laid eyes on him that I was going to do no less than to entrust him with the truth.

'After all, I had finally made it… I was talking to the right man, wasn't I?!' I case you need it spelled out, this guy was the Head of Human Resources for the entire shootin' match!

Sitting there cross legged on the garage floor, I dug deep as our eyes occasionally met as he bent over polishing the little gem. As I laid my heart open, I would occasionally pull my hand through the little waves of white beach sand gathered about the floor. 'Surely, I must of hit a vein of gold,' I thought, as my heart unfolded before this mighty company man. The moment left me truly awed!

I filled his head with Dianne and Peter; Barter and Price. I let him know how Bjelde had treated me like a piece of discarded trash, making no attempt to gloss over his unprofessionalism towards me.

For the first time ever, I exposed the engineers and their buffoonery during the birthing process. On the other end of the spectrum, I wasn't the least bit bashful, as I exalted Kevin and all he had been to the Company and project. Even going so far as to suggest they hunt him down and bring him back as the new President of Fram.

From time to time, while in the midst of all that puttering on the Austin, he would just stop dead. He'd put all that brushing and rubbing aside and cock his head towards the floor, and stare at me like a baffled hound dog at a raccoon. Most of the time, all he could get off would be a labored, "Would you mind repeating that one again Steve?"

I hit him hard on the ethics thing, figuring if anything, that was his area of expertise, personnel and communications. For God's sake man…! I had the highest ethics officer in the entire Company corralled in his vacation home's garage! Now just think of that one for a moment!

And this day I wasn't bashful about the area of "Best Efforts" and specific performance either, giving that area nearly as much weight. Unfortunately, over the course of our little soirée, it had become more than apparent that he wasn't the slightest bit aquatinted with this filter, making me wonder. As always, these people were always making me wonder.

'And who would have known better?' There he was, in his tidy beach house garage, polishing a collector's automobile, most certainly a tribute afforded him by his position within the Company, but as to my filter? Well, he was drawing somewhat of a blank!

You would of thought that since my filter had been the featured achievement for the Automotive Division that year, displayed in the middle of page fifteen of the Company's Annual Report would have given him an edge, but it didn't. And I guess, just to add insult to injury, there was a top of the line Beamer in the drive as well, sitting next to a new Mercedes and I'll bet you the farm that a Double Guard wasn't found amongst them! Out of sheer exasperation I have to quote from the 96' Annual Report:

"In 1996, the new Fram Double Guard premium oil filter was introduced in North America and has since sold more than 2.4 Million units through such outlets as Walmart, Chief auto Parts, Track Auto and Pep boys."

This was all done of course with a beautiful rendering of the filter and the box, the only illustration to grace that page. In no uncertain terms, I got across to him, that for each and every day that this project languished, the Company would be losing an incredible sum of money, and in turn, so would I!

Well let me tell you something, that certainly got his attention in a hurry! A guy with, I don't know how many umpteen stock options just waiting to be exercised at the most profitable opportunity.

I was talking money now… And he knew the score on that one far better than I could of imagined, his handsome net worth was surely proof enough for that argument.

"Steve," putting his arm around my shoulder as we reached the end of his driveway, "This is about money. Making lots of money. It's about the both of us making money and of course you being treated fairly along the way too, you know."

In a moment of deadly seriousness, I shared this little insight with him… I could only hope that it would register with him, because so far it hadn't worked too well on the rest of the crew. "Mr. Redlinger, you are correct sir. This is about money. It's about me being able to provide for myself and for my family's future. You are absolutely correct sir; it has always been about the money. And may I add something else sir?"

"Sure," he said, sporting a big smile, as I stared up into his big friendly face.

"I don't want to make an issue out of it at this time, but Mr. Redlinger, your Company has been holding back on a portion of my royalties since the second quarter of 96' sir."

"What?!!! What do you mean Steve?"

"Oh, we can get into that one later sir. It has to do with all the filter thefts which have been occurring at Walmart," I offered carefully, not wanting to overload this good man's plate. You know Mr. Redlinger, Allied' has had to repackage this filter in the theft-proof packaging for sale in Walmart to combat all the theft and pilfering which has been going on, or else the filter would no longer be welcomed for sale there again. "Did you know that sir?"

"As a matter of fact, Steve, I'm hearing of this for the very first time! he offered completely baffled.

My heart just sank then, and I hated myself for being so right, but it was true. My filter was floating adrift, in obscurity, amongst the confines of the great behemoth. I had to do something to get someone's attention, and I was now beyond desperate!

"Not for anything sir, but I'm telling you that I have been deeper inside of your Company than any paid consultant you'd ever hope to find… And all I can tell you sir, is that your Company, at least from what I've experienced, is cancerous!

"At this point, I want nothing more than to be able to show you how to go about cutting it out. I want to settle our differences privately, because I certainly don't want to write a book about all that I've witnessed so far, and believe me, I could. And by the same token sir, I certainly don't want to get any lawyers involved either."

With that, he jumped in. "Steve I'll make sure you get a fair hearing on all of this…, you can trust me. And as for the lawyers! Well, I can assure you that we really don't want to get them involved either, it'll end up just costing the both of us a lot of money.

"So, this is what I'd like for you to do for me. You have just told me so much that I can't possibly keep all of it straight. So, if you wouldn't mind, would you please jot your thoughts down for me. I don't even care if its handwritten on a piece of scrap paper, so long as I can have something in front of me to look at."

"I be glad to do that for you sir. I'll certainly do that for you and I can assure it won't be done on scrap paper either, it'll be typed. I want to do this right.

"I really appreciate all you've done for me. I'll do my utmost to get it to you by next week.

"Where should I send it?

"Should I send it to your office in Morristown? I'll be more than happy to do it that way."

"No…, no! That won't be necessary at all Steve! I'm here nearly every weekend. Why don't you just call the house and drop it on by when you're done. That'll be just fine."

Just so you know, as an upcoming retirement present to self, Mr. Redlinger would move out of this modest beach house located across the street from the blue Atlantic. He's since moved on to much better digs. Today, Mr. R's beach house is more of a small mansion, a little something he had custom built. It's directly on the beach this time, and it's resale value clocks in somewhere around 10 million bucks. I told you that land values in these parts do nothing but appreciate.

CHAPTER 27
IT'S A MATTER OF TRUST

I couldn't wait to get home and call Kevin, 'and why wouldn't I?'
Ring, ring… "Hello…
"Hey Kev! Boy have I got something to tell you! Do you have a minute?!"
"Yeah sure Stevie! How goes the battle?"

As I made mention earlier, Kevin and I still kept in touch, we had become fast friends. He still had his ear on the railroad track and would discretely feed me things he could trust me with from time to time. And for my part, I was out there alone now, armed with a machete, blazing my own trail. He knew darn well I was commin' at em'; just like he also knew that my struggle would be an incredible upstream paddle that would last until whenever. And at this point, neither one of us had any idea how long whenever meant.

"Guess who I just got done meeting with?"
"Oh, this ought to be good," he said sarcastically. Who?"
"Redlinger," I said.

There was total silence, then… "Don Redlinger! Get outa here!" tangled up in his own disbelief he began sputtering, lost for words.

"Kevin! he only lives a couple of miles from my house. I must have surfed and fished at his beach a hundred times."

"So, what's that supposed to mean! I only worked for the Company for thirteen years and I have never even seen the guy! You know something, you really are amazing! So, tell me, how'd you pull this one off!

"Stevie…, honestly man, you just don't have any idea how powerful that guy is."

"Relax Kevin would you! I live in a place that's crawling with ten cent millionaires. I've sold houses to guys like him. What's the big deal anyway?"

"You really don't get it do you man? For all I know, he and Larry might have adjoining offices," he said.

"Now you're talkin', 'cause the way I'm being treated I hope they do."

Let me tell you something Kevin, if this guy bombs out on me, Larry's going to be next the one on my hit parade. Because if the Company doesn't turn this thing around now Kev, it'll all be over, but the cryin'. They're really wetting the bed on this one, you know."

"Your right, you have no other choice but to go for it. I guess if I was in your shoes I'd be doing' the same thing.

"Hey, looking on the bright side. If you've tapped this guy, you could very well be on your way my good man, and you might not have to go to Larry. 'Cause let me tell you something right now Stevie, you're not going to be able to reach Larry as easily as you just reached that guy.

Believe me, that's going to be quite another story."
"Yea I know.
"So, have you ever met him? I mean Redlinger," trying to fix a line on the top gun.
"Well personally no. But I've run into him once at a Company function. I think he might vaguely know who I am."

"Good."

"So why is that? What the heck did you do now!"

"Oh nothing." I didn't have to see his face; I could tell he was smiling over the phone. I loved Kevin.

"I just told him that if Allied wanted to turn the Fram Division around, he should bring you back immediately and make you the President of the Division, is all."

"You what! You're damn madman! Do you know that?!"

"Not really Kev. You're up for the job. You could run that division a lot better than it's now being run. Anyway, quit arguing with me. I was just handing out a good lead to the head of personnel is all. And you know what?"

"No, I don't," came his befuddled reply.

"What I told him about you today, I'm gonna put in writing with the rest of the stuff I'm gonna give to him next week..., just so he won't forget.

"All I can say to you Kev, is that I sure hope he takes me seriously."

"So, do I Buddy. So, do I!"

That following weekend, just like I had promised, I visited with Mr. Redlinger at the shore house, it was sometime after lunch. When he came to the phone he told me that I'd have to make it fast, because he had a tee time to keep and a house full of guests. But if I could swing by in the next fifteen minutes or so, he'd be glad to take my papers.

There went flying out the window any fantasy I might of had about sitting on his front porch while sipping pink lemonade, going over my papers. I was in a hurry to get the ball rollin', so for the sake of expedience, I placed my total trust into his care. I was going to sacrifice any would-be review session and place my very real complaint into his total charge, leaving it completely up to him to do the right thing without the benefit of my personal involvement.

As I pulled up to the curb, the back deck was filled with some serious cocktailer's. I could feel their eyes, as they glared at me over the rail..., rocks glasses in hand. As I reached for the satchel of papers, my only guess was that the golf course that they were about to tackle must have required a bit of lubrication beforehand.

I got out of my car and greeted Redlinger on the stones, and handed him a legal pouch, containing my best shot at justice.

As he received it from my outstretched hand, I thanked him once again for getting involved. For his part, he left me with, "I'll call you, once I've gone over this. Thanks for all that you've done, Steve."

I was working myself up to the point of frenetic. It was now Memorial Weekend and I hadn't heard a word back from Mr. Redlinger as of yet. He had been in possession of my papers now for nearly a month!

Now I want you to realize something, when we first had spoken in the garage, he told me that he would have accepted my complaint on the back of a cocktail napkin. Yet, true to form, I decided to do a little better than that. So, I wrote him a personal letter of thanks, as well as another letter extolling the performance of Kevin Gill. Then there was a five-page transcript, highlighting the shoddy performance I had received at the hands of Fram's General Counsel, Richard Bjelde. Then there was another four-page document I referred to as the "Marketing Plan Overview," detailing the marketing fiasco in the making.

At this point I have to make something crystal clear to all of you reading this. AlliedSignal did not give a tinker's damn about my ethics charges. They were non-existent as far as they were concerned!

'Do you read me?!'

Yet, I still couldn't allow myself to walk away from that allegation, not by any stretch. But what I did however, was to begin playing the game by their rules. Which was to cry with an exceedingly loud voice about "Best Efforts" and the specific failure to perform from a marking aspect!

Then the last document to be entrusted into his care, was the twelve-page time line with the sixteen corroborating exhibits attached. These exhibits were a compilation of both Company documents as well as that of my own, which had been generated through our business association.

And to think I had delivered all this to him in a timely and professional manner, requiring only a one-week turnaround! But what he hadn't realized, was that I had painstakingly gone over every detail to the extent that I had even sought out the counsel of Bill Herbert at the cost of a grand…, doubly insuring that what he was about to receive was the best it could be. I had gone just short of having Bill send it out himself! And to think, I did all this in a week! And of course, I left my attorney out of it, just like Redlinger had suggested that I do.

'So, I guess you wanna know what happened?'

No phone call, no nothing, except a very thin letter which had arrived, dated May 20,1997, signed John Donofrio; Associate General Counsel and Chief Intellectual Property Counsel. I can't resist, I just have to quote you from this letter…

Dear Mr. Moor:

Thank you for the recent communication you sent to Mr. Don Redlinger and all the materials attached to that letter. I am the Chief Intellectual Property Counsel for AlliedSignal and thus, Mr. Redlinger passed the materials you sent on to me for investigation.

"I have reviewed all of your materials you sent to Mr. Redlinger at some length and talked with Rick Bjelde and others here at AlliedSignal concerning the issues that you raised. I also reviewed the time line that you prepared. After careful study we have concluded that, for the reasons outlined below, the agreement between you and AlliedSignal was fair, and arm's length transaction. We will of course, abide by the terms of the agreement but will not renegotiate the terms of the agreement or give you any additional compensation.

*Specifically, by your own account you approached AlliedSignal in early 1994 and sent AlliedSignal a copy of your patent. Over approximately the next eighteen months **you worked sporadically** with various AlliedSignal employees in an attempt to interest AlliedSignal in your patent. Nevertheless, AlliedSignal entered into a licensing agreement with you that provided for an up-front payment and an ongoing royalty. AlliedSignal certainly doesn't owe you anything more than what is provided for in the license agreement.*

We are sorry in retrospect you are not satisfied with the terms of the licensing agreement. However, the written record of what transpired demonstrates that there was no "duress" when you entered into that agreement, as you state in your letter to Mr. Redlinger."

I'm of course still at this very moment lost for words..., well maybe not. There is a little word called trust. An accurate definition of the word goes something like this. "Trust is the resting of mind, on the integrity, veracity, justice, friendship, and sound principals of another person." In this particular case, we could include that to be, persons and or corporation. There was absolutely no hint of that word amongst the ranks at Allied.

Before I get onto the next jewel, I think it's time to introduce two major facts I'd been holding out on you. Please don't lose sight of the fact the Peter Ross, Vice President of Marketing for Fram; Richard Bjelde, General Counsel for Fram; Steven Price, President of Fram; John Barter Senior Vice President AlliedSignal Automotive; Donald Redlinger, Senior Vice President of Personnel, AlliedSignal; and now John Donofrio Associate General Counsel and Chief Intellectual Property Counsel, AlliedSignal; could not have all been blind to a couple of items which still happened to be sticking in my craw.

Let's start off with this one...

"The Wall Street Journal, July 10th, 1996; front page under the "What's News" section, the fifth featured story read as follows:

"An AlliedSignal Internal memo from the chairman describes a "serious issue in cash flow" and exhorts top managers to improve matters."

Then continuing on page C 1:

"The Money and Investing" page the article continues:

"Conglomerate bosses from Harold Genteen of ITT to Jack Welch of GE have a long history of tirelessly exhorting their division managers to post better and better results.

But a recent example of the genre raises questions about current business conditions at AlliedSignal, the aerospace-automotive-engineered materials conglomerate in Morristown N.J.

"We have a serious issue in cash flow and need your immediate attention and focus,'" AlliedSignal Chairman Lawrence Bossidy **wrote to his unit general managers and sector presidents** in a June 13 internal memo obtained by this newspaper." The one-page memo concluded:

"Cash flow is a critical issue for the Company. Not only is it the fuel for our growth but is an indication of operational efficiency. Our second-quarter cash flow, coupled with the results of the first quarter, **may cause the analysts who follow AlliedSignal to question our performance... Please make cash flow a priority."**

Of course, I'm not a true insider, but I want you all to know something. The marketing funds for the Double Guard mysteriously came to a screeching halt, right about the time of this memo's release! No matter what, the old adage held true whether Bossidy wanted to change the rules to suit his particularly fickle needs of the moment or not. 'You gotta spend money to make money!'

So, there you have it! The unit general managers including sector presidents were told to cut back any unnecessary cash drain in an effort to please the ever-vigilant street watchers. And one other point of interest.

'How thoughtful for someone at the 'Signal to leak this to the Journal! Don't get me wrong, I'm eternally thankful! Because if it hadn't been for that article, I'd be out the only rational explanation I could proffer for the wholesale gutting of the Double Guard marketing campaign!

The marketing funds had been cut off before the filter had been out on the market a full quarter! At the point in which I had contacted Redlinger, ten months long months had already lapsed passed since the marketing funds for this BILLION-DOLLAR BABY had been cut off. …And merely, because Larry got a little nervous about his cash flow!

Hey you guys! I'm speaking to the thirty or forty of you at the top of the food chain over at Allied, and specifically, you six I just mentioned. Show me what you mean by "Reasonable Efforts," for the biggest and best oil filter manufacture in the world!

Oh, and one last point, just so you don't think that I'm being hardheaded or inflexible.

Say my marketing funds got cut off cold, which they did. 'So how come they never got turned back on when things turned around for Allied the following quarter?

'I was just wondering.'

'So, what got cut off you might wonder?'

The fabulous commercial which happened to be featured during the Yankee's home games in the Metro N.Y. area…, all had been cut off.

'And you know what?'

The Yank's went on that season to win their division, then went on to become the World Series Champs! It's funny, but I can somehow remember being promised that the commercial would be featured during such an event as the World Series, Super Bowl or NBA Playoffs. Oh well…

Then there were the radio spots, of which I can only say I had been told about. It appears they hadn't even been around quite long enough for this radio fanatic to hear one personally!

'And what about the huge two-story inflatable oil filter made in the image and likeness of the Double Guard, I saw featured at some of the NHRA drag races on TV?'

It had been deflated and most likely abandoned in a disheveled heap, left somewhere to dry rot, never to be seen on the racing circuit again.

The print adds which I followed diligently, had suddenly all disappeared as well. And while I'm on that subject, let's focus in on the print ads for just a moment, shall we? I never saw any of the beautiful full page adds appear in Car and Driver, Road and Track or any of the heavy muscle car magazines which had been promised me.

'But you know where I saw them?'

Certainly not where you would think they should of been featured. I only caught them in Outdoor Life and The Handyman! They occurred ever so briefly, almost like a rare cactus blooming in the dessert. The print ad campaign lasted for two consecutive issues, then no more.

Now I don't have anything against those publications, but you've got to ask yourself, 'is that where your gonna spend your advertising budget, when your trying to launch a brand new automotive product?

'Are those the types of publications that a brand loyal do it yourselfer, or a gear head is going to read?' I didn't think so!

I promised you two things, so hang onto your seat.

Before I let you in on a very well-kept secret, allow me to warn you armchair coaches of something beforehand. Hopefully you were able to read in-between the lines as to how Allied's Chief Patent Attorney had already viewed the whole thing.

So, have fun going to court against the likes of these people. I hoped I was smarter than that, by choosing not to venture it. The chances of obtaining justice were slim to nil in light of their unrepentant attitude. So, call me pessimistic, but I wasn't up for being made wrong, and wasn't about to be dragged through the court system for the next ten or fifteen years of my life either!

'Remember the Walmart theft?'

And believe me, I know for a fact the filters were being switched or stolen from every place they were being sold! So, in the second quarter of 96' I got a little surprise. Without a hint of notice, AlliedSignal started holding back my royalty payments due to me under the contract! I had been penalized for the thefts which had been going on at the retail level. Clearly, a real violation of my contract!

And just for the record, I told Ross about it at our Christmas meeting…, and Bjelde at our new year's opener…, and to Redlinger right at the time the dogwoods came into bloom. And all of it to their faces!!!

'But did that matter?'

Apparently not. That's if you can recall their chief patent lawyers letter to me. "We will of course abide by the terms of the agreement…

CHAPTER 28
ETHICS FROM A SPEEDING CAR

After the letter had arrived from Allied's patent heavy, I was left no choice to but to track down Mr. Redlinger, his betrayal was as blatant as was my naïveté to trust a man of his position. What a fool I was, having entrusted him with my defense and dropping those papers off at his shore house like I did. Looking back, I should have gone over this matter in his Morristown office face to face and page for page.

Well…, I guessed that might not of mattered anyway. If it wasn't in his heart to conduct himself as the Head of Personnel wearing a pair of Bermuda's in his garage, I don't think a suit and a change of venue would have been enough to change the outcome much either.

I began calling his office, wanting to speak with him. And it wasn't my plan to berate, nor chastise him for his barefaced sellout of my soul. No, that wasn't my job. My job was to get him on the phone, that's if he would come, 'cause if you can remember, most of them wouldn't, once we had our first date. If I ever got him on the other end, it would be up to me to choose my next shot based upon what dance step he preferred.

Around seven one evening, near the tail end of May, he called from his cell phone, while racing down the turnpike headin' for home. He was polite but hurried, and I knew it would have to be fast.

"Oh, did you receive the letter from our patent counsel, Steve?"

"Yes sir, I did."

"Very good then. I just thought it best, that he review your file. What you brought to my attention really isn't within the scope of my department," politely giving me the brush off.

"What about the ethics part," I asked, lost for words.

He proceeded to do a good bit of dancing, so I knew not to press him, since I was already onto my next move, up the food chain.

"What about Mr. Bossidy?"

"What about him?" he asked, rhetorically.

"I want to see him about this matter, is all."

"Well…," he said, knowing darn good and well that the deck had already been stacked in his favor. Nevertheless, it was my sworn duty to press onward for the sake of the mission, as if for nothing else!

"You can surely try Steve, and I don't have any problem with that whatsoever. But just keep in mind that he's an extremely busy man!"

"Why don't you just sit down and write him a letter? I know that he reads his mail."

"I understand that sir, but one last thing before I let you go. Is there any such thing as an ethics committee? After all, that is one of the primary reasons why I had sought you out in the first place."

"And why was that Steve?" 'Now for sure I realized that I was up against a real political animal,' as I carefully weighed his every response.

"So perhaps I could get a fair and sound hearing in front of some live bodies, that's why. I'd even be willing to abide by their decision and drop this whole matter if it came down to that. You know Mr. Redlinger, this letter writing stuff is getting me nowhere, if you know what I mean?"

"Hum… I'm sorry Steve. I'll tell you what! Call my office and speak with my secretary Ellie in the morning. Hopefully, she might be able to better-guide you than I can. I know we must have something in place that you might be able to avail yourself of, but it just escapes me now.

"And Steve, call me back and let me know how you're making out, would you? Because I would like to keep our lines of communication open."

The very next morning I reached Ellie and after some rooting around, she was able to refer me an eight hundred number to call. To make a long story short, it was an outside agency, totally independent of AlliedSignal, located in Florida. Apparently, this firm worked in the capacity of liaison for AlliedSignal screening out complaints. Let me explain.

The lady who answered my call, immediately informed me to put my complaint in writing, including as much detail as possible, for which I told her I had already done that. Before too long, I found myself explaining everything all over again to her supervisor and that's when I let him know what I had already done on my own. With that he was left sort of speechless, admitting I had just about taken this matter farther than he could have ever of hoped to!

So out of good conscience and knowing there wasn't a thing he could do for me, he was at least honest enough to offer me the name and phone number of a contact within Allied's Automotive Compliance Department in Southfield, Michigan.

I certainly appreciated his candor, but it was beginning to appear that I would just be heading down another dead-end trail if I followed through with his advice. Surely it didn't require a genius to figure out that I was already operating at a level above any compliance officer in the Company! After all, Mr. Redlinger was one short rung from the top and it was looking like a decision had all but been rendered. So, in an attempt not to beat my head any further against the wall, and eat up any more of the clock, I decided to hold off on making that call.

I opted to make one more attempt at getting to the bottom of the ongoing marketing debacle, before continuing to stir pot any further.

CHAPTER 29
FRAM BRAND MANAGEMENT

I had a lot of stuff kicking 'round inside my head. Simultaneous with the goings on with Redlinger, I was doing my best to meet with somebody from marketing. NASCAR, along with the entire world of motor sport was at long last coming into its own. Racing, was absolutely taking the civilized world by storm and I had to ask myself as I stared at the TV set, 'where in God's name was Fram? And more importantly, where was my filter?' The market was exploding!!!

I had to get to the bottom of the pathetic excuse of *"Reasonable Efforts"* and at this point I was about to stop at nothing. My royalty check amounts had dropped through the basement, and like a tomato on the vine, with no water out in the baking hot sun, was doomed. And you see, I knew it!

Though Peter and I had patched things up between us, I had no further desire to meet with him after our last go 'round in December. It wasn't that I didn't like him, it had nothing to do with something as touchy-feely as that, it was just that the man had lost the fire in his belly. And by the same token, I'm sure he was doing his best to stand clear of me as well, certain that I was on the brink of mounting another campaign.

'And you know what?' By this point I don't think he gave two hoots who I might call, because he finally woke up to the fact that I wasn't about to take all of this lying down.

And you know something, he was right! So, I shot for Mr. Steven Price the President of Fram, figuring he still owed me from the last time. In classic fashion, he wouldn't take my call.

In case I failed to mention this earlier, Redlinger at one point had mentioned that Price was a good man, and that I should give him a call about any marketing concerns I might of had. Though Mr. Price apparently didn't feel I merited a visit, nonetheless through his secretary, he was inclined to kick me down a notch, to a guy named John Ympa, the Senior V.P. of Marketing. As far as I could gather, Mr. Ympa was just another wonder, hired from the outside, who had been brought in to fill Jack McGrath's old job.

I think it's appropriate at this point to explain a couple of things. For instance, why Kevin had left Fram. Naturally, there were several reasons why he parted ways when he did, but one of the motivating factors behind his brash move was that he aspired to leapfrog over Peter Ross and land Jack McGrath's slot as Executive V.P. of Marketing.

But of course, that wasn't to be. Though at least in my mind, he was certainly qualified for the brass ring. However, John Corey, the President of Fram; at the time felt otherwise and turned him down. Kevin, the wonderful thoroughbred that he was, started looking and before very long…, was gone.

Likewise, Peter, who no doubt had been stalking the vacancy of Jack's old job for himself, had been stepped over by a new hire taken from another field as well! Keeping all that in mind, you can easily imagine how a man's fire can get extinguished in pretty short order, around a place like Fram. Anyway, Ympa wouldn't see me either.

'Remember I just got done telling you I wanted to get to the bottom of the failed marketing plan for Fram's Double Guard oil filter project, 'didn't I?'

Admittedly…, by now I had most of the stuffing kicked out a me, but I didn't say that the fire in my belly had been extinguished yet, nor had I lost my incredible ability to read the writing on the walls of Allied!

Ympa's secretary shook me loose and kicked me down to a very nice guy that held the title of Manager of Fram Brand Marketing. As best I could tell, it was a sort of a watered-down version of Kevin's old job. Anyway, I was thankful that the guy was at least brave enough to meet with me. His name was Jeff Bye and I had to hustle him a bit over the phone, to wrangle out luncheon date, but he finally acquiesced, and we met on June 12th of 1997. The simple fact was, I wouldn't hesitate to jump in the car and drive the five to six hours one-way, in hopes of speaking to anyone who'd listen!

And so, once again, I dared let my hopes rise, determined to see my Phoenix rise out of the ashes! No longer would I allow myself to be constrained to wait the normal four to six months to see this fella, this meeting only took only about a month to be arranged!

I hadn't been waiting in the familiar surroundings of the foyer very long before these two young guys came bouncing through the security doors to meet me. You know something, ever since Kevin had left, it seemed quite evident that I was never to pass through the glass doors again and find my way upstairs. That was unless I had a good reason to do so, like I had to use the men's room.

We ended up at a pleasant restaurant, by now that had become the drill every time I came up. It seemed the Company was more than happy to feed me lunch, but not much else worth mentioning. Apparently, Jeff must have felt that it might be to his advantage, if he brought someone else along for Company.

'And you know something?' He was right. Because he had unwittingly afforded me a much better peek under the tent, as I made the acquaintance of Mr. Brian Mcinerney; the new point man for Autolite Spark Plugs. Brian had just been brought in from the outside, to shepherd the spark plug group, drawing his raw talent from a stint at Kraft foods! If I can remember correctly, I think he said that he was in dairy. And if our initial conversation meant anything, this boy who by my recollection was barely a man, seemed to be receiving a good deal of his marching orders from Jeff. A prospect I had already begun to find frightening.

And as for Mr. Bye himself, well he was an outside hire himself, fresh from another non-related industry! Mr. Bye had just come from Stanley Tool Works out of nearby Connecticut, at least he had relocated within relative proximity to his old employer, but that's where the similarities ended. He had come out of hardware to sell oil filters!

I was nothing less than cordial, taking copious mental notes. So please indulge me for a moment, I think it would be beneficial.

I'm a salesman, and I'm convinced, a pretty darn good one at that. However, my expertise is limited to the field of Real Estate sales with an emphasis on residential and light commercial. I also happened to be skilled in the art of technical sales as well but limited for the moment to oil filters. Period. Just because I may know how to sell a house or two, doesn't by virtue allow me to sell Co-op space on New York City's Fifth Avenue. At best, I could only be a trainee! 'Don't ya get it?!!'

Though on the other hand, I'm very familiar with class-eight trucks. But the reality of the matter is, I lack actual selling experience! So once again, limited by experience, I could only be considered as a new trainee; albeit one with a good aptitude perhaps…, but nonetheless a trainee!

Now I find myself sittin' across the table, havin' lunch with these two very nice chaps and all with the best of intentions, I'm sure. But if the truth be known, both of them were utterly devoid of hands on experience for the positions entrusted them! I was more of an expert that day in their respective fields than they could ever hope to pretend, not the other way around! And just because they might of been toting an MBA in Business Administration or some similar degree, to the guys in the blood and guts world of the automotive aftermarket that wouldn't count for squat!

So, I listened on, as my amazement turned to horror.

"Steve... Did you hear that Peter Ross left the Company?" Jeff offered cordially, after I had brought his name up.

"Yes, I know. I already heard something to that effect. From what I understand, he left around April to go and work for a milk company."

As you might have expected, I had brought Dianne's name up as well, but these guys were way too fresh on the job to fathom the passing of that notorious individual to be any the wiser. So, I didn't mind filling a couple of blanks for them, letting 'em know that after she tore up Fram, she had miraculously landed a job for a recognized subcontractor of Allied's. Though it was incredible to my way thinking, Dianne had managed to stay in the automotive business, landing employment at a major player in the filtration media business, Parker Hannifin!

As lunch progressed, I recited the entire litany of the failed marketing debacle to both gentlemen, so they could at least be brought up to date.

I had to! 'And my rational?' Barely a year had gone by since the launch and not a soul that had anything to do with the grass roots of marketing of this product was left to take over the helm! My baby had been entrusted to the care of this unseasoned, unsuspecting recruit who was used to selling door knobs for a living! Like I said before, Peter's boiler had grown cold long ago and when he got the chance, he was so desperate he jumped ship to go and sell milk!

I couldn't help but notice, but Mr. Bye just sat there kinda amused, listening to me expound upon the ins and outs of how to market an oil filter. I guess all along he had to of been wondering, just who the heck I might have thought who I was..., talking the way I did with such confidence. Apparently though, my discourse had left him unimpressed.

"You know Steve, you ought to consider yourself lucky that I wasn't around when this marketing plan for Double Guard was first formulated. You might not realize it, but I'm telling you that the Fram Brand name is in trouble, and all of our marketing emphasis has to be directed toward that effort! Be patient, Double Guard will come up to speed in about four or five years and then at best, it will occupy only a small niche."

Now I have to tell you, right about then I fought back my emotions with every fiber.

'What was this guy talking about? Did he know?'

"Jeff, I don't understand? Have you seen my contract? I have less than five years remaining on it now!!!"

"Yes, I'm aware of that. I've read it, but there's nothing I can do about the deal you've struck for yourself."

"But that's why I'm here meeting with you guys! So, I can explain to you about what's been promised, in light of what's actually been going on!"

"Sorry Steve, I can't help you out there," he said, sporting a rather vindictive sort of grin.

"What about the theft in Walmart?" I asked, trying to make sense of his position.

"Yeah, so what about it?" he asked, as if I was purposely trying to be an annoyance.

"If this filter was a dog, which the facts have already proven otherwise, then how come people have been stealing it from the get go, despite an incredibly limited marketing campaign?

"And another thing, let me ask you a question, Jeff; and you too Brian, for that matter. What has either Kraft Foods or Stanley Tools brought to market recently that required theft proof packaging, because the consumer was willing to chance a police record for the stealing it?!"

Just so you know, as I was bringing these two very green horns up to speed, because over 750,000 oil filters had already been stolen out of Walmart alone!

He couldn't resist an explanation, "You've gotta be referring to the situation Walmart has blown way out of all proportion!" snickering as if he had actually been around for that one first hand.

"Walmart is more trouble than they're worth, a pain in the neck to deal with. The Double Guard theft was nil! Come on Steve, what are you talking about. They're making much to do about nothing, 'cause they can't manage their own damn inventory system and you know that! If I had my way, we would get out of all our retail accounts and just focus on the automotive retailers."

What I couldn't believe was how much he already sounded like Peter on that score! And he had the gall to think that I sounded cocky?

Well you could have fooled me! Because for a guy who had only been in the business a few months, he sure sounded like someone who had already made a career of it.

"So Jeff, tell me, how could that be possible?" I asked puzzled. "Since you guys are only featuring this filter in only a few specialty merchants now as it is. And I shouldn't have to remind you, but Pep Boys has reported its share of thefts as well!"

I must have hit a nerve or something because he suddenly stopped and just stared at me. There was no mistaking it, something was coming. "If I may Steve, let me enlighten you. We are supporting your filter! If my memory serves me correctly, we just sent our licensing fee out to DuPont not very long ago."

"What are you talking about Jeff?" I grimaced, totally caught off guard.

"We have to pay DuPont for the privilege of using their trademark on our product now," he offered sourly…, like I should have known.

"I still don't follow you Jeff? This has got to be something new? DuPont didn't require any such payment when we first started out, I can assure you! That would have been enough to kill the project from the very beginning with this tight-fisted outfit!"

"Tight fisted outfit huh…! Well I can't speak about the arrangements of the past. All I know is that we just sent DuPont a quarter of a million dollars to rent their trademark for the upcoming year!"

Horrified, I couldn't do anything much, but ponder the entire mix. 'But that was only one tiny rat hole he was talking about!' I reasoned. What I really needed to locate was the big black hole which had been responsible for gobbling up the millions and millions supposedly earmarked for the annual marketing budget.

'So, if they were willing to pay a quarter of a million bucks just for the sake of keeping the logo on the packaging the same, then how could they justify allowing this billion-dollar baby rot on the vine unsupported?' It just wasn't adding up.

The more I thought about it, the more I realized that he wasn't telling me anywhere near the whole story. And if you asked me, it was more because he didn't know what was going on, more than anything else.

"If you don't mind Jeff, I'm gonna call DuPont tomorrow and get to the bottom of this licensing fee you're telling me about."

His reply was metered, as his angst towards me came glaring through. "Hey Steve, you just go ahead and do what you want."

It was more than obvious we had arrived at the stage where we were just going to argue now. So, I did just enough to keep him going, certain he still had other valuable insights that would surface before we parted ways. That's if I hadn't ticked him off completely by now.

"What about the racing circuit?" I asked. "That sport is taking the world by storm! Anybody who's anybody has got their logo slapped across the hood of one of those cars! And now that you've already told me that you're willing to rent the trademark for all that money, how come you guys don't jump headlong into the racing circuit like you already should have! Just like you promised…, before I signed on the dotted line!"

"Steve, the racing circuit is way too expensive to advertise in, and besides, race fans aren't that brand conscious nor are they that loyal to brands anyway. It's not a very cost-effective way to advertise for us."

'Out of the mouth of babes!' By now that was about all that would register.

I hit him with one more item before I had to get the heck out of there. By this point I was nearly physically sick, having gotten what I had come for…, the Truth, at least the way Mr. Bye interpreted it to be.

"So, what about the display case back at headquarters?" I see that someone finally thought it important enough to have tossed a lone filter in there this time around. Do you realize that nearly twenty-one months have lapsed before it finally went on display?"

"Ah the display case at Fram's headquarters isn't very important for the divisions image nor their morale. With that, I pressed him for the reason why Larry Bossidy touted the Double Guard in the last annual report.

To be honest with you Steve, having the Double Guard featured in the 96' Annual report wasn't very meaningful either. That was just Larry filling up space for the stockholders, because he didn't have anything else to stick in there. So, if I were you, I wouldn't put much stock in that either."

You know, I really had to hand it to him. He was beginning to sound a lot like Rick Bjelde on that one, except Rick being a lawyer, was a bit more pragmatic when we had touched upon that subject, as I began to recall his philosophical rational for my predicament. I can clearly recall that it went something like this, "You know Steve, you really ought to be happy. You've already made over a quarter of a million dollars so far!

"Do you have any idea how long it takes people who have to work for a living, to make that kind of money?"

Just so you know, I did call Walmart regarding the thefts and I spoke with both their legal and accounting departments on this subject. And you want to know something, the upper management of Walmart were both concerned and upset for me..., the little inventor who happened to be selling his wares throughout their entire chain..., nationwide.

They not only confirmed the theft numbers, they were thoughtful enough to send me the proof that I required on a CD. They gladly complied to my request, since I was representing myself Pro se in in this lawsuit against Honeywell. The opposing attorney for Honeywell, vehemently insisted that I have the contents of that CD printed out immediately for his viewing pleasure, since I didn't ask for his permission to obtain it ahead of time. A rookie mistake, for sure. But here's a little something you may of never come across, and it's a good one. It's a little phrase that lawyers love using amongst themselves when they routinely break the rules... "It's easier to obtain forgiveness, then it is to get permission." Now think on that a while.

Anyway, by the time Kinko's was done, they had spit out a ream, nearly a foot and a half thick. I sent it off in a nice cardboard box as a present to my sparring partner..., David Brafman proving to Honeywell itself, that I knew the facts behind the thefts & returns in Walmart.

Just so you know, in these sorts of fights, "What's good for the Goose isn't necessarily good for the Gander." It's rather amazing, but I formally requested under the Federal Rules of Civil Procedure on seven different occasions for Honeywell to hand over some very important "Documents and Things", all of which were necessary in order to conduct a lawsuit based upon the evidence. To say they were non-compliant would be a high compliment. But don't get me started...

During my fifth year of pretrial, my young attorney deposed Honeywell's trademark accounting department regarding various matters that Honeywell had yet to cough up during the Discovery process. Though I had passed the reins over to this young buck, I was still an integral part of our two-man legal team, so as you might expect, I was in the room and present during the festivities.

Rather surreptitiously, Jeff Bye just happened to be slated to be questioned that day. 'So, what did an inept marketing guy have to do with Honeywell's trademark department, anyway?'

Before his deposition concluded, he offered that both he and Brian Mcinerney were terrified of me. Somehow, the doors to my Suburban had mysteriously locked us all in, as we sat in Fram's parking lot, saying our good byes that fateful day. He then began to paint me as some sort of a religious kook and that these two grown men had feared for their very lives, "Because they thought I may have had a gun in my briefcase."

Just so you know, during that period in my life I didn't possess or own a gun of any caliber, not even a BB gun. The kids were small and that was my rational for not owning one. Today, things are a bit different, the kids are grown and I'm a licensed gun owner.

It just so happened, that this was a long-distance telephone deposition, so the audio was recorded. Of course, Honeywell had to get that little soundbite on the record. My jury trial was heading down the tracks, and it was heading straight for them. ...And they were powerless at this point to derail it.

Besides..., wouldn't it be a nice touch, to paint me as a crazy, with the eminent potential to do mortal harm? Just thought you'd like to know.

CHAPTER 30
AN INDEPENDENCE DAY LETTER

I had come away from that luncheon devastated. The arrogant stupidity of this Company was beginning to make Dianne's nightmare seem almost like an afternoon daydream. As the parade of careless employees marched on past, it was time to take it to the chief. I had warned them all, big and small alike, but I guessed nobody took me seriously. Think about it! Nobody was left!

'Who could I turn to, lawyers?'

Na…! Call me stupid, call me naïve, but I wasn't about to get myself embroiled in that world. So off to Larryland I went. When I could take it no longer I sat down and began to write. It was Independence Day of 97', when I sat down and began to pen my heart….

Dear Mr. Bossidy,

I am addressing you as a partner in business with AlliedSignal's Fram Oil Filter Division. Other than yourself and the Aftermarket Division, I am the largest stakeholder in the Double Guard Oil Filter venture.

I would like to refer to the 1st quarter report of 1996, page 13. "…and strong sales of the new Fram Double Guard oil filter offers unsurpassed protection against engine wear and tear." And a quote from yourself, repeated by an associate, at a significant marketing meeting I attended in April of 1995…, "Larry is really into this filter, he thinks the box should be gold." [per Diane Newman]

Well Mr. Bossidy, "your sales forecast for 1997 for the Double Guard will be at least half the volume achieved in 1996… and that will be achieved purely on the product's own merit." 'You wanted a gold box?' Well I'm endeavoring to reach you before you need to change your color scheme to clear… Clear as in AlliedSignal's version of a Clear Pepsi marketing debacle.

Your stock value is at an all-time high, plus you just bolstered your position in the Aftermarket with the acquisition of Prestone, just in time to fall flat on your faces with what you called "the most significant innovation in oil filtration history." I find myself after all that I have witnessed of your Company, left in utter amazement.

Notwithstanding, and much to my dismay, what had started out to be an honorable, positive and open exchange of ideas and confidential information, has become a devastating and frustrating ordeal of denial and subterfuge.

I understand how busy you are as the Chief Executive Officer of such a large company, and I am sure that no time would be convenient to approach you personally on this matter. However, I have been very patient with this entire situation for over two years and now is the time for me to act. I have endeavored to straighten these matters out with various individuals within the Company, working within the prescribed framework of hierarchy and protocol. To no avail. I have been bantered about by bureaucratic rebuff and legal postulation about contract law and the validity of my patent. I take offense to these tactics, as they are disingenuous to say the least.

At this time, I am going to alert you personally about two pressing issues that are crucial to our mutual success and prosperity in going forward with the Double Guard.

Ethics and Honorable Conduct During the Pursuit of Business

The Badly Flawed and Faltering Double Guard Marketing Plan *Personal Background:*

I am the individual that brought the formative marketing, manufacturing and production plans to Fram. I laid the groundwork for Fram to co-trademark Double Guard with the DuPont Fluoropolymer Division and incorporate the Teflon trademark on the packaging, as well as several other key attributes that are now part of the finished product. I have well over a decade of experience in the fields of tribology, oil filter function and manufacture, and have a keen understanding of the various markets in which they play a part. I hold two United States patents on oil filters and my approach to oil filtration is unique and specific to me. In regard to the heavy-duty filter market, I have extensive hands on knowledge backed by real time test studies conducted with some of the nation's premiere trucking fleets. I have gathered the knowledge to market the fleet owner, fleet manager, their OEM's and the owner operator.

Ethics

On May 31, 1995 in the presence of Kevin Gill, the Manager of Product Marketing Filter Products and Dianne Newman, Director of Business Planning and Development, I had agreed to a licensing and royalty rate agreement with all the necessary parameters discussed and agreed upon.

Kevin Gill was the point man for the Company on this project and we jointly co-birthed the Double guard Project. I have nothing but praise and admiration for the person he is and the job he performed. Kevin left the Company for another employment opportunity two days after that meeting. I was left in the hands of Dianne Newman, who was my nemesis. Dianne managed to take what we had agreed to in that room and pervert it into a document that had little resemblance to what we three had given our words of honor to. I was then subjected to an expensive and prolonged three months of "them against me."

Your Company in the form of this person and the individuals meant to monitor her actions betrayed the trust and made a mockery of the Company's business code of ethics as stated in your Vision, Values and Mission Statement. In short, they did their very best to steal my idea. Dianne's employment was terminated with the Company in July of 1996.

A Faltering Rollout

The marketing debut of Double Guard got off to a poor start.

I placed a call to your office in October of 1995 and attempted to speak with you on the fact that the Company was going to miss the opportunity to properly unveil the Double Guard at Industry Week. I was told at least six months prior that the Double Guard was to headline for Fram at the trade show. Mr. Barter phoned me, we spoke for fifteen minutes and I detailed him succinctly concerning my displeasure about my contract negotiations and the Faltering Rollout of Double Guard.

Subsequently, the planogram dates were all missed, and the product never made it to the shelves until May of 1996; over six months behind schedule.

Let me elaborate on the only Premier aspect of this product that I have witnessed. The box, the filter itself, the graphics, the infomercial for the vendors and the commercial for the consumers. The "material stuff" of this project are superlative and so far, that is all.

I could lament about the cutting off of marketing capital for a market that is approaching a half-billion dollars in scope, and over a billion dollars if the full impetus was to be weighed. But much to my chagrin, that is just symptomatic of the problem. The root cause of the problem is the Division lacks a cohesive battle plan with proven market and product experience in this area. They just don't get it! In the meantime, racing is taking the civilized world of sport by storm. The market is exploding with opportunities never before seen in this industry with awesome upside potential and growth. The Company's lack of participation is indicative of a flawed marketing plan.

I assure you that I possess an inspired marketing plan that will transform your Fram Filter Division as you presently know it... I have certainty on this. The Fram brand could become a household name and this situation could go a long way toward building your legacy among your many other achievements at the Company.

Summary

I would like to state in closing that my main objective is to meet with you personally. I would like you and I to put our business relationship back on track. I would like to brief you on any of these areas that are of importance or interest to you.

Your words are prophetically accurate, "The Double Guard is the most significant innovation in oil filtration history." I can most assuredly help the division make those words come to pass. Unfortunately, the personnel running Fram are incapable of doing so, or have already decided to fail. Please call me."

I wanted so much for this letter to hit its intended target. I had gone to the trouble of calling Mr. Bossidy's office for the second time in my life. And with nearly the same care and trepidation, I spoke to one of his personal secretary's, an Ilene Powell. I let her know that I had a letter that I wanted to hand carry to her boss personally. So, after great persuasion on my part, that I wasn't a deranged bomber or craven gunman, she acquiesced and allowed me to bypass the mail system.

It was desperate beyond measure. If there was a vestige of a bridge left at all, I had willfully and knowingly chosen to blow it! There was nothing left standing between me and a courtroom, except Bossidy. All the other foolish hires had let me down. I was truly on my own now.

So, on the morning of July 8th, 1997 Patti and I made the trip to Mecca, hoping to be received. I wore my best suit with a white cotton shirt, along with my burgundy wingtips. All I can remember was that I was sweating and scared, as the sweet young secretary broke away from her handsome escort whom she had brought along with her…, just in case.

She had done me a big favor that morning, pressing her flesh against mine, feeling my pulse and gazing into my eyes. We exchanged a few kind words. All I could do was hope, that along with my letter, she could bring back just a little bit of my humanity as she delivered what I was convinced would be my last plea to her boss.

CHAPTER 31
FOCUS ON THE CUSTOMER

You know, the more I had thought about it, the more I realized that Jeff Bye wasn't just kidding. The Fram Brand name was in trouble..., big trouble! Oh, it wasn't something as simple as a good name that had gone bad on its own. It was something more complex than that, like the management behind the name. My only apprehension was that the mayhem didn't run all the way to the top!

'It couldn't,' I reasoned, 'Larry liked money too much to have ever allow that to infect him.' Mr. Bossidy as it turns out, is one of the most highly paid CEO's in the country, his salary often causing a sore point amongst the various groups of people that monitor such matters. What's more, Mr. Bossidy had instituted something called "Six Sigma" at the Company where manufacturing defects are kept to a bare minimum, with the target being zero defects. He prided himself on communication and the integration of processes, which equates to more efficiency, more innovation, and of course, higher profit margins. The world is his audience, the street being his judges..., the loyal shareholders his cheering band.

Keeping that in mind, upon my return from Morristown that afternoon I made a side trip, so I could stop at my real estate office to check my mail box. And there it was to greet me, the 1st Quarter report for 97'. Upon opening it, I nearly had a fit! It commandeered all of page 8, under "Customer Focus", and the customer was none other than Walmart!

Remember I had dreams of being compensated with stock options just like the big boys get? Well, after the thrashing I had received at the hands of the Company, I just couldn't bring myself to purchase even one share of Allied's stock, it was matter of principle. Kinda like back in the 80's, when people didn't purchase stock in South African based companies, because of their stand against Apartheid.

As a matter of fact, it took all I could do, to ask The Lord to bless them after what they had done to Our Dream. But of course, I prayed for them, and the result was nothing short of miraculous. The Double Guard continued to sell over the 500,000 units necessary to keep both me and The Lord in the game. Sales were being propped up by the two of the best stores in the world in their respective categories, Walmart and Pep Boys.

Jeff Bye's stout words against Walmart were still swirling around in my head along with Peter Ross's, turned the 'milkman'. As I read the Company line as portrayed in the quarterly report my milk started getting hot, to the point that I had to go home and pen an addendum to the letter I had just got done delivering to Larry's secretary. I knew sending him a second letter in the space of a couple days would certainly be pushing the envelope, but I had no choice, we were crashing and so was Fram!

Again, allow me to quote this piece from the 1st quarterly report of 1997...

*"Glance at the list of AlliedSignal Automotive's largest customers and you'll see some well-known names: Ford, Chrysler, Fiat, Caterpillar, Walmart. Walmart? Indeed, from its humble beginnings in Arkansas 35 years ago, **Walmart today is the world's largest retailer-and AlliedSignal's largest automotive aftermarket customer. Last year, the 2300 store giant sold over $60 million worth of Fram filters and Autolite spark plugs.***

"Walmart's business philosophy is simple: offer customers a wide variety of quality merchandise at everyday low prices, backed by the friendliest service in the business. **Behind Walmart's folksy charm, however, lies one of the world's most sophisticated inventory and distribution systems.**

"Traditionally, suppliers delivered their products to retailers in the same quantities each month, with little regard for actual consumer demand. This "push" system often left retailers out of stock on popular items, while forcing them to dedicate valuable shelf and warehouse space to products that weren't selling so well. "Walmart pioneered the use of continuous replenishment systems in which purchase data - captured electronically at the cash registers of individual stores - are used to determine precisely when additional product shipments are needed from suppliers and in what quantities.

"Walmart has begun placing increased responsibility for the success of its continuous replenishment systems into the hands of suppliers, asking them to make ordering, inventory and distribution decisions traditionally handled by the retailer itself. **To date, only 24 of Walmart's 5000 suppliers have been invited to move to this "vendor managed inventory' approach; AlliedSignal is one of them.**

"To ensure the highest level of customer satisfaction, AlliedSignal has put a dedicated Walmart account team in place, including sales and marketing, purchasing and logistics professionals. *The new process has gone smoothly so far, and AlliedSignal is applying the lessons learned from its work with Walmart to improve the service it provides to other large aftermarket retailers such as Kmart, Auto Zone, Pep Boys and Western Auto".*

'So, is this what both Peter and Jeff meant when they said that "Walmart was a pain in the ass, and that they're more trouble than they are worth?"'

'Don't you think it only fair to provide a degree of service to a vendor that is enabling you to sell $60 million dollars' worth of oil filters and spark plugs per year?

'And let me ask another foolish question? If your largest and most sophisticated retailer tells you that there is a theft problem with a specific item, why wouldn't you as the vendor remedy it immediately!

'Why would you wait to be kicked out six months later like AlliedSignal did over the theft of the Double Guard?

'Then you take an entire quarter to remedy something as simple as blister packaging a rectangular box! You call that cutting edge?' I didn't think so either!

'So, what about my Italian friend, Giuseppe?'

Didn't we just read back there that Allied was giving Walmart their highest level of service by providing them with a "dedicated account team." Giuseppe didn't mention seeing a dedicated account team. As a matter of fact, when I asked him about how this product was being overseen, all he could tell me was that it wasn't being overseen at all! Especially, not by anybody from AlliedSignal!

CHAPTER 32
A FOLLOW UP, TO A PLEA

Unable to wait for even that fastest overnight courier, I faxed Ilene Powell a copy of my second letter.

In the process of letting her know to be on the lookout for my letter, I asked her if Mr. Bossidy had received my first correspondence yet. To which she replied, "Most definitely." Ilene let me know that Mr. Bossidy had already referred the matter along to his Chief General Counsel, a Mr. Peter Kriendler. Then Ilene went on to assure me that he would be contacting me in the next few days.

"*Dear Mr. Bossidy,*

I want to thank you for a quick response and directing my letter to Mr. Kriendler. In like fashion, I will not contact your office again on this matter.

I received a copy of the 1st quarter report of 1997 after I had delivered your letter and I would be remiss if I didn't furnish this additional material to you after reading that report. You spoke about the importance of brand building, the buying of significant companies with vast product lines, your own recognition of the important role that the Aftermarket plays and customer focus with high praise for Walmart.

The overriding intent of my first letter was to guarantee that we didn't have a marketing failure on our hands. I was perhaps a little too discrete, and the ethics issue may have diverted your attention from the main focus of the letter, which was marketing. I hope a few of these quotes from individuals that are/were in positions in your Division that I have personally met with, will enlighten you more than I can:

"Walmart is a pain in the neck to deal with, they are more trouble than they are profitable. The theft with Double Guard was nil, they made much to do about nothing because they can't manage their own inventory system. We should consider exiting that account along with the other large mass merchants and just focus on the specialty retailers; they create less headaches for us." V.P. Product Management. "The display case at Fram's headquarters isn't important for the Divisions image nor morale. Your featuring Double Guard in the 96' Annual Report..., isn't very meaningful and that was just Larry filling up space for the stockholders, because he didn't have anything else to stick in there." Director of Marketing.

"We failed the installed test study because the fellow who owned the test sites has been against additives his whole life. Anyway, these guys are just too busy selling other stuff like anti-freeze to get involved with an oil filter." Both the V.P. of Product Management and the Director of Marketing.

"The racing circuit is too expensive to advertise in and besides, race fans aren't that brand conscious nor that loyal to brands. It's not a cost-effective way for us to advertise." Both.

"The Fram Brand name is in trouble, and all of our marketing emphasis has to be directed toward that effort. Be patient, Double Guard will come up to speed in about four to five years and will occupy a small niche." Director of Filter Product Marketing.

These are just a few of the gems that I have been carrying around privately with me. It should be obvious that the Fram marketing team isn't on the same page as you or I. Nor are they in line with the philosophy that you have been proudly sharing with your stockholders. It would be very easy at this moment for you to dismiss me as a disgruntled inventor or some quack that desires your special attention.

I can most assuredly tell you that this is not the case. I am very uncomfortable bringing this matter before you, but I will shoulder the burden of proof. The truthful irony at this point Mr. Bossidy, is that I am painfully aware of the situation at hand and you are not; because it has been skillfully hidden from you for the moment."

CHAPTER 33
A MESSAGE FROM THE ARMOR-BEARER

I let a few days' pass before I started hunting down Peter Kriendler. I had faxed Ilene the letter on July 11th at 9:45 A.M. and it was now the 16th. With absolute resolve, I determined not to get caught up in the same waiting games like I had done so in the past.

Let me make this clear. I was none too happy about the way in which Larry had responded to my letter, kicking it over to his Chief Attorney like that, instead of reaching out for me himself.

I was looking for an open ear, a dialogue…, a hear me out session. The last thing I was looking for, was to involve myself with some hair-splitting expert who was about to hide behind all the ins and outs of corporate law. And I gotta be frank, what I had to say didn't involve the laws they were so intent upon hiding behind! It had more to do with Murphy's Law! And as far as I was concerned, O'l Murphy was staring us, right in the face!

So as a result of my calls, and in particular, a message I had carefully delivered to his secretary, Mr. Kriendler in turn, called my house one evening, leaving the sort of a message that could only make me wonder.

And if you can believe it, the message he left on my answering machine was quite peculiar. Mr. Kriendler, as it appeared, felt it was more expedient to focus on what I had spoken to his secretary than what I had written to his boss! His reply was astonishingly devoid of anything to do with the contents of my two letters!

'So, what put him on the defensive you might ask?'

Well, take a look at what I had told his secretary and perhaps maybe you can figure it out.

As always, I had identified myself immediately, as Stephen Moor; the inventor of The Double Guard oil filter. And as was usually the case, the lady on the other end of the line, responsible for picking up the phone, was a pleasant and a non-confrontational professional.

So, I can assure you, there was no need, nor justification to for me to have even considered having an attitude. Besides, I was too darn nervous to cop an attitude, it was just that darn simple. To be honest about it, these phone calls and letters that I was writing had more of a chilling effect of scaring the heck out of me…, not them!

After informing Karen that I had recently written two letters to Mr. Bossidy, I let her know that in his wisdom, Mr. Bossidy had decided to pass this matter along to her boss.

I then told her that it was important that I now speak with Mr. Kriendler concerning the letters and that I desired to have a personal dialog with him. I politely expressed my desire that I didn't want to have our communication relegated to just a phone conversation or letter, and that I wanted a personal meeting with him.

I informed her that I had already been put off by the Company thus far and had received the brush off treatment. Going a little further, I went on to say that all I wanted to do was air my heart and that I had come in a spirit of peace.

I was as humble and as genuine as I could make it come out when I spoke with this lady and I have every confidence she was capable of taking down my words as well as my intent. In truth, I nearly begged her to have her boss call me, so that we could arrange for an open and honest face to face hearing, privately amongst ourselves, handled in a spirit of peace and cooperation.

Now that's how I left it with her, and that's the truth. There wasn't a lick of double meaning interspersed amongst my words. So here is what Mr. Kriendler deemed appropriate to leave on my answering machine, the evening of July 16th, at 6:15 P.M.

"Ah..., Mr. Moor... This is Peter Kriendler from AlliedSignal, returning your call. I saw your letter to Mr. Bossidy and I had also talked to Mr. Redlinger when you first approached him, and I asked John Donofrio, our Chief Patent Counsel to take a look at the matter.

"I believe he sent you a letter. Frankly I'm not sure what there is to talk about after that. I see no basis for you're being upset or dissatisfied in any respect, and I certainly don't see any potential claims against AlliedSignal.

"But if you want to talk with me... But frankly, when you tell me you come in peace... I'm not sure how to interpret that?

"Obviously there is an implicit threat in that. And frankly, we think it's a fair contract that we've entered into, and we intent to abide by it.

I don't know what else we can do?"

Obviously, there was plenty they could have done.

There's a bit more to come, so we'll have to just wait and see if he was telling me the truth…

CHAPTER 34
WHY DON'T YOU JUST DROP IT?

'So, it's Thursday night around a quarter past six, the question being, 'do I dare call the Chief General Counsel of AlliedSignal back?'

His message sounded so ominous, so cold, so final. He didn't want to talk, at least not the way I wanted to. And I'd be lying, if I didn't fess up and tell you that the tone of his voice alone was enough to wanna make me crawl under a big rock and forget about the whole damn thing.

Larry got my letters all right, that was for sure! But I certainly wasn't reaping any of the benefits for my honesty. It took great amount of courage on my part, to tell this vaunted captain of industry that there was indeed a great problem running around loose in the bowels of his mighty ship.

Duty called. I had no choice, and before I knew it, he was on the other end of the line foaming at the mouth, like a good junk yard dog, guarding the rusting hulks of my once shinny dream. Try as I might, I knew full well that I didn't possess the necessary powers to be doing a whole lot of disarming of this fella.

"What can I do for you?" he asked, agitated to the core that I would have the unmitigated gall to return his call. I don't know, perhaps he was just a bit upset at himself, like he lost his touch or something.

"I wrote two letters to Mr. Bossidy, and before that, I gave Mr. Redlinger a whole bunch of papers and I can tell right up front that you guys are doing your best to turn this thing into a patent issue."

He never acknowledged or hinted at my letters, not even for a single moment, but he was trigger quick to let me know that he was busy now and that he had an important dinner engagement to attend. And that was fine by me, 'cause I would have gladly of dropped off the phone and picked it up at a more convenient time, except for one thing. He still kept talking!

In-between the asking of why I had called, his conversation was laced with innuendo, letting me know that I didn't even have even a good wooden leg to stand on.

"At the moment, Mr. Bossidy and I are working on much more important matters than this Mr. Moor. Do you have any idea of how big a Company like AlliedSignal really is? Do you…, Mr. Moor?"

I was dumfounded, but I gave it my best shot, "Ah yeah. I think so. You're a Fortune 38 Company, and certainly the largest oil filter manufacturer in the Northern Hemisphere. I believe that's why I finally settled on picking you as my business partner. And now that I'm having a problem with you guys, all I seem to be getting around here is lip service."

It was coming… It was telegraphed long before he ever put it into words. "But didn't you sign a contract with us?" he growled.

"Of, course I signed a contract! What should I have done? Your Company told me that they were gonna go on without me! So…, let me ask you. What was I supposed to do? Let 'em go on without me? I gotta tell you, what you guys did was tantamount to extortion!"

The was no reaction on the other end of the line, this guy was used to fighting dirty, therefore my feeble cry meant squat.

"Did you sign it, Mr. Moor?" he asked, as if questing me in front of a jury that he was about to sway.

I was trumped for the moment, he was hiding behind the queen of hearts, and the best I could do for the moment was to repeat myself like a helpless schoolboy in the face of such a cowardly query.

"Well then..., it's a valid contract Mr. Moor. We are going to uphold our end of the bargain. I'm sorry you're upset that you're not making as much money as you had hoped for. And quite frankly I think it's a very fair contract, and frankly I think that you've been adequately compensated."

He had me pinned against the ropes now and he hit me with a solid shot of double speak to the body. At that moment, Bill Herbert's words came ringing true. Kriendler let me know in no uncertain terms, that if this contract had risen to his level during the time of our negotiations, I most certainly wouldn't of fared as well as I had. There's no doubt they "would have gone without me," leaving me no other option, but to sue them in Federal Court.

I was battling now. "Now I know you are a huge Company," I started in. "But there's something I don't quite understand, perhaps you can straighten it out for me. Like I already pointed out, I had a proprietary information and joint technology sharing agreement with the Company that we were supposed to adhere to. As a matter of fact, I had a working relationship with the Company for over a year and a half. So, I guess, after I gave you guys all you needed, you then found it okay to up and tell me at 12th hour that you're gonna go on without me.

"So, tell me something sir, how come Allied found it convenient to do so after we had already passed three or four versions of the contract back and forth, in good faith?

"You guys strong armed me! And I have a witness," I cried. "A former employee of the Company! He was in the room the day we had all agreed, to agree!

"And you know what happened?

"After he left, the other individual decided to turn this into an agonizing three-month ordeal for me..."

There, I had said it! I had relieved my heart of its heavy burden, it was now up to him to decide what to do with it.

"Did you sign the contract Mr. Moor?" Then, sneering, he once again asked me if the Company had been paying me.

I froze like a deer in the headlights, on that one. That was way too complicated an issue to get into before his dinner date. They were paying me all right. But then again, I didn't call holding back on my royalties for returns and inventory adjustment paying me! As a matter of fact, neither did my contract!

Not wanting our little conversation to end, I broke through the silence and squeaked out a feeble "Yes... but the returns."

"Good! Then we intend on upholding our end of the contract," sounding more final than ever.

There was never going to be a meeting between us, I could feel it in my bones. And as for the letter writing campaign in all of its grand futility, that was all but over as well! I had perhaps a remaining minute left, perhaps two at the outside, before his kettle would boil over, so I began pleading my case one last time.

"Mr. Kriendler, I just want to bring out into the open what's been going on, like how we've gotten to this point. Questions like, what did I experience at the hands of Allied's employees up until the point of signing.

"Questions like why did I sign the contract to begin with in the first place?

"I gotta tell you something sir. Your marketing guys aren't even on the same page as Mr. Bossidy! Didn't you read my letters?!!"

…Silence…

"Sir, I've been told to my face by the senior management over at Fram that Allied should exit accounts such as Walmart, because it's too much of a hassle to manage!!!"

"Hmm… Well, I think that if you have a problem, you should be calling the people over there in Aftermarket, don't you? Why don't you write Mr. Price a letter?"

I could hear myself laughing at the gall. He hadn't read my letters! Nah…., the closet he ever got to them was perhaps waving good-bye, before they found their way into an obscure filing cabinet meant to house the correspondence from all the nuts like me.

"Call Mr. Price!" It was out of the shoot before I had a chance to muzzle it, "I just got done dealing with those guys for the last two years. That's why I went over all of their heads!! And that's exactly why I'm trying to speak with you."

"I think you should write Mr. Price a letter," he insisted. "I feel that he's doing a fine job over there and they surely know what they're doing."

Now he was so screwed up, he began to really repeat himself. He had no basis from which to argue, and I knew it. All because he hadn't taken the five minutes necessary to prep himself before calling my little ranch house to defend the Company's honor. At this point, all he cared about was that the Company didn't have any liability.

Then for a guy who was about to run out the door for dinner, he really asked for it by sarcastically inferring that I was just some ignorant outsider, that didn't know a damn thing about what I was talking about!

So, I let em' have it both barrels. He wasn't getting to dinner now, unless he hung up on me!

"I brought these guys the concept in its entirety! They didn't have a clue until I showed up!" I could see that terrible trait of mine had made its way clear past the surface. I was in the full-blown act of defending myself. Against some guy who didn't even have enough respect to know what in the world he was supposed to be talking about.

I began to back off on the throttle a bit, looking for a way out now. Unable to resist, he took a parting shot, reminding me that this was a clear-cut patent issue and nothing else. With that, he pulled me back into the ring one last time.

"It's not a patent issue and it never was!" I told him. "I told you it's about a business contract, about specific performance! It's about ethics! I'm not talking about whether my patent is valid or not, 'cause as far as I'm concerned it's valid! Or you guys wouldn't have paid me a dime for it in the first place! It's about a Teflon treated oil filter isn't it? Well, what are you guys making anyway? A Teflon treated oil filter!

"That's right, a Teflon treated oil filter!

"I'd like to remind you of something Mr. Kriendler. A Fortune 38 like yours, shouldn't behave like this. If you are gonna tell me that my patent isn't any good, you should have told me right up front, now shouldn't of you?

"How come AlliedSignal didn't tell me right away that my patent wasn't worth the paper it was written on?

"How come you didn't bother to tell me that until right before you were preparing to go to market? Holding back on a matter as important as the validity of someone's patent that you intended on developing an entirely new product line around! And what about my trade secrets? Your making this product with all of my trade secrets! Shouldn't have all of this of been researched in a timely fashion, in let's say the first couple of months?!"

He was about to boil over, as he hit me with, "How come you never bothered to respond to our Chief Patent Counsel, Mr. Donofrio?" he sniped, like a maddened bully.

"Because it would a been to discuss nothing more than a moot point. Mr. Kriendler, did you read his letter?" my teeth were now showing over the phone.

"Yes, as a matter of fact I had," he replied, with a renewed sense of calm.

"I found it offensive," I charged back. "And where does he get off telling me that my experience with your Company was sporadic at best?"

CHAPTER 35
THE LAST ATTEMPT & SEVEN GOOD REASONS

It was now early December 97' and I had this uncontrollable urge to remind Larry that I was wasn't about to fade out of the picture, no matter how ridiculous he might make it for me. Six long months had passed since I had been in contact with anyone from Allied.

Oh, I still had a person or two that would take my call, but they were in accounting. And as what had become my custom, I would call my contact in the accounting department shortly after the end of every quarter, just to make sure.

'Sure, of what?'

Well, to make sure of a couple things. For starters, to make sure that they knew that I still was in the system, so I'd get my royalty check.

'You have got to be kidding! Really now Steve! Had your little storm driven you into the depths of paranoia?'

Well from my perspective, the accounting department at Fram seemed to be about as fragile as the marketing department. In the span of a year and a half, from the time in which my first check was cut, I had been through a succession of five, yes count 'em…, five accountants!

Even the bean counters were not immune from leaving the Company for greener pastures! Not unlike my other experiences with the Company, it seemed to befall me that every time a new recruit arrived, it was incumbent upon me to teach them how to pay me. Nobody seemed to be embarrassed, least of all the accounts, but the new blood never arrived at their post able to generate an intelligible sales report which was supposed to accompany my check each quarter.

If you don't mind, I'd like to give you a bit of an example. 'Remember the returns charged against my royalties?'

Well they had started being charged against my account shortly after I had received my very first check! I can recall stumbling upon this phenomenon quite innocently, during a conversation I was having with a very nice man in accounting department, named Robert Meyer. This conversation took place a good year ago, back in December 96', as we were discussing the Walmart theft fiasco.

I'm telling you, out of the blue, he gently brought to my attention that I was going to share the pain that quarter to the tune of eight grand in chargebacks! I didn't make the slightest deal out of it, and just let him talk, doing my best to pump him for any additional info along the way. All the while, my blood ran cold, thinking of the next chapter that I was about to involuntarily enter into.

And for those of you who might have forgotten that my royalty rate was calculated on a dime per filter, that would equate to 80,000 filter returns from Walmart alone. And that was just the first wave of many more returns to come!

In case you may be thinking, 'well that's not very many returns, Steve!'

You wanna bet, 'cause it was big enough to put an oil filter on every seat of the two largest football stadiums in America!

Now what I'm about to tell you, is the solemn truth. Up until this point, I had never had received any communication whatsoever from the Company that I was going to be involved with any chargebacks whatsoever, whether it be in writing or verbal. Bob just happened to of slipped that day, and I just happened to be alert enough to catch him.

And the proof. Well, I happened to be the one who asked if he wouldn't mind making sure that my sales reports from here on out would clearly spell out the returns and so from that time onward my returns were clearly spelled out for me on every statement! So, from that time forward, you would at least think that I had somewhat of a handle on the returns, but then again, you'd be wrong.

I was having a chat with my newest handler over in accounting one day, this time with a fellow by the name of Paul Mello. It was late August of 97' and Kriendler's double speak was still fresh on my mind... "Are we paying you? Well then it's our intention to uphold our end of the contract Mr. Moor."

Typically, the second quarter produced the largest royalty checks of the year and I was hoping against hope, that the sales for this quarter had turned the corner and would begin climbing up. I was flat out hoping for my God to perform a miracle, because The Double Guard oil filter had all but been cast off by the Company at this point.

I waited for the news, as he pulled it up on his screen, letting me know that the Company had shipped 253,528 units, for the quarter ending June 30th, 1997.

'Hmm,' I thought. 'It was sure puny enough in the scheme of things, but nonetheless I thanked The Lord above that I was at least making a living for the time being.

"Hey Paul, what about the returns?" I asked, hoping their numbers had finally stabilized and were on the way down.

I could hear him swallowing hard on the other end of the line, then came, "I don't really understand this Steve, but the returns look like they're in the neighborhood of 246,185 for this quarter."

Silence on both our parts as I grabbed my calculator off the counter and began doing the math. Muttering under my breath, 'Dear Jesus we're looking at a 97% return rate!'

"What's going on here Paul," I asked, barely able to speak.

"From what I'm told Steve, the stores are shipping back the unpopular models, in exchange for the models they sell more of. We call it inventory adjustment. Anyway Steve, it looks like we'll be owing you a check for $743.30 this quarter. I'll get it out to you right away..."

Naturally I called Kevin and told him of the goings on and he went just short of going ballistic. I called Bill Herbert and paid him another three grand for him to tell me the obvious. His assessment was that Allied was in violation of my contract. Not only that, but they had gone well beyond the conventional guidelines for this sort of thing! Please understand something, even if I was to be held accountable for any returns at all, regardless of the cause, the maximum percentage under any such generally accepted guidelines in a licensing agreement is limited to between 1 and 1½%!

In no time Bill had a letter drafted, ready to head out to Mr. Price, but once again I put him off, opting to keep my lawyer out of it, still trying to fix this on my own. You see, Bill was a patent prosecution attorney, he wasn't a litigator! Nor did he even try and conduct himself like one. Besides, suing an outfit the size of Texas was still something that I was totally incapable of wrapping my brain around.

So, I still had to try... On December 8th, 1997 I sent out my third letter to Mr. Bossidy. This letter was much different in tone, as compared to the previous ones fired across his bow, because I started off by directly quoting my licensing agreement for his review.

Dear Mr. Bossidy

"This letter is a follow up to my previous communications with yourself and / or AlliedSignal regarding the "License Agreement" entered into with AlliedSignal on September 1,1995, the representations leading up to the formation of that Agreement and the subsequent performance thereunder or absence thereof.

Section 1.(h) "Licensed Heavy-duty Products." I was given assurances that the Company would participate in this market shortly after the debut in automotive. Hence the notation of a 20 cent royalty for every unit sold; 3.(b). Not one sale has occurred as of this date and I am not aware of any marketing that has taken place.

Section 3.(h) "AlliedSignal shall use "Reasonable Efforts" to promote the sale of licensed products." I was openly given confidential Company documents delineating a detailed marketing and action plan. In addition, there was made strong verbal assurances concerning a rather comprehensive and aggressive marketing plan, including Heavy-duty and Installed Sales.

Section 4.(b) "Licensor makes no representation or warranty, express or implied, regarding the merchantability of licensed products…" I have been recently informed that I am to bear the full brunt of "Returns generated by various accounts due to normal stock adjustments."

Section 4.(c) "Licensor assumes no liability or responsibility under this agreement with respect to the use sale, or disposition by AlliedSignal… of Licensed Products… including any failure in production, design, operation or otherwise." I am shocked that the Company would be holding back royalty monies due to packaging, restocking or any other problems that I have absolutely nothing to do with.

Section 8.(a) "All payments which shall become due under any provision of this Agreement shall be made by AlliedSignal… without discount or offset…" In the 2nd quarter of 1997, I had 97% of my royalty monies due me held back without so much as a forewarning.

Section 8.(b) "Within sixty (60) days after the end of each Reporting Period, AlliedSignal or such sub-licensed Affiliates as the case may be shall render to the Licensor an accounting statement showing the quantities of the Licensed Products…sold…during the applicable period…"

Returns were not brought to my attention by the Company in compliance with the reporting procedure specified under the sixty-day clause. Returns are not part of my contract!

Section 8.(d) "… the correctness of any such payment shall be conclusively presumed unless questioned within one (1) year from the date of receipt thereof."

The rest of the letter read as follows:

"I was contract bound to notify the Company as soon as the information was brought to my attention, and that's what I had done. I received that information via fax on 11/20/97.

The enumeration of these deficiencies are in no way limited to just those issues brought forth in this letter, nor the contract that I have signed. There is an additional body of promises that the Company had made to me dealing with business plans that helped to cement our relationship. I went forward from the beginning of my relationship with AlliedSignal convinced by the Company's promissory intent. I did so with great faith in with whom I was doing business.

Somewhere along the way however, the marketing team and others with whom I had been involved were disbanded. Marketing strategies which were essential to the products dissemination and acceptance were abandoned.

The result is reflected in a decrease in sales by over fifty percent from 1996 to 1997!

Pep boys, the nation's second largest specialty retailer in gross sales is now hawking Purolator's "Pure Oil" filter in the most prominent area of the filter department of the stores that I have seen. The shelf space allotted Purolator, eclipses that of AlliedSignal's flagship, the Fram Extra Guard.

The Double Guard does not enjoy the benefit of that type of focused advertising. To the contrary, in the local Walmart stores in my area there is a total absence of advertising, (a photograph of the area in which the product is displayed is attached). The remedy would be simple, cost effective and readily implemented to ensure that our message would be picked up by the targeted consumer.

The Double Guard was not conceived to just be another filter item on the retailer's shelf. All of us who worked on the project at the time knew that. It was meant to have a second life in the installed sales market as well as in the heavy-duty market.

It was our feeling then, and my feeling now that the installed sales market was going to be the next boom in oil filter sales. Installed sales is steadily taking market share from the retail DIY market. I feel the Company is unrealistically limiting its potential for substantial future growth by just limiting its commitment to the retail DIY market despite steadily losing ground in this arena.

At the same time, the Company has not recognized consumer preference towards service. The Double Guard concept is futuristic compared to the present competition....., from both a step-up vantage point, as well as from a technological one. The concept targets the discerning installed sales consumer as well as the present DIY retail customer.

WITH YOUR ACQUISITION OF PRESTONE..., PRESTONE'S INTIMATE KNOWLEDGE OF THE AUTOMOTIVE RETAIL SECTOR..., THEIR PRESENCE ON THE NASCAR RACING CIRCUIT, AND THEIR UNDERSTANDING AND PARTNERING WITH JIFFY LUBE IN THE INSTALLED SALES MARKET..., I FEEL STRONGLY THAT THIS IS AN UNPRECEDENTED OPPORTUNITY FOR US ALL TO SIT DOWN TOGETHER. I WOULD REQUEST THE OPPORTUNITY TO MEET WITH THE PRESENT ALLIED MARKETING TEAM ALONG WITH THE PRESTONE STAFF IN ORDER TO EXAMINE THE MARKETING STRATEGIES AND TO HELP FORMULATE THOSE FOR THE FUTURE.

I conservatively estimate that a market of six to seven million units can be generated in a short period of time if we all work together.

When that accomplishment is realized, the next projection would be substantially higher.

I would like to go from this day forward into a new relationship with Allied and the Prestone team to help realize the promise that The Double Guard holds.

I will be available to you at your earliest possible convince..."

Fram was still hemorrhaging uncontrollably from all facets of the operation and now my greatest fear was that Bossidy would put her on the open market and sell her for scrap! That's if he could bring himself to weather such a terrible financial beating. And if that were to ever be the case, it would surely spell the end for my pursuit of justice.

But once again, the Lord had spared me…, it wasn't to be. There'd be no takers for Larry's cast off the Division, simply because it was too unprofitable to sell. And from what I could see, Prestone hadn't done a thing for the ailing sector either, obviously this wasn't working out to be the shot in the arm that Larry had been fantasizing about. No, like I had pointed out earlier, it boiled down to the basics, there were foundational problems to be dealt with first, before anything good could come about.

So, as it turned out, there would be more casualties jumping out from amongst the flames of the behemoth run aground. Rick Bjelde, Fram's attorney jumped over the rail sometime after I had met with Redlinger in the spring. To this day, I'm still not certain if he had jumped, or if he was pushed. And as for the Head of Fram Brand Management, I was told that Jeff Bye left of his own volition, shortly after the double album I sent over to Mr. Bossidy earlier that July.

And to think of the irony of it all… 'Remember Mr. Kriendler's advice to me six months ago?' Admonishing me, "That I should write Mr. Price, because he was such a good man and on top of things…"

Well…, before '97 was over, so was he! No longer the of President of Fram, but instead of being fired, he was absorbed by Prestone. Look out boys here comes another favored son being tossed over the side!

It was certainly coming down to wire. God was about to show me that He was in control, not I. And most certainly…, not Larry!

CHAPTER 36
A MORNING WITH THE STAKEHOLDERS

The mountain that I'd been eyeing off in the distance was now looming larger than I ever imagined it could. It goes by the name of Mount Intellectual Property Lawsuit. Let me tell you, it's truly a terrible place to be…, frightening beyond your wildest imagination.

This leg of the journey is about to conclude and another one of much higher magnitude is just about ready to get underway…, but first, we have just a bit further to travel before you get off this merry-go-round.

You know…, they say the pit of Hell resides in the belly of the earth. Well I can tell you that there's a high-speed elevator, that runs from this pit, and it will take you to the very top of this mountain. It is an express run, with no stops along the way. When you get to the top, the heavy doors clang open with a metallic thud…, then without warning, a sinister force pushes you out and before you know it, you land flat on your face amongst the rubble that's strewn upon this evil ground. The smell of war…, and the lies and deceit that started those many wars, hangs heavy in the air. The deceit is so thick, it's spawns mini-dirt devils that swirl amongst the carnage. Your gut tells you that many a battle has been waged here and that you're just another statistic in a never-ending succession of combatants.

As you drag yourself up, your first impulse is to wipe the dust of incredulity from your eyes. Suddenly, you see something terrifying out of the corner of you eye. It's appears to be a giant demon, straight out of central casting from the Book of Revelation. As you run for cover, and tuck under an outcropping, he whisks on by…, but before he does, you catch a glimpse, a visage if you will. Tattooed across his chest, he wears his name like a perverse badge of honor. His name is Misappropriation of Trade Secrets. Soon, another beast whooshes on by, it goes by the name of Patent Infringement… and so, they march on by. All dressed for war and ready to take on any unsuspecting visionary with a dream. …Breach of Contract, Tortious Interference with Advantageous Business Relationships, Falsifying the Oath of Inventorship…, a total of nine ugly counts would pass on by before I could come out into the feeble light.

After taking such a long journey together, it just wouldn't of been right for me to hold back my winning cards from you. This whole story would have ended up being nothing more than a polished lie if I kept my personal brand of faith from you. It not only gave me the strength to forge ahead, but it definitely enabled me to play a game that was way above my intellectual capacity. It framed my view of reality during this arduous climb, and to this day, I can't separate myself from that. Each one of us has our own brand faith, and as such, each one of us will carry that until we no longer walk this earth. We're only here for the briefest of moments. I certainly respect your absolute right to justify or explain any of the events that you've lived through, and it's your choice as to what lens you want to view it through. But since this is my story, I'm duty-bound to be true to self and use my lens.

When you're in the midst of a storm, it can have only one of two possible effects on a human being's heart. The buffeting can so devastate one as to crush that person's soul until the point of death, or it can have the quite the opposite effect. In any case, the choice lies strictly with the individual, as to which path will be chosen.

As unimaginable as it may seem, I chose to draw strength from my storm. The deeper it pressed, the bigger it grew, the more hopeless it seemed, the more it drew me into the arms of my dearest friend…, Jesus.

The key is patience, perhaps the hardest of human traits to work with, but that's what He requires, so I wasn't about to fight with Him about that one. He allowed nearly four years to pass from the time of the signing of my contract. During this time, I had an inner confidence that He had been hard at work for me, each and every day. He was quietly moving behind the scenes, working within the confines of our human frame work…, shaping the events that I had been sharing with you and the ones that I'm about to pull back the wraps on.

Oh…, and one last thing, my particular brand of faith promises that no matter the obstacle, when God's on your side, "No weapon formed against you can prosper." That's just His way of saying, "Steve…, we'll just keep on playing this game until you either win or you quit. The decision is ultimately yours as to how things will turn out in the end!"

I think you might be primed for a couple more examples to see if what I just said back there really has any merit…, other than just being a pleasant coincidence.

April '98, The Senior Vice President of The Automotive Division for AlliedSignal steps down. Mr. John Barter was let out to pasture and shortly after his departure, the Automotive Division Head Quarters in Southfield Michigan is shut down and moved to Morristown, N.J. There is no successor appointed for the vacant position and it is declared that Larry Bossidy will personally assume the role of Head of the Automotive Sector.

Kevin once told me in a moment of brutal honesty, "That the only difference between Fram and the Titanic, was that at least the Titanic had a band playing as she slipped under." It wasn't much after our conversation that Fram and Autolite had closed down its Rumford operations and was sent packing over to the care of Prestone in Darien, Connecticut. The hemorrhaging at Fram had now turned into bloodletting.

Around this very same time frame, the press had begun to hammer Larry on the performance of his Company and the heavy drag that the Automotive Sector's lackluster performance was putting on the whole corporate operation!

'But what had he done about my letters?'

Nothing! As it turned out, he never even bothered to dignify my December 8th, 1997 correspondence with a response.

Like it or not, my letters were prophetic! And sadly, I could see this man wasn't about to respond to them like someone who really wanted something fixed. My best guess was that Larry didn't believe in prophesy… Although he once proclaimed… *"And since prophesy isn't one of our core competencies, our operating plan contains detailed contingency measures for unforeseen events."* Larry Bossidy, February 6th, 1996 "To Our Shareowners," pg. 6.

Well I knew a little bit about prophesy myself, and as far as his Automotive Division was concerned, apparently so did the Forbes April 20, 1998 article entitled; *Bleeding Arm, but no Bleeding Heart,* by Bruce Upjohn. The article talks about how Larry summons 150 of his top managers to

Morristown headquarters twice a year and projects onto a darkened wall what he calls his "leakers" list.

"A Division gets on the list if it fails to earn 11%, which is what Bossidy figures capital costs Allied. Make the list once, shame on you. Make it twice and you may no longer be with the Company. Not long after the last such session, the President of Allied's North American replacement car parts got yanked from his post."

'Remember what happened to Mr. Barter and Mr. Price?' They never returned my calls either…

The article goes on to say that the automotive replacement parts business has been on his black list for two years running. Just to be clear, "This Division sells Fram oil filters, Autolite spark plugs and Bendix friction materials (brake pads) to retailers like Auto Zone and Walmart. It will likely gross 1.6 billion worldwide this year, excluding recent acquisitions."

Just so you know, when I entered the licensing agreement with them, this Division was eclipsing 5.5 billion dollars. Now it was down to an embarrassing 1.6 Billion dollars, an astonishing 71% gutting in less than 3 years' time. Surely the locusts were busy, eating away at Larry's crop.

What the article didn't say, was that Fram's flagship orange filter, The Extra Guard got kicked out of Pep Boys around the start of the 1998 season!!! So apparently, the marketing team at Fram couldn't even get that one right.

I can only guess as to why one of the top automotive retailers on the face of the planet would kick out the leading orange filter maker. But there's an irony to the whole story! Pep Boys has kept nearly the entire Double Guard line and continues to offer 22 models of the original 24 for sale. The further irony, that this was all happening on Larry's watch, now that he was in charge of calling the shots for the entire Automotive Division! And he was running her into the ground in the mist of my letter campaign!

But there's more! The Automotive Division, once Allied's crown-jewel…, their biggest and most profitable division, had now fallen into third place, behind it's much more profitable aerospace and chemicals groups.

Now here's a good one, *"Bossidy wants more of his car parts business to be in the sale of replacement parts, a business where he is not at the mercy of the sharp penciled carmakers. The auto parts group is now 65% aftermarket, but Bossidy wants to see that percentage grow to 80% by the year 2000."*

I'm compelled to ask once again, 'what about the installed sales and the heavy-duty filter markets left virtually untapped and impenetrable by the Fram logo?'

You surely can't call my filter a dog. That argument had been diffused long ago by the two premiere retailers in the world, who would continue to give this the product shelf space, despite a total lack of support from AlliedSignal.

The piece goes onto say that Allied acquired Prestone Products U.S. operations as well as their European counterpart for a cool $550 Million dollars. 'For what, you might ask?'

According to the article, *"Both were smart strategic buys. Selling into the retail market rather than the car manufacturing market, they come with operating margins double those of Allied's other auto parts businesses. Prestone brings with it marketing smarts that Allied sorely lacked."*

Just so you know, Prestone Products Company is a NASCAR approved sponsor and its antifreeze product is the official antifreeze of NASCAR. So, let me ask a stupid question, 'why wouldn't Fram ride their coattails into this new bonanza?'

Again…, what the article doesn't tell you, is that the Double Guard oil filter already brought to market by Allied was purposely created to double the Company's profit margins over its standard premium filter line. I hope you're starting to get it.

That's precisely why it still had a life in both Pep Boys and Walmart! Because from its inception, these retailers were included in the plan of sharing the wealth, making at least twice the profit margin on the sale of every Double Guard filter sold! And as the adage goes, I guessed they must of been selling, or they wouldn't of been taking up valuable shelf space in such a hotly contested market.

"Bossidy has plenty of work to do cleaning up an inefficient distribution network. The Aftermarket auto parts business has been accustomed to selling to small distributors who in turn sell to service stations. Those days are over. Now fast-growing retailers like AutoZone and the service station chains like Jiffy Lube cut out the middle man..."

You can't say that I didn't tell you that before.

And now magically, you're hearing it after the fact from Forbes.

'Remember the installed sales market and Jiffy Lube?'

The article closes out by saying that Larry is a no-nonsense sort of guy, tough as nails. *"A guy like that doesn't waste a lot of sympathy on well paid executives who don't deliver."*

It was quite an enigma to me, all this public relations bunk. I was still left with a question that was burning deep down inside of me…

If all this be so, and I've read several pieces parroting the same line, including the stuff which comes directly off of Larry's pen or out of his mouth, then how come such a lover of money and the bottom line, never gave me, the inventor of a billion-dollar baby…, a moment of his time?!!

Any fool could see that the mighty Signal's Automotive empire was imploding. I realize that I was a simple outsider at first, but then again…, I eventually did make inside. I got far enough inside and spoke to enough incompetent fools…, enough times to know, what writing would soon appear on their wall. Before it was over, I had amassed more firsthand dope than any high-priced efficiency expert could ever hope to uncover. It's scary, but if you tally it up, nearly everyone I had ever talked to, or tried to work with in order to salvage what could have been a winner…, had either jumped over the rail, quit, or gotten fired.

I truly believe that if Larry and I would of teamed up and approached this ongoing disaster intelligently, we could have kept that mighty ship from running headlong onto the reef. In the end I guess Larry was just too stubborn and far too arrogant for his own good.

I came bearing a billion-dollar gift and the best they could do, was to let it slip below the surface. Oh well…

In protest, I never bought a single share of AlliedSignal stock…., that was until April 1st, 1999.

I had to reach Larry, I was still hot on his trail, so…

It was the morning of April 26th, 1999 and I was on my way to my first real shareholders meeting ever! I was heading for Morristown, to see Larry. I had gained entrée to this prestigious event by purchasing a single share of common stock, the minimum requirement to gain admittance to this gala. I had done so, just three weeks prior to the event.

As I entered the highly secured facility, I whisked my way past several elderly jet setters, up from Miami no doubt, pulling their portable oxygen tanks behind them.

Dear God! I had to marvel at their loyalty and the homage they were bestowing on the Chief, making perhaps their last fateful trip to this stakeholders Mecca. If someone had lit a match, there was enough pure oxygen in that room to have blown the building apart.

I had arrived a good half hour early, just in case there was a glitch getting in. From way in the back of the room, I could see him up at the front table with Kriendler, that faithful sergeant at his side. Upon sighting the duo, my galvinistic readings went off the chart. …And boy, those bottles of oxygen being towed about the room started looking good. You gotta realize something! I knew what they all looked like from seeing their faces in the annual reports for the last three years, but no one in the room knew what I looked like, but him… For those of you who may of forgotten, 'The Betrayer at the Beach', the VP of Human Resources, Don Redlinger was the only person who could finger me!

And there he was! Glad handing with one of the stakeholders, my betrayer from the beach. Our eyes caught for just a split second as I made my way on through the crowd. I would have gladly of talked with him, but it was too late. He was already cowering from my gaze, and in one smooth move, turned his back on me, like a dog who just got done soiling the oriental rug in the living room.

I blew past him and took a seat on the end of the second row, right in front of Kriendler. We were so close we could almost shake hands if he would have permitted it. But instead, we proceeded to exchange glances for the next half hour or so. It was turning out to be just like old home week, the three of us…, me, Larry and Peter.

During the exchange of glances, I got a good feeling for Larry and believe it or not, I still yearned to get on with our business despite all his evasive maneuvers of the past. However, I'm sure he never even considered it for a moment. Nonetheless, I still harbored many points for which there could be no reconciliation on my part. That was unless he was able to see his way through, by manning-up and doing the right thing by both me and The Double Guard.

It was going to be his shot now. So, if he wasn't capable of taking a cold hard look at his once respected Automotive Division now in tatters, and wholeheartedly resurrect my billion-dollar baby, I would indeed declare war on him! Through it all, I was still able to forgive his arrogance and yearned for nothing more than to have a talk with him without any more games on his part.

As for Kriendler, he was your typical well-educated hit-man type. Though I could have mopped the floor with him, his piercing glances were cold enough of to ward off any such foolish thoughts. He was part and parcel as to why Larry wouldn't risk speaking with me, careful to make sure that his boss didn't venture outside the bounds of the facade of the cold-hearted law that they took so much comfort in hiding behind.

If I was ever gonna meet Larry, this morning was going to be it! I'd be afforded no other chance, and I would of certainly of been within my rights as a shareholder of record to have gone up and introduced myself to the Chief. It was all part of the show, because for the next two hours, the Chief Executive Officer of AlliedSignal belonged to his Stakeholders, adoring or otherwise.

But I had a slight problem... I was precluded from going up and introducing myself to him. During my hour and half ride up to Morristown, I had a non-stop talk with the Lord and I made Him a solemn promise..., a promise that I was intent on keeping. I promised that I would not talk with any individual, shareholder or otherwise concerning my plight! And don't think for a moment I wasn't desperate enough to search out for a powerful shareholder or two, begging for the opportunity to enlighten anybody who would be willing to listen as to why their beloved shares weren't appreciating like they ought.

And there was another part to this promise. I swore off that I wouldn't go up to Bossidy and introduce myself to him. As a matter of fact, he'd have to come to me, or not at all. So, I just sat there nearly able to touch him, while my head kept screaming amidst the palpitations of my heart, 'go for it you fool, you'll never get another shot like this for as long as you live! Go for it!'

I had no choice but to sit there, determined to let God be God. I wasn't in control, that much had already been proven. So, I let it ride.

About ten minutes before show time, with speech in order, he got up one last time to work the crowd. At first, he went over to the far side of the room, my eyes never left him as the minutes ticked away, wondering if I'd ever get my chance. He seemed so darn genuine, so truly interested! My heart pined to meet him, knowing that if he gave me a chance, we could turn this terrible thing around in a heartbeat!

Without so much as a hint, he changed course and headed directly towards me! I wanted nothing more than to stand up and thrust out my hand, but I was duty bound..., I couldn't! I couldn't break my oath, and if ever I was tempted, that moment would of qualified. I was certain that this morning would be my last shot, 'cause I had plans on never coming back.

Just so you know, up until this moment, I had intentionally passed on making any kind of a public stand. I had purposely boycotted the previous three shareholder's meetings, avoiding any opportunity for a personal showdown. I never went to the newspapers or the media. I always attempted to deal with Allied/Honeywell privately like man ought. So, I was counting on this being my last time on Allied's soil, unless..., something miraculous took place!

And one last thing, social media, the thing that everybody so whimsically runs to in order to air their butt-hurt feelings..., well it hadn't been invented yet. As of this writing, I've never used it. And I've been sitting on this story for over twenty years...

You see, in my heart of hearts, I had this terrible premonition. In 1999, if the sales of Double Guard fell below the 500,000-unit mark, I'd be out altogether! Out for good! It was truly an Act of God that he hadn't managed to sell her off yet, I mean the Fram Division or even the whole damn Automotive Business like I had heard rumored about so often.

As he strolled out front, he suddenly turned and stopped by me seat! Looking down from his imposing six-foot frame he thrust out his big hand my way, offering a warm smile. "Hi I'm Larry Bossidy."

It was my turn now, as I rose to my feet, looking him square in the eye, all signs of nervousness gone. "Hi Larry, I'm Steve Moor, the inventor of The Double Guard oil filter."

Not the least bit flapped, his smile broadened, "So where're you from?"

For a split second, I thought about the question, only to realize that I'd already caught the man acting. "Jersey," I said, doing my best to project that I was already onto his game. While our hands were still intertwined, I looked up into this giant of man and asked him straight out, "Did you read all my letters? I sent you three of them, you know?"

"Yes I did," came his metered reply. His smile hadn't changed one bit, belying the fact that he was still acting. "Steve if you have a problem, please…, please feel free to come in and speak with our attorneys."

Well that was an awful nice invite, but he was way late on that offer. So, I replied, pulling my hand out of his, "I already tried that Larry, and wasn't afforded that opportunity. Anyway, I don't want to talk to those guys now. I want to talk to you! Just give me twenty minutes of your time, that's all."

Still trying to disarm me, he offered real nice, "Well why don't you come in and talk with our people [lawyers]."

"No thanks sir. I want you…, twenty minutes."

Then switching tact, he offered, "You know Steve…, if you have a problem, please feel free to air it this morning during the open floor period. You'll have three minutes to say whatever you'd like…"

"No thanks Mr. Bossidy. If I wanted to have done something like that, I would have showed up a year or two before. Nah…, what I want to say, I want to say to you…, man to man in private, no lawyers, no crowd."

With that, he unhooked and offered me one last compromise. "Well why don't you come up and speak with our people, then when you've finished, you can come in and see me."

I had to think to myself, 'where had I experienced that tactic before?' And besides, his people would have been all lawyer's, because by my count, he had a couple of hundred of them on staff.

I fell back into my seat wanting to scream my thanks to God at the top of my lungs. Never in a million years did I expect what had just happened. I was euphoric. I felt like removing myself from the room, because at this point, my seat could barely contain my joy. As I was gathering my stuff, readying to leave… I heard His gentle voice, telling me to just settle back down and take it all in. I wasn't going anywhere. Besides, I had a lot to learn…

So, for the next hour and a half, I sat there and took in the workings of a first-class shareholders meet. You could tell, given the opportunity, Larry wouldn't let a chance like this get by. There he was, behind the podium with Kriendler at his side, espousing upon the marvels of his beloved "Six Sigma" doctrine and the like.

I couldn't help but marvel how The Double Guard had been mysteriously swallowed up into an industrial black hole with so fervent a captain at the helm. It was all I could do to watch, as he preached the crowd wild with his vision of a near perfect environment of productivity and creativity.

As I digested his every word, I tried not to be bitter, doing my best to weigh his intentions, taking it all in as he made it clear to the masses that he wanted to exit the Original Equipment end of the Automotive Business, due to the tight reigns that the car makers held on his Company. In a fleeting moment of fantasy, I wished that it was somehow possible for him to realize that's exactly what he had been doing to me. The very thing he had been suffering at the hands of the automakers, was precisely the same thing he'd been doing to me!

But seemingly the more I studied him, the more my heart began to lose hope. The man was a consummate actor…, as good as the best politician. I knew that underneath that blue suit and lovable exterior of his, operated one of the world's most brutal captains of industry.

'Would he meet with me, after I came up and spoke with his people?'

I came away believing that he couldn't be trusted on that one. Especially not after the three letters I sent to him, pointing out that the shiny corporation on the hill, wasn't quite so shiny.

Of course, he talked about the development of new products and their crucial introduction into the public arena. Of the vital roles that they played, in order to propel the Company forward, into the ever-changing market place. The sermon was laced with lots of that double speak, intended to pacify the faithful that was now gathered. Not a soul in the crowd knew what I knew. Therefore, I had no choice, but to follow my gut to the end, after all, that's why I had made the pilgrimage here in the first place. I didn't come to dine on the pabulum, the others were lapping up.

'If they only knew,' I thought, as he boasted about the millions being made here and about the millions being made there. And all the while, our billion-dollar baby lay on an abandoned siding, rusting away like some ancient steam locomotive. I couldn't take it, as my mind conjured up the plethora of vehicles already out there, from beat up pick trucks to glistening new SUV's donning the signets of loyalty. If one more car drove by me with a NASCAR sticker on their bumper or the number of their favorite driver neatly displayed on the back window, I was gonna scream! The NASCAR emblem had found its way into the mainstream and it wasn't just for rednecks anymore, not by a long shot! Amazingly enough, it's powerful advent occurred simultaneously with the birth of The Double Guard!

And yet I had to keep asking myself that maddening question, 'where was Fram in all of this, let alone where was The Double Guard?!!

Peter told me back in December of 96' when a flood of potential sponsorship was jockeying for position, that Allied had decided to pass on Fram becoming officially sanctioned as a NASCAR sponsor, allowing someone in the hamburger business pick up on their lost opportunity. So, McDonald's did!

We could a been riding that wave, obviously others were! The smart money had run out and sponsored a car long ago; Caterpillar, Home Depot, Lowes, just to name a few. Even a toy company in the form of Mattel had the smarts to seek out the son of legendary Richard Petty to drive its Hot Wheels car! No longer was The Winston Cup and Bush series the domain of tobacco pushers and beer peddlers, as sponsors began showing up in droves!

Perhaps Allied could have tagged along with DuPont or even Prestone. Ironic as it might seem, one of the most highly regarded racers on the planet, Jeff Gordon drove the infamous #24 Dupont car! But I guess the match already forged out in Heaven, between Fram Filters and DuPont's Teflon was not to be…, no matter how obvious! In the end, Larry chose not to pony up the million or two out of the billions the Automotive Division was earning, to join in on what the chairman of Lowes called the "bleeding edge of marketing."

To be an active part of NASCAR would have earned Fram the right to be out there with the big boys, where all the heads were getting turned. Estimates were coming in, that there was some

50,000,000 loyal fans! All of them buying product, and lots of them buying shares of stock in their favorite sponsors to boot!

So, if I witnessed another 140,000-seat racing arena packed to the gunwales devoid of Allied's presence or another NASCAR logo on a box of chicken or on a pair of sneakers I was gonna have to write a book…

As it turned out, I was already steaming toward the end of my thirteenth chapter, as I sat in my seat pondering the finale. I was certainly far enough along with the piece to of shared it with him, and let me tell you flat out, that's exactly why I undertook this exercise over a year and a half ago in the first place! To get the truth of the matter into Larry's hands!

I can only imagine what you must be thinking of me by now. Perhaps before, you may have entertained the thought that I might of been a little bit idealistic for my own good, but by now you might be a little bit more certain. Maybe you might think that I'm a bit wacky as well…, and just maybe…, I am. But I was in love darn it! I still am. With my God, with my wife and children, with my dream and yes…, with my Double Guard!

With all that said, I think now would be a good time for me to share with you, how all of this had come about…, the book I mean.

It was a typical morning, late spring sometime. I don't remember the exact day nor the hour, and believe me, that's not what's important. All I know was that it was 1997 and I had lawyers on my mind. I had had about enough of all the games and broken promises and I was gonna take Allied to court and sue them for a whole host of things.

Pulling up to the traffic light my mind was going a mile a minute, formulating another plan of attack. It was really weird. Trust me when I tell you, the word sue was in the darkest recesses of my mind until I got run over by this outfit. So… I'm sittin' there, waiting for the light to change so I can make it across the highway to get a cup of coffee at Seven Eleven, …my mind in a total upheaval. Remember now, I didn't have a lawyer, nor a law firm picked out at the time yet, but I was diligently hunting for one. And the challenge, just try finding a qualified lawyer or firm willing to go up against AlliedSignal and their vast billions and you've just created a needle in a haystack mission for yourself, especially if you're short the up-front, two-million-dollar cash retainer!

The light seemed to have stayed red for an eternity. Then out of nowhere, it was Him! He was talking to me again… "You have to write a book."

'I hadn't even had my coffee yet and I was way too busy trying to fix my own problems. I gotta grab a cup of coffee and head home to continue this maddening search for a lawyer,' that's at least what I'm thinking….

"What?!!" as I broke the silence.

As soon as I spoke, the invisible Voice surfaced again… "You have to write a book."

"I don't want to," I cried out. I had enough of school, I hate that sort of stuff. I can't, and I won't! I want to go the easy route for once I tell Ya! I want to find an attorney who'll do all the fighting for me. I'm so tired of fightin', this whole thing has exhausted me Lord. I can't possibly write a book!"

Believe me when I tell you, I knew full well who I was arguing with…, it was The Holy Spirit.

The light changed, and I was on my way through the intersection when I heard Him one last time. "You must write a book."

I can still remember being disobedient and wanting to argue further with the gentle Lover. "…But I can't write… I never… It's too much work… I'm not strong enough to pull it off. Yet I got out of my car knowing what His will for my life was. And I sure can tell ya that I wasn't too pleased at all about the assignment.

'So, what did I do?'

What nearly anyone of us would have done. I spent the next several months looking for lawyers! Because, I certainly wasn't about to write any stupid book, especially not for someone who wasn't going to read it!

And so, what did I get for the trouble, you might ask? Well, I learned a bunch of stuff about the legal system and believe me, what I found out was more than a little bit disheartening. Spent some more of my hard-earned royalties and for the most part, had every single law office door slammed squarely in my face. That's what being out of line with God's will, will produce for you every time!

And the consensus…. they all wanted their money. A suit like the one I'd been shopping could make for a gold rush. Yet on the other hand, they were terrified of Honeywell's unlimited billions and their top tier defense firm. And they knew them by name…, Kirkland & Ellis.

Just so you know, when God talks to us mere mortals it's not necessarily audible, though for some, it certainly could be. For me, I hear Him in my head and gut simultaneously. It is the softest of all prodding's. Yet, it's so firm there can be no denying that it didn't originate from the synaptic maze of my brain. It's so sudden. It comes out of left field. It always catches me off guard every time, and there's never an explanation given, nor a follow up. And it's definitely something that you can't argue with. All I can say, is that when it occurs and if you're sensitive to it…, you'll know. And for me, it's only happened but a few times in my life.

'So if He's God, why can't He talk to us when we need his help?'

Something to think about.

When Patti went back to school that fall, I began to write. At first, I tried tackling the feat longhand, but that didn't last very long. It would of been absolutely impossible to yellow pad this piece, unless I had the next ten years to myself or better yet, was confined to a jail cell to do it.

'Would someone please convince me that God doesn't plan things?'

All you need to do is give Him a little credit, then look! He's always at work for you, even if you don't believe in Him!

As it turned out, for the last nine months, I'd been going to bed staring at this five-thousand-dollar computer setup in the corner of my bedroom, wondering if my seven-year-old daughter was ever gonna learn how to use it. Upon my wife's insistence, we just had to get Jackie ready for the computer age. So, there it sat, taking up a sizable part of our bedroom, beckoning to be turned on by somebody, anybody. 'But who would do it?' We were all kinda scared of it! I know that I certainly was.

And as fate would have it, the impressive setup had somehow had made its way into our bedroom where I couldn't even lie in bed without it staring at me! I for one, was scared of the thing, even though I had the mechanical aptitude to of set it up! And that's about where both my bravery and computer savvy ended, knowing virtually nothing about the operation of the horrid machine!

I was so put off by the whole computer age that I didn't even bother to venture out onto this new thing that they called the Internet.

But if I had any hopes of writing, that would have to change, and indeed over time, it would. So, after some much-needed pointers, I was finally able to begin my second great journey…, the book. And by January of 98', I had five chapters fairly well pounded out.

Then it happened… After six or seven months I couldn't take it any longer, because writing is hard work. 'So, what did I do?' I started looking for lawyers of course, and all with the same result I might add. Nonetheless, I blew the next nine months in disobedience, looking for what I perceived was my way out. Aside from some gained insight, I wasted a lot of precious time by not doing what I had been told to do in the first place. So now, after being totally disillusioned with my search, I started to sit down and finish the race, vowing not to stop writing until I got to the end this time.

So, there I was. Sitting there in the executive cafeteria of AlliedSignal's Worldwide Headquarters and Larry's winding up his rendition of Westminster's dog and pony show, when one of the stakeholders stands up and asks Larry if he would stay on… 'Stay on?'

'What's going on here?!' I wondered. I hadn't heard a thing about his leaving!

Then he dropped the bombshell. He was retiring in April of the year 2000 and that was etched in stone, as per Mrs. Bossidy as well as the Company's mandatory retirement age of sixty-five.

'My God,' I thought, 'If I was ever gonna reach him, I'd have to work fast. For all I knew he was a lame duck and a successor had already been picked! And if that were the case I'd be thrown out…, and this time for good!

The madding question and answer session had finally concluded, and the room was quickly emptying out. The Chief was hunched over the table out front, in the process of tidying up his papers readying for the trip back up to his lair. I'm sure he was relieved, 'cause just like a queen bee caught outside the hive, he had been subjected to about enough of the publics poking and prodding. At long last, he could go back upstairs to his office and assume his position of being unreachable.

By this point, a couple of reporters and photographers rushed the podium to start the fanfare off once again. Suddenly, I found myself not too far behind them, as I edged my way towards the front.

"Hey nice job Larry!" I said, as the big man raised his head to greet a fan. Smiling, I stuck out my hand, as I repeated the accolade once more. Grabbing his big paw, I said, "Twenty minutes, right? Just you and me. No lawyers."

It didn't take a rocket scientist to figure out that Kriendler was going nuts right about then, wondering who had the unmitigated nerve to be accosting his boss like that. But it was only me, the inventor of The Double Guard oil filter. I had turned up once again like a bad penny and wasn't going away anytime soon, except nobody around there could get that through their impenetrable egos.

He just stood there a moment looking at me. I don't know…, perhaps for the very first time he began to put himself in my position.

Maybe I intrigued him? I certainly didn't intimidate him, that was for darn sure. For me to of entertained a thought like that, would have been idiotic. One things for sure, Larry was accustomed to dinning on much larger fare than me, before he even had breakfast in the morning.

He just looked down at me and smiled, "Call my office young man. You can do that…"

This what I brought to Honeywell...

A couple of Benchmark patents & the extremely valuable trade secrets behind them...
I brought them the manufacturing, the marketing, and the entire business plan...
Everything necessary in order to make this product a huge success where nothing like it had ever existed before.
The stuff that dreams are made of..., not nightmares.
In the end, it would take a full-blown lawsuit and two self-diagnosing books in order for me to comprehend why Honeywell chose to focus on wrestling away my IP, instead of capitalizing on the billion-dollar opportunity I had gift wrapped for them.

My two patents plaques.

These two patents launched the journey that I'd set out on.
The '842 patent on the left has been cited 37 times and genesised The Double Guard.
The '901 patent on the right has been cited 122 times and genesised the TRT.
These two patents are responsible for launching the 'additive treated oil filter' category.
Today they are benchmark citations, making me the most cited inventor in the field of oil filtration.

During my Intellectual Property battle, Honeywell was never able to have either of these two patents declared invalid. Instead, my patents & IP would only serve as a spring boards for the dozens of related patents that Honeywell would go on to file without my knowledge nor my consent.

Just so you know, the PTO receives approximately a half-million patent applications annually.
The PTO rejects approximately 50% of all patent applications they receive.
It takes on average, 2 to 2 ½ years to receive a patent grant.

CHAPTER 37
PREACHING AGAINST THE CHOIR

It was rather hard to believe, but I wasn't dreaming…

I found myself hunkered down on the third row, surveying my surroundings from the safety of a pedestrian version of a winged back chair. Once again, I found myself in the executive cafeteria of AlliedSignal…, it was September 1st, 1999. And to think, less than six months had passed, since I had attended my first Shareholders meeting, back in May. Yet this time, it was somehow different.

What was about to go down was big…, really big. I was attending a Special Meeting of the Shareholders and it billed as the last one Larry would ever give. Larry was not only retiring, but he was merging the Company with that of another giant!

Just like the last meeting, I'd have to settle for a window seat, because after a month and a half of calling…, Larry in his wisdom had declined to grant me a personal meeting.

My only recourse to his disingenuous invite was to fire off what would end up being my last and final letter to him…, and that's what I'd like to tell you about.

Though I wrote it, I decided against personally sending it. This time, I opted to entrust that small detail to an attorney friend of mine. The very notion that I had finally selected somebody from amongst the local legal talent to do my bidding, would have surely have brought a smile to Dianne's maw. And one could have hardly of lumped Ray Bogan in amongst the clam diggin' real estate closers that dotted the shoreline of my backyard either.

Na…! I knew firsthand that Ray was more than qualified to lob this shell across Allied's bow, especially that I had finally decided to declare war on Larry and his band of merrymakers! Mind you, I might have hated doing it, but Larry had quickly whittled down my available options, and it would now only be a matter of time before I'd meet up with his band of merrymakers in Federal Court.

I had found out by complete surprise, and so did most of the civilized world when it was announced on Monday June 7th, 1999, that AlliedSignal was to acquire the giant thermostat maker, Honeywell for 13.8 billion dollars, creating an aerospace parts and electronics mega-giant. Larry had pulled off the deal in near secrecy by meeting with Michael Bonsignore, the CEO of Honeywell for what was said to have been three solid days of secret talks in a New York City hotel room. In the deal, the heir apparent to Larry's post, Mr. Frederick Poses became one of the first major casualties of the mega merger. I felt for him, since the post of CEO had already been promised him. Yet by the same token, he'd float back to earth ok, lick his wounds and be just fine, for the golden parachute to which he'd been attached, would provide him a rather comfy landing.

It was a bonanza, all the boys net worth's would undoubtedly double. Honeywell for its part, would have to leave its Minneapolis headquarters of the last 104 years and AlliedSignal would have to trade its stodgy sounding industrial name and would be known going forward as Honeywell.

Larry would have to sever the arm of his best man and amongst other things and give away the Company's long held moniker. All in the name of future growth, since he had been unsuccessful during his tenure to organically grow the Company himself. The result being, from here on out, the new thirty-billion-dollar giant would be known as the new Honeywell Corporation.

Oh…, and just to be fair, you can understandably see why he didn't have the time to meet with me this last go-round, since he was in the process of making the biggest clandestine deal of his career.

But, if only I had of known! Because during that time frame, I still hadn't given up on calling his office. So when I called, I was simply told that he was extremely busy. Like jetting off to the Paris Air Show one week, and off again the next to the Symposium on Excellence held in London.

In my good patience, I let well over a month of excuses go by the boards until one morning I could take it no longer. The four years of frustration in trying everything I knew to reach him had risen to a such a level, that I felt justified when I passed along to his personal secretary that Larry had given me his word at the May shareholders meeting that he would see me. I told her straight out to remind her boss, 'that if he was a man of his word, he'd meet with me as promised!'

Boy, now that one got results! Two days later, Kriendler had surfaced on my answering machine once again, wanting to go over the details of the little discussion which had transpired between the both of us at the head table last time. 'Wouldn't you know it?'

Oddly, the last time I spoke with his boss, Kriendler had only been separated by an arm's length at best. Apparently, the morning that Larry promised to meet with me, he had somehow managed to stay out of earshot of our conversation. And you know something, I thought that rather bizarre…, since I didn't recall speaking to his boss like I was a church mouse.

However, as for this go 'round…, I chose to not to dignify the Armor Bearer with a return call, so I guessed that the war between us was finally on!

The next day I grabbed a hold of my attorney friend and gave him a quick five hundred dollars' worth of what had befallen me. Without a doubt, I could have easily gone on for thousands and thousands more, but I passed on that option.

Well, I just had one last letter to write the boys over at Allied. At this point all I needed from Ray, was his professional guidance and understanding. In return, he was quick to lend a hand, promising to keep me out of trouble, as he said, "Just write the letter Steve. Put in there what you want, and I'll make sure you don't cross any lines."

Just so you know, during that five-hundred-dollar soirée, I couldn't resist popping the question… 'So Ray, do you want to help me sue these bastards?'

He didn't even need to give it a second thought… "Steve I'm happy to help you fine-tune this letter of yours, that's certainly no problem. But to sue a company like Honeywell is way beyond my ability. For starters, I'd need a fleet of attorneys and more than a few back-office paralegals. I'd have to drop all my other clients in order to focus just on them. And I'd need to be doing just that for the next several years. I'd starve out. You couldn't find enough money to keep an operation like that afloat."

"Ok," I replied, crushed by the enormity. The lawsuit mountain that I was still determined scale, was doing nothing more than just getting bigger and bigger.

"So how about, just preparing the Complaint for me? Can you do something like that?"

"Steve… the time…, the research into doing something like that from scratch would be immense. I'd have to study your entire case from both a factual standpoint, and legal grounds. Then there's the intellectual property side of this case, which is huge. I'm not anything close to an intellectual property attorney, you know that! Remember, I specialize in Real Estate, Contract and Maritime law."

"I don't care Ray, would ya just ball park-it for me? So at least I'd know, 'cause I've never priced this out before."

"Well if I could even do it, which I can't… I'd have to say in the neighborhood of ninety-thousand dollars."

From here on out, the manuscript that I had been slaving over for the last year and a half would have to do the talking for me…, since I couldn't find anybody to walk up to the plate.

To put it mildly, I was just plain old sick and tired of trying to explain myself to every lawyer that happened to come down the pike wanting to diagnose my ailment.

You see, every lawyer I ever called and some of them were world renowned… Well, they'd all come to the phone and we'd talk. Many would saber rattle while others would make promises. They'd call me back on the week-ends and some, would even give me their home numbers. But in the end, Honeywell and the enormity of such an undertaking scared them.

Nobody had to tell me, I already knew it, The Double Guard was being propped up now by only two retailers and if it hadn't been for the continuing Grace of God, this filter would have never have been able to fend for itself on the shelves alone. Believe me, the hand of God was definitely upon this filter for it to be selling all by itself to the tune of around a million units per year without any sort of marketing support! I cannot begin to stress enough how things like that just do not happen all by themselves in the natural world, simply because they don't!

'So, why'd you bother to pen your story Mr. Inventor?' After all, a hundred grand a year for sitting on your backside would seem a pretty good deal to nearly anybody. Oh, I don't know…

Maybe 'cause by now I should of been pulling a check out of my mailbox every quarter for about million bucks, and that shoulda been happening by mistake! That's all! 'It was about the money, remember?'

It was always about the money for me. It was never about going to court to enforce my contract. It was never about writing a book. Never about something as stupid as notoriety… and it was never about me! It was never about nothin', but the money and the principal of the thing! And by this time, in case you might have missed the point, it was about the money due both me and God!

As always, I still had a plan. I simply wanted to get my finished manuscript into Larry's hands so that he could read in detail, how his Company had fallen far short of his delusional Six Sigma status and prove to him text book style that he was all wet with regard to this "excellence mantra" that he was espousing all around the world.

Just like a high-priced efficiency consultant, it was my strongest desire to hand him this piece, unabridged and just the way I had penned it. All because my Double Guard was very dead now and it was only fair that the Company do the right thing and hear me out after destroying ***"the most significant oil filter innovation in history!"***

On June the 14th, 1999, Raymond Bogan, sent out my first letter ever, to wear the signet of a lawyer since their breaking of my contract. With as much fury as legal etiquette would allow, it hurtled towards Larry full at full speed. The missile was out of the silo and I could only hope that my honesty wouldn't draw an accusatory response, like I was extorting them or something as equally ridiculous. Even if I wanted to give them a taste of their own medicine, I wasn't driven to the point of doing something that asinine. So, I was very, very careful! Because whenever you challenge one of these mega-corporations, just understand that it is just like throwing a rock at a bull elephant while your locked in its paddock.

───────────────

Late one afternoon about a week later, Kriendler got a hold of Ray Bogan and according to Ray, Kriendler was calling from Brussels, Belgium. It was sometime around 11 P.M. over there when he had paced the call. Naturally when Ray had first contacted me about the particulars my heart soared! The Chief General Counsel of one of the largest companies in the world doesn't bother to personally call the attorney representing some tiny gnat after dining on five-star cuisine nestled in the jewel of Europe for no good reason... 'does he?'

No, of course not! He'd call his wife and kids to tuck them in, that was for certain, but to call the lawyer of some irritating pest before bedtime just to be social...? I didn't think so. Understandably, I couldn't wait for Ray to fill me in, this guy was calling from Europe in the middle of the night!

Unfortunately, Ray's tone was a dead giveaway, immediately setting me up for the impending letdown which was soon to follow. "He danced a lot Steve. Feeling me out and flexing his muscle a bit, while all at the same time asking me if I realized just how big and powerful a Company like AlliedSignal was..."

'Now where have I heard that line before?' as my hope immediately began to grow cold.

As Ray poured out the few precious details he had gleaned from the posturing giant, Kreindler went on to say that Larry was much too busy to read my manuscript and that I could just forget about any possibilities of it ever being read by anyone at Allied.

"Steve, we can still try, but like I warned you from the very beginning, I know how these guys all operate. I've dealt with the likes of them before, they're tough. They've got lots of money and lots of high priced lawyers behind them."

So being an idealistic dreamer..., and if you must know..., I much prefer viewing myself more a man of faith, I instructed my competent and trusted friend to pursue this avenue wholeheartedly for the remainder of the summer. That was going to be the allotted time in which I'd allow them to respond. Because after that..., I was prepared to sail on the evenings tide.

'And the result?'

Allied summarily stopped all communication with my attorney.

'And my recourse to enforce my contract for which they were in direct violation under the "Reasonable Efforts" clause and the withholding of my royalties?'

Well according to Ray, there was but one answer to get them to respond, "Court Steve! You have to file a complaint and take them to court, they are under no obligation to respond to you any further about the matter," was his final assessment.

Please re-read that one sentence and reflect upon all that I've already laid out. There is never any recourse..., just a hellacious lawsuit waitin' on you, once you get enough nerve to pull the trigger. So, keep that in mind the next time you get slighted in life or in business.

"Well what about the 750,000 thousand filters that have been stolen outa Walmart? They haven't paid me for that Ray? Seventy-five grand at this point would go a long way right about now!"

"Sue 'em Steve! That's about all I can tell you. I'm ready," he offered in a moment of false bravado.

It was obvious, I had nowhere else to turn, but God. Now more than ever, I made it a point to walk the shoreline of the Atlantic every morning before I would start the day and talk with my Friend and my Counselor. He would lead me…, of that I was confident. It was just up to me now to seek His face and be open to the gentle prodding of His Holy Spirit. I wasn't scared, I wasn't nervous, nor was I upset…, just determined to play on until I won and that's about the size of it.

There can be no denying it. I wrote this book for Honeywell. And now the Chief General Counsel of the entire shootin' match was telling my attorney that Honeywell didn't want any part it. Well… what he was really telling the man, was that they didn't want any part of me…, and that certainly wasn't going to fly, not after all they had put me through.

If they had bothered to consider all that my relationship with them had churned up, it may not of been necessary to drag them into court, kicking and screaming. And perhaps if they had just read it, at the time in which it had been given, maybe they would have righted their listing ship and fixed it.

But that wasn't to be…

As I was writing this book there was yet another force at work, and of course they were blind to it. I sorely wanted to let this story have a life of its own. I was falling dangerously in love with the notion of putting this book out there. It's quite natural you know. 'Who in their right mind writes a book, only to shelve it?' To be frank, it's something that I've struggled with from the very moment I put a cover on it.

Just so you know, I've sat on this story for 17 long years… Then one day, not too long ago, I pulled it out and began reading. Once again, I had stepped into the dream and was whisked away…, overtaken by the dream and the enormity of the journey. Once again, I found myself its prisoner…, a prisoner of this rather insane journey. That's when I knew that I could deny it no longer, it was going to come out into the light of day.

At this fork in the road, Allied wasn't talking to me, and as it appeared, God wasn't so quick to spell it out for me either. So, I'll let you in on a little secret, thankfully by this point in my life I had matured sufficiently enough to realize that it was best not to place absolute trust in my own abilities to handle something as complex as this situation. At least from my vantage point, I was left no real option other than to just continue on patiently with my writing and of course, walk the beach every day and pray!

Looking back now, I had no other compass to follow but my faith, most importantly my faith in His Word. So, if you think about it, it was really the only thing I needed anyway. The answer would have to show itself before too long, because the whole situation was so pregnant and just about ready to burst! Then during one of my walks it hit me! The thought came rushing in like the unbridled tide on a full moon!

Allied was calling a special meeting on September the 1st, 1999 at 10 A.M. at the headquarters in Morristown, N.J., to formally ratify the merger between themselves and Honeywell.

I was to go! I didn't want to, but I had to, so I ran it by Ray hoping to come away with his legal blessing for my shiny new plan. "Sure Steve, go along…, nothing ventured nothing gained," he said, building me up. At this point, Ray was quick to remind me that nobody from Allied was ever going to talk with me, certainly not after the call he had with Kreindler. He also let me know, that if I went, it could turn out to be the opportunity of a lifetime…, or it could just fizzle and end up being a waste of time. So, the choice was mine to make. But, as was always the case, I was obliged to show up in order to see how the chips would fall. You see, if you want to play the Faith Game, showing up is never an option, rather, it's always a requirement.

My wife and the few people I chose to confide in told me the exact same thing. I had to go, but I didn't want to. I was just so sick and tired of the whole thing and just wanted to stop all the madness. 'And if I went, I'd have to sit on the front row. Surely the big boys would surely spot me this time, thinking that I was just some sort of cry baby…, there to cause trouble.'

Just the notion of showing up was enough to get my adrenaline to run. Because for what it's worth, I knew that if I bothered to go, I'd be duty-bound to make a stand, come hell or high water. And let me tell you, the thought of doing that in front of a few hundred people and in front of all the higher-ups at Allied wasn't something I'd relish.

If you can believe it, I even called Allied's shareholder relations to see if I would be out of order if I addressed the Chief about anything other than the merger, that's how bad I was looking for an out!

'And the response?'

Predictably it came back that all questions and comments were to be strictly focused on the business at hand, the merger and acquisition of Honeywell.

Now I ask you, 'how was that for being dumb, scared and downright stupid for sabotaging my own plan before it could ever get off the ground!?' Obviously, I had caught a bad case of stage freight, because there was a performance of sorts coming.

Before launching into the final showdown, I'd like to tie up a couple of loose ends. I'd also like to share something that was percolating just beneath the surface. Something diabolical…, something you'd never catch, unless I bothered to point it out… Something of which, at the time of this final face-off, I had no earthly knowledge of!

You see, totally unbeknownst to me, Gary Bilski, Charlie Probasco and Robert Franklyn Voigt had already sworn an oath of inventorship for a patent application that they had knowingly falsified. As for Mr. Voigt, he was a janitor for cryin' out loud! 'So, what might his contributions be?'

On August 1st, 1996, AlliedSignal filed a patent on behalf of this trio that violated the Oath of Inventorship, 35 U.S.C. §115 & 116. This means that both Allied and these inventor's knowingly lied to the United States Patent Office. Allied also stole my trade secrets, so they were in violation of the Misappropriation of Trade Secrets and other related statutes as well. Keep in mind, the ink on my licensing agreement barely had time to dry before they filed this beaut of a patent. If you can believe it, only eleven months had passed since my license had been signed, and they were scurrying behind my back, filing their first in a succession of submarine patents!

On March 10, 1998, AlliedSignal was granted a patent for a Teflon treated oil filter 5,725,031 based upon my trade secrets. And I didn't have clue, until I spotted it that night in Walmart while strolling with Pat and the kids. This sighting was the tipping point for me. Because of it, I'd end up filing suit against them.

Let me explain….

Just so you know, up until November 29, 2000; the U.S. Patent Office kept all patent applications a strict secret until such time that it was either granted or denied. So, monitoring this situation was absolutely impossible!

In addition to that, Allied waited two years before ever printing their patent numbers on the Double Guard. The '031 issued in early March of 1998. However, it wasn't until late 1999 or early 2000, before they ever marked the product with their patent number. That's when I first saw it.

So, yet another key detail had been hidden from me in plain sight.

Just so you know, when it comes to big companies, patents and marking requirements, either the 'patent pending' identifier or the patent numbers are typically put on a product right away, and it's done so for a reason. Marking a product serves to alert the public that the product is registered under U.S. patent law and is accorded the protection and privileges that come with that registration. Second, and just as important, it establishes a starting point from which to begin calculating damages should an infringement occur. It has to do with a legal provision known as 'constructive notice' and rarely are big companies lax about flexing their muscle when it comes to marking requirements.

The Double Guard had never been marked with my patent number!

If you go back to the licensing negotiations, Allied had agreed to mark The Double Guard with my patent number. And they promised to do so through six separate versions of the licensing agreement. However, after Allied told me, **"that that they were going to go on without me"**, they made it clear that they had decided *not to mark* the Double Guard with my patent number. Here's what's so off the charts, they left the Double Guard unmarked for approximately 5 years! That's beyond contradiction, not marking a product that was hailed as **"the most significant innovation in oil filtration history."**

'Was it because they were waiting out my 5-year contract to run out?' Now you tell me?

Here's where I found myself…

It was September 1st, 1999 and Larry was in the midst of merging AlliedSignal with Honeywell. And as sure as I was breathin', Allied wasn't about to stick their new patent numbers on the Double Guard, at least not until the big merger had taken place. Not with me snoopin' around like I had.

'Don't you think I would have included it my last letter to Larry, had I of known? Can you imagine the storm I would have created if I had accused them of Misappropriating my trade secrets and filing a patent behind my back during the biggest shareholders meeting in the Company's history!'

And of course, I would have. … If only I had the proof!

Here's my point… AlliedSignal/Honeywell had already ventured deep into Misappropriating my trade secrets. They had violated my Licensing Agreement and of course, my Test Marketing Agreement which had governed my trade secret contributions. The Automotive Division and their intellectual property department had been aware of it, and they weren't neophytes by any stretch. AlliedSignal had more than a few thousand patents under management in their portfolio and this wasn't their first rodeo when it came to handling this sort of stuff. They were world-class intellectual property experts, and they had no doubt assayed every detail of both my patents down to their molecular level. And you know what, they'd have to, in order to overcome the prior art that both my '842 & '901 had already established as benchmark citations in this field.

Then there was this sticky subject of my intimate relationship with the Company. 'How could they under any circumstance, get around the oath of inventorship, 35 U.S.C. §115 & 116? And how could they possibly get around my trade secret agreement[s]?' The answer to that one is simple. They couldn't, unless they were lying and involved in a massive cover up.

So, that's why their Chief Patent Counsel of the entire shootin' match bothered to put something like this in writing. Donofrio wrote…

"…you approached AlliedSignal in early 1994 and sent AlliedSignal a copy of your patent. Over approximately the next eighteen months **you worked sporadically** with various AlliedSignal employees in an attempt to interest AlliedSignal in your patent.

It was a veiled attempt at providing a smoke screen, but you gotta wonder…, who he might have been writing to?

Now I gotta ask a question…, 'was my interaction sporadic?'

The process of getting this patent application past the PTO's watchful eye must have been quite an undertaking, since I had already tried to get a non-time-released Teflon treated oil filter past my examiner and been denied. A minor detail of which, I had openly shared with Bliksi and the engineering crew, as I disgorged not only my trade secrets, but the inner workings behind both my patent applications. The application for a non-time-released Teflon Treated oil filter, utilizing Acheson Colloids SLA 1612 was my trade secret. It was my idea and it always had been, and I could devote an entire chapter on how they pulled this one off.

So, picture this…. AlliedSignal was in both a license and a trade secret agreement with me, the very inventor that they are now citing not only once, but twice for this particular patent application. Yet somehow, they felt it proper to exclude me, their full-fledged business partner as the co-inventor. They chose to lie to the PTO, and instead, they opted to replace me with a janitor. Hum…?

Again, as I pursed this bunch for equitable treatment, I hadn't a clue from an evidentiary standpoint. And before I could establish that any sort of a crime had been committed, I'd have to sue Honeywell in Federal Court, in order to depose Bilski & Voight and the others. And that wouldn't be happening yet for another few years.

So, let's have a look at the cast of characters who I'm convinced had intimate knowledge of what was going on. Let's begin with Hampilos, without question he knew. He drew the license agreement, and I credit him for being one of the early masterminds of the whole caper. Then there was Diane, she was certainly in cahoots, so was Barter, Cory, Mishal, Price, Ympa, Ross, Rohrbach and Bjelde. You know the whole damn engineering department knew of it, even down to the man who swept the floors at night. As demonstrated, the crime made its way up the food chain past Redlinger, to Donofrio & Keindler and now all the way to Bossidy! The whole friggin' team knew it! And please forgive me if I left anyone out, because I would have been happy to name them. It seems, the only one who didn't know what heck was going on at the time, was me! 'So why did this happen?'

As I've been telling you from the start, this was a *'billion-dollar marketing idea that was capable of repeating itself each and every year for the next decade and it was protected by a patent & trade secrets.'* The bottom line was, they wanted it for their own and didn't want me tagging along.

However, there was a simple catch before all this money could come rollin' on in…, proper execution & support!

So, let's put this in perspective. For the last couple of years, I had been front and center on Kreindler's radar screen, so when I would occasionally pop up, he was capable of identifying the pesky little dive bomber. He certainly was aware of the false filing[s] since I had already bent back most of the feathers of the higher-ups in both Rumford and Southfield. There's no doubt, it had long since gotten back to him. There wasn't a snowballs chance in hell that he didn't know about the games that were being played with both my contract and my IP.

And now come to think of it, that goes a long ways towards explaining why his tone towards me was always so damn nasty, and why he was doing his best to try and scare me off.

You got to understand, Kreindler's highest duty in life was to not only shield…, but to protect Larry from any and all unpleasantries that might come his way! So, I'm convinced now more than ever that Larry knew of what had been going on as well, because Kreindler would have told him why he could never meet with me, under any circumstances. I was deemed to be radioactive, 'who knew?'

Now here's where it begins to get really spicy.

The ink on my licensing agreement hadn't been dry, before Allied violated every IP law on the books known to man by filing this application! So, it only stands to reason that they had been conspiring to do this deed during the great summer shakedown of 1995, when they had threatened, *"to go on without me."* Apparently, they weren't bluffing…, they were actually laying the groundwork to do just that.

Just so you know, they didn't just stop with just my Teflon treated oil filter either, because they went on and pulled the same exact same maneuver with my '842, the one that genisised the additive treated TRT. And that patent would issue as my lawsuit was under a full head of steam. However, do to extenuating circumstances, it wasn't possible to amend my complaint and add this additional crime to their already mounting list of sins.

Here's the reason why we let that count go by the wayside...

I was midway into my lawsuit before I had found a lawyer brave enough to team up with me. He was young…, ten years my junior and was fairly green. After parting ways with his firm, in a bold move, he agreed to represent me. He was a strapped for funds, so he took out a home equity to set up shop in a hundred-year-old converted horse stable. His newly acquired photocopier, had seen better days, having already logged a couple of million copies and at times, could be quite temperamental.

We were on the brink of trial and it was just the two of us, manning the battle stations in a converted stable in south Jersey. We rather had our hands full, preparing for the impending onslaught. During the incoming, I'd do long stints with him and I'd sleep in his basement for days at a time.

We were now facing a super transmuted Fortune 38 Company, with over 250 in-house attorneys. They were buttressed by an additional separate thirty-man law firm who knew the judicial swampland in the Newark vicinage like the back of their hand. Bringing up the rear was Goliath. It would be the ninth largest of its kind on the face of the earth…, Kirkland & Ellis; fielding an army of 1,100 armed combatants.

Remember when Bossidy at the May Shareholders meeting, had invited me to meet with the Company's lawyers, then dodged meeting with me personally. Well, I hope it's starting to make sense to you now! His knowledge of what had been going on, made him an accessory to this crime. So, if Larry had met with me, and it was later discovered that he had foreknowledge that his Company embezzled my IP, it would of been beyond a scandal! So, Larry could never chance a meeting between he and I…, even if it meant saving our billion-dollar baby or straightening out his failing multi-billion-dollar Automotive Division. It simply would of been way too dangerous for him. He had to let both my project and my deep insights as to their shoddy Automotive operation slip below the turbulent waves.

And just for illustrative purposes, think of how I'd become like an untouchable when it came to Redlinger after the handoff. And you all thought that the big boys at the top didn't talk to one another. Hum…?

Now just understand something, I pieced this all together long after this book was written and after it was in the can.

Just so you know, I would need the added luxury of enduring a crushing four-years' worth of pretrial against multiple law firms, in order to distill what I just presented to you!

So, here's my attempt of a final assessment. Power, deceit, corruption and the like will blind the soul's inner ability to see straight. As it was, I was incapable of persuading them to see my side, because they had crossed over the golden line and they all knew it. Everyone at the top knew what had gone down and they just couldn't chance it.

In reality, they were terrified that I had already figured it out, and that there was a remote chance that I could make my way upstream and present this madness in court. Surely it was a long shot that I'd ever get there, yet by this time, it couldn't be discounted.

Come to think of it, that's one of the reasons why they hired one of the most powerful law firms on earth to go against me as a Pro se litigant. Perhaps, that's why they had selected one of the most politically connected law firms that did business at the edge of the Judicial swamp and carefully set up the chess pieces the way they had. Perhaps that's why they ended up paying me millions on the eve of trial. All I can say, is that I came damn close to spilling my guts.

And for all the arrogance… They took a full four years to settle with me, knowing what I already knew…, and believe me, they knew a heck of a lot more that they weren't sharing!

As for my sanity during this period of reaching out to them… Well, I was really starting to develop a complex back then. Nobody from Allied wanted to talk with me from the moment that this licensing agreement was presented! And once I signed it, things really went dark.

You know, I could never quite figure out as to why. Luckily though, I had finally put it all together, 'cause I was really beginning to think that there was something terribly wrong with me.

Arriving a good half hour early, déjà vu stuck. I whizzed past Redlinger, my betrayer from the beach, just in time to catch him do a quick two-step, so as to avoid the mad inventor and his solitary share of stock. Undeterred from the mission at hand, I found my way onto the third row that morning, only steps away from one of the five floor microphones pressed into service for the folks who might be needing to vent.

The lure of the microphone drew me inexorably close, like a moth to the flame. Yet unlike the unsuspecting moth, I knew well in advance that I could wind up like an over cooked pork chop if my plan backfired.

Bossidy and Kriendler were slow-moving this morning, as they prematurely basked in the afterglow of the mega-merger that was about to make them rich beyond their wildest dreams.

Then it happened, I was spotted! Larry bent his tall frame down and began whispering into the ear of his ever-attendant Mr. Kriendler, who was seated beside him. All of a sudden there seemed to be an awful lot of frenetic whispering going on up there between the two giant killers, as they happened upon the field hand armed with a sling shot.

I'm telling you, in-between their chatter and the glaring looks intended to scare the stuffing out of me…, I had the audacity to fantasize that one of them would be man enough to approach me before the festivities got underway. At the moment, I wanted a cease-fire more than anything else in the world that I could think of, but like I said…, that was pure fantasy.

Before long, the meeting got underway and we rolled along at a noticeably faster clip than the previous shareholders meeting I had attended back in the spring. Larry had all but finished his merger spiel and the room found itself patiently waiting-out an elderly gent as he wrapped up his rather obtuse ditty from behind one of the microphones. All I could do was sit in my seat and consider my next move, trying to figure out if I had guts enough to carry out my intended mission.

Every so often I'd look up, only to be met with one of the boss's scowls as he stared down front and center at me. I'm sure the very last thing he wanted, was for me to be interfering with his biggest day and I didn't blame him one bit for the occasional glare. We were at war now and I'm sure that he knew it, but it wasn't of my doing! It was his! That's precisely why I had found myself here once again amongst the crowd of stakeholders.

All that kept running through my mind, 'was what a foolish man he was! This was a war he most certainly could of avoided.'

Well, it was too late now…

He'd never know what was up my sleeve, that was, until it was too late!

The open forum as predicted meandered like a silt clogged river, as the entire room suffered through our second helping of an elderly shut-in with way too much time and money on his hands. I could also sense that Larry's patience was wearing thin as well, fearing he'd soon tire of all this madness and announce last call. All I could do was wonder, as to what was to about to happen… The last thing I needed was to be denied my only shot, because of a couple of old wind bags.

Preceding the start of this morning's meeting, Larry had made himself quite clear, "No commentary unless it pertained specifically to the business at hand." He even went so far as to repeat himself a couple of times and I tell ya, coincidence or not, he was staring directly at me when he said it! And that's what got me movin' now in a hurry.

Before I knew it, I broke loose from the bonds of trepidation and was firmly ensconced behind one of the microphones I had strategically spied out. Scarcely able to believe what I was about to do, I cried out inside, 'Dear Lord, here I come!' I then reached inside of my jacket for the neatly folded pages of the letter I had safely tucked away.

Yes! The night before due to a combination of writer's block and perhaps just plain old common sense, I had decided to enter my letter of June the 14th into the official record! I was gonna make my plan public now and at long last I was going to expose AlliedSignal and its flagrant mistreatment towards one of its smallest business partners as well!

All can I say was that my left knee shook uncontrollably as it rattled around inside the baggy leg of my Khaki's, as I drew a bead on Bossidy.

"I am the inventor of The Double Guard oil filter. My invention was put in the first quarter report of 1996 and was also featured in the Annual Report of 1996 as well. It was one of the high-water marks of the Automotive Division that year. Allied in its own words has referred to my improvement as '"the most significant innovation in oil filtration history.'"

Believe it or not, even I was blown away by the resolve that came pouring out of me as I addressed the gallery brimming full of the faithful. My eyes roamed the room as if I had just graduated from Emily Post's school of public speaking and I found myself very much alone now, as I made my stand. Naked as a Jay bird, there wasn't much shielding me from the glare of the crowd as I stood behind the skinny chrome rod holding up the mike.

I was scared, but I was more determined than ever to blow the bridge as I caught sight of the two neatly packed rows of Senior Vice Presidents that sat off to my left. It was truly bizarre, but all of a sudden, this sense of self-satisfaction came over me, as I studied all their frozen faces caught in this curious time warp. Immediately it had become crystal clear, I had their undivided attention as I began to preach against the choir. There was little doubt left in my mind that my plight had never circulated very far outside the reaches of Larry's inner sanctum. The obvious shock etched across their faces only served to fuel my resolve as I forged ahead.

From time to time, my eyes would meet up with Larry's. There wasn't time, but his eyes were a dead giveaway that this deed of mine was a twisted act of betrayal. Realizing I had no time to analyze his misguided feelings, I continued on…

"With that being prefaced, I just wanted to introduce into the record a letter I sent to the Company through my attorney and a situation I am dealing with Allied at the moment. I want the Shareowners and anybody else interested to know what I have been going through. I will skip the formality part."

That left leg of mine was still quivering and most assuredly so was my voice and I'm sure I must have sounded like I was about to cry at any moment, but I was far from doing that. Continuing to survey the room, the Board of Directors were conspicuously absent this go 'round, unlike the last time, when they were seated so close to me…, I could have reached out and grabbed them.

Oh…, how I had restrained from myself during this entire last year from sending them all a big fat letter, wanting to let them know what Larry was doing to my project, all in the name of shareholder value. So perhaps rather foolishly, I let that opportunity go by the wayside, yielding once again to the higher virtues of patience, protocol, and peace. Now I found myself addressing the room, feeling this same thing, forever sorry that I hadn't spoken out publicly much sooner.

After having skipped over my attorney's introduction, I dove into the meat of the letter…

"Mr. Moor has informed me that he has made many attempts to communicate with your office over the course of the last four years regarding this issue. In addition, he had a brief discussion with you at the shareholders' meeting of April 26,1999, at which time you had agreed to meet and discuss the issues."

"This was about communication; I'd been trying to reach Mr. Bossidy over the last four years," I lamented, raising my head just in time to lock onto Kreindler's pair of heat seeking eyes.

Reading on, *'Still of paramount concern to Mr. Moor was his treatment suffered both during and after the licensing process of his patent, which is now embodied in The Double Guard oil filter. With regard to the contract, Mr. Moor feels the Company is in violation of its 'Reasonable Efforts' clause."*

"That has to do with marketing," I said, trying once more to drive my point home.

"This breach began long before the product's initial rollout and subsequent campaign follow-through. Also, in violation of the contract, the Company has, in the area of royalties, penalized Mr. Moor for returns due to theft, packaging and inventory adjustments. Beyond that, there is a duty to act in good faith, which he feels Allied has breached.

"Taking into consideration that the Company has summarily dismissed Mr. Moor's repeated strenuous attempts to communicate, he has taken it upon himself to meticulously document his experience first-hand with the Company. Mr. Moor to date has chronicled in the form of a 197,000-word manuscript his ill-fated treatment at the hands of the Company.

"By the way, I didn't do that overnight. It has taken me a year and four months to do that, six hours a day, six days a week," I said, wanting to let the onlookers know that I hadn't just decided to take on their illustrious Company, solely on a whimsical basis.

At last the nerves were shaking out, I was on what you'd call a roll.

"That treatment flies in the face of AlliedSignal's Mission, Vision and Values statements, and falls incredibly short of the Company's lofty standards of professionalism, communication and efficiency from several critical aspects. Mr. Moor's ardent desire is to place this document into your hands for careful review with the hope you might realize what he has had to endure, watching his life's work so inappropriately managed by your Company over the course of the last several years.

"Additionally, it is Mr. Moor's hope that this document may better direct this Company, of which he has become a part."

At this point there stood only one paragraph between me and finishing out what I had purposed to do. And according to Allied's three-minute clock, I still had plenty of time left to do a proper close. Larry just stood there and took it. I could feel his anguish as he gazed at me, restrained by his very own rules of engagement to hear me out, knowing full well that an interruption on his part would have made him look all the more the bully.

Nearly overcome by emotion I threw myself upon the mercy of the court. "I'm not just a shareholder, I'm a stakeholder. I have ten years of my life invested in this venture and I'm not happy with what has gone on! That filter, if properly marketed, would have positioned this Company into a billion-dollar a year repeatable business in the oil filtration arena. And it has sorely been mishandled!

"I hate coming up here and pouring out my heart, reading my lawyers letter to Mr. Bossidy, but I have been stonewalled and I just wanted the shareholders to know. I did not want to go to the newspapers or do anything different. I wanted to do this in house…, I wanted to do it as family. And I have been rebuffed and I am angry! I do not have too much more patience. I just want to finish this."

Nearly blown out, I raced against the ticking clock to enter the last paragraph of the manifesto.

"Additionally, it is my hope that this document may better direct this Company, of which I have become a part, and perhaps become a grounding rod for any future situations where honesty and integrity are conveniently pushed aside in the pursuit of business."

Finally, it was the Chief's turn...

"Thank you, Mr. Moor. I want to remind people that the questions should relate to the two issues of the meeting today. We have a very different disagreement with this young man about the product he talks about. He has elected to take legal means to protect himself, which we think is fine. At the end of the day the truth will come forward, and if he is in fact entitled to something... He will indeed get something!"

The
End

Epilogue, End Notes & A Stream of Consciousness

After reading my story, I trust that you might be better able to relate to the complex intellectual property law suit that would soon follow. I would file a nine-count complaint against Honeywell on July 1st, 2002. I won seven of those nine counts. Being able to win each count is a mega accomplishment in of itself, which entails having to endure a battle of magnanimous proportions in order to win each and every one. I've already foreshadowed the legal tidal wave that I was about to face from the opposing side, so I'm not going to get too long-winded.

Just so you know, in legal terms; each *count* is referred to a *cause of action*. Each cause of action is a separate lawsuit unto itself and the aggrieved party must win each separate cause of action in order for it to proceed to trial. Pending Federal Court matters can easily take four years or more in order to ripen for trial. After a final verdict has been rendered on the counts, it can easily take another five years or more to go through the Appeals Court process where the judgment is relitigated in front of a bank of judges! It's not unheard of for this madness to rage on for a dozen years or more. If ones not careful, this quagmire can completely swallow up a decent man's/woman's life. As the battle rages on…, *Murphy's War* plays incessantly in the background, on a never-ending loop in the back of one's head.

Honeywell settled with me on Friday September 1st, 2006; just before the start of the Labor Day weekend for a multi-million-dollar settlement as the judge was scooting around in his car doing errands.

During the last couple of chaplets, it may have appeared that there was lots of saber rattling about going to court. It was never my intention to come off like a sword brandishing version Manuel Noriega. I was just lamenting about the prospect of a game that you'd never want to play. So, in many ways, the very tail-end of the Aftermath is a birds-eye view of what a run-up to suing one of the biggest companies on the planet looks like from the inside of your gut.

Truth is, I had to be spit on enough…, I had to be taunted enough… I had to be stolen from enough in order to pull the trigger. I never really knew when and if I was going to do it. Until one day I sat behind the keyboards and started pounding out a thirty-two-page Complaint, replete with 26 exhibits.

Here's a ditty you may enjoy. The day I filed this Complaint, was three days before the July 4th weekend. I was so scared, that I didn't even drive the sixty miles to the Federal Courthouse in Newark, NJ. Instead, I would take the train and walk the few blocks to the courthouse. That's right, a fearless over-the-road-trucker who was too scared to drive his big black Suburban on a blue-sky day and on a flat road. I was about to throw a rock at a bull-elephant and apparently, I was temporarily short circuiting. It was my hope that the hour and a half train ride could fix that. Filing a Complaint against such an adversary isn't easily retractable…, 'you know that, right?' I'm sure you don't.

When I finally made it to the intake window to pay my $220 filing fee, the clerk who took my six identical copies, had time… Plenty of time to thumb through it, 'cause the processing unit was in a virtual state of animated suspension due to the upcoming holiday. As she thumbed through it, she lifted her head, her eyes meeting mine. "So, you're suing Honeywell, huh young man… are you?" she said, as if it was a big deal, even to someone who had taken-in virtually every kind of complaint under the sun.

I swallowed hard, "Well yes I am," trying to act the part.

"What law firm are you with, because I don't see one listed here," she said, testing me.

"Well..., I'm not with anybody, Mam. It says it right there," as I put my pointer finger on the cover page. "I'm representing myself Pro se. I did it right..., didn't I Mam?"

"Well..., yes you did, young man. Yes, you did indeed! You know that what you're about to do is a massive undertaking..., now don't you?" she said with look of motherly seriousness.

"Yes, I know, but it's something I have to do, they stole my invention..." I said with finality.

"Well young man..., you got the jurisdiction and venue right. Do you know how many practicing attorneys still can't seem to get one right! Do you mind if I take another quick look?" a smile now broke out across her face. "I see that you bothered to take the time to include some well-thought-out exhibits. A very nice touch, I might add," craning her neck, to take in my whole face. She didn't try and hide it now, as she tried her best to peer into this young 'echo warriors' soul.

"Yes mam. The judge has got to know what I'm talking about and he's got to take me seriously."

"Oh..., he will Mr. Moor, I'm sure of it." Just then, she pivoted to the side, turning her entire body around. She gave a call to the crew who were sitting in the back doing their work and having their early morning coffee. "Guy's come here..., come quick! You aren't going to believe it..., this young fella's an inventor and he's about to sue Honeywell, Pro se! Come take a look! You're not gonna believe it! It's one of the best Complaints that this window has seen in a very long time!"

The story that you just finished is virtually the one that I sent off to Honeywell. Yes, I updated parts and revised others to make it flow better. I also expounded upon many of the facets that were yet a total mystery even to myself, as I penned the first edition. Of course, I took the liberty to lay bare some of the finer details that only suing one of the largest companies on planet through four years of the most grueling pre-trail can bring to the fore. So, if you're looking for the verbatim copy of the one that I sent to Honeywell, this isn't the one. However, it's worth noting, that I left the overwhelming majority of the original version untouched. Good enough.

One last rambling... Now mind you, it not only took the tome of this book, but it also took a full-blown lawsuit and yet another book after that, for me to finally put this puzzle together. Strangely, what had started out as a pleasant stroll to the fair, would wind up being a full-blown archeological dig. Therein lies the answer as to why the legal community refers to these cases as complex intellectual property litigation and that's why there are few precious souls walking the earth today who will step-up and take something like this on for a contingency fee.

IN THE UNITED STATES DISTRICT COURT
FOR THE DISTRICT OF NEW JERSEY

STEPHEN E. MOOR)
)
Plaintiff,) CIVIL ACTION NO.
)
v.) 02W3142 (FSH)
)
HONEYWELL INTERNATIONAL INC.,)
f/k/a ALLIEDSIGNAL INC., AUTOMOTIVE)
AFTERMARKET, AND DOES 1-100, INCLUSIVE,) COMPLAINT
) JURY TRIAL DEMAND
Defendants.)

PARTIES

1. Stephen E. Moor ("Moor") is the inventor and the owner of record of patent 5,209,842, "OIL ENHANSING MULTIFUNCTION FILTER" (" '842 patent") a Teflon treated oil filter.

2. AlliedSignal, ("Allied") merged with Honeywell International ("Honeywell") in or about September 1999, and changed its name to Honeywell. Honeywell is a Delaware Corporation with its Corporate Headquarters located in Morristown, NJ. The Company referred to herein at all times will be known as Honeywell.

Cover page of my 9 count 32-page Complaint

After a five-year campaign of phone calls, letter writing and futile meetings..., Honeywell would prove incapable of owning up to their actions and come clean. Exasperated beyond words..., I'd end up throwing a rock at a vengeful bull elephant. *"Murphy's War"* had begun in earnest, and it would rage on for the next four-plus years.

Court filings & Pleadings can be found on www.pacer.gov

Every story has a moral, 'so why should this one be any different?' During my only day of arbitration, the Arbiter, who had recently done an eleven-year stint as the Dean of Seton Hall's law school, posed a question to me. He was feeling rather fulfilled, as the measly two-hundred bucks an hour had lined his pockets just enough to justify his sworn duty to the court. As the arbitration session was winding down and the requirements for trial had been fulfilled, he turned to me and asked one of the dumbest questions I'd ever heard. "What if Honeywell wanted to give you back your patents? Would you settle, because Honeywell has standing a million dollar offer on the table that's good through trial?"

By now, any fool could see that what I had brought them was much greater than how he phrased it..., so I thought I'd help him out. "You know, here's how I feel about the whole thing," as I took in his Spring Lake oceanfront tan and all of his ridiculous gold bobbles. "You've got to be kidding..., Honeywell, not only stole my stuff... but they were stupid enough to destroy a billion-dollar a year repeatable market."

"How so, Mr. Moor, I don't quite understand what you're trying to say here?"

"Well let me explain it to you in terms you might understand. You see, Honeywell not only destroyed the opportunity, but along with it, all of my IP. It's now soiled goods! The biggest Company in the world, stole something of mine and then they were stupid enough to destroy it in the process. They weren't even smart enough to capitalize on it! So now they want to give it back to me after they screwed it up! No thanx! They can keep it. I don't want it back. But I'll tell you what..., I'll be glad to meet them in the courthouse down the street as soon as it can be arranged!"

A few closing thoughts…
Never in my life did I ever want to write books…, hopefully, I've written two good ones.
I never wanted the conflict, I hate conflict with a white-hot passion.
I just wanted the money that I had earned and that was due me for the work I had put up.
I never wanted to sue anybody, let alone Fortune 38 like Honeywell.
I never wanted to be the most cited oil filter inventor in perhaps the whole entire world. By the way, that title is worthless, it gets you absolutely nothing…, not even bragging rights.

I never wanted to ever try and publish a book and have to deal with the indifference and the insane smugness of literary agents. I gave it my best shot on two prior occasions and met with abject failure. As a result, I was barred from going main steam. Had I succeeded, I would have wound up under someone else's thumb again, and as you've already figured out, that wouldn't of been a good place for me.

As you can see, I failed at something. And I promise you…, I've failed at more things, than I've succeeded at!

I failed at this lawsuit, because I had to settle. The Judge who had been strategically hand-picked to preside over my case, in concert with the big boys from Honeywell, beautifully manipulated the inner workings of the judicial chessboard, making it impossible for me to have a fair and impartial jury trial. This judge pulled many evil stunts during my pretrial and if you don't mind, I'd like to share a low-light with you.

Just so you know, on the very eve of trial, the judge granted Honeywell permission to begin the process of clawing back some of the precious counts I had already won! And no, it wasn't legal at all! It was all done over the phone, and once again, by some jack ass taking control of my destiny from behind the wheel of a speeding car.

Though I slaved and devoted four long years for my big day, I didn't dare paddle out under those conditions. I was destined to get off this merry-go-round…, so I did.

Just like an Olympian who trains his whole life and breaks an ankle on the eve of the event… that's what it was like for me to have settled. To me, settling was just like quitting, and it nearly killed me. Caving-in, based upon the dictates of a lopsided judicial system, and not based upon the facts was almost more than I could bear. I had a spectacular jury case and I would have mopped the floor with 'em.

It took me a long time to heal from that wound, but we all know, life goes on…

This was Us back then.   summer 2001   photo Vincent La Fata

A family portrait taken during the interminable run-up to lawsuit madness.

This photo was on the back cover of *The Greed of a Dime (1st edition)*.
In early autumn of '01, I hand delivered a copy to the CEO's personal assistant in the main lobby of Honeywell's World-Wide Headquarters in Morristown, NJ.

The following summer, I would file suit.

We were a young family back then.
Today, we're thankful for each other, and we're still very much intact.

You know... All I ever wanted was the money that was due me. All I wanted was to take some of my earnings and go out and buy a brand-new tractor-trailer, so that I could drive around this great country of ours, making pick-ups and deliveries and doing some charity hauls. That was it. I didn't want any part of this madness.

Now at sixty, many years have passed since I was in my thirties when I first launched out on this chapter. So, I'm going public now with two pretty heavy books.

Let's see how it goes..., because I know I've got a third book living inside of me if I chose to breathe life into it. The lawsuit book..., and you can't possibly imagine that one...

I'm an author and publisher now, so I can't very well remain anonymous as I take on this new role and this next big mountain. I won't be afforded the luxury of climbing this mountain alone and in secret, like the others I've scaled. As I said when we first met..., the climb is going to be 'arduous and it's going to be gritty,' nonetheless I'm committed to this newest adventure.

I'd like to thank you all for taking this journey with me.
So, from the bottom of my heart...
Thanks for taking the ride.

Stephen Moor

www.ingramcontent.com/pod-product-compliance
Lightning Source LLC
Chambersburg PA
CBHW060526010526
44107CB00059B/2609